Practical Marko

Progressive HTML Rendering and Micro Front-Ends

Damodaran Chingleput Sathyakumar

Foreword by Hassan Djirdeh and Ryan Carniato

Apress®

Practical Marko: Progressive HTML Rendering and Micro Front-Ends

Damodaran Chingleput Sathyakumar
West Jordan, UT, USA

ISBN-13 (pbk): 979-8-8688-1482-2   ISBN-13 (electronic): 979-8-8688-1483-9
https://doi.org/10.1007/979-8-8688-1483-9

Managing Director, Apress Media LLC: Welmoed Spahr
Acquisitions Editor: Anandadeep Roy
Editorial Project Manager: Jessica Vakili

Cover image by Freepik (www.freepik.com)

Distributed to the book trade worldwide by Springer Science+Business Media New York, 1 New York Plaza, New York, NY 10004. Phone 1-800-SPRINGER, fax (201) 348-4505, e-mail orders-ny@springer-sbm.com, or visit www.springeronline.com. Apress Media, LLC is a Delaware LLC and the sole member (owner) is Springer Science + Business Media Finance Inc (SSBM Finance Inc). SSBM Finance Inc is a **Delaware** corporation.

For information on translations, please e-mail booktranslations@springernature.com; for reprint, paperback, or audio rights, please e-mail bookpermissions@springernature.com.

Apress titles may be purchased in bulk for academic, corporate, or promotional use. eBook versions and licenses are also available for most titles. For more information, reference our Print and eBook Bulk Sales web page at http://www.apress.com/bulk-sales.

Any source code or other supplementary material referenced by the author in this book is available to readers on GitHub. For more detailed information, please visit https://www.apress.com/gp/services/source-code.

If disposing of this product, please recycle the paper

To Swathi, Avyukth, Mom, and Dad for the countless hours put into this work that caused me to stay away from you.

Table of Contents

About the Author

 **Damodaran CS** is a staff engineer at eBay and the author of two of eBay's largest traffic platforms. Both are horizontal UX platform-as-a-service apps that drive over a billion impressions in site traffic for eBay. He was recognized for the same by the 2024 Titan International Business Awards. He is also a winner of the 2024 American Business Awards by Stevie and was also honored with Utah's Best of State Award for web development. He holds three patents for similar use cases built around this approach. Besides contributions to the industry, he also contributes to academia via international IEEE conference papers on UX engineering and software engineering. He won the Best Paper Award at the 2024 IEEE International Conference on Software Engineering and Artificial Intelligence (SEAI) for presentation engineering. Damodaran also actively contributes in mentoring and reviewing international conference papers by being on the technical review committee of conferences like IEEE SEAI and IEEE JCICE.

About the Technical Reviewer

 **Sanjeev Subedi** is a staff frontend developer at eBay, specializing in developing web applications. His expertise spans architectural design, leading a team, and frontend implementation utilizing JavaScript, Node, CSS, HTML, and a variety of frameworks. He also dedicates time to educating and mentoring aspiring frontend developers and students around the world.

Acknowledgments

This book wouldn't have been possible without the support and guidance of the super busy folks on the Marko dev team—**Dylan Piercey** (Senior Staff Engineer, Marko Platform), **Michael Rawlings** (Senior Staff Engineer, Marko Platform), **Luke Lavalva** (Senior Engineer, Marko Platform), and **Ryan Turnquist** (Staff Engineer, Marko Platform).

Despite its greatness, Marko as a framework wouldn't have gained its adoption without the support offered by the associated core UX team of eBay led by **Ian McBurnie** (Principal Engineer, Web Platform) and **Andrew Gilga** (Staff Engineer, Marko and Web Platform) for their pioneering work in responsive, accessibility-first UX components along with the core UX theming framework—*Skin*—that drives eBay's brand and trust.

Thanks to my initial mentors for getting me interested in web development—**Suresh Ayyasamy** (Staff Engineer, eBay Live Auctions) and **Pranav Shekar Jha** (Principal Engineer, Roblox). A special thanks to Marko's first author **Patrick Steele-Idem** (for getting me interested in Marko over other frameworks) and **Ryan Carniato** (for SolidJS and showing the world it is possible to love and work for more than one framework—you are awesome).

A special thanks to **Senthil Padmanabhan** (VP Fellow, Platform and Infrastructure Engineering) for always being a great mentor, a source of support, and someone to always look up to. Thanks to Dmytro Semenov (Senior Architect, Node JS platform) for inspiration. A special thanks to my engineering leaders—*Prashanth Patlolla, Paul Stathacopoulos, Vidya Lingineni, Ganesh Talele, Lakshimi Duraivenkatesh, Rajesh Pinapala, Shikha Aggarwal, Manohar Shankara, Venkat Bathula, Julie Cheng*, and *Srikanth Rentachintala*—for the trust, the support, and for offering me with great work.

I'd also like to thank the reviewers of this book (engineers from the Marko team) and other awesome engineers (**Sanjeev Subedi**, Staff Engineer, eBay's Seller Experiences) for their contributions into reviewing this work.

Thanks also to **Hassan Djirdeh** (author of *Building Large Scale Web Apps: A React Field Guide*) and **Ryan Carniato** (author of SolidJS) for offering to provide a foreword for the book.

Foreword

With so many frontend frameworks and libraries out there, it's easy to overlook one that's quietly doing something a bit different. Marko JS might not be the loudest in the room, but it's one of the few frameworks that's truly built with server performance in mind.

Damodaran takes years of hands-on experience building at scale and distills it into a guide that's both practical and easy to follow. From concepts like progressive rendering and HTML streaming to building apps with Marko-run and server-side micro frontends, this book walks you through how to build for performance on both the server and client.

If you're already familiar with frameworks like React, Vue, or Svelte, there's a lot here that'll feel new in the best way. Marko's approach challenges some common assumptions and opens up new ways to think about rendering, composition, and performance. The techniques and mental models shared throughout this book are valuable beyond just the Marko ecosystem; they can change how you approach frontend architecture in general.

Whether you're exploring Marko for the first time or just looking for new ideas to push your applications further, this is a book well worth your time.

—Hassan Djirdeh

I still remember the first time I saw Marko. It took me all of five seconds to realize the team had put together something unprecedented. What they had accomplished in 2014 was still bleeding edge even in 2020—fully compiled reactivity, islands, and out-of-order streaming. The framework was ten years ahead of its time. And the best part? It was open source for anyone to use. I knew immediately I needed to join the team at eBay, if only just to learn about this incredible technology.

Marko has completely reshaped the way I think about solutions in the web space. It has changed the meaning of web performance for me and broadened my horizons to the potential of where developer experience could go in the future. The journey has been amazing.

Through my time at eBay, I met Damodaran, a seasoned veteran, working on some of the largest Marko codebases. I can't think of a better person to lead you on the next steps of your journey into the Marko framework.

—Ryan Carniato (Creator of SolidJS)

Introduction

This book is intended to be a handbook to get you started, interested, and become a practitioner of Marko JS. Marko? What's that you may wonder. Marko is the view framework that powers the majority of eBay's pages. We are talking at the scale of a billion renders while solving for the server and SEO. Built within eBay, now open sourced and part of the OpenJS Foundation, Marko remains one of the most remarkable and consequential frameworks of its time, powering some of the mainstream ideologies like progressive rendering, streaming, micro frontends, React Suspense–like and server-only component-type features, tackling for SEO, and handling efficient hydration, long before these terms even had those names.

"But I've never heard of it," you may say. True. The team is small, and there isn't generally time and resources available for large-scale marketing. However, Marko has been quietly gaining traction in the recent years with its deeper integrations into the open source frontend tooling ecosystem, its adoption of the Babel AST, the progressive interest spike in server-side rendering, streaming, adoption of meta frameworks, etc. While view frameworks like Solid, React, Vue, Angular, Svelte, and their related ecosystem are widely known among the mainstream web developer community ecosystem, Marko is now gaining the much-needed attention it deserves.

With Marko looming for a major upcoming release (bringing in resumability, reactivity, and isomorphic progressive renders), Marko 6 is sure to gather a lot more attention. In this book, we will be dealing with Marko v5 which already has a lot of the aforementioned greatness, a vibrant developer experience, and superior performance that the framework offers out of the box. While the rest of the world took the known path with React, Solid, Svelte, Angular, Vue, etc., eBay took a bold and a different approach with Marko that stands the test of time to this day alongside its competitors. As a developer, it's been a joy to watch this unfold over the years, and this book is an attempt to shout out the great work being done by the Marko dev team to the world.

This book is by no means a comparison between frameworks, nor does it serve to answer questions like why Marko is better than React, Svelte, Solid, etc. That isn't the focus point of this book, although occasional parallels are unavoidable. This book's purpose is to solely have you embrace Marko and highlight some of the great patterns it brings into the developer workflow. It also offers a great perspective into its philosophy of multi-page, server-rendered applications, tackling apps with a server-first approach. It also offers insights into some of the incredible things that Marko does because of its advantage of being a compiler at its core.

By the end of this book, you will come to appreciate Marko and its unique take on authoring apps (no JSX here) and how you can benefit from it with a great developer experience that is seamless and hassle-free, making building apps extremely fun, without compromising on performance. Also, the hope is that you give the Marko team a shout-out, spread the word among the community about it, and support the awesome work being done by the Marko team!

CHAPTER 1

Introduction

This book is a practical introduction to Marko JS—the framework you may have never come across! This book contains a number of concepts and principles that are core to Marko, along with practical examples showcasing the same, besides sample applications with Marko JS. In the following chapters, we will look at what Marko JS is, what it has to offer, and why it is turning out to be one of the most compelling and consequential JS view frameworks of its time.

Background (What This Book Is About)

For starters, Marko JS (https://www.markojs.com) is an eBay open source (https://github.com/marko-js/marko), isomorphic, and high-performance view framework that makes building performant web apps easy and fun. It not only enhances developer productivity but also supercharges application efficiency and performance. It is also a part of the OpenJS Foundation (https://openjsf.org/projects) and delivers over a billion view renders at scale for eBay. Since its inception in 2012–2013, Marko has come a long way and is currently into its fifth iteration, with version 6 coming soon!

Marko is one of the very few frameworks to have solved for the server side first. Marko was written by *Patrick Steele-Idem*, its first author and maintainer, during eBay's Node JS adoption journey that began in 2012. While today's frameworks solved for the client initially, and then are taking steps to solve for the server, Marko was developed at eBay to solve for server-side rendering in a performant manner—something that the mainstream frameworks didn't.

Today, Marko is more performant than ever, thanks to the brilliant minds behind it—*Michael Rawlings* (@mlrawlings), *Dylan Piercey* (@dylan_piercey), *Ryan Carniato* (@RyanCarniato) (of SolidJS fame), *Ryan Turnquist* (@rturnq), and *Luke Lavalva* (@

LukeLaValva)—who continue to push the boundaries toward unlocking extreme performance, highly efficient, and microsized bundles alongside a great developer experience.

What Does Marko Offer?

Marko JS is one of the very few frameworks that comes out of the box with the following features:

- Declarative authoring of views. No fancy JSX, just plain augmented HTML

- Clear separation of markup and behavior (template files and component files)

- Streaming, asynchronous rendering, progressive rendering

- Isomorphic rendering with automatic partial hydration when rendering on server

- Multiple compilation outputs for highly efficient renders—strings on the server and VDOM nodes on the browser (this is an implementation detail that will change over time)

- Support for TypeScript

- Babel AST and therefore automated framework migrations

- Hot module reloads and support for bundlers—Vite, Webpack, and Rollup

- Editor and IDE tooling support (VS Code plugin and Marko Language Server for syntax highlighting, autocompletion, and hyperlink in files that can be clicked to reach references)

- A meta framework called *Marko-run* that helps in scaffolding Marko apps easily to get you hit the ground running

- Single-file and multi-file components to suit your code styles

- Server-only components, also referred to as split components (one of the first 0KB JS frameworks)

- Performant and efficient (13KB Gzipped runtime)

- Compatible for MPA (multi-page applications), SPA (single-page applications), and SSG (static site generation) development

- Extreme performance on the server and on the client

- Unparalleled developer experience

- Upcoming in Marko 6: resumability, reactivity, and scoped css

- Modular and tree-shakeable runtime

- A smart compiler that detects and sends only those dependencies that are needed for execution on the browser

- Funded and backed by eBay. Scalable, trusted, and battle tested at eBay with over one billion rendered views and counting, along with 13,000+ stars on GitHub

- Decoupled micro frontends via *@micro-frame/marko*

- Support for GraphQL with *@marko/urql*

- Fully loaded with features like portals, context, subscribe, match-media, and client-side routing with router5 (not out of the box)

- Compatible with industry standard solutions like Jest, ESLint, LESS, SASS, Prettier, Vitest, Testing Library, Storybook, Redux, and CSS Modules

- Component-based development and installable artifacts

- A supported theming and core UX component toolkit provided by eBay that is 100% accessibility compliant

- Reduced memory consumption on the server, which is crucial for server-side performance

Another Javascript Framework? Why Marko?

While the Javascript fatigue is understandable and given there are a ton of frameworks—React, Angular, Vue, Solid, Svelte, and so on—it is important we address this question. To answer this, we will look at the top facets related to Marko's design philosophy, which sheds some light on why this framework is compelling.

Built for the Server and the Browser

Marko had its beginnings within eBay at about the timeframe of 2012–2013, right when eBay was beginning its Node JS adoption journey. While eBay initially relied on the Dust templating engine (of LinkedIn) as the render engine of choice for its views, Dust did not offer the option of streaming HTML from the server. Besides, eBay also wanted to solve for minimal memory usage on the server. So, Marko began under the vision of *Patrick Steele-Idem* (*@psteeleidem*), its original creator, to solve streaming HTML, asynchronous rendering, progressive rendering, and a reduced in-memory footprint on the server.

The server side has always been important for a large-scale ecommerce site such as eBay because it has the use case of solving renders that were compatible for SEO purposes (which meant majority of the render was from the server). Moreover, eBay as an application is an MPA (multi-page application). This meant every page had its own production pools, code repositories, and teams that operated on them. This also implied that the framework had to be operable within an MPA context from the start. The main reasons for this are scalability, failure isolation, decoupled code release cycles, easier debugging, and tracing and tracking.

Besides all the aforementioned goodness of server and render performance, Marko is also very performant on the client side. It achieves this by performing batched updates, declarative event binding, efficient event delegation, offering stateful widgets, isomorphic renders, and DOM diffing and patching based on state changes by relying on a unidirectional data flow model and a great algorithm (check out Marko's *warp10* module) for serializing server-side data to reuse on the client side (a process known as hydration).

Not Opinionated

Marko is not opinionated about a specific router for you to use, although on the server it does offer the Marko-run meta framework. But you can always spin up a simple Express server with your own router of choice to render views on the server, while a solution like *router5* can be used for routing on the client. Similarly, Marko does not enforce a specific tool or framework. You are free to use a tool of your choice; however, in terms of industry standards, Marko does offer integrations with standard tools like Vite, Vitest, Webpack, Rollup, Jest, Storybook, TypeScript, and Testing Library. However, most of the examples in this book will focus on using the latest and greatest—Vite and Vitest.

Similarly, Marko is not opinionated about placing logic within the template files vs. component files. Unlike React, where *.jsx* lets you author structure and behavior together, Marko offers the concept of single-file and multi-file components, meaning you can author HTML within the templates (**.marko files*) and wire behavior within the **.component* files. Marko takes care of wiring them together. However, if you choose to have it all together in one file, Marko lets you place structure and behavior within the same template, but with well-defined boundary constructs that let you achieve clear separation between concerns in the same file. However, it does not restrict you from using Javascript inline expressions, interspersed within HTML as you wish. It is also not restrictive about whether less or more logic should go into the templates and leaves that as a decision to be made by the developers.

Compile-Time Checks

Since every piece of code that you write will be inspected and transformed by the compiler, you get the goodness of compile-time type checking and syntax checking, attributes, custom tags, installed tag libraries, and imports with informative error messages that help you resolve them. So the chances of something blowing up in production are next to none, except for Javascript-related uncaught runtime errors—which should be resolved with the usage of TypeScript for the most part. This also means that every tag gets validated at compile time, with its suite of compile-time checks. Also, being a more natural extension of the HTML language unlike JSX, Marko parses every attribute as if it were a Javascript expression. This lets you pass arrays and objects as attribute values, which Marko takes care of resolving.

Readable, Debuggable, and Modular Outputs

Marko templates (*.marko* files) are compiled by the compiler to output JS modules that are very close to the source templates and are easily debuggable since they are Javascript. Source-mapped outputs configured through the bundler settings help to remap the output JS modules back to the right lines on the Marko template files to facilitate easy debugging. Yes, you can step through the template files.

The outputs by the compiler are also modular JS modules in nature. This means Marko will only include those runtime dependencies in the bundle that will be required to run the code, nothing extra. In the event you don't require any JS, with the page being just a static page, no Javascript will be shipped to the browser (0KB of JS). Marko's compiler performs code eliminations such that it only sends that code that is needed for the interactivity of the component. This means less code to download, parse, and execute.

Given that the runtime of Marko is modular as well (only those runtime dependencies of the framework that are required will be included), it does not therefore get to be distributed as a single file.

Progressive Rendering

Marko is one of the few frameworks that offers progressive server rendering out of the box, which implies you get HTML streaming and asynchronous rendering by default for all of your templates, to unlock superior server-side rendering performance. Language constructs are available by default in the Marko language to help you achieve this (read about the **<await>** tag later), provided your downstream API systems or microservices also support this by streaming data in chunks (like JSON streams or text/event-stream APIs). True progressive rendering implies that the framework under the hood has solved for both asynchronous rendering and streaming—Marko does it all. This also means Marko is perhaps the only framework that does *in-order flushing* and *out-of-order flushing* of HTML from the server while also ensuring *in-order paint*. We will elaborate more on this in the subsequent chapters.

Custom Installed Tag Libraries Do Not Require Importing

Marko has a way to scan directories at compile time to determine tags that are either within the project or installed within the project as part of the *node_modules* directory. This means you do not have to manually *import* them every time it gets used in one of your templates. Neither do you have to import "marko" into your code every time. You can also import other Javascript modules and CSS modules just as you would into any Javascript file. Marko also provides custom registrations that let you import *.marko* templates into your JS/TS files for the purpose of invoking the render.

Rich API to Get You Started

Marko has a set of prebuilt language constructs for handling conditionals, looping, asynchronous rendering, building small reusable template partials, including external HTML directly, and a rich context API similar to React for global state while also providing global access to server-side whitelisted variables on the browser (which get serialized to the browser). Every Marko component is an instance of the Node JS event emitter package, which means you can emit events to parent components without the need for passing down functions from parent to child. Most of these APIs appear to be augmentations of HTML or appear to be adding support to existing HTML syntax, like a natural extension of the HTML language for building reactive and dynamic user interfaces.

Integrations (Tooling)

Marko has integrations and support for many industry-leading solutions and tooling, like Redux, Storybook, Webpack, Rollup, Vite, Jest, Testing Library, Vitest, ESLint, GraphQL, and editor plugins, and support for editors like VS Code.

Internally, Marko's language extends the Babel AST (look up the Babel plugin handbook: `https://github.com/jamiebuilds/babel-handbook/blob/master/translations/en/plugin-handbook.md`), which means you can build custom solutions and integrations with ease, given the underlying AST representation, being Babel, is also an industry standard.

Marko therefore also has you fully covered for upgrades in the form of a migration tool that lets you perform automated framework upgrades without a hassle.

Superior Performance

Marko's compiler produces two different outputs that target the respective environments in which the code will be executed—the server and the browser. On the server, it outputs HTML as strings, while on the browser, it outputs VDOM nodes (this is an implementation detail that could change over versions). However, you will write your components only once, and Marko takes care of producing optimized code for the respective environments. Moreover, if a component is initially rendered on the server and then will re-render on the browser, Marko takes care of handling this switch all by itself, freeing you from any environment setup, thereby letting you focus on your code.

When you compare this to JSX-based solutions that produce VDOM nodes for rendering on the server, they are required to build the entire VDOM tree once before serializing the tree to stringified HTML to be sent over the wire (two passes). Marko, however, with multiple compilations can render directly to the HTTP stream, without the need to build out the component render tree.

For many frameworks, they re-render the full page back again on the client after server rendering (replayable frameworks). But Marko does not require doing this, as it is able to serialize the input and state so that it can pick up on the client side exactly where it left off on the server, with this serialization being automatic. Marko v5 is technically not resumable yet (something that is coming in Marko 6). This is because, although it serializes component boundary markers and component state data, etc., it still doesn't serialize the framework state or embed listeners into the HTML to ensure instant interactivity and fully avoid the process of hydration upfront by progressively doing it. So, Marko can be said to reconcile with the server-rendered HTML.

The Compiler

The presence of a compiler means that Marko does maximum work at the compile time itself. Marko's modular runtime is the result of this smart compiler, which helps to size down on the framework's runtime by eliminating needless framework-related dependencies.

Moreover, the compiler also detects static subtrees (that do not change with every render) and static attributes (values that do not change with every render) and is able to optimize for the same. By detecting these static attributes and static subtrees, Marko can fully skip the diffing and patching operations for them.

Marko's compiler is also able to offer numerous hints to the Marko runtime (which the runtime can utilize at execution time) for optimized renders. Moreover, the presence of the compiler means Marko is able to achieve backward compatibility between versions. The compiler is able to output Javascript modules that also export the renderer API along with it (this means you do not require something like *ReactDOMServer. renderToString(myComponent)*.

In comparison to JSX, which is syntactic sugar that translates elements to createElement() function calls, the Marko compiler has full control over how things are compiled and optimized. The presence of a compiler offers additional hooks for running compile-time transformations.

Partial Hydration

Hydration will be touched upon briefly in the subsequent chapters. However, Marko, with version 5, performs progressive hydration to some extent (Marko 5 hydrates components as they are flushed out from the server render). However, Marko is not a resumable framework as of version 5. But this changes with version 6 with the introduction of fine-grained reactivity and resumability that will place Marko alongside the framework Qwik and offer avenues for unlocking subcomponent hydration (further efficient serialization of data).

However, Marko with the presence of a smart compiler is able to achieve partial hydration with version 5. This means the compiler is able to detect the interactive portions (components) of the page-level template and serialize the required data only for those portions. Besides the smart compiler being able to detect parts of the page that need to be hydrated (by eliminating those portions that do not have interactivity), Marko utilizes a very efficient algorithm to serialize the server data while maintaining a mapping between references of this single source of data and those components deep within the hierarchy. This greatly helps Marko in achieving superior server rendering performance (refer to the server benchmarks here: `https://www.infernojs.org/benchmarks`).

So, in short, Marko performs partial hydration out of the box, thereby reducing unnecessary JavaScript, which minimizes client-side download time, parse time, and processing time, resulting in faster page interactivity and improved performance, particularly on mobile devices with limited resources. It also progressively hydrates chunks as they are being server rendered and flushed.

Decoupled MPAs (and Micro Frontends)

Marko has out-of-the-box extended support for achieving decoupled multi-page applications (server-based micro frontends) through the use of its official *@micro-frame/marko* (`https://github.com/marko-js/micro-frame`). If your application is the one using this tag, it will be referred to as the host application, while the application you are attempting to reach will be the provider application. This tag helps to invoke other Marko-based web applications (provider apps) in your enterprise server environment and transclude its rendered content into your application's (host application's) source. Given the runtime of Marko is very small, this helps you to achieve decoupled micro frontends in comparison to solutions like module federation. This uses the *writeableStream* API to stream raw HTML into existing DOM nodes.

Why Is Performance So Important?

There are numerous measurements done by many high-traffic and large-scale websites that support the theory of page speed and performance being directly correlated with the conversion and success of a given product. You can read more about this at `https://www.builder.io/c/performance-insights`, where Steve from *builder.io* gives multiple examples of websites that increased their conversions through the improvement of web page speed and performance. In short, they translate to reduced bounce rates and increased engagement time, which translates to increased conversions and better revenue. So, having established that performance (render speed, memory consumption, and load time—bundle sizes) is so crucial, it becomes important to have a very good view framework solution that is able to solve these.

The Approach Followed by This Book

This book is intended to be a starter guide on building applications using Marko. This book introduces concepts, followed by examples to build on the concepts to develop a mental model, followed by more concrete examples, such as building out a sample application toward the end. The version of Marko used in this book is version 5 or higher.

The book has numerous illustrative examples along with code blocks that can be tried out as you read the book. You can also find the code examples in a GitHub repository, which will be linked next to the example.

The goal of this book is to be your go-to place toward building applications using Marko JS and have you enjoy it in the process. It shall also help you better appreciate the numerous intricate design decisions employed by Marko JS that help it stand out among a sea of Javascript frameworks.

While this book aims to be a starter reference for Marko, it does not aim to be a complete reference, nor offers details into the design of the compiler, nor does it compare Marko with other frameworks out there in terms of architecture, syntax, design decisions, and benchmarks.

The book is also intended for an intermediate-level audience who have prior experience working with Javascript, TypeScript, HTML, CSS, and a view framework such as React, Angular, Vue, Svelte, and Solid. That would help to better appreciate the intricacies and tiny nuances that come along in learning a framework such as Marko. However, that would in no way limit you from understanding the content of this book if you do not have prior expertise in any view framework.

The examples followed in this book will utilize one of Vite or Webpack (Vite mostly) and Vitest/Jest alongside the Marko Testing Library. Also, this book expects a reasonable basic understanding of Node JS and its ecosystem of using NPM, Yarn, and the terminal. The examples mentioned in this book utilize Mac OS.

By the end of this book, you shall have a firm grasp about authoring applications using Marko and come to appreciate it for being one of unparalleled frameworks out there that blazed its own path, which many of the existing frameworks are attempting to discover.

What Does the Community Think About Marko JS?

The following snippets shall showcase some of the sentiments captured on the X platform (formerly Twitter) from other engineers and developers who have had the chance of using Marko JS.

Saulo Vallory ✔ @svallory_en · Apr 11   ···

This is NOT why I've invested almost all my spare time in Marko over the last six months.

It is pretty great. But the DevX is unparalleled. Just go to component-party.dev (If you are feeling lazy, check the next tweet)

> **Marko** @MarkoDevTeam · Apr 11
>
> Benchmarks are misleading. But...
>
> ```
> > ssr-benchmark@1.0.0 start
> > cross-env NODE_ENV=production node src/index.js
> ```
>
> | (index) | name | ops/sec | average (ms) | samples | body (kb) | duplication | relative to marko |
> |---|---|---|---|---|---|---|---|
> | 0 | 'marko' | 6158 | '0.162' | 61589 | '96.74' | 'x1.00' | ' ' |
> | 1 | 'react' | 730 | '1.369' | 7303 | '97.28' | 'x1.00' | '8.44 x slower' |
> | 2 | 'sveltekit' | 545 | '1.834' | 5453 | '184.46' | 'x2.00' | '11.30 x slower' |
> | 3 | 'solid' | 527 | '1.896' | 5275 | '215.93' | 'x2.00' | '11.69 x slower' |
> | 4 | 'remix' | 428 | '2.332' | 4288 | '189.10' | 'x2.00' | '14.39 x slower' |
> | 5 | 'vue' | 259 | '3.850' | 2598 | '96.72' | 'x1.00' | '23.78 x slower' |
> | 6 | 'nuxt' | 238 | '4.195' | 2385 | '97.57' | 'x1.00' | '25.87 x slower' |
> | 7 | 'next-pages' | 100 | '9.992' | 1001 | '187.67' | 'x2.00' | '61.58 x slower' |
> | 8 | 'mfng' | 66 | '14.977' | 668 | '317.31' | 'x2.50' | '93.30 x slower' |
> | 9 | 'next' | 51 | '19.607' | 511 | '284.64' | 'x2.00' | '120.75 x slower' |

Figure 1-1. *Tweet mentioning Marko's dev experience*

 Saulo Vallory ✔ @svallory_en · Aug 25, 2023   ···

Honestly, I can't believe that markojs.com from @MarkoDevTeam isn't the framework EVERYBODY is using. I'm in love with it. It's the most well-rounded framework I've seen in years. Amazing DevX, fast to write, and fast on runtime. I guess they need a Dev Rel

💬 1   🔁 2   ♡ 10   ılıl 1K   🔖 ⬆️

Figure 1-2. *Tweet mentioning Marko's dev experience*

Austin Gil @heyAustinGil · Apr 21, 2023   · · ·
Starting to sound more and more like we all should have just gone with
@MarkoDevTeam to begin with.

💬 2   🔁 1   ♡ 7   ⅈⅈ 2K   🔖 ⬆

Figure 1-3. *Tweet about Marko*

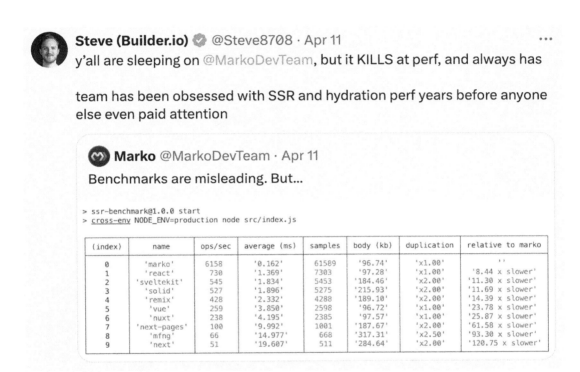

Figure 1-4. *Tweet about Marko's performance*

Filip Rakowski ✔ @filrakowski · Sep 27, 2022   ...

It blows my mind that a framework like @MarkoDevTeam was out there for
years, powering eCommerce giants like @ebay with all the"current cool
things" like partial hydration or streaming.

It looks like it takes more than just a good solution to a problem to start a
revolution

💬 3   ↻ 6   ♡ 39   ılıl   🔖 ↑

Figure 1-5. *Tweet celebrating Marko's performance*

Shelton Louis @SheltonLouisX · Feb 24, 2023   ...

@MarkoDevTeam is the first framework to propely synchronize HTML CSS
and Typescript. Typescript. Wow. What a truly advanced framework.

Generic Inputs

Generic Types and Type Parameters on Input are recognized throughout the entire .marko
template (excluding static statements).

For example, if you set up a component like this:

```
components/my-select.marko
export interface Input<T> {
  options: T[];
  onSelect: (newVal: T) => unknown;
}
static function staticFn() {
  // can NOT use `T` here
}
${
  const instanceFn = (val: T) => {
    // can use `T` here
  };
}
// can use `as T` here

select on-input(evt => input.onSelect(options[evt.target.value] as T))
  for|value, i| of=input.options
    option value=i -- ${value}
```

Figure 1-6. *Tweet about Marko and TypeScript*

Anthony Campolo (ajcwebdev) ✔ @ajcwebdev · Nov 3, 2022   ···
Replying to @saucedopen @RyanCarniato and 2 others
Amazing interview front to back, but want to highlight specifically the
section on how @MarkoDevTeam was years ahead of the game.

> 🖼 youtube.com
> Another JavaScript Framework | Ryan Carniato | The ?
> Ryan Carniato is a frontend performance enthusiast
> and Fine-Grained Reactivity super fan. Author of th...

Figure 1-7. *Tweet about Marko and TypeScript*

 Magne @magnemg · Nov 30, 2022   ···
Qwik vs. Marko:

This talk between @steve8708 from @QwikDev and @dylan_piercey from
@MarkoDevTeam explains the differences.

"Marko: the fastest framework you've been sleeping on" youtu.be/7XR5-
qDhqGY via @YouTube

#qwik #marko #nextgen #js #javascript #fullstack #webdev

> 🖼 youtube.com
> Marko: the fastest framework you've been sleeping
> on

Figure 1-8. *Tweet about Marko and Qwik*

Steve (Builder.io) ✔ @Steve8708 · Aug 19, 2022   •••
Added throughput to the benchmark

Wow, @MarkoDevTeam KILLS at SSR

As always, this is very early, send feedback: github.com/builderio/fram…

(index)	name	1%	2.5%	50%	97.5%	99%	Avg	Std Dev	Min	Max
0	'marko'	3651	3651	5547	6107	6107	5485.73	692.71	3650	6107
1	'fresh'	1765	1765	2097	2107	2107	2059.31	100.46	1765	2107
2	'hydrogen'	891	891	1665	1786	1786	1541.46	292.01	891	1786
3	'svelte'	813	813	1255	1286	1286	1193.37	134.82	813	1286
4	'solid'	699	699	1169	1213	1213	1105.41	153.32	699	1213
5	'nuxt2'	367	367	626	681	681	600.28	83.56	367	681
6	'astro'	432	432	601	626	626	583.6	55.01	432	626
7	'remix'	330	330	400	473	473	392.5	40.85	330	473
8	'gatsby'	178	178	228	263	263	226.9	24.36	178	263
9	'next-bun'	171	171	233	242	242	225.9	20.11	171	242
10	'next'	136	136	183	214	214	186.1	22.96	136	214

Figure 1-9. *Tweet about Marko's server rendering performance*

Pier @pierbover · Jan 13, 2022   •••
The most underrated JS framework of all time is definitely Marko.

Most people have never heard of it, and yet it powers Ebay's front end. Has been doing partial hydration and streaming since 2017 IIRC.

@MarkoDevTeam @RyanCarniato

github.com/marko-js/marko

> 🔥 **Fireship** ✔ @fireship_dev · Jan 12, 2022
> What are some underrated open source libraries that deserve more exposure?

Figure 1-10. *Tweet celebrating Marko*

What Will You Accomplish at the End of Every Chapter?

- **Chapter 1—Introduction**: The introduction to Marko JS.

- **Chapter 2—Prerequisites**: Learn about the different application types, rendering paradigms, and their pros and cons. Get introduced to buffers, streams, character sets, character encoding, Server-Sent Events, and the EventSource API. Understand the performance issues associated with client-side renders and single-page applications, the benefits of MPAs and server renders, the cost of hydration for server renders, how server rendering can be improved, and the need for further advanced and efficient server-side rendering techniques for optimizing page load time through progressive HTML rendering.

- **Chapter 3—Introduction to Progressive Rendering**: Imperatively understand the mental model behind progressive rendering and the various techniques through a module called async-writer and a sample application declaratively with Marko.

- **Chapter 4—Introduction to the Marko Language and API Reference**: Learn the basics of Marko in terms of its syntax and usage through examples.

- **Chapter 5—The Marko-Run Meta Framework**: Learn about the Marko-run meta framework in the context of connect and non-connect-style applications.

- **Chapter 6—Marko Ecosystem and Developer Experience**: This chapter walks you through all the essentials needed for a great DevEx and how it works with Marko—TypeScript, ESLint, Storybook, Stylelint, and IDE tooling.

- **Chapter 7—Testing Marko Components and Pages**: This chapter walks you through testing Marko components using the state-of-the-art testing frameworks like Vite and Testing Library.

- **Chapter 8—The Marko RealWorld App**: This chapter offers a sample application using all the knowledge we have learned.

- **Chapter 9—Decoupled MPA Micro Frontends: App Federation via @micro-frame/marko**: Learn the need for decoupled and distributed application design. Learn how decoupled render micro frontends are possible through micro-frames. Accomplish all the learnings via a sample application using these techniques.

- **Chapter 10—App Federation–Based Micro Frontends with Marko**: Build a sample application with Marko utilizing all the aforementioned learning.

- **Chapter 11—Recipes with Marko**: This chapter showcases samples of Marko in various scenarios.

Your First Page Using Marko!

Let's get started with a simple default starter that is offered by Marko JS to get our hands dirty!

The following steps assume you have Node JS and NPM installed on your system. In the terminal or command prompt, type

```
> npx @marko/create
```

This will show a list of options.

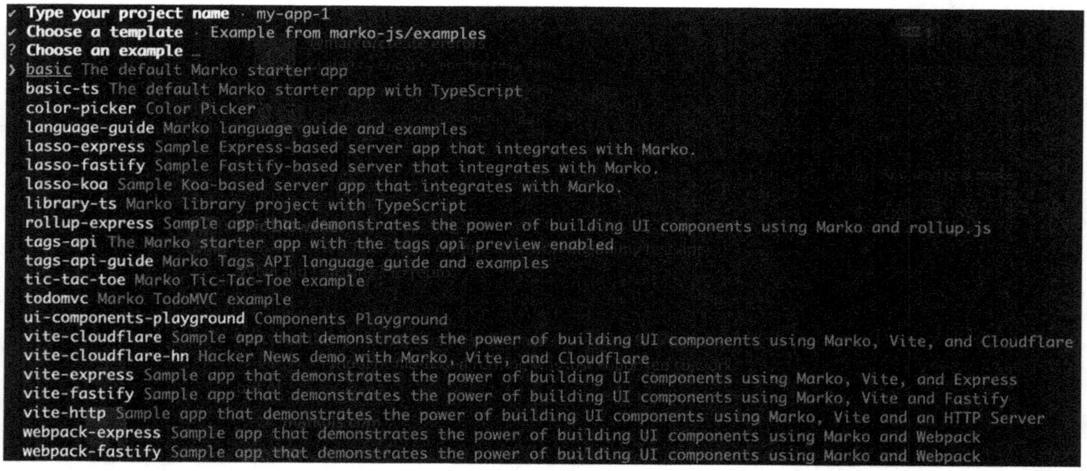

Figure 1-11. *Marko's project scaffolder*

Choose the **basic**. You should next see the associated dependencies getting installed.

```
✓ Type your project name · my-app-1
✓ Choose a template · Example from marko-js/examples
✓ Choose an example · basic
⁞ Installing npm modules... (this may take a minute)
```

Figure 1-12. *Marko's project scaffolder template selection*

And finally, the project is created.

```
✓ Type your project name · my-app-1
✓ Choose a template · Example from marko-js/examples
✓ Choose an example · basic
✓ Project created! To get started, run:

    cd my-app-1
    npm run dev
```

Figure 1-13. *Marko's project scaffolder project creation*

Next, execute the steps in the order mentioned!

```
> cd my-app-1
> npm run dev
```

Figure 1-14. *Marko project creation complete*

Navigate to http://localhost:3000 to view the page now!

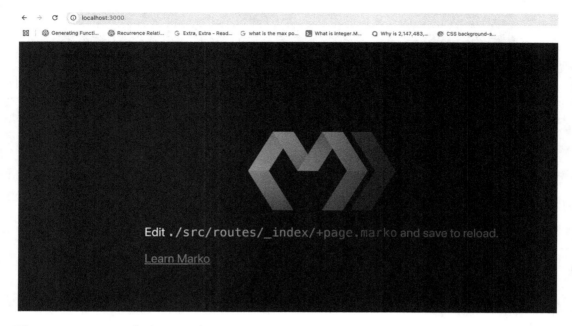

Figure 1-15. *Marko's sample project page*

That's it! You have built your first sample Marko application. We will delve into the specifics of this in the subsequent chapters with more examples, some theory about streaming, progressive rendering, the mental model behind it, the syntax basics of Marko, and finally back to this example.

However, for the sake of curiosity, if you peek into the app folders you will notice that it all starts with the file *+layout.marko*, which includes the *+page.marko* within it. *+page.marko* utilizes the component *mouse-mask.marko*. You will notice that Marko files are named with the extension *.marko*. You will also notice that routing for this application is handled by default, and the file names appear in a peculiar fashion—with a + sign at the start. This is because the basic application uses Marko's new meta framework called Marko-run that utilizes Vite as the bundler for local development and hot module reloads. Marko-run does file directory structure–based routing that requires this naming convention. We will revisit Marko-run in the subsequent chapters.

If you peek into the file *mouse-mask.marko*, you will notice three pieces—a **class {}** block, a **style {}** block, and lastly the HTML itself **<div.mouse-mask>** that represents the behavior (widget), formatting (styling), and the structure (template).

About Multiple Compilation Outputs...

Before heading to the next chapter, it's helpful to understand what Marko means by the term "multiple compilation outputs." For this, under the root folder my-app-1, create a *sample.js* file similar to the code in Figure 1-16.

```
import * as compiler from "@marko/compiler";
compiler.configure({ output: "dom" });

const result = compiler.compileFileSync("./sample.marko", {
  modules: "cjs",
});

console.log(result);
```

Figure 1-16. *Code to show multiple compilation outputs*

This imports Marko's compiler and sets it to output for the browser environment. Next, include a *sample.marko* file with the content in Figure 1-17, colocated to *sample.js*.

```
<div>
    This is a sample Marko template!
</div>
```

Figure 1-17. *Code to show sample Marko template*

Next, run

```
> node sample.js
```

You will see the compiled output logged to the IDE console.

```
{
  ast: null,
  map: null,
  code: '// Compiled using marko@5.36.0 - DO NOT EDIT\n' +
    '"use strict";\n' +
    '\n' +
    'exports.__esModule = true;\n' +
    'exports.default = void 0;\n' +
    'var _index = require("marko/src/runtime/vdom/index.js");\n' +
    'var _renderer = _interopRequireDefault(require("marko/src/runtime/components/renderer.js"));\n' +
    'var _registry = require("marko/src/runtime/components/registry.js");\n' +
    'var _defineComponent = _interopRequireDefault(require("marko/src/runtime/components/defineComponent.js"));\n' +
    'function _interopRequireDefault(e) { return e && e.__esModule ? e : { default: e }; }\n' +
    'const _marko_componentType = "sample.marko",\n' +
    '  _marko_template = (0, _index.t)(_marko_componentType);\n' +
    'var _default = exports.default = _marko_template;\n' +
    '(0, _registry.r)(_marko_componentType, () => _marko_template);\n' +
    'const _marko_component = {};\n' +
    '_marko_template._ = (0, _renderer.default)(function (input, out, _componentDef, _component, state, $global) {\n' +
    '  out.be("div", null, "0", _component, null, 0);\n' +
    '  out.t("This is a sample Marko template!", _component);\n' +
    '  out.ee();\n' +
    '}, {\n' +
    '  t: _marko_componentType,\n' +
    '  i: true,\n' +
    '  d: true\n' +
    '}, _marko_component);\n' +
    '_marko_template.Component = (0, _defineComponent.default)(_marko_component, _marko_template._);',
  meta: {
    id: 'sample.marko',
    deps: [],
    tags: [],
    watchFiles: [],
    diagnostics: [],
    ___marko_component_files___: {
      styleFile: undefined,
      packageFile: undefined,
      componentFile: undefined,
      componentBrowserFile: undefined
    },
    hasComponent: false,
    [Symbol()]: Set(1) { 'div' },
    [Symbol()]: Map(3) {
      'marko/src/runtime/components/renderer.js' => [NodePath],
      'marko/src/runtime/components/registry.js' => [NodePath],
      'marko/src/runtime/components/defineComponent.js' => [NodePath]
    }
  }
}
```

Figure 1-18. *Code indicating compilation in browser VDOM mode*

Notice that this output contains VDOM nodes. Next, modify the compiler options to "**html**" instead of "**dom**". This implies we are instructing the compiler to output code for the server land.

Rerun the same command and check the console now. You will notice a different compilation output consisting of HTML strings rather than VDOM nodes.

```
{
  ast: null,
  map: null,
  code: '// Compiled using marko@5.36.0 - DO NOT EDIT\n' +
    '"use strict";\n' +
    '\n' +
    'exports.__esModule = true;\n' +
    'exports.default = void 0;\n' +
    'var _index = require("marko/src/runtime/html/index.js");\n' +
    'var _renderer = _interopRequireDefault(require("marko/src/runtime/components/renderer.js"));\n' +
    'function _interopRequireDefault(e) { return e && e.__esModule ? e : { default: e }; }\n' +
    'const _marko_componentType = "sample.marko",\n' +
    '  _marko_template = (0, _index.t)(_marko_componentType);\n' +
    'var _default = exports.default = _marko_template;\n' +
    'const _marko_component = {};\n' +
    '_marko_template._ = (0, _renderer.default)(function (input, out, _componentDef, _component, state, $global) {\n' +
    '  out.w("<div>");\n' +
    '  out.w("This is a sample Marko template!");\n' +
    '  out.w("</div>");\n' +
    '}, {\n' +
    '  t: _marko_componentType,\n' +
    '  i: true,\n' +
    '  d: true\n' +
    '}, _marko_component);',
  meta: {
    id: 'sample.marko',
    deps: [],
    tags: [],
    watchFiles: [],
    diagnostics: [],
    __marko_component_files__: {
      styleFile: undefined,
      packageFile: undefined,
      componentFile: undefined,
      componentBrowserFile: undefined
    },
    hasComponent: false,
    [Symbol()]: Set(1) { 'div' },
    [Symbol()]: Map(1) { 'marko/src/runtime/components/renderer.js' => [NodePath] }
  }
}
```

Figure 1-19. *Code indicating compilation on the server for SSR mode*

Upon inspection of both these outputs, you will notice that Marko only includes those specific framework dependencies that it requires, making its runtime modular. Also, notice that you had authored the code only once; however, Marko produced two different outputs that were optimized for the respective environments. Marko is also a great example of the "dependency injection" pattern on the frontend side of things. Some required dependencies and variables are made available in the code for you to access always, magically. It is also a great example of the "inversion of control" implementation, where the framework code calls your code.

About 0KB of JS

Firstly, is this a big deal? Not really for most of your everyday practical use cases, unless of course you are just building static pages. By 0KB JS, we mean that when your application is an MPA and is fully server rendered and if you do not have any interaction on your page, then why send any Javascript at all? Your components are all being rendered on the server and should not ideally contribute to the bundle size.

Marko does this with ease because firstly it produces two compilation outputs, and in the case of the server land, it outputs HTML as strings. Secondly, Marko's compiler is super optimizing in the sense it precisely knows which components are required to be bundled to the client side. The reason for highlighting the 0KB JS is that Marko's compiler is optimizing so much that it removes away the runtime when there is no need for it. An important part of this is when you use third-party libraries, you no longer have to be worried about pulling them to the client side when they are not being used.

Also, server-only components do not carry any state that requires to be serialized (as part of hydration) to the browser to pick up, on the browser, where the server left off. Marko also implements the islands architecture as mentioned earlier.

With the islands architecture, what they imply is that instead of building the app as an application that controls the rendering of an entire page, use multiple entry points for individual interactive points of the page. The JavaScript for these tiny islands of interactivity can be sent to the client side on demand (progressive enhancement) and hydrated independently, thereby letting the rest of the page serve the initial static SSR HTML quicker that requires minimal to no Javascript upon page load.

And this is easier done when your app is envisioned as a multi-page app. Partial hydration also helps achieve this architecture. The difference lies in how the app gets developed/built. With the previous method, you have multiple entry points related to the app or page's interactivity. With partial hydration, your application development experience stays the same. You don't indulge in doing all these manual wirings. Instead, you write the app as you always will and the underlying framework does the magic for you.

You can read more about these here:

```
https://www.patterns.dev/vanilla/islands-architecture/
https://dev.to/this-is-learning/is-0kb-of-javascript-in-your-future-48og
https://jasonformat.com/islands-architecture/
```

We shall look at this via a simple example of a Hacker News demo. This has been done quite a few times by the Marko team, and we shall just showcase it here for you to gain initial insights.

To begin with, we shall scaffold a new application using the scaffolder we previously saw:

```
>> npx @marko/create
```

Provide a name for this new sample marko app. In our demo, we have named it marko-hacker-news. Choose the **basic** template from the list of template options provided by the scaffolder and then wait for it to initialize the app and install the modules. Once that is done

```
>> cd marko-hacker-news
>> npm run dev
```

This should get the app running on http://localhost:3000. Now go to the *src/routes/_index* folder and replace the contents of the +***page.marko*** with the following. The section highlighted in purple is a reusable fragment within a given template called **macro**. The yellow section is a custom Marko component, and the blue section is the core **<await>** tag that can be used to handle any async behavior on the server.

```
src > routes > _index > ≡ +page.marko > ⚎ macro > ⚘ main > ⚘ ui
  1    $ const getStories = $global.getStories;
  2    $ const pageNumber = $global.pageNumber;
  3    $ const storyType = $global.storyType;
  4
  5    <macro|{ storiesList }| name="stories-section">
  6      <main class="stories-list">
  7        <ul>
  8          <for|story| of=storiesList>
  9            <hn-story storyData=story/>
 10          </for>
 11        </ul>
 12      </main>
 13    </macro>
 14
 15    <div class="container">
 16      <div class="stories-list">
 17        <await(getStories) client-reorder>
 18          <@then|storiesList|>
 19            <hn-pagination
 20              pageNumber=pageNumber
 21              storyType=storyType
 22              storiesList=storiesList
 23            />
 24            <stories-section storiesList=storiesList/>
 25          </@then>
 26          <@placeholder>
 27            <div class="loading">
 28              Loading...
 29            </div>
 30          </@placeholder>
 31          <@catch|err|>
 32            $ console.log("err occurred.", err.message);
 33          </@catch>
 34        </await>
 35      </div>
 36    </div>
```

Figure 1-20. *src/routes/_index/+page.marko*

To this, we will add a +**handler.js** file within *src/routes/_index*. This will look for specific URL params in the incoming request. You can think of this as a Controller/ Servlet. The folder is structured in a certain way, and the files are named in a certain way too, per the naming convention of Marko's meta-framework called marko-run. We will look into all those in detail later. For now, you can think of this as the scaffolder having produced a basic marko-run template, and we are filling in some code to illustrate the 0KB phenomenon.

```
src > routes > _index > JS +handler.js > ...
1     import { getSpecificStories } from "../../services";
2
3     export async function GET(context, next) {
4         const { searchParams } = context.url;
5         const storyType = searchParams.get("storyType") || "top";
6         const pageNumber = parseInt(searchParams.get("pageNumber"), 10) || 1;
7         context.getStories = getSpecificStories(storyType, pageNumber);
8         context.pageNumber = pageNumber;
9         context.storyType = storyType;
10        return next();
11    }
```

Figure 1-21. *src/routes/_index/+handler.js*

Let's include some styles specific to this page through a **+page.style.css** under *src/routes/_index*.

```
src > routes > _index > # +page.style.css > ⌗ .next
1
2     .container .stories-pagination, .stories-list  .loading {
3       min-height: 50px;
4       font-size: 20px;
5       margin: 0 auto;
6       justify-content: center;
7       display: flex;
8       align-items: center;
9     }
10    .prev {
11      margin-right: 15px;
12    }
13    .next {
14      margin-left: 15px;
15    }
```

Figure 1-22. *src/routes/_index/+page.style.css*

Next, let's update the *src/routes/+layout.marko*. The **<${input.renderBody}/>** is used to transclude the contents of the previous *src/routes/_index/+page.marko* into this template. This is automatically done by Marko. It helps to segregate page-specific main contents and focus on building page-generic layouts in a separate template and have them composed together.

```marko
src > routes > ☰ +layout.marko > 🔧 html > 🔧 body
 1   <!doctype html>
 2   <html lang="en">
 3     <head>
 4       <meta charset="UTF-8">
 5       <meta name="viewport" content="width=device-width, initial-scale=1.0">
 6       <meta name="description" content="Marko Hackernews">
 7       <title>Marko JS - Hacker News Sample</title>
 8     </head>
 9     <body>
10       <header>
11         <nav>
12           <a href="/"><b>Hacker News</b></a>
13           <a href="/?storyType=new"><b>New</b></a>
14           <a href="/?storyType=show"><b>Show</b></a>
15           <a href="/?storyType=ask"><b>Ask</b></a>
16           <a href="/?storyType=job"><b>Jobs</b></a>
17           <a.github
18             href="http://github.com/marko-js/marko"
19             target="_blank"
20           >
21             Built with Marko &hearts;
22           </a>
23         </nav>
24       </header>
25       <${input.renderBody}/>
26     </body>
27   </html>
```

Figure 1-23. src/routes/+layout.marko

Next, we shall include a *src/routes/+layout.style.css* file to include styles that are common to all pages. Overall, there will be three pages—the generic stories with all the related news, then a page to view the individual story, and finally the user page to view the user.

After this, let's also look at the component **<hn-pagination/>** and **<hn-story/>** that was used within *src/routes/_index/+page.marko* and their associated component styles (if any) in the following figures.

```
src > routes > # +layout.style.css > ⅀ header nav a
 1    body {
 2        font-family: "Arial", sans-serif;
 3        font-size: 15px;
 4        background-color: ■#f2f3f5;
 5        margin: 0;
 6        color: □#34495e;
 7        overflow-y: scroll;
 8    }
 9    a {
10        color: □#34495e;
11        text-decoration: underline;
12    }
13    ul {
14        margin: 0;
15        padding: 0;
16    }
17    li {
18        list-style: none;
19    }
20
21    header {
22        background-color: ■#ff6602;
23        min-height: 50px;
24    }
25    header nav {
26        max-width: 800px;
27        margin: 0 auto;
28        padding: 20px 0;
29        display: flex;
30        justify-content: space-around;
31    }
32    header nav a {
33        display: inline-block;
34        vertical-align: middle;
35        font-weight: 800;
36        color: ■#FFF;
37        font-size: 20px;
38    }
39    .container {
40        font-size: 18px;
41    }
```

Figure 1-24. *src/routes/+layout.style.css*

29

For context, marko in this setup with its meta framework marko-run automatically picks up these files when running the dev server on Vite and also when running production builds. Marko is all for componentization and supports single-file, split-file, and multi-file components, as we will see in the examples that come along and also in detail in Chapter 4, where you will be introduced to the Marko language and syntax.

Next lets look at src/components/hn-pagination/index.marko.

```
src > components > hn-pagination > ≡ index.marko > ⚘ div > ⅗ <${...}>
1    $ const { pageNumber, storyType, storiesList } = input;
2
3    <div class="stories-pagination">
4        $ const prevHref = (
5            pageNumber > 1
6                ? `?${new URLSearchParams({
7                    storyType,
8                    pageNumber: pageNumber - 1,
9                })}`
10               : undefined
11       );
12       <${pageNumber > 1 ? "a" : "span"} class="prev" href=prevHref>
13           < Prev
14       </>
15
16       <span class="current">
17           {${pageNumber}}
18       </span>
19       $ const nextHref = (
20           storiesList.length >= 28
21               ? `?${new URLSearchParams({
22                   storyType,
23                   pageNumber: pageNumber + 1,
24               })}`
25               : undefined
26       );
27       <${storiesList.length >= 28 ? "a" : "span"} class="next" href=nextHref>
28           Next >
29       </>
30   </div>
```

Figure 1-25. *src/components/hn-pagination/index.marko*

```
src > components > hn-story > # style.css > ⟨⟩ .title
 1    li.story {
 2        padding: 15px;
 3        border-bottom: 1px solid ■#eee;
 4        background: ■#FFF;
 5        line-height: 25px;
 6        display: flex;
 7    }
 8    li.story .points {
 9        color: ■#f60;
10        font-weight: bold;
11        font-size: 20px;
12        min-width: 100px;
13        display: flex;
14        justify-content: center;
15        align-items: center;
16    }
17    .title .host {
18        margin-left: 10px;
19        font-size: 18px;
20    }
21    .title {
22        font-size: 20px;
23        color: □#34495e;
24    }
25    .title a {
26        text-decoration: none !important;
27        color: □#34495e;
28    }
29    .meta-inf, .meta-inf a {
30        color: ■#828282;
31        font-size: 17px;
32    }
```

Figure 1-26. *src/components/hn-story/style.css*

```
src > components > hn-story > ☰ index.marko > 🔧 li > 🔧 div > 🔧 span > 🔀 if > 🔧 a
  1    $ const { storyData } = input;
  2
  3    <li class="story">
  4      <div class="points">
  5        <span>${storyData.points}  </span>
  6      </div>
  7      <div class="">
  8        <span class="title">
  9          <if(storyData.url)>
 10            <a href=storyData.url target="_blank">
 11              ${storyData.title}
 12            </a>
 13            <span class="host">
 14              (${storyData.domain})
 15            </span>
 16          </if>
 17          <else>${storyData.title}</else>
 18        </span>
 19        <br>
 20        <span class="meta-inf">
 21          <if(storyData.type !== "job")>
 22            by
 23            <a href=`/users/${storyData.user}`>
 24              ${storyData.user}
 25            </a>
 26            ${` ${storyData.time_ago} | `}
 27            <a href=`/stories/${storyData.id}`>
 28              ${storyData.comments_count
 29                ? `${storyData.comments_count} comments`
 30                : "discuss"}
 31            </a>
 32          </if>
 33          <else>
 34            <a href=`/stories/${storyData.id}`>
 35              ${storyData.time_ago}
 36            </a>
 37          </else>
 38        </span>
 39      </div>
 40
 41      <if(storyData.type !== "link")>
 42        <span class="label">
 43          ${storyData.type}
 44        </span>
 45      </if>
 46    </li>
```

Figure 1-27. *src/components/hn-story/index.marko*

Next, we will include the services file, which invokes the call to the Hacker News API via ***undici***. This will be placed in *src/services/index.js*.

```
src > services > JS index.js > ...
  1    import { fetch } from 'undici'
  2
  3    const storyTypes = {
  4      top: "news",
  5      new: "newest",
  6      show: "show",
  7      ask: "ask",
  8      job: "jobs",
  9    };
 10
 11    export function getSpecificStory(storyId) {
 12      return getData(`https://node-hnapi.herokuapp.com/item/${storyId}`)
 13    }
 14    export function getSpecificUser(userId) {
 15      return getData(`https://hacker-news.firebaseio.com/v0/user/${userId}.json`);
 16    }
 17    export function getSpecificStories(type, page) {
 18      const storyType = storyTypes[type];
 19      const result = getData(`https://node-hnapi.herokuapp.com/${storyType}?page=${page}`);;
 20      return result;
 21    }
 22
 23    async function getData(url) {
 24      const res = await fetch(url, {
 25        headers: { "User-Agent": "chrome" },
 26      });
 27      return res.json();
 28    }
```

Figure 1-28. *src/services/index.js*

Now, run

```
>> npm run build
>> npm run preview
```

With the above command, we have instructed Marko-run to work with Vite (the bundler) under the hood to generate a production build for the application. This will cause it to output the generated assets (CSS, Javascript) into a **dist**/ folder.

Then, the next command instructs it to spin up a preview server to preview the app in production mode. Open the page at http://localhost:3000/, and you will see the initial Hacker News page with all the stories.

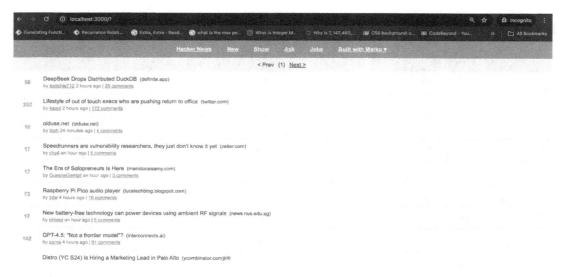

Figure 1-29. *Hacker News stories landing home page*

Now for the best part: Open the sources tab to check for Javascript in this—0KB of JS. This is actually the right thing to do because we absolutely have no interactivity and have server-rendered the page. When there is no interactivity, Marko does not need to send its runtime and any data for initialization. Marko understands that no part of the server data is now required to be hydrated on the client side, because there are no re-renders involved.

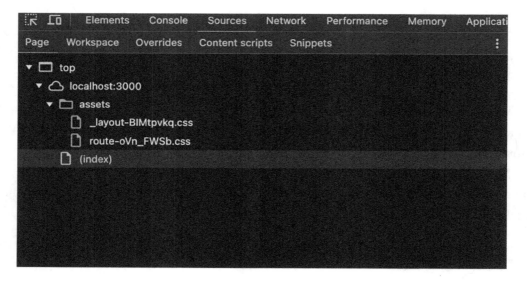

Figure 1-30. *Hacker News page sources*

Let's next proceed to create the user page and the individual story page. We will have two separate pages for them under the **src/routes** folder named *src/routes/stories.$storyId* and *src/routes/users.$userId*. This basically means *src/routes/stories/$storyId* and *src/routes/users/$userId*. This is the meta framework naming convention, which we will get to later. Place the handler files as shown in Figure 1-31.

```
src > routes > stories.$storyId > JS +handler.js > ...
1      import { getSpecificStory } from "../../services";
2
3      export function GET(context, next) {
4          context.getStory = getSpecificStory(context.params.storyId)
5      }
6
```

Figure 1-31. *src/routes/stories.$storyId/+handler.js*

```
src > routes > users.$userId > JS +handler.js > ...
1      import { getSpecificUser } from "../../services";
2
3      export function GET(context, next) {
4          context.getUser = getSpecificUser(context.params.userId)
5      }
```

Figure 1-32. *src/routes/users.$userId/+handler.js*

Next, under *src/routes/users.$userId*, place the ***+page.style.css*** file.

```
src > routes > users.$userId > # +page.style.css > ⅊ .user-about
 1    .user-info {
 2        background:  ■#FFF;
 3        padding: 25px 25px 25px 55px;
 4    }
 5    .user-meta {
 6        font-size: 20px;
 7    }
 8    .user-links {
 9        font-size: 18px;
10    }
11    .user-about {
12        margin-top: 20px;
13    }
```

Figure 1-33. *src/routes/users.$userId/+page.style.css*

Next, under *src/routes/users.$userId*, place the +page.marko file.

src > routes > users.$userId > ☰ +page.marko > 🖉 div > ⅋ await

```marko
1      $ const getUser = $global.getUser;
2
3      <div class="user-info">
4          <await(getUser)>
5              <@then|user|>
6                  <h1>User: ${user.id}</h1>
7                  <ul class="user-meta">
8                      <li>
9                          <span class="user-sku">
10                             Created:
11                         </span>
12                         ${user.created}
13                     </li>
14                     <li>
15                         <span class="user-sku">
16                             Karma:
17                         </span>
18                         ${user.karma}
19                     </li>
20                     <if(user.about)>
21                         <li class="user-about">
22                             $!{user.about}
23                         </li>
24                     </if>
25                 </ul>
26                 <p class="user-links">
27                     <a href=`https://news.ycombinator.com/submitted?id=${user.id}`>
28                         submissions
29                     </a>
30
31                     <a href=`https://news.ycombinator.com/threads?id=${user.id}`>
32                         comments
33                     </a>
34                 </p>
35             </@then>
36         </await>
37     </div>
```

Figure 1-34. *src/routes/users.$userId/+page.marko*

Next, under *src/routes/stories.$storyId*, place the **+page.style.css** file.

```
src > routes > stories.$storyId > # +page.style.css > ᗶ .stories-story__con
 1    .stories-story__header {
 2        background: ■#FFF;
 3        padding: 20px 20px 20px 30px;
 4        box-shadow: 1px 2px □#0000001a
 5    }
 6    .stories-story__header p {
 7        font-size: 18px;
 8    }
 9    .stories-story__comments {
10        padding: 20px 20px 20px 30px;
11        background: ■#FFF;
12        margin-top: 20px;
13    }
14    .stories-story__comments-header {
15        font-size: 20px;
16    }
17    .stories-story__comment-children {
18        font-size: 18px;
19    }
```

Figure 1-35. *src/routes/stories.$storyId/+page.style.css*

Next, under *src/routes/stories.$storyId*, place the +page.marko file.

src > routes > stories.$storyId > ☰ +page.marko > 🔧 div > 🔗 await > 🔗 h

```marko
1     $ const getStory = $global.getStory;
2
3     <div class="stories-story">
4         <await(getStory)>
5             <@then|story|>
6                 <div class="stories-story__header">
7                     <h1>
8                         <a href=story.url target="_blank">
9                             ${story.title}
10                        </a>
11                    </h1>
12                    <p class="meta">
13                        ${story.points} points | by
14                        <a href=`/users/${story.user}`>
15                            ${story.user}
16                        </a>
17                        ${` ${story.time_ago}`}
18                    </p>
19                </div>
20                <div class="stories-story__comments">
21                    <p class="stories-story__comments-header">
22                        ${story.comments_count
23                            ? `${story.comments_count} comments`
24                            : "No comments yet."}
25                    </p>
26                    <ul class="stories-story__comment-children">
27                        <for|comment| of=story.comments>
28                            <hn-comments commentData=comment/>
29                        </for>
30                    </ul>
31                </div>
32            </@then>
33            <@catch|e|>
34                Err occurred! ${e.message}
35            </@catch>
36        </await>
37    </div>
38
```

Figure 1-36. *src/routes/stories.$storyId/+page.marko*

There are two components that we need to add for the two **+*page.marko*** files that we have included. These are custom marko components, and we will place project-specific components under the src/components folder. This is the same as how we placed the **<hn-pagination>** and **<hn-story>** components previously.

First, let's look at *src/components/hn-comments/index.marko*.

```
src > components > hn-comments >  ☰ index.marko > ...
  1      $ const { commentData } = input;
  2
  3      <li class="comments__comment">
  4        <div class="by">
  5          <a href=`/users/${commentData.user}`>
  6            ${commentData.user}
  7          </a>
  8          ${` ${commentData.time_ago}`}
  9        </div>
 10        <div class="text">
 11          $!{commentData.content}
 12        </div>
 13        <if(commentData.comments.length)>
 14          <hn-toggle-comment>
 15            <for|nested| of=commentData.comments>
 16              <hn-comments commentData=nested/>
 17            </for>
 18          </hn-toggle-comment>
 19        </if>
 20        </li>
```

Figure 1-37. *src/components/hn-comments/index.marko*

Notice how **<hn-comments>** gets recursively invoked within itself.

Next lets look at src/components/hn-comments/style.css

```
src > components > hn-comments > # style.css > ✂ li.commen
1    li.comments__comment {
2        border: 1px solid ■#eee;
3        padding: 10px;
4    }
```

Figure 1-38. *src/components/hn-comments/style.css*

Next, let's look at *src/components/hn-toggle-comment/index.marko*.

```
src > components > hn-toggle-comment > ☰ index.marko > …
1    class {
2      onCreate() {
3        this.state = { expanded: true };
4      }
5      toggle() {
6        this.state.expanded = !this.state.expanded;
7      }
8    }
9
10   <div class=[
11     "toggle-comments",
12     {
13       expanded: state.expanded,
14     },
15   ]>
16     <a on-click('toggle')>
17       ${state.expanded ? "[-]" : "[+]"}
18     </a>
19   </div>
20   <ul class="comment-children" style={ display: state.expanded ? "auto" : "none" }>
21     <${input.renderBody}/>
22   </ul>
```

Figure 1-39. *src/components/hn-toggle-comment/index.marko*

Now run the production build and start the preview server again. Click any username or the comments, and it will take you to the respective pages. Even the user page has no interaction, and absolutely no JS asset is loaded. However, in the comments page, we have an expand-collapse component, which has state and interactivity, and this is where Marko loads some Javascript for the first time.

41

User: mritchie712

Created:1426517825
Karma:2283

Founder at Definite (https://www.definite.app/).

Definite is ETL, a data warehouse and BI in one app.

Previously founded SeekWell (https://seekwell.io/), acquired in 2021.

twitter: https://twitter.com/thisritchie

email: mike@definite.app

meet.hn/city/us-Philadelphia

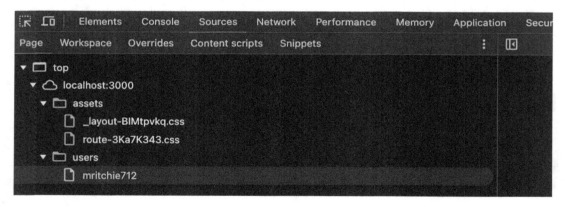

Figure 1-40. *The user page*

The individual story page, which loads the comments, has the expand-collapse interaction, and you will notice that now the assets folder includes JS assets as well, which brings in the Marko runtime, gzipped at 13KB (pretty tiny in comparison to many other frameworks), and the component-specific JS and template.

DeepSeek releases distributed DuckDB

114 points | by mritchie712 2 hours ago

37 comments

memco an hour ago

Love this straightforward analysis of use cases:

> Using smallpond and 3FS depends largely on your data size and infras

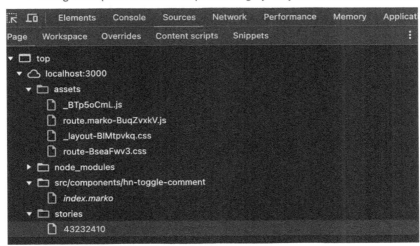

Figure 1-41. *The individual story page*

The view seen in Figure 1-41 is the one you get with source maps turned on for better debugging. The *node_modules* folder is mimicked based on the source maps. Do not be alarmed!

The overall folder structure is shown in Figure 1-42.

Conclusion

In the subsequent chapters, we will look at more aspects of this amazing framework!

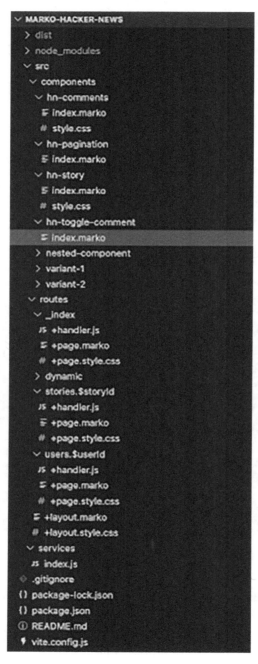

Figure 1-42. *Marko Hacker News project layout*

CHAPTER 2

Prerequisites

Introduction

In this chapter, we will look at some of the prerequisite concepts that will help to better understand and appreciate this journey on Marko in the server land via Node JS. As part of this, various rendering techniques, application types, hydration, and resumability will be touched upon. Moreover, a few other background concepts such as Buffers, Streams, Server-Sent Events, and the EventSource API will be explored.

Different Application Types

At a high level, application types can be categorized as follows.

Single-Page Apps (SPAs)

In this, the initial render happens on the server, where the server responds with a shell of HTML that contains the minimal HTML resources—scripts, styles, etc.—where the entire app lives. The main content of the page is however not rendered yet. This is the traditional single-page application with full client-side rendering (CSR), where you would initially notice a blank screen with a loading indicator, such as a spinner.

The browser proceeds to download the scripts (provided from the server as part of the shell HTML), followed by parsing and execution of the script. The same is done for the styles. As the script is executed, it makes further API or service calls to fetch the data that is required for the HTML render. Once the data is fetched, the app renders the main content HTML on the client browser, followed by wiring up the event listeners and triggering the mount of the app, which implies the page is now ready.

© Damodaran Chingleput Sathyakumar 2025
D. Chingleput Sathyakumar, *Practical Marko*, https://doi.org/10.1007/979-8-8688-1483-9_2

Subsequent interactions on the page will trigger further service calls that may either refresh the existing view with new data or fully replace the existing view, for example, refreshing the shopping cart when a new item is added to it vs. navigating to an entirely new view, such as from the search results to the profile page. *However, all of these view updates happen without reloading the entire page* while also updating the browser's history object. Therefore, when you navigate back in the browser, the app is able to take you to the previous state (since the URL is now within the history).

To avoid the initial blank screen with the loading indicator, this application model then proceeded to improve it in a few ways:

1. Couple CSR with some minimal render on the server (at runtime). For example, render the header and footer.

2. Depending on the use case, statically generate the pages (known as static site generation) via pre-rendering through a build step.

3. Fully server-render the initial view, thereby making it a hybrid app.

For example, if you initially land on a search results page (*/results* on the URL), notice a pagination component, and click page 2, the app utilizes a client-side router solution to update the URL and the history object. This means you may see the URL getting updated to */results?page=2*, *without a page load*, via the *history* API. The results for page 2 are fetched and painted. Given that the URL is updated, they can now be bookmarked and shared.

So, if someone else loaded the page with the URL ending with */results?page=2*, they are expected to see page 2 of the search results. Depending on the technique of render used above, one may entirely server-render page 2 or perform the initial basic server rendering of the shell page and load page 2's contents on the client side.

The components involved in this application are

1. A client-side router and a server router

2. A global state management solution on the client side

3. A data fetcher component

4. A view framework that is able to maintain local state, sync with the global state, handle user interactions, and re-render the associated view in response to a state change while also working well with the first three components.

And, the important part is that there is no hydration involved when fully rendering on the client. For the most part, the browser performs the heavy lifting. However, this may vary with hybrid rendering or hybrid apps.

The benefits of SPAs include faster load times - TTFB (Time to First Byte). Depending on the improvised type of render, FCP (First Content Paint) may be immediate or delayed. TTI (Time to Interact) is however still an issue.

Multi-page Apps (MPAs)

In contrast to the SPAs, from an architectural standpoint, MPAs are those apps that require a full page reload for any navigation. This implies more roundtrips to the server with every page being a fresh render on the server. With MPAs, the general setup involves a more enriched server-side routing solution, followed by most of the data fetching that happens on the server side. On the client side, besides interactivity, there will be minimal data fetches to refresh or update portions of the page. Such a solution doesn't usually require an elaborate global state management solution or a client-side routing solution because there is usually not much happening in terms of updating the browser history to maintain backward navigation and so on. However, some applications start as MPAs but, on specific pages, contain a lot more navigation within them and build those sub-navigations as SPAs. We will next look at this.

The usual talk for MPAs is that they are slow because of full render happening on the server and also because of full page reloads. When using frameworks not optimized for this, they delay the TTFB.

Hybrid Apps

These are a combination of MPAs and SPAs. For example, for a large-scale ecommerce website such as eBay, all its top-level navigations, such as the home page, item page, search page, product page, and checkout page, are individually server-rendered pages. This means as you navigate between these pages, they all require a full page load. However, within the context of one of these pages, such as a seller metrics page, internal navigations within that page may be built as a SPA, with its various views grouped into different shell pages that operate as a SPA. With hybrid applications, in the SPA context, it is worth noting that such newer views may be entirely rendered on the server with the DOM being updated by raw HTML itself, rather than just fetching data to render on the client. This is partly because of a larger server presence. Hybrid apps have a strong server- and client-side routing system, and depending upon the complexity of the sub-navigations, they may or may not choose to use a global state management and data fetcher solution.

Hybrid apps require careful selection of the view framework, just as MPAs. They need to be optimized for server rendering and for re-render on the client. Marko is a framework that makes achieving this simple.

History Behind the Application Types

In the olden times, applications used to be traditionally fully server rendered—via Rails, JSPs, PHP, Python, and so on. They had minimal interactivity in the form of solutions like jQuery. However, this caused code duplication in different languages—Javascript for the client and the respective server language to sync the application state.

To avoid code duplication, SPAs became the hot favorite where the majority of the code was moved from the server land to execute on the browser, and Javascript became the de facto language of choice. This was also the time when Node JS was gaining traction, and frameworks began realizing its potential for isomorphic rendering—rendering on the client and server with the same code written in Javascript.

Moreover, when issues such as the blank screen during initial load, the lack of HTML for SEO optimizations, harder debugging, poor scalability, etc., came up, practitioners realized the mistake and began advocating for moving code back from the client side to the server land, transforming application architectures from traditional SPAs to MPAs and hybrid applications. However, this time, with the usage of Node JS as the backend for the frontend, code duplication was no longer an issue as apps could still do isomorphic rendering.

In practice, high-performance applications are MPAs that tend to be hybrid applications. This is because it helps with scaling individual apps as pages, failure isolation, decoupled code releases and release cycles, maintainability, and much more.

Different Rendering Techniques

In this section, the history of rendering on the web and the different rendering paradigms will be revisited. The aforementioned application types utilize one of the following render techniques.

Traditional Server-Side Render (SSR)

In traditional server render, the server responds to incoming HTTP requests with server-rendered HTML. The render technology used on the server could be anything (PHP, Rails, and so on). Ultimately, it responds with HTML as a string. On the client side, scripts are downloaded by the browser that adds minimal interactivity. This is how the olden days were. With the advent of AJAX, minimal page refreshes were done, with the thin JS client used for wiring up interactivity and managing minimal state, while subsequent HTTP requests still reached the server where majority of the render happened. This was the time when frameworks like jQuery and various MV* frameworks like Knockout and Ember gained popularity.

Client-Side Rendering (CSR)

Soon, as apps became more interactive with the usage of more state, the problem of code duplication on the server and client began surfacing. With the server-render technology being different, client-side rendering with Javascript gained prominence. All of the render and the associated view logic were pushed to the client-side Javascript world. Javascript on the client browser was where the heavy lifting was being done.

This was the time when frameworks like React and Angular began gaining serious prominence. In CSR, the HTML delivered by the server in response to an incoming HTTP request is very basic, consisting of styles and script tags and some very basic HTML (as we saw earlier). Once the HTML arrived, the browser proceeded to download the scripts, execute the code to trigger data fetch, and then finally render the application view fully on the client browser. This was also the time when Node JS was gaining mainstream adoption.

Progressively over time, other frameworks like Ivy, Hyperapp, Vue, Riot, Inferno, Svelte, Solid, Glimmer, Preact, Mithril, newer versions of Angular, and React joined this space. They competed heavily over syntax, routers, features, APIs, community, ease of use, performance, benchmarks, bundle sizes, bundler support, associated plugins, state management solutions, community support, etc. This was also the time when terms like Virtual DOM (React, Vue), memoized DOM (Lmba), and incremental DOM (Angular) became popular.

Static Site Generation (SSG) or Pre-rendering or Static SSR

Traditional client-side rendering had many issues as outlined earlier in the SPA section. The important piece was the heavy lifting on the client. Moreover, depending upon the device and its memory, apps were sluggish and slow, despite having an initial fast response time. They were not good for SEO and state management, and debugging was hard. To overcome this, tricks like pre-rendering were used.

Static site generation is a form of pre-rendering which works for predominantly static pages. The HTML was generated as part of a build step, deployed or hosted. With solutions using Node JS gaining prominence, this was easy. This allowed for pages to be instantly served to the users when requested, resulting in faster load times and improved user experience. This was beneficial for SEO as well, as the HTML being available was something that the search engines could crawl. However, this wasn't great for dynamic content.

To solve for dynamic content, these frameworks allowed for the rendering to happen on the server land of Node JS. However, they were not really made for server-side rendering as most of these frameworks used solutions like Virtual Dom nodes. But server-side HTML had to be emitted in the form of strings that required one extra pass.

While SSG and pre-rendering were used to augment CSR solutions to improve the user's perceived load time by having some parts of the HTML painted on the screen, dynamic SSR solutions (for real-time requests that generated dynamic content) were slow, given that these frameworks were not optimized for the same.

Server-Side Render with Hydration

While SSG and pre-rendering helped augment CSR and alleviate some of its pain points to a certain extent, server-side rendering was the answer to solving for dynamic content. However, this delayed the page loads as the server render process was slow, causing slower numbers on TTFB. Still, many felt this was better than the blank screen with the loading indicator and was also good for SEO.

With this approach, the server fetched all the data on the server land, performed the render of the entire view on the server, and responded with HTML just as the traditional server-side rendering approach. However, in order to pick up on the client exactly where the app left off on the server, the app state was serialized to the browser. On the browser, the DOM tree was rebuilt with this app state, and the original view rendered on the server was swapped for the new view rendered on the client side. Basically, the framework replayed the app (re-rendered) on the client side.

This was the problem with the server-side render and hydration—the framework replayed the app. This caused slow numbers on the TTI as illustrated by Paul Lewis with his uncanny valley representation (`https://aerotwist.com/blog/when-everything-is-important-nothing-is/`). Solutions such as progressive hydration and partial hydration helped alleviate this to a large extent. This was further improved by frameworks like Marko v5, which reconciled with the server-rendered HTML rather than fully tossing it away like some other frameworks. However, it was not something that could be fully eliminated.

But Marko at this point was perhaps one of the first frontend frameworks that already had a compiler and was able to perform smart optimizations, while other frameworks still had not figured out the server part of the render equation. Marko with its compiler was able to produce optimized output for both server and client while also solving the TTFB problem in server-side rendering with HTML streaming and progressive rendering.

Reactivity and Resumability

While frameworks were attempting to solve their shortcomings regarding server-side rendering performance, other frameworks on the client side made major strides. First was Svelte that dropped the Virtual DOM solution approach, showing it to be an overhead. Next was SolidJS that took a completely different approach and supercharged client-side performance with the introduction of a fine-grained reactive render model via Signals. This meant that state updates were no longer tied to entire components doing a top-down re-render. Instead, state data were atomic signal values that were tied to the respective DOM nodes, causing only the specific DOM nodes to be updated. This model helped unlock serious performance gains on the client side.

However, for server-side rendering, time spent on hydration was still an issue. This is where the Qwik framework introduced the concept of resumability (O(1) framework). With resumability (as discussed in the introduction), the framework no longer replays the app on the client side by reconstructing the DOM representation from the serialized app state. Instead, knowledge of the app state, framework state, listener information, and much more was embedded into the HTML itself, enabling the app to instantly bootstrap and become interactive on the client side.

So with resumable frameworks, the initial code sent to the browser is considered to be constant, irrespective of the size of the app. This reduces the amount of code run for bootstrap. Following this, as and when the user interacts, code for the different sections of the page is downloaded and run. Therefore, the app progressively boots. This is based on the principle that the user is not going to interact with every feature on the page.

Marko 6 will have reactivity and resumability, with still great server-side performance of streaming HTML and progressive rendering. You will get this upgrade for free with Marko's migration tools.

Issues with CSR

In summary, while CSR offers benefits like flexibility, improved UX (no full page reloads), faster initial load time, and reduced server load, it also introduces challenges related to performance, development complexity, and operational management. Good TTFB, not so great TTI and FCP. More are listed below.

Performance Considerations

1. **Initial Load Time**

   a. **JavaScript Download and Execution**: The browser needs to download and execute JavaScript files before rendering the page content. This can lead to longer initial load times compared to server-side rendering (SSR), especially on slower networks or devices.

   b. **Rendering Delay**: Since the content is rendered on the client side, users may experience a delay before seeing any content, often referred to as a "white screen" effect.

2. **Time to Interactive (TTI)**: CSR can delay the time it takes for a page to become interactive because the browser has to parse and execute JavaScript before the user can interact with the page.

3. **Caching:** While static assets like images and stylesheets can be cached, dynamic HTML content generated by JavaScript might not benefit as much from traditional caching strategies, potentially leading to more frequent data fetching.

4. **SEO Challenges**: Search engines may have difficulty indexing content that is rendered on the client side, although this has improved with advancements in search engine technology. Still, CSR can be less SEO-friendly than SSR if not handled properly.

5. **Resource Usage**: CSR can be resource-intensive, as it offloads the rendering process to the client device. This is an issue for users on devices with limited processing power or memory, rendering the app slow and sluggish.

Operational Challenges

1. **Complexity in Development**: CSR often requires a more complex development setup, including client-side routers, server-side routers, client-side global state management, a data fetching solution, and a view framework with its own plugins for all the aforementioned tasks, which can increase the development and maintenance overhead.

2. **State Management**: Managing application state on the client side can become complex, especially in large applications. This often necessitates the use of state management libraries like Redux, Vuex, MobX, and Recoil.

3. **Debugging and Testing**: Debugging CSR applications can be more challenging due to the asynchronous nature of JavaScript and the complexity of the client-side code and its associated tooling.

4. **SEO and Social Sharing**: CSR can complicate SEO efforts due to the lack of HTML for the main content initially. Additionally, ensuring that social media platforms can generate previews from dynamically rendered content requires additional configuration, such as using server-side rendering for certain routes or pre-rendering.

5. **Security Concerns**: With more logic and data processing
    occurring on the client side, CSR can expose more attack vectors
    for client-side vulnerabilities, such as XSS (Cross-Site Scripting).

However, the bigger problem with CSR was that the client side did the heavy lifting, while the server did little to no work. The issue with both render modes—CSR and SSR—was that one of the sides did most of the heavy lifting. With SSR, it was the server.

Benefits of Server-Side Rendering

Having seen the benefits and concerns for CSR and the slow pushback to the server, server-side rendering presents us with a number of benefits in terms of better FCP metrics, great TTFB metrics (when using a framework like Marko JS), improved SEO performance, better performance on low-powered devices, and improved accessibility. The other usual cons stated are not so great TTI numbers (due to hydration) and increased server load. SSR does have its other cons—developers need to know what code can run on the server only vs. code that can run in both environments. Besides deciding on the above, developers must also decide on.

But, What Do We Really Need?

The issue with both render modes—CSR and SSR—was that one of the sides did most of the heavy lifting. With SSR, it was the server, and with CSR it was the browser. With hybrid apps, these techniques get used in an equal measure. However, the golden rule here is to ensure that while the server is doing work to fetch the data and build the HTML, the browser isn't staying idle, but is processing the HTML rendered from the previous chunk. By processing, we mean downloading the resources, parsing the script code, and executing them. This is possible through HTML streaming. This ensures that both the server and client are doing work simultaneously.

What Is Hydration?

Hydration is the process of bootstrapping or initializing the app on the client side by adding interactivity to server-rendered HTML. This also means that it has to resupply the associated data that was used by the components while rendering on the server so that they are available for reuse on the client side, for purposes of re-rendering, when the state data associated with a component changes in response to some user interaction.

As part of this process, the framework is required to dehydrate the data (serialize) that was used for the server render (extracting out the data associated with every component, deep within the component tree hierarchy, with references of the respective data parts, to the respective components mapped out) and then, on the client side, resupply (rehydrate) the data back to those components on the client. The cost associated with this is CPU cycles spent in processing the data such that only one copy is serialized, with references to it for the respective deep subcomponents being maintained. This also means no circular data references or duplication of data.

Originally, to avoid the white doom screen that occurred in fully client-rendered applications, frameworks resorted to pre-rendering or server-rendering the HTML (to paint the view quickly so as to improve perceived load time). However, as part of this bootstrap, they would re-render the whole app on the client side, essentially throwing away the HTML that was originally generated on the server.

However, as frameworks got smarter, they chose to reconcile with the server-rendered HTML rather than do a full render. This process, now referred to as hydration, was progressively made smarter by various popular frameworks on the market today. This process results in the uncanny valley popularized by Paul Lewis (`https://aerotwist.com/blog/when-everything-is-important-nothing-is/`) where the app is not interactive yet, even though the server-rendered view has been painted on the screen. The smaller this uncanny valley is, which is the time taken for the app to become interactive, the quicker is the interaction time for the application.

Frameworks today tackle this bootstrap or initialization process in one of the four ways: traditional hydration, partial hydration, progressive hydration, and resumability. While the first three are said to be what replayable frameworks do, the latter is about what resumable frameworks do.

Talking about the different techniques of hydration, *traditional or full hydration* involves serializing all of the app state—nothing smart about this. *Progressive hydration* is mostly about the *timing—when* does the framework hydrate? This is usually tied to either during the app's idle state or as components come into the viewport or upon user interactivity. This means the app is bootstrapped progressively over time—instead of downloading all of the data required for the app in one go, they are downloaded in chunks and processed as and when needed.

Partial hydration is about *what* pieces of the data get hydrated—this means those template fragments (components) that have no interactivity or no variable state will not have their associated data serialized. Partial hydration helps achieve the *component islands architecture*—a term coined by Jason Miller (`https://jasonformat.com/islands-architecture/`).

Ryan Carniato (of SolidJS fame) talks about a more efficient paradigm called *subcomponent hydration* (or islets), for which there are no known frameworks that offer this at the time of writing this book, although Marko 6 is expected to solve this (`https://dev.to/ryansolid/fluurt-re-inventing-marko-3o1o`). This involves breaking the individual components into further small isles of interactivity as opposed to partial hydration that broke a page into islands (components) of interactivity. For more information on partial hydration, Anthony Campolo delves deep into this (`https://ajcwebdev.com/what-is-partial-hydration/`) and credits Marko for many of its incredible firsts.

While the various forms of hydration aim at reducing the uncanny valley, they aren't able to fully eliminate it. This is where resumability comes in. Resumability is a different paradigm where the associated view framework aims to not replay the render (to regain the framework state) or reconcile with the server-rendered HTML. It aims to recover the state of the application instantly without all the re-execution on the client side, thereby nearly eliminating the uncanny valley. This, when done progressively alongside fine-grained reactivity to update the DOM directly rather than re-render all the components top-down based on a state object, results in extremely performant server and client performance (fast) alongside tiny bundles (referred to as O(1) frameworks). You can read more about it at `https://www.builder.io/blog/our-current-frameworks-are-on-we-need-o1`.

As mentioned in the introduction, Marko v5 (the version used in this book) does progressive hydration to some extent and partial hydration out of the box automatically. This means only those interactive components will be hydrated and its data sent to the browser. This also means streamed HTML chunks will be hydrated progressively as they appear. This changes with version 6, where Marko moves to the resumable paradigm. You get this automatically as part of the provided migration tools. Coupling reactivity (fine-grained state management), you can see how Marko 6 is poised to transform the landscape of frameworks.

Areas of Improvements for Server-Side Rendering

In the previous sections, it was highlighted how server-side rendering overcomes the various downsides of pure client-side rendering. This is represented in Figure 2-1, where you will notice a great amount of time spent waiting for Javascript and CSS to be downloaded. Although the first byte appears, in terms of this initial shell page, you will notice the page immediately shows up with a giant spinner as work is being done behind the scenes to download the CSS and JS.

Once the JS is downloaded, the render process begins, where the entire HTML render is being done on the client browser. Even at this point, the end user will not notice anything on the page.

This is because further service calls are being made from the client browser to the API endpoints to fetch data for the render. Once these calls are resolved, the render process completes when the associated templating and widget system is able to bind the data needed for the various components on the page to render.

Once the page is fully rendered, it is then mounted onto the browser DOM, and only then you will notice the spinner going away and being replaced by the actual HTML, which was fully rendered on the client browser.

In this technique, the browser does all the heavy lifting of the render process, while the server just does some initial work of handling the request and sending the client page down to the end user's client browser. But you will notice the giant amount of time when nothing happens and both the server and the browser are idle.

This is the result of rendering the entire page on the client side. Most of the existing SPA (single-page application) architectures make use of this. This is for the initial page load. Subsequent page loads may be faster depending on how much content is being replaced and rendered afresh. Some architectures speed this up by performing some form of pre-rendering to ensure that the page loads fast.

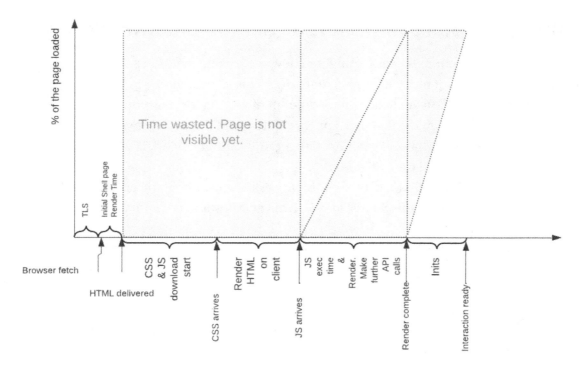

Figure 2-1. *Pure client-side rendering*

When you contrast this with rendering on the server, in Figure 2-2, you will notice it is a drastic improvement from the previous figure for client-side rendering. The idle time, or wasted time, is substantially reduced. Most of the service calls to API endpoints now happen on the server itself, as the render process occurs on the server which requires all the data there.

Also, once the HTML arrives, a small portion of time is spent downloading CSS, and the view is immediately ready for the end user. But it's important to note that while the view is painted, it's not ready for interaction yet. This is because the JS download will be progressing. Once the JS download completes, it is executed and initialization is performed to wire event handlers to the painted view.

Only at this point, the view painted is ready for interaction. However, you will notice that when you compare it with the previous figure, the red-shaded areas are minimal, which indicates that the work is now shared between the browser and the server. This is a major improvement when compared to client-side or client-only rendering.

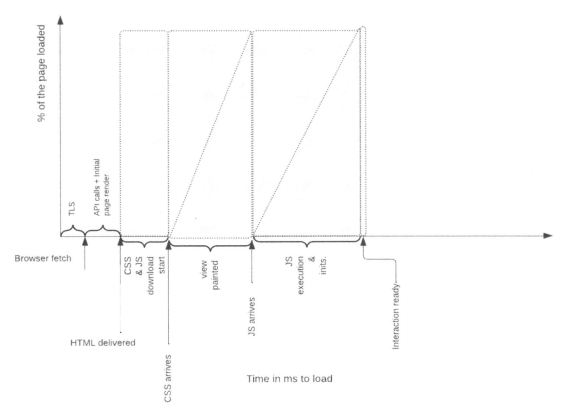

Figure 2-2. *Pure server-side rendering*

But the question is this: Is it really efficient yet? You will notice that it is not completely efficient. This is because the entire view is buffered on the server until the full render is complete. Once the full render of the page or the fragment is complete, the rendered HTML is then sent to the client side.

This is not efficient because the client browser does not get any head start to do any work until the entire render is completed on the server. A lot of things could have been accomplished by the client browser if it had a head start—for example, downloading the CSS.

But to achieve that, the templating system being used to render the HTML will have to resort to some tricks and unlock some advanced mechanisms to achieve the same, because sending some information to the browser to let it download the CSS and then sending the HTML means we are talking about sending responses multiple times.

The aforementioned discussion is illustrated in Figure 2-3.

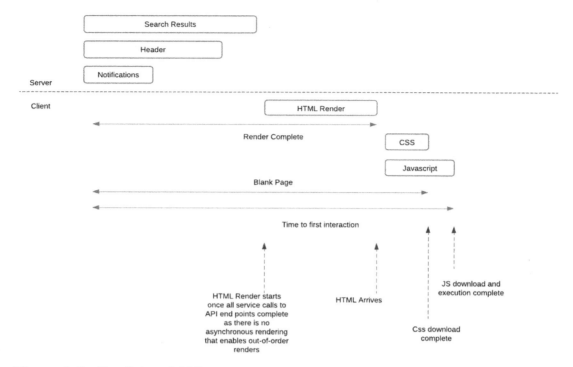

Figure 2-3. *Traditional SSR*

What Is Asynchronous Rendering?

In the previous case of traditional server rendering shown in Figure 2-3, we notice how the render process starts once all the associated service calls to the various API endpoints are complete. This is an inefficient usage of render time, because a top-level page template that builds out a page is dependent on a number of other templates, which build out the various sections of the page (talking about componentization).

These do not have to wait if the associated data needed for their render is available. That is what asynchronous rendering attempts to solve. If a page has a header section and a notification section, then the latter does not have to wait on the former to begin the render process. If a templating system implemented asynchronous rendering, it would help achieve something called out-of-order render, where the system will not have to wait for the header to complete render, then start on the search results fragment, just because the page was ordered that way. If the search results data arrived before the data for the header section, it would proceed to render that fragment. This can be seen in Figure 2-4.

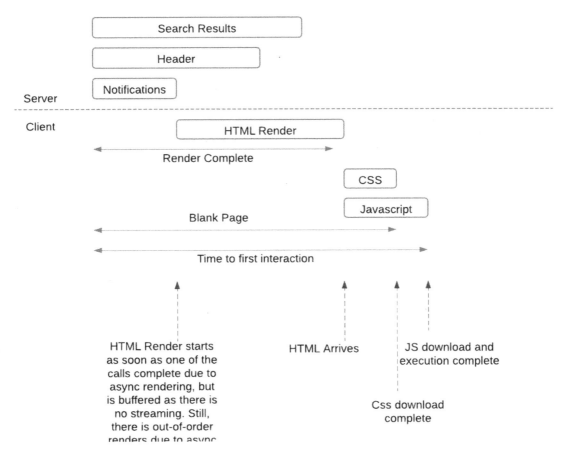

Figure 2-4. *Asynchronous rendering*

Compare it with the previous figure, and you will notice the timeline of where the HTML render begins. In this case, it starts off the moment the first response arrives—for the notifications. The render for the associated fragment begins right there. Contrast this with the previous figure, where you will notice that the render process begins only when all the three service calls—search results, header, and notifications—are complete, thus saving precious wait time.

Can this be improved? Yes, it can be. How can this further be improved? The answer to this lies in an age-old technique called progressive HTML rendering. When streaming is introduced, alongside with asynchronous render, it helps achieve progressive rendering.

What Is Progressive Rendering?

You may want to skip to the section of "Buffers and Streams" in this chapter to aid in the mental model of what is happening. In simple terms, it involves flushing the buffer. That is, sending the data in multiple chunks, as they become available, instead of building it all up and flushing them as one single chunk finally. This technique has a few variants to it, depending on how deeply it is implemented. The answer lies in the implementation.

A) First Flushing the <head>?

For example, if the <head> section of the HTML document that contains the external CSS resources is first flushed, it would give the browser a head start in downloading those resources. Therefore, the browser is doing work, while the server is also doing work in rendering the HTML when the data from an API endpoint or service call arrives. This differs from the original server-side rendering approach where the entire HTML arrived in one chunk, during which the browser was idle, and after the entire chunk arrived, the browser began working on downloading the said resources.

This is made possible because browsers can parse and respond to the HTML content, as it is being streamed from the server, even before the entire response stream is terminated. This therefore improves the perceived load time for the end user while also enhancing the core vital metrics like FCP (First Content Paint) and TTFB (Time to First Byte).

This practice of flushing the head early is one of the primitive implementations of progressive rendering. This is illustrated in Figure 2-5. Note that we have only mentioned about first flushing the <head> section. While the rest of the <body> arrives as they get rendered on the server and become available, the browser will have to perform work in downloading and executing the associated external script files, to make it interaction ready.

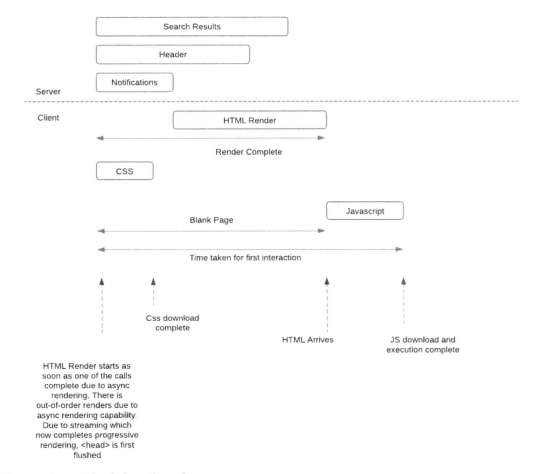

Figure 2-5. *Flush head early*

B) Can We Flush Multiple Times?

In the previous case, the <head> was one of the first fragments to be flushed. It was about early flushing, to get the browser to also do some work while the server was doing work to render the HTML. But, just as the <head> section, what if we can flush multiple times as and when HTML for different fragments get rendered and become available? A page can be broken down into multiple fragments depending on their data sources as indicated in Figure 2-6.

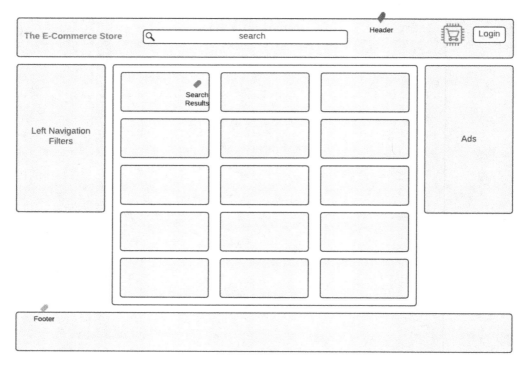

Figure 2-6. *A simple ecommerce store page*

In the figure, you will notice a header section, left filters section, right ads section, bottom footer section, and lastly the central river section containing the search results. Each of them is tied to different data sources. For example, if the data for the filters section is obtained, it can be used to render the associated filters fragment asynchronously, while the other fragments wait for their data. Next, if the render is completed, and if the order is right, then the filters section doesn't have to wait for all the other fragments to complete. They can be sent to the browser. So, they are flushed out.

C) In-Order Flushing

It's important to remember two pointers for this case:

1. Either the order in which the HTML is flushed will have to be maintained or the order of painting HTML has to be maintained. This is to ensure that the order of the HTML is maintained and remains consistent so as to avoid disastrous layout issues occurring.

2. The actual render can be out of order. For example, in the aforementioned case, if the ads section receives the data first, the associated fragment is rendered. It does not have to wait for the left filters fragment and the central river search results fragment to finish their renders. This is what we called out-of-order render which is accomplished by a framework that supports asynchronous renders of their template fragments.

If maintaining the order involves flushing the fragments in the right order, then this is handled by the server, which buffers the rendered content until it's ready to be sent. Earlier solutions like buffers and streams in the Node JS world help to achieve them. The result of performing multiple flushes can be seen in Figure 2-7.

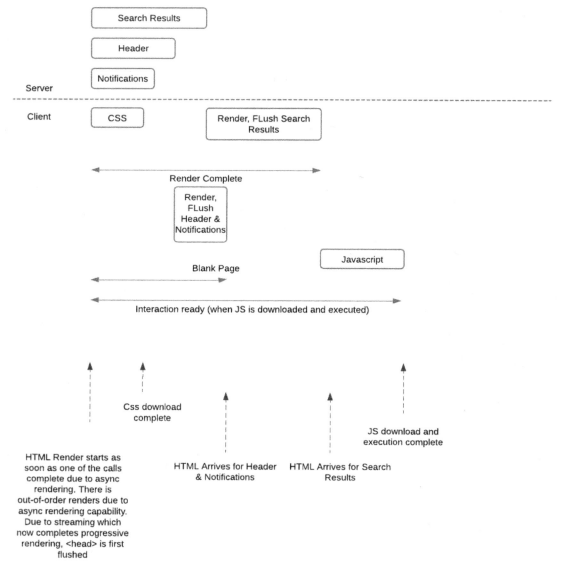

Figure 2-7. *Flushing multiple times in order*

In this example, you will notice that, as before, the render begins immediately as soon as one of the responses arrives. Next, as before, you will notice that the <head> is first flushed, thereby enabling the browser to do work, by downloading the resources. Following this, the header and notifications are first rendered. Since the order in the buffer is right and follows the document order, they are flushed next. Following that, the render of the search results completes. It is then flushed and so on. The HTML responses are flushed multiple times in this case. Yet, the order is maintained on the server. If, for instance, the search results response had arrived first and its render had completed, it would not be flushed and instead would have been buffered until the header and notifications completed their render, so as to maintain the document order.

D) Out-of-Order Flushing

In the previous section, we discussed the benefits of flushing multiple times from the server, in order. While this preserved the final order of the HTML in the document, it was still slightly inefficient in that some portion of the rendered fragments had to be buffered on the server, so that order was maintained in the final output. This is because there may be fragments on the page that depend on each other.

For example, the footer may have to show up only after ads, left nav, and search results are rendered, even though it may have finished rendering. Then, for instance, even between adjacent fragments, the search and ads fragment may need to wait, even though ads may have been rendered, just because the search service took a long time, causing it to be buffered until the rest was available. So, the previous use case had out-of-order asynchronous renders but in-order flush.

To get rid of those minor inefficiencies, in this scenario, we will flush out of order so that there is no major buffering involved. Fragments are flushed as they are rendered, even though they may not be in the right order. But, however, before they are surfaced on the browser client, known as the paint operation, they are painted in the right order. The only caveats for this approach are the following:

1. It requires Javascript to move the out-of-order rendered and out-of-order flushed fragments to the right locations in the DOM; therefore, they are painted in the right order.

2. This may cause reflows if not done properly. Prior knowledge of the fragment dimensions in the layout of the page will be useful in building temporary placeholders that are displayed until the fragments arrive.

The important benefit in this case is highlighted in Figure 2-8.

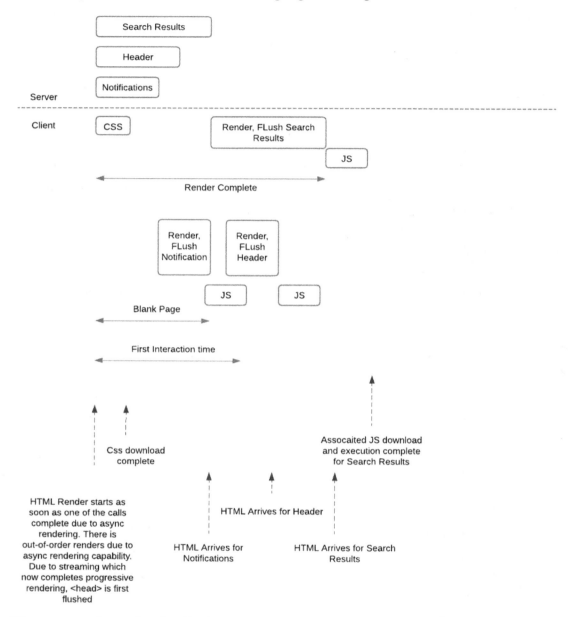

Figure 2-8. *Out-of-order flush*

While the server is fetching data, performing the render and flushing the HTML, the browser is able to download the resources for the fragments that arrive while also initializing the fragments to ensure they are interaction ready.

Revisiting Progressive Rendering

Progressive rendering is thus made possible via two must-haves:

1. **Asynchronous Rendering**: Being able to render fragments of the templates asynchronously, out of order, thereby ensuring that no template fragment is waiting on another.

2. **Streaming**: Being able to flush the rendered HTML, as soon as it's available. Therefore, the output is made available in multiple chunks. Suppose your templating solution had asynchronous rendering but did not support streaming, it would have to buffer in all the rendered content before doing a single flush.

The following illustrations revisit the concepts from the previous pages once more. Let us consider a page that displays

1. Search results

2. Notification count on the header

3. Cart count on the header

The first scenario is without asynchronous rendering and streaming, where every service call to the various API endpoints is waited upon until they complete, before beginning the render process. This is the old traditional server-side rendering. As the templating solution did not support asynchronous renders, it has to wait for all the data to arrive before starting the render. Also, as it does not have streaming support, it has to wait for all the template fragments to finish rendering before flushing them as one chunk.

The second scenario is when the templating solution supports async rendering but still does not support streaming. In this case, you will notice that the render operation does not wait for all the data from the API endpoints to be available. It begins rendering when the associated data for that specific fragment is available. So there is no wait on the render process. However, it isn't able to flush the data as it becomes available, since there is no streaming support. So, it finally goes out as one chunk.

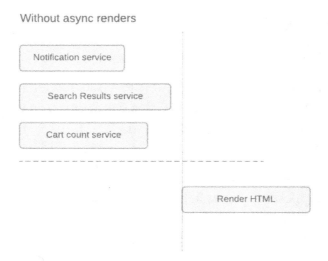

Figure 2-9. *Without async renders*

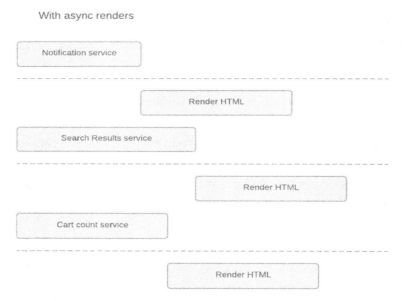

Figure 2-10. *With async renders*

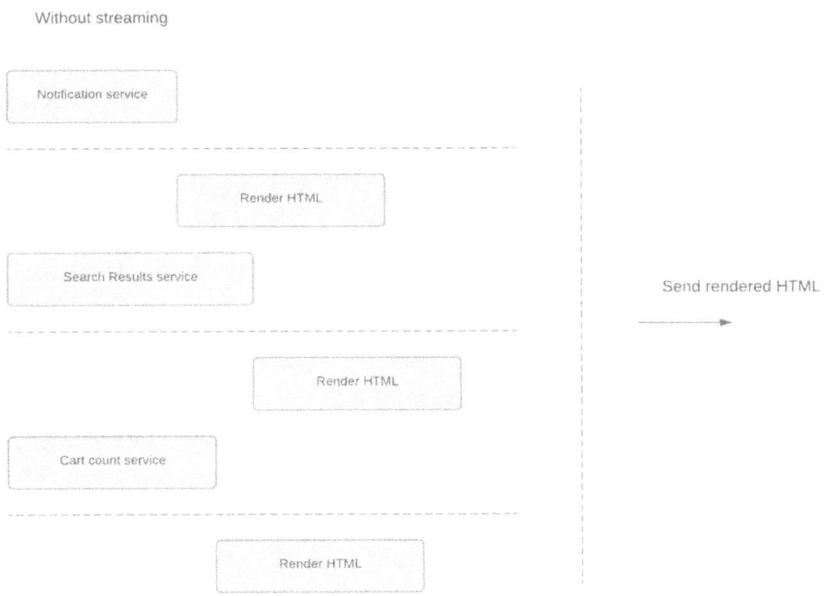

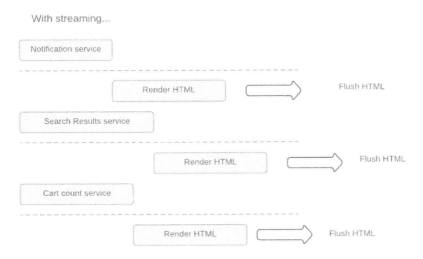

Figure 2-11. *With async renders and no streaming*

Figure 2-12. *Async renders and streaming*

The third scenario is when the templating solution supports both asynchronous rendering and streaming. In this case, you will notice the chart representing that it not only doesn't wait for all the data to be available to start the render but also doesn't wait for all the render to be completed before sending the response. Instead, the response content is sent immediately as it gets available. This is the best-case scenario.

The only variation here is in-order flush and in-order paint vs. out-of-order flush and in-order paint. The former relies on the server to ensure that the order is right before the content is sent out, while the latter relies on Javascript to ensure that the paint order is maintained on the client side, by moving fragments to their right locations.

The four scenarios are illustrated in Figures 2-9 to 2-12.

Now that we have seen the benefits of server rendering over client-side rendering, the issues with traditional server rendering, and where progressive rendering—powered by HTML streaming and asynchronous rendering—helps to speed things up, we will revisit the original illustration that showed the benefits of server rendering over client-side rendering and the inefficiencies of traditional server rendering. But, this time, however, we will revisit the illustration with updates from our newly gained knowledge of progressive rendering. This can be seen in Figure 2-13.

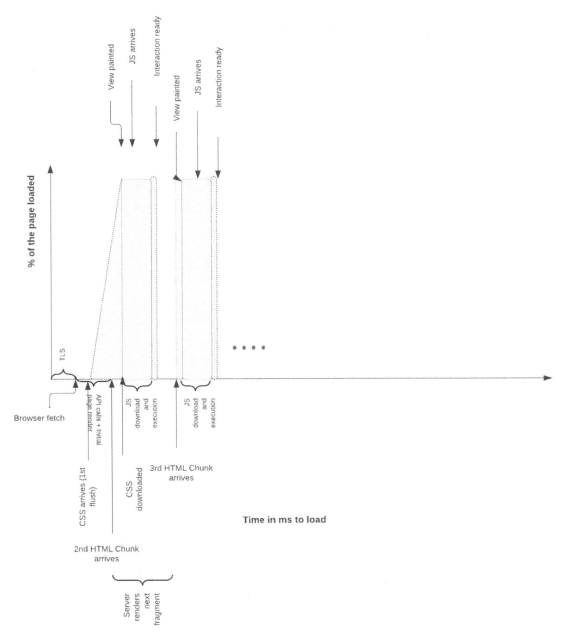

Figure 2-13. *Progressive rendering*

You will notice how much the wasted areas have been reduced. There are further tricks that can be done to reduce the size of the Javascript, which now becomes the only bottleneck, as it has to be downloaded, parsed, and then executed. If the modules or components that show up on the page are not too dynamic, the Javascript assets can also be sent via the early hints API. In a similar manner, common UX component libraries and framework code can also be sent via the early hints API, thereby leaving only the associated component code for execution. Properly organizing the Javascript assets via code splitting, lazy loading, and tree-shaking also helps reduce the time spent in parsing and execution. Note that download, parse, and execute are directly a function of the size of the Javascript. So, utilizing lean frameworks and the aforementioned techniques greatly reduces the time spent on Javascript.

In the following sections, we will explore a few concepts as a 101 that will help build this mental model around HTML streaming, progressive rendering, and asynchronous rendering.

Buffers and Streams

You can think of a buffer as a temporary spot for holding data, while the data is being transferred or moved around. It is limited in size and is temporary. Data can be written into and read out of it. It's not a spot to hold data for too long though. It can be thought of as a spot to aggregate data as we do work and, once it's full, move it along so that the next set of data can come in. This is shown in Figure 2-14.

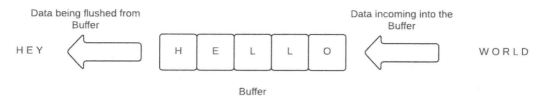

Figure 2-14. *Buffers*

Given that data is being moved into and out of it, a buffer is usually tied to a construct known as a Stream from which data is either coming in from or going out to. You can think of this as a sequence of data that is available over a period of time as shown in Figure 2-15. They are not available all at once, at the same instant. But they are data that keeps arriving and gets moved into the buffer over a period of time while being read out of the buffer or cleared from the buffer once it is full. Eventually, these pieces of data combine to form the entire message or data that was transferred around.

Next Destination   A stream   Data from source

Figure 2-15. *Streams*

If Streams and Buffers were not there, the source would have to transmit the entire data in one go, while the destination would have to receive it in one go. In the context of, for example, reading a file, consider the use case of reading and writing from one file to another, with a size of a few GB. This would require us to have a considerable amount of memory, without crashing the system. But, with the usage of Buffers and Streams, this process happens over a period of time, as data is being read from one end—usually a readable stream—while also being transferred around, stored in a buffer. As the Buffer gets filled, it's flushed while being written into a writable stream—the destination file. This is shown in Figure 2-16.

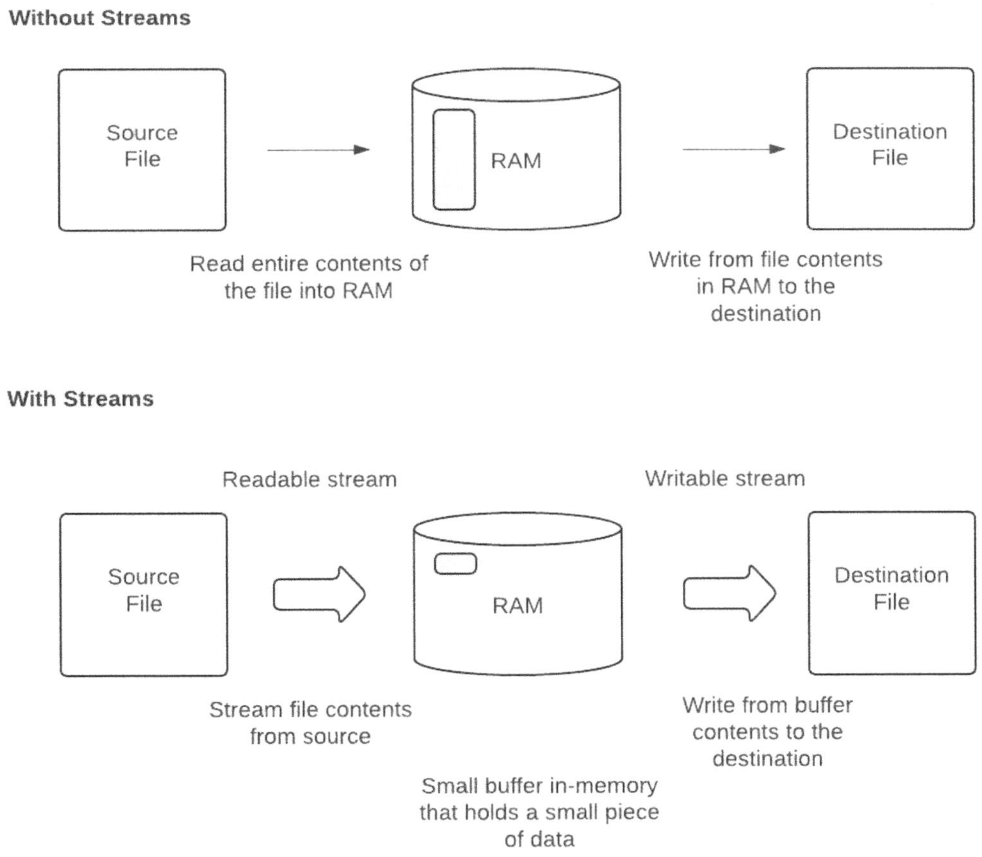

Without Streams

| Source File | → | RAM | → | Destination File |

Read entire contents of the file into RAM

Write from file contents in RAM to the destination

With Streams

Readable stream   Writable stream

| Source File | ⇒ | RAM | ⇒ | Destination File |

Stream file contents from source

Write from buffer contents to the destination

Small buffer in-memory that holds a small piece of data

Figure 2-16. *With and without streams*

75

Another example related to this is watching a movie online. With streaming providers, you aren't downloading the entire movie. You are watching it as small portions of the movie load. This way, you are not waiting for the entire movie to be downloaded and then watched. Small portions of the movie are downloaded and played.

Besides the aforementioned reasons for using Buffers and Streams, one other reason for moving data via streams, through buffers, is the need to process data along the way. Instead of processing entire datasets, small fragments of data can be processed via the usage of Buffers and Streams. Data is being read, gathered, and processed, with decisions being made on it or it's being stored somewhere. And in most of these use cases, streams and buffers tend to be used in tandem. Data comes via the stream. This data is gathered in a Buffer. Once the buffer is full, it's cleared for processing and then further moved around to its destination. This is shown in Figure 2-17.

Figure 2-17. *Streams and Buffers together*

So, in the context of Node JS when talking about Streams and Buffers, it's the idea of data being moved around. These are small packets of data at any instant, occurring over a period of time, with Buffers being areas in the memory that serve as temporary pockets for storage, intentionally limited in size, that are able to hold these packets of data so that some work (processing) can be done over them, as the data arrives in chunks. They enable splitting a large dataset into multiple chunks and efficiently move them around, with reduced memory requirements. This is shown in Figure 2-18.

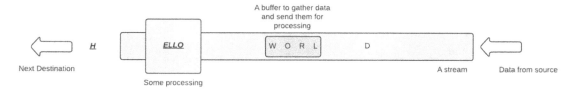

Figure 2-18. *Streams and Buffers in the context of Node JS*

Character Encoding and Character Sets

Before looking at character encoding and character sets, we have to take a look at binary data. Binary data is data represented by 0s and 1s—via the binary number system—and it basically means data is stored in 0s and 1s. Each "1" or "0" is called a bit—a binary digit. It's the foundational math upon which computers are built.

A binary number, say 0101, is representing some data, with only two digits. We say 0101 is the binary system representation of the number 5, which is based on the decimal system. How do we say this? This can be illustrated through the computation in Figure 2-19.

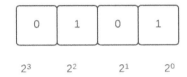

Figure 2-19. Binary place value representation

Each place is computed based on the place value that is raised to the power of 2, due to binary being a base 2 system—two digits being used to represent all the numbers. It's the base 2 representation of a given number that requires only two digits to represent. This is just the same as how we would represent any other number. Let's consider 35; how do we know it is 35?

It's 35 because we are able to show the same value through the base 10 number system (also called the decimal system) that requires ten digits to represent a number in that system, going from 0 to 9.

For example, 35 can be represented in the decimal system (base 10) as shown in Figure 2-20.

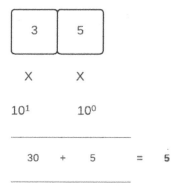

Figure 2-20. *Decimal system place value representation*

For example, 5 can be represented in the binary system (base 2) as 0101.

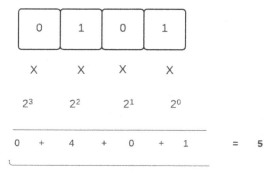

Figure 2-21. *Converting binary to decimal*

In contrast to the decimal system, the binary number system requires only two digits to represent any number, making it great for computer-related math and operations. This is also because we can represent these binary digits physically. For example, in a DVD or a blu-ray disc, the 1s can be represented via the bumps and the other areas as 0s. So, as it spins, with the lasers bouncing off of it and reading it, it is able to transition from a bump to an area without a bump, which helps it interpret and register the data as 1s and 0s.

So, based on the presence and absence of these physical formations, the interpretation of the data happens. The earlier was about storage. But, inside computers, they have transistors that, at a high level, are switches that regulate the flow of electricity. The ON state can be interpreted as a 1 and the OFF state as a 0. The same is true with other forms of storage like a flash drive, etc. They are just different ways to represent either an ON state or an OFF state, that is, a 0 or a 1. This lets us store these numbers physically. And that lets us store data.

Now that we have had a short walk-through of the binary number system, the number of digits, and how it helps to store the data physically, let's look at character encoding and character sets. We have established above how data is stored. It is done so numerically in its physical form via 1s and 0s that are representations of an ON or OFF state. But then how does one store non-numeric data? So, in order to store other kinds of data that are non-numeric, we have to represent everything that we store as numbers.

A character set is a representation of characters as numbers. You can think of it as a code. Every character gets mapped to a number. For example, Unicode and ASCII are types of character sets. Characters get assigned a number in these character sets.

For example, consider the word HELLO. Every letter is mapped to a number and so is every character being typed. Now they are represented by numbers. What number each character gets defines a particular character set. In this case, HELLO is represented by the Unicode character set. All a character set does is map a number (numeric value) to a specific character.

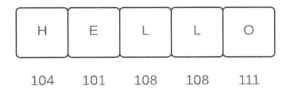

Figure 2-22. *Mapping HELLO to its Unicode charset*

Unicode is very popular because it exhaustively encompasses characters from other languages, like Japanese and Chinese, which require a lot more characters. So we need larger character sets, which means we need bigger numbers. That is, more numbers are required to represent all of these characters. That translates to having more bits for every character. While these characters are mapped to numeric values, these values are inherently stored in the binary format.

Character encoding determines how these numbers are stored in the binary format. Those numeric values that are mapped to every character are referred to as code points. These are converted and stored in binary. But there are different ways in which this can be converted and stored. For example, the character encoding UTF-8 determines how these code points are converted and stored in binary.

You may think that there is only one way to store a number from another system in binary—via 0s and 1s. That is true, but in the context of encoding, what we are talking about is how many bits we use to represent each number. In the case of UTF-8, there are 8 bits—that is, eight digits—to represent a number in its binary form. Each number gets allocated 8 bits to it, even if some numbers may not require it. They would be filled with 0s on the far left. This is because the more bits, the larger the numbers we can represent, which in turn can be used to map to a larger collection of characters, making it well suited for international usage. Therefore, now, we know that every 8 bits represent a new piece of data in the sequence. Since it's character-encoded in UTF-8, we know it's 8 bits and therefore can determine the number. This number belongs to a character set—in this case, Unicode—that maps it to a character, and from that, the character can therefore be determined. This helps us determine what the character is.

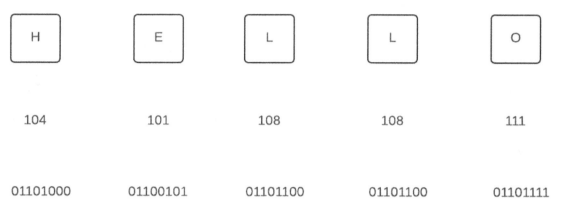

Figure 2-23. *Unicode to UTF-8*

The importance of Buffers in this context is that it serves as a placeholder for storing binary data and offers a number of methods for working with binary data—for example, converting between buffers and strings, storing strings as binary data in the buffer object, with a particular character encoding as seen above.

A chunk of data is a piece of data sent through a stream that may be held temporarily in a buffer for aggregation or for further processing. This stream in the context of rendering is an HTTP response stream, while the data we are dealing with is string-based HTML.

Server-Sent Events

Server-Sent Events are one of the ways for APIs to stream responses (updates from the server) to the frontend or to the backend for the frontend (BFF). The great part about SSE is that they also have the *EventSource* API on the browser for consuming them. They are still HTTP requests and are unidirectional (server to client) instead of bidirectional (like WebSockets).

In the case of a BFF pattern where the BFF serves as a place to do server-side rendering, the BFF server on Node JS acts as the SSE consumer, while the backend APIs act as the SSE provider. The APIs are expected to set the *content-type* as *text/event-stream* over a *Keep-Alive* type *connection* and *no-cache* as the *Cache-control* header.

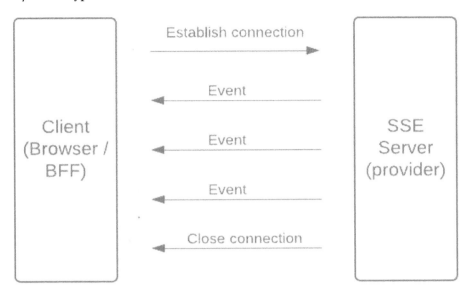

Figure 2-24. *Server-Sent Events*

With SSE

1.   The client (browser/BFF) makes the initial HTTP request to establish a connection.

2.   The server returns an event-stream response and keeps the connection open (aforementioned headers).

3.   The server uses this connection to send text messages at any point as Events.

4.   The incoming data raises a JavaScript event on the client. An event handler function can parse the data and resolve it.

5.   The SSE provider terminates the connection.

All major browsers support this, and on Node JS, you can use it via the EventSource NPM package. EventSource serves as the client browser's interface to SSE. It helps open a persistent HTTP connection to the SSE provider.

How Do These Tie in Together to Achieve Progressive Rendering?

While the earlier sections discussed the importance of Buffers and Streams in the context of operating upon binary data and character sets and character encoding for using binary data to represent characters, this lays the understanding for many of the foundational parts of chunked responses and streaming.

With progressive rendering, in the context of rendering using Node JS as the server technology, we are looking at ways to hold the rendered data, hold it temporarily, and write it down the stream in chunks.

The earlier sections talked about progressive rendering and its various forms. The common underlying factors that enabled all of it were

1. The ability to asynchronously render different fragments independently

2. Buffer their responses (aggregate)

3. Stream the responses (write it to the response stream)

4. The ability of the framework runtime to process this on the client side as chunks of data arrive

5. The ability of the framework to simplify all of this and provide a declarative abstraction.

While 2, 3, 4, and 5 rest on the view framework (in the case of this book, Marko), 1 depends on how the underlying services or APIs return responses. Sometimes, an entire page can be powered by one API on the backend, or different sections of a given page could be powered by different APIs. However, the important ability of these services is to be able to stream responses (chunk them progressively over time). This is where techniques like Server-Sent Events or traditional JSON streaming help.

A view framework template usually renders in response to an input model. In this case, this input data model contains properties that are all pending promises—pending on the APIs. These APIs can chunk responses. When this input model containing props, which are pending promises, is passed to a template, they (pending promises) are mapped to the respective fragments within the template that are waiting on these promises to be resolved, so that data becomes available for the render.

By mapping the promises to the respective template fragments, a view framework is expected to render these async parts of the template independent of each other. For example, when the search results API responds, it should render the search results fragment. It should not be waiting on the left navigation API to respond. This is what a framework like Marko accomplishes. Similar to mapping promises, you can map readable streams directly into the template to read chunks of data and render the different chunks of the template. So, this basic understanding of binary, Buffers, and Streams will help us better understand the Streams API and its usage in Chapters 10 and 11.

Another Example to Understand the Different App Types and the Associated Rendering Techniques

Let's consider the example of a simple todo app:

- You have to load an initial UX that displays the "Active" screen.

- There is a text field for adding the TODO, along with an "Add."

- You also have to display the previously added todos.

- There is a tabbed view to display "Active" and "Completed" TODOs.

- When clicking "Completed," it switches to the "Completed" view that lists the completed TODOs.

Client-Side Rendering and SPAs

With pure client-side rendering, you will have the following workflow.

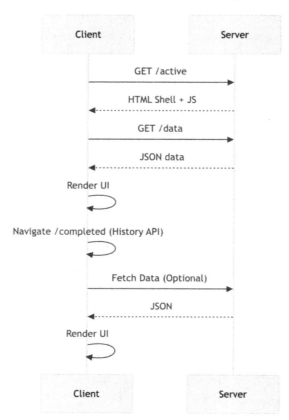

Figure 2-25. *TODO app envisioned as a SPA with CSR*

Here, the initial request is responded with the JS and CSS assets, along with a shell HTML. The server does not really care if you loaded the app with /active or /completed URL path fragments. The browser then proceeds to download, parse, and execute the associated Javascript and CSS. It realizes it will need to fetch the data from the server for rendering the UX. The server responds with data to the HTTP request made by the client for the data, and the app, which has now bootstrapped, uses this data to render the UI. Subsequent navigations will either fetch more data and render or fetch other dynamic bundles and the data to render. This is a pure client side–rendered application. This is also a great example of a SPA. When switching to the "Completed" view, you will notice that the URL changes. If you now copy this URL and load it into another browser tab, the same workflow will continue, and this time it will fetch the data needed to render the "Completed" view. The server does not understand the client URLs. So, it does not understand when you do /completed or /active in the URL path fragment.

Server-Side Rendering and MPAs

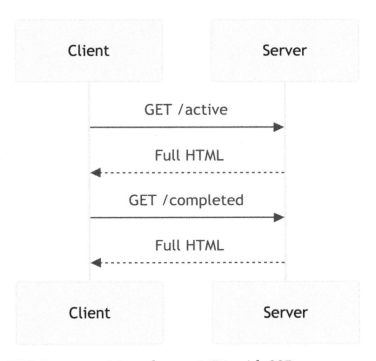

Figure 2-26. *TODO app envisioned as an MPA with SSR*

In this setup, you will render the initial page under /active or /completed. The server has full knowledge of what this means and what UI will be rendered. API orchestration for data fetching happens on the server side, and it will respond with full rendered HTML (with the TODOs). On the client side, interactivity is sprinkled for the client-side interactions. This could be adding a TODO, saving a TODO, moving a TODO to its completed state, etc. When clicking the /completed route, there will be a page reload, and the page for the / completed view will be rendered on the server side and flushed to the client browser in a similar fashion. There are techniques like streaming, progressive rendering, etc., that will help speed this up, and Marko is a champ in handling these. Newer technologies like cross-document view transitions can help smooth this experience greatly. This setup may or may not involve a hydrate phase depending on the type of the view framework being used.

Hybrid Rendering (Combo of MPAs and SPAs)

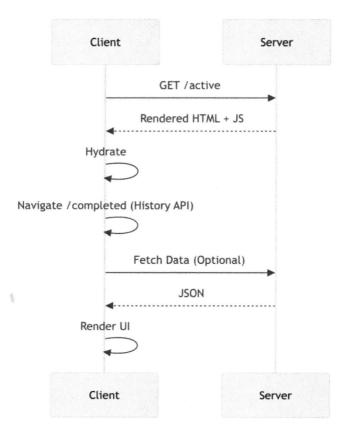

Figure 2-27. *Hybrid app with hybrid rendering*

In this setup, /active will render the UX initially similar to the MPA SSR type setup. Subsequent interactions on the client side will be the same as the SPA setup. Meaning, when you click the "Completed" tab, it will route on the client side, fetch data, update the URL, and work the same way as the CSR SPA application. However, if you now copy the updated URL or bookmark it and load it directly, the server understands you want the "Completed" view and will render that directly on the server and load the page directly with that view. In that sense, both the server and the client are "aware" of the context.

There are slighter variations to the hybrid setup where applications indulge in custom rendering. As in Step 2, when fetching data to render the "Completed" view on the client side, the application routes like a SPA, but instead of fetching data to render the view on the client, it fetches server-rendered HTML and swaps out the view. This is also included in Figure 2-28.

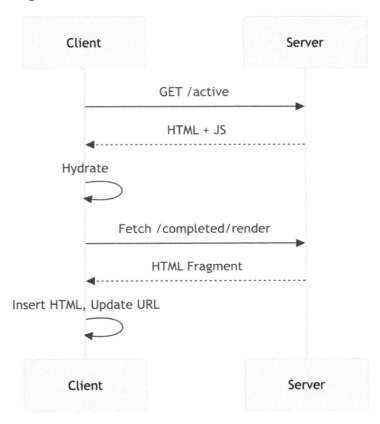

Figure 2-28. *Hybrid app with customized rendering*

Depending on the use cases and their efficacies, you will usually resort to one of these techniques. Marko plays well with all these use cases; however, it advocates for MPAs for better maintainability and operability. We will learn more about these in the upcoming chapters.

CHAPTER 3

Introduction to Progressive Rendering

Introduction

In this chapter, let's delve deeper into the concept of progressive HTML rendering, what it is, its subtypes, what it takes to achieve it, and how Marko helps in achieving it with ease on the server and client. We will also look at a sample application and a custom implementation of a tag that helps achieve isomorphic progressive HTML rendering.

Native HTTP HTML Streaming

The standard understanding of the HTTP protocol is the regular request-response pattern. But, HTTP offers advantages such that a sender can possibly send data beyond the holding memory limit of the sender, in the form of chunks progressively, while the receiver can act on this data, as it arrives, instead of waiting for the entire data to arrive and then act on it. Streaming is also the basis for Server-Sent Events (only the HTTP protocol; websockets are not discussed here).

The *Content-Length* HTTP header contains the byte length of the request/response body. If not specified, HTTP servers add the *Transfer-Encoding*: *chunked* header. *Content-Length* and *Transfer-Encoding* headers are mutually exclusive—cannot occur together. The receiver doesn't know the length of the body and therefore cannot determine the download completion time. The *Content-Length* header, when set, must match the entire body in bytes. When incorrectly set, the behavior of the receiver is undefined. The *Content-Length* header will not allow streaming. With HTTP/2, this header is no longer needed and supported as HTTP/2 supports chunking inherently.

© Damodaran Chingleput Sathyakumar 2025
D. Chingleput Sathyakumar, *Practical Marko*, https://doi.org/10.1007/979-8-8688-1483-9_3

HTTP HTML streaming is one of the core underlying concepts behind progressive HTML rendering to improve web performance. Given that the HTTP is a response stream, server technologies like Node JS with native implementation of buffers and streams can be utilized to stream the rendered HTML as it becomes available, instead of buffering the entire rendered HTML of the page, until the render is complete and then sending it down the response stream. By streaming the content, TTFB metrics are improved, and by flushing chunks multiple times (writing to the response stream multiple times), we can send chunks of server rendered HTML to the browser, thereby improving the FCP metrics as well.

Node JS has great support for HTTP streaming. The native HTTP module does streaming by default for both incoming requests and outgoing responses. Every time *response.writeHead* or *response.write* is invoked, it is just writing a chunk of data to the response stream.

However, streaming has to be implemented effectively to see real performance gains. The page and the associated services that power them must be broken up into smaller pieces. For example, instead of writing 1KB ten times, it's better if 10KB is written once into the response stream. Browsers also have a render buffer limit. So, anything small, the browser also buffers the contents until either the connection is closed or the buffer is filled.

Imperative Mental Model for Progressive Rendering

As mentioned in the previous chapters, progressive rendering is a technique to render fragments of a given page (that is made up of several templates), quicker; thereby it is able to improve on the TTFB (*Time to First Byte*) and FCP (*First Content Paint*) core vital metrics and perceived page load time. To develop a mental model for progressive rendering, it would be beneficial if we delved deeper into its workings via imperative and rudimentary examples.

These sets of experiments will help unravel the various forms of progressive rendering. The example being used is a very basic setup and makes use of Node JS. This assumes you already have Node JS installed and is operational.

```
1    const http = require('http');
2    const server = http.createServer();
3    const port = 8080;
4
5    server.on('request', (req, res) => {
6        res.setHeader('Content-Type', 'text/html; charset=utf-8');
7        res.statusCode = 200;
8        res.write(`
9        <!DOCTYPE html>
10           <html>
11               <head>
12                   <title>Marko v3 Server Side Rendering</title>
13               </head>
14               <body>
15                   <h1>------Before everything--------</h1>
16                   Hello Frank! You have 30 messages!
17                   <ul>
18                       <li style="color: red"> Red </li>
19                       <li style="color: green"> Green </li>
20                       <li style="color: blue"> Blue </li>
21                   </ul>
22                   <h1>------After everything--------</h1>
23               </body>
24           </html>`);
25       res.end();
26    });
27
28    server.listen(port, () => {
29      console.log(`Successfully started server on port ${port}`);
30    });
```

Figure 3-1. *Writing as a single chunk (everything is buffered)*

The snippet of code in Figure 3-1 just uses the native HTTP module in Node JS to spin up an instance of an HTTP server that listens for HTTP requests on port 8080. Let's save this file as *index.js*. Go to the command prompt (Windows) or terminal (if Mac/Linux) at the location of this file. Now run *node index.js*. When you open the browser and hit http://localhost:8080, you will see the page up. The important thing to note here is that we have written the response once to the output HTTP response stream as one chunk via *res.write*. You will notice the entire HTML being written out correctly.

But, everyday practical use cases are far from this kind of a setup. A page will be powered by many microservices that requires writing into the response stream multiple times. This can be simulated in the following way.

```
1    const http = require('http');
2    const server = http.createServer();
3    const port = 8080;
4
5    server.on('request', (req, res) => {
6        res.setHeader('Content-Type', 'text/html; charset=utf-8');
7        res.statusCode = 200;
8        res.write(`
9    <!DOCTYPE html>
10        <html>
11            <head>
12                <title>Marko v3 Server Side Rendering</title>
13            </head>
14            <body>
15                <h1>------Before everything--------</h1>`);
16        res.write(`Hello Frank! You have 30 messages!
17    <ul>|
18        <li style="color: red"> Red </li>
19        <li style="color: green"> Green </li>
20        <li style="color: blue"> Blue </li>
21    </ul>`);
22        res.write(`    <h1>------After everything--------</h1>
23    </body>
24    </html>`);
25        res.end();
26    });
27
28    server.listen(port, () => {
29        console.log(`Successfully started server on port ${port}`);
30    });
```

Figure 3-2. *Writing multiple times sync*

In this example in Figure 3-2, you will notice that the response stream is being written multiple times. This is similar to receiving responses from different microservices to render various template fragments that are dependent on it. Ultimately, these template fragments (whatever templating system be it) will output HTML. You will notice that the HTML is being written out correctly in the way it was coded.

But, while this simulates the ideal world scenario, real-world use cases are far from this. This is because different microservices return responses at different times. So, although our previous example was writing multiple times to the response stream, the data for all the writes were readily available, which seldom happens in the real world.

So, to simulate more of the real world, we will write multiple times as before, but in an async fashion, meaning the data is not readily available all at the same time.

```
1    const http = require('http');
2    const server = http.createServer();
3    const port = 8080;
4
5    server.on('request', (req, res) => {
6        res.setHeader('Content-Type', 'text/html; charset=utf-8');
7        res.statusCode = 200;
8        res.write(`
9    <!DOCTYPE html>
10       <html>
11           <head>
12               <title>Marko v3 Server Side Rendering</title>
13           </head>
14           <body>
15               <h1>------Before everything--------</h1>`);
16       setTimeout(() => {
17           res.write(`Hello Frank! You have 30 messages!
18           <ul>
19               <li style="color: red"> Red </li>
20               <li style="color: green"> Green </li>
21               <li style="color: blue"> Blue </li>
22           </ul>`);
23       }, 3000);
24       res.write(`    <h1>------After everything--------</h1>
25       </body>
26       </html>`);
27       res.end();
28    });
29
30    server.listen(port, () => {
31      console.log(`Successfully started server on port ${port}`);
32    });
```

Figure 3-3. *Writes multiple times with async ops*

The example in Figure 3-3 is mostly unchanged as the previous, except that there is a block of HTML being written to the response stream while being wrapped in a *setTimeout.* This helps emulate the practical scenario of responses being async. When running this, you will notice that "<h1>-------After everything—-------</h1>" is written out, but the block of HTML wrapped in the *setTimeout* is not written out. Now, Why did this happen? This happened because the *res.end* triggered before the async *res.write*, causing the response stream to be ended.

93

In a large-scale system that may contain many tens of template fragments that together build up a page, with each of them waiting on their respective service calls to return responses, we will need a way to effectively organize and coordinate, writing into the response stream, while terminating them when everything completes. So, what does this entail? At a high level, this requires accomplishing the following:

1. Know when to terminate the stream.

2. Render template fragments asynchronously, out of order.

3. Store the rendered output temporarily.

4. Know the ordering of the fragments.

5. Clear the buffer automatically when the order of rendered fragments is correct or when there is a manual prompt to send (flush).

6. While the aforementioned points ensure out-of-order render and in-order flush, provide for the ability to flush out of order (order not maintained on the server) while ensuring in-order paint (order managed on the client side).

Elaborating on the aforementioned points, we would need a solution that is able to perform the following:

1. Have an overall understanding of the order of the fragments. For example, per the ordering of the HTML and the template, if the left navigation section is to be sent (flushed) before the central body or river section of the page, the overseeing templating mechanism must be able to hold off on flushing the central body section, even though it may be rendered and available, until the left navigation section is finished rendering. In doing so, it is able to adhere to the order in which the final HTML in the document is organized.

2. Being able to render template fragments out of order as and when data arrives. For example, rendering the footer section, while the rest of the template fragments wait on their respective data to arrive. This is also called asynchronous rendering of the template fragments.

3. Being able to write the rendered output into a temporary in-memory storage buffer and hold off on flushing it until the order is correct for the HTML that is already rendered.

4. Being able to flush the buffer as and when needed, automatically, when the order is right.

5. Being able to terminate the response stream once all writes are complete. This includes monitoring the various template fragments and their respective calls while dealing with timeouts, errors.

6. Being able to flush the HTML out of order, but utilize Javascript to move the fragments to their correct places (in-order paint). For example, if the central body/river section is rendered, it can be flushed. Then the left navigation section can be rendered and flushed. Earlier, it was mentioned about maintaining the order on the server through a buffer. Thereby ensuring that when flushing the buffer, left navigation went ahead of the central body/river section, thereby ensuring the HTML order. However, this can be handled in another way by flushing the fragments out of order. Therefore, we will be flushing the central river/body section first, followed by the left navigation. However, when surfacing them on the page, the system will ensure they are in the right order. This is accomplished via Javascript and is called in-order paint.

Unless you have a mechanism to be able to buffer in async writes and properly queue them so that their order is maintained in the final output, async writes will not show up in the output stream! Our approach is very primitive, and let's attempt to fix it for now using a module called the async-writer. *Async-writer* (now used internally within *Marko* as *AsyncStream*) helps us to write asynchronously to the output stream, out of order, while ensuring it emits bytes in the correct order! This is illustrated in Figure 3-4.

```
1   const server = require('http').createServer();
2   const port = 8080;
3
4   server.on('request', (req, res) => {
5       res.setHeader('Content-Type', 'text/html; charset=utf-8');
6       var out = require('async-writer/debug').create(res, {
7           shouldBuffer: true
8       });
9       out.write('<h1>A</h1>');
10      var asyncOut = out.beginAsync();
11      setTimeout(function () {
12          asyncOut.write('<h1>B</h1>');
13          asyncOut.end();
14      }, 1000);
15      out.write('<h1>C</h1>');
16      var asyncOut2 = out.beginAsync();
17      setTimeout(function () {
18          asyncOut2.write('<h1>D</h1>');
19          asyncOut2.end();
20      }, 4000);
21      out.end();
22  });
23  server.listen(port, () => {
24      console.log(`Successfully started server on port ${port}`);
25  });
```

Figure 3-4. *Fixing the async op output order with async-writer*

When you run this, you will notice the four letters ABCD rendered in the right order, although they are written into the output stream at different times, with the *setTimeout* again being used to simulate some async behavior. Now, what is happening here with this example? Let's break it down.

This is a classic example that illustrates the *async-writer* module.

As before, the incoming response writable stream of HTTP is wrapped by the Async-Writer to become an Async output writeable stream. This happens via the line

var out = require('async-writer').create(res);

Then, "A" is first written into it. Next, we want to write "B", but we sense some delay in the response to "B". So, we wrap into inside an Async operation via

var asyncOut = out.beginAsync()

The end of this Async operation will be marked by a

`asyncOut.end();`

The end of the writeable stream will be marked by a

`out.end()`

So, for now, to simulate an async op, we use a *setTimeout* and then write "B" into it. We then follow it up by writing "C", then another async op, where we write "D". After completing writing "D", we just end the async operation via

`asyncOut.end().`

But note that we have still invoked *out.end* much ahead of *asyncOut.end*.

This implies, when *out.end* executes, there is nothing more to write; you can end the stream if there are no async ops. But, we have created an async operation, so we wait. Upon invoking *asyncOut.end*, we see if there is anything further left to write. There is nothing as the response stream has already been marked with *out.end()*. So it's the end of the stream.

This gives the output "ABCD".

You may have noticed we wrote into the response stream in different order. Yet, our output is still rendered out in the right order as mentioned above: "ABCD". How is this possible?

- The **Async-Writer** makes it possible to flush bytes to the output stream out of order, while still flushing out bytes in the correct order finally.

- So, you can write parts of the stream out of order. But the bytes will be flushed in the right order.

- Content that is written after an async op will be kept in a buffer, and after the async op is done, the output is buffered out properly in the right order.

So far, we have seen that

1. Writes are possible asynchronously to the response stream, thereby enabling out-of-order renders, while asynchronously rendering the data.

2. The response is buffered so that the final HTML order is maintained in the response.

Now, while the order of the writes is maintained in the output, you will notice that the server load takes a moment. This is because we are waiting for the responses to be buffered in, so as to maintain the order while flushing out the fragments. This, in many instances, can impact the metrics like TTFB and FCP. In real-world scenarios, this could be a service call that is delayed, which ends up having a cascaded effect, delaying the page load. So, how does one avoid this? This can be avoided by flushing the buffer as we get data.

Let us look at further updating our example of Figure 3-4 in Figure 3-5.

```
1       const EventEmitter = require('events').EventEmitter;
2       const server = require('http').createServer();
3       const port = 8080;
4
5       /**
6        * This function serves like an SSE end point which pushes data.
7        * Data is emitted in chunks here.
8        */
9       function getDataEmitter() {
10          const ee = new EventEmitter();
11          let i = 0;
12
13          function getData() {
14              i = i + 1;
15              ee.emit('data', i);
16              if (i < 5) {
17                  setTimeout(getData, 1000);
18              } else {
19                  ee.emit('end');
20              }
21          }
22
23          process.nextTick(getData);
24          return ee;
25      }
```

Figure 3-5. *Simulating flushing the buffer early but order is messed up*

```
26
27      server.on('request', (req, res) => {
28          res.setHeader('Content-Type', 'text/html; charset=utf-8');
29          const out = require('async-writer').create(res);
30          const asyncOut = out.beginAsync({
31              timeout: 0
32          });
33          const dataEmitter = getDataEmitter();
34          asyncOut.write('<h1>Hello world!</h1>');
35          dataEmitter.on('data', function (data) {
36              console.log('data!');
37              asyncOut.write('<h3>' + data + '</h3>');
38              asyncOut.flush();
39          });
40          dataEmitter.on('end', function () {
41              asyncOut.end();
42          });
43          asyncOut.write('<h1>Bye world</h1>');
44          out.end();
45      });
46
47      server.listen(port, () => {
48          console.log(`Successfully started server on port ${port}`);
49      });
```

Figure 3-6. *Simulating flushing the buffer early but order is messed up (continued)*

The above code snippet introduces the **getDataEmitter** function that contains an *EventEmitter*, which is designed to serve as a sample endpoint that emits data just as a service endpoint that emits data in chunks, akin to Server-Sent Events. Most of it follows the previous example. The new portion is the line

asyncOut.flush()

This is invoked every time data is emitted and a write is done to the output stream. This line informs the *async-writer* module to clear the buffer. Now when this example is run, you will notice that the page loads with data as it arrives. There is no wait. Data keeps arriving until the end of the EventEmitter. But on the flip side, you will notice that the order is incorrect. This is what we call out-of-order render, out-of-order flush, and out-of-order paint.

While the previous example helped with the FCP and TTFB, they obviously were incorrect because the order of the HTML gets impacted. This can cause disastrous layout issues on pages and is something that is not desirable, requiring to be fixed. But it was useful in showcasing as a step to better appreciate the benefits and the issues with the various techniques of progressive rendering. In the following example, the issue seen with the previous example will be fixed. However, the caveat is that Javascript is required for this to be fixed.

We are leaving the EventEmitter setup getDataEmitter as is, same as the previous example. The modification is only in the subsequent portion as illustrated in Figure 3-7.

```
26
27    server.on('request', (req, res) => {
28        const out = require('async-writer').create(res);
29        const asyncOut = out.beginAsync({
30            timeout: 0
31        });
32        const dataEmitter = getDataEmitter();
33        asyncOut.write('<h1>Hello world!</h1>');
34        dataEmitter.on('data', function (data) {
35            console.log('data!');
36            asyncOut.write('<noscript><h3>' + data + '</h3></noscript>');
37            asyncOut.flush();
38        });
39        dataEmitter.on('end', function () {
40            asyncOut.write(`
41                <script>
42                    console.log('executing script...');
43                    (function(){
44                        const noscripts = document.getElementsByTagName('noscript');
45                        const placeholder = document.querySelector('#placeholder');
46                        let data = '';
47                        console.log(placeholder);
48                        Array.from(noscripts).forEach(function (noscript) {
49                            data = data + noscript.innerHTML;
50                        });
51                        if (placeholder) {
52                            placeholder.innerHTML = data;
53                        }
54                    })();
55                </script>
56            `);
57            asyncOut.flush();
58            asyncOut.end();
59        });
60        asyncOut.write('<div id="placeholder"></div>');
61        asyncOut.write('<h1>Bye world</h1>');
62        out.end();
63    });
64
65    server.listen(port, () => {
66        console.log(`Successfully started server on port ${port}`);
67    });
```

Figure 3-7. *Fixing the order of paint*

In this updated version of the code, you will notice that the change lies in the *data* and *end* event of the data emitter. As and when a chunk is emitted, it is written into a <noscript> tag and does not display on the page immediately. However, once the last chunk of data is emitted, a small script snippet is added, which contains the required logic to access the content from within the <noscript> tags and move them into the required placeholder, thereby displaying them in the correct order on the page. That is, they are painted back on the page, in the right order, despite being rendered and flushed out of order. As you notice, this technique has a caveat that it requires Java script for it to work. One more issue with this approach is that there is a possibility of reflows occurring due to elements being moved around, resulting in some jank. There are techniques to avoid this, like creating placeholders with the reserved dimensions, if those dimensions are previously known. Loading silhouettes also serve a similar purpose in helping reduce the jank.

Basic Need for a Framework Like Marko

This journey was about unraveling the various intricacies involved with progressive rendering and help develop a mental model for it while understanding the various problems any framework would require to solve to achieve this. This does not however delve into the initialization part of it yet, referred to as hydration. Hydration is being tackled by different frameworks in different ways. Even Marko, which is the topic of this book, is attempting to handle it in a different way in their new upcoming V6. This is however an implementation detail that the framework practitioner wouldn't have to concern themselves with.

But the larger issue is we did all of this in an imperative fashion. Our examples were small and the scope was intentionally limited to better understand the inner workings. However, real-life projects are seldom this simple and would usually involve hundreds of template fragments, with a ton of service calls made in a microservice environment, with some being rendered on the server, while others on the client, with data fetching happening on the server and from the client and so on, adding to the complexities that we have discussed above. Thus, you begin to see the need for a framework to be able to handle all of this and offer an out-of-the-box solution. More importantly, the framework must abstract away all the imperativeness and offer us a simple interface to be able to invoke it and perform all of the above in a declarative fashion. This is where a framework like Marko shines.

Revisiting the Progressive Rendering Techniques

1. **Synchronous Single Chunk Render**: Write the whole chunk one time. This is similar akin to waiting for all the service calls to have completed before beginning to render the data.

2. **Synchronous Multi-chunk Render**: This is attempting to write multiple times under the assumption that data is readily available all at the same time, which is an ideal case scenario.

3. **Asynchronous Multi-chunk Render**: Which had errors with the async writes not working. This is a scenario that mirrors the real world, where service calls can receive responses at different times.

4. Using the async-writer to primitively emulate what a large-scale framework will do to handle async operations.

   a. **Out-of-Order Render In-Order Flush**: This highlights the concept of buffering the response to maintain order. While this fixed #3, this however impacted the TTFB and FCP metrics.

   b. **Out-of-Order Render and Out-of-Order Flush**: The order was messed up in this case. But the learning here is that TTFB and FCP are improved.

   c. **Out-of-Order Render, Out-of-Order Flush, but In-Order Paint**: This fixes the problem encountered in the previous step—the incorrect ordering of rendered fragments. However, the fix involves relying on Javascript while taking into account measures that will avoid jank.

Now that we have a robust mental model of progressive rendering and the various intricacies involved around it that any framework will be required to solve for, let us take a look at Marko and see what it has to offer. Note that whatever was discussed so far is about achieving progressive rendering on the server side. Progressive rendering can be achieved on the client side too. The Event Source API is one of the ways to consume a Server-Sent-Event stream. Moreover, the calling API must also be able to emit data in chunks for the frontend application to consume. We will look into this as we build out an example.

What Marko 5 Offers for Progressive Rendering?

Marko JS offers an out-of-the-box solution to progressive rendering and HTML streaming, besides a lot of other things that any general framework on the frontend landscape will be required of. At a high level, Marko offers the following:

1. Streaming and async rendering.

2. Full TypeScript support for development.

3. Automatic partial hydration of server-rendered HTML.

4. Babel AST internally offers tools for running automated migrations to framework upgrades (isomorphic progressive rendering expected with version 6).

5. Multiple compilation outputs—VDOM on the client side, strings on the server.

6. Support for bundler integrations—Vite, Rollup, and Webpack with local development support with hot module reloads.

7. Extremely performant streaming server-side rendering. Marko was built with server rendering performance from the ground up.

8. Scalable, trusted, and battle tested. It serves over 1B views on websites like eBay, delivering on their pages that have the highest traffic like home page, search results, item page, and product page.

9. Reduced memory consumption on the server.

10. A meta framework called Marko-run that makes scaffolding and building a progressively rendered Marko application extremely easy.

11. Editor and IDE tooling support (VS Code and Language server support)

12. Server-only components. This results in 0KB of Javascript sent to the browser if no interactive components are present.

13. Multi-file components and single-file components.

14. Extremely performant due to having a bundle size of 13KB upon gzip. The version being discussed in this book is v5 which is the recommended LTS (Live to Site) version at the time of authoring this book. However, the Marko dev team has V6 out on beta that has a further reduced runtime to about 7KB upon gzip.

15. Integrations with all the industry standard tooling.

Sample Project Explaining Progressive Rendering with Marko on the Server

In the following examples, using Marko, we will look at the three scenarios:

1. Single chunk

2. Out-of-order render but in-order flush (and therefore in-order paint)

3. Out-of-order render and out-of-order flush (and in-order paint)

The sample application used here is a marko, express, and webpack app. The first file here is the *package.json* file, shown in Figure 3-8, which is basically equivalent to a manifest file, which describes the projects, its dependencies.

```
1    {
2      "name": "marko-progressive-renders",
3      "description": "Sample app that demonstrates the power of Progressive Rendering using Marko and Webpack",
4      "version": "1.0.0",
5      "dependencies": {
6        "@marko-tags/subscribe": "^0.5.1",
7        "@marko/express": "^1.0.0",
8        "compression": "^1.7.4",
9        "express": "^4.17.1",
10       "marko": "^5.17.2",
11       "raptor-pubsub": "^1.0.5"
12     },
13     "devDependencies": {
14       "@marko/compiler": "^5.16.1",
15       "@marko/webpack": "^9.2.0",
16       "css-loader": "^6.5.0",
17       "css-minimizer-webpack-plugin": "^3.1.1",
18       "marked": "^3.0.8",
19       "mini-css-extract-plugin": "^2.4.3",
20       "spawn-server-webpack-plugin": "^6.1.0",
21       "webpack": "^5.60.0",
22       "webpack-cli": "^4.9.1",
23       "webpack-dev-server": "^4.3.1",
24       "webpack-node-externals": "^3.0.0"
25     },
26     "private": true,
27     "scripts": {
28       "build": "rm -rf ./dist && NODE_ENV=production webpack --progress",
29       "dev": "webpack serve",
30       "dev:inspect": "INSPECT=1 npm run dev",
31       "start": "NODE_ENV=production node dist/main.js"
32     }
33   }
```

Figure 3-8. *The package.json file*

In the above file, the ***scripts*** section contains numerous commands that can be executed from the terminal or command line over this project. The ***build*** command is used to build the application for production purposes. By building the app, what we mean here is compiling the marko template files in the project, which transforms them from .marko files to .js files. This is done by the bundler, which invokes the compiler plugin of marko, as part of the build process. As part of the process, CSS is also bundled and output. In case LESS or other style solutions are used, their corresponding plugins are to be included, which can be picked up by the bundler, and used to compile the LESS files to CSS files and then resolve variables and bundle them. The ***dev*** command starts a development server, which is the local server that starts the application on port 3000. The ***dev:inspect*** starts the server in the debug mode. Finally, the ***start*** command starts the server in production mode and will serve the production bundle. We will use

webpack as the bundler for this example. The difference between production mode and development mode is that live reloads will work in the development mode.

In the ***dependencies*** list, ***express*** is used to start a Node JS web server. ***Compression*** is for performing response compression such as GZIP. ***Marko*** is the dependency name for Marko JS that lets us use it. ***@marko/express*** helps to render Marko templates into an express web application. ***Raptor-pubsub*** is a small utility that helps to use the publish-subscribe pattern to emit events and act on it. Marko uses this for inter-component communication as it piggybacks on the native EventEmitter interface. ***@marko/subscribe*** is a marko tag that lets us subscribe and unsubscribe to global events that are triggered on global event emitter objects such as the window or document object.

The ***devDependencies*** list consists of those modules that will be used for bundling the application. They include Webpack-related plugins and the marko compiler plugin that will be used by webpack to compile Marko templates to Javascript files. This process is known as precompiling the templates. The following file is the ***webpack.config.js*** placed at the project root that tells webpack how the bundling is to be done and what the plugins are to be used for the same.

The output of the build process is dumped into the ***dist*** folder, found under the project root.

Usually in large-scale projects, the build process is triggered as part of the CI pipeline. Thereby, if any failure occurs, like a missed dependency or a missed import, it would error out immediately before deployment. This is also usually the step where, if TypeScript was used, additional stages with additional plugins would be included in the bundler, to compile away TypeScript, before creation of the final manifest. The Babel compiler would also be used in these stages to target different execution environments by transpiling them to different browser targets via the ***browserlist*** module. Figures 3-9 to 3-12 indicate the webpack config used.

```
1    const path = require("path");
2    const webpack = require("webpack");
3    const nodeExternals = require("webpack-node-externals");
4    const CSSExtractPlugin = require("mini-css-extract-plugin");
5    const MarkoPlugin = require("@marko/webpack/plugin").default;
6    const SpawnServerPlugin = require("spawn-server-webpack-plugin");
7    const MinifyCSSPlugin = require("css-minimizer-webpack-plugin");
8
9    const markoPlugin = new MarkoPlugin();
10   const { NODE_ENV = "development" } = process.env;
11   const isDev = NODE_ENV === "development";
12   const isProd = !isDev;
13   const filenameTemplate = `${isProd ? "" : `[name].`}[contenthash:8]`;
14   const spawnedServer =
15     isDev &&
16     new SpawnServerPlugin({
17       args: [
18         "--enable-source-maps",
19         // Allow debugging spawned server with the INSPECT=1 env var.
20         process.env.INSPECT && "--inspect",
21       ].filter(Boolean),
22     });
23
24   module.exports = [
25     compiler({
26       name: "browser",
27       target: "web",
28       devtool: isProd
29         ? "cheap-module-source-map"
30         : "eval-cheap-module-source-map",
31       output: {
32         filename: `${filenameTemplate}.js`,
33         path: path.join(__dirname, "dist/assets"),
34       },
35       optimization: {
36         runtimeChunk: "single",
37         splitChunks: {
38           chunks: "all",
39           maxInitialRequests: 3,
40         },
41       },
42       devServer: isProd
```

Figure 3-9. *The Webpack config*

```
43              ? undefined
44              : {
45                  hot: false,
46                  static: false,
47                  host: "0.0.0.0",
48                  allowedHosts: "all",
49                  port: parseInt(process.env.PORT || 3000, 10),
50                  headers: {
51                    "Access-Control-Allow-Origin": "*",
52                  },
53                  ...spawnedServer.devServerConfig,
54              },
55          module: {
56            rules: [
57              {
58                test: /\.css$/,
59                use: [CSSExtractPlugin.loader, "css-loader"],
60              },
61              {
62                test: /\.(jpg|jpeg|gif|png|svg)$/,
63                type: "asset",
64              },
65            ],
66          },
67          plugins: [
68            markoPlugin.browser,
69            new webpack.DefinePlugin({
70              "typeof window": "'object'",
71            }),
72            new CSSExtractPlugin({
73              filename: `${filenameTemplate}.css`,
74              ignoreOrder: true,
75            }),
76            isProd && new MinifyCSSPlugin(),
77          ],
78        }),
79        compiler({
80          name: "server",
81          target: "async-node",
82          devtool: "inline-nosources-cheap-module-source-map",
83          externals: [
84            // Exclude node_modules, but ensure non js files ar
```

Figure 3-10. *The Webpack config (continued)*

```
85              // Eg: `.marko`, `.css`, etc.
86              nodeExternals({
87                allowlist: [/\.(?!(?:js|json)$)[^.]+$/],
88              }),
89            ],
90          optimization: {
91            minimize: false,
92          },
93          output: {
94            libraryTarget: "commonjs2",
95            path: path.join(__dirname, "dist"),
96            devtoolModuleFilenameTemplate: "[absolute-resource-path]",
97          },
98          module: {
99            rules: [
100             {
101               test: /\.(jpg|jpeg|gif|png|svg)$/,
102               generator: { emit: false },
103               type: "asset/resource",
104             },
105            ],
106          },
107          plugins: [
108            spawnedServer,
109            markoPlugin.server,
110            new webpack.IgnorePlugin({
111              resourceRegExp: /\.css$/,
112            }),
113            new webpack.DefinePlugin({
114              "typeof window": "'undefined'",
115            }),
116          ],
117        }),
118      ];
119
120    // Shared config for both server and client compilers.
121  ∨ function compiler(config) {
122      return {
123        ...config,
124        mode: isProd ? "production" : "development",
```

Figure 3-11. *The Webpack config (continued)*

```
125        stats: isDev && "minimal",
126        cache: {
127          type: "filesystem",
128        },
129        output: {
130          ...config.output,
131          publicPath: "/assets/",
132          assetModuleFilename: `${filenameTemplate}[ext][query]`,
133        },
134        resolve: {
135          extensions: [".js", ".json"],
136        },
137        module: {
138          rules: [
139            ...config.module.rules,
140            {
141              test: /\.marko$/,
142              loader: "@marko/webpack/loader",
143            },
144          ],
145        },
146        plugins: config.plugins.filter(Boolean),
147      };
148    }
```

Figure 3-12. *The Webpack config (continued)*

The source code will be contained in the ***src*** folder. The following is the piece of code (Figure 3-13) that creates an HTTP Express server and starts it. It is placed under the ***src*** folder as ***src/index.js***.

```
1     import express from "express";
2     import compressionMiddleware from "compression";
3     import markoMiddleware from "@marko/express";
4     import indexPage from "./pages/index";
5     import iframePage from "./pages/iframe";
6
7     const port = parseInt(process.env.PORT || 3000, 10);
8
9     express()
10     .use(compressionMiddleware()) // Enable gzip compression for all HTTP responses.
11     .use("/assets", express.static("dist/assets")) // Serve assets generated from webpack.
12     .use(markoMiddleware()) // Enables res.marko.
13     .get("/", indexPage)
14     .get("/iframe", iframePage)
15     .listen(port, err => {
16       if (err) {
17         throw err;
18       }
19
20       if (port) {
21         console.log(`Listening on port ${port}`);
22       }
23     });
```

Figure 3-13. *src/index.js*

This code snippet basically uses the express module to start a HTTP server on port 3000. As part of the server startup, it uses the ***compression middleware*** and the ***marko middleware*** that helps to render marko templates into an express web application while also getting the **response.marko** method that renders the template directly into the output stream. It also designates two routes—the first being *"/", **the default route**, and /* **iframe which loads the embedded page.** To serve the static assets like Javascript and CSS, it also uses the express.static construct to serve the generated assets, which can be found in the ***dist*** folder, directly under the project root. The **src** folder will look like the following figure, for our example. It contains ***pages*** and ***components. Components*** folder contains individual atomic Marko templates that are basically used to render small HTML fragments, along with wiring up an associated widget. ***Pages*** folder contains top-level Marko templates that will contain these components to build out entire pages. In our example, we have two pages—the default page (accessed by /), which contains another page, via an iframe (accessed by **/iframe**), embedded in it. These are represented as two folders within the ***pages*** folder.

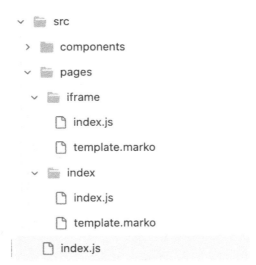

Figure 3-14. *Sample server-side progressive render project layout*

The components folder is further expanded as shown below to contain atomic components, which are those HTML fragments that were mentioned earlier. This is shown in Figures 3-14 and 3-15.

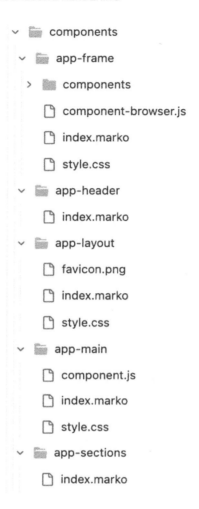

Figure 3-15. *Expanded sample server-side progressive render project layout*

Here, we have five components named as ***app-main***, ***app-sections***, ***app-layout***, ***app-header***, and ***app-frame***. If you notice, ***app-frame*** has its own components folder, which contains components used by them as shown in Figure 3-16. By default, Marko's compiler will look for the ***components*** folder within or a ***marko.json*** metadata file to resolve the various tags as it compiles them.

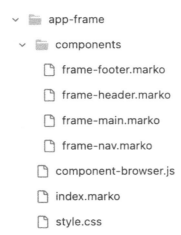

Figure 3-16. *Contents of app-frame/components*

The snapshot above shows the expanded view of the **app-frame** component folder, which contains the **components** folder within it. Assuming you have completed the prerequisite of having Node JS installed, as a first step, in the terminal or command prompt, we will run

```
> npm i
```

This will install all the dependencies and drop in a generated package-lock.json file, which is a file that pins the dependencies via the current install. Before we go over the code, we will then do the following commands:

```
> npm run build
> npm run start
```

The first command builds the project while the second one starts it. Once these are complete, you will see the page up when you access it on *http://localhost:3000*. The following is the snapshot of the page as seen in Figure 3-17.

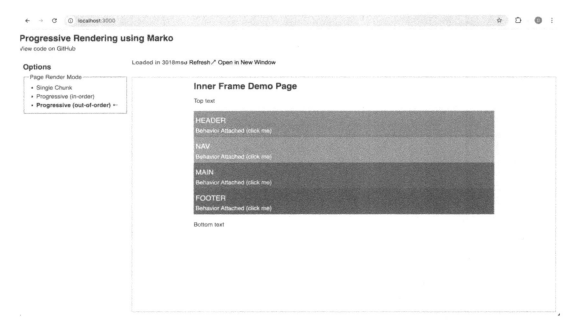

Figure 3-17. *Our sample application*

The main page can be found under ***pages/index***, while the embedded iframe page can be found under ***pages/iframe.*** As options are selected on the left navigation, we will see the embedded page perform different types of loads based on the selections.

When

- The first option ***Single Chunk*** is selected, you will notice that the entire page is buffered until all the fragments complete render and is then flushed in one shot.

- The second option ***Progressive (in-order)*** is selected, you will notice that the entire page is NOT buffered as before, but they are flushed as soon as some fragments are available in the right order. This is the out-of-order render, in-order flush, or in-order paint type.

- The third option ***Progressive (out-of-order)*** is selected, you will notice that not only is the entire page NOT buffered as option 1, but neither do they wait for a set of fragments to be rendered complete to maintain the order on the server, before being flushed. Instead, as and when fragments are complete, they get flushed. Still, the order is maintained on the client side by using Javascript to move the fragments to the right locations. This is what we call out-of-order render, out-of-order flush, and in-order paint.

Now let's go over the code. The first file which serves as the entry point to the application is the **src/pages/index/index.js** file that responds to the default route http://localhost:3000/.

```
1    import template from "./template.marko";
2
3    export default (req, res) => {
4      const renderMode = req.query.renderMode || 'progressive-out-of-order';
5      res.marko template, {
6        renderMode
7      });                         Provided by @marko/express
8    };
```

Figure 3-18. *src/pages/index/index.js*

The ***res.marko*** is the utility offered by the ***@marko/express*** package which hooks up this method on the response stream to render Marko JS templates via Express JS. This basically checks the query to see if any selection was made, if not, it loads the page with the default view '*progressive-out-of-order.*' The next file is the associated template, in the same folder, named ***template.marko.*** This is a top-level template that will be rendered on the server and will not be bundled to the client browser by webpack.

```
1    <app-layout
2      renderMode=input.renderMode
3      showHeader
4      showSections
5    >
6      <@head>
7        <title>Progressive Rendering using Marko</title>
8      </@head>
9      <@body>
10        <app-main renderMode=input.renderMode/>
11      </@body>
12    </app-layout>
```

Figure 3-19. *src/pages/index/template.marko*

This tells us that there is another template fragment called ***app-layout*** (which you can find under the ***src/components*** folder). This tag refers to that component ***app-layout.*** So, the ***app-layout*** component can be considered to be a dependency of ***src/pages/index/template.marko.*** Next, the **<@head>** and **<@body>** are attribute tags of Marko. Meaning, the contents within the **<@head>** and **<@body>** will go into specific placements within the ***<app-layout/>.*** They are referred to as attribute tags because, while they are tags, they serve as attributes to the app-layout component, which offers us a way to pass in some parameters as inputs. In the react world, we call it props. Also, if you noticed, ***app-layout*** takes in a couple of other attributes—***renderMode***, ***showHeader***, and ***showSections***. In those, ***showHeader*** and ***showSections*** do not take in any values, meaning they are boolean attributes. So, just having them included in the tag inputs gives them a ***true*** value. Let us look at ***src/components/app-layout*** next. Once we have finished exploring ***app-layout***, we will get to the second tag— ***src/components/app-main***—included within the attribute tag **<@body>**.

```
1    import favicon from "./favicon.png";
2    <!doctype html>
3    <html lang="en">
4      <head>
5        <meta http-equiv="content-type" content="text/html; charset=UTF-8">
6        <meta
7          itemprop="description"
8          name="Description"
9          content="Progressive Rendering using Marko"
10       >
11       <meta
12         name="description"
13         content="An example progressive rendering application showcasing Webpack & Marko."
14       >
15       <meta name="viewport" content="width=device-width, initial-scale=1.0">
16       <link rel="icon" type="image/png" sizes="32x32" href=favicon>
17       <link
18         href="https://fonts.googleapis.com/css?family=Open+Sans:300,400,700"
19         media="all"
20         rel="stylesheet"
21       >
22       <${input.head}/>
23     </head>
24     <body>
25       <if(input.showHeader)>
26         <app-header/>
27       </if>
28       <if(input.showSections)>
29         <app-sections renderMode=input.renderMode/>
30       </if>
31       <div class="container">
32         <if(input.showHeader && input.showSections)>
33           <main id="main">
34             <${input.body}/>
35           </main>
36         </if>
37         <else>
38           <${input.body}/>
39         </else>
40       </div>
41     </body>
42   </html>
```

Import web dependencies

Content within <@head> is included here

Content within <@body> is included here

Figure 3-20. *src/components/app-layout/index.marko*

The biggest difference you will notice here is in the syntax—the absence of JSX-style syntax popularized by React, Solid, and many other frameworks. In the Marko world, interspersing Javascript within the HTML is generally frowned upon. This is why you see Marko JS having clear separation of concerns between HTML, CSS, and Javascript code via the *style { }, class { }* sections where styling and behavior for the associated component can be placed, while the HTML is seldom disturbed.

In this case, to achieve conditional rendering, instead of writing Javascript alongside the HTML, like what JSX does, Marko offers built-in conditional rendering support via the core *<if>*, *<else>*, and *<else-if>* tags, making decisional control flow appear natively within the HTML language. They also offer looping support via the *<while>* and *<for>* tags. In the aforementioned figure, the showHeader and showSections are booleans that conditionally render the *app-sections* and *app-header* components. You will also notice that whatever was passed via the attribute tags *<@head>* and *<@body>* from the src/pages/index/template.marko will now be transcluded into this component via the *<${input.body}/>* and *<${input.head}/>*.

The next file is *src/components/app-header/index.marko*.

```
1    <header>
2        <h1>Progressive Rendering using Marko</h1>
3        <a
4            href="https://github.com/dsathyakumar/marko-progressive-renders"
5            target="_blank"
6        >
7            View code on GitHub
8        </a>
9    </header>
```

Figure 3-21. *src/components/app-header/index.marko*

This is a simple marko template that renders the header element. Following this, let's look at *src/components/app-sections/index.marko.* This is also a simple Marko template that renders a section fragment. But the new tag here is the *macro* tag. Macros are reusable fragments within a template itself. They may not be big enough to be pulled out into a template of its own but rather contain some HTML that forms a small reusable part of the existing template. Here, *render-mode* is a macro that renders either a link to go to the next selection or a plain text for the current selection.

Macros are part of Marko's core tags like <if>, <else>, <for>, <while>, <else-if>, <include-text>, <include-html>, <html-comment>, and <await>. *<await>* is the tag that abstracts away the magic of progressive rendering under it (by offering the ability to make the response wait for, buffer and stream it, while rendering the various template fragments (index.marko templates) asynchronously.

The important thing here is all the components we saw so far —*app-layout, app-header*, and *app-sections*—all have an **index.marko** file. This is the renderer and the widget for the component. They are of type single-file components, which may contain both the markup and the behavior. While still being single file, they will still have clearly demarcated separation of concerns by placing the widget (behavior) placed under *class { }.*

```
1     <section class="options">
2         <h2>Options</h2>
3         <macro|{ type, desc }| name="render-mode">
4             <if(input.renderMode === type)>
5                 <span>
6                     <b>${desc}</b>
7                     ↵
8                 </span>
9             </if>
10            <else>
11                <span>
12                    <a href=`/?renderMode=${type}`>
13                        ${desc}
14                    </a>
15                </span>
16            </else>
17        </macro>
18        <fieldset>
19            <legend>Page Render Mode</legend>
20            <ul>
21                <li>
22                    <render-mode type="single-chunk" desc="Single Chunk"/>
23                </li>
24                <li>
25                    <render-mode
26                        type="progressive-in-order"
27                        desc="Progressive (in-order)"
28                    />
29                </li>
30                <li>
31                    <render-mode
32                        type="progressive-out-of-order"
33                        desc="Progressive (out-of-order)"
34                    />
35                </li>
36            </ul>
37        </fieldset>
38    </section>
```

Figure 3-22. *src/components/app-sections/index.marko*

The last tag we will look at before wrapping up **src/pages/index** is *app-main.* This tag or component under *src/components/app-main* will contain an index.marko and a component.js. This is what we call split file components. The HTML markup for this specific fragment or component is well placed under *index.marko*, while the *component.js* contains the behavior which attaches the widget to the associated markup in the *index.marko* file. Marko takes care of wiring them, giving clear separation of concerns, while still ensuring better maintainability and readability. The other files you will notice are a *style.css* or a *style.less* file under the respective component folders. You can place the associated component styles in these, and they will be processed by the bundler of choice—*Webpack/Vite/Rollup*—when the associated plugins are provided.

```
1    <div>
2      <subscribe to=window on-load("refreshPage")/>
3      <h2 key="loading" class="loading">            Once the main index page load
4        <span key="loadingMessage">                 upon the load event, call
5          Page loading...                           this function refreshPage
6        </span>
7        <button type="button" key="refreshButton" on-click("refreshPage")>
8          ↻ Refresh
9        </button>
10       <button type="button" key="newWindowButton" on-click("newWindowClick")>
11         ↗ Open in New Window
12       </button>
13     </h2>
14     <div class="iframe-container">                 Iframe loads the different
15       <iframe                                      pages based on the options
16         title="results-frame"                      we select
17         src=state.iframeUrl
18         key="iframe"
19         on-load("handleOnload")
20       />
21     </div>
22   </div>
```

Figure 3-23. *src/components/app-main/index.marko*

Keys are identifiers given to specific elements or custom Marko components within the template. They help us to query them from Javascript. Every Marko template has four keywords to it:

1. **Input**: This includes component input or props.

2. **Out**: This provides access to the output response stream on server and Marko's *AsyncVDOMBuilder* on the client side. The type of this out stream in the client side is an implementation detail that is bound to change in the upcoming newer versions of Marko.

3. **State**: This provides access to state props.

4. **Component**: This provides access to specific functions within the component.js or class { } which are basically utilities that we may want to use.

It's also important to note that Marko's performance in V5 is made possible because of two different compilation outputs—string on the server and VDOM nodes on the client side. Marko's compiler takes care of having the right outputs depending on the environment based on some heuristics, which we will look at in the upcoming chapters.

```
1
2     export default class {
3  ∨    onInput(input) {
4         this.state = {
5           renderMode: input.renderMode || 'progressive-out-of-order',
6           startTime: Date.now(),
7           iframeUrl: 'about:blank'
8         };
9       }
10      newWindowClick() { // this is fine
11        const url = '/iframe?renderMode=' + this.state.renderMode;
12          window.open(url, '_blank');
13      }
14  ∨   refreshPage(url) { // window load and refresh button handler
15        const loadingEl = this.getEl('loading');
16        const loadingMessageEl = this.getEl('loadingMessage');
17
18        loadingMessageEl.innerHTML = 'Page loading...';
19        loadingEl.className = 'loading';
20
21        this.setState('startTime', Date.now());
22
23        if (typeof url !== 'string') {
24          url = '/iframe?renderMode=' + this.state.renderMode +
25            '&ts=' + this.state.startTime;
26        }
27        this.setState('iframeUrl', url);
28      }
29  ∨   handleOnload() { // iframe load handler
30        const loadingEl = this.getEl('loading');
31        const loadingMessageEl = this.getEl('loadingMessage');
32        const elapsedTime = Date.now() - this.state.startTime;
33        loadingMessageEl.innerHTML = 'Loaded in ' + elapsedTime + 'ms';
34        loadingEl.className = 'loading-done';
35      }
36    };
```

setup component state based on incoming input

The new window click functionality

The refresh functionality wired to a button and on index page on load event

accesses specific elements in the template that are given unique identifiers via the "key" prop

updates the startTime prop in state

updates the iframeUrl prop in state

Compute load time of iframe upon iframe onload event

Figure 3-24. *src/components/app-main/component.js*

The state is set up within ***onCreate*** or the ***onInput*** methods if the ***state*** has to be derived from the ***input*** props. In this case, we set up the state of the component within ***onInput*** as it has to be derived from the input. ***newWindowClick*** and ***refreshPage*** are two event handlers that are wired up to two buttons within the ***index.marko*** file. Finally, ***handleOnLoad*** is the on-load event handler for the embedded iframe element to compute load time.

Most importantly, there is no wiring needed for tying up the template file (***index. marko***) to the widget/behavior file (***component.js***). It just works and is magically handled for you by Marko and the associated web bundler behind the scenes. Marko follows the inversion of control principle, where the framework calls your code and not the other way around.

Next, let us look at the embedded iframe page, which can be found under **src/pages/ iframe**. In this **template.marko** file (a top page-level template is sometimes also named **template.marko**). Most importantly, when a file is named **index.marko**, it can act as the **renderer** (a construct that performs the rendering). However, when you have a **template. marko**, you can have an **index.js** file alongside it, which in turn invokes the rendering by using the **template.marko**'s render method.

```
1    <app-layout
2        renderMode=input.renderMode
3        showHeader=false
4        showSections=false
5    >
6        <@head>
7            <title>Progressive Rendering Page using Marko</title>
8            <script>
9                function clearPage() {
10                   document.body.innerHTML =
11                       "Reloading page... Waiting for server...";
12               }
13           </script>
14       </@head>
15       <@body>
16           <app-frame
17               headerDataProvider=input.headerDataProvider
18               navDataProvider=input.navDataProvider
19               footerDataProvider=input.footerDataProvider
20               mainDataProvider=input.mainDataProvider
21               renderMode=input.renderMode
22               reorderEnabled=input.reorderEnabled
23           />
24       </@body>
25   </app-layout>
```

Figure 3-25. *src/pages/iframe/template.marko*

You will notice there are no functions present here, just the HTML markup. However, in the associated **index.js** file, which we will see next, it will import this template as just another JS file and invoke the **render** function present in it. The importing of **.marko** files into JS files is made possible by Marko JS internally which patches the require and import system of Node JS and Javascript to be able to require extensions of **.marko** into JS files.

Everytime a Marko template is compiled, it will output a **.JS** file. We can choose to keep this in memory or have them output to the disc locally. However, for local development, these are held in memory, making them easy to update for hot module reloads or live reloads based on the bundler system. However, if you noticed, when we started the project we ran npm run build, which ran the build for production mode, thereby providing the output to the dist folder. The files in this folder can then be uploaded to any custom CDN or Amazon S3 instance and then be written out to the disc and be used to render the CDN files in production.

```
 1   import template from "./template.marko";
 2
 3 ∨ const getAPromise = (sectionName, delay) => {
 4       const renderPromise = new Promise((resolve, reject) => {
 5           setTimeout(() => {
 6               resolve({
 7                   sectionName
 8               });
 9           }, delay);
10       });
11       return renderPromise;
12   }
13
14   export default async (req, res) => {
15       const renderMode = req.query.renderMode || 'progressive-out-of-order';
16       const reorder = renderMode === 'progressive-out-of-order';
17       let viewModel = {
18           headerDataProvider: getAPromise('header', 2000),
19           navDataProvider: getAPromise('nav', 500),
20           mainDataProvider: getAPromise('main', 3000),
21           footerDataProvider: getAPromise('footer', 1000),
22           renderMode: renderMode,
23           reorderEnabled: reorder
24       };
25
26       if (renderMode === 'single-chunk') {
27           template.render(viewModel, (err, html) => {
28               if (err) {
29                   console.log(err);
30                   console.log('erroed!');
31                   res.end(err.toString());
32                   return;
33               }
34               res.end(html.toString());
35           });
36       } else {
37           res.marko(template, viewModel);
38       }
39   };
```

Marko patches the import and require system to be able to require compiled Marko JS files into

A function that returns a promise that resolves after the specified delay.

A function present on the compiled Marko JS template that lets do a render as a single chunk

@marko/express offers this method to render Marko templates in Express

Figure 3-26. *src/pages/iframe/index.js*

In this piece of code snippet, various promises are utilized to simulate the case of the components relying on different API endpoint services that will return responses at different times, thereby simulating real-world use cases. If you look at the previous figure, the code within the ***template.marko*** file contained an ***app-frame***. The ***render*** function is present in the compiled output of every Marko template. Marko does not have strong opinions about your data fetchers. You're welcome to use *node-fetch/Axios* or any service client library of your choice here to fetch data.

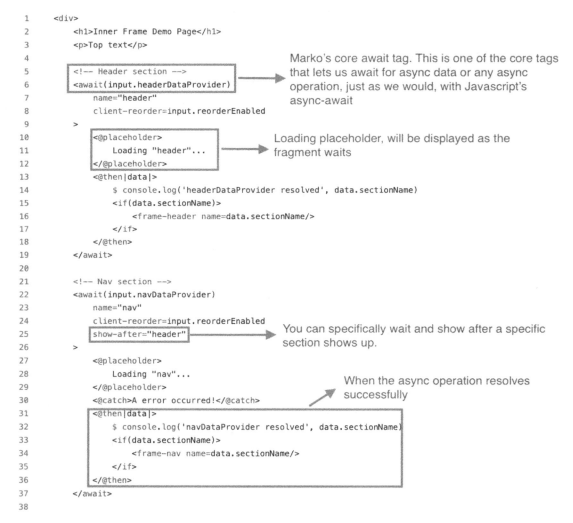

Figure 3-27. *src/components/app-frame/index.marko*

The *<await>* tag is one of Marko JS's core tags, offered out of the box by the framework, that lets you await for async data and operations, similar to the Javascript style async-await syntax. In this example, we map various promises like the *headerDataProvider*, *navDataProvider*, *mainDataProvider*, and *footerDataprovider*. These are reminiscent of the real-world scenario where a page is composed of many component fragments that wait for the associated API service endpoints to return responses. These tags come with the

1. *<@then>* that will be rendered once the data is available. Note that it takes a parameter called *data* which contains the resolved data.

2. *<@catch>* that will be displayed in the event the async operation or data load fails.

3. *<@placeholder>* attribute tags that lets you specify any specific loading placeholders.

```
39        <!-- Main section -->
40        <await(input.mainDataProvider)
41            timeout=20000
42            name="main"
43            client-reorder=input.reorderEnabled
44        >
45            <@placeholder>
46                Loading "main"...
47            </@placeholder>
48            <@catch>A error occurred!</@catch>
49            <@then|data|>
50                $ console.log('mainDataProvider resolved', data.sectionName)
51                <if(data.sectionName)>
52                    <frame-main name=data.sectionName/>
53                </if>
54            </@then>
55        </await>
56
57        <!-- Footer section -->
58        <await(input.footerDataProvider)
59            name="footer"
60            client-reorder=input.reorderEnabled
61        >
62            <@placeholder>
63                Loading "nav"...
64            </@placeholder>
65            <@catch>A error occurred!</@catch>
66            <@then|data|>
67                $ console.log('footerDataProvider resolved', data.sectionName)
68                <if(data.sectionName)>
69                    <frame-footer name=data.sectionName/>
70                </if>
71            </@then>
72        </await>
73        <p>Bottom text</p>
74    </div>
```

When client-reorder is enabled, it means out-of-order render and flush, and use JS on the client for in-order paint

In the event the async operation errors out

Figure 3-28. *src/components/app-frame/index.marko (continued)*

The ***await*** tag also takes a ***timeout*** prop which can be provided to it, that will timeout after the said amount of milliseconds, the operation and render the error. The ***name*** prop helps with debugging and also when you want to make use of the prop ***show-after*** prop. The ***show-after*** prop is used to make sure that the said fragment renders alongside or after the fragment mentioned in ***show-after.*** For example, in the previous figure, the nav section will be rendered alongside or after the header section is rendered. Next, the client-reorder is a boolean prop, which, when true, will enable you to move around sections on the client side using Javascript.

So, per this template, we have the entire iframe page's contents dependent on the loading of these four fragments that have some async behavior tied to it to resolve them at different time instances, simulating real-world scenarios of accessing service API endpoints. Before we go to the individual child components, we will also look at this file *component-browser.js*. Earlier we saw a *component.js* that helped maintain separation of concerns, such that the markup was in the *index.marko* file, while the widget/component behavior was placed within the *component.js* file and we called this setup split file components. But what is this *component-browser.js* file? Well, these are files that have two use cases:

1. If you have some piece of code that you want to exclusively run on the client side, that is on the browser, you can place it within the ***component-browser.js*** file.

2. If you want your component not to have the renderer, then you place a ***component-browser.js*** file in this fashion. When saying not to have a renderer, what we imply is that if you are sure that this component will not re-render on the client side and so does not require its renderer or the template to perform the render, then you can go ahead with the ***component-browser.js*** file.

Moreover, there are some things to remember when you use a ***component-browser.js*** file:

1. If your parent component was capable of performing a re-render, then even if you only had a ***component-browser.js*** file, it will still send the *renderer —that is the template* because the parent component can receive props, which will require to re-render itself, and, in the process, re-render this child component as well.

2. If you have a ***component.js*** file alongside a ***component-browser.js*** file, only the ***component-browser.js*** will be sent to the browser or be bundled to the browser. The ***component.js*** will not be sent as long as there is no parent component that does a re-render. If your component is the child of a parent component that does a re-render, then all the three files—***component.js***, ***component-browser.js***, and ***index.marko***—will be compiled and bundled to the browser.

Most importantly, component-browser.js helps to isolate code that may run exclusively on the client and the server.

```
1    export default class {
2        onMount() {
3            console.log('AppFrame mounted');
4        }
5    }
```

Figure 3-29. *src/components/app-frame/component-browser.js*

We will next look at the four components—***frame-header***, ***frame-footer***, ***frame-nav***, and ***frame-main***. The following is the code for ***frame-header.marko***. All these can be found under the **components/** folder found in ***src/components/app-frame/***.

You will notice the **class { }** block alongside the HTML markup. These are the single-file components that were mentioned earlier. They contain both the markup and the behavior. However, despite having them both in the same file, they have clear separation of concerns.

```
1    class {
2        onMount() {
3            const headerMessage = this.getEl('header-message');
4            headerMessage.innerHTML = 'Behavior Attached (click me)';
5        }
6        click() {
7            const headerEl = this.getEl('header');
8            const headerMessage = this.getEl('header-message');
9            headerEl.style.backgroundColor = '#2c3e50';
10           headerMessage.innerHTML = 'Clicked!';
11       }
12   }
13
14   <header key="header" once-click('click')>
15       <h2>${input.name}</h2>
16       <span key="header-message">
17            
18       </span>
19   </header>
```

Figure 3-30. *src/components/app-frame/components/frame-header/ index.marko*

The following is the code for *frame-nav.marko*.

```
1    class {
2        onMount() {
3            const navMessage = this.getEl('nav-message');
4            navMessage.innerHTML = 'Behavior Attached (click me)';
5        }
6        click() {
7            const navEl = this.getEl('nav');
8            const navMessage = this.getEl('nav-message');
9            navEl.style.backgroundColor = '#2c3e50';
10           navMessage.innerHTML = 'Clicked!';
11       }
12   }
13
14   <nav key="nav" once-click('click')>
15       <h2>${input.name}</h2>
16       <span key="nav-message">
17            
18       </span>
19   </nav>
```

Figure 3-31. *src/components/app-frame/components/frame-nav/index.marko*

The methods we say earlier—*onInput* and *onMount*—are some of the lifecycle methods of Marko JS. *onInput* triggers every time a component receives new input via props. *onMount* triggers only once, on the client side, when the component mounts for the first time. Subsequent re-renders triggered by state changes or new props will not trigger the *onMount* method. This is an indication that the component is interaction ready. Most importantly, *this* keyword is accessible only within the onMount and associated client-side event handlers.

```marko
1    class {
2        onMount() {
3            const footerMessage = this.getEl('footer-message');
4            footerMessage.innerHTML = 'Behavior Attached (click me)';
5        }
6        click() {
7            const footerEl = this.getEl('footer');
8            const footerMessage = this.getEl('footer-message');
9            footerEl.style.backgroundColor = '#2c3e50';
10           footerMessage.innerHTML = 'Clicked!';
11       }
12   }
13   <footer key='footer' once-click('click')>
14       <h2>${input.name}</h2>
15       <span key="footer-message">
16            
17       </span>
18   </footer>
```

Figure 3-32. *src/components/app-frame/components/frame-footer/index.marko*

```marko
1    class {
2        onMount() {
3            const mainMessage = this.getEl('main-message');
4            mainMessage.innerHTML = 'Behavior Attached (click me)';
5        }
6        click() {
7            const mainEl = this.getEl('main');
8            const mainMessage = this.getEl('main-message');
9            mainEl.style.backgroundColor = '#2c3e50';
10           mainMessage.innerHTML = 'Clicked!';
11       }
12   }
13
14   <main key="main" once-click('click')>
15       <h2>${input.name}</h2>
16       <span key="main-message">
17            
18       </span>
19   </main>
```

Figure 3-33. *src/components/app-frame/components/frame-main/index.marko*

This completes our walkthrough of all the project files within this sample project that illustrated the various techniques of progressive rendering. As you play around with these samples more, you will begin to better appreciate progressive rendering and develop a solid mental model around the same.

It's important to note that at this point of time of writing this book, which is based on v5, Marko JS does not perform isomorphic progressive renders. You can either do it from the server by consuming an API endpoint that emits either a JSON stream or Server-Sent Events or on the browser via the EventSource API that talks to an API endpoint that emits data in the Server-Sent Events format.

Sample Project Explaining Progressive Rendering with Marko on the Client

Firstly, the core **<await>** tag discussed here does not have support for performing progressive rendering on the client side. It's a server-side only tag, however, that shouldn't hold you from doing it on the client, just with a custom Marko component and state. However, this is changing with Marko v6 where **<await>** is expected to be truly isomorphic. One of the issues with isomorphic **<await>** is taking care not to replay those calls on the client that may have already been triggered on the server. We will update our previous example with a client-only progressive render. The only caveats with respect to this example is that we are not doing the **show-after** and **name.** This being an example, we intend to keep it simple. However, they are additions you can always add but will complicate our setup. Firstly, the following are the files we are either adding to the setup or modifying.

src/components/app-client-frame/components/client-frame-footer.marko ⊞

☑ src/components/app-client-frame/components/client-frame-header.marko ⊞

☑ src/components/app-client-frame/components/client-frame-main.marko ⊞

☑ src/components/app-client-frame/components/client-frame-nav.marko ⊞

☑ src/components/app-client-frame/index.marko ⊞

☑ src/components/app-client-frame/style.css ⊞

☑ src/components/app-main/component.js ⊡

☑ src/components/app-sections/index.marko ⊡

☑ src/components/client-await/index.marko ⊞

☑ src/index.js ⊡

☑ src/pages/client-iframe/index.js ⊞

☑ src/pages/client-iframe/template.marko ⊞

☑ src/pages/client-index/index.js ⊞

☑ src/pages/client-index/template.marko ⊞

Figure 3-34. *File diff for the sample progressive rendering on client project*

src/index.js

```
src/index.js                                                                    ⚙ ▾ ⊡

    ↑         @@ -2,7 +2,9 @@ import express from "express";
  2   2       import compressionMiddleware from "compression";
  3   3       import markoMiddleware from "@marko/express";
  4   4       import indexPage from "./pages/index";
✓     5    +  import clientIndexPage from "./pages/client-index";
  5   6       import iframePage from "./pages/iframe";
✓     7    +  import clientIframePage from "./pages/client-iframe";
  6   8
  7   9       const port = parseInt(process.env.PORT || 3000, 10);
  8  10
  ⋮           @@ -11,7 +13,9 @@ express()
 11  13         .use("/assets", express.static("dist/assets")) // Serve assets generated from webpack.
 12  14         .use(markoMiddleware()) // Enables res.marko.
 13  15         .get("/", indexPage)
✓    16    +    .get("/client", clientIndexPage)
 14  17         .get("/iframe", iframePage)
✓    18    +    .get("/client-iframe", clientIframePage)
 15  19         .listen(port, err => {
 16  20           if (err) {
 17  21             throw err;
  ⋮
```

Figure 3-35. *src/index.js*

136

src/pages/client-index/index.js

```
src > pages > client-index > JS index.js
1    import template from "./template.marko";
2
3    export default (req, res) => {
4      const renderMode = req.query.renderMode || 'progressive-out-of-order-client';
5      res.marko(template, {
6        renderMode
7      });
8    };
```

Figure 3-36. *src/pages/client-index/index.js*

This page is similar to the **src/pages/index/index.js**, and the following is the associated template.marko file in **src/pages/index/template.marko**.

```
src > pages > client-index > ☰ template.marko > ⛓ app-layout
1    <app-layout
2      renderMode=input.renderMode
3      showHeader
4      showSections=true
5    >
6      <@head>
7        <title>Progressive Rendering using Marko</title>
8      </@head>
9      <@body>
10       <app-main renderMode=input.renderMode/>
11     </@body>
12   </app-layout>
```

Figure 3-37. *src/pages/client-index/template.marko*

The next are some changes to **src/components/app-sections**.

```
src > components > app-sections > ≡ index.marko > ℘ section > ℘ fieldset > ℘ ul > ⁑ if > ℘ li > ⁑ render-mode
 1    <section class="options">
 2        <h2>Options</h2>
 3        <macro { type, desc } name="render-mode">
 4            <if(input.renderMode === type)>
 5                <span>
 6                    <b>${desc}</b>
 7
 8                </span>
 9            </if>
10            <else>
11                <span>
12                    <a href=`/?renderMode=${type}`>
13                        ${desc}
14                    </a>
15                </span>
16            </else>
17        </macro>
18        <fieldset>
19            <legend>Page Render Mode</legend>
20            <ul>
21                <if(input.renderMode === 'progressive-out-of-order-client')>
22                    <li>
23                        <render-mode type="progressive-out-of-order-client" desc="progressive-out-of-order-client"/>
24                    </li>
25                </if>
26                <else>
27                    <li>
28                        <render-mode type="single-chunk" desc="Single Chunk"/>
29                    </li>
30                    <li>
31                        <render-mode
32                            type="progressive-in-order"
33                            desc="Progressive (in-order)"
34                        />
35                    </li>
36                    <li>
37                        <render-mode
38                            type="progressive-out-of-order"
39                            desc="Progressive (out-of-order)"
40                        />
41                    </li>
42                </else>
43            </ul>
44        </fieldset>
45    </section>
```

Figure 3-38. *src/components/app-sections/index.marko*

The next are some changes to **src/components/app-main/component.js** to handle different frame URLs.

```
src > components > app-main > JS component.js
1   const getPath = (renderMode) => {
2     let path = 'iframe';
3     if (renderMode === 'progressive-out-of-order-client') {
4       path = 'client-iframe'
5     }
6     return path;
7   }
8   export default class {
9 >   onInput(input) {…
15    }
16    newWindowClick() { // this is fine
17      const url = `/${getPath(this.input.renderMode)}?renderMode=` + this.state.renderMode;
18        window.open(url, '_blank');
19    }
20    refreshPage(url) { // window load and refresh button handler
21      const loadingEl = this.getEl('loading');
22      const loadingMessageEl = this.getEl('loadingMessage');
23
24      loadingMessageEl.innerHTML = 'Page loading...';
25      loadingEl.className = 'loading';
26
27      this.setState('startTime', Date.now());
28
29      if (typeof url !== 'string') {
30        url = `/${getPath(this.input.renderMode)}?renderMode=` + this.state.renderMode +
31          '&ts=' + this.state.startTime;
32      }
33      this.setState('iframeUrl', url);
34    }
35 >  handleOnload() { // iframe load handler…
41    }
42  };
```

Figure 3-39. *src/components/app-main/component.js*

Given that we have a different URL for the iframe page for client-side progressive renders, here is **src/pages/client-iframe/index.js**.

```
src > pages > client-iframe > JS index.js
 1    import template from "./template.marko";
 2
 3    export default async (req, res) => {
 4        const renderMode = req.query.renderMode || 'progressive-out-of-order-client';
 5        const reorder = renderMode === 'progressive-out-of-order-client';
 6        let viewModel = {
 7            headerDataProvider: null,
 8            navDataProvider: null,
 9            mainDataProvider: null,
10            footerDataProvider: null,
11            renderMode: renderMode,
12            reorderEnabled: reorder
13        };
14
15        res.marko(template, viewModel);
16    };
```

Figure 3-40. *src/pages/client-iframe/index.js*

This is followed by the associated template **src/pages/client-iframe/template.marko**.

```
src > pages > client-iframe > ☰ template.marko > ...
 1    <app-layout
 2        renderMode=input.renderMode
 3        showHeader=false
 4        showSections=false
 5    >
 6        <@head>
 7            <title>Progressive Rendering Page on Client using Marko</title>
 8            <script>
 9                function clearPage() {
10                    document.body.innerHTML =
11                        "Reloading page... Waiting for server...";
12                }
13            </script>
14        </@head>
15        <@body>
16            <app-client-frame
17                headerDataProvider=input.headerDataProvider
18                navDataProvider=input.navDataProvider
19                footerDataProvider=input.footerDataProvider
20                mainDataProvider=input.mainDataProvider
21                renderMode=input.renderMode
22                reorderEnabled=input.reorderEnabled
23            />
24        </@body>
25    </app-layout>
26
```

Figure 3-41. *src/pages/client-iframe/template.marko*

140

But note that all the **providers** are **null** to begin with. **<app-layout>** is the same as before for both the new pages. The only new component we have is **<app-client-frame>**.

```
src > components > app-client-frame >  ≡ index.marko > ...
  1    class {
  2        onCreate(input) {
  3            console.log('AppClientFrame created');
  4            this.state = {
  5                headerDataProvider: input.headerDataProvider,
  6                navDataProvider: input.navDataProvider,
  7                mainDataProvider: input.mainDataProvider,
  8                footerDataProvider: input.footerDataProvider,
  9            }
 10        }
 11        getAPromise = (sectionName, delay) => {
 12            const renderPromise = new Promise((resolve, reject) => {
 13                setTimeout(() => {
 14                    resolve({
 15                        sectionName
 16                    });
 17                }, delay);
 18            });
 19            return renderPromise;
 20        }
 21        onMount() {
 22            console.log('AppClientFrame mounted');
 23            this.replaceState({
 24                headerDataProvider: this.getAPromise('header', 2000),
 25                navDataProvider: this.getAPromise('nav', 500),
 26                mainDataProvider: this.getAPromise('main', 3000),
 27                footerDataProvider: this.getAPromise('footer', 1000),
 28            });
 29        }
 30    }
```

We are simulating async behavior here. This could very well be client side fetch to APIs

Figure 3-42. *src/components/app-client-frame/index.marko*

The same file is continued below showing the template.

Given that our custom await tag is not provisioned to accept tag arguments, we pass the promise in as part of the **value** prop. So we don't have **<client-await(promise)>** but instead do **<client-await value=promise>**.

```
src > components > app-client-frame > ☰ index.marko > ...
 31
 32
 33    <div>
 34        <h1>Inner Frame Demo Page</h1>
 35        <p>Top text</p>
 36
 37        <!-- Header section -->
 38        <client-await value=state.headerDataProvider>
 39            <@placeholder>
 40                Loading "header"...
 41            </@placeholder>
 42            <@then|data|>
 43                $ console.log('headerDataProvider resolved', data.sectionName)
 44                <if(data.sectionName)>
 45                    <client-frame-header name=data.sectionName/>
 46                </if>
 47            </@then>
 48        </client-await>
 49
 50        <!-- Nav section -->
 51        <client-await value=state.navDataProvider>
 52            <@placeholder>
 53                Loading "nav"...
 54            </@placeholder>
 55            <@catch>A error occurred!</@catch>
 56            <@then|data|>
 57                $ console.log('navDataProvider resolved', data.sectionName)
 58                <if(data.sectionName)>
 59                    <client-frame-nav name=data.sectionName/>
 60                </if>
 61            </@then>
 62        </client-await>
 63
 64        <!-- Main section -->
 65        <client-await value=state.mainDataProvider>
 66            <@placeholder>
 67                Loading "main"...
 68            </@placeholder>
 69            <@catch>A error occurred!</@catch>
 70            <@then|data|>
 71                $ console.log('mainDataProvider resolved', data.sectionName)
 72                <if(data.sectionName)>
 73                    <client-frame-main name=data.sectionName/>
 74                </if>
 75            </@then>
 76        </client-await>
 77
 78        <!-- Footer section -->
 79        <client-await value=state.footerDataProvider>
 80            <@placeholder>
 81                Loading "nav"...
 82            </@placeholder>
 83            <@catch>A error occurred!</@catch>
 84            <@then|data|>
 85                $ console.log('footerDataProvider resolved', data.sectionName)
 86                <if(data.sectionName)>
 87                    <client-frame-footer name=data.sectionName/>
 88                </if>
 89            </@then>
 90        </client-await>
 91
 92        <p>Bottom text</p>
 93    </div>
```

Figure 3-43. *src/components/app-client-frame/index.marko (continued)*

We have copied (not moved!) the contents of

- src/components/app-frame/components/frame-header

- src/components/app-frame/components/frame-footer

- src/components/app-frame/components/frame-main

- src/components/app-frame/components/frame-nav

and put them here

- src/components/app-**client**-frame/
  components/**client**-frame-header

- src/components/app-**client**-frame/components/**client**-frame-footer

- src/components/app-**client**-frame/components/**client**-frame-main

- src/components/app-**client**-frame/components/**client**-frame-nav

Now load the page as http://localhost:3000/client and you will see. Upon initial load, there will be nothing. However, upon initialization (mount), you will see the same progressive rendering behavior done using just state. The providers are filled with promises upon **mount**, and they get resolved one by one based on their timeout. These can be considered to be API calls made with fetch on the client side.

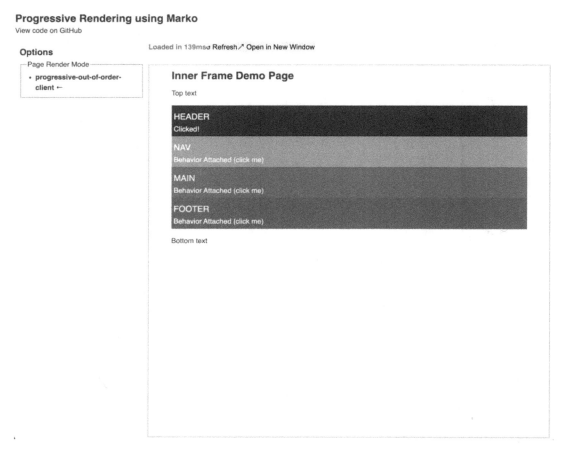

Figure 3-44. *Client side progressive rendering example with Marko*

Revisiting the Examples

In the *first* sample project that discussed progressive rendering, the render was done on the server. When you inspect the webpack source files, you will notice those templates that used the **<await>** in that case, namely, *<app-frame>/index.marko*, will not be found in the webpack sources on the client. They don't get bundled. However, we were able to do the three different versions of server-side progressive rendering:

1. Single-Chunk (async render, buffered on server, and flushed once as a single chunk).

2. Multi-Chunk In-order (async render, buffered on the server to maintain order, but flushes if the buffer has the right order up to whatever was rendered— out-of-order render, in-order flush, and page painted in order since flush was in order). Page flushed in multi-chunks.

3. Multi-Chunk Out of Order (async render, not buffered on the server to maintain order, flushed as fragments are rendered, out-of-order render, out-of-order flush, and page painted in order through the use of Javascript to get the fragments in the right order). Page flushed in multi-chunks.

The core **<await>** is not supported for use on the client side. You will incur errors of not supported on the client side. Client re-order relies on using the Marko runtime to fix the order of said fragments on the client.

In the *second* sample project that discussed progressive rendering, the render occurred on the client side (assuming fetch or other API calls happened on the client side). When you inspect the webpack source files, you will notice those templates that used the *<client-await>* in that case, namely, *<app-client-iframe>* will be found in the webpack sources on the client, along with the *<client-await>* component. Since they are required for re-render on the client, these are bundled to the browser. However, we were able to do the following form of progressive rendering by default:

1. Multi-chunk Out of Order (async render, not buffered on the server/client, nothing flushed but just involves setting the state once the data arrives, causes the associated components to render and update their associated views, out-of-order state sets and out-of-order renders, page ultimately painted in order)

Also, the current way we have done it for the second example is for the respective fragments to *"appear"* out of order, but the final order of the page is maintained due to their location in the DOM. But if you wanted them to *"appear"* in order, then you can have a parent component that controls the setting of state based on the order in which data arrives.

Let's look at the rendered sources on the browser for Example 1 (server-side progressive rendering). You will notice that

1. **<app-layout>** component is not sent (Marko detects there is nothing to re-render and does not send the template). Only the style file is sent.

2. The components contained within **<app-layout>**, namely, **<app-header>** and **<app-sections>**, are also not sent since there is no state involved and the parent **<app-layout>** does not have any re-renderable pathways.

3. **<app-main>** belongs to the main page rendered when accessing / and its template and component is sent to the browser as it involves state and needs to re-render when choosing options on the left navigation section.

4. **<app-frame>** template (*index.marko*) is not sent. This contains the server-side core **<await>** tags.

5. **<app-frame>** *component-browser.js* is sent. This is built as a split component and only the behavior is sent (we will look at what are split components in the subsequent chapters). The associated style file is sent.

6. *app-frame/components*, namely, **<frame-footer>**, **<frame-header>**, **<frame-main>**, and **<frame-nav>**, are sent. This is because although they only have a click function wired on to the server-rendered HTML and that there is no re-render involved, they are still built as single-file components (the template *index.marko* file contains both the template and the behavior). If we had built it as a split component the same way as *<app-frame>* (template within *index.marko* and client-side behavior within a *component-browser.js*), the template would not have been sent to the browser.

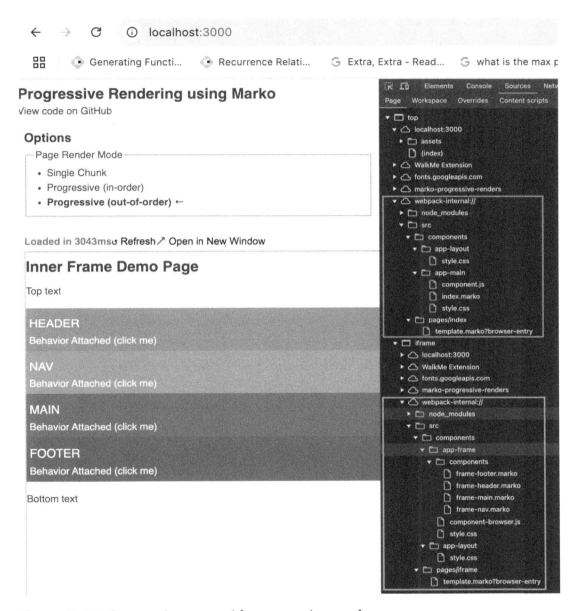

Figure 3-45. *Sources in server-side progressive render*

Next, let's look at the rendered sources on the browser for Example 2 (client-side progressive rendering). You will notice that

1. **<app-layout>** component is not sent (Marko detects there is nothing to re-render and does not send the template). Only the style file is sent.

2. The components contained within **<app-layout>**, namely, **<app-header>** and **<app-sections>**, are also not sent since there is no state involved and the parent **<app-layout>** does not have any re-renderable pathways.

3. **<app-main>** belongs to the main page rendered when accessing / and its template and component is sent to the browser as it involves state and needs to re-render when choosing options on the left navigation section.

4. **<app-client-frame>** is sent. This contains the client-side **<await>** tags. Notice again this is built as a single-file component. Even had it been built as a split file component, this would have had its associated template (*index.marko)* file sent to the browser as there is state involved and Marko realizes this component has a pathway for a re-render.

5. All *app-client-frame/components*, namely, **<client-frame-footer>**, **<client-frame-header>**, **<client-frame-main>**, and **<client-frame-nav>**, are sent. This is because irrespective of whether or not they are built as single-file or split file components, their template will be sent since the parent component **<app-client-frame>** has a pathway for a re-render, causing the child components to be sent.

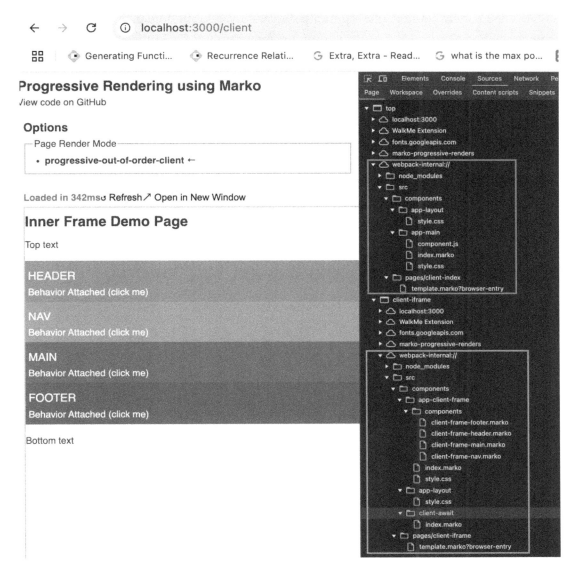

Figure 3-46. *Sources in a client-side progressive rendered page*

Given all this, would it be nice if we had some isomorphic form of an **<await>** tag where we could perhaps send the contained HTML fragment to the client, start a promise for the data on the server, resolve the promise on the server once the data arrives, and observe the resolution on the client by causing to contained HTML fragment to render on the client (and not on the server)?

This is the ideal isomorphic experience we would like. But note that we can still achieve the first example, (2) Multi-Chunk In Order, **but not** (3) Multi-chunk Out of Order. This is because to get (3) Multi-chunk Out of Order working, we require deeper support from Marko's internals itself (in terms of re-ordering on the client and syncing with Marko's server-side runtime) (to serialize the hydrated data of server render); however, we can still achieve (2) Multi-chunk In Order just with some promises and using the existing behavior of Marko's server-side runtime, which buffers the fragments so that order on server is maintained by default. We will look at this next and call it as **<iso-await>**. However, note that full isomorphic support for the core **<await>** to achieve (3) Multi-chunk Out of Order is expected to land with Marko v6. And as mentioned earlier, you will get this for free via Marko's migration utility.

Isomorphic <await> Without client-reorder

As always, we begin with *src/index.js* to create separate routes for this isomorphic await experience within our project as shown in Figure 3-47.

```
src/index.js

           @@ -3,8 +3,10 @@ import compressionMiddleware from "compression";
    3    3  import markoMiddleware from "@marko/express";
    4    4  import indexPage from "./pages/index";
    5    5  import clientIndexPage from "./pages/client-index";
         6 + import isoIndexPage from "./pages/iso-index";
    6    7  import iframePage from "./pages/iframe";
    7    8  import clientIframePage from "./pages/client-iframe";
         9 + import isoIframePage from "./pages/iso-iframe";
    8   10
    9   11  const port = parseInt(process.env.PORT || 3000, 10);
   10   12
           @@ -16,6 +18,8 @@ express()
   16   18    .get("/client", clientIndexPage)
   17   19    .get("/iframe", iframePage)
   18   20    .get("/client-iframe", clientIframePage)
        21 +  .get("/iso", isoIndexPage)
        22 +  .get("/isoiframe", isoIframePage)
   19   23    .listen(port, err => {
   20   24      if (err) {
   21   25        throw err;
```

Figure 3-47. *src/index.js file diff*

Separate routes are wired on for the initial page load and the embedded iframe that displays the experience.

Next let's look at src/pages/iso-index/index.js

src/pages/iso-index/**index.js**

```
@@ -0,0 +1,8 @@
1  + import template from "./template.marko";
2  +
3  + export default (req, res) => {
4  +   const renderMode = req.query.renderMode || 'iso-progressive-out-of-order';
5  +   res.marko(template, {
6  +     renderMode
7  +   });
8  + };
```

Figure 3-48. *src/pages/iso-index/index.js*

Next let's look at src/pages/iso-index/template.marko

src/pages/iso-index/**template.marko**

```
@@ -0,0 +1,12 @@
1  + <app-layout
2  +   renderMode=input.renderMode
3  +   showHeader
4  +   showSections
5  + >
6  +   <@head>
7  +     <title>Progressive Rendering using Marko</title>
8  +   </@head>
9  +   <@body>
10 +     <app-main renderMode=input.renderMode/>
11 +   </@body>
12 + </app-layout>
```

Figure 3-49. *src/pages/iso-index/template.marko*

151

```
src > components > app-main > JS component.js > [∅] getPath
  1    const getPath = (renderMode) => {
  2      let path = 'iframe';
  3      if (renderMode === 'progressive-out-of-order-client') {
  4        path = 'client-iframe'
  5      } else if (renderMode === 'iso-progressive-out-of-order') {
  6        path = 'isoiframe'
  7      }
  8      return path;
  9    }
 10  > export default class {
 44    };
 45
```

Figure 3-50. *src/components/app-main/component.js*

```
src > pages > iso-iframe > ≡ template.marko > ...
  1    <app-layout
  2        renderMode=input.renderMode
  3        showHeader=false
  4        showSections=false
  5    >
  6        <@head>
  7            <title>Progressive Rendering Page using Marko</title>
  8            <script>
  9                function clearPage() {
 10                    document.body.innerHTML =
 11                        "Reloading page... Waiting for server...";
 12                }
 13            </script>
 14        </@head>
 15        <@body>
 16            <app-frame-iso
 17                headerDataProvider=input.headerDataProvider
 18                navDataProvider=input.navDataProvider
 19                footerDataProvider=input.footerDataProvider
 20                mainDataProvider=input.mainDataProvider
 21                renderMode=input.renderMode
 22                reorderEnabled=input.reorderEnabled
 23            />
 24        </@body>
 25    </app-layout>
```

Figure 3-51. *src/pages/iso-frame/template.marko*

```
src > pages > iso-iframe > JS index.js > ...
  1    import template from "./template.marko";
  2
  3    const getAPromise = (sectionName, delay) => {
  4        const renderPromise = new Promise((resolve, reject) => {
  5            setTimeout(() => {
  6                resolve({
  7                    sectionName
  8                });
  9            }, delay);
 10        });
 11        return renderPromise;
 12    }
 13
 14    export default async (req, res) => {
 15        const renderMode = req.query.renderMode || 'iso-progressive-out-of-order';
 16        const reorder = renderMode === 'iso-progressive-out-of-order';
 17        let viewModel = {
 18            headerDataProvider: getAPromise('header', 2000),
 19            navDataProvider: getAPromise('nav', 500),
 20            mainDataProvider: getAPromise('main', 3000),
 21            footerDataProvider: getAPromise('footer', 1000),
 22            renderMode: renderMode,
 23            reorderEnabled: reorder
 24        };
 25
 26        res.marko(template, viewModel);
 27    };
```

Figure 3-52. *src/pages/iso-frame/index.js*

```
src > components > app-sections > ☰ index.marko > ...
  1    <section class="options">
  2        <h2>Options</h2>
  3 >      <macro { type, desc } name="render-mode">
 17        </macro>
 18        <fieldset>
 19            <legend>Page Render Mode</legend>
 20            <ul>
 21 >              <if(input.renderMode === 'progressive-out-of-order-client')>
 25                </if>
 26                <else-if(input.renderMode.startsWith('iso'))>
 27                    <li>
 28                        <render-mode type="iso-progressive-out-of-order" desc="iso-progressive-out-of-order"/>
 29                    </li>
 30                </else-if>
 31 >              <else>
 47                </else>
 48            </ul>
 49        </fieldset>
 50    </section>
 51
```

Figure 3-53. *src/components/app-sections/index.marko*

153

```marko
src > components > app-frame-iso > ≡ index.marko > ...
 1    class {
 2        onCreate(input) {
 3            console.log('sample-wrapper-parent created', input);
 4            input.name = "app-frame-iso"
 5            this.state = {
 6                name: input.name || "app-frame-iso"
 7            }
 8        }
 9        onMount() {
10            console.log('sample-wrapper-parent mounted');
11        }
12        toggle() {
13            if (this.state.name === "app-frame-iso") {
14                this.state.name = "iso-app-frame"
15            } else {
16                this.state.name = "app-frame-iso";
17            }
18        }
19    }
20    <div>
21        <h1>Inner Frame ${state.name} Page</h1>
22        <p>Top text</p>
23        <nested-component ...input/>
24        <p>Bottom text</p>
25        <button on-click('toggle')>Change text</button>
26    </div>
```

Figure 3-54. *src/components/app-frame-iso/index.marko*

In this, we are just keeping a top-level parent component that contains the awaits within them.

```
src > components > app-frame-iso > # style.css > ⅔ h1
  1   h1 {
  2       font-size: 1.5em;
  3   }
  4
  5   h2 {
  6       font-weight: normal;
  7       font-size: 1.2em;
  8       text-transform: uppercase;
  9   }
 10
 11   body {
 12       font: 12pt/1.5em sans-serif;
 13   }
 14
 15   header {
 16       background-color: ▢#16a085;
 17       padding: 5px;
 18       color: ■white;
 19   }
 20
 21   nav {
 22       background-color: ▢#e67e22;
 23       padding: 5px;
 24       color: ■white;
 25   }
 26
 27   main {
 28       background-color: ▢#c0392b;
 29       padding: 5px;
 30       color: ■white;
 31   }
 32
 33   footer {
 34       background-color: ▢#8e44ad;
 35       padding: 5px;
 36       color: ■white;
 37   }
```

Figure 3-55. *src/components/app-frame-iso/styles.css*

Now that we have got all of the basic setup ready, we come to the important files. src/
components/app-frame-iso/index.marko contains a **<nested-component>** which is the
one containing our isomorphic ***await*** tag named **<iso-await>**.

This is shown in the next file src/components/nested-component/index.marko. In
this file, you will notice the **<iso-frame-header>**, **<iso-frame-footer>**, **<iso-frame-
nav>**, and **<iso-frame-main>** which are the same components found in the earlier
example for server-side and client-side progressive rendering; they are locally scoped

and placed within the **components**/. Since these are the same files in terms of their content and have just been renamed, they have been skipped from being included in the following figures. They have been renamed for clarity.

The aforementioned components **<iso-frame-header>**, **<iso-frame-footer>**, **<iso-frame-nav>**, and **<iso-frame-main>** are placed with the <@then> block of the <iso-await> component as part of its body content.

```
src > components > nested-component > ☰ index.marko > ⌀ div > ⫴ iso-await > ⫴ n > ⫴ if >
  1    class {
  2       onCreate(input, out) {
  3          console.log('sample-nested-component created', input);
  4          this.state = {
  5             headerDataProvider: input.headerDataProvider,
  6             navDataProvider: input.navDataProvider,
  7             mainDataProvider: input.mainDataProvider,
  8             footerDataProvider: input.footerDataProvider
  9          }
 10       }
 11       onInput(input) {
 12          console.log('sample-nested-component input', input);
 13       }
 14       onMount() {
 15          console.log('nested component mounted!')
 16       }
 17    }
 18
 19    <div>
 20       <!-- Header section -->
 21       <iso-await provider=input.headerDataProvider
 22          name="header"
 23       >
 24          <@placeholder>
 25             Loading "header"...
 26          </@placeholder>
 27          <@then|data|>
 28             $ console.log('headerDataProvider resolved', data.sectionName)
 29             <if(data.sectionName)>
 30                <iso-frame-header name=data.sectionName/>
 31             </if>
 32          </@then>
 33       </iso-await>
 34
 35       <!-- Nav section -->
 36       <iso-await provider=input.navDataProvider
 37          name="nav"
 38       >
 39          <@placeholder>
 40             Loading "nav"...
 41          </@placeholder>
 42          <@catch>A error occurred!</@catch>
 43          <@then|data|>
 44             $ console.log('navDataProvider resolved', data.sectionName)
 45             <if(data.sectionName)>
 46                <iso-frame-nav name=data.sectionName/>
 47             </if>
 48          </@then>
 49       </iso-await>
 50
```

Figure 3-56. *src/components/nested-component/index.marko*

```
51         <!-- Main section -->
52         <iso-await provider=input.mainDataProvider
53             timeout=20000
54             name="main"
55         >
56             <@placeholder>
57                 Loading "main"...
58             </@placeholder>
59             <@catch>A error occurred!</@catch>
60             <@then|data|>
61                 $ console.log('mainDataProvider resolved', data.sectionName)
62                 <if(data.sectionName)>
63                     <iso-frame-main name=data.sectionName/>
64                 </if>
65             </@then>
66         </iso-await>
67
68         <!-- Footer section -->
69         <iso-await provider=input.footerDataProvider
70             name="footer"
71         >
72             <@placeholder>
73                 Loading "nav"...
74             </@placeholder>
75             <@catch>A error occurred!</@catch>
76             <@then|data|>
77                 $ console.log('footerDataProvider resolved', data.sectionName)
78                 <if(data.sectionName)>
79                     <iso-frame-footer name=data.sectionName/>
80                 </if>
81             </@then>
82         </iso-await>
83     </div>
```

Figure 3-57. *src/components/nested-component/index.marko (continued)*

Finally comes the **<iso-await>** component, which we shall look into in detail. If you will notice, the setup has three files—a template in an *index.marko* file, a *component.js* file for the Marko's lifecycle handlers, and a utils.js file. The **<iso-await>** is used within the **<nested-component>** that we earlier saw. Its body content includes templates that need to be rendered if the **<iso-await>** successfully resolves whatever async task it is bound to.

157

The *index.marko* file conditionally executes server-side code and client-side code. In the server-side code, you will notice that it takes in a **then**, **catch**, and **timeout**. The values to these are what we passed within the body of **<iso-await>**. They are available on the props input.catch and input.then (both passed via attribute tags) and input.timeout (passed via attribute values). Besides this, it also takes the async object that it has to wait for. After that, it's the usual core **<await>** tag that works its magic internally. However, notice that nothing is rendered on the server here. This is telling Marko to execute the async task on the server, serialize the resolved data from the server to the client, observe the resolution on the client side, and proceed to render on the client.

There is also an isBrowserEnv to distinguish the rendering between server and client. It imports a few things from the associated *utils.js*.

For the browser part of the execution, it observes the resolution of the promise that was resolved/rejected on the server. This promise is made available by storing it in the component's state object. The browser part of the execution is able to observe the resolved/rejected value here because Marko serialized the result from server to client. Based on the resolution of the promise, the associated renderer— input.then/input. catch/input.loading—is used and that renders the corresponding body content that was placed within <iso-await>. You will notice that in the next set of images, before resolving/ rejecting, the promise has a default value. So, if in case the promise is neither resolved/ rejected on the server and there was a timeout or a serialization failure, by default, the placeholder will execute.

```
src > components > iso-await >  ≡ index.marko > ⅔ else
 1    import {
 2        PROMISE_STATUS_RESOLVED,
 3        PROMISE_STATUS_REJECTED
 4    } from "./utils"
 5
 6    static var isBrowserEnv = typeof window !== "undefined";
 7
 8    <if(isBrowserEnv)>
 9        $ console.log('-----START: browser-----');
10        $ {
11            let renderer = input.placeholder;
12            if (state.settled === PROMISE_STATUS_RESOLVED) {
13                renderer = input.then;
14            } else if (state.settled === PROMISE_STATUS_REJECTED) {
15                renderer = input.catch;
16            }
17            renderer && renderer.renderBody && renderer.renderBody(out, state.value);
18        }
19        $ console.log('-----END: browser-----');
20    </if>
21    <else>
22        $ console.log('-----server: start-----');
23        <await(input.provider)
24            then=input.then
25            catch=input.catch
26            timeout=input.timeout
27        >
28            <${input.placeholder.renderBody}/>
29        </await>
30        $ console.log('-----server: end-----');
31    </else>
```

Figure 3-58. *src/components/iso-await/index.marko*

```
src > components > iso-await > JS component.js > ...
1    import {
2        makeAsyncDataSerializable,
3        isPromise,
4        maybeSyncServerState,
5        PROMISE_STATUS_LOADING,
6        PROMISE_STATUS_RESOLVED,
7        wireThen
8    } from "./utils"
9
10   const isBrowserEnv = () => typeof window !== "undefined";
11
12   export default class {
13       onCreate(input) {
14           console.log('create: iso-await', input)
15           var value = input.provider;
16           if (isBrowserEnv()) {
17               this.state = { settled: PROMISE_STATUS_LOADING, value: undefined };
18           } else if (isPromise(value)) {
19               // if not browser env, make the async value serializable.
20               makeAsyncDataSerializable(value);
21           }
22       }
23       onInput(input) {
24           console.log('oninput: iso-await', input)
25           if (isBrowserEnv()) {
26               var value = input.provider;
27               if (!maybeSyncServerState(this.state, value)) {
28                   console.log('im entering the !maybeSyncServerState block', this.state, value);
29                   if (isPromise(value)) {
30                       console.log('im entering the isPromise block on client', value)
31                       this.state.settled = PROMISE_STATUS_LOADING;
32                       wireThen(value, this.state);
33                   } else { // if its not a promise, we just set the value
34                       console.log('im entering the else block', value)
35                       this.state.settled = PROMISE_STATUS_RESOLVED;
36                       this.state.value = value;
37                   }
38               }
39           }
40       }
41   }
```

Figure 3-59. *src/components/iso-await/component.js*

The next image is the associated *component.js* file that contains Javascript (behavior) associated with the template (*index.marko*). You will notice two lifecycle handlers of Marko—**onCreate** and **onInput**. While we will cover these in depth in Chapter 4, the TL;DR version of this is that

1. **onCreate**—a good place to set up the state of the component— executes before onInput.

2. **onInput**—a good place to set up the state when the input is dependent on the state.

3. **onCreate** fires before **onInput**.

So, in the **onCreate** section, on the server side, serialization support is added to this pending async value through the *makeAsyncDataSerializable* function, which adds serialization support for the async task/promise via a **toJSON** method. When Marko serializes the data associated with this component, for hydration purposes, it will trigger this method. Following this, it wires on the then handlers to handle resolution of the promise or rejection of the promise. The default value is an object that contains the value of the promise and a flag that indicates the status—Pending/Resolved/Rejected. The default value is initially set to undefined and status is marked as loading. If the async task/promise resolves, this will be updated to status Resolved and value being the resolved value. If the async task/promise rejects, this will be updated to status Rejected and value being the error. Next, the **onInput** event fires on the server, but the check **isBrowserEnv** prevents it from executing anything.

On the client side, the initial value of the state object is set to

```
this.state = { settled: PROMISE_STATUS_LOADING, value: undefined };
```

This is set within the **onCreate** handler within the **isBrowserEnv**() check. Once the async task is settled on the server side, the original data on the server, which is also
{ settled: PROMISE_STATUS_LOADING, value: undefined }, is updated to either
{ settled: PROMISE_STATUS_RESOLVED, value: value } or
{ settled: PROMISE_STATUS_REJECTED, value: err } and serialized via the
toJSON() method.

Next, on the client side, onInput fires and this time *maybeSyncServerState* executes to sync the state of the promise on the client with the serialized promise from the server. If this is successful, then the check if (!maybeSyncServerState(this.state, value)) evaluates to a falsy value and does not execute. Now, the template re-renders as the state is updated, this time executing only the browser side of the template via the conditional isBrowserEnv, displaying the content.

What Does *maybeSyncServerState* Do?

The *maybeSyncServerState* function is designed to handle server-side rendering (SSR) synchronization for promises. In an SSR context, the server pre-renders your component and sends the initial HTML along with serialized data to the client. When the client hydrates (re-initializes) the component, it needs to reconcile the server-rendered state with what it expects to manage on the browser side. This is where *maybeSyncServerState* comes in. Let's delve a bit into what it does:

1. **Check for Serialized Promise Data**: It checks if **value** (the **input. provider** passed to the component) is an object with a **_settled** property. This property indicates that the value was serialized on the server using *makeAsyncDataSerializable*. The serialization process attaches **_settled** and **_value** to the promise's JSON representation.

2. **Handle Unresolved Promises**: If **_settled** === 0 (i.e., PROMISE_ STATUS_LOADING), it throws an error. This makes sense because, during SSR, the server should have awaited the promise to completion (resolved or rejected) before sending it to the client. A still-loading promise at this point indicates a serialization failure or timeout or other issues on the server side.

3. **Sync the State**: If **_settled** is either 1 (resolved) or 2 (rejected), it updates the component's state.settled and state.value with the serialized values (**value._settled** and **value._value**). *This ensures the client picks up exactly where the server left off—no need to re-fetch or re-resolve the promise.*

4. **Return Value**: It returns true if server-client synchronization happens, signaling that the client state has been successfully aligned with the server's serialized data. If the condition isn't met (e.g., value isn't a serialized promise), it implicitly returns undefined (falsy). So, *maybeSyncServerState* is a bridge between server-rendered promise data and the client-side state, ensuring hydration works seamlessly when the server has already resolved or rejected the promise.

What Does if (!*maybeSyncServerState*(state, value)) Do?

This check in the **onInput** method determines whether the client needs to handle the promise itself. Let's delve a bit into it:

1. *maybeSyncServerState*(**state, value**) **returns true**: If the server serialized the promise data (e.g., _**settled** and _**value** are present), *maybeSyncServerState* updates the state and returns **true**. The if (!*maybeSyncServerState*(state, value)) condition evaluates to **false**, and the block is skipped. This means the client doesn't need to do anything further—the state is already in sync with the server's result.

2. *maybeSyncServerState*(**state, value**) **returns undefined** (**falsy**): If **value** isn't a serialized promise object (e.g., it's a fresh promise or a plain value), *maybeSyncServerState* doesn't update the state and returns **undefined**. The condition if (!*maybeSyncServerState*(state, value)) becomes **true**, and the block executes. This is where the client takes over to handle the promise or value dynamically.

3. **Inside the block**

   a. If value is a promise (isPromise(value)): The client sets **state.settled** to PROMISE_STATUS_LOADING and attaches **.then** and **.catch** handlers to update the state when the promise resolves or rejects. This is for cases where the promise wasn't pre-resolved by the server (e.g., client-side-only data fetching).

   b. If value isn't a promise: The client assumes it's a resolved value, sets **state.settled** to PROMISE_STATUS_RESOLVED, and assigns **state.value** directly. This handles static or synchronous data passed to the component. In short, if (!*maybeSyncServerState*(state, value)) acts as a fallback, it runs when the server didn't provide pre-serialized promise data, forcing the client to resolve the promise or process the value itself.

Why Is This Useful?

This setup enables isomorphic behavior (hence "iso-await"): the component works consistently whether rendered on the server or client.

1. **Server Side:** The **<await>** tag resolves the promise, and *makeAsyncDataSerializable* serializes the result into a JSON-compatible format (with **_settled** and **_value**) that's sent to the client.

2. **Client Side:**

   a. If the server already resolved it, *maybeSyncServerState* syncs the state, avoiding redundant work.

   b. If not (or if the promise is client only), the !*maybeSyncServerState* block kicks in to handle it dynamically. The *maybeSyncServerState* function and its associated check ensure the client doesn't reprocess promises unnecessarily during hydration while still supporting dynamic promise handling when needed. It's a key part of making SSR and client-side rendering play nicely together.

   Next, let's get to the **utils.js** file. We have already seen *maybeSyncServerState* and *makeAsyncDataSerializable*. One thing here is the use of Symbol.

Why Is a Symbol (ASNYC_SERIALIZATION_MARKER) Used?

In JavaScript, a Symbol is a primitive type introduced in ES6 that guarantees uniqueness. Unlike strings or numbers, every Symbol created with Symbol() is distinct even if they have the same description.

The ASNYC_SERIALIZATION_MARKER symbol is used as a unique property key on promise objects to mark them as having been processed by *makeAsyncDataSerializable*. Here's why this is valuable:

1. **Avoiding Collisions**: Promises are often third-party objects or native JavaScript objects you don't fully control. If you used a string key like "*isSerializable*", there's a risk of clashing with existing properties on the promise (e.g., from a library or user code). A Symbol ensures the property is unique and won't conflict with other keys.

2. **Private-Like Behavior**: Symbols aren't enumerable in for...in loops or Object.keys(), so ASNYC_SERIALIZATION_MARKER won't accidentally show up in serialization or debugging unless explicitly accessed. This keeps it out of the way of generic object traversal while still being usable in your logic.

3. **Marking Intent**: The symbol acts as a flag to indicate that the promise has been augmented with serialization logic (via toJSON). This lets *makeAsyncDataSerializable* check if it's already processed the promise, avoiding redundant work. In this case, ASNYC_SERIALIZATION_MARKER is essentially a "processed" marker for promises, ensuring the serialization logic is applied only once and can be reliably detected.

What if Multiple Instances of <iso-await> Use the Same Symbol?

Given that this ASNYC_SERIALIZATION_MARKER appears to be initialized once, the observation is very natural; however, the short answer is "it's not a problem." Let's explore why:

- **Single Symbol Instance:** ASNYC_SERIALIZATION_MARKER is defined once as a constant in the utils module. Since it's exported, every instance of **<iso-await>** (or anything imported from "./utils") shares the same Symbol reference. This is intentional and by design.

- **Why It's Fine for Multiple Instances:** The ASNYC_SERIALIZATION_MARKER symbol isn't tied to a specific instance of **<iso-await>**. Instead, it's a marker attached to individual promise objects passed to *makeAsyncDataSerializable*. Each promise gets its own property: value[ASNYC_SERIALIZATION_MARKER] = true. When multiple **<iso-await>** components process different promises, each promise is independently marked with the same ASNYC_SERIALIZATION_MARKER symbol. Since the symbol is just a key, and JavaScript objects (like promises) store their own properties, there's no overlap or conflict between instances. Each promise is a distinct object, and the ASNYC_SERIALIZATION_MARKER property is set on each one separately.

- **What if the Same Promise Is Used by Multiple Instances?:** If two **<iso-await>** components receive the same promise object (e.g., input.provider is the same reference), *makeAsyncDataSerializable* will only process it once. The if (value[ASNYC_SERIALIZATION_MARKER]) check ensures that subsequent calls skip reprocessing, reusing the already-serializable promise. This is efficient and prevents duplicate **.then/.catch** handlers from being attached.

- **No Instance-Specific State:** The symbol doesn't store instance-specific data—it's just a flag. The actual serialized data (_settled and _value) lives in the **finalData** object, which is scoped to each promise via its **toJSON** method. So, multiple **<iso-await>** instances sharing the same symbol doesn't cause crosstalk. In summary, because ASNYC_SERIALIZATION_MARKER is a single, shared Symbol used as a property key on promise objects—and not a counter or instance-specific value— it works perfectly across multiple iso-await instances without issue.

Why Is There an if-check in makeAsyncDataSerializable?

- **Efficiency and Idempotency:** The if (value[ASNYC_SERIALIZATION_MARKER]) check determines if the promise has already been processed by this function. If value[ASNYC_SERIALIZATION_MARKER] is true, it means the promise already has the toJSON method and handlers set up. Returning early avoids reapplying the serialization logic, which would

  - Create a new finalData object (wasting memory).

  - Overwrite the existing toJSON method (potentially losing updates to finalData).

  - Attach additional .then/.catch handlers (causing multiple redundant callbacks when the promise resolves).

- **Preventing Side Effects:** Without this check, calling *makeAsyncData-Serializable* multiple times on the same promise would pile up handlers, leading to unpredictable behavior (e.g., **finalData** being updated inconsistently by different handlers). The early return ensures the function is idempotent—calling it repeatedly on the same promise has the same effect as calling it once.

- **How It Ties to SSR:** During server-side rendering, *makeAsyncDataS-erializable* is called on the **input.provider** promise. If the same promise is reused (e.g., cached or passed to multiple components), this check ensures it's only serialized once, maintaining consistency when the serialized data is sent to the client.

```
src > components > iso-await > JS utils.js > [@] wireThen > ⊕ asyncValue.then() callback
 1    export const ASNYC_SERIALIZATION_MARKER = Symbol();
 2    export const PROMISE_STATUS_LOADING = 0;
 3    export const PROMISE_STATUS_RESOLVED = 1;
 4    export const PROMISE_STATUS_REJECTED = 2;
 5
 6    export const wireThen = (asyncValue, finalData) => asyncValue.then(
 7        (resolvedVal) => {
 8            finalData._settled = PROMISE_STATUS_RESOLVED;
 9            finalData._value = resolvedVal;
10        },
11        (err) => {
12            finalData._settled = PROMISE_STATUS_REJECTED;
13            finalData._value = err;
14        },
15    ).catch((err) => {
16        finalData._settled = PROMISE_STATUS_REJECTED;
17        finalData._value = err;
18    });
19
20    export function isPromise(val) {
21        return val && val.then;
22    }
23    export function maybeSyncServerState(state, value) {
24        if (value && typeof value === "object" && "_settled" in value) {
25            if (value._settled === 0) {
26                throw new Error("Was unable to serialize promise data from server");
27            }
28            state.settled = value._settled;
29            state.value = value._value;
30            return true;
31        }
32    }
33    export function makeAsyncDataSerializable(asyncValue) {
34        if (asyncValue[ASNYC_SERIALIZATION_MARKER]) {
35            return asyncValue;
36        }
37
38        asyncValue[ASNYC_SERIALIZATION_MARKER] = true;
39
40        asyncValue.toJSON = function () {
41            console.log('serializing....', finalData);
42            return finalData;
43        };
44
45        const finalData = { _settled: PROMISE_STATUS_LOADING, _value: undefined };
46
47        wireThen(asyncValue, finalData);
48
49        return asyncValue;
50    }
```

Figure 3-60. *src/components/iso-await/utils.js*

In the next image, the sources folder for this isomorphic await is showcased.

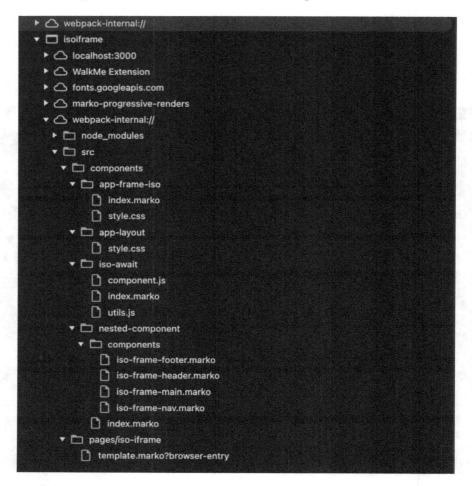

Figure 3-61. *Sources for <iso-await> use cases*

It pretty much mirrors examples 1 and 2. The only difference here is that with
<iso-await> the template also gets sent to the client, along with its parent **<nested-
component>**, therefore enabling it to observe on the client side, the resolution of the
task that happened on the server and re-render accordingly after setting the received
value in its state.

Note that when using the **<await>** within **<iso-await>** we passed in the **then** and
catch via attributes. These are actually attribute tags, but we passed them as attributes.
We shall read about attributes and attribute tags in depth in Chapter 4. But you can also
replace them with their attribute tags as shown in Figure 3-62.

```marko
src > components > iso-await >  ☰ index.marko > ⅋ else > ⅋ await > ⅋ h
 1    import {
 2        PROMISE_STATUS_RESOLVED,
 3        PROMISE_STATUS_REJECTED
 4    } from "./utils"
 5
 6    static var isBrowserEnv = typeof window !== "undefined";
 7
 8    <if(isBrowserEnv)>
 9        $ console.log('-----START: browser----');
10        $ {
11            let renderer = input.placeholder;
12            if (state.settled === PROMISE_STATUS_RESOLVED) {
13                renderer = input.then;
14            } else if (state.settled === PROMISE_STATUS_REJECTED) {
15                renderer = input.catch;
16            }
17            renderer && renderer.renderBody && renderer.renderBody(out, state.value);
18        }
19        $ console.log('-----END: browser----');
20    </if>
21    <else>
22        $ console.log('-----server: start----');
23        <await(input.provider)
24            timeout=input.timeout
25        >
26            <@then|data|>
27                <${input.then.renderBody} ...data/>
28            </@then>
29            <@catch|err|>
30                <${input.catch.renderBody} ...err/>
31            </@catch>
32            <@placeholder>
33                <${input.placeholder.renderBody}/>
34            </@placeholder>
35        </await>
36        $ console.log('-----server: end----');
37    </else>
```

Figure 3-62. *src/components/iso-await/index.marko*

This completes our dive into building an isomorphic await tag. But wait.

Is It Really Isomorphic? Let Us Revisit

1. Executes an async task on the server

2. Waits for the async task to settle on the server

3. Serializes the settled async task value to the client

4. Observes resolution of the settled task value on the client side

5. Renders UX on the client side

On the surface, it does appear to. But hold on. Rerun the example on the http://localhost:3000/iso route (that we had configured in *src/index.js*), and you will notice that the placeholder text never showed up. Well! Well! What is happening?

The first render never happened on the server. Marko just waited for the task on the server to resolve and sent the serialized value on the client side because we added a toJSON method. One other reason for the toJSON method is that **<iso-await>** is within the **<nested-component>**, a class component, with state, that may re-render. This requires the templates of itself and all its child components to be bundled and data be hydrated (requiring the associated hydration data of the child component **<iso-await>** to be serializable as well.

The placeholder text also doesn't render because they are intended for client-side hydration scenarios. On the server side, Marko assumes the promise would resolve quickly, thus rendering the resolved content directly without the placeholder. If the promise resolves within the same tick as rendering, the placeholder won't show because Marko processes resolved states immediately. This is visible even when executing Example 1's Single Chunk and Progressive In-order use cases.

So, How Do We Fix It?

Let's give it a shot with a custom **<server-await>** component. We have already seen that using **<await>** doesn't offer us much help with this scenario, so we ought to use the Async APIs of Marko.

We first start with src/components/server-await and drop in a *marko-tag.json* file. We will read about *marko-tag.json* files in Chapter 4, but they are tag descriptor files for Marko. In this, we mention that the renderer is a special file called *renderer.js*—a sibling to *marko-tag.json*.

```
src > components > server-await > {} marko-tag.json > ...
    1   {
    2           "renderer": "./renderer.js"
    3   }
```

Figure 3-63. *src/components/server-await/marko-tag.json*

Next comes the contents of the *renderer.js*. Next, let's update the *src/components/iso-await/index.marko* to use the **<server-await>** instead of the core **<await>**.

```
21   <else>
22       $ console.log('-----server: start----');
23       <server-await
24           key="await"
25           dataProvider=(input.provider)
26           then=input.then
27           catch=input.catch
28           timeout=input.timeout
29       >
30           <@placeholder>
31               <${input.placeholder.renderBody}/>
32           </@placeholder>
33       </server-await>
34       $ console.log('-----server: end----');
35   </else>
```

Figure 3-64. *src/components/iso-await/index.marko*

```
src > components > server-await > JS renderer.js > ⊗ <unknown> > ⊗ exports > ⊗ finally() callback

  1    module.exports = function (input, out) {
  2        const emitter = input.dataProvider;
  3
  4        let isFinished = false;
  5
  6        // This async fragment doesn't have timeout handling
  7        const asyncOut = out.beginAsync({timeout: 0, name: input.name});
  8
  9        emitter.then((data) => {
 10            console.log('isnide then', data);
 11            renderFragment(input.then, data);
 12        }, (err) => {
 13            console.log('isnide err');
 14            renderFragment(input.catch, err);
 15        }).finally(() => {
 16            isFinished = true;
 17            closeFragment();
 18        })
 19
 20        function closeFragment() {
 21            if (isFinished) {
 22                console.log('closing...');
 23                asyncOut.end();
 24            }
 25        }
 26
 27        function renderFragment(renderer, data) {
 28            console.log('render frag');
 29            if (!isFinished) {
 30                if (renderer) {
 31                    console.log('render fragment....');
 32                    renderer.renderBody(asyncOut, data);
 33                }
 34                asyncOut.flush();
 35            }
 36        }
 37
 38        renderFragment(input.placeholder);
 39    };
```

Figure 3-65. *src/components/server-await/renderer.js*

In the *renderer.js*, you will see this code which we got ourselves familiarized with
when learning what progressive rendering is. Basically, what this does is it

1. Begins an async stream for the render.

2. Wires another **.then** block besides whatever was wired on by **<iso-await>,** which was used for serializing the value of the async task. This is to observe resolution and make decisions.

3. When the async task is pending, it flushes the placeholder tag by invoking renderFragment that contains an *asyncOut.flush().*

4. In the **.then** success handler, it renders the **<@then>** tag by invoking renderFragment and flushing it.

5. In the **.then** failure handler, it renders the **<@catch>** tag by invoking renderFragment and flushing it.

6. Finally, when the task settles, it is serialized by the parent and the existing async stream is shut.

On the client side, in **<iso-await>**, the state is set and it re-renders, effectively removing the default placeholder texts and re-rendering **<iso-await>** to showcase the updated UI.

Let us look at the logs next.

```
create: iso-await {
  provider: Promise { <pending> },
  name: 'header',
  placeholder: {
    renderBody: [Function: renderBody],
    [Symbol(Symbol.iterator)]: [GeneratorFunction: selfIterator]
  },
  then: {
    renderBody: [Function: renderBody],
    [Symbol(Symbol.iterator)]: [GeneratorFunction: selfIterator]
  }
}
oninput: iso-await {
  provider: Promise {
    <pending>,
    toJSON: [Function (anonymous)],
    [Symbol()]: true
  },
  name: 'header',
  placeholder: {
    renderBody: [Function: renderBody],
    [Symbol(Symbol.iterator)]: [GeneratorFunction: selfIterator]
  },
  then: {
    renderBody: [Function: renderBody],
    [Symbol(Symbol.iterator)]: [GeneratorFunction: selfIterator]
  }
}
-------server: start-----
render frag
render fragment....
-------server: end-----
```

Figure 3-66. *Logs with updated <server-await>*

```
create: iso-await {
  provider: Promise { <pending> },
  name: 'nav',
  placeholder: {
    renderBody: [Function: renderBody],
    [Symbol(Symbol.iterator)]: [GeneratorFunction: selfIterator]
  },
  catch: {
    renderBody: [Function: renderBody],
    [Symbol(Symbol.iterator)]: [GeneratorFunction: selfIterator]
  },
  then: {
    renderBody: [Function: renderBody],
    [Symbol(Symbol.iterator)]: [GeneratorFunction: selfIterator]
  }
}
oninput: iso-await {
  provider: Promise {
    <pending>,
    toJSON: [Function (anonymous)],
    [Symbol()]: true
  },
  name: 'nav',
  placeholder: {
    renderBody: [Function: renderBody],
    [Symbol(Symbol.iterator)]: [GeneratorFunction: selfIterator]
  },
  catch: {
    renderBody: [Function: renderBody],
    [Symbol(Symbol.iterator)]: [GeneratorFunction: selfIterator]
  },
  then: {
    renderBody: [Function: renderBody],
    [Symbol(Symbol.iterator)]: [GeneratorFunction: selfIterator]
  }
}
-----server: start-----
render frag
render fragment....
-----server: end-----
```

Figure 3-67. *Logs with updated <server-await> (continued)*

```
create: iso-await {
  provider: Promise { <pending> },
  timeout: 20000,
  name: 'main',
  placeholder: {
    renderBody: [Function: renderBody],
    [Symbol(Symbol.iterator)]: [GeneratorFunction: selfIterator]
  },
  catch: {
    renderBody: [Function: renderBody],
    [Symbol(Symbol.iterator)]: [GeneratorFunction: selfIterator]
  },
  then: {
    renderBody: [Function: renderBody],
    [Symbol(Symbol.iterator)]: [GeneratorFunction: selfIterator]
  }
}
oninput: iso-await {
  provider: Promise {
    <pending>,
    toJSON: [Function (anonymous)],
    [Symbol()]: true
  },
  timeout: 20000,
  name: 'main',
  placeholder: {
    renderBody: [Function: renderBody],
    [Symbol(Symbol.iterator)]: [GeneratorFunction: selfIterator]
  },
  catch: {
    renderBody: [Function: renderBody],
    [Symbol(Symbol.iterator)]: [GeneratorFunction: selfIterator]
  },
  then: {
    renderBody: [Function: renderBody],
    [Symbol(Symbol.iterator)]: [GeneratorFunction: selfIterator]
  }
}
-----server: start-----
render frag
render fragment....
-----server: end-----
```

Figure 3-68. *Logs with updated <server-await> (continued)*

```
create: iso-await {
  provider: Promise { <pending> },
  name: 'footer',
  placeholder: {
    renderBody: [Function: renderBody],
    [Symbol(Symbol.iterator)]: [GeneratorFunction: selfIterator]
  },
  catch: {
    renderBody: [Function: renderBody],
    [Symbol(Symbol.iterator)]: [GeneratorFunction: selfIterator]
  },
  then: {
    renderBody: [Function: renderBody],
    [Symbol(Symbol.iterator)]: [GeneratorFunction: selfIterator]
  }
}
oninput: iso-await {
  provider: Promise {
    <pending>,
    toJSON: [Function (anonymous)],
    [Symbol()]: true
  },
  name: 'footer',
  placeholder: {
    renderBody: [Function: renderBody],
    [Symbol(Symbol.iterator)]: [GeneratorFunction: selfIterator]
  },
  catch: {
    renderBody: [Function: renderBody],
    [Symbol(Symbol.iterator)]: [GeneratorFunction: selfIterator]
  },
  then: {
    renderBody: [Function: renderBody],
    [Symbol(Symbol.iterator)]: [GeneratorFunction: selfIterator]
  }
}
-----server: start----
render frag
render fragment....
-----server: end----
isnide then { sectionName: 'nav' }
render frag
render fragment....
navDataProvider resolved nav
closing...
isnide then { sectionName: 'footer' }
render frag
render fragment....
footerDataProvider resolved footer
frame-footer created
closing...
isnide then { sectionName: 'header' }
render frag
render fragment....
headerDataProvider resolved header
closing...
isnide then { sectionName: 'main' }
render frag
render fragment....
mainDataProvider resolved main
closing...
serializing.... { _settled: 1, _value: { sectionName: 'header' } }
serializing.... { _settled: 1, _value: { sectionName: 'nav' } }
serializing.... { _settled: 1, _value: { sectionName: 'footer' } }
serializing.... { _settled: 1, _value: { sectionName: 'main' } }
```

Figure 3-69. *Logs with updated <server-await> (continued)*

This completes the server render. On the client side, when the page loads, you will notice the loading placeholders show up (being rendered on the server). Then, when the server side serializes the promise, you will initially see the following logs.

```
sample-wrapper-parent created
  ▶ {headerDataProvider: {…}, navDataProvider: {…}, footerDataProvider: {…}, mainDataProvider: {…}, renderMode: 'iso-progressive-out-of-order', …}
sample-nested-component created
  ▶ {headerDataProvider: {…}, navDataProvider: {…}, footerDataProvider: {…}, mainDataProvider: {…}, renderMode: 'iso-progressive-out-of-order', …}
sample-nested-component input
  ▶ {headerDataProvider: {…}, navDataProvider: {…}, footerDataProvider: {…}, mainDataProvider: {…}, renderMode: 'iso-progressive-out-of-order', …}
create: iso-await ▼ {provider: {…}, name: 'header', placeholder: {…}, then: {…}} i
                    name: "header"
                  ▶ placeholder: {renderBody: f, Symbol(Symbol.iterator): f}
                  ▶ provider: {_settled: 1, _value: {…}}
                  ▶ then: {renderBody: f, Symbol(Symbol.iterator): f}
                  ▶ [[Prototype]]: Object
oninput: iso-await ▶ {provider: {…}, name: 'header', placeholder: {…}, then: {…}}
-----START: browser----
headerDataProvider resolved header
-----END: browser----
create: iso-await ▶ {provider: {…}, name: 'nav', placeholder: {…}, catch: {…}, then: {…}}
oninput: iso-await ▶ {provider: {…}, name: 'nav', placeholder: {…}, catch: {…}, then: {…}}
-----START: browser----
navDataProvider resolved nav
-----END: browser----
create: iso-await ▶ {provider: {…}, timeout: 20000, name: 'main', placeholder: {…}, catch: {…}, …}
oninput: iso-await ▶ {provider: {…}, timeout: 20000, name: 'main', placeholder: {…}, catch: {…}, …}
-----START: browser----
mainDataProvider resolved main
-----END: browser----
create: iso-await ▶ {provider: {…}, name: 'footer', placeholder: {…}, catch: {…}, then: {…}}
oninput: iso-await ▶ {provider: {…}, name: 'footer', placeholder: {…}, catch: {…}, then: {…}}
-----START: browser----
footerDataProvider resolved footer
frame-footer created
-----END: browser----
⊗ ▶ [Deprecation] Listener added for a 'DOMNodeRemoved' mutation event. Support for this event type has been removed, and this event will no longer l
   https://chromestatus.com/feature/5083947249172480 for more information.
  nested component mounted!
  sample-wrapper-parent mounted
```

Figure 3-70. *Client-side logs with <server-await>*

Only the browser part of the execution pathway is run, and the server-side generated HTML is thus removed from the DOM.

This completes the solution with full isomorphic renders (in order). For out-of-order flush (similar to Example 1), we will require deeper bindings with Marko's internals. This is expected to land in Marko v6. The critical piece of this execution, as you would notice, is avoiding re-executing the same work that was done on the server on the client side. Our implementation is crude, but you get the point.

CHAPTER 4

Introduction to the Marko Language and API Reference

Introduction

In this chapter, we will explore through simple examples the various features of the Marko language. While Marko JS contains the *.marko* template files, you can still throw in HTML to render it. Marko template files are just an extension of HTML files—in that, they let you build dynamic and reactive user interfaces by augmenting HTML, so that you are able to do it declaratively.

However, for being able to render dynamic HTML and achieve highly performant reactive user interfaces that can re-render itself and stay updated in response to any change in data (state associated), Marko introduces augmentations to HTML in the form of being able to handle conditionals, async data, loops, small reusable in-template fragments, data within tag body, event handling and subscriptions, state, and styles. These are offered via the Marko core tags that are already authored and available for you, the developer, to use. They are ingrained into the Marko language and are handled by the compiler, supercharging your ability to build code fast.

Marko JS is a big supporter of componentization of the UI and therefore natively offers ways to build custom tags that encompass business logic. They also offer different render pathways as mentioned earlier—components that could be rendered exclusively on the server, isomorphically on the server and browser, and so on. Additionally, they

© Damodaran Chingleput Sathyakumar 2025
D. Chingleput Sathyakumar, *Practical Marko*, https://doi.org/10.1007/979-8-8688-1483-9_4

offer numerous attributes, ways to handle dynamic text, inline Javascript, functional parameters, dynamic tags, importing external components, files (including static HTML files), and a rich render API for handling different render modes.

Under a given component folder, Marko knows what is to be done to handle the *.marko* files, the *component* file, the *component-browser* file, and any style files—offering a clear separation of concerns (HTML—structure, formatting—style, behavior— Javascript). Even within the behavior, it helps you separate those that will be handled on the browser and server.

By the end of this chapter, you will be accustomed and fluid with the Marko language and its syntax. If it helps, you can head out to the `https://markojs.com/try-online/` feature and select the language guide in the drop-down to play around with many of the language features.

Setting Up Our Sample Workspace

There are a couple of commands one can use to scaffold marko projects from a basic template. This is done in Figures 4-1 to 4-4.

`>> npx @marko/create`

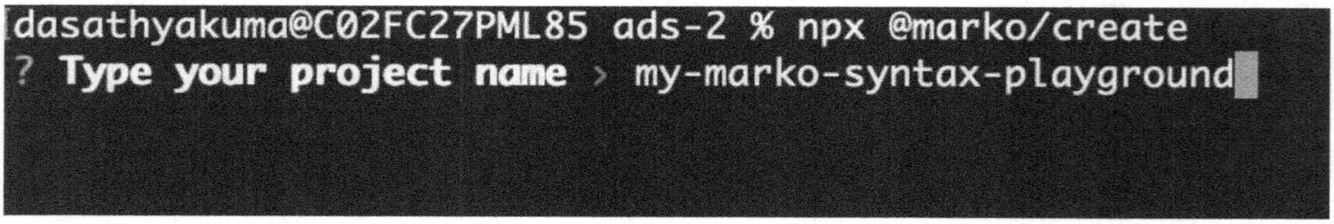

Figure 4-1. *Using the npx @marko/create command to scaffold a marko app*

Or the other command is

`>> npm init marko`

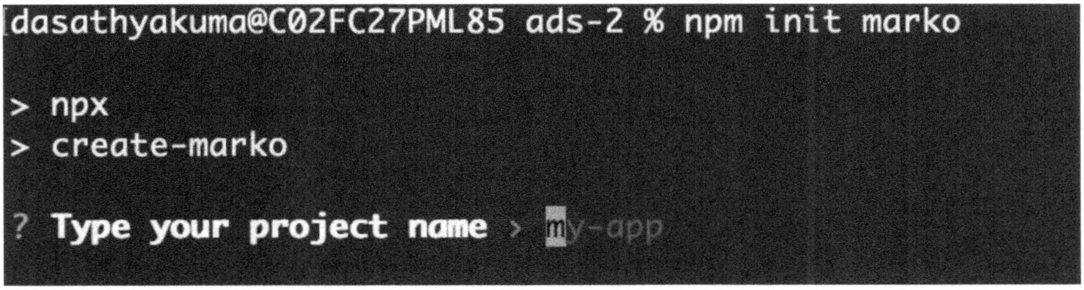

```
dasathyakuma@C02FC27PML85 ads-2 % npm init marko

> npx
> create-marko

? Type your project name > my-app
```

Figure 4-2. *Providing the project name*

This will internally call the first command.

We are naming our sample *app my-marko-syntax-playground*.

```
dasathyakuma@C02FC27PML85 ads-2 % npx @marko/create
✓ Type your project name · my-marko-syntax-playground
? Choose a template … Use ↑ and ↓. Return ⏎ to submit.
> Default starter app
  Example from marko-js/examples
```

Figure 4-3. *Choosing from a preexisting template*

The scaffolder asks what the type of the app is—either the default starter or if we want to pick from an array of samples already provided to us. We will go with the second option—*example from marko-js/examples*.

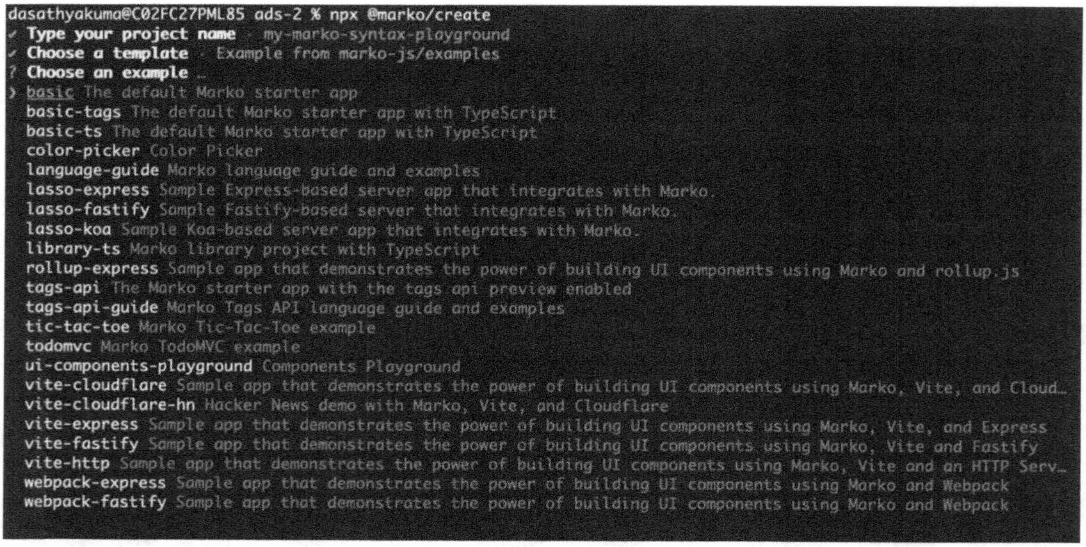

Figure 4-4. *Selecting from a list of available templates*

As you can see, there are a number of default starter apps provided to us by the marko dev team to learn or play around with the various aspects or integrations of external frameworks and libraries with Marko. We will choose the ***basic*** template.

The project scaffolder scaffolds the project and provides you with instructions to enter the directory and then do a

```
>> npm run dev
```

This should bring the server up on http://localhost:3000/ as shown in Figure 4-5.

Figure 4-5. *The sample app is up!*

When you open the project in your IDE (Integrated Development Environment), you will notice the *src* folder and the *routes/_index* folder. The page is being served from there. Now, we will just duplicate the *_index* folder and rename it *playground*, with the same contents.

The project directory will look like this as shown in Figure 4-6.

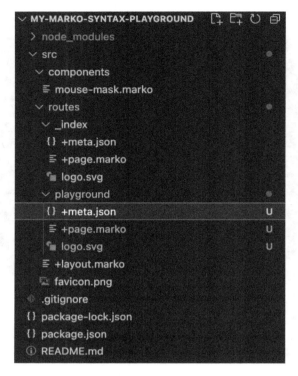

Figure 4-6. *The sample project layout and adding a new page under playground/*

This was done with VS Code, and you can use an editor or IDE of your choice. Marko has nice bindings and a language server built for VS Code to handle TypeScript, so you would be better off when trying this on VS Code. The files indicated in green are the ones we have included anew. With VS Code, Marko offers the Marko VS Code plugin that helps with syntax highlighting and works with the language server to bring in type suggestions and autocomplete.

You will also notice a different naming convention being used, with the files named *+page.marko*, etc. This is the naming convention followed by Marko's meta framework called *marko-run*. We will look at the *marko-run* meta framework in depth in the subsequent chapters. It's because of this that we were able to spin up a new server route under */playground* by just duplicating the *_index* directory and renaming it. *Marko-run* supercharges development with Marko and helps to easily scaffold Marko applications.

As a next step, let's kill the server and rerun:

```
>> npm run dev
```

This will bring up the same earlier page on the */playground* route (URL).

Our First Marko Component

In this, we shall author our first Marko component—a simple counter that increments and decrements. The original code under *src/routes/playground/+page.marko* is now modified as shown in Figure 4-7.

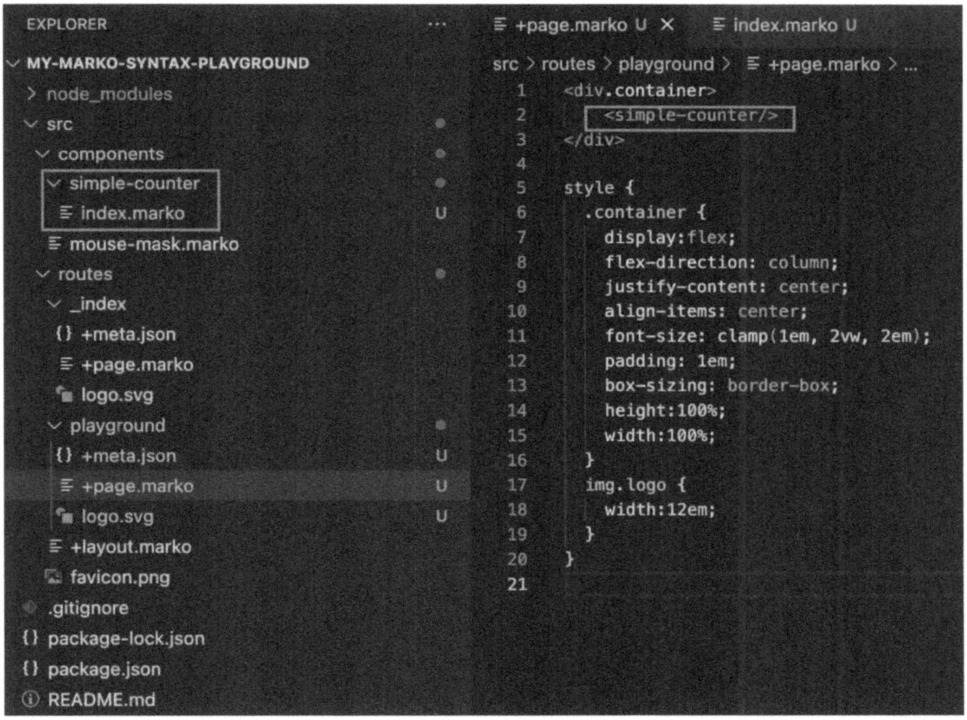

Figure 4-7. *A simple counter at src/routes/playground/+page.marko*

You will notice the original code being replaced by *<simple-counter/>* and a folder called *simple-counter* under *src/components/simple-counter* with the file *index.marko*. This folder represents a component in Marko.

What Is a Component?

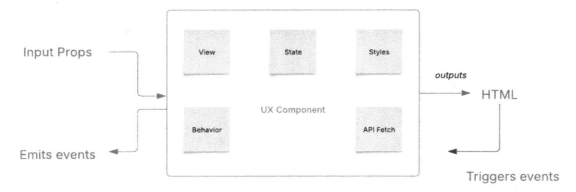

Figure 4-8. *The component*

By a component, as shown in Figure 4-8, Marko implies

1. A unit that contains structure (*HTML*, the *view*, or the *DOM*), formatting (*styles*), and behavior (*Javascript* or the *widget*).

2. These units can be independently tested.

3. They can be composed within other components to build composite components.

4. They can be independently published to the NPM registry for reuse in other applications.

5. Marko compiles them into Javascript modules that encapsulate view and behavior.

6. They emit events to their parents and also listen to events from interactions made on the DOM elements contained within them.

7. Every component in Marko is an instance of the event emitter.

8. The outcome (HTML) is dependent on the kind of the input passed in.

9. The input can influence the value of the state, internal to the component.

10. The output changes (component re-renders HTML) upon any change to the input or the internal state. With Marko v5, Marko relies on a Virtual DOM implementation to diff and patch the state. But this is just an implementation detail that will change with v6.

11. The data flow is unidirectional—user interactions cause events to be emitted, the associated event handlers modify the component state in response to the user action, and the change of state causes the component to re-render. Or the parent component re-renders, causing new input to be passed, thereby causing the component to re-render.

12. The view is always a function of the input and the state.

A Note on Naming

In the aforementioned example, *<simple-counter/>* contains a single template file— index.marko. In this case, Marko looks for a *component.{js, ts}*, *component-browser.{js, ts}*, and *style.{css, less, scss, stylus}* depending on the CSS preprocessor. This can also be named *simple-counter.marko*. In that case, it would look for a *simple-counter.component.{js,ts}*, *simple-counter.component-browser.{js,ts}*, and a *simple-counter.style.{css, less, scss, stylus}*.

Component Authoring Flavors

Next, when looking into the *<simple-counter/> index.marko* template file, you will notice that this uses the flavor of single-file components. As mentioned in an earlier chapter, Marko supports three flavors of authoring components, namely:

– **Single-File Components**: The markup, behavior, and formatting are all contained within one file. This may be familiar to those from the React world with JSX. Even within the single file, Marko clearly is able to separate the concerns with separate blocks for styling (formatting) and behavior (the widget Javascript).

- **Split-File Components**: This is a render-based differentiation. If there is certain computation to be done only on the server, Marko offers a way for executing code exclusively on the server (with the *component.js* file) while handling only interactive behavior on the client (with the *component-browser.js* file). But, please note that if your split component is part of the render tree of a parent component that is stateful, then there is not much gain, as everything is sent to the browser. This is because, as the parent re-renders, it may have to re-render all its children (including the split component, which otherwise may not have re-rendered). So don't overoptimize unless it makes a difference.

- **Multi-file Components**: These have a contrasting flavor to the single-file components. Here, markup, behavior, and formatting are all placed in separate files, having clear separation of concerns. This is usually favored by purists who want clear separation of concerns.

Let's Look at a Sample

The snapshot in Figure 4-9 shows the *src/components/simple-counter/index.marko* file.

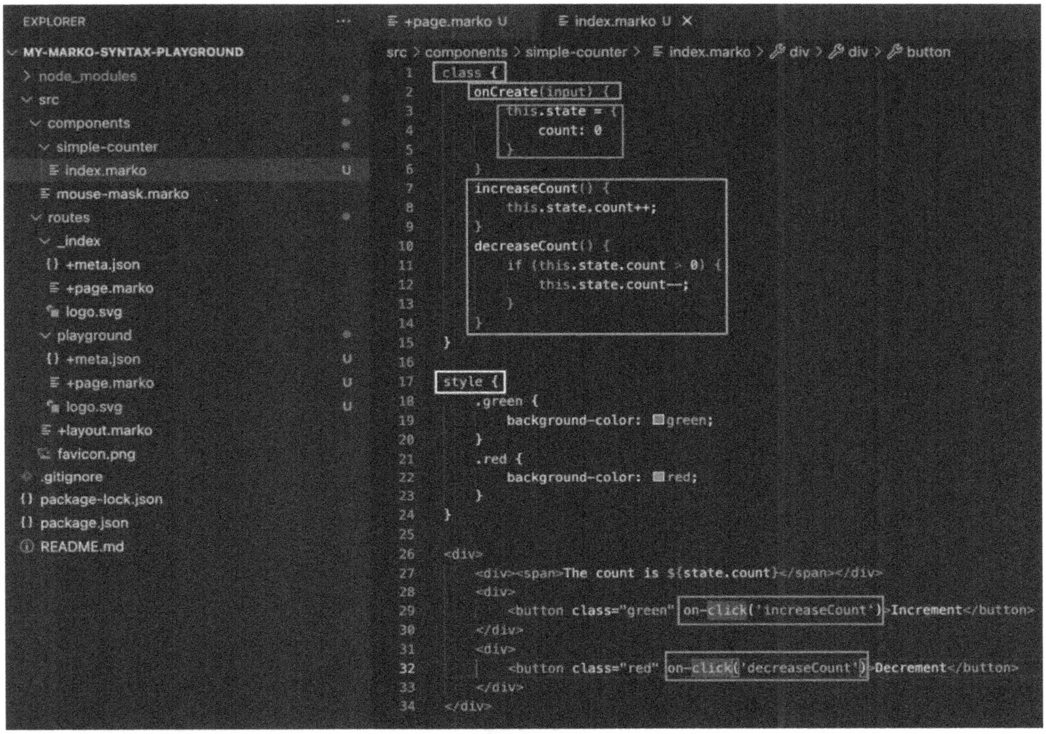

Figure 4-9. *src/components/simple-counter/index.marko*

Let's break down this piece of code:

1. The *style {}* block encapsulates the styles for the component. Marko lets you define styles within your component while still maintaining separation of concerns. Note that, at this point, with Marko v5 there is no scoped CSS as in Svelte. However, you can still use CSS modules. This is expected to change with Marko v6.

2. The *class {}* block encapsulates the behavior for the component. Marko lets you define behavior within your component while still maintaining separation of concerns. In the React world, these are functions within the functional component before returning JSX.

189

3.   The markup has its own place and doesn't get mixed with the others.

4.   Within the component behavior, you will notice the two event handlers: *increaseCount* and *decreaseCount*. These are wired by Marko to the HTML declaratively via the *on-click* directives.

5.   The *onCreate()* function is where the *state* is created or initialized. Note that the *state* can be initialized via the *input* props as well, which is why it takes the argument *input*. The *onCreate()* function is one of the lifecycle functions of Marko. This is the first function to trigger in the lifecycle of a Marko component. More on the lifecycle in the subsequent pages.

6.   Lastly, the *${state.count}* is the means by which Marko embeds dynamic values (either from the state or from the input) into the rendered HTML.

7.   When accessing state values from the markup portion, ${state.count} is used, but within the behavior section ${this.state.count} is used. ***this*** is accessible within the behavioral section.

The output is as follows:

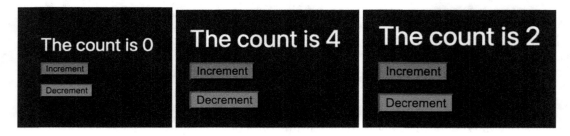

Figure 4-10. *Output of the <simple-counter> component*

Every time there is a change to the value of *count* (in the state), *the view re-renders to stay updated.*

With this basic component, we have accomplished the following:

1.   Adding simple styles

2.   Initializing/creating state and updating it

3. Basic componentization

4. Basic event handling

In the next sections, we will look deeper into how Marko handles state and events.

How Marko Handles State?

State management is a crucial part of any view framework/library. Most of these libraries have the view as a function of the state data. The state data is usually derived from the Input props.

Deriving State from Input

In the earlier Marko component example, the creation/initialization of state was shown. **State can also be derived from the input (props).** For example, if a modified variant of the same component had a use case of beginning the count at a specific value, then when the *<simple-counter/>* tag is used, we are also required to pass some input props to inform the component what the initial value is. This can be something like *<simple-counter startsWith=5/>*.

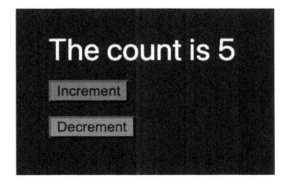

```
class {
    onCreate(input) {
        this.state = {
            count: input.startsWith || 0
        }
    }
    increaseCount() {
        this.state.count++;
    }
    decreaseCount() {
        if (this.state.count > 0) {
            this.state.count--;
        }
    }
}
```

Figure 4-11. *Deriving state from the input props within src/components/ simple-counter/index.marko*

The only change is this highlighted piece of code, but you get it; here, the state is being derived from the input, and so, when you save and the changes get reflected (auto-reload), the component shows a default value of 5.

Handling State Updates

State updates are performed via the following ways:

1. *this.state.count = this.state.count + 1*

2. *this.state.count++*

3. *this.setState("count", this.state.count + 1)*

When the syntax is updated to use the one listed above, the component still works.

```
class {
    onCreate(input) {
        this.state = {
            count: input.startsWith || 0
        }
    }
    increaseCount() {
        this.state.count = this.state.count + 1;
    }
    decreaseCount() {
        if (this.state.count > 0) {
            this.setState("count", this.state.count - 1)
        }
    }
}
```

Figure 4-12. *Updating the state props in src/components/simple-counter/index.marko*

How State Updates Are Done?

When a property on the state object is updated (like *this.state.count*), the component is said to be scheduled for an update. This is because all the updates are batched together. This means you can update multiple state properties, but the update will be scheduled only once and applied once.

Next, state updates that schedule a component update by Marko occur only in a shallow manner. That is, the properties are watched only one level deep. This means if you tried updating inner or nested properties on an *Object* type, or push a new item into a property which is of *Array* type, Marko will not be able to detect it.

For example, the following will not work:

```
this.state.count.value++;
this.state.count.value = this.state.count.value + 1
this.state.menu.push("mashed potatoes")
```

This is purely for efficiency's sake—how quick a component is able to diff and produce an update. To help with these cases, Marko offers the *this.setStateDirty(propName)*.

By marking a property "dirty," you are telling the Marko runtime to force-schedule an update.

Let's see an example.

```
class {
    onCreate(input) {
        this.state = {
            count: {
                value: input.startsWith || 0,
                name: input.name
            }
        }
    }
    increaseCount() {
        this.state.count.value = this.state.count.value + 1;
        this.setStateDirty('count');
    }
    decreaseCount() {
        if (this.state.count.value > 0) {
            this.state.count.value = this.state.count.value - 1;
            this.setStateDirty('count');
        }
    }
}

style {
    .green {
        background-color: green;
    }
    .red {
        background-color: red;
    }
}

<div>
    <div>
        <span>The ${state.count.name} is: </span>
        <span>${state.count.value}</span>
    </div>
    <div>
        <button class="green" on-click('increaseCount')>Increment</button>
    </div>
    <div>
        <button class="red" on-click('decreaseCount')>Decrement</button>
    </div>
</div>
```

Figure 4-13. *Example of setStateDirty*

Try removing the lines *this.setStateDirty*, and you will notice that clicking the *Increment* and *Decrement* buttons does not work. We are passing the prop name as "*Age*" in the input when using the <simple-counter/> tag from within *src/routes/ playground/+page.marko*.

Inter-component State Management

Every instance of a Marko component being an event emitter, it emits events to its parents. The parent component can then listen and act on it, doing its own state updates and triggering a re-render of itself or any other action. But there are always cases of deeply nested subtrees, and to reach a leaf, it begins to get cumbersome in emitting from the grandchild component to the grandparent component and so on.

In such cases, a solution like React's *<context>* is something we may look forward to. Marko also offers this solution via its *<context>* tag API. This can be found at `https://github.com/marko-js/tags/tree/master/tags/context`. This is an installable tag via NPM. It is not a core Marko tag that is available by default as part of the Marko language itself. Let us look at an example with this. The tag can be installed by NPM as

```
>> npm install @marko-tags/context
```

Next, let's modify *simple-counter.marko* to use the *<context>* tag. Existing portions of the code are collapsed and displayed.

```
class {
>    onCreate(input) {…
    }
>    increaseCount() {…
    }
>    decreaseCount() {…
    }
    handleCouponCopy() {
        alert('Coupon selected');
    }
}

> style {…
}

<div>
>    <div>…
    </div>
>    <div>…
    </div>
>    <div>…
    </div>
    <div>
        <context couponvalue=55 couponcode="ABC12345" on-copy("handleCouponCopy")>
            <!-- Somewhere nested in the container will be the buy button -->
            <nested-component/>
        </context>
    </div>
</div>
```

Figure 4-14. *Modified code showcasing <context> in src/components/simple-counter/index.marko*

The use case is the *simple-counter.marko*, which now uses a *<nested-component/>* to display some coupons. *couponValue* and *couponCode* are passed in from *simple-counter. marko* into the *<context>* tag. The contents of the <nested-component/> are shown in Figure 4-15.

```
src > components > nested-component >  ≡ index.marko > 𝄞 coupon
   1        <coupon/>
```

Figure 4-15. *src/components/nested-component/index.marko containing <coupon/>*

This just invokes another tag *<coupon/>*. You will notice that no value is being passed from *<simple-counter/>* -> *<nested-component/>* -> *<coupon/>*. There are no input props flowing around. The contents of the *<coupon/>* tag is a component.

```
src > components > coupon >  ≡ index.marko > 𝄞 context
   1      <context|{ couponvalue, couponcode }, emit| from="simple-counter">
   2          <span>Coupon: ${couponvalue}% off.</span> <button on-click(emit, "copy")>${couponcode}</button>
   3      </context>
```

Figure 4-16. *src/components/coupon/index.marko*

Here, the value that was set in the grandparent component *<simple-counter/>* is accessed—specifically, the two values *couponValue* and *couponCode*. This is made possible via the *from* attribute. *<context/>* also offers an *emit* function to emit events back.

Here, upon clicking, a "copy" is emitted. Again, if you notice, events are not emitted back to the immediate parent, which then emits it to the grandparent—which is the usual flow of Marko. Instead, if you revisit the code for *<simple-counter/>*, you will notice the event being emitted directly to *<simple-counter/>*, which now has an *on-copy* handler, to listen to this event specifically on the *<context/>* tag, which may have been emitted from the component deep within that subtree.

Clicking the button, we get the "Coupon Selected."

Using a Global State Management Solution like Redux

If your app's state is simple, or you only need to share state between a few components, Marko's Context API, or even local component state, may suffice without introducing the complexity of Redux. In short, use Redux only when the **scale and complexity of your**

app's state management justify it. While Redux can be a powerful tool for managing complex state in large applications, it is not always necessary. Developers should first consider whether the complexity of their application truly warrants the additional overhead that comes with implementing Redux. Dan Abramov offers a great article to help you with this: `https://medium.com/@dan_abramov/you-might-not-need-redux-be4360cf367`.

At eBay, we have relied on simpler solutions like using **CustomEvents**, a publish-subscribe utility (`https://github.com/raptorjs/raptor-pubsub`) to handle our needs of cross-component communication, without having to resort to patterns like Redux or lifting the state up. However, there are complex use cases that bring the need of a global state management solution like Redux. We will later look at an example of Marko with Redux.

Other State Management Pattern Recommendations

This is a recommendation I usually give engineers. While all the view frameworks like React, Solid, Svelte, Vue, and Marko provide a declarative API to build reactive and dynamic user interfaces that are interaction-rich, you may notice that state management is still imperative. What I mean by that are the *.setState* calls.

This can be overcome via a solution like **Finite State Machines (FSM)**. Through the FSM, state management becomes declarative, and the business logic is separated from the component lifecycle hooks, enhancing maintainability and readability. You will no longer be required to trigger *.setState* calls imperatively. Instead, events sent to the FSM will cause the FSM to transition from one state to the next.

XState (`https://xstate.js.org/`) is a great library that implements the W3C Finite State Machine spec, along with some additional features that offer this experience. XState offers a neat visualizer that can be integrated into the component storybook to supercharge developer velocity even for newcomers into your project. Zag (`https://zagjs.com/`) is a UI component library that is built on this concept.

The brilliance of using an FSM to manage state externally is that your project can fully switch to a new framework tomorrow without worrying about replicating the biz logic. This is because using an FSM helps to abstract out the biz logic from state management. This helps you freely switch between frameworks. Your only change will be the FSM adaptor. Next, FSM helps you with auto-generation of tests, ensuring that your code is 100% covered, requiring no maintenance.

Marko's State Management API

With Marko, you get the following state management APIs:

1. **setState(propName, propValue)**

   – This is used to update the value of a particular prop within the state object.

2. **setState(newStateObj)**

   – This can be used to update the value of a subset of state properties. This is like Partial<State>. The properties are merged into the existing state object, overriding any existing ones and retaining the old ones. This removes the need to spread the old state properties into a new object and then merging.

3. **this.state.x = <newValue>**

   – This is the same as (1) and is used to update the value of one state prop. You can access nested props in this manner like **this.state.x.y.**

4. **replaceState**

   – This is used to fully replace the value of the existing state object. This can be thought of as **this.state** = **<newstate>**. So, when using this, ensure that the new state being used to replace the previous state contains values for all the props.

5. **setStateDirty**

   – The important thing to note is that only the properties directly under **state { },** the first time it is created (usually within the **onCreate(input)**), will be watched for changes, at the first level (one level deep). This means setting **this.state.x = <newValue>** will queue the component for a state update and a possible re-render; however, doing **this.state.x.y = <newValue>** will not. The state is watched one level deep, and the comparison is shallow. So, for example, if you had initially done ***this.state. numArr = [1,2,3]*** and then you do ***this.state.numArr.push(5)***, this will not cause a re-render as the original value of the prop *numArr* remains the same array, although a new element was pushed into it. So, to force the component to queue a state update, you can mark the property as "dirty" by doing *this.setStateDirty("numArr")*. In this case, although the new value of the state property (same **numArr** object) equals its old value (at a shallow level), the component is still re-rendered. This is useful when a state property contains a complex nested object, which may go undetected by a shallow compare. So, doing setStateDirty, in such cases, will skip the equality checks.

this.state.x vs. state.x

- *this.state.x* is used when accessing component state within the *class { }* portion of the Marko component (where behavior is defined). In this part of the Marko component, you can both read the state value and mutate the state properties.

- *state.x* is used when attempting to access a property on the state within the template or HTML portion of the Marko component (where structure is defined). Note that, in the HTML portion of the Marko component, you can only read off state values and not mutate them.

- Similar to *this.state.x* and *state.x*, input is accessed as *this.input* and *input.x*, respectively.

The aforementioned ones are described and highlighted in the sample in Figure 4-17 and can be found within our *simple-counter/index.marko* file.

```
    decreaseCount() {
        if (this.state.count.value > 0) {
            this.state.count.value = this.state.count.value - 1;
            this.setStateDirty('count');
        }
    }
    handleCouponCopy() {
        alert('Coupon selected');
    }
}

<!-- style {
    .green {
        background-color: green;
    }
    .red {
        background-color: red;
    }
} -->

<div>
    <div>
        <span>The ${state.count.name} is: </span>
        <span>${state.count.value}</span>
```

Figure 4-17. *Accessing state props from within the class {} and from within the template src/components/simple-counter/index.marko*

Immutable State Updates Through Immer vs. setStateDirty

Earlier, we mentioned that if you wanted to mutate a state property (perhaps push a new item into an array), you can mark it as dirty with ***setStateDirty.*** Else, Marko will not detect this, as the new object is identical and is not detected by a shallow compare, and the properties are watched only one level deep. However, the Marko dev team considers **setStateDirty** as an anti-pattern and recommends using immutable data structures like Immer JS.

The following example is a simple todo-mvc app that uses a **<marko-todo/>** component under *src/components/marko-todo/index.marko* and a *src/routes/todo/+page.marko*, which is the top-level server-rendered page that hosts this component.

The component uses **Immer** for doing immutable state updates and does not resort to using ***setStateDirty*** in this case. You can see the page at http://localhost:3000/todo.

```
src > routes > todo > ≡ +page.marko > 🔧 div
  1    <div.container>
  2        <marko-todo/>
  3    </div>
```

Figure 4-18. *src/routes/todo/+page.marko*

In the **<marko-todo/>** component, notice that we have used Immer as the library to perform immutable state updates via its ***produce*** function, which takes in the original state, applies the updates to a draft state, and finally returns the new state. This new value is then set to the specific property of our state object that we originally intended to modify.

```
src > components > marko-todo > ☰ index.marko > ...
  1   import {produce} from "immer"
  2
  3   class {
  4       onCreate() {
  5           this.state = {
  6               todos: ['Goto the bank', 'Buy book for kid'],
  7               task: ""
  8           }
  9       }
 10       updateTaskValue(evt) {
 11           this.state.task = evt.target.value;
 12       }
 13       addTodo() {
 14           if ((this.state.task || "").trim()) {
 15               const nextTodos = produce(this.state.todos, (draftTodos) => {
 16                   draftTodos.push(this.state.task)
 17               });
 18               this.state.todos = nextTodos;
 19               this.state.task = "";
 20           }
 21       }
 22       removeTask(index) {
 23           if (index < this.state.todos.length) {
 24               const nextTodos = produce(this.state.todos, (draftTodos) => {
 25                   draftTodos.splice(index, 1);
 26               });
 27               this.state.todos = nextTodos;
 28           }
 29       }
 30   }
 31
 32   <div>
 33       <h1>Todo List:</h1>
 34       <input
 35           type="text"
 36           value=state.task
 37           on-change("updateTaskValue")
 38           placeholder="Add a new task"
 39       />
 40       <button on-click("addTodo") disabled=(state.task === "")>Add Task</button>
 41       <ul>
 42       <for|todo, index| of=state.todos>
 43           <li key={index}>
 44               ${todo}
 45               <button on-click("removeTask", index)>Remove</button>
 46           </li>
 47       </for>
 48       </ul>
 49   </div>
```

Figure 4-19A. *src/components/marko-todo/index.marko*

A Little More on \<context>

We learned about the **\<context>** tag in an earlier example. An important part of the **\<context>** tag is that it will re-render its body content (we will look at what this means in depth) alone without causing the template in which it is placed to re-render. This means it will not cause its ***onRender*** and ***onUpdate*** lifecycle event handler hooks to trigger for the component in which it is embedded.

Only the ***renderBody*** is re-rendered when a tag parameter associated with the \<context> that is being watched changes. So it won't trigger the ***onUpdate*** or ***onRender*** (covered later) for the whole component. If it's just to have a derived value, then you should do derivations inside a $ scriptlet, in the **\<context>**'s ***renderBody.*** But do not use the scriptlets to compute derivations that set mutations in the component where ***\<context>*** is used/embedded. You won't be able to change the state of the current component based on ***context*** changing. If you need state based on context, then what you're looking for is to wrap the said component with the **\<context>** tag, as shown in Figure 4-19B.

```
<context|{couponValue}| from="coupon-parent">
        <my-stateful-component value=couponValue />
</context>
```

Figure 4-19B. *Using Marko's context tag API*

Even when debugging, you will notice that the debugger in the Marko template comes only within the \<context> body and will not come anywhere else in the template that contains the **\<context>.**

For our example, we will use a *src/components/coupon-code.*

```
src > components > coupon-code > ≡ index.marko > ⵊ context
 1    class {
 2        onRender() {
 3            console.log('coupon-code: render')
 4        }
 5        onUpdate() {
 6            console.log('coupon-code: update')
 7        }
 8    }
 9    <context {couponCode} from="coupon-parent">
10        <span>${couponCode}</span>
11    </context>
```

Figure 4-20. *src/components/coupon-code/index.marko*

We will use a *src/components/coupon-text.*

```
src > components > coupon-text > ≡ index.marko > 🔧 span
 1    <span>Your coupon code is ABCDEFGH</span>
```

Figure 4-21. *src/components/coupon-text/index.marko*

We will use a *src/components/coupon-value.*

```
src > components > coupon-value > ≡ index.marko > ⵊ context
 1    class {
 2        onRender() {
 3            console.log('coupon-value: render')
 4        }
 5        onUpdate() {
 6            console.log('coupon-value: update')
 7        }
 8    }
 9    <context {couponValue} from="coupon-parent">
10        <span>${couponValue}</span>
11    </context>
```

Figure 4-22. *src/components/coupon-value/index.marko*

For our example, we will use a *src/components/coupon-parent.*

```
src > components > coupon-parent >  ≡ index.marko > ...
  1   class {
  2       onCreate() {
  3           this.state = {
  4               couponCode: "",
  5               couponValue: ""
  6           }
  7       }
  8       updateCouponCode() {
  9           this.state.couponCode = Math.random().toString()
 10       }
 11       updateCouponValue() {
 12           this.state.couponValue = Math.random().toString()
 13       }
 14   }
 15
 16   <context
 17       couponValue=state.couponValue
 18       couponCode=state.couponCode
 19   >
 20       <!-- Somewhere nested in the container will be the buy button -->
 21       <coupon-code/>
 22       <coupon-value/>
 23       <button on-click("updateCouponCode")>
 24           Update coupon code
 25       </button>
 26       <button on-click("updateCouponValue")>
 27           Update coupon value
 28       </button>
 29       <coupon-text/>
 30   </context>
```

Figure 4-23. *src/components/coupon-parent/index.marko*

The **<coupon-parent>** will be included in a top-level server template under src/routes/context.

```
src > routes > context >  ≡ +page.marko > ⅋ coupon-parent
  1       <coupon-parent/>
```

Figure 4-24. *src/routes/context/+page.marko*

Now load the page at http://localhost:3000/context and click the button "Update coupon code."

Figure 4-25. *Click "Update coupon code" to update the coupon code*

The "Update coupon code" button is part of **<coupon-parent>**. So, you will notice the state changes, and that causes change for that text fragment. But the update state variable value is passed as a prop to the context tag parameter **couponCode**.

Now, the **<coupon-code>** component is subscribed to the **<context>** tag for this property value. And you will notice that the program halts at the debug point we have placed.

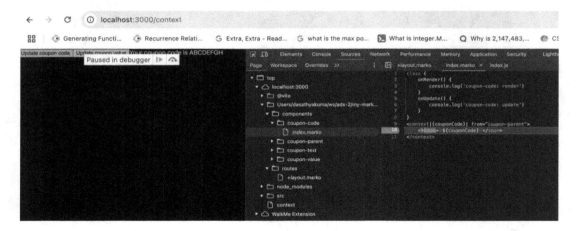

Figure 4-26. *The breakpoint triggers within <context> for the listened values but not the lifecycle handlers*

Once the value has updated and you check on the console logs, you will not see any of the logs for **onRender** and **onUpdate** lifecycle handlers within **<coupon-code>**.

How Marko Handles Styles

Organizing Component Styles

Marko offers two ways of working with styles:

- **Placing the Styles Within the Same File**: When you are authoring your component as a single-file component, to maintain separation of concerns within the same file, Marko lets you put the styles related to the component in a *style { }* block. In Figure 4-27, you will notice the styles placed within the *style { }* block and how they are applied to the component's buttons.

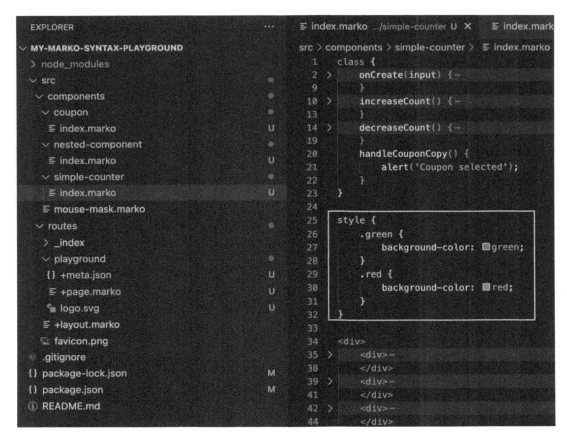

Figure 4-27. *src/components/simple-counter/index.marko showcasing placing styles within the same component*

– **Placing the Styles External to the Component**: In this case, you can have a *style.{css, less, stylus, scss}* file, and the bundler you use with your Marko project can be configured to pick up these styles. This is the usual approach in case of authoring components using the multi-file approach. In Figure 4-28, the styles found earlier within the component's *.marko file is now moved out to an external style.css file, which gets picked and handled by the bundler. You will see the styles still getting applied to the component's buttons upon page refresh.

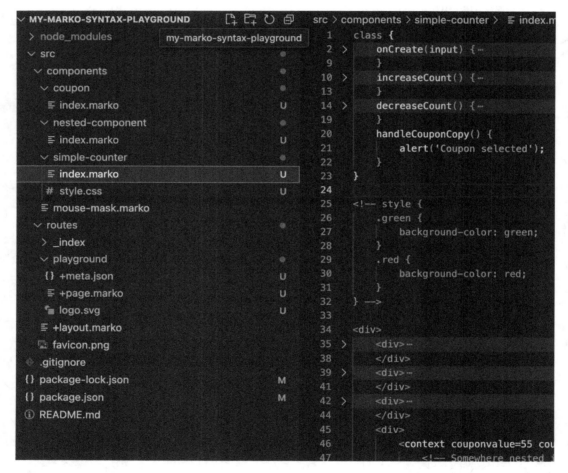

Figure 4-28. *src/components/simple-counter/index.marko showcasing placing styles externally in a style.css file*

At the time of writing this book, with Marko v5, the recommendation by the Marko dev team is to use CSS modules. However, scoped CSS will be addressed in the upcoming version of Marko 6.

The Style and Class Attributes

In Marko, attributes are parsed as Javascript expressions, instead of just strings. This means you can use dynamic values to control your attribute values.

```
<div style={display: "inline", background: false, marginRight: "0px"}></div>
<div class=["divClass", {specialDivClass: false}]></div>
<div class={divClass : true, specialDivClass: true, superSpecialDivClass: false}></div>
```

Figure 4-29. *The style and class attribute variants in Marko*

The output of the above code is shown in Figure 4-30.

```
<div style="display:inline;margin-right:0px"></div>
<div class="divClass"></div>
<div class="divClass specialDivClass"></div>
...
```

Figure 4-30. *Output of the syntax seen in Figure 4-29*

But you may wonder, why would I require something to be explicitly set to be true or false? It's a contrived example just to illustrate how style and class attributes can take on values that can be set dynamically, which brings us to the next one—dynamic values.

How Marko Handles Dynamic Values via *${ }*

In Marko, you can evaluate JavaScript expressions (variables holding values) within your templates using the *${ }* syntax. These can be thought of as placeholders that can evaluate Javascript expressions or variables. They accept any JavaScript expression, and the result of the expression will be inserted into the HTML output. Or they can be used to evaluate the variables that decide the values of CSS/style or any attribute property values. Figure 4-31 showcases how we had used the *${ }* placeholder in our simple counterexample.

```
∨ MY-MARKO-SYNTAX-PLAY...    src > components > simple-counter > ≡ index.marko > �'s div > �'s div
  > node_modules             23     }
  ∨ src                 ●    24
    ∨ components        ●    25     <!-- style {
      ∨ coupon          ●    26         .green {
        ≡ index.marko   U    27             background-color: green;
      ∨ nested-compo... ●    28         }
        ≡ index.marko   U    29         .red {
      ∨ simple-counter  ●    30             background-color: red;
        ≡ index.marko   U    31         }
        # style.css     U    32     } -->
      ≡ mouse-mask.marko     33
    ∨ routes            ●    34     <div>
      > _index               35         <div>
      ∨ playground      ●    36             <span>The ${state.count.name} is: </span>
      {} +meta.json     U    37             <span>${state.count.value}</span>
      ≡ +page.marko     U    38         </div>
      🖼 logo.svg       U    39         <div>
      ≡ +layout.marko        40             <button class="green" on-click('increaseCount')>Increment</button>
      🖼 favicon.png         41         </div>
    ◆ .gitignore            42         <div>
    {} package-lock.json M   43             <button class="red" on-click('decreaseCount')>Decrement</button>
    {} package.json     M    44         </div>
    ① README.md             45         <div>
                             46             <context couponvalue=55 couponcode="ABC12345" on-copy("handleCouponCopy")>
                             47                 <!-- Somewhere nested in the container will be the buy button -->
                             48                 <nested-component/>
                             49             </context>
                             50         </div>
                             51     </div>
```

Figure 4-31. *How marko handles or reads dynamic values*

Terminology: Things to Note

1. **Rendering**: Components can be rendered on the browser and the server. For performance, Marko produces two different compilation outputs—strings on the server and VDOM nodes for the browser. However, the VDOM nodes are an implementation detail that can change anytime (expected to change in Marko v6). Just like React, Marko is usually used in the Javascript land, with technologies like Node JS or Deno to render on the server.

2. **Renderer**: The part of your Marko component that can perform re-rendering of the component in response to change in the input props or the component state. For performing re-rendering, the Marko component needs to send the template to the browser. If, however, there are not going to be changes to the state or the

input, then it may be performant to author your component as a split file component (aforementioned in this chapter), so that the component's template is not shipped (bundled) to the browser. However, if your component is part of the render tree of a parent, which re-renders, then the bundler, as instructed by Marko, will include the split component's template to be bundled. Every time you make a decision not to send the template, check to see if it's really worthwhile, as the performance gains will be minimal unless the render tree is quite large.

3. **render()**: This is a function exposed by the renderer, which, when invoked, can be used to render the component. The act of rendering is to cause the component to refresh itself in response to a state update or new input props. By re-rendering, the component's view remains in sync with its state and input props. Earlier versions of Marko had an explicit renderer.js file tied in with every template. But with **Marko v5** and **Marko-run** meta framework onward, your ***index.marko** (template)* becomes the renderer for the component.

4. **index.marko** vs. **template.marko** vs. **+page.marko**: As we explore various examples in the subsequent chapters by scaffolding off the various starter packages under **npx @marko/create**, you may notice the files **index.marko**, **+page.marko**, and **template.marko**. Among these, **Index.marko or <component-name>.index.marko** is the naming convention used for individual components. Legacy versions of Marko and associated Legacy apps that operated directly upon the server template in terms of importing and rendering them used the **template.marko** to distinguish between top-level server page templates and individual components. Now, with the introduction of Marko's meta framework **marko-run**, **+page.marko** assumes the role of **template.marko**, with the enhancement of you, the developer, not having to manually **import** or take care of their render. For example, the sample progressive rendering app in Chapter 3 would have used the **webpack-express** scaffolder that still contains the **template.marko** file, with the **src/index.js** used for

setting up express JS, routes, and middleware and the *src/pages/ index/index.js* and *src/pages/iframe/index.js* used to serve as the controller or the incoming request handler.

How Marko Handles Events

The Types of Events That Marko Handles

Marko supports wiring event handlers to listen to

- Native events emitted by the browser from core HTML elements

- Custom events emitted by other custom Marko tags when composing components

Wiring DOM Event Handlers

Native events are those events defined on every core HTML element tag by the W3C spec, for example, the on-scroll, on-change, on-keypress, on-keydown, on-keyup, on-change, on-input, on-click, on-drag, and so on.

```
<div>
    <button class="green" on-click('increaseCount')>Increment</button>
</div>
<div>
    <button class="red" on-click('decreaseCount')>Decrement</button>
</div>
```

Figure 4-32. *Wiring event handlers for DOM-native events*

In the figure, you will notice the ***on-[eventName]*** being added declaratively to the core HTML elements. This simply means *increaseCount* and *decreaseCount* event handlers present within the **class { }** will be called when the respective buttons are clicked due to ***on-click***.

Wiring Custom Event Handlers

Custom event handlers are those that are made available because of the custom event spec. They are not W3C-native events and are any events emitted by a custom Marko tag or component.

Similarly, in *src/components/coupon/index.marko*

```
src > components > coupon >  ≡ index.marko > ⁢ context
 1    context { couponvalue, couponcode }, emit  from="simple-counter"
 2        <span>Coupon: ${couponvalue}% off.</span> <button on-click(emit, "copy")>${couponcode}</button>
 3    </context>
```

Figure 4-33. *Emitting a custom event*

In this case, you will notice there is a similar button; however, this has no event handlers being wired on to listen to the click event. There is an ***on-click*** attached, but it contains the ***emit***. This basically means that when there is a click, just emit it upward for the parent component to listen and handle as it sees fit. So, the button, when clicked, emits a ***copy*** event.

However, in this example, the component **<coupon/>**, although within the **<nested-component/>**, is within the **<context/>** tag. Due to the nature of the **<context/>** tag, to make values deeply available within a component tree while also being able to listen to events emitted deep within the component tree, we can now wire on a listener, on the **<context/>** tag, to listen to the emitted ***copy*** event.

```
src > components > simple-counter > ≡ index.marko > 🔧 div > 🔧 div > ↳ context > ↳ nested-component
  1    class {
  2  >     onCreate(input) { …
  9      }
 10  >     increaseCount() { …
 13      }
 14  >     decreaseCount() { …
 19      }
 20      handleCouponCopy() {
 21          alert('Coupon selected');
 22      }
 23    }
 24
 25  > <!-- style { …
 32    } -->
 33
 34    <div>
 35  >     <div> …
 38      </div>
 39  >     <div> …
 41      </div>
 42  >     <div> …
 44      </div>
 45      <div>
 46          <context couponvalue=55 couponcode="ABC12345" on-copy("handleCouponCopy")>
 47              <!-- Somewhere nested in the container will be the buy button -->
 48              <nested-component/>
 49          </context>
 50      </div>
 51    </div>
```

Figure 4-34. Wiring event handlers to listen to emitted custom events

Values That on-* Can Take

The **on-*<eventName>*** declarative attribute can take one of the three values:

- An inline arrow function or an anonymous inline non-arrow function

- A variable reference to a function defined within the ***static { }***

- A method name, with the method defined inside the **class { }**

Let us look at these via the following examples. Here, we are including a **<display-name/>** component, within **+page.marko**, that allows for editing names and displaying a welcome message and basic information.

```
src > routes > playground > ☰ +page.marko > ...
  1    <div.container>
  2        <display-name name="John" notifCount=5/>
  3        <simple-counter startsWith=5 name="Age"/>
  4        <div style={display: "inline", background: false, marginRight: "0px"}></div>
  5        <div class=["divClass", {specialDivClass: false}]></div>
  6        <div class={divClass : true, specialDivClass: true, superSpecialDivClass: false}></div>
  7    </div>
  8    |
  9  > style {…
 24    }
 25
```

Figure 4-35. *src/routes/playground/+page.marko*

Using an Inline Event Handler via an Arrow Function

```
> class {…
  }

> static function changeName (event) {…
  }

> style {…
  }

<div>
    Hello
    <div.name on-input((event) => {
        component.state.name = event.target.textContent;
    }) contenteditable="true">${state.name}</div>
    <div>You have ${state.notifCount}</div>
    <div>Click here to view ${state.name}'s messages</div>
</div>
```

Figure 4-36. *src/components/display-name/index.marko showcasing inline event handler via an arrow function*

This produces the output shown in Figure 4-37 when edited.

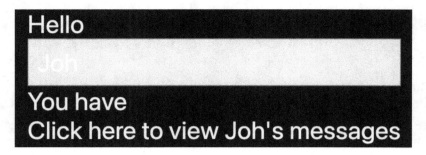

Figure 4-37. *Output after including <display-name>*

Using an Inline Event Handler via an Anonymous Non-arrow Function

```
<div>
    Hello
    <!-- <div.name on-input((event) => {…
    }) contenteditable="true">${state.name}</div> -->
    <div.name on-input(function (event) {
        this.state.name = event.target.textContent;
    }) contenteditable="true">${state.name}</div>
    <div>You have ${state.notifCount}</div>
    <div>Click here to view ${state.name}'s messages</div>
</div>
```

Figure 4-38. *Using an inline event handler via an anonymous non-arrow function*

This is a slight modification to the earlier inline arrow function that could not access **this**. While this is available, the general practice of including event handlers within the view imperatively is not generally recommended.

Using a Variable Reference to a Static Function

In this case, we can have a variable that references a static function or a direct reference to the static function as shown here. Static functions inside static blocks are only run once per template and not once per instance. Yet, they do receive access to this and therefore the component state. However, static blocks and functions within them (essentially static functions) do not execute every time the template executes a re-render for the component to be rendered again.

This is a good pattern that will help your components scale over time. This helps to abstract out the business logic and keep your component code to just manage the lifecycle and the state of the component while moving complex business logic out in a manner that can make it independently testable.

```
> class { …
}

static function changeName (event) {
    this.state.name = event.target.textContent;
}

> style { …
}

<div>
    Hello
>   <!-- <div.name on-input((event) => { …
    }) contenteditable="true">${state.name}</div> -->
    <!-- <div.name on-input(function (event) {
        this.state.name = event.target.textContent;
    }) contenteditable="true">${state.name}</div> -->
    <div.name on-input(changeName) contenteditable="true">${state.name}</div>
    <div>You have ${state.notifCount}</div>
    <div>Click here to view ${state.name}'s messages</div>
</div>
```

Figure 4-39. *Variable reference to a static function*

217

Using a methodName with the methodName Defined in the Class { }

This was the same as the first example with *increaseCount* and *decreaseCount*.

```
<div>
    Hello
    <!-- <div.name on-input((event) => {
    }) contenteditable="true">${state.name}</div> -->
    <!-- <div.name on-input(function (event) {
        this.state.name = event.target.textContent;
    }) contenteditable="true">${state.name}</div> -->
    <div.name on-input('editName') contenteditable="true">${state.name}</div>
    <div>You have ${state.notifCount}</div>
    <div>Click here to view ${state.name}'s messages</div>
</div>
```

Figure 4-40. *Using a method name that has its definition in the class { }*

To summarize the aforementioned examples

1. In the **view** part of the template, **${state.xyz}** is to be used to only **access** the state. There are **no mutations allowed** from the view.

2. For *inline event handler functions*, defined as *arrow functions*, **component.state.xyz** is to be used to **access and mutate** the state here.

3. For *inline event handler functions*, defined as *anonymous non-arrow functions*, **this.state.xyz** can be used to **access and mutate** the state here.

4. For *static event handler functions*, **this.state.xyz** can be used to **access and mutate** the state.

Binding Arguments to the Event Handlers

You can bind additional dynamic arguments to the event handlers declaratively. Additional arguments can be bound as follows:

```
<button on-click((name, event, el) => {
    console.log(name);
    console.log(event);
    console.log(el);
}, state.name)>Say Hello</button>
```

Figure 4-41A. *Passing args to the event handlers besides the event object*

```
John
▶ PointerEvent {isTrusted: true, pointerId: 1, width: 1, height: 1, stopPropagation: f, …}
  <button>Say Hello</button>
```

Figure 4-41B. *Logs of Figure 4-41A*

{state.name} is dynamic here and is declaratively bound to the event handler. It is also the first argument that shows up in the event handler. The logs are also included above.

If there are more arguments, an equal number of parameters will show up. For example, refer to Figure 4-42.

```
<button on-click((name, location, companyName, event, el) => {
    console.log(name, location, companyName);
    console.log(event);
    console.log(el);
}, state.name, "Texas", "SpaceX")>Say Hello</button>
```

Figure 4-42. *When there are more arguments*

```
John Texas SpaceX
▶ PointerEvent {isTrusted: true, pointerId: 1, width: 1, height: 1, stopPropagation: f, …}
  <button>Say Hello</button>
```

Figure 4-43. *Logs of Figure 4-42*

The logs above are included for the same, which now log additional parameters. However, the final two parameters will be the ***event*** and ***el***.

Arguments for Native Event Handlers

- **...args**

  - By this, what we mean is the entire list of parameters is made available as arguments in the function definition.

    For example, *on-click("sayHello", name, location, company)* will translate to the method definition *sayHello(name, location, company, event, el)*.

- **eventArgs**

  - The native DOM event object.

- **el**

  - The DOM event on which the event handler was attached to.

For *custom* events, as discussed earlier with the **copy** event emitted from *src/components/coupons/index.marko*

```
src > components > coupon > ☰ index.marko > ⅋ context > ⚙ button
  1    <context|{ couponvalue, couponcode }, emit| from="simple-counter">
  2        <span>Coupon: ${couponvalue}% off.</span>
  3        <button on-click(emit, "copy", "John", "texas", "SpaceX")>${couponcode}</button>
  4    </context>
```

Figure 4-44. *Emitting "copy" custom event upon click*

The most important thing to note here is that the **emit** isn't part of **this** and belongs to the **<context>** tag. But every component also gets its own **emit** made available on the component's instance, that is, on **this**. So, you can do **this.emit**.

On src/components/simple-counter/index.marko

```marko
src > components > simple-counter > ☰ index.marko > ...
  1    class {
  2 >     onCreate(input) {…
  9       }
 10 >     increaseCount() {…
 13       }
 14 >     decreaseCount() {…
 19       }
 20       handleCouponCopy(name, location, company, event, instance) {
 21           console.log(name);
 22           console.log(location);
 23           console.log(company);
 24           console.log(event);
 25           console.log(instance);
 26           alert('Coupon selected');
 27       }
 28    }
 29
 30 > <!-- style {…
 37    } -->
 38
 39    <div>
 40 >     <div>…
 43       </div>
 44 >     <div>…
 46       </div>
 47 >     <div>…
 49       </div>
 50       <div>
 51           <context couponvalue=55 couponcode="ABC12345" on-copy("handleCouponCopy")>
 52               <!-- Somewhere nested in the container will be the buy button -->
 53               <nested-component/>
 54           </context>
 55       </div>
 56    </div>
```

Figure 4-45. *Listening to the copy event and handling it via handleCouponCopy*

The output is shown in Figure 4-46.

```
John
texas
SpaceX
▶ PointerEvent {isTrusted: true, pointerId: 1, width: 1, height: 1, stopPropagation: f, …}
  <button>ABC12345</button>
```

Figure 4-46. *Logs for Figure 4-45*

Arguments for Custom Event Handlers

- **...args**

  - By this, what we mean is the entire list of parameters is made available as arguments in the function definition.

    For example, when **this.emit("copy", "John", "Texas", "SpaceX")** is emitted, the receiver (parent or context) will receive it via the **on-copy(handleCopy)**. Here, **handleCopy** is the eventHandler for the "**copy**" event. The function definition for **handleCopy** will now be **handleCopy(name, location, company, event, el)**.

- **EventArgs**

  - The arguments passed into **this.emit()** by the target UI custom Marko component.

- **componentInstance**

  - The instance of the component to which the handler was wired. In this case, it would be the **<coupon/>** component's instance.

Binding event handlers for native events and custom events are similar, albeit with some minor differences as illustrated above.

One-Time Event Handlers via once-*

Many times, it may be required to bind a handler to listen to an event or an interaction just one time. This is where *once-** comes in. Marko wires on this handler to fire only one time and takes care of cleaning up the handlers.

In terms of binding additional parameters and making them available as additional arguments in the event handler function definition, **once-*** also follows the same pattern as **on-***, depending on what event you are wiring the handler for—*native event* or *custom event*.

For example, in the **<display-name/>** component, if the **"Say Hello"** button is wired with **once-click** instead of the previous **on-click**

```
<button once-click((name, event, el) => {
    console.log(name);
    console.log(event);
    console.log(el);
}, state.name)>Say Hello</button>
```

Figure 4-47. *Handlers that trigger only one time*

Then, despite clicking numerous times, the handler executes only one time, logging the said values only once.

Emitting Events via this.emit

We saw in the previous paragraphs about the **emit** function. However, that belonged to the **<context/>** tag. The **emit** we talk about in this section is the one provided by Marko, on the component instance itself, to emit events to the surrounding parent component. For example, if we are trying to emit some event from **<coupon/>** to the **<nested-component/>**

```
src > components > coupon > ≡ index.marko > ...
  1    class {
  2        getNew() {
  3            this.emit("new", "John Doe", "Texas", "SpaceX");
  4        }
  5    }
  6
  7    <context|{ couponvalue, couponcode }, emit| from="simple-counter">
  8        <span>Coupon: ${couponvalue}% off.</span>
  9        <button on-click(emit, "copy", "John", "texas", "SpaceX")>${couponcode}</button>
 10        <button on-click('getNew')>Get a new coupon</button>
 11    </context>
```

Figure 4-48. *Emit event to the parent via **this.emit** from within src/components/ coupon/index.marko*

```
src > components > nested-component > ≡ index.marko > ...
  1    class {
  2        callThis(name, location, company, event, el) {
  3            console.log(name, location, company, event, el);
  4        }
  5    }
  6
  7    <coupon on-new('callThis')/>
```

Figure 4-49. *The parent src/components/nested-component/index.marko listens to this event emitted by the child component <coupon/>*

This is made possible because every Marko component extends the EventEmitter and is thus capable of emitting events to the parent component. For cross-component communication, solutions like publish-subscribe (`https://github.com/raptorjs/ raptor-pubsub`) or custom events can be used. Resort to solutions like Redux only if it is absolutely beneficial. Read `https://medium.com/@dan_abramov/you-might-not-need- redux-be46360cf367` to decide if your use case really benefits from a solution like Redux.

Using this.subscribeTo to Handle Global Subscriptions

There will arise use cases where it will be required to subscribe to global objects like **window**, etc., for events such as **scroll** and so on. For these use cases, Marko offers a simple API abstraction via the ***this.subscribeTo*** (made available on the ***this*** object of every component instance) to connect with such event targets or event emitters and listen to specific events from them. By using this, you do not have to deal with unregistering the handlers from these eventTargets or global objects. Marko handles it for you.

```
src > components > nested-component > ≡ index.marko > ...
1    class {
2        onMount() {
3            this.subscribeTo(document).on('mousemove', (e) => {
4                console.log(e.pageX, e.pageY);
5            });
6        }
7        callThis(name, location, company, event, el) {
8            console.log(name, location, company, event, el);
9        }
10    }
11
12    <coupon on-new('callThis')/>
```

Figure 4-50. *Imperatively using this.subscribeTo for listening to events on global objects*

Figure 4-51. *Logs of Figure 4-50*

Using the Custom <subscribe> Tag

The **<subscribe>** tag is similar to the ***this.subscribeTo()*** API, except that the former is imperative, while the latter is declarative and can be wired in the view instead of from within the component, as in ***this.subscribeTo()***.

The tag information can be read here: `https://github.com/marko-js/tags/tree/master/tags/subscribe`. But this is not a core tag, and Marko has provided this abstraction as a custom tag that is available to be installed from the NPM registry via

```
>> npm install @marko-tags/subscribe
```

This will install the module. Next, let's modify the code to use the **<subscribe>** tag to see the differences.

```
src > components > nested-component > ☰ index.marko > 🔀 subscribe
 1    class {
 2        onMount() {
 3            // this.subscribeTo(document).on('mousemove', (e) => {
 4            //     console.log(e.pageX, e.pageY);
 5            // });
 6        }
 7        mouseMove(e) {
 8            console.log(e.pageX, e.pageY);
 9        }
10        callThis(name, location, company, event, el) {
11            console.log(name, location, company, event, el);
12        }
13    }
14
15    <subscribe
16        to=document
17        on-mousemove("mouseMove")
18    >
19        <coupon on-new('callThis')/>
20    </subscribe>
21
```

Figure 4-52. *Declaratively using <subscribe> for listening to events on global objects*

When running the code, you will notice the same output as before.

However, when using the **<subscribe>** tag, care must be taken to ensure that the **EventTarget** or the **EventEmitter** (in this case, "**document**" assigned via the "**to**" attribute) is available in the environment of render. For example, when the aforementioned template is rendered on the server, it will error out, since "**document**" is not available in the Node JS world.

However, if ***this.subscribeTo()*** is used, you have the ability to wrap it in a check for window, as if (typeof window !== "undefined").

Marko's Core Tags

Overview

In this section, let us look at the core tags of Marko that are made available in Marko by default. So, there is no need for you to explicitly install them. They include

1. **Conditional Tags**: Marko lets you author conditional-style *if*, *else-if*, and *else* syntax right into the HTML through the provision of these core tags. Just like any other Marko tag or HTML tag, <if> now becomes a part of the HTML syntax. This is made possible by Marko expanding upon the HTML syntax to provide a truly dynamic HTML authoring experience. This removes the need for having JSX-style expression syntax interspersed with the HTML when authoring conditional-style code.

   a. **<if>**

   b. **<else-if>**

   c. **<else>**

2. **Looping Tags**: Similar to the conditionals**, Marko** lets you author looping-style code by directly expanding upon the HTML language to offer you the <for> tag and the <while> tag, just as how you would write loop-style code in the Javascript language via the for and while statements. This removes the need for having JSX-style expression syntax interspersed with the HTML when authoring looping-style code.

    a.   **\<for>**: The \<for> tag has a few variations depending on what it is iterating.

        i.   When iterating over an array

        ii.   When iterating over an object with properties

        iii. When iterating over a range

    b.   **\<while>**

3. **Local Reusable Template Partial:** These are small HTML repeatable fragments within the context of a larger template or component. They may not necessarily qualify to require a template or component of their own, but help to neatly author code to achieve better reusability, maintainability, and readability within the template.

    a.   **\<macro>**

4. **Async Tags:** This is the tag that helps Marko do all the magic of asynchronous rendering and progressive HTML rendering.

    a.   **\<await>**

5. **\<html-comment> Tag:** Marko removes any comment included in the HTML. Marko includes comments in the HTML, which are mostly generated by it for determining component boundaries and are referred to as component boundary markers. However, if you do require comments to show up in your HTML source, then this is the tag, within which you place your comments.

6. **Include Static HTML File:** There will be times that while rendering a larger page template, there may be smaller sections that are static and are composed of other teams in your organization. These teams just share these static HTML fragments so that they can be included within the larger page. This tag helps you achieve it—link a static HTML into your template (inlines the contents of the static HTML file). This means the special HTML characters will not be escaped.

    a.   **\<include-html>** tag

7. **Include Static Text File**: While the previous example mentioned including static HTML files, this tag helps to include static text files (inlines the contents of the text files). This will escape HTML syntax characters.

    a.   **<include-text>** tag

Next, we will look at some examples that illustrate these core tags.

Conditional Tags

Conditional programming is a basic construct of any programming language, and Marko is no different here. While JSX-styled solutions let you use the traditional if, else if, and else syntax within the JSX-style syntax, they intersperse HTML and Javascript, eroding the separation of concerns. However, Marko makes it cleaner by instead expanding upon the HTML language to provide similar constructs as core tags—<if>, <else-if>, <else>—just as a natural extension of the HTML language. They all evaluate Javascript expressions and execute the contained HTML partial only when they are respectively truthy. Let us look at this with an example. Consider the use case of showing a greeting message for the following three different users:

1. A guest user

2. A logged-in user

3. A logged-in recognized user but session expired

Figure 4-53. *The <if>, <else-if>, and <else> core tags*

In our +page.marko, we have used this tag as

```
<greeting userName="Joseph" isRecognizedUser=true />
```

Figure 4-54. *The greeting component*

Based on the input props, one of the <if>, <else-if>, and <else> tags evaluates to a truthy and renders the content controlled by it within its body.

Looping Tags

As previously mentioned, Marko does looping via the **<for>** and the **<while>** tags. The **<for>** tags can handle iterations on *arrays*, *array-like* structures, *object properties*, and between *ranges*. The **<for>** is pretty universal in the sense that it can iterate over any *iterable*—Strings, NodeLists, Sets—and any object that is indexed from zero and has a *.length* property. It can be considered to be similar to the *for..of* and the *for..in* loops in Javascript.

<for> Tag to Iterate over Arrays (Similar to for..of)

In the following example, our *state* object has a *student* property of type Array. Here, we use the *for..of* variant of the <for> tag to iterate over this.

The syntax is

```
<for|item, index, array| of=array>
```

This will render the contained body within the for tag for each item of an array.

The tag gets the current array item, the current index under iteration, and the overall current array.

Figure 4-55. *Using <for> to iterate over arrays*

Figure 4-56. *Output of Figure 4-55*

<for> Tag to Iterate over Object Properties

In the following example, our *state* object has a *universitiesAndFees* property of type Object. Here, we use the ***for..in*** variant of the <for> tag to iterate over this.

The syntax is

```
<for|key, value| in=object>
```

The tag will get the current key and value as the tag parameters.

`<for>` Tag to Iterate over Objects

This will render the contained body within the for tag for each property of the object.

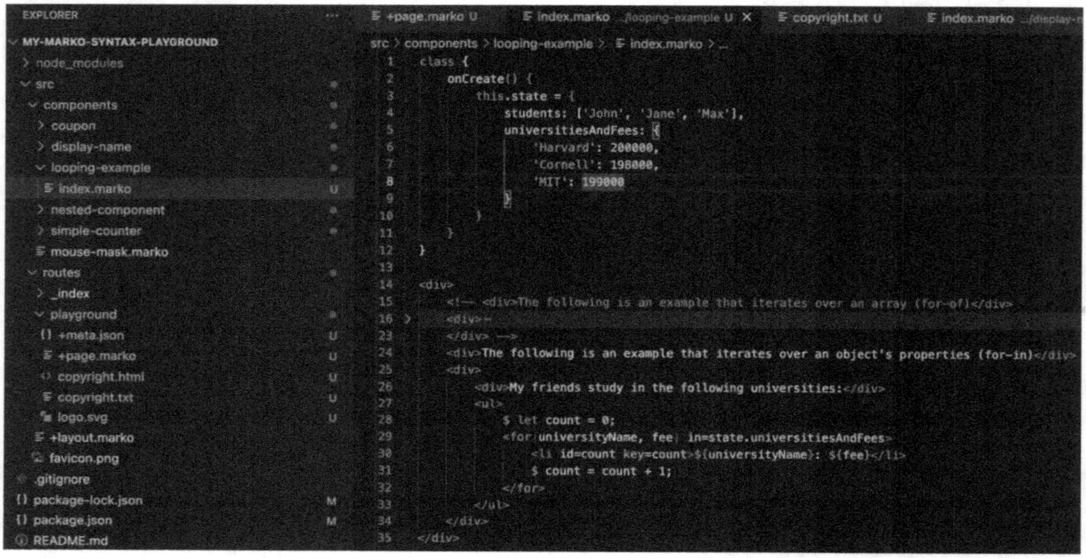

Figure 4-57. *Using <for> to iterate over objects and its properties*

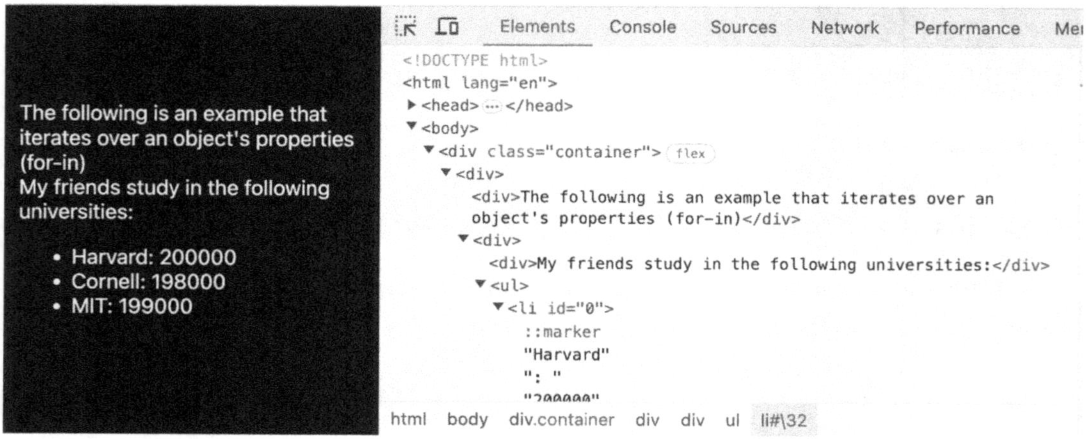

Figure 4-58. *Logs for Figure 4-57*

\<for> Tag to Iterate over a Range

This basically helps to achieve a traditional for loop.

The syntax is

```
<for|value| from=first to=last step=increment>
```

This will render its body for each value in between and including from and to, proceeded forward or backward by the step. The current value will be provided as the tag parameter.

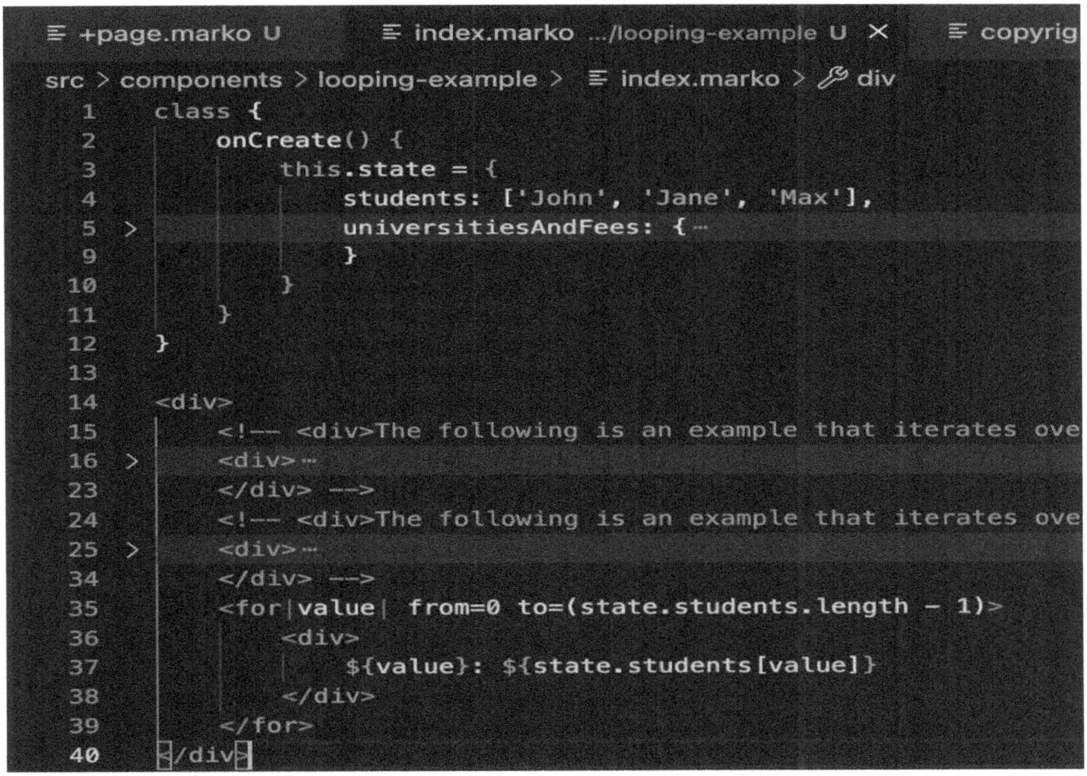

Figure 4-59. *\<for> tag to iterate over a range*

Figure 4-60. *Logs for Figure 4-59*

<while> Tag

The `<while(expression)>` tag is equivalent to the while keyword in Javascript. Marko's `<while>` takes an expression that must evaluate to a truthy for the loop to progress. Once the expression evaluates to a false, the looping is stopped. In doing so, Marko removes the need for a JSX-style syntax that intersperses Javascript and HTML.

Let us repeat the <for> range iteration example with <while>.

```
$ let flag = 0
<while(flag <= state.students.length - 1)>
    <div id=`num-list-${flag}`>
        ${flag}: ${state.students[flag]}
        $ flag = flag + 1;
    </div>
</while>
```

Figure 4-61. *The <while> tag*

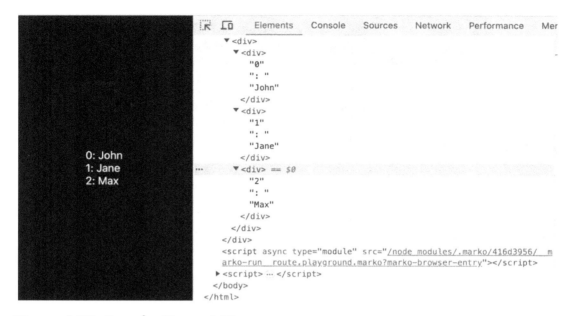

Figure 4-62. *Logs for Figure 4-61*

The three variants of <for>—used as a traditional for loop to iterate over a range of values, for..of to iterate over arrays, and for..in to iterate over objects—along with the <while> tag, comprise Marko's language features to help you achieve repeated content easily without having to write it in JSX style.

Setting a Key

In the earlier examples, you will have noticed we set something called a ***key***. This is specifically recommended by Marko, in cases of repeated content. Specifying keys gives Marko a way to identify items in a list that produce repeated content and helps it keep track of which items in the set of repeated content have been modified, updated, added, or removed. The basic requirement of a *key* is that the value has to be unique. It can be a Number or a String type. If there are multiple repeated tags, within the body of the <for>, then only the first such tag needs to be provided with a *key*.

```
<ul>
    $ let count = 0;
    <for|universityName, fee| in=state.universitiesAndFees>
        <li id=count key=count>${universityName}: ${fee}</li>
        $ count = count + 1;
    </for>
</ul>
```

Figure 4-63. *Setting a "key" for elements*

There are some more use cases for the **key** that we shall look at while looking at **directives** later in this chapter.

Macros

Macros are reusable template partials within a given template that are used in the same template itself. They are not something that can be exported out and used elsewhere. That would require it to be built as a component. However, <macros> help to achieve separation of constructs within a larger template. For example, when building a table, with different types of rows for different records, each record type can be extracted out as a <macro>. This is obviously a contrived example, but you get the point. One thing to note is you cannot emit an event from within a handler of the macro and expect the same component to catch it. It will be emitted to the parent, since Macro is not a separate component, but part of the same component.

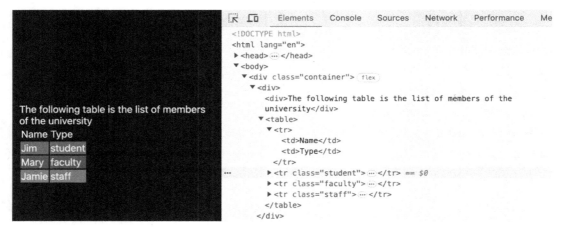

Figure 4-64. *Output using <macro>*

The code for this is shown next.

```
src > components > macros-example >  ≡ index.marko > ...
 1   style {
 2       .student td {
 3           background-color: ▦green;
 4       }
 5       .faculty td {
 6           background-color: ▦brown;
 7       }
 8       .staff td {
 9           background-color: ▦grey;
10       }
11   }
12
13   class {
14       onCreate() {
15           this.state = {
16               members: [
17                   { type: 'student', name: 'Jim' },
18                   { type: 'faculty', name: 'Mary' },
19                   { type: 'staff', name: 'Jamie' }
20               ]
21           }
22       }
23   }
24
25   <macro|{member}| name="build-student">
26     <tr.student>
27       <td>${member.name}</td>
28       <td>${member.type}</td>
29     </tr>
30   </macro>
31
32   <macro|{member}| name="build-faculty">
33     <tr.faculty>
34       <td>${member.name}</td>
35       <td>${member.type}</td>
36     </tr>
37   </macro>
38
39   <macro|{member}| name="build-staff">
40     <tr.staff>
41       <td>${member.name}</td>
42       <td>${member.type}</td>
43     </tr>
44   </macro>
45
46   <div>
47       <div>The following table is the list of members of the university</div>
48       <table>
49           <tr>
50               <td>Name</td>
51               <td>Type</td>
52           </tr>
53           <for|value, index| of=state.members>
54               <if(value.type === "student")>
55                   <build-student member=value key=index/>
56               </if>
57               <else-if(value.type === "faculty")>
58                   <build-faculty member=value key=index/>
59               </else-if>
60               <else>
61                   <build-staff member=value key=index/>
62               </else>
63           </for>
64       </table>
65   </div>
```

Figure 4-65. *Code showcasing <macro>*

Also, you can wire event handlers onto elements within the <macro> tag. You can also use custom Marko tags within the <macro> tags. Let us look at the following example that wires a click onto the rows. You will notice that due to the lack of a separate component definition, they refer to handlers within the component definition of the same template.

```
src > components > macros-example > ☰ index.marko > ⅀ macro
  1 > style {…
 11   }
 12
 13   class {
 14 >     onCreate() {…
 22     }
 23     getName(index) {
 24         console.log(this.state.members[index].name);
 25     }
 26   }
 27
 28   <macro|{member, index}| name="build-student">
 29     <tr.student on-click('getName', index)>
 30       <td>${member.name}</td>
 31       <td>${member.type}</td>
 32     </tr>
 33   </macro>
 34
```

Figure 4-66. *Using event handlers for elements within <macro>*

Including HTML Comments

In the **+page.marko**, let's include a comment.

```
☰ +page.marko U  ✕      ☰ copyright.txt U        ☰ index.marko

src > routes > playground > ☰ +page.marko > ⅋ div > ⅀ html-c
  1   <div.container>
  2     <html-comment>
  3       This is our playground page!
  4     </html-comment>
```

Figure 4-67. *Code showcasing <html-comment>*

In the output, you will be able to see this as a comment when inspecting the HTML source.

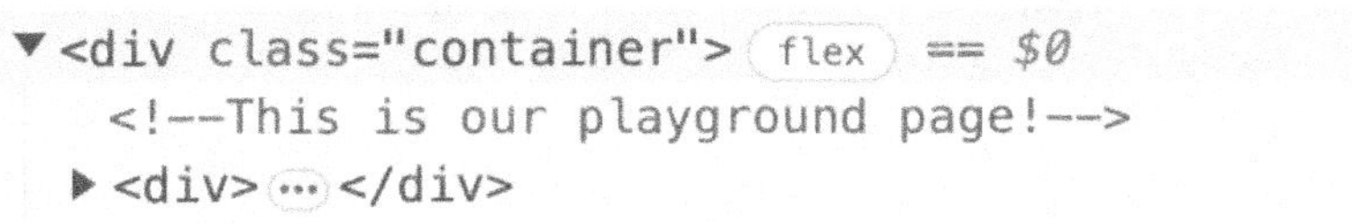

```
▼ <div class="container"> ( flex ) == $0
    <!--This is our playground page!-->
  ▶ <div> ⋯ </div>
```

Figure 4-68. *Seeing the comments in the output HTML*

Including Static Files

There are two types of files you can include: text and HTML. Let's look at their syntaxes.

Including Static Text Files

In the following example, we just include an external **copyright.txt** into the main **+page. marko** that we have been working with. You will notice how the static text file gets inlined into the page; however, the HTML tags do get escaped.

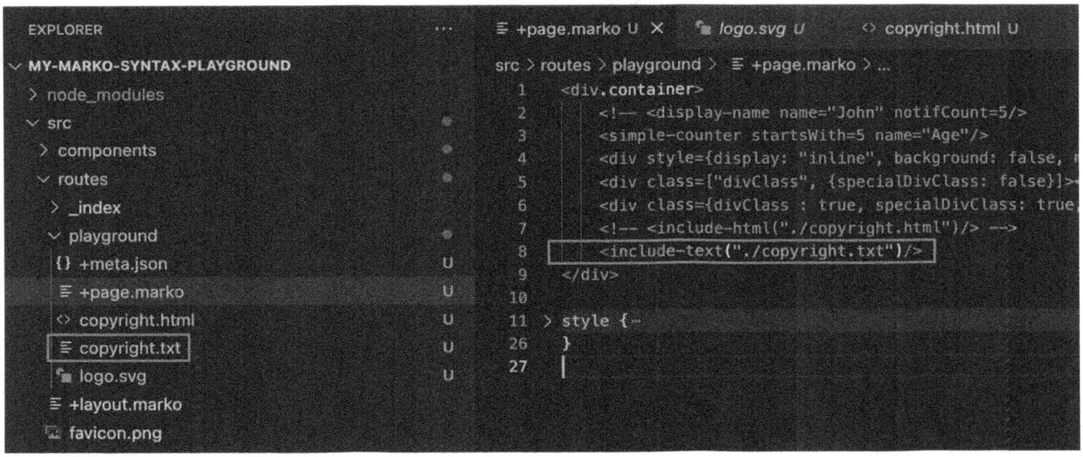

Figure 4-69. *Example showcasing including static text files*

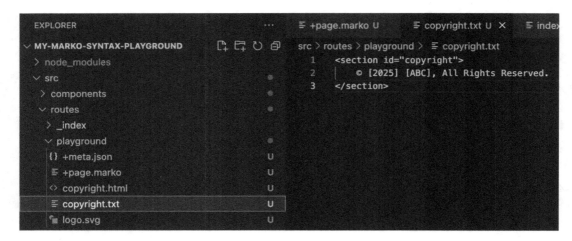

Figure 4-70. *The static text file*

Figure 4-71. *The output of including the static text file*

Including Static HTML Files

In the following example, we just include an external ***copyright.html*** into the main ***+page.marko*** that we have been working with. You will notice how the static HTML gets inlined into the page, along with maintaining HTML tags (they do not get escaped).

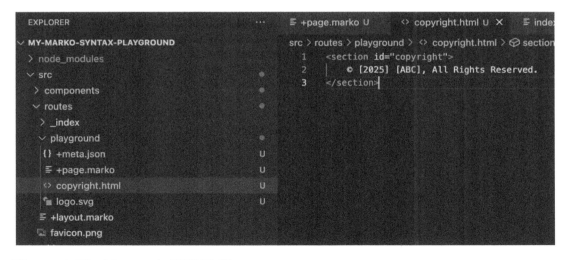

Figure 4-72. *Including static HTML files*

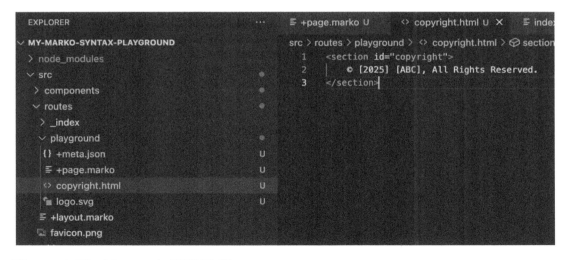

Figure 4-73. *The static HTML file*

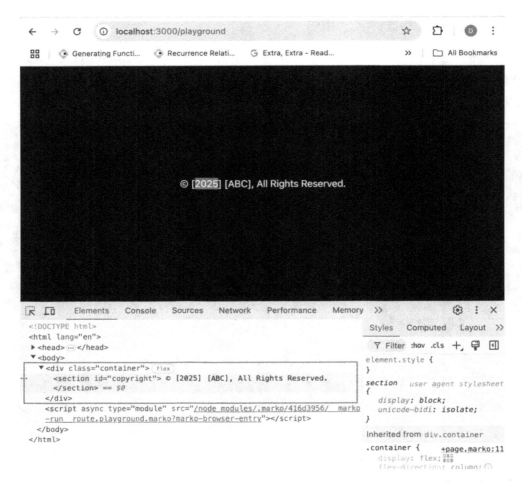

Figure 4-74. *Output showcasing the static HTML file*

Handling Async

Although we have seen this in our simple application for progressive HTML rendering on the server, let's formally introduce the ***<await>*** tag. This tag helps you to treat HTML fragments or partials as pending promises. What this means is it offers a way for you to mark view fragments as pending. To recap, for example, if you have a section on the page, like the left navigation, waiting on a service call, your entire page template does not have to wait for the left nav service to respond before beginning rendering the entire page template. Instead, it proceeds to render other sections of the template that already have data available. This is what we refer to as asynchronous rendering.

Similarly, it also offers a mechanism to stream or flush the rendered data (on the server) to the browser, without having to wait for other pending sections to be render complete. This means it offers hooks to do both of the following:

– Preserve the render order of the HTML on the server (referred to as *in-order flush*) and then fully flush the rendered HTML from the server in the right order.

– **Not** preserve the render order of the HTML on the server (referred to as *out-of-order flush*). In this case, the HTML is no longer buffered on the server to preserve order, but they are flushed as soon as they are rendered. However, on the client side, Javascript is used to move the rendered elements back to the right places (referred to as *in-order paint*). This is done so to preserve the order of the HTML fragments.

Attributes on *<await>*

Attribute Name	Type	Description
timeout	Number	A timeout value up to which the await tag shall wait. Beyond this value, it rejects the promise, wrapping the HTML partial, with a Timeout Error.
name	String	When you have multiple fragments that depend on each other. For example, show Fragment A after Fragment B and so on, this helps to identify the fragment. Also, helps with debugging.
show-after	String	Similar to name, but has the value of the "name" of another fragment after which, the current fragment has to show up, although it may be ready.
client-reorder	Boolean	When **true**, any HTML fragments after the **<await>** tag will be server-rendered before the Promise associated with the **<await>** completes. Once the **<await>** completes, then the fulfilled Promise's result is used to render the body content of the **<await>**'s **<@then>** tag. The position of the rendered contents will then be updated into the DOM with client-side JavaScript (*out-of-order flush* & *in-order paint*). Note that with Marko v5, **<await>** is server only.

Figure 4-75. *Table with details about the <await> tag attributes*

Attribute tags on **<await>** are shown in Figure 4-76.

Attribute tag name	Description	Parameters
<@placeholder>	A loading placeholder HTML fragment. Anything within the body of this tag, will be displayed while the content is being loaded / rendered.	None
<@then>	HTML Content within this tag, will be displayed once data is available (render and load complete). It usually depends on data that is available. It is parameterized and gets the **data** object as the parameter.	The resolved **data** object that is required for rendering the underlying HTML partial.
<@catch>	When the **<await>** tag fails - rejected promise, thrown error or an upstream service call failure etc., what is the fallback UX to be rendered? That is placed within the body of this attribute tag. This is a parameterized tag and receives the **error** object as a tag parameter.	The **error** object that contains the error information. This helps to distinguish between specific types of errors - like a 404, 500 or a timeout error and so on.

Figure 4-76. *Table with details about the attribute tags of <await> tag*

Revisiting our sample project in Chapter 3, which explained progressive rendering, you will better appreciate the example now.

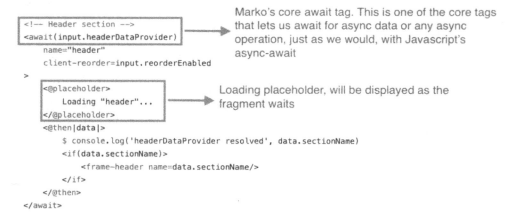

Figure 4-77. *Example from Chapter 3, showcasing the <await> tag*

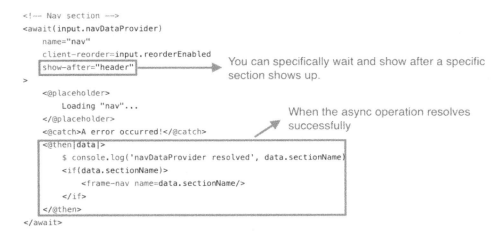

Figure 4-78. *Example from Chapter 3, showcasing the <await> tag*

Global APIs and Keywords in Marko Templates

The following are some keywords specific to the Marko language that is available universally in all the templates:

1. **out**: This is the output stream associated with the template. It offers access to some specific properties. This can be any async stream—WHATWG Response stream on server vs. an Async Node Stream on the browser.

2. **input**: This is the input received by the template. Properties on the input can be accessed as *input.xyz*. We have seen this in earlier examples.

3. **state**: This is the state associated with the template. State properties can be accessed as *state.xyz*. We have seen this in earlier examples.

4. **component**: This is the component instance. You can invoke methods present on the component instance. For example, *component.getStudentName()*. Here, **getStudentName()** will be defined within the *class { }*. *this* will be available here.

5. **$global**: This is a feature in Marko that lets you make data
    available to all the templates on the server side. If there are any
    universal data props that are accessed across all templates, they
    can be placed within this.

6. **out.global**: This is a property on the *out* keyword. This is used to
    whitelist a set of values to make them available to all templates on
    the client side. This is similar to *$global*, but for the client side.
    This is specifically offered, so as to avoid serializing all the data
    that may have been globally present for the server render.

It's worthwhile to remember that the **this** keyword is not available for access in
the view or template. It's available only within the *component* (class or no class). So,
from within the view / HTML, you wouldn't be able to do *this.xyz*. While we haven't
yet discussed Marko's meta framework—Marko-run—it shouldn't be a blocker in
understanding **$global** and **out.global**.

To the *+handler.ts*, we include the code shown in Figure 4-79.

```
src > routes > playground > JS +handler.js > ⊗ GET
1    export async function GET(context) {
2        context.globalMessage = 'hello-world';
3        context.serializedGlobals.globalMessage = true;
4    }
5
```

Figure 4-79. *Setting a prop on $global and whitelisting it for hydration to client*

The first line informs Marko that the property *globalMessage* is to be made available
up to every leaf node/component during the server render. The second line informs
Marko to serialize the global property *globalMessage*. The only reason you may want to
serialize this value is when you think this value will be required on the client side when
any component re-renders.

Next, to access this *globalMessage* on the server side in the top-level template, you
can access it via the *$global* keyword.

246

```
src > routes > playground >  ☰ +page.marko > 🔧 div
  1      $ const message = ($global).globalMessage;
  2
  3      $ console.log("====================");
  4      $ console.log(message);
  5      $ console.log("====================");
  6
  7      <div.container>
  8          <section>
  9              ${message}
 10          </section>
```

Figure 4-80. *What is set on context is accessible on $global*

But you will notice, we are accessing this within the **+*page.marko***, which is the top-level server template used while rendering the /playground route on the server. Let's try accessing this in one of the included components, **<macro-example/>**.

```
☰ +page.marko U        JS +handler.js U      ☰ index.marko .../macros-example U  ✕    ☰ index.marko .../greeting U      ☰ co
src > components > macros-example > ☰ index.marko > ...
  1  > style { …
 11    }
 12
 13  > class { …
 26    }
 27
 28  > <macro|{member, index}| name="build-student"> …
 33    </macro>
 34
 35  > <macro|{member, index}| name="build-faculty"> …
 40    </macro>
 41
 42  > <macro|{member, index}| name="build-staff"> …
 47    </macro>
 48
 49    <div>
 50      <div>${out.global.globalMessage} The following table is the list of members of the university</div>
 51  >     <table> …
 67      </table>
 68    </div>
```

Figure 4-81. *Accessing the value from out.global*

Here, within subcomponents (not top-level template), we access it like *out.global. globalMessage*. Suppose this component had a state change within the on-click handler ***getName***.

```
class {
    onCreate(input, out) {
        this.state = {
            members: [
                { type: 'student', name: 'Jim' },
                { type: 'faculty', name: 'Mary' },
                { type: 'staff', name: 'Jamie' }
            ]
        }
    }
    getName(index) {
        console.log(this.state.members[index].name);
        this.replaceState({
            members: [
                { type: 'student', name: 'Tom' },
                { type: 'faculty', name: 'Jerry' },
                { type: 'staff', name: 'Goofy' }
            ]
        });
    }
}
```

Figure 4-82. *Accessing global values from out.global on the client*

You will notice that after re-render, ***globalMessage*** is still available.

Figure 4-83. *Output for the earlier example*

Click the rows, you will find the state being changed, and the component re-renders, but "hello-world" is still available during the re-render.

Figure 4-84. *"Hello world" is available after re-render*

Global APIs on *this* in Marko Components

The ***this*** keyword is the component instance and is available within the ***class { }*** (referred to as the widget/behavior part of the component). The following are the APIs available on the ***this*** keyword:

1. **this.state** (available on the view/template as just state, and one can access *state* props as **state.<propertyName>** in the view layer). Setting this or modifying the first level of properties within it will queue up the component to re-render (component gets nominated for a re-render). Note that only those properties initially set within *onCreate* will be watched over for changes, one level deep. If you did not want a property initially, you can always have the property set to *null*. As stated earlier, if you had an array and pushed new elements into it, you could use *setStateDirty* to mark that the specific state property was indeed modified (else, this won't be detected by shallow compare—great for performance) or use an immutable structure like *Immer*.

2. **this.input** (available on the view/template as just *input*, and one can access *input* props as **input.<propertyName>** in the view layer). Setting this will cause the component to re-render.

3. **this.id**: The unique ID associated with this component instance. It's a string for the root HTML element that the component is bound to. It's not the ID attribute.

4. **this.el**: The root Node/Element associated with a given Marko component.

5. **this.els**: The collection of root Nodes/Elements associated with a given Marko component. This is useful at times when the component doesn't have one single root Node, but rather a collection of Nodes (siblings) that are all root nodes.

6. **Event Handling:** We have seen these in the state management section. Event handling is best done with ease declaratively via the *on-<eventName>(Function Declaration | Function reference | Method name as a string) or once-<eventName>(Function Declaration | Function reference | Method name as a string)* declaratives.

   a. **this.emit(eventName: string, ...args?: any)**: Can be used to emit a custom event or any event that can be captured by the surrounding parent component. In Marko, every component is an instance of an event emitter that can emit events to its parent.

   b. **this.subscribeTo(eventEmitter: EventEmitter)**: Can be used to subscribe to an instance of an EventEmitter such as a Node JS–style event emitter or a DOM object like window or document that is usually global.

   c. **this.once(eventName: string, handler: Function)**: Can be used to wire an event handler to run just once.

   d. **this.on(eventName: string, handler: Function)**: Can be used to wire on an event handler. Adds the listener function to the end of an internally maintained listeners array for the eventName. Does not check to see if the listener has already been added. Multiple calls passing the same combination of eventName and handler will result in the listener being added and called multiple times.

7. **Method or property access** via **this.<methodName>**() or **this.<propName>** (available on the view via just *component*, and one can access component instance methods as **component.<methodName>** in the view layer).

8. **Accessing native HTML tags within the component**

   a. **this.getEl(key?, index?)**

   b. **this.getElId(key?, index?)**

   c. **this.getEls(key)**

9. **Accessing other custom Marko components within a component**

   a. **this.getComponent(key, index?)**

   b. **this.getComponents(key, index?)**

10. **State APIs**

    a. **this.setState(propName, propValue) || this.setState(statePartial or newstateObject)**: **statePartial** here means that a subset of the original state properties can also be passed, and Marko does an additive update. Any existing properties not passed in will be retained, while those passed in will override the existing, avoiding having to spread the old properties into the new state object.

    b. **this.replaceState(newstateObject)**: Fully replaces all the state properties. So, be sure to include all properties here. No additive updates.

    c. **this.setStateDirty(propName)**: Helps to mark deeply nested state properties that they have changed. Usually an anti-pattern and not recommended. The Marko dev team recommends doing immutable updates via solutions like **Immer**. State properties, part of **onCreate**, are the ones that will be watched and only one level deep. So, for anything that will not be detected by shallow comparison, this is the way to get Marko to notice it.

    d. **this.isDirty()**: This returns a **true** if a given component's **state** properties are changed and if the component requires to be re-rendered.

11. **Forcing a rerender**

    a. **this.rerender(inputProps?)**

12. **Force updating the DOM and the state**

    a. **`this.forceUpdate()`**

    b. **`this.update()`**

13. **Component destruction**

    a. **`this.isDestroyed()`:** This returns **true** if the component was destroyed via **`this.destroy()`**. Else, it returns a **false**.

    b. **`this.destroy()`:** A lifecycle event handler on the component. The **destroy** event is first emitted, followed by **onDestroy** being called, whenever the component is to be unmounted from the DOM and be cleaned up. Any event handlers wired via **`this.subscribeTo`** or via **<subscribe>** will be auto-cleaned by Marko. This event handler can be used by the developer to clean up any third-party libraries that were setup within this component or to listen to any elements within a given component.

14. **DOM manipulation methods**

    a. **`this.appendTo(parentTargetNodeOrElement)`**

    b. **`this.prependTo(parentTargetNodeOrElement)`**

    c. **`this.insertAfter(childTargetNodeOrElement)`**

    d. **`this.insertBefore(childTargetNodeOrElement)`**

    e. **`this.replace(childTargetNodeOrElement)`**

    f. **`this.replaceChildrenOf(parentTargetNodeOrElement)`**

We may have seen some of them already, specifically 1, 2, 6, 7, and 10. Also, there isn't too much detail to dive into 3, 4, 5, and 13, and they have been therefore explained inline above. We will look at 8, 9, 11, 12, and 14. The **?** next to the arguments, in the function definition, denotes that they are optional, similar to TypeScript optional function arguments.

this.getEl(key?, index?)

Syntax	`this.getEl(key?, index?)`	
Description	Returns a nested DOM element within the given template, that is referenced by a **key**. If a key isn't passed, it returns the root Node of the template. In the case when there are multiple root nodes, it returns the first.	
Parameter	**Type**	**Description**
key	String	The scoped identifier for the element
index	number	The index of the element, if the key references a repeated element within a **\<for\>**
returns	HTMLElement	The element matching the key, or `this.el` if no key is provided

Figure 4-85. *Table explaining this.getEl*

this.getEls(key)

Syntax	`this.getEls(key)`	
Description	Returns a collection of nested DOM elements within the given template, that is referenced by a **key**. Repeated DOM elements must have a value for the key attribute that ends with `[]`. For example, **key**=`"items[]"`.	
Parameter	**Type**	**Description**
key	String	The scoped identifier for the element
returns	HTMLElement`[]`	The element matching the key, or `this.el` if no key is provided

Figure 4-86. *Table explaining this.getEls*

this.getElId(key?, index?)

Syntax	`this.getElId(key?, index?)`	
Description	Same as `this.getEl(key?, index?)` but returns the string ID of the nested DOM element within the given template, that is referenced by a **key**. Or, if no **key** is passed, it returns `this.el.id`	
Parameter	**Type**	**Description**
key	String	The scoped identifier for the element
index	number	The index of the element, if the key references a repeated element within a **<for>**
returns	String	The ID of the element matching the key, or `this.el.id` if no key is provided

Figure 4-87. *Table explaining this.getElId*

this.getComponent(key, index?)

Syntax	`this.getComponent(key, index?)`	
Description	Returns a nested custom Marko component within the given template, that is referenced by a **key**.	
Parameter	**Type**	**Description**
key	String	The scoped identifier for the Custom Component
index	number	The index of the component, if the key references a repeated custom component within a **<for>**
returns	Component	A reference to a nested Component for the given **key**. If an *index* is provided and the target component is a repeated component (i.e. **key**=`"items[]"`), then the component at the given index will be returned.

Figure 4-88. *Table explaining this.getComponent*

this.getComponents(key)

Syntax	`this.getComponents`(key, index?)	
Description	Returns a collection of nested custom Marko components within the given template, that is referenced by a **key**. In this case, it is something referenced as **key**=`"items[]"`	
Parameter	**Type**	**Description**
key	String	The scoped identifier for the Custom Component
returns	Component	An array of repeated Custom Marko Component instances for the given **key**.

Figure 4-89. *Table explaining this.getComponents*

this.rerender(input?)

Syntax	`this.rerender`(input?)	
Description	It is used within a component to trigger a re-render of that specific component instance with new input. If new input is not passed, the component will do a rerender based on the existing input and state. If new input is passed, the state may be re-derived from the new input within onInput(). This is typically used in scenarios where the component needs to be updated based on internal changes or state updates that aren't automatically captured by Marko's reactive handling of state or input changes. For example, if a component needs to update based on an asynchronous operation or a complex calculation that doesn't directly involve state mutations.	
Parameter	**Type**	**Description**
input	Object	The input object

Figure 4-90. *Table explaining this.rerender*

this.forceUpdate()

Syntax	`this.forceUpdate()`
Description	Queues the component to rerender. It causes Marko to skip all the associated checks to see if a re-render is actually needed. In comparison to `this.rerender()` it does not let you pass in any input. Also, the DOM update post re-render will be queued up. If you want to immediately update the DOM then call this.update() after calling `this.forceUpdate()`

Figure 4-91. *Table explaining this.forceUpdate*

this.update()

Syntax	`this.update()`
Description	Immediately executes any pending updates to the DOM, rather than following the normal queued update mechanism for rendering as in the case of `this.forceUpdate`. This can be used to immediately update the DOM after every **setState** operation. This may particularly be helpful in some scenarios where the DOM update has to be reflected immediately, because a collection of **setState** operations are usually batched and may not be the intended result required in those cases.

Figure 4-92. *Table explaining this.update*

While most of the earlier methods helped in accessing the elements, components, IDs, helped fiddle around with the component updates and re-render, the next set are exclusively related to DOM manipulation—where a given Marko component can be inserted.

this.insertAfter(childNode)

Syntax	`this.insertAfter(childNode)`
Description	Moves the current Marko UI component's DOM elements into the position **after** the target DOM element.

Figure 4-93. *Table explaining this.insertAfter*

this.insertBefore(childNode)

Syntax	`this.insertBefore`(childNode)
Description	Moves the current Marko UI component's DOM elements into the position **before** the target DOM element.

Figure 4-94. *Table explaining this.insertBefore*

this.prependTo(parentNode)

Syntax	`this.prependTo`(parentNode)
Description	Moves the Marko UI component's DOM elements into the position **before** the target element's **first** child.

Figure 4-95. *Table explaining this.prependTo*

this.appendTo(parentNode)

Syntax	`this.appendTo`(parentNode)
Description	Moves the Marko UI component's DOM elements into the position **after** the target element's **last** child.

Figure 4-96. *Table explaining this.appendTo*

this.replace(targetNode)

Syntax	`this.replace`(targetNode)
Description	Replaces the **target element** with the Marko UI component's DOM elements.

Figure 4-97. *Table explaining this.replace*

this.replaceChildrenOf(targetNode)

Syntax	`this.replaceChildrenOf(targetNode)`
Description	Replaces the **target element's children** with the Marko UI component's DOM elements.

Figure 4-98. *Table explaining this.replaceChildrenOf*

Declaratives Available in the Marko Template

Declaratives are special attributes in Marko that offer you hooks with special powers for optimizations. They are usually applied over to native tags, native tag attributes, or custom Marko tags. We have seen a few before. The following are a list of such directives:

1. Key

2. Wiring native and custom event handlers via **on-**
   <eventName>/once-<eventName>

3. The ***:scoped** attribute directive

4. The **no-update** directive

5. The **no-update-if()** directive

6. The **no-update-body** directive

7. The **no-update-body-if()** directive

8. The **:no-update** attribute directive

We have seen (2) previously, in the event handling section of this chapter. Let us look at the rest of the directives.

Key: Other Uses

The key attribute in Marko does a couple of things:

1. It helps you get references to native HTML elements within your template and even references to other custom components within your template. This is via the **this.getEl, this.getEls, this.getComponent, this.getComponents,** and **this.getElId** APIs offered on the component instance: **this**.

2. It helps in cases of looping by maintaining a reference and matching the corresponding elements in case of diffing and patching after a re-render. So, after the re-render, while updating the DOM with the modified snapshot generated during the re-render, keyed elements and components are matched and reused instead of being thrown away and rebuilt.

Internally, Marko will assign a unique key to all the HTML elements and UI components in a given template, based on the order of appearance. If there are repeated elements as in the case of a <for> or a <while>, or elements that move between locations in the DOM, then it is best to assign a custom key by adding a key attribute that is unique. The key attribute can be applied to both HTML elements and custom tags.

You can do an **array** when iterating over an array using a **<for>**. The suffix (e.g., **key="colors"**) tells Marko that the element shall be repeated multiple times with the same key. This helps you reference all the <li>s in a collection, together, which would not have been possible had you assigned unique keys using the index. For example, you can query this via **this.getEls('colors')**. Marko internally takes care of making the keys unique while also making it available to you via the aforementioned *this* APIs.

```
src > routes > directives >  ≡ +page.marko >  🔧 div >  🔧 ul > ⁐ for
1    class {
2        onCreate() {
3            this.state = {
4                colors: ['red', 'blue', 'yellow', 'green']
5            }
6        }
7        onMount() {
8            console.log(this.getEls('colors'))
9        }
10   }
11   <div>
12       <ul>
13       <for|color| of=state.colors>
14           <li key="colors[]">${color}</li>
15       </for>
16       </ul>
17   </div>
```

Figure 4-99. *The usage of "key" in loops*

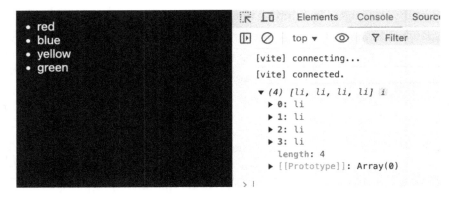

Figure 4-100. *Logs for Figure 4-99*

The other one is what we saw using the **<for>** tag earlier. If we had a collection of *users* to iterate over and display, and if every user had a unique ID, this ID can be used over the index to key the individual users. That way, if the order of the users changed for some reason due to sorting or filtering, Marko can more efficiently re-render the list.

*:scoped

This helps to create unique IDs that tie up a couple of elements together. For example:

1. Tying a **<label>**'s **for** and the ID of an associated element

2. Tying an **<a>**'s **href** to a section ID to jump to that section

3. Tying aria-* properties of an element to another element, for example, **aria-describedBy**

```
src > routes > directives >  ≡ +page.marko > 🔧 label
  1    <label for:scoped="Age">Age</label>
  2    <input id:scoped="Age" value="55"/>
  3    <button
  4        aria-describedby:scoped="LearnMore">Learn More</button>
  5
  6    <p id:scoped="LearnMore">
  7        Learn more about www.ebay.com
  8    </p>
  9
 10    <a href:scoped="#FVF">Jump to Final value Fees</a>
 11    <section id:scoped="FVF"></section>
```

Figure 4-101. *The usage of scoped*

The output is shown in Figure 4-102.

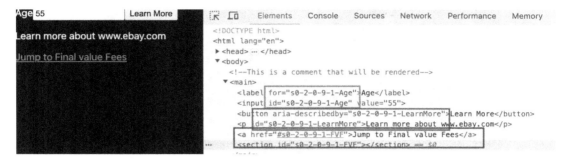

Figure 4-102. *Output logs for Figure 4-101*

no-update Directives

The no-update directives are **no-update, no-update-if(), no-update-body, no-update-body-if()** and lastly the attribute **no-update**.

In the following example, **no-update** is applied to the custom Marko tag **<update-example/>** under *src/components/update-example/index.marko*. This is included into the directives page at *src/routes/directives/+page.marko*.

```
src > components > update-example > ≡ index.marko > ...
  1    class {
  2        onCreate() {
  3            this.state = {
  4                name: 'Mark'
  5            }
  6        }
  7        onRender() {
  8            console.log('I was rendered')
  9        }
 10        onUpdate() {
 11            console.log('Im about to be updated!')
 12        }
 13        changeName() {
 14            if (this.state.name === "Mark") {
 15                this.state.name = "Jim"
 16            } else {
 17                this.state.name = "Mark"
 18            }
 19        }
 20    }
 21    <div>
 22        <div>My name is: ${state.name}</div>
 23        <button on-click("changeName")>Toggle Name</button>
 24    </div>
```

Figure 4-103. *src/components/update-example/index.marko*

You may wonder if the template of a child component (marked with **no-update**, when used inside a stateful parent) gets sent, even if it doesn't have a class { }.

The answer is yes. If a child component marked with ***no-update*** is used inside a stateful parent, and even if it does not have a **class { }**, its template is still sent. The ***no-update*** directive prevents the DOM subtree associated with the element or component from being modified during re-rendering, but it does not affect the initial sending of the template. Anything under a class template is bundled (as it's considered to potentially become an island per the island's architecture).

Refer to https://www.patterns.dev/vanilla/islands-architecture.

```
src > routes > directives > ☰ +page.marko > 🔧 div
 1    import {produce} from "immer"
 2
 3    class {
 4        onCreate() {
 5            this.state = {
 6                randomNumbers: [Math.random(), Math.random(), Math.random()]
 7            }
 8        }
 9        onMount() {
10            console.log(this.getEls('randomNos'))
11        }
12        addRandomNos() {
13            const nextRandomNos = produce(this.state.randomNumbers, (draftRandomNos) => {
14                draftRandomNos.push(Math.random())
15            });
16            this.state.randomNumbers = nextRandomNos;
17        }
18    }
19    <div>
20        <update-example no-update/>
21        <ul>
22            <for|randomNumber| of=state.randomNumbers>
23                <li key="randomNos[]">${randomNumber}</li>
24            </for>
25        </ul>
26        <button on-click("addRandomNos")>Add some Random Numbers</button>
27    </div>
```

Figure 4-104. *no-update on <update-example> component*

The **onRender()** and **onUpdate()** are two of Marko's core lifecycle event handlers. Please read the section "A Deeper Look into Marko Components: The Lifecycle" at the end of this chapter. In short, these serve as event handlers for Marko's lifecycle events— **update** and **render**, respectively. These events are triggered whenever the component re-renders and whenever the re-render is going to produce an update to the DOM. This tag **<update-example>** is included within the parent with a **no-update** directive. Notice that, as we add random numbers to the list, within the parent component, the console logs inside **onRender()** and **onUpdate()** of <update-example> will not trigger. The re-render of the parent component, caused by state updates due to adding random numbers, did not trigger a re-render on the child **<update-example>**. Now when you toggle the names inside **<update-example>**, you will notice that **<update-example>** re-renders perfectly fine.

So having understood with a basic example of what these no-update* directives do, we can summarize them in the table, as the others are just an extension of this basic idea.

Directive	Description
no-update	Preserves the DOM subtree associated with the element or component, so it won't be modified when the parent rerenders
no-update-if(conditionalExpression)	Same as no-update but takes a conditional expression and evaluates based on the result of the expression, whether or not it has to re-render the element / component.
no-update-body	Same as no-update but preserves the descendant / children nodes
no-update-body-if(conditionalExpression)	Same as no-update-body but again takes in a conditional expression similar to **no-update-if** and evaluates based on the result of the expression, whether or not it has to re-render the element's / component's descendant / children nodes.

Figure 4-105. *Table for no-update*

These are specifically useful if an element/component has a massive subtree that you are better off optimizing when it has to re-render or whether it has to re-render. Some further examples are listed below:

```
<!-- Don't re-render this table without table data -->
<table no-update-if(input.records == null)> ... </table>

<!-- Never re-render any nested DOM elements -->
<div no-update-body> ... </div>

<!-- Never re-render any nested DOM elements without table data -->
<table no-update-body-if(input.records == null)> ... </table>

<!-- Never modify the `class` attribute -->
<div class:no-update=input.className> ... </div>
```

Marko's Additional Non-core Tags

In this section, let us look at some other tags offered by Marko. These are not core tags and so aren't available by default. They will have to be installed as need be.

The list includes

1. **<subscribe>**

2. **<context>**

3. **<match-media>**

4. **<portal>**

5. **<destroy-when-detached>**

Note that we have already visited **<subscribe>** and **<context>** when going over state management in Marko. In this section, let us look at **<portal>** and **<match-media>**. We will visit **<destroy-when-detached>** while visiting the chapter on micro-frames.

Let's look at these with an example. First, let us install the two tags:

```
>> npm install @marko-tags/match-media @marko-tags/portal
```

Let's include a new page under *src/routes/customtag*. The first tag we will look at is **<match-media>**. They bring in media queries directly into your template declaratively.

```
src > routes > customtag > ≡ +page.marko > ⁊$ .container
  1   <match-media{ mobile, tablet, desktop }|
  2     mobile="(max-width: 600px)"
  3     tablet="(min-width: 601px) and (max-width: 767px)"
  4     desktop="(min-width: 768px)"
  5   >
  6       <if(mobile)>
  7         <section class=['container', 'mobile']>
  8             <greeting userName="Jane" isRecognizedUser=true />
  9         </section>
 10       </if>
 11       <else-if(tablet)>
 12         <section class=['container', 'tablet']>
 13             <greeting userName="Jane" isRecognizedUser=true />
 14         </section>
 15       </else-if>
 16       <else>
 17         <section class=['container', 'desktop']>
 18             <greeting userName="Jane" isRecognizedUser=true />
 19         </section>
 20       </else>
 21   </match-media>
 22
 23
 24   style {
 25 >   .container {-
 33     }
 34     img.logo {
 35       width:12em;
 36     }
 37     section.tablet {
 38       border: 5px solid ▣green;
 39     }
 40     section.mobile {
 41       border: 5px solid ▣red;
 42     }
 43     section.desktop {
 44       border: 5px solid ▢purple;
 45     }
 46   }
 47
```

Figure 4-106. *The match-media tag*

The outputs when the screens are resized are shown in Figures 4-107 to 4-109.

Hello (Jane)! Session expired. Login again

Figure 4-107. *Large screen output*

Figure 4-108. *Medium screen output*

Figure 4-109. *Small screen output*

Next, let's look at the **<portal>** tag. They can be read here: `https://github.com/ marko-js/tags/tree/master/tags/portal`. The only caveat with **<portal>** is that they are best used only within components and not in the top-level page server template.

Let's modify **<greeting/>** slightly to wrap the contents of the template within a **<portal>**.

```
src > components > greeting > ≡ index.marko > ⁂ portal
  1 > style { …
  7   }
  8   <portal>
  9 >     <div.greeting> …
 19     </div>
 20   </portal>
```

Figure 4-110. *The portal tag*

Portals are a means to render elements into a DOM node that exists outside the hierarchy of the parent component. In this case

- **<greeting>** is included in *src/routes/customtag/index.marko*.

- Contents of the *src/routes/customtag/index.marko* are included within **<main>** of *src/routes/+layout.marko*.

267

We have modified *src/routes/+layout.marko* to include its contents within a **<main>**.

```
src > routes > ≡ +layout.marko > 𝓅 html > 𝓅 body > 𝓅 main
  1        <!doctype html>
  2        <html lang="en">
  3    >   <head> …
  9        </head>
 10        <body>
 11          <main>
 12            <${input.renderBody}/>
 13          </main>
 14        </body>
 15        </html>
 16
 17    >   style { …
 32        }
```

Figure 4-111. *src/routes/+layout.marko file*

- Now, using **<portal>** in **<greeting>** moves the rendered contents of the **<greeting>** tag directly to be under **<body>**.

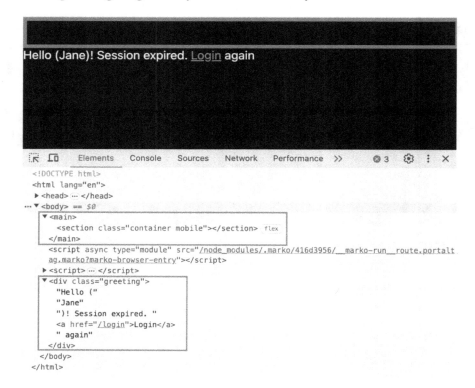

Figure 4-112. *Output of Figure 4-111*

\<portal> takes a ***target*** attribute where the ID of another DOM node can be specified.

Body Content Within Marko Tags

Firstly, What Do We Mean by Body Content?

To understand this, let's say, for example, we have a custom Marko tag **\<hello-world>**. Whatever is included between the start and closing tags of **\<hello-world/>** is what we call body content of a custom Marko tag. This is present even in HTML, in the case of **\<summary>** and **\<details>** tags.

How Do We Render Body Content in Our Custom Tag?

For example, let's say there is a **\<fancy-content>** custom Marko tag that is invoked within *src/routes/fancy-content/+page.marko*. And it's being invoked as

```
<fancy-content>
    My awesome content goes here
</fancy-content>
```

Now, within the **\<fancy-content>** tag found at *src/components/fancy-content/index.marko*, the body content "My awesome content goes here" will be rendered via the special **renderBody** property on the **input**: **<${input.renderBody}/>**.

```
<p class="fancycontent"><${input.renderBody}/></p>
```

The output is

```
<p class="fancycontent">My awesome content goes here</p>
```

\<fancy-content> can choose whether or not to render its body content. The body content can be rendered multiple times as well. Thus, it provides a way for the custom marko component to give control to the end user about what is being rendered. However, when and where to render are fully at the discretion of the custom Marko tag. This gives a way to compose components and its contents, offering a separation of ownership.

Can You Pass Attributes to Body Content?

We have seen this with the **<for>** core Marko tag itself. The **<for>** tag provides the body content with the current element, index, and the entire array itself.

```
<for|color, index| of=colors>
    <li>${index}: ${color}</li>
</for>
```

In this case, the body content of the **<for>** is the **<li>** tag, which gets the **index** and the **color** as tag parameters. You can think of this as follows: when Marko would perhaps have invoked **<${input.renderBody}/>** somewhere within the **<for>** tag, it would have invoked it as

```
<${input.renderBody} index=currentIdx item=currentItem />
```

Named Body Content

The previous examples with **<for>** and **<fancy-content>** were just plain body content. But when passing such body content, we may want different parts of the body content to go into different specific places or to be based on the use cases. Say, you have a custom tag and you want to render something when there is data or show a fallback message when there is an error, you basically need to specify different body content under different circumstances. This is what named body content helps achieve.

This is very evident with the core **<await>** tag itself, where the body content has named tags: **<@then>**, **<@catch>**, **<@placeholder>**, and so on. So, if we had a special loading message, it could be placed with **<@placeholder>**, fallback message within the **<@catch>** named body content, and so on. These are also called ***attribute tags***. They are basically attributes, but take the form of a tag, so as to enable you to pass specific content. Let us update the **<fancy-content>** tag with some attribute tags:

```
<fancy-content>
    <@heading>Delete Listings</@heading>
    <@content>
        To delete your listing, go to the My products page.
    </@content>
    <@footer>
```

```
        Tip: Instead of deleting your listing, end your listing!
    </@footer/>
</fancy-content>
```

When attempting to render these named body sections or attribute tag contents, you can access them via their name followed by the *renderBody* property, for example, in the case of our updated <fancy-content> example, **<${input.heading.renderBody}>**, **<${input.content.renderBody}>**, and **<${input.footer.renderBody}>**, or you can just drop the renderBody prop and access it as **<${input.heading}>**, **<${input. content}>**, and **<${input.footer}>**. The contents of the <fancy-content> may perhaps be something like

```
<section class="fancy-content">
    <div class="fancy-content__heading">
        <${input.heading.renderBody}>
    </div>
    <div class="fancy-content__body">
        <${input.content.renderBody}>
    </div>
    <div class="fancy-content__footer">
        <${input.footer.renderBody}>
    </div>
</section>
```

As before, each of these named tag attributes can still receive tag parameters.

Repeated Body Content

When multiple similar attribute tags are present within the body of a custom Marko tag, this becomes repeated body content. In such cases, these attribute tags are available as an iterable to the custom Marko tag. For example, in the case of building a data table UI component, this allows its user to specify any number of columns, yet still provides the user control over how every column is rendered. Let us look at this with an example of the same data table component under *src/components/data-table/index.marko*.

```
src > components > data-table > ☰ index.marko > 🔧 table
  1    <table class="data-table">
  2        <for|row| of=input.rows>
  3            <tr>
  4                <!-- Iterate by number of <@column> tags -->
  5                <for|column| of=input.column>
  6                    <td>
  7                        <${column.renderBody} ...row/>
  8                    </td>
  9                </for>
 10            </tr>
 11        </for>
 12    </table>                        Pass in every row
```

Figure 4-113. *src/components/data-table/index.marko to showcase repeated content*

Let us create a separate page for this example at *src/routes/repeatedbody/+page.marko*.

```
src > routes > repeatedbody > ☰ +page.marko > 🔧 div
  1    <div.container>
  2        <!-- New way -->
  3        <data-table rows=[
  4        {
  5            name: "Patrick",
  6            age: 63,
  7        },
  8        {
  9            name: "Austin",
 10            age: 12,
 11        },
 12        ]>
 13        <!-- Number of columns per row -->
 14        <@column|column|>
 15            Name: ${column.name}
 16        </@column>
 17        <@column|column|>
 18            Age: ${column.age}
 19        </@column>
 20        </data-table>
 21    </div>
```

Figure 4-114. *src/routes/repeatedbody/+page.marko*

272

The output is shown in Figure 4-115.

```
▼<div class="container"> flex
  ▼<table class="data-table">
    ▼<tbody>
      ▼<tr>
          <td>Name: Patrick</td>
          <td>Age: 63</td>
        </tr>
      ▼<tr> == $0
          <td>Name: Austin</td>
          <td>Age: 12</td>
        </tr>
      </tbody>
    </table>
  </div>
```

Figure 4-115. *Output of Figure 4-114*

Attributes on Attribute Tags

In the previous example, you would have noticed the Name and Age keep showing up for every column in a given row. That is not something we would ideally want. We saw how attribute tags help position specific content—when and where. Next, we saw how attribute tags can be repeated and how they receive parameters. We also saw initially that body content can receive parameters—tag parameters. In the same way, we can specify attributes on attribute tags, besides the parameters they already receive. Let us modify the earlier example.

```
src > routes > repeatedbody > ≡ +page.marko > 𝒫 div
  1    <div.container>
  2        <!-- New way -->
  3        <data-table rows=[
  4        {
  5            name: "Patrick",
  6            age: 63,
  7        },
  8        {
  9            name: "Austin",
 10            age: 12,
 11        },
 12        ]>
 13        <!-- Number of columns per row -->
 14        <@column|column| header="Name">
 15            ${column.name}
 16        </@column>
 17        <@column|column| header="Age">
 18            ${column.age}
 19        </@column>
 20        </data-table>
 21    </div>
```

Figure 4-116. *Attributes on attribute tags*

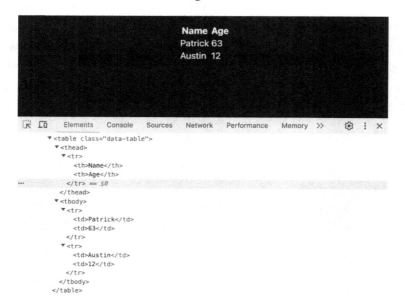

Figure 4-117. *Output of Figure 4-116*

```
src > components > data-table >  ≡ index.marko >  𝓟 table >  𝓟 tbody
  1    <table class="data-table">
  2        <thead>
  3            <!-- Header row -->
  4            <tr>
  5                <!-- Iterate by number of <@column> tags & use the header message to create the header row -->
  6                <for|column| of=input.column>
  7                    <th>
  8                        ${column.header}
  9                    </th>
 10                </for>
 11            </tr>
 12        </thead>
 13        <tbody>
 14            <!-- Iterate by number of rows (from the input) -->
 15            <for|row| of=input.rows>
 16                <tr>
 17                    <!-- Iterate by number of <@column> tags -->
 18                    <for|column| of=input.column>
 19                        <td>
 20                            <${column.renderBody} ...row/>
 21                        </td>
 22                    </for>
 23                </tr>
 24            </for>
 25        </tbody>
 26    </table>
```

Figure 4-118. *src/components/data-table/index.marko*

Nested Attribute Tags

From the previous improvement, we can now give a column name/header separately. However, what if we required further fine-grained control on how the column header is to be rendered. These are scenarios where nested attribute tags help. Let's create **<data-table-nested>** under src/components/data-table-nested/index.marko and src/routes/nested-attribute-tags/+page.marko. This new page can be accessed at http://localhost:3000/nested-attribute-tags.

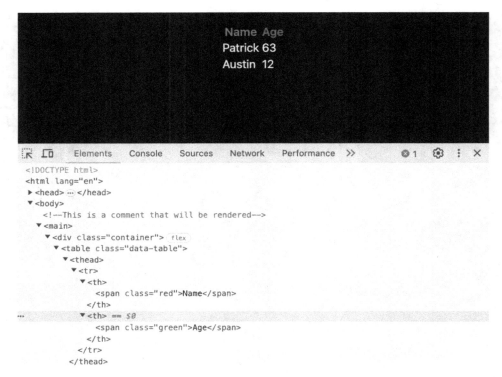

Figure 4-119. *The output of Figure 4-120*

```
src > components > data-table-nested > ≡ index.marko > 𝒫 table
 1    <table class="data-table">
 2        <thead>
 3            <!-- Header row -->
 4            <tr>
 5                <!-- Iterate by number of <@column> tags & use the header message to create the header row -->
 6                <for|column| of=input.column>
 7                    <th>
 8                        <${column.header.renderBody}/>
 9                    </th>
10                </for>
11            </tr>
12        </thead>
13        <tbody>
14            <!-- Iterate by number of rows (from the input) -->
15            <for|row| of=input.rows>
16                <tr>
17                    <!-- Iterate by number of <@column> tags -->
18                    <for|column| of=input.column>
19                        <td>
20                            <${column.cell.renderBody} ...row/>
21                        </td>
22                    </for>
23                </tr>
24            </for>
25        </tbody>
26    </table>
```

Figure 4-120. *src/components/data-table-nested/index.marko*

```
src > routes > nested-attribute-tags > ☰ +page.marko > ⛫ .green
 1    <div.container>
 2        <!-- New way -->
 3        <data-table-nested rows=[
 4        {
 5            name: "Patrick",
 6            age: 63,
 7        },
 8        {
 9            name: "Austin",
10            age: 12,
11        },
12        ]>
13        <!-- Number of columns per row -->
14        <@column>
15            <@header><span class="red">Name</span></@header>
16            <@cell|column|>
17                ${column.name}
18            </@cell>
19        </@column>
20        <@column>
21            <@header><span class="green">Age</span></@header>
22            <@cell|column|>
23                ${column.age}
24            </@cell>
25        </@column>
26        </data-table-nested>
27    </div>
28
29    style {
30      .red {color: ◼red; font-weight: 600;}
31      .green {color: ◼green; font-weight: 600;}
32 >    .container { …
40      }
41    }
```

Figure 4-121. *src/routes/nested-attribute-tags/+page.marko*

Now we can perform specialized treatments for the header cells.

Dynamic Attribute Tags

In the previous two examples, we were obviously trying to showcase the language features and hence kept the complexity to a minimum. But when you think of it, for large data tables, you obviously cannot put in that many **<@column>** tags within the body content, hard-coded. It has to be dynamic. That is what we will look at doing now.

In Figure 4-122, you will notice the **<@column>** tag is used only one time under a **<for>** loop. The for runs thrice, once for each property, to build three columns for every row, while the row iteration is within the **<data-table-nested>**.

```
src > routes > dynamic-attr-tags >  ☰ +page.marko > ...
 1   $ const data = [ // 3 records or rows
 2       {
 3           name: "Patrick",
 4           age: 63,
 5           location: "NC",
 6       },
 7       {
 8           name: "Austin",
 9           age: 12,
10           location: "TX",
11       },
12       {
13           name: "Dylan",
14           age: 12,
15           location: "AZ",
16       },
17   ];
18
19   <div.container>
20       <data-table-nested rows=data>
21           <!-- Number of columns per row -->
22           <for|colKey| in=data[0]>
23               <@column>
24                   <@header><span class="red">${colKey}</span></@header>
25                   <@cell|column|>
26                       ${column[colKey]}
27                   </@cell>
28               </@column>
29           </for>>
30       </data-table-nested>
31   </div>
```

Figure 4-122. *src/routes/dynamic-attr-tags*

Generic Syntax/Features in Marko

The following are some basic generic syntax and features in Marko:

1. Dynamic Text

2. Attributes

3. Handling Complex Javascript Expressions

4. Boolean Attributes

5. Dynamic Attributes

6. Style Attributes

7. Class Attributes

8. Shorthand Attributes

9. Tag Parameters

10. Arguments

11. Dynamic Tag Names

12. Dynamic Custom Marko Components

13. Dynamic Body Content

14. Attribute Tags

15. Inline Javascript

16. Static Javascript

The next set of subsequent sections will explore each of them.

Dynamic Text

We have seen this earlier. This is the basic manner in which Marko reads dynamic data within the view HTML. There are two versions to this as shown below.

The **escaped version** (*${ }*) is used by Marko to insert dynamic data.

```
<div>
    Hi ${"Welcome ".trim()}
</div>
```

Figure 4-122A. *Usage of $ { }*

The values are automatically escaped to avoid inserting malicious content. This placeholder can take in any Javascript expression and insert the result of the execution into it. You can invoke functions to include their result within the HTML.

The **unescaped version** (*$!{ }*) is used by Marko to insert dynamic data without escaping.

```
<div>
    Hello $!{"<b>World</b>"}
</div>
```

Figure 4-122B. *Usage of $!{ }*

This can be thought of as being similar to React's *dangerouslySetInnerHTML*.

Inserting $

There will be times when $ is to be part of the text, and to do that, you just use a backslash.

```
The following code snippet includes a placeholder text
<code>
  Dynamic values are included as \${someValue}
</code>
```

Figure 4-123. *When $ is needed and not to be evaluated*

```
The following code snippet includes a placeholder text Dynamic values are
included as ${someValue}
```

Figure 4-124. *Output of Figure 4-123*

Attributes

In marko, attributes are parsed as just another JS expression. This means all the following are valid, and you can go pretty wild with it:

```
<div class=myClassName/>
<input type="checkbox" checked=isChecked/>
<my-custom-tag string="Hello"/>
<my-custom-tag number=1/>
<my-custom-tag template-string=`Hello ${name}`/>
<my-custom-tag boolean=true/>
<my-custom-tag array=[1, 2, 3]/>
<my-custom-tag object={ hello: "world" }/>
<my-custom-tag variable=name/>
<my-custom-tag function-call=user.getName()/>
```

With *functions as attributes*, there are some caveats to remember, although you can pass down functions through attributes. To pass functions via attributes, your components (current parent component calling the said child component and the child component itself) have to be rendered exclusively either only on the server or only on the client. When you use this with components where one renders on the server and others on the client, or where the initial render was on the server and then subsequently re-renders on the client, Marko is required to serialize these as part of the hydrated data. With Marko 5, there are some limitations around that. This is expected to be seamless with Marko 6.

Attributes that are passed in the aforementioned manner to the **<my-custom tag>** are received within it, and they are available on the special input keyword accessible within the **view** as **input** and within the **class { }** as **this.input**.

A Note: Although mostly you won't notice a difference, strings are parsed as JS strings and not as HTML strings. This is noticeable, for example, when using the *pattern* attribute with the *<input>* tag, where you are required to "**double-escape**" the regex escape sequences, just as if you were passing a string to the RegExp constructor (or you can use a literal /**regex**/).

For example:

```
<input pattern="\\w+" type="text"/>
<input pattern=/\w+/ type="text"/>
```

This produces

```
<input pattern="\w+" type="text" />
```

Handling Complex Javascript Expressions

Any JS expression is a valid attribute value, provided it meets the following criteria:

1. It should not have spaces nor any > <.

2. If you require > <, then wrap them in a ( ), and it can contain
    spaces when placed within ( ).

The following are thus valid:

```
<ebay-compute sum=1+2 difference=3-4/>
<ebay-compute sum=(1 + 2) difference=(3 - 4) greater=(1 > 2) />
```

Boolean Attributes

HTML spec mentions that the presence of a boolean attribute on an element represents a true value, and the absence of the attribute represents a false value. With Marko, when an attribute value evaluates to **false**, **null**, or **undefined**, the attribute is not included in the output. If an attribute value is **true**, only the attribute name is included in the output. For example:

```
<input type="checkbox" checked=true>
<input type="checkbox" checked=false>
```

The above produces the following:

```
<input type="checkbox" checked />
<input type="checkbox" />
```

Similarly, when the attribute name alone is included, it's equivalent to specifying it with a true value.

```
<!-- The following are the same  ->
<ebay-menu expanded/>
<ebay-menu expanded=true/>
```

You can use this to conditionally render attributes:

```
<div class=(active && "tab-active")>Hello</div>
```

The above will produce the following when **active** is **true**:

```
<div class="tab-active">Hello</div>
```

The above will produce the following when **active** is **false**:

```
<div>Hello</div>
```

Dynamic Attributes

There will be cases where you have to build attributes for a given tag dynamically based on a number of requirements (variables that handle business constraints). Marko lets you construct the attributes like an object and spread them into the tag. With spread attributes, the order matters. You can use this to have a set of default attributes and override them with specific attributes based on the values those constraints take at render time. For example, in a given template, you could do the following:

```
$ {
    const shouldOpenInNewWindow = !!input.externalLink;
    const linkAttrs = {
        class: `active ${input.linkType}`,
        href: input.url,
        target: `${shouldOpenInNewWindow ? '_blank': null}`
}

<a ...linkAttrs>${input.label}</a>
```

This will produce the following given the **input.url** is https://www.ebay.com/, the **input.linkType** is **fancy**, **input.label** is **eBay**, and **input.externalLink** is **true**:

```
<a class="active fancy" href="https://www.ebay.com/"
target="_blank">eBay</a>
```

You can provide undefined to a spread attribute, and it will output nothing.

Style Attributes

We have seen this earlier in the styles section. However, to recap, you can assign Javascript expressions consisting of dynamic variables that will eventually result in an array or Javascript object of truthy values that Marko uses to build out the style attribute.

```
<!-- As a string: -->
<div style=`display:${displayValue}; margin-left:20px`/>

<!-- As an object: -->
<div style={ display: "flex", color:${hasColor}, marginLeft: 20 }/>

<!-- As an Array: -->
<div style=["display:flex", null, { marginLeft: 20 }]/>

<!-- All this results in: -->
<div style="display:flex; margin-left:20px;"></div>
```

In this case `displayValue` is **flex**, while `hasColor` is **false**.

Class Attributes

We have seen this earlier in the styles section. However, to recap, you can assign Javascript expressions consisting of dynamic variables that will eventually result in an array or Javascript object of truthy values that Marko uses to build out the class attribute.

```
<!-- As a string: -->
<div class="mweb touch"/>

<!-- As an object: -->
<div class={ mWeb: isMweb, touch: isTouch, webKit: isWebKit }/>

<!-- As an Array: -->
<div class=["mWeb", null, { touch: isTouch }]/>

<!-- All this results in: -->
<div class="mWeb touch"></div>
```

In this case **isMweb** and **isTouch** are **true**, while **isWebKit** is **false**.

Shorthand Attributes

Marko lets you mention native HTML attributes in a shorthand format. Some examples of this are

```
<div.feature-class/>
<span#feature-id/>
<button#submitForm.primary.small/>
<button.button--${variant}></button>
```

Marko will render these in the right manner:

```
<div class="feature-class"></div>
<span id="feature-id"></span>
<button id="submitForm" class="primary small"></button>
<button class="button--fancy"></button>
```

Tag Parameters

We have already seen this in the section "Body Content Within Marko Tags" within this chapter. To recap, body content is the content (text or HTML or other custom marko components) that can be present within the opening and closing braces of a custom Marko tag. For example, in some template

```
<greeting|cautionMessage| message="Good morning!">
    <!-- body content -->
    <span>John ${cautionMessage}</span>
</greeting>
```

Here, *cautionMessage* is the tag parameter passed to the body content.

When a Marko custom tag renders its body content, it can provide data to this body content, which can be received in the form of tag parameters after the tag name. Note that contained named body sections (attribute tags) can also receive tag parameters exclusively for themselves.

This is a powerful feature that allows components to provide functionality and data while giving you, the invoker, full control over what gets rendered, while the component chooses to control where, when, and how to render it. We saw this earlier with the data table example. One of the simplest examples of this feature can be seen in the core **<for>** tag.

Note that tag parameters, |parameters|, are just regular JavaScript function parameters. This means you can destructure, set default values, etc. This can be thought of as

- **Tag attributes** are a means for you to inform the underlying component (**pass data to**).

- **Tag parameters** are a means for the underlying component to inform you (**receive data from**).

For example, if there was a **<position>** component that tracked the mouse coordinates, you would invoke it as

```
<position|{x,y}|>
    The mouse is at ${x}, ${y}!
</position>
```

Internally, **<position>** would render its body and provide the position similar to this: `<${input.renderBody} x=0 y=0/>`.

Arguments on Core Tags, Attributes, and body-only-if

Some core tags and core attributes accept Javascript function-like arguments. Arguments are denoted by parentheses that follow a given tag or attribute. Arguments are a way to pass data to a tag or an attribute.

```
$ {
   const content = isPremiumUser ? input.premiumContent : 'You need to
   subscribe!'
}
<if(isPremiumUser)>
    <h1>
       See more recipes ${isPremiumUser ? '' : 'when subscribed'}
    </h1>
    <section body-only-if(!isPremiumUser)>
       ${content}
    </section>
</if>
```

In the aforementioned example, the core **<if>** gets an argument to evaluate the truthiness of the condition, while the **body-only-if** attribute also takes arguments to evaluate the condition.

Dynamic Tag Names

Depending on various requirements, you may have to conditionally render native HTML tags dynamically. Marko lets you do this with ease. The **<${dynamic}>** syntax is used to render a tag or component that isn't determined until runtime. It can also be used within a custom tag to render body content that was passed to that tag.

```
$ {
    const label = isPremiumUser ? 'Premium content' : 'Subscribe'
    const href = isPremiumUser ? 'https://www.ebay.com' : '';
}

<${href ? 'a' : 'button'} href=href>${label}
```

You can also do

```
$ {
    const label = isPremiumUser ? 'Premium content' : 'Subscribe'
    const href = isPremiumUser ? 'https://www.ebay.com' : '';
    const awesomeTag = href ? 'a' : 'button';
}
```

The following are then valid:

```
<${awesomeTag/>
<awesomeTag/>
```

If you come across a use case where you need a wrapper element that is conditional, but whose body should always be rendered, then you can use a null dynamic tag. For example, to only render a wrapping **<a>** tag if there is a valid URL, then you could do the following:

```
<${href ? 'a' : null} href=href>
    Some content that will always be rendered
</>
```

In this case, when a valid href exists, the **<a>** will be rendered. Else, the **<a>** will be skipped and only the contained body content will be displayed.

Dynamic Custom Marko Components

Depending on various requirements, you may have to conditionally render components or choose components to render at runtime dynamically. This is the only time you will have to explicitly have the components imported—be it local components or those installed via NPM.

For example, within *./components/some-template.marko*

```
import fancyTable from "<fancy-table>";
import simpleTable from "<simple-table>";

<${isPremiumUser ? fancyTable : simpleTable}/>
```

You can toggle between a native HTML tag and a Marko component:

```
import fancyTable from "<fancy-table>";

<${isPremiumUser ? fancyTable : 'table'}>...
```

Note that one cannot reference a Marko custom tag or macro via the name as a string. So, the following will not work:

```
<${isPremiumUser ? "<fancy-table>" : "<simple-table>"}/>
```

Dynamic Body Content

We have already seen this in the previous sections. When a custom Marko tag contains body content (content between the opening and closing of its tags), it is passed and made available via the special **renderBody** property. To render this content, you can pass the renderBody as the dynamic tag name. For example, in some template

```
<greeting>
     <span>John</span>
</greeting>
```

```
Within greeting/index.marko
```

```
<div>
    This is a special greeting to <${input.renderBody}/>
</div>
```

Will output:

```
<div>
    This is a special greeting to <span>John</span>
</div>
```

Attribute Tags

We have already seen this in body content, but to recap, **<@attribute-tags>** are special attributes that take the form of tags. They let you pass named body sections to a custom tag.

For example, if you had a **<page-layout>** tag and you had named body sections like **<@page-header/>**, **<@left-nav>**, **<@footer>**, **<@main-content>**, etc., this will let the caller of your tag pass the respective sections under the corresponding attribute tags. For example:

```
<page-layout>
    <@page-header>This is my page header</@page-header>
    <@left-nav>This is my left Nav</@left-nav>
    <@main-content>This is my main content of page</@main-content>
    <@page-footer>This is my page footer</@page-footer>
</page-layout>
```

The core **<await>** tag also lets you pass named body sections within it in the form of **<@placeholder>**, **<@then>**, **<@catch>**, and so on. As seen before, these named attribute tags can be accessed via the **input.pageHeader.renderBody** or **input.pageHeader** and can be used to have named body sections by just invoking them as tags like **<${input.pageHeader.renderBody}/>** or **<${input.pageHeader}/>**.

These attribute tags can also receive parameters, but they cannot access the parameters handed to their parents. Check the "Body Content Within Marko Tags" section within this chapter for more elaborate examples.

Inline Javascript

If you require to run/execute any instance-dependent Javascript code snippet within your template, this would be the way to do it. You can even use a ***debugger*** statement here to debug the template as it renders. The way to do it is via the **$** syntax. A line that begins with a **$** and a space will be considered as executable Javascript. Multiple statements can be grouped within a **$ { }**. This also means you can do **input.xyz** and **state.xyz**. Let's include the code shown in Figure 4-125 in **<countdown-timer/>** and use it within a new page *src/routes/inlinejs/+page.marko*.

```
src > components > countdown-timer > ≡ index.marko > ...
  1    $ {
  2        let flag = 0;
  3        console.log('--- BEGIN ---);')
  4        console.log(input.start);
  5        console.log(state.timeLeft);
  6        console.log(flag);
  7        console.log('--- END ---);')
  8    }
  9    class {
 10        onCreate(input) {
 11            console.log('Create');
 12            this.state = {
 13                timeLeft: input.start || 3
 14            }
 15        }
 16  >     onMount() { ⌄
 28        }
 29        onDestroy() { console.log('destroy');}
 30        onRender() { console.log('render');}
 31        onUpdate() { console.log('update');}
 32        onInput() { console.log('input');}
 33    }
 34
 35    <div>
 36        <h1>Countdown Timer</h1>
 37        <p>${state.timeLeft} seconds remaining</p>
 38    </div>
```

Figure 4-125. *Inline Javascript*

An important part to note is that these inline JS expressions with the $ can be interspersed within the view template markup in the same file, and it will just work!

Figure 4-126. *src/routes/staticjs/+page.marko*

A subset of the logs is shown in Figure 4-127. You will notice the BEGIN and END logs every time the template is re-rendered. The page is accessed at http://localhost:3000/staticjs. It just follows the folder name.

```
Create
input
render
--- BEGIN ---);
1
1
0
--- END ---);
Create
input
render
--- BEGIN ---);
2
2
0
--- END ---);
mount
render
--- BEGIN ---);
2
1
0
--- END ---);
update
render
--- BEGIN ---);
```

Figure 4-127. *Logs for code in Figure 4-126*

Static Javascript

The JavaScript code within **static** blocks will just run one time when the template is loaded. It must be declared at the top level and does not have access to values passed in at render time, such as **this.input.xyz** and **input.xyz**. Multiple static statements can be put together inside a **static { }** block. In the following example, we have *src/routes/staticjs/+page.marko* that includes the **<countdown-timer/>** twice. You will notice, in the logs, that the static blocks will execute altogether once even though there are multiple instances of the template. They will not re-execute for any of the re-renders. They serve as good spots to place any instance-independent utility functions or their instantiations. Say, you have an output formatter specific to a template. You can place it inside the static block, because just one instance of the formatter is really needed for multiple instances of the template.

```
src > routes > staticjs >  ☰ +page.marko >
1      <countdown-timer start=1/>
2
3      <countdown-timer start=2/>
```

Figure 4-128. *src/routes/staticjs/+page.marko*

And within *src/components/countdown-timer/index.marko*

```
src > components > countdown-timer >  ☰ index.marko > ...
  1    static let count = 0;
  2    static {
  3        console.log('———— START ————');
  4        console.log(count);
  5        console.log('———— END ——————');|
  6    }
  7
  8    class {
  9        onCreate(input) {
 10            console.log('Create');
 11            this.state = {
 12                timeLeft: input.start || 3
 13            }
 14        }
 15  >     onMount() { …
 27        }
 28        onDestroy() { console.log('destroy');}
 29        onRender() { console.log('render');}
 30        onUpdate() { console.log('update');}
 31        onInput() { console.log('input');}
 32    }
 33
 34    <div>
 35        <h1>Countdown Timer</h1>
 36        <p>${state.timeLeft} seconds remaining</p>
 37    </div>
```

Figure 4-129. *Static blocks in src/components/countdown-timer/index.marko*

The associated console logs are shown in Figure 4-130.

```
[vite] connecting...
[vite] connected.
---- START ----
0
---- END -------
Create
input
render
Create
input
render
mount
render
update
render
update
destroy
render
update
destroy
```

Figure 4-130. *Logs for code in Figure 4-129*

Notice the START and END logs only appear once for multiple instances.

Importing External Files

The **import** statement is used in Marko to import external components or utilities. It follows the same syntax as the Javascript **import** statement. For example, in Figures 4-130A and 4-130B, a file *diff*.{js/ts}, which provides a diff function, is being imported and used within a given template.

```
import diff from '../utils/diff';
<div>The diff of 5 - 3 is ${diff(5, 3)}</div>
```

Figure 4-130A. *import syntax in Marko*

Components can be imported in a similar fashion. Note that under normal scenarios, you do not have to import custom tags/components to use them in the template. Marko will automatically discover them through its automated tag discovery process, which we will see in the subsequent sections. However, when using dynamic Marko components—deciding between a couple of components based on some parameters/variables—Marko will require all the associated components to be imported upfront within the template. This aids Marko in the compilation process—to help the compiler compile ***.marko*** files to JS.

```
import MyCustomComponent from "<my-custom-component>"
```

Figure 4-130B. *import syntax for components*

The HTML tag name is the one exposed by the associated component, through its marko.json file, wrapped in < >.

Output Comments vs. Code-Level Comments

You can use plain HTML comments within the template code. They will not be output in the final result. Marko will strip away comments from the rendered HTML. However, if you require comments to show up in the HTML source, use the **<html-comment>** tag as discussed previously.

```
src > routes >  ☰ +layout.marko > 🔧 html > 🔧 body > ⟨ᵗᵍ html-comment
 1      <!doctype html>
 2      <html lang="en">
 3    >   <head> …
 9      </head>
10      <body>
11        <!-- This is a comment that will not be rendered -->
12        <html-comment>
13          This is a comment that will be rendered
14        </html-comment>
15    >     <main> …
21        </main>
22      </body>
23    </html>
```

Figure 4-131. *Generic HTML comments won't be output; only those within*
<html-comment> will be

```
 R  ⟨⟩     Elements    Console    Sources    Network    Performance    Memory

<!DOCTYPE html>
<html lang="en">
▶ <head> … </head>
… ▼ <body> == $0
      <!--This is a comment that will be rendered-->
  ▶ <main> … </main>
    <script async type="module" src="/node_modules/.marko/416d3956/__marko-ru
  ▶ <script> … </script>
  ▶ <div class="greeting"> … </div>
  </body>
</html>
```

Figure 4-132. *Output for code in Figure 4-131*

We have just included two comments in *src/routes/+layout.marko* to show how
comments are handled. The one within **<html-comment>** alone will be rendered while
the other one won't be.

What Is a Custom Tag?

As earlier mentioned, Marko fully supports componentization and a component-based architecture for pages, similar to other mainstream frameworks. Custom tags/components are individual Marko components, which are small individual units of UX that do one thing—help you build and manage atomic functionality encompassing view, behavior, and styling. Many times, you will have a separate repository of components that you may want to pull in and use within your project—like Core UX/UI components. Other use cases include breaking down larger UX in your own repository into smaller, reusable, functional, and atomic modules. These components will live within your repository.

Marko supports all the native HTML tags and attributes. It also offers a set of core tags as seen earlier. Besides this, you can also build your own custom tags and install third-party tags published to NPM.

Let's say you have a top-level page template with the content shown in Figure 4-133.

```
<!doctype html>
<html>
<body>
    <h1>Welcome to the Bookshop Jane!</h1>
</body>
</html>
```

Figure 4-133. *A top-level page template*

Slowly, the page grows and becomes unmanageable. It's time to break this down into smaller pieces. We could move the greeting message out to a separate component. It could perhaps later handle other greeting use cases—user logged in, user recognized but session expired, and user logged out.

First, the greeting message is moved to its own component under ***components/welcome-message***.

```
<h1>Welcome to the bookshop ${input.name}!</h1>
```

Figure 4-134. *A simple welcome-message component*

Then it's included in the top-level page template.

```
<!doctype html>
<html>
<body>
    <welcome-message name="John"/>
</body>
</html>
```

Figure 4-135. *Including the welcome-message custom tag in the top-level template*

That's all! You now have a custom Marko tag and component. This is however within the same app/repository. In a similar manner, you can have installed components.

Using Custom Tags Installed As NPM Modules

We have already seen this with an example via the **<context>** and the **<subscribe>** tags in the state management and event handling sections of this chapter. These tags are not core Marko tags. They are not available by default. They are built by the Marko team and published to NPM and are available for anyone to install and use. The only thing Marko needs in the case of using custom tags is for it to be a part of the project's *package.json (installed)*. For example, to use the **<context>** tag

```
>> npm install @marko-tags/context
```

Looking back at the *src/components/simple-counter.marko*.

```
class {
    onCreate(input) {~
    }
    increaseCount() {~
    }
    decreaseCount() {~
    }
    handleCouponCopy() {
        alert('Coupon selected');
    }
}

style {~
}

<div>
    <div>~
    </div>
    <div>~
    </div>
    <div>~
    </div>
    <div>
        <context couponvalue=55 couponcode="ABC12345" on-copy("handleCouponCopy")>
            <!-- Somewhere nested in the container will be the buy button -->
            <nested-component/>
        </context>
    </div>
</div>
```

Figure 4-136.   Looking back at the src/components/simple-counter.marko

Notice that we have *not* explicitly imported the tag. This is true for the most part unless we resort to deciding which tag to use at runtime dynamically. In those cases, Marko needs the tags to be imported explicitly. This is because, as a compiler, Marko needs prior information about the tag to compile the template to Javascript code and ensure the compile is successful.

Authoring Custom Tags and Publishing Them

Let's go back to the application scaffolder. Marko provides a means to scaffold projects via the **@marko/create** package. We have seen this earlier. Choose the **library-ts** example and give the sample application a name. I have the **library-ts** starter scaffolded into a sample project called **lib-marko**. This comes with a default <**counter**/> example. However, we shall create a modified version of the <**countdown-timer**> here.

The first thing to note is that this **library-ts** comes with Typescript support as standard. Marko is advocating heavily for the usage of Typescript and has full support for Typescript in the template and component files, which we shall look at in subsequent chapters. To begin with, let us create a **count-down-timer** folder under src/components to hold our **<count-down-timer>** component. The template, index.marko, is placed under src/components/count-down-timer.

```
src > components > count-down-timer >  ≡ index.marko >  🔧 div
1     import style from "./styles.module.css";
2     <div>
3         <h1>Countdown Timer</h1>
4         <p>Timer originaly began from ${input.start}</p>
5         <p class=style.test>${state.timeLeft} seconds remaining</p>
6         <!-- Reset the counter as long as count is not 0 -->
7         <button on-click("resetCounter")>
8             ${(state.timeLeft === 0) ? "Restart counter" : "Reset counter"}
9         </button>
10    </div>
```

Figure 4-137. *src/components/count-down-timer/index.marko*

The component definition is placed under src/components/count-down-timer/component.ts.

```
src > components > count-down-timer > TS component.ts > ᛏ default > ⊘ resetCounter
 1    export interface State {
 2        timeLeft: number;
 3    };
 4
 5    export interface Input {
 6        start: number;
 7    };
 8
 9    export default class extends Marko.Component<Input, State> {
10        timerId: NodeJS.Timeout | undefined;
11        onCreate() {
12            this.state = {
13                timeLeft: 0
14            }
15        }
16        onInput(input:Input) {
17            this.state.timeLeft = input.start || 0;
18        }
19        beginCounter() {
20            this.timerId = setInterval((() => {
21                if (this.state.timeLeft === 0) {
22                    if (this.timerId !== null && this.timerId !== undefined) {
23                        clearInterval(this.timerId);
24                    }
25                } else {
26                    this.state.timeLeft = this.state.timeLeft - 1;
27                }
28            }, 1000);
29        }
30        onMount() {
31            this.beginCounter();
32        }
33        resetCounter () {
34            if (this.timerId !== null && this.timerId !== undefined) {
35                this.emit("reset");
36                clearInterval(this.timerId);
37            }
38            this.state.timeLeft = this.input.start;
39            this.beginCounter();
40        }
41    }
```

Figure 4-138. *src/components/count-down-timer/component.ts*

Some styles are under src/components/count-down-timer/styles.module.css.

```
src > components > count-down-timer > # styles.module.css > ...
 1    .test {
 2        color: ☐blue;
 3    }
```

Figure 4-139. *src/components/count-down-timer/styles.module.css*

Let's include a default story to it, placing the stories under src/components/count-down-timer/stories.ts.

```
src > components > count-down-timer > TS stories.ts > [∅] default
 1   import type { Meta, Story } from "@storybook/marko";
 2
 3   import type { Input } from "./component";
 4   import Template from "./index.marko";
 5
 6   export default {
 7     title: "count-down-timer",
 8     component: Template,
 9     argTypes: {
10       start: {
11         control: {
12           type: "number",
13         },
14       },
15     },
16   } as Meta<Input>;
17
18   export const Default: Story<Input> = {
19     args: {
20       start: 10,
21     },
22   };
```

Figure 4-140. *src/components/count-down-timer/stories.ts*

We can now run storybook via

```
>> npm run storybook
```

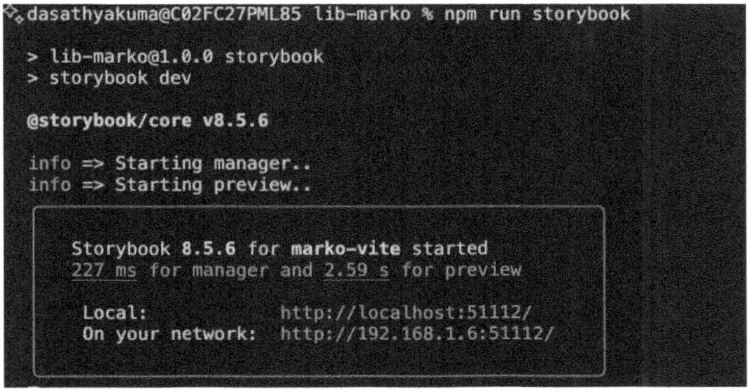

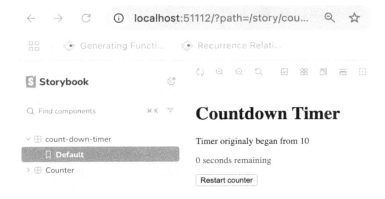

Figure 4-141. *Storybook up and running*

This should open a storybook for this project in a browser tab, and you will notice the countdown timer begins to count down to zero. You can reset as the countdown is happening. Or, once it completes, you can reset it again to start from ten.

Figure 4-142. *Storybook page of count-down-timer*

An important thing to note here is the "**files**" property in **package.json** under the project root. This property tells what files will be included when this package is published.

```json
{} package.json > {} peerDependencies
 1  {
 2    "name": "lib-marko",
 3    "version": "1.0.0",
 4    "description": "Marko library project with TypeScript",
 5    "license": "MIT",
 6    "type": "module",
 7    "files": [
 8      "dist",
 9      "marko.json",
10      "!**/*.test.*",
11      "!*.tsbuildinfo",
12      "!**/{,*.}stories.*"
13    ],
     ▷ Debug
14    "scripts": {
15      "@ci:build": "npm run build",
16      "@ci:lint": "npm run lint",
17      "@ci:test": "CI=true vitest --no-color",
18      "build": "mtc && postcss ./src/**/*.css -d dist --base sr
19      "clean": "rm -rf coverage dist node_modules/.{cache,vite,
20      "format": "eslint --format unix --fix .; stylelint --form
21      "lint": "mtc && eslint --format unix . && stylelint --for
22      "prepare": "husky",
23      "storybook": "storybook dev",
24      "test": "vitest"
25    },
```

Figure 4-143. *Package.json "files" prop*

We can include a couple of server and client tests (we shall look at unit testing in depth in the subsequent chapters). For this, we shall add a couple of tests—**server.test.ts** and **browser.test.ts**—under *src/components/count-down-timer*.

The important thing here is how the stories get used within the tests. We shall look at it in depth in the subsequent chapters.

```
src > components > count-down-timer > TS browser.test.ts > ⊙ test("Default") callback
  1   import { fireEvent, render, screen } from "@marko/testing-library";
  2   import { composeStories } from "@storybook/marko";
  3
  4   import * as stories from "./stories";
  5
  6   const { Default } = composeStories(stories);
  7
  8
  9   test("Default", async () => {
 10     const { emitted } = await render(Default);
 11
 12     const $btn = screen.getByRole("button");
 13     expect($btn).toHaveTextContent("Reset counter");
 14
 15     await fireEvent.click($btn);
 16
 17     expect($btn).toHaveTextContent("Reset counter");
 18     expect(emitted("reset")).toHaveLength(1);
 19   });
```

Figure 4-144. *src/components/count-down-timer/browser.test.ts*

```
src > components > count-down-timer > TS server.test.ts > ...
  1   import { render, screen } from "@marko/testing-library";
  2   import { composeStories } from "@storybook/marko";
  3
  4   import * as stories from "./stories";
  5
  6   for (const [name, story] of Object.entries(composeStories(stories))) {
  7     test(name, async () => {
  8       await render(story);
  9       expect(screen.getByText("Timer originaly began from 10")).toMatchSnapshot();
 10     });
 11   }
```

Figure 4-145. *src/components/count-down-timer/server.test.ts*

In short, what this component does is take in an input and begin a countdown from the input value passed via the prop *start* until it reaches zero. During this, you have the option to reset the counter back to the input value (before the countdown reaches zero) or restart the countdown once it has reached zero. When there is a reset, it emits a **reset** event.

As part of the tests, the server tests generate snapshots for the given story, and we assert a few things there. The snapshots are generated for the first time and placed under the __**snapshots**__ folder in src/components/count-down-timer. Subsequent runs of the server test will cause it to compare it with the existing snapshots that were first generated and error out if something has changed. For the browser tests, we click Reset and check to see if the reset event was emitted.

The tests can be executed by running the following command, which causes them to use **vitest** to execute:

```
>> npm run test
```

Figure 4-146. *Executing all tests of count-down-timer*

Now that we have built the component, dev tested it with storybook, and validated it with our test suite, we are ready to publish our awesome component! For this, we need to enable a production build. To do this, we run

```
>> npm run build
```

Running this will trigger Marko's type checker package via the **mtc** terminal command configured in the NPM scripts for **build** and cause it to output the compiled output into the **dist** folder. **This is what we will be publishing.**

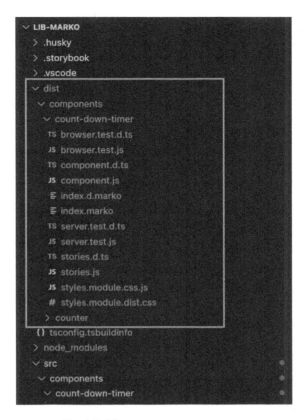

Figure 4-147. *The output dist/ folder*

Notice the enormous amount of files that have been generated. The ***.d.ts** files are declaration files that have been generated from our type definitions for use by those who will install the **lib-marko** package and use the **<count-down-timer>** component. In this, the **test** files and the **stories** will be excluded in the published package as they are of no use to the consumer of our modules. Only the **marko**, **component**, and **css** will be published. Another important file, not a part of the **dist** folder currently but which will however be included in the final published folder, is the **marko.json** file under **lib-marko/.** This provides the path to the compiler about its directory of components. It acts as a project/component descriptor. We shall learn more about this in the subsequent sections. Note that it's configured to load from **dist/components**.

```
{} marko.json > ...
1    {
2        "exports": "./dist/components"
3    }
4
```

Figure 4-148. *The marko.json*

To publish this module, first log in to the NPM registry. If you do not have an account, please create an account in NPM.

```
dasathyakuma@C02FC27PML85 lib-marko % npm login --registry=https://registry.npmjs.org/

npm notice Log in on https://registry.npmjs.org/
Login at:
https://www.npmjs.com/login?next=/login/cli/31addab7-2d5c-48f1-b417-824840b127bf
Press ENTER to open in the browser...

Logged in on https://registry.npmjs.org/.
```

Figure 4-149. *Log in to your NPM account*

Once logged in, do >> npm publish.

```
> lib-marko@1.0.0 prepare
> husky

npm notice
npm notice      lib-marko@1.0.0
npm notice Tarball Contents
npm notice 484B README.md
npm notice 327B dist/components/count-down-timer/component.d.ts
npm notice 912B dist/components/count-down-timer/component.js
npm notice 0B dist/components/count-down-timer/index.d.marko
npm notice 386B dist/components/count-down-timer/index.marko
npm notice 75B dist/components/count-down-timer/styles.module.css.js
npm notice 40B dist/components/count-down-timer/styles.module.dist.css
npm notice 190B dist/components/counter/index.d.marko
npm notice 282B dist/components/counter/index.marko
npm notice 75B dist/components/counter/styles.module.css.js
npm notice 34B dist/components/counter/styles.module.dist.css
npm notice 37B marko.json
npm notice 2.0kB package.json
npm notice Tarball Details
npm notice name: lib-marko
npm notice version: 1.0.0
npm notice filename: lib-marko-1.0.0.tgz
npm notice package size: 2.2 kB
npm notice unpacked size: 4.8 kB
npm notice shasum: 31a891e4fce91edf68a6472834ea0492842d591f
npm notice integrity: sha512-sFxsUrcNGA1eI[...]9YAwKhBR5oHvg==
npm notice total files: 13
npm notice
npm notice Publishing to https://registry.npmjs.org/ with tag latest and default access
+ lib-marko@1.0.0
```

Figure 4-150. *Publish module*

Now our module is successfully published. Let's go back to the project **my-marko-syntax-playground** and create a new page under the *src/routes/installed* folder and put a *+page.marko* there.

We shall install the package into **my-marko-syntax-playground** project via

```
>> npm i lib-marko
```

This will install our newly created package. Now go to *my-marko-syntax-playground/node_modules/lib-marko,* and you will find this component along with the exported **marko.json** file. This helps the current project's Marko compiler find this component.

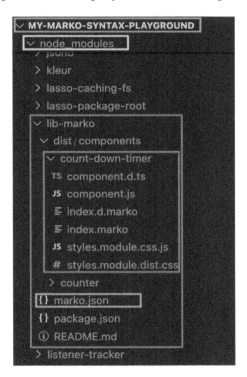

Figure 4-151. *Install into the my-marko-syntax-playground*

Now in *src/routes/installed/+page.marko,* let's include this component.

```
src > routes > installed >  ≡ +page.marko >
  1      <count-down-timer start=20/>
```

Figure 4-152. *Use the installed component*

Next, let's start the project via npm run dev and access the page at http://localhost:3000/installed to see our installed component. This is how we author and install Marko UX components to use.

Marko's Tag Discovery Mechanism

The first thing to note is that you do not have to explicitly import custom Marko tags/components for it to be used. Marko does it automatically. The only exception is when you have dynamic tags—tag names being decided at runtime. This is because Marko is a compiler, and the compiler needs upfront information about the tags being used in the render of a given template for it to be able to compile down the templates into Javascript code. So, that is the only time you would be explicitly required to **import** the tag. This is an implementation detail that could change.

Otherwise, Marko finds out components relative to any given *.marko* template file whenever a custom tag is used within a *.marko* file. Starting at this file, Marko walks up directories recursively until it finds a *components/* folder which contains a folder with a name that matches the name of the custom tag. If it has reached the project root without being able to discover the said tag, it will proceed to look into the *node_modules/* folder for the same.

For example, refer to Figure 4-153.

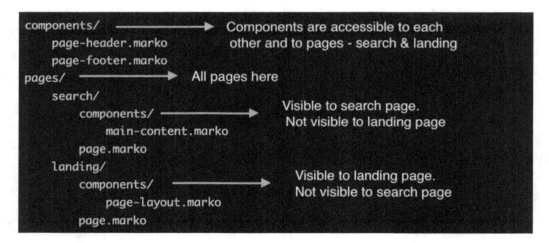

Figure 4-153. *Tag discovery in Marko*

By using nested ***component/*** directories, the page-specific components are scoped to be visible to the respective pages. You can use this to have nested ***components/*** directories to create so-
called subcomponents, which are only visible to the component that contains them.

Individual Marko components under ***components/*** can have their own directories with ***index.marko***, ***component.{js,ts}***, ***component-browser.{js,ts}***, and ***style.{css/less/stylus}***. For component naming convention, refer to the beginning of this chapter.

While this is the naming convention for Marko. Marko-run is a meta framework that brings in the naming convention like ***+page.marko*** and so on. We will look at this in detail in the next chapter, where Marko-run helps you to instantly bootstrap Marko MPA and SPA applications through a file directory–based routing mechanism that makes it seamless to scale Marko applications into large applications, aiding maintainability and readability.

With installed modules, you can also modify the directories to look at by specifying the same within the **marko.json** file, which we shall look at next.

marko.json vs. marko-tag.json

Marko uses configuration files to describe components to the compiler and to the editor/IDE tooling. This is specifically useful when you run custom validations, want to enable experimental features, or have custom parsing, translating, and migration logic that you would like to run over specific components during specific phases of the Marko compiler, at the time of the compilation process (the compilation lifecycle, not the component lifecycle).

Besides that, they are also a way to configure the compiler to look at custom paths to a directory of components (thereby aiding the tag discovery mechanism). They also serve as descriptors for components, in that you can specify what attributes and tags the respective components take, what their types are, and so on. These become useful because they get picked up by tooling—the editor plugins, IDE, etc.—to offer useful hints to the developers.

Overall, Marko supports two configuration files

1. **marko.json**: This describes an entire suite of Marko components.

2. **marko-tag.json**: This describes a single Marko component.

marko-tag.json

Marko will automatically look for a **marko-tag.json** file within every single component directory. This is autowired into Marko, and there is nothing you will have to do to enable this. They serve as a descriptor for the said Marko component, in that you can mention the attributes list that component supports, the type of those attributes, whether it supports body content, whether it's an HTML tag or a custom tag, whether it's self-closing, and so on. Specifying attributes and their types helps in Marko doing compile-time checks.

```
{
  "html": true, // Treat as a native HTML tag, not a custom tag.
  "htmlType": "svg", // Optimizes for specific types of native tags (currently only `svg` and `html`).
  "open-tag-only": true, // Forbids passing body content to this tag.
  "featureFlags": [ "feature-a" ], // Enable beta features by passing feature flags.
  "nested-tags": { // This section configures attribute tags.
    "tab": {
      "target-property": "tabs", // Puts `<@tab>` tags into `input.tabs`.
      "is-repeated": true,  // Allow more than one nested `<@tab>`.
      "attributes": {
        // Same as the "Attributes" section below.
      }
    }
  }
}
```

Figure 4-154. *A sample marko-tag.json file*

```
{
  "attributes": {
    "heading": "string"
  }
}
```

Figure 4-155. *Attributes list and types*

The above code ensures that the **heading** attribute is the **only** attribute supplied to the said tag. The string value is used as documentation for the custom Marko tag. It may be picked up by tooling, like Marko's editor plugins, to provide hints to the user.

The recommended list of attribute types is as follows:

1. Expression (any JavaScript expression)

2. String

3. Number

4. Boolean

5. RegExp

6. Date

7. Object

8. Array

9. Function

In the previous figure, the attribute **heading** was mentioned as a type **String**. But you can also specify an object for every single attribute definition to describe every attribute in greater detail.

```
{
  "attributes": {
    "heading": {
      "type": "string", // Same as setting "string" above.
      "default-value": 0, // The attribute will default to this value.
      "required": true, // Error during compilation if this attribute is undefined. (Mutually exclusive with "default-value"
      "preserve-name": true, // By default component attributes are camelCased; this disables that feature.
      "remove-dashes": true, // By default native tag attributes are dash-cased; this disables that feature.

      // The following attributes do nothing, but are picked up by tooling.
      "deprecated": true,
      "description": "The component's heading text" // Describes the attribute's purpose.
    }
  }
}
```

Figure 4-156. *marko-tag.json*

We can also describe a pattern of **attributes** to match a number of attributes to a definition. In Figure 4-157, all attributes prefixed with a **data-** are configured to be of type **String**.

```
{
    "attributes": {
        "data-*": {
            "type": "string",
            "pattern": true
        }
    }
}
```

Figure 4-157. *The attributes list*

Following the above, there are many options that override the default discovery of component files, such as the template. In Marko, every template (***.marko**) can itself serve as the renderer, but there may be some cases, such as a top-level server template, where you want to specifically include a ***renderer.js*** to handle the incoming input (massage it) before invoking ***res.marko*** or ***template.render*** (check the **webpack-express** starter package in the application scaffolder **npx @marko/create**). Typically, you should let Marko find these files automatically, but here is a reference in case you encounter these settings in the wild.

```
{
    "template": "./template.marko", // Custom path to the `.marko` template.
    "renderer": "./renderer.js", // Custom path to the `renderer.js` file.

    // Compiler file hooks
    "parse": "./parse.js", // Used to augment parsing.
    "migrate": "./migrate.js", // Used for migrating deprecated features.
    "transform": "./transform.js", // Used to modify the AST before generating it.
    "analyze": "./analyze.js" // Used to analyze metadata the entire ast before beginning to translate it.
    "translate": "./translate.js" // Used to generate custom JS.
}
```

Figure 4-158. *Other props in marko-tag.json*

What you see described above as property keys (specifically ***parse***, ***migrate***, ***transform***, ***analyze***, and ***translate***) are the names of the various phases (hooks) in the compilation process of Marko. The template and renderer are related to the user land, where the user can mention alternate paths or file names for the associated renderer and the component's template.

marko.json

Next is the ***marko.json*** file that can be used to configure an entire directory of components. Similar to ***marko-tag.json***, this file is discovered if placed within a tag directory (like src/ lib/ components/). It will also be discovered at the root directory of a project or in a node_module package (published NPM modules that are reusable, shareable Marko components). The options are listed in Figure 4-159.

```
{
  "taglib-id": "my-custom-tag-library", // Names the component library, for better errors.
  "exports": "./dist", // Where to export the compiled components.
  "tags-dir": "./ui-modules", // What directory to crawl to autodiscover components. Default: './components/'
  "taglib-imports": ["./some-folder/marko.json", "./other-folder/marko.json"], // Creates a _combined_ tag library by referencing others.

  "tags": { // Definitions for individual tags.
    "my-tag": {
      // Same options as "marko-tag.json".
    }
  },

  "attributes": {
    // Defines attributes on all tags.
    // Options are the same as the "attributes" section in "marko-tag.json".
  },

  // Compiler file hooks (run on all templates)
  "migrator": "./migrator.js", // Hooks into the migration stage for migrating deprecated features.
  "transformer": "./transformer.js", // Used to modify the AST before generating it.
  "text-transformer": "./text-transformer.js", // Used to transform all static text in the template.
}
```

Figure 4-159. *The generic marko.json file*

The **tags** and **attributes** sections are similar to **marko-tag.json**, in that you can place the information of all the tags and their associated attributes in this one **marko.json** file itself, instead of having to maintain individual files in every component directory. However, if your component definition is pretty complex, then you may be better off maintaining individual component-level tag definition files via separate **marko-tag. json**. Both configuration files—***marko.json*** and ***marko-tag.json***—support the usage of shorthands for defining **tags** and **attributes**. For example, in this ***marko.json*** file

315

```json
{
  "taglib-id": "my-custom-tag-library",
  "tags": {
    "my-layout": {
      "attributes": {
        "name": "string",
        "age": "number"
      },
      "nested-tags": {
        "heading": {
          "attributes": {
            "color": "string"
          }
        },
        "body": {
          "attributes": {
            "color": "string"
          }
        }
      }
    }
  }
}
```

Figure 4-160. *Listing tags in marko.json*

You will notice the tags and attributes section. This can be replaced by the usage of "**@attributeName**" and "**<nested-tag>**", as shown in Figure 4-161.

```json
{
  "taglib-id": "my-custom-tag-library",
  "<my-layout>": {
    "@name": "string",
    "@age": "number",
    "<heading>": {
      "@color": "string"
    },
    "<body>": {
      "@color": "string"
    }
  }
}
```

Figure 4-161. *Listing tag attributes in marko.json*

The heading and nested body content tags are now modified to their shorthand versions. You may recall in the "Body Content Within Marko Tags" section that named body content can be repeated. This can also be specified in the configuration files, as shown in Figure 4-162.

```json
{
  "<my-layout>": {
    "@sections <section>[]": {
      "@color": "string"
    }
  }
}
```

Figure 4-162. *Named body sections*

This example assumes that **<my-layout>** contains a nested repeated body content fragment called **section**. For nested-tags, there is an equivalent via the **is-repeated** and **target-property**. This can, therefore, also be represented as shown in Figure 4-163.

```
{
  "tags": {
    "my-layout": {
      "nested-tags": {
        "section": {
          "target-property": "sections",
          "is-repeated": true,
          "attributes": {
            "color": "string"
          }
        }
      }
    }
  }
}
```

Figure 4-163. *Repeated props*

Marko's Render API

While we do not use these directly, Marko uses them under the hood. However, if you want to build custom apps for your use case, where you are required to interface with Marko closer, you may want to look at this. The following are the render APIs offered by Marko:

1. **renderSync(input)**

2. **render(input)**

3. **render(input, callback)**

4. **render(input, stream)**

5. **render(input, out)**

6. **renderToString(input)**

7. **stream(input)**

What Does Render Mean?

Some basics were covered in this chapter's "Terminology: Things to Note" section. To recap, ***render*** is the process of passing in requisite input data to the template, which causes Marko to convert the plain template, containing HTML with a placeholder for dynamic values, into actual HTML, with the required parts of the input data inserted into the right placeholders.

That is, let's say we have a **<color-button>** component, with the following content:

```
<button>${input.label}</button>
```

It converts the above to output

```
<button>Learn more.</button>
```

when the following is done:

```
import ColorButton from "./components/color-button.marko";
const html = ColorButton.renderToString({ label: "Learn more." });
console.log(html);
```

As part of the render, Marko also returns an **instance** of the component (the behavior/Javascript associated with the HTML), which helps you interact with and operate upon the output by inserting it into the DOM or using it in the scenario of a test case where you would like to assert on the output and so on. Also, Marko's compiler is able to output Javascript modules that also *export the renderer API along with it* (this means you do not require something like *ReactDOMServer. renderToString(myComponent)*). Also, one of the first things to remember when importing Marko templates on the server, in a traditional setting (i.e., not through one of the starter packages provided by the application scaffolder—**npx @marko/create** or the **Marko-Run** framework), is to have the Marko-node require extension installed and invoked, so that you are able to require/import Marko files just as any other Javascript module.

A Short Aside on Marko-Node Extension and the Compiler API

The Marko-node extension is given by

```
// The following line installs the Node.js require extension
// for `.marko` files.  This should be called once near the start
// of your application before requiring any `*.marko` files.
require("marko/node-require");
```

Whether or not the Node.js extension is to be used is completely up to you. If you prefer to not use the Node.js require extension, then you will need to precompile all of the marko templates using Marko dev tools at `https://github.com/marko-js/cli` or directly from the CLI via the compiler package available at **@marko/compiler** or, even better, just go ahead with one of the starter packages provided by the application scaffolder or the Marko-Run meta framework.

```
>> npx markoc your/template/to/compile.marko
```

The **markoc** command comes with a number of options which can be found by just doing

```
>> npx markoc
```

The full list of options available with the **markoc** command is shown in Figure 4-164. If you check out the marko-js CLI Dev Tools package at `https://github.com/marko-js/cli`, they offer two packages—**@marko/build** and **@marko/serve**—that contain dev tools with *serve* to assist with hot module reloads and developer experience. **@marko/build** also contains additional utilities for achieving production builds, etc. But while this is to give you additional information about existing packages and utilities available to help you build Marko projects, this is however not recommended by the Marko dev team going forward.

```
npx markoc
Usage: markoc <pattern> [options]

Examples:

  Compile a single template:
    markoc template.marko

  Compile all templates in the current directory:
    markoc .

  Compile multiple templates:
    markoc template.marko src/ foo/

  Delete all *.marko.js files in the current directory:
    markoc . --clean

Options:

            --help Show this help message [boolean]

--files --file -f * A set of directories or files to compile [string]

        --ignore -i An ignore rule (default: --ignore "/node_modules" ".*") [string]

      --clean -c Clean all of the *.marko.js files [boolean]

          --force Force template recompilation even if unchanged [boolean]

        --paths -p Additional directories to add to the Node.js module search path [string]

        --quiet -q Only print warnings and errors [boolean]

      --migrate -m Run any migrations that exist for the provided template and write changes to disk
[boolean]

    --strip-types -t Strip all type information from the compiled template [boolean]

        --browser -b Browser output [boolean]

    --source-maps -s Output a sourcemap beside the compiled file. (use --source-maps inline for an
inline source map) [string]

        --version -v Print markoc and marko compiler versions to the console [boolean]
```

Figure 4-164. *Marko compiler options*

Marko-run is the updated and latest recommendation by the Marko team into building Marko applications that are seamless, hassle-free, and super fast. Marko-Run is indeed positioned as a recommended starting point for new Marko projects, as it simplifies the setup process with minimal configuration. It handles building, bundling, and serving web applications, which aligns with the functionalities provided by **@ marko/build** and **@marko/serve**. Therefore, "Marko-Run" can be seen as a more streamlined and integrated approach, replacing the need for separate **@marko/build** and **@marko/serve** commands. While these packages might still be in use for existing projects, the emphasis is on using marko-run for new projects due to its comprehensive approach to building, bundling, and serving Marko applications. This is also stated by the Marko dev team here: `https://github.com/marko-js/run?tab=readme-ov-file#what-about-markoserve`.

In addition to the above *markoc* command, **@marko/compiler** also offers some API-level utilities for compiling Marko templates, if you may have any custom scenarios in doing the same. The **@marko/compiler** provides functions like **compileFile()** and **compileFileSync()** for loading templates from disk and compiling them into JavaScript, as well as **compile()** and **compileSync()** for compiling templates provided as string inputs. These functions return a **CompileResult** interface that includes the compiled JavaScript code, source maps for debugging, and other related metadata.

Next, coming back to the render function, the kind of output returned by the render function will depend on the environment. Most of them return a **RenderResult** interface which contains the following methods that let you operate on the DOM. These APIs mirror the earlier DOM manipulation methods we saw on the component instance *this.* They include

1. **appendTo(parentTargetElementNode)**

2. **insertBefore(childTargetElementNode)**

3. **insertAfter(childTargetElementNode)**

4. **prependTo(parentTargetElementNode)**

5. **replaceChildrenOf(parentTargetElementNode)**

6. **replace(childTargetElementNode)**

Besides the above DOM manipulation utilities, they also return the following methods:

1. **getOutput()** - *deprecated*

2. **getComponent(selector/key?, index?)**

3. **getComponents(selector/key?, index?)**

4. **afterInsert(selector?)**

Let us next look into the previously mentioned list of ***render*** functions slightly deeper. The associated examples assume you have a simple HTTP/Express server up and running, with an associated route that is able to render these templates. Else, you can just scaffold the **vite-express** or **vite-http** starter packages provided by **@marko/create** by doing an **npx @marko/create**. For instance, our progressive rendering example in Chapter 3 was based on the **webpack-express** starter that used one of these **render** functions.

renderSync(input)

Parameter	Type	Description
input	Object	The input passed to the template to render the view
return	**RenderResult**	The result of the render op, with the methods above

Figure 4-165. *Table about renderSync*

```
import searchResults from "./search-results/index.marko";
const renderResult = searchResults.renderSync({});

renderResult.appendTo(document.body);
```

Figure 4-166. *Usage of renderSync*

render(input)

Parameter	Type	Description
input	Object	The input passed to the template to render the view
return	**AsyncStream / VDOMBuilder**	The async output as a promise. This can generate HTML on server & VDOM nodes on the browser.

Figure 4-167. *Table about render*

```
import searchResults from "./search-results/index.marko";
var resultPromise = searchResults.render({});

resultPromise.then((result) => {                    Template input
  result.appendTo(document.body);
});
```

Figure 4-168.   *Usage of render*

render(input, callback(err, result))

Parameter	Type	Description
input	Object	The input passed to the template to render the view
callback	Function	A function that is called when render is completed
err	Argument in callback function	The error object when the render errors out
result	**RenderResult**	The result of the render op, with the methods above

Figure 4-169.   *Table about render*

```
import searchResults from "./search-results/index.marko";

searchResults.render({}, (err, result) => {
  result.appendTo(document.body);
});
```

Figure 4-170.   *Usage of render*

render(input, stream)

Parameter	Type	Description
input	Object	The input passed to the template to render the view
stream	Writable stream	A writable stream into which Marko streams output
return	**AsyncStream / VDOMBuilder**	The async output as a promise. This can generate HTML on server & VDOM nodes on the browser.

Figure 4-171. *Table about render*

```
import http from "http";
import searchResults from "./search-results/index.marko";

http.createServer((req, res) => {
  res.setHeader("content-type", "text/html");
  searchResults.render({}, res);
});
```

Figure 4-172. *Usage of render*

render(input, out)

Parameter	Type	Description
input	Object	The input passed to the template to render the view
out	**AsyncStream / VDOMBuilder**	The async out to render into.
return	**AsyncStream / VDOMBuilder**	The async output as a promise. This can generate HTML on server & VDOM nodes on the browser.

Figure 4-173. *Table about render*

From the earlier examples on the explorations of progressive rendering via the async-writer, when the asyncOut is created by you, then you are responsible for ending it.

```
import searchResults from "./search-results/index.marko";
var out = searchResults.createOut();

searchResults.render({}, out);

out.on("finish", () => {
  console.log(out.getOutput());
});

out.end();
```

Figure 4-174. *Usage of render*

renderToString(input)

Parameter	Type	Description
input	Object	The input passed to the template to render the view
Return value	String	The rendered HTML as a string

Figure 4-175. *Table about renderToString*

```
import searchResults from "./search-results/index.marko";
const html = searchResults.renderToString({});

document.body.innerHTML = html;
```

Figure 4-176. *Usage of renderToString*

renderToString(input, callback(err, html))

Parameter	Type	Description
input	Object	The input passed to the template to render the view
callback	Function	A function that is called when render is completed
err	Argument in	The error object when the render errors out
	callback function	
html	String	The rendered HTML as a string

Figure 4-177. *Table about renderToString*

```
import searchResults from "./search-results/index.marko";

searchResults.renderToString({}, (err, html) => {
  document.body.innerHTML = html;
});
```

Figure 4-178. *Usage of renderToString*

stream(input): *For Use on Server*

Parameter	Type	Description
input	Object	The input passed to the template to render the view
Return value	Node JS stream	A Node JS type output stream that you can pipe to another output stream or a File Stream

Figure 4-179. *Table about stream*

```
import fs from "fs";
import searchResults from "./search-results/index.marko";
const writeStream = fs.createWriteStream("result.html");

searchResults.stream({}).pipe(writeStream);
```

Figure 4-180. *Table about stream*

This is equivalent to writing the output to a static HTML file. However, you can also see how stream is used at runtime in the **vite-http** starter package.

Note that you wouldn't have to be working with these directly if you provision/scaffold your app through one of the starter packages that employ Marko-run with Vite. While Marko has support for bundler integrations like Rollup, Webpack, Lasso (now deprecated and in maintenance), and Vite, Vite is now fully the recommended bundler by the Marko dev team for building Marko web applications.

While we had seen the list of DOM manipulation APIs, such as this.getComponent(key?, index?) and this.getComponents(key, index?), in the section "Global APIs on *this* in Marko Components," in this chapter, *getOutput()* and *afterInsert(selector?)* are ones we have not seen as much.

API	Status	Description
getOutput()	Deprecated	Returns a string based HTML output.
afterInsert(selector?)	Active	Triggers the mount lifecycle of a component without necessarily attaching it to the DOM.

Figure 4-181. *getOutput and afterInsert*

Earlier, Marko provided getOutput() as a means to get the stringified output HTML, load it into a solution like *Cheerio* for easier asserting of the HTML, and then use it with its in-house solutions like marko dev-tools for testing purposes. However, this is no longer used, given that Marko now supports other sophisticated contemporary solutions like **Testing-library**.

Serializing Server-Rendered Data for Use on Client Side

We have already seen this with *out.global* and *$global* through setting the properties that we require for the entire server render on the ***context*** object. In case we require this for re-render on the client, those properties are required to be whitelisted on the *serializedGlobals* property. This was seen in the context of a marko-run app (refer to the section "Global APIs and Keywords in Marko Templates"). But let's also look at this in the case of a plain old Marko and Express example.

Let's go back to the terminal and do

>> npx @marko/create

```
dasathyakuma@C02FC27PML85 marko-express % npx @marko/create
✓ Type your project name · marko-express
? Choose a template … Use ↑ and ↓. Return ↵ to submit.
  Default starter app
> Example from marko-js/examples
```

Figure 4-182. *Scaffolding a marko app*

Give a name and choose "*Example from marko-js/examples*". Choose the ***vite-express*** starter package. Once the dependencies are installed, cd into the project folder and do

>> npm run dev

The page should come up at http://localhost:3000.

Note that this is not a marko-run app. This uses the Native rendering APIs of Marko. One of them is the method ***res.marko*** that is provided by the ***@marko/express*** package.

Note that the view engine associated with Express, while asynchronous, doesn't support streaming. So, by using ***@marko/express***, we bypass the view engine of Express. The ***@marko/express*** package adds the ***res.marko()*** to Express's response object. This is similar to ***res.render()***, but removes the restrictions of Express's view engine, offering full support for Marko's streaming.

Now go to *src/pages/index/index.js*. As part of this example, we are looking to learn how to use **$globals** and **serializedGlobals** in a non-marko-run setting. Let's think of a use case where you display a different UI based on whether the screen is for mobile or desktop. If there is a hypothetical function like ***isDweb*** that returns whether or not the associated render is for a large-screen device and if you require that info to be passed down to a leaf-node component, you do not have to do props drill down or other related things.

Just set them on ***$global***. The associated object passed into ***res.marko*** is the input for the template and mirrors the API of ***template.render*** (which we looked at earlier). Within the input object, place those properties that you want all components to have access to, within ***$global***. Next, if you think these properties will be used by the respective templates, while re-rendering on the client side (due to a state change or new input), you can whitelist those properties. For example, here we have whitelisted dWeb, within **serializedGlobals**. This makes the property dWeb available for use on the client side as Marko will now serialize it to the browser.

```
2
3    function isDWeb() {
4        return "Desktop";
5    }
6
7    export default (req, res) => {
8        res.marko(template, {
9            $global: {
10               dWeb: isDWeb(),
11               serializedGlobals: {
12                   dWeb: true
13               }
14           }
15       });
16   };
17
16   };
17
```

Figure 4-183. *$global and whitelisting props for client-side usage inside serializedGlobals*

In the top-level page template under *src/pages/index/template.marko*, you can access the property **dWeb** either via **$global** or **out.global**.

```
src > pages > index > ≡ template.marko > ⭐ app-layout > ⭐ y > ⭐ app-main
 1    static function getToggleModeName(mode) {
 2      if (mode === "Desktop") {
 3        return "Mobile";
 4      } else {
 5        return "Desktop";
 6      }
 7    }
 8
 9    <app-layout>
10      <@head>
11        <title>UI Components Playground</title>
12        <link
13          href="https://fonts.googleapis.com/css?family=Open+Sans:300,400,700"
14          media="all"
15          rel="stylesheet"/>
16      </@head>
17      <@body>
18        <h1>
19          You are viewing the screen in ${out.global.dWeb} mode.
20          To view the page in ${getToggleModeName($global.dWeb)}, try it on inspect element.
21        </h1>
22        <app-main/>
23      </@body>
24    </app-layout>
```

Figure 4-184.   *Accessing serialized globals from out.global*

This is a top-level page template—used on the server for rendering and that will not be shipped to the browser. However, next, within the **<app-main>** component included in this top-level page server template, as the body content of **<app-layout>**, you will see a number of components being included. One such component is **<app-button>.**

Let's try a contrived action of setting state here upon every click to update a ***data-value*** prop while also accessing the ***dWeb*** property for setting a class value.

Every time the button is clicked, the ***value*** property within the state is updated, causing the button to be re-rendered to update the ***data-value*** property while still accessing the ***dWeb*** property within ***out.global*** to set a class value. Inspect any random button on the page, and you will be able to see this in action.

Note that if you have installed the Marko VS Code extension, you will be able to Command-click the tag and navigate to the associated template/component.

Using ***res.marko()*** makes properties from Express JS ***app.locals*** and **res.locals** to be automatically available on **$global**. However, to serialize some of them, you will have to whitelist them on ***serializedGlobals***. Only those properties that can be serialized will be.

While the example we have used forks off the vite-express starter, Marko, as part of the samples, also offers starter packages with Express that use Webpack and Rollup to suit your convenience. However, Marko-run defaults to using Vite as the underlying bundler.

```marko
src > components > app-button >  ☰ index.marko > 🔧 button
 1    class {
 2      onCreate() {
 3        this.state = {
 4          value: Math.random()
 5        }
 6      }
 7      handleClick(event) {
 8        // Every Widget instance is also an EventEmitter instance.
 9        // We will emit a custom "click" event when a DOM click event
10        // is triggered
11        this.setState('value', Math.random())
12        this.emit("click", {
13          event: event // Pass along the DOM event in case it is helpful to others
14        });
15      }
16    }
17
18  > $ const {⋯
24    } = input;
25
26    <button
27      ...attrs
28      class=[
29        className,
30        "app-button",
31        out.global.dWeb === "Desktop" ? "dweb": "mweb",
32        variant !== "primary" && `app-button-${variant}`,
33        size !== "normal" && `app-button-${size}`
34      ]
35      data-value=state.value
36      onClick("handleClick")>
37  >   <span>⋯
44      </span>
45    </button>
```

Figure 4-185. *Out.global is accessible during re-renders*

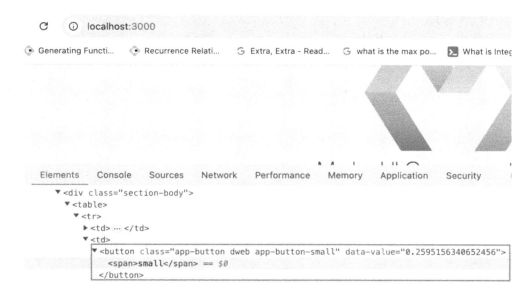

Figure 4-186. *Output of code in Figure 4-185*

A Deeper Look into Marko Components: The Lifecycle

Marko has the following lifecycle events:

1. Create

2. Input

3. Render

4. Mount

5. Update

6. Destroy

These events are emitted at various phases of the lifecycle, as described in Figure 4-187.

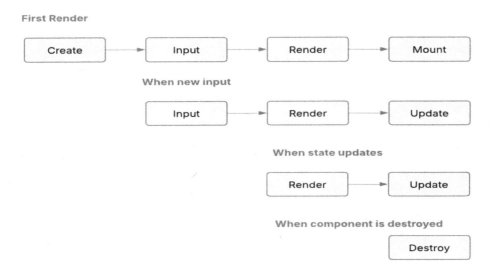

Figure 4-187. *The Marko lifecycle events and phases*

Now that these events are emitted by the component, at respective phases of the lifecycle, Marko gives you lifecycle methods (or hooks) that enable you to tap into these handlers to do things you would want to for your component. These handlers are shown in Figure 4-188.

```
1    class {
2        onCreate(input, out) {}
3        onInput(input, out) {}
4        onRender(out) {}
5        onMount() {}
6        onUpdate(){}
7        onDestroy(){}
8    }
```

Figure 4-188. *The marko lifecycle event's handlers*

If the aforementioned events are emitted, then these handlers are invoked next. Next, let's look at the event handlers in detail.

Event Name	Create	
Parameters		
	Input	The input data passed into the component to render it
	out	The async stream used to render the component. This can be an async WhatWG Response stream on the server or an AsyncNodeStream on the browser.
Description	This is the place to set the state for the component. This event is emitted only once, upon the first render when the component is created for the first time. If rendered on the server, it will not fire in the browser. This means the component is being created.	
Method Signature	onCreate(input, out)	

Event Name	Input	
Parameters		
	Input	The input data passed into the component to render it
	out	The async stream used to render the component. This can be an async WhatWG Response stream on the server or an AsyncNodeStream on the browser.
Description	This is emitted whenever there is input to the component - be it new input or the initial input. This means the component has received input. When the **state** is derived from the **input**, this can also be used to set the state. This is particularly useful when a parent component passes **input** props to a child and those **input** props were part of the parent component's **state**	
Method Signature	onInput(input, out)	

Event Name	Render	
Parameters		
	out	The async stream used to render the component. This can be an async WhatWG Response stream on the server or an AsyncNodeStream on the browser.
Description	This is emitted whenever the component is about to render or rerender.	
Method Signature	onRender(out)	

Figure 4-189. *The marko lifecycle event's details*

Event Name	Mount
Parameters	None
Description	When a component is rendered on the server, this will be the first event emitted when the component is serialized from the server to the browser. This is emitted when the component is first mounted to the DOM. Subsequent rerenders will not fire this event. This is the point at which you will be able to query elements belonging to this component like **this.el** (root element of the component), **this.els** (when there are multiple root elements) etc., Also, this is a good spot to wire on / initialize any third party libraries you may want to use. For example, when you want to wire on an event listener for listening to window scroll via *this.subscribeTo* imperatively. Note that onMount triggers recursively from the leaf node, bottom up. This means, when the onMount for a parent component triggers, then the onMount of all its children is first triggered, before triggering the onMount of the parent.
Method Signature	*onMount()*

Event Name	Update
Parameters	None
Description	Note that the *update* event is triggered only when there was render / rerender that resulted in an update to the DOM. It fires after the update has been applied to the DOM. If suppose there was a rerender but no associated DOM with the component was updated, this will not trigger.
Method Signature	*onUpdate()*

Event Name	Destroy
Parameters	None
Description	When a component is about to be killed, the **destroy** event is emitted by Marko, for the component. This means that the component is about to be unmounted from the DOM. However, this method offers another hook for the developer to clean up any related event handlers belonging to 3rd party integrations, that the component may have been relying on. If there are any events wired on via Marko, then, cleaning them up will be done by Marko itself.
Method Signature	*onDestroy()*

Figure 4-189. *(continued)*

We can check this with the simple counterexample that we had. Let's look at an example.

```
src > components > countdown-timer > ≡ index.marko > ...
1  ∨ class {
2  ∨     onCreate() {
3            console.log('Create');
4  ∨         this.state = {
5                timeLeft: 5
6            }
7        }
8  ∨     onMount() {
9            console.log('mount')
10 ∨         const timerId = setInterval(() => {
11 ∨             if (this.state.timeLeft === 0) {
12                    clearInterval(timerId);
13                    this.destroy();
14 ∨             } else {
15 ∨                 this.setState({
16                        timeLeft: this.state.timeLeft - 1
17                    });
18                }
19            }, 1000);
20        }
21        onDestroy() { console.log('destroy');}
22        onRender() { console.log('render');}
23        onUpdate() { console.log('update');}
24        onInput() { console.log('input');}
25 }
26
27 ∨ <div>
28        <h1>Countdown Timer</h1>
29        <p>${state.timeLeft} seconds remaining</p>
30 </div>
```

Figure 4-190. *Example with countdown-timer*

The above code snippet is a simple **<countdown-timer/>** component that begins at five and ends at zero and destroys the component. This is included within the *+page.marko* under *src/routes/playground*.

The logs for this are shown in Figure 4-191.

```
Create

input

render

mount

render

update

render

update

render

update

render

update

render

update

destroy
```

Figure 4-191. *Logging the lifecycle events timeline*

Now let's include a class {} in the parent +*page.marko* page template. Notice how we are retrieving the underlying **<countdown-timer/>** component via the *key* and getComponent().

```
class {
  onMount() {
    console.log('parent mount');
    const timer = this.getComponent('timer');
    timer.on('mount', () => {
      console.log('listening child mount from parent');
    });
    timer.on('input', () => {
      console.log('listening child input from parent');
    });
    timer.on('render', () => {
      console.log('listening child render from parent');
    });
    timer.on('update', () => {
      console.log('listening child update from parent');
    });
    timer.on('destroy', () => {
      console.log('listening child destory from parent');
    });
  }
}

<div.container>
  <section>
    ${message}
  </section>
  <countdown-timer key='timer'/>
```

Figure 4-192. *Accessing the events of timer component from its parent*

The logs for this are shown in Figure 4-193.

```
Create
input
render
mount
parent mount
render
listening child render from parent
update
listening child update from parent
render
listening child render from parent
update
listening child update from parent
render
listening child render from parent
update
listening child update from parent
render
listening child render from parent
update
listening child update from parent
render
listening child render from parent
update
listening child update from parent
render
listening child render from parent
update
listening child update from parent
destroy
listening child destory from parent
```

Figure 4-193. *Child mount followed by parent mount*

Notice how the **mount** for the *<countdown-timer/>* is first triggered, followed by the **mount** of the parent *+page.marko*. Also, we have listened to the lifecycle events emitted on the child component from the parent component.

Conclusion

As we come to the end of this chapter, you will now be very familiar with marko's syntax and APIs. You can use the **try-online** feature of Marko to test these out and further familiarize yourself with it. This will help you navigate code samples in the subsequent chapters with much more ease and confidence. It shall also help you to better appreciate the various features and design decisions made by the framework.

CHAPTER 5

The Marko-Run Meta Framework

Introduction to Meta Frameworks

What Are They?

Meta frameworks in Javascript are frameworks usually built around an underlying core framework to facilitate the use of the underlying framework that they wrap. For example, in Javascript, when thinking of React as the view framework, React has its own solution— the create-react-app. But then, there are numerous use cases beyond the simple scaffolder create-react-app that a large-scale enterprise will want to build.

What Do They Help With?

This will require support for many of the following tasks:

- Server-side rendering (partial, pre-render, streaming, async rendering)

- Server-side routing and route configuration

- Centralized state management on the client

- Client-side routing

- Data fetching—server and client (GraphQL support)

- Presets for linting, formatting, and unit testing

- SEO support

© Damodaran Chingleput Sathyakumar 2025
D. Chingleput Sathyakumar, *Practical Marko*, https://doi.org/10.1007/979-8-8688-1483-9_5

– Integrated bundlers

– Serializing state from server to client (seamless hydration on client)

– Rendering optimizations

– Tooling

– Auth

– Middleware support

– Animations and transitions

– Scoped CSS and styling

– Hot module reloads for development

– Internationalization

– Static site generation

– Session and cookie management

– Custom hooks to handle the aforementioned functionality with ease

– Error handling

– Easier configuration

– Easier handling of environment variables

– Easier TypeScript support

– Support for multipart uploads

– Support for handling forms

– Deployment hooks—Netlify, Vercel, etc.

– Accessibility support

– Backend for frontend support

– Interfacing with different JS runtimes—Node/Deno

– Easier debugging

– Interfacing support with different resource servers (think Amazon S3)

What Are Some Meta Frameworks Available Today?

These are some of the tasks that meta frameworks aim to solve. In the React world, you have Next.js, Remix, and Gatsby, which are some of the most popular ones. Solid has Solid Start, Svelte has Svelte Kit, Vue has Nuxt.js, and Marko has Marko-run.

What Are the Benefits?

These frameworks handle configuration, performance optimizations, and data integration challenges to offer a more cohesive developer experience. Instead of you making all the decisions yourself and having to deal with a ton of configuration files, environment variables, and plugin systems scattered everywhere, a meta-framework guides you. *Note that not all of the aforementioned frameworks handle all of the listed functionalities. You can think of them as the many responsibilities that the various frameworks handle to make your life easier. What each individual framework does is something best looked up in their documentation. In this chapter, we will specifically focus on Marko-run.* By the way, there is another one, Nest JS, which is said to be a progressive node framework—a complete backend solution for the Node JS backend world. It can also be thought of as a meta framework solution given that it supports Express and Fastify under the hood.

Life Before Meta Frameworks

Before meta-frameworks, developer life when using any specific view framework to build applications was messy. They had to choose between different routing solutions, state management solutions, bundlers, bundler plugins, etc. A lot of time was being spent on the compatibility of the different modules with each other. Developers would spend more effort integrating, configuring, and plumbing these various tools together to make them work, handling their upgrades rather than building the actual application.

Life After Meta Frameworks

Meta-frameworks arrived as the intended solution to simplify and streamline the whole process and experience. Your code lives within a well-defined structure. This means the onboarding process for new developers becomes easier, consistency is maintained across large codebases, and it helps to keep pace with evolving best practices without constantly switching between different tools, plugins, configurations, etc. Most importantly, it also makes migrations a breeze.

Some meta frameworks like Remix and Redwood JS are full-stack solutions for the React world. Redwood JS is also a meta-framework that comes with batteries included, with Prisma ORM, GraphQL support, etc. Some of these meta frameworks do the server-side routing via a file-based routing solution to make life much easier. Some frameworks that focus on MPA, (multi-page applications) like Marko, do not offer a client-side routing solution. Here, additional routing solutions like router5 help in building SPAs with Marko. Also, Marko offers a seamless integration with GraphQL APIs via the @ *marko/urql* package—a plugin to use Marko with URQL under the hood.

Meta frameworks are higher-level frameworks that wrap an underlying framework, abstract it away, and offer a lot of structure, opinionated conventions, additional features on top of the underlying framework, and abstractions to simplify complex application development. They make it easier to build these large-scale apps without having to lose sleep on making them performant. Overall, the additional benefit of these is the great developer experience that improves developer efficiency. They are opinionated implementations for specific frameworks and can seriously speed up development while enabling you to scale if need be in the future. They're designed to provide a lot of convenience out of the box. As with most things, you need to embrace their way of doing things for the best results.

Vite's Role in the Evolution of Meta Frameworks

Meta-frameworks wouldn't have been possible the way it is today without the surge in the popularity of *Vite*—a supercharged module bundler. Vite tracks changes and makes them instantly available without requiring a complete re-bundling of the dependencies or reload of the page or a restart of the server, thereby revolutionizing the role of the bundlers in meta-frameworks.

Marko-run is powered by Vite under the hood. Earlier, Marko used and relied on a setup that was powered by Webpack. However, Webpack doesn't have great support for server-side rendering, causing a lot of custom work to be done to get the Marko setup up and running. This was a maintenance burden and led to issues such as no Hot Module Reloads (HMR) support (just live reload in dev). By switching to Vite with its first-class SSR support, Marko is able to offer a more seamless experience to developers, who can now focus on the joy of building the intended app instead of haggling with the bundler under the hood.

Benefits to Developer Experience

One of the core tenets of every meta-framework is a better developer experience (DX/DevEx). That often includes the following:

- **Rapid Setup Time**: You no longer have to spend hours plumbing different parts of your stack to get them up and running. Through a meta-framework, you can initialize an app within minutes and have file-based directory structure type server-side routing, live reloads, type checking, linting, Storybook, and testing frameworks ready to go. This rapid startup lets developers focus on just building their features entrusted to them rather than fighting configuration quirks.

- **Code Organization**: Meta-frameworks are opinionated and enforce a specific project structure. Good news, that is uniform throughout. So when your company adopts a meta-framework, you no longer have to deal with the quirks of every single codebase. With a mandated framework, you just can hop between codebases and fix code. They clearly mandate where pages go, where components go, specific locations for configuration files, etc. While these conventions eliminate guesswork and personal biases in organizing the codebase, they might make customization hard and reduce flexibility as mentioned. This consistency slashes down on enormous time spent in understanding a codebase's quirks.

- **Optimized for Performance**: Previously, some meta-frameworks offered built-in techniques to handle code splitting by default, tree shaking, caching headers, and SSR/SSG optimizations. However, with Vite, this advantage between frameworks has been blurred. While they all still free up developer time spent haggling over configurations, if your app requires something very specific, then you still have to fiddle with them. Also, most of them offer a lot of these server optimization techniques, like asynchronous rendering, streaming, etc., by default, out of the box, which enable building faster pages from day one, with SEO in mind.

- **Data Fetching APIs for the Frontend and Backend:** Meta-frameworks make the integration between frontend and backend concerns pretty seamless by providing patterns and tooling for handling server-side logic and client-side logic. Along with this, they offer automatic serialization of data from the server to hydrate on the client for easier SSR. Moreover, others like RedwoodJS couple React components with GraphQL easily. This tight integration reduces data fetching and state management friction, making the process more straightforward and less error-prone.

Disadvantages

While the benefits are massive, just like any tool, meta frameworks have their own set of challenges, issues, or limitations, as you would like to call them. The first is the learning curve. Every meta framework comes in opinionated, and you obviously have a lot of initial learning involved. Each meta framework has its own set of concepts and features that must be thoroughly understood to make app building easier. Therefore, they demand a certain amount of time in getting used to.

Also, they are not a fit for all use cases, although some frameworks come with default presets for the different use cases—SSG, SSR, etc. If you have a very specific custom use case, then you are better off starting with the bare-bones example app provided by the respective view framework and slowly adding solutions as the need presents itself. This is also the reason Marko provides the developer with the many default starter templates, which we scaffolded earlier via the command *npx @marko/create*.

Additionally, meta frameworks sometimes introduce complexities that could have been avoided by using a simpler, language-specific bare-bones app. They may also add unnecessary abstraction layers or bloat to a project, steering it away from the optimal performance path. And finally, as developers rely heavily on a specific meta framework, it can lead to the risk of tight coupling and reduced flexibility. This is a downside when the framework becomes obsolete or brings in major updates.

Marko-run

Marko-run is Marko's answer to the question of meta frameworks. However, it may very well be the simplest meta framework out there. This is because Marko originated within eBay and was eBay's answer to server-side rendering on Node JS. It was designed for massive ecommerce pages that served a lot of content and traffic and was tailor-made for performance from the start. This also means that the creators of Marko understand that the right balance between flexibility (coupling) and features has to be offered.

What It Does Not Offer?

Marko-run was thus designed with this in mind—the bare-bones essentials required to get you started from the ground up and running, instilling in you the concept of MPAs and why they are better for maintainability and performance. You can read more about the mindset shift to MPAs here: `https://medium.com/@mlrawlings/maybe-you-dont-need-that-spa-f2c659bc7fec`.

Marko-run thus offers only the bare-bones essentials required to build a Marko app because, from their experience of building and delivering large-scale apps within eBay, the Marko dev team understands that many aspects of meta frameworks, like the following, invariably tend to get replaced by enterprises/teams as the companies/teams/products evolve.

These include

- **Centralized State Management on the Client**: Marko-run *doesn't offer a solution like Redux here (if that is what you are looking for). However, it does offer the **<context>** tag, provided by the Marko framework as earlier seen. But you are free to plug and play whatever state management library you see fit. We will see a Marko-redux app example later.*

- **Client-Side Routing and History Management**: Marko-run *envisions apps as MPAs. This doesn't mean you cannot build SPAs, but they do not offer a dedicated client-side router out of the box. **router5** plays well with Marko and can be used here. However, this can change in the near future with the release of Marko 6.*

- **Data Fetching—Server and Client**: Marko-run *makes no assumptions about your data fetching needs. You are free to use any library of your choice to fetch data. The moment the data is passed into the component via props, they re-render. However, as aforementioned, they do offer GraphQL support via **@marko/urql**.*

- **SEO Support**: *In most frameworks, this is offered as an abstraction to render* **<meta>** *tags, while others offer some form of a Helmet type component that also does this. However,* Marko-run *makes no assumptions, and you are free to insert them into your top-level server-rendered page template. The responsibility is left to the developer.*

- **Tooling**: *At this point, there is no additional tooling for this.*

- **Auth**: Marko-run *makes no assumptions about your auth solution. You are free to plug and play whatever solution you wish to use.*

- **Animations and Transitions**: *While this is offered by Svelte,* Marko-run *makes no assumptions about the kind of animations and transitions you would need in your UI modules as there are a ton of UI frameworks out there for developers to choose from. You are free to author whatever you wish to.*

- **Scoped CSS and Styling**: *As mentioned earlier,* Marko-run *does not offer a focused scoped CSS solution similar to Svelte. This is changing with Marko 6. However, it does support CSS modules that help you achieve the same.*

- **Internationalization**: Marko-run *makes no assumptions here, and you are free to use any library here.*

- **Session and Cookie Management**: Marko-run *makes no assumptions here, and you are free to use any library here to operate on cookies and sessions.*

- **Error Handling**: *Marko doesn't support something like error boundaries. This is expected to land with Marko 6.*

- **Easier Handling of Environment Variables**: Marko-run does not offer specialized support for handling env files. However, you can pass env files via the Marko-run CLI commands using the -e or --env flag, and Marko will load them with dotenv.

- **Support for Multipart Uploads**: Marko-run *makes no assumptions here, and you are free to use any library here to handle multipart uploads.*

- **Support for Handling Forms**: Marko-run *makes no assumptions here, and you are free to use any library here to handle forms.*

- **Accessibility Support**: Marko-run *does not offer accessibility support out of the box like what Svelte does. Marko believes in leaving it to the underlying core UI modules to deal with accessibility.*

- **Interfacing with Different JS Runtimes—Node/Deno**: *Right now, Marko-run is well tested with Node JS.*

- **Interfacing Support with Different Resource Servers** (think Amazon S3): Marko-run *makes no assumptions here, and you are free to use any library of your choice to upload Vite-generated bundles to any resource server of choice.*

Given that we have stated what Marko-run doesn't offer, let's look at what it offers in the next section.

What Does It Offer?

Marko-run is intentionally designed to be lean and simplistic, aiming to solve only those essential facets, absolutely required for rapidly bootstrapping a Marko-run. The marko team picks on these specific features because they are closely tied with the workings of Marko itself—in terms of loading, compiling, and rendering a Marko template—and therefore have closer integration with Marko's core. But the ones stated above are something not necessarily closely tied to the finer inner workings of Marko and are therefore left to the choice of the developer, to pick and fit what best works for them.

Marko-run offers the following:

- Server-side rendering (partial, pre-render, streaming, async rendering)

- Easy access to route config, request headers, response header, query params, route parameters, etc.—a file directory–based routing mechanism

- Server-side routing and route configuration

- Presets for linting, formatting, unit testing, and Storybook support

- Ships with default support for Vite as the bundler

- Serializing state from server to client (seamless hydration on client)

- Rendering optimizations

- Middleware support

- Hot module reloads for development

- Static site generation

- Easier configuration

- TypeScript support with declaration files auto-generated for components, routes, etc.

- Deployment hooks—Netlify and Cloudflare

- Backend for frontend support

- Easier debugging (source map support with Vite and Node JS inspector)

- Automated route-based code splitting

With Marko-run solving the most essential ones required for a meta framework, Marko-run makes building with Marko a breeze. It helps you rapidly develop applications, letting you focus on your code with Marko-run doing the heavy lifting behind the scenes. By focusing on important facets of what a meta framework offers, Marko-run provides developers with the much-needed loose coupling and flexibility to use solutions of their choice for the other pieces, thereby striking a good balance.

In short, Marko-run

- Is the quickest way to build a marko application.

- Supercharges developer experience with Vite under the hood. File changes are tracked and refreshed instantly.

- Hyper-focused on performance from the start.

- Helps you begin a marko project with ease, with zero configuration.

- When there is absolutely no interactivity on your page, 0KB of JS is sent over.

- Ensures route-based code splitting.

– Automatic partial hydration with streaming, async, and progressive rendering.

– Easy setup to access global data accross, ismorphically.

– Doesn't make assumptions and offers the right balance between flexibility and functionality.

Marko-Run in Depth

Scaffolding a Marko-Run App

A Marko-run app can be scaffolded from the default Marko scaffolder package **@marko/create**, by choosing the **basic** template or **basic-ts** template—depending on whether or not you like to have TypeScript incorporated into the package.

For now, however, we will be going ahead with the example that uses TypeScript, given the prevalence and popularity of TypeScript and the benefits of strong type checking:

```
>> npx @marko/create
```

We scaffold an app with the name *marko-run-ts-app*. The project structure of the application is shown in Figure 5-1. In the figure, the red boxed section displays the development dependencies used by this application, and you will notice that it only uses **marko-run**. You will also notice that there are no configuration files.

However, you are free to use a ***vite.config.ts*** file to include your configuration changes specific to **Vite**. Marko-run, as mentioned earlier, uses **Vite** as the bundler under the hood. Marko-run configs are additive. This means they will add to the inner configs maintained by the framework.

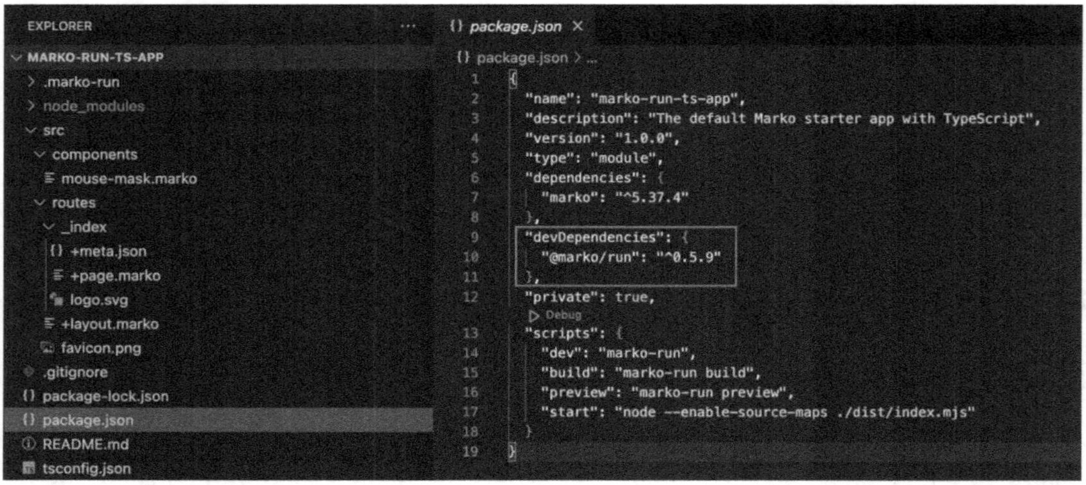

Figure 5-1. *Project layout after scaffolding the sample app via @marko/create*

One thing to note is that the Marko-run starter app scaffolded above is a **non-connect-style** application. **Connect** is a middleware framework for Node.js, which provides a collection of high-performance "plugins" referred to as middlewares. These middlewares are modular functions that are used to handle incoming HTTP requests and outgoing HTTP responses sequentially and in a modular way.

Examples of Connect-style servers include Express.js, which is built on top of Connect and uses the same middleware pattern. If you are looking for a Connect-style Marko starter, the ***vite-express*** or ***vite-http*** starter packages are a nice place to start. Marko-run also offers an adapter (**@marko/run-adapter-node**) which helps to build and preview Marko-run apps for Connect-style environments.

The Routes Directory

By default, **Marko-run** looks for the **src/routes** as the folder structure and the folder within which the pages of your multi-page app are present. You can modify this configuration to any directory of your choice, as shown in Figure 5-2, via a **vite.config. ts** file placed in the project root. The router recognizes certain naming conventions which are prefixed with a +. The list of file names mentioned in the next section will be discovered in any directory inside your application's routes directory (assuming **src/routes**). If you had renamed it to something like **src/pages**, through a **vite.config.ts file**, then it will look for these files in it.

```
  ⚡ vite.config.ts > [∅] default
                                                                        > routes
  1    // vite.config.ts
  2    import { defineConfig } from "vite";
  3    import marko from "@marko/run/vite"; // Import the Vite plugin
  4
  5    export default defineConfig({
  6      plugins: marko({
  7        basePathVar: "__MY_ASSET_BASE_PATH__",
  8        routesDir: "src/pages",
  9      })
 10    });
```

Figure 5-2. Providing a new top-level dir instead of the defaults

Individual Route-Specific Files and Folders in a Marko-Run App

In this section, let's look at the various files that the *marko-run* framework understands. As mentioned earlier, meta frameworks are opinionated and usually insist on a certain naming convention, folder, and directory structure.

+page.marko

By including a *+page.marko* under any folder within *src/routes*, you are informing Marko to treat it as a page or a top-level server template that can be served in response to an HTTP GET. Only one *+page.marko* top-level server template can exist for any path. For example, you may find a *+page.marko* in *src/routes/welcome-page/+page.marko* that can be accessed via *<project_base_url>/welcome-page*.

+layout.marko

While the *+page.marko* contains crucial page-specific markup, the surrounding markup that builds the layout, etc., can be placed in an optional *+layout.marko* file. This file includes the *+page.marko* within it as its body content. These files are a layout component that wraps all nested layouts and pages while also getting wrapped by other layouts that will nest this.

Layouts are just as any other Marko component receiving the same request, request path params, URL params, and route metadata as input, along with a *renderBody* which refers to the nested (contained) page that is being rendered.

+middleware.{js/ts}

These files can be thought of as a *+layout.marko* file, but they are for the *handlers.ts* files instead. So, they are called before the handlers and let you execute arbitrary work before and after, similar to Connect-style middleware, except that these are route specific or can be set at the *src/routes* or *src/pages* directory level to execute for all the routes.

Connect-style frameworks like Express JS utilize a similar series of middleware functions to process HTTP requests. They let you build custom server-side logic by chaining middleware functions. These middlewares manage request pipelining in a file-based routing setup. This approach integrates server-side logic within the file structure without needing external server frameworks.

The difference lies in their integration and structure. Marko's *+middleware.ts* is tightly integrated with its file- or directory-based routing solution, while Connect-style servers focus on running standalone server customization or workflows to be executed on HTTP request/response cycles using middleware chains.

Similar to Connect-style middlewares, these run for all the HTTP requests.

It contains a default export that can be one of the following:

- A handler function

- An array of handler functions that are called in the order in which they are defined

- A promise that resolves to a handler function or an array of handler functions

This definition is slightly different from the function definitions that can be authored within a *handler.ts* file.

Handler functions can be sync or async. They take two arguments as part of their function definition:

- **context**: This contains the WHATWG Request, URL params, path params, search params, and the associated route metadata.

- **next**: This calls the next downstream process/task. In the context of **handler.ts**, this means rendering the *+page.marko* or *+layout.marko* (for GET functions) and returning a 204 for others if the other handlers do not have anything else. As mentioned above, if nothing is provided (when undefined is returned), next will be invoked. So, returning nothing is the same as doing return next().

+handler.{js/ts}

These files act as your principal controller for the route (defined by the folder structure) at the current path. They contain methods named after the HTTP verbs, which serve to handle requests for the GET, POST, PUT, and DELETE HTTP methods.

In the earlier chapters, we discussed how earlier versions of Marko had a *renderer.js* or an *index.js* that received the incoming request, required the associated top-level template, and manually invoked the *.render* function on it. This follows a similar pattern, except that you do not have to import and manually invoke the render of the template. That is done internally by Marko.

This file is just used to receive the incoming request like a proper HTTP servlet/controller. So, this usually serves as the place to run server-side logic, exclusive to the specific route. This may include making API calls to other services that return data in your ecosystem. The data returned is set on a ***context*** object that is now available to be queried from within the **+*page.marko*** and **+*layout.marko***.

Like pages, only one handler may exist for any served path's HTTP verb. Exported functions should be named after the HTTP verbs. It accepts a WHATWG Request and returns a WHATWG Response. Every export can be one of the following:

- A handler function named after an HTTP verb

- An array of handler functions that are called in the order in which they are defined

- A promise that resolves to a handler function or an array of handler functions

Handler functions can be sync or async. They take two arguments as part of their function definition:

- **context**: This contains the WHATWG Request, URL params, path params, search params, and the associated route metadata.

- **next**: This calls the next downstream process/task. In the context of ***handler.ts***, this means rendering the +*page.marko* or +*layout.marko* (for GET functions) and returning a 204 for others if the other handlers do not have anything else. As mentioned above, if nothing is provided (when undefined is returned), next will be invoked. So, returning nothing is the same as doing `return next()`.

+meta.{js/ts}

These files represent the static route–specific metadata that is to be attached to the given route represented by the directory/folder path structure. They will be made available to the developer on the route context when invoking a route. You will be able to access this from the context object inside the handler.ts file. For example, at eBay, this route-specific metadata is used to mark which routes are behind the auth wall, which contain some modules (like internationalization bundles) that require to be preloaded, etc.

WHATWG

A "WHATWG Request-Response" refers to the standard way of describing a data exchange between a client and a server on the web, as defined by the Web Hypertext Application Technology Working Group (WHATWG), where a "request" is the data sent by the client to the server, and a "response" is the data sent back from the server to the client, following the established protocols outlined in the WHATWG Fetch Standard; essentially, it's a structured way to send and receive information on the web, with specific details like headers and status codes included.

Generic Top-Level Route-Agnostic Special Files

Beside the aforementioned files that can be defined within any directory (that represents a route path) under, for instance, the *src/routes/welcome-page* or *src/pages/welcome-page* directory, some special files can only be defined at its top level, that is, within *src/pages* or *src/routes*. These include the following.

+404.marko

This special page responds to any incoming HTTP request where the **Accept** request header includes **text/html**, and there is no other handler or page that is available to render the request. Responses with this page have an HTTP 404 status code.

+500.marko

This special page responds to any incoming HTTP request where the **Accept** request header includes **text/html**, and there is an uncaught error that occurs while processing the request (be it a render or any random runtime error). Responses with this page have an HTTP 500 status code.

These files basically serve the purpose of handling unforeseen runtime errors gracefully. You can think of them as error pages.

Order of Execution of the Files

In our sample project structure as shown in Figure 5-3, we have the following files.

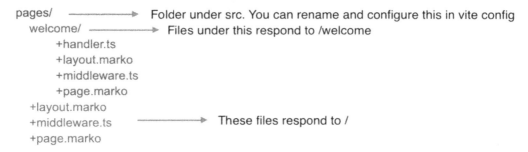

Figure 5-3. *Marko-run project folder and files*

Any calls to just **<baseURL>/** will be answered by the files directly under **pages/** highlighted by green font. Calls to **<baseURL>/welcome** will be answered by the files within the folder **welcome/** highlighted in blue font. However, the *middleware.ts* present directly under the **pages/** will also be invoked and so will the *+layout.marko*.

The order of execution is described in Figure 5-4.

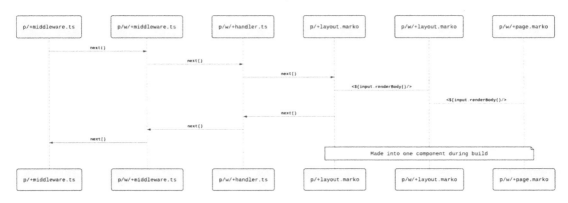

Figure 5-4. *Order of execution sequence diagram*

When the path **/welcome** is requested, the files are executed in the following order:

1. *+middleware.ts* files from root-most to leaf-most path

2. *+handler.ts* at the leaf route path

3. *+layouts.marko* files from root-most to leaf-most path

4. *+page.marko* at the leaf route path

In Figure 5-4, the *pages/welcome* is replaced with the prefix letters *p/w* for the sake of space.

Commands in a Marko-Run App

Marko-run provides four commands in being able to control the application.

Build

This lets you trigger a production mode build. It will not start the server. It only generates the resources after compiling the marko templates in the project, resolving all the dependencies.

```
>> npm exec marko-run build
```

The generated assets/files will be output under the **dist/public** folder directly beneath the project root directory. This will be used by Marko when it starts the server in production mode.

An important step of your production build process or non-dev mode process would be to upload the generated bundles to the resource server of your choice. You can do that after this step, once the assets are generated.

Preview

This triggers a build in production mode and spins up the preview server to preview the app in production mode.

```
>> npm exec marko-run preview
```

Dev

This lets you spin up a dev server with the watch mode on. Vite tracks your changes and instantly updates it via hot module refresh, supercharging developer productivity.

```
> npm exec marko-run
> npm exec marko-run dev
```

Both these commands achieve the same thing.

358

Start

This is a command to start the server in production mode in CI-based environments via the node command. In production mode, your application will usually rely on process managers, like PM2, to start the server in a clustered manner.

```
> npm run start
```

Controller Function Namings Based on HTTP Verbs

As mentioned earlier, *handler.ts* files export functions sync/async that are named based on HTTP verbs. *middleware.ts* files export default functions sync/async. Both of them have the option of exporting an array of functions as well as a promise from the previously mentioned function options.

Related Packages

There are a group of packages that enable all this magic behind the scenes. They are listed below:

1. @marko/vite

2. @marko/run

3. @marko/run/vite

4. @marko/run-explorer

5. @marko/run-adapter-node

While **@marko/run (https://github.com/marko-js/run/tree/main)** is the meta framework that helps you build Marko apps at a blazing pace, it relies on a couple of other packages/plugins under the hood. We shall look at the aforementioned list next.

For example, to plumb Vite with Marko, it relies on the **@marko/vite** plugin (**https://github.com/marko-js/vite**) that helps Vite understand *.marko* files and use the Marko compiler for loading and compiling them while building bundles. They also deal with injecting the assets into the compiled Marko templates and loading them correctly.

@marko/run/vite is a separate Vite plugin that wraps around the **@marko/vite** plugin and provides a few marko-run-specific things such as finding the application's route files and creating type-safe routing code.

One thing to note is that, in our examples related to passing **routesDir** and **basePathVar** to the Vite Marko plugin, **@marko/run/vite** is the one that is used. Any configuration to **@marko/vite** can be passed via **@marko/run/vite**, and it will pass it through. Refer to the types exported by them as you try examples. This is also explained in Figure 5-4A.

Some other options provided by **@marko/vite** are

- babelConfig

- runtimeId

```
plugins: [
    marko({
        babelConfig: {
            presets: ["@babel/preset-env"],
        },
        runtimeId: "MY_MARKO_RUNTIME_ID"
    })
],
```

Figure 5-4A. *Optional configs into @marko/run/vite through vite.config.ts*

babelConfig, as the name suggests, lets you pass in an optional babel configuration object that will override whatever is maintained by marko-run internally. If no babel configuration is specified, babel-related config files will not be considered.

Given that we are talking about MPAs and that Marko helps you build MPAs with ease, there are always use cases where you may want to *embed* UX built elsewhere into your page. Let us also assume that this embeddable UX is also built with Marko. In such cases, there will be multiple isolated copies of the Marko runtime on the page, potentially conflicting with each other. The conflict is because Marko relies on some *window* properties to initialize (perform hydration), and this can cause issues. For example, by default Marko will read the server-rendered hydration code from ***window.$components***. So, when there are multiple copies of Marko, each attempting to read from the same variable, it results in unwanted issues that are hard to debug. To avoid this, Marko provides you with an option to change these *window* properties by rendering with

```
{
  $global: {
    runtimeId: "MY_MARKO_RUNTIME_ID"
  }
}
```

Figure 5-4B. *runtimeID into @marko/run/vite through vite.config.ts*

as input on the server side. This plugin offers you a way to achieve it in the Marko-run setup via this ***runtimeId*** option. It automatically sets the ***$global.runtimeId*** to whatever you have provided, in the options, on the server side and adds initialization code to correctly read from this property, in the browser, ensuring there are no conflicts.

However, note that you would never need to operate/use these plugins. The information related to this is just provided to you so as to keep you informed about the various packages at play here to be able to achieve this seamless developer experience. We shall look at packages (4) and (5) in the subsection "Other Ecosystem of Packages."

Resource Servers and Marko-Run Non-connect-Style Apps

One of the important steps before starting your server in production mode would be to upload the generated assets of the current build to your resource servers of choice. This is required so that Marko can now serve the respective assets, inlined into the compiled template, along with the CDN server's base URL prepended. While Marko with Vite under the hood generates assets with unique URL fingerprints (usually a hash of the content), resource servers may also provide unique URL subpaths (to the resource, after it's uploaded).

At eBay, our usual practice has been to trigger the build as part of the CI manifest creation. This shall generate the required assets in production mode. Once the assets are generated at build time, the upload of the assets to the resource server happens before application bootstrap on the production VM. This usually happens within a resource server upload client that uploads the entire **dist/** folder to the resource server. The resource server then responds with a CDN URL path (to the uploaded directory on the resource server), which is to be appended to the resource generated.

Once this URL has been received from the resource server upon upload of the directory of assets (generated from the current build), this would be written out to a flat file and cached for use between the three PM2 workers that would be spun off (eBay uses Process Manager 2 in production to manage the three Node workers per VM). For example, in our sample marko-run app, when running the build command, the files generated are shown in Figure 5-5.

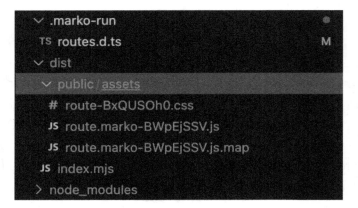

Figure 5-5. *Project folder structure*

So, if the file is **route-BxQUSOh0.css** and if the resource server URL is, for instance, `https://my-resource-server.com/somewhere/deep/within/myorg/uploads/ someRandomHash,`then this has to be appended to all the resources to generate a final URL as `https://my-resource-server.com/somewhere/deep/within/myorg/uploads/ someRandomHash/route-BxQUSOh0.css`

When running our project in dev mode locally, Vite takes care of serving all the files locally. However, when executing the app in production mode, the Vite dev server is not running in the background, and marko-run has to inject/inline these assets into the compiled Marko templates correctly and also append the base URL that was received after uploading the generated assets to the resource server.

For this, marko-run offers an option via the @marko/run/vite plugin. We saw this plugin in Figure 5-2 where we used it to provide an alternate path to the *src/routes* folder by setting the *src/pages* folder in it. The same plugin can be used here to set a property in its options called **basePathVar**. Note that this **basePathVar** property can be used to set the name of the property that will be used by Marko-run to query the CDN base paths from. This is shown in Figure 5-6.

```
vite.config.ts > [ø] default > 🔌 plugins > 🔌 basePathVar
1    // vite.config.ts
2    import { defineConfig } from "vite";
3    import marko from "@marko/run/vite"; // Import the Vite plugin
4
5    export default defineConfig({
6      plugins: marko({ basePathVar: "__MY_ASSET_BASE_PATH__" })
7    });
```

Figure 5-6. *Vite config showcasing the usage of basePathVar*

We set the **basePathVar** as __MY_ASSET_BASE_PATH__. This means, when you look up the generated server-side code under dist/index.mjs, you will notice references to this __MY_ASSET_BASE_PATH__ variable. This variable will be queried by the marko-run runtime, in its generated code, to compute the final asset URL to be included in the compiled template, so that when the template outputs HTML, it includes the correct asset URL (either <scripts> or <link> or <img>, etc.) in the respective tags.

Now that we have instructed marko-run to look up the asset information from this property __MY_ASSET_BASE_PATH__ , we are required to set this variable. Ideally, we would want to set this variable as part of some app startup or bootstrap code or some entry file. With the marko-run Connect-style setup, marko-run currently is configured to deal with an index entry file where it lets you configure the Connect-style module like Express JS and deal with it. Take a look at the vite-express starter for this.

However, if you have noticed, the existing marko-run setup (non-connect style, the one we are currently looking into) as of semver ^0.5.9 version of marko-run doesn't offer a way to execute code as a one-off bootstrap or setup. This is because Marko-run mostly considers itself to be a zero-configuration starter. So, there isn't a way to currently run code during application startup/bootstrap. This is expected to change in the upcoming versions. So, if you wanted to run some code before the application bootstraps, the best place right now is the root *middleware.ts* file, where you could do an IIFE to execute some code and return what is to be used as the middleware function. Since the ESM *imports* are cached, this will be executed only once and serves as a good place to set the __MY_ASSET_BASE_PATH__ variable. This is indicated in Figure 5-7.

```
src > routes > TS +middleware.ts > ...
  1    declare global {
  2        var __MY_ASSET_BASE_PATH__: string;
  3    }
  4    // replace this assignment with getCdnpaths() function that will maybe read off a written
  5    // file that contains the asset base path url information
  6    globalThis.__MY_ASSET_BASE_PATH__ = "https://www.example.com/rv/z/1/"
  7    export default async function (context: any, next: any) {
  8        return await next();
  9    };
```

Figure 5-7. *Using the variable set in basePathVar within the src/routes/ middleware.ts*

Route Path Parts

Earlier, we mentioned that marko-run looks up specific directories within your **src/** folder, called the "**routes**" folder, which it looks up by default. You can have this configured to some other directory via the **routesDir** prop within the Vite marko plugin invocation, within **marko()**, inside the *vite.config.ts* file. And any folder within this is usually considered a route where marko-run looks for files like *+page.marko*, *+layout. marko*, *+middleware.ts*, and *+handler.ts*. Well, there are some caveats around the folder naming. Let us look at the different patterns of directory names and what they all mean.

Static Directories

These are the ones we have seen so far. They contribute their name to the URL path. As we saw earlier with the /**welcome** route, which was mapped to the *src/pages/welcome* when the **routesDir** optional property within **marko()** in the **marko-vite** config. So, if it's not one of the following patterns, then this is the default behavior. Note that it is not absolutely necessary that you need all of the following files, but for a given default static directory, you atleast require the *+page.marko* file to serve HTML for the given route. This is illustrated in Figure 5-8.

```
pages/
   terms/
         +handler.ts
         +layout.marko
         +middleware.ts
         +page.marko
   welcome/
         +handler.ts
         +layout.marko
         +middleware.ts
         +page.marko
   +layout.marko
   +middleware.ts
   +page.marko
```

Figure 5-8A. *Default static route directories*

However, notice that marko-run, while acting as a server-side router for your app, is not just a router for your marko files. There will always be the case when you may want to run additional HTTP verb requests (PUT/PATCH/DELETE), etc., that do not necessarily render HTML. In such cases, you can still have these static routes to handle the incoming request, make your API calls, and return nothing (same as doing return next()) which will return a 204.

Pathless Directories

These directories won't contribute their name to the URL path. Directory names that are prefixed with an underscore _ will be ignored when parsing the route. Their main purpose is scoping and code organization without impacting URL path fragments. They allow you to nest files and folders without contributing to the route structure, meaning the enclosed files can be scoped without creating new routes. This approach aids in structuring code cleanly while maintaining the routing hierarchy.

When we talk about scope here, for example, if you want to indicate logically and organize a subset of routes to be under auth, via an auth middleware, you can organize them logically under an **_auth** folder. In the URL path parts, there will not be an **_auth** fragment. The available set of routes will therefore be

- pages/home

- pages/search

- pages/messages

- pages/profile

This is indicated in Figure 5-8B.

```
pages/
    home/
        +page.marko
    search/
        +page.marko
    _auth/
        +middleware.ts
        messages/
            +page.marko
        profile/
            +page.marko
```

Figure 5-8B. *Pathless directories*

In this case, *+middleware.ts* under **_auth** will be used to process incoming requests to check for auth and maybe send the user to an error page.

Dynamic Directories

These are directories that are prefixed with a **$**. In doing so, the text following the **$** acts as a dynamic parameter part of the URL path and will match any value at that fragment of the URL path.

Any directory name that starts with a single dollar symbol (**$**) is considered a dynamic directory, and the following text (remaining directory name) will be the parameter name at runtime. If the directory name is exactly **$**, without a following text, then the parameter will not be captured, but it will be matched.

For instance, we have a route that can be accessed at **/personal/$user** to provide a personalized greeting message to the user.

```
pages/
    personal/$user/
        +handler.ts
        +page.marko
```

Figure 5-9. *Dynamic directories ($user)*

Our *+handler.ts, +page.marko,* and *+meta.ts* files are shown in Figures 5-10 to 5-12.

```
src > pages > personal > $user > TS +handler.ts > ⬡ GET
1    export async function GET(context: any, next: () => any) {
2        console.log(context);
3        context.greetingMessage = `Hello world ${context.params.user}`;
4        return next();
5    }
```

Figure 5-10. *src/pages/personal/$user/+handler.ts*

```
src > pages > personal > $user > Ξ +page.marko > 🔧 html
1    $ const message = ($global as any).greetingMessage || "Default Greeting Message";
2
3    $ console.log("==================");
4    $ console.log(message);
5    $ console.log("==================");
6    <html>
7        <head>
8            <title>
9                Welcome to the personalized greeting page.
10           </title>
11       </head>
12       <body>
13           <div>${message}</div>
14           <div>Welcome to the personalized greeting page.</div>
15       </body>
16   </html>
```

Figure 5-11. *src/pages/personal/$user/+page.marko*

```
src > pages > personal > $user > TS +meta.ts > [∅] default > 🔧 description
1    export default {
2    💡   description: "This is a test route to understand the {$urlpart}"
3    }
```

Figure 5-12. *src/pages/personal/$user/+meta.ts*

When logging the context argument within the GET HTTP method found in *+handler.ts*, we get the logs shown in Figure 5-14. The output is shown in Figure 5-13.

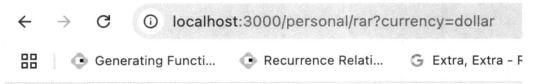

Hello world rar
Welcome to the personalized greeting page.

Figure 5-13. *The test page*

```
{
  request: Request {
    method: 'GET',
    url: 'http://localhost:3000/personal/rar',
    headers: Headers {
      host: 'localhost:3000',
      connection: 'keep-alive',
      'sec-ch-ua': '"Not A(Brand";v="8", "Chromium";v="132", "Google Chrome";v="132"',
      'sec-ch-ua-mobile': '?0',
      'sec-ch-ua-platform': '"macOS"',
      'upgrade-insecure-requests': '1',
      'user-agent': 'Mozilla/5.0 (Macintosh; Intel Mac OS X 10_15_7) AppleWebKit/537.36 (KHTML, like Gecko) Chrome/132.0.0.0 Safari/537.36',
      accept: 'text/html,application/xhtml+xml,application/xml;q=0.9,image/avif,image/webp,image/apng,*/*;q=0.8,application/signed-exchange;v=b3;q=0.7',
      'sec-fetch-site': 'none',
      'sec-fetch-mode': 'navigate',
      'sec-fetch-user': '?1',
      'sec-fetch-dest': 'document',
      'accept-encoding': 'gzip, deflate, br, zstd',
      'accept-language': 'en-US,en;q=0.9',
      cookie: 'marko-run-client-id=j378la9d'
    },
    destination: '',
    referrer: 'about:client',
    referrerPolicy: '',
    mode: 'cors',
    credentials: 'same-origin',
    cache: 'default',
    redirect: 'follow',
    integrity: '',
    keepalive: false,
    isReloadNavigation: false,
    isHistoryNavigation: false,
    signal: AbortSignal { aborted: false }
  },
  url: URL {
    href: 'http://localhost:3000/personal/rar',
    origin: 'http://localhost:3000',
    protocol: 'http:',
    username: '',
    password: '',
    host: 'localhost:3000',
    hostname: 'localhost',
    port: '3000',
    pathname: '/personal/rar',
    search: '',
    searchParams: URLSearchParams {},
    hash: ''
  },
```

Figure 5-14. *src/pages/personal/$user/+handler.ts logs for **context** argument*

```
platform: {
  request: IncomingMessage {
    _events: [Object],
    _readableState: [ReadableState],
    _maxListeners: undefined,
    socket: [Socket],
    httpVersionMajor: 1,
    httpVersionMinor: 1,
    httpVersion: '1.1',
    complete: true,
    rawHeaders: [Array],
    rawTrailers: [],
    joinDuplicateHeaders: null,
    aborted: false,
    upgrade: false,
    url: '/personal/rar?currency=dollar',
    method: 'GET',
    statusCode: null,
    statusMessage: null,
    client: [Socket],
    _consuming: false,
    _dumped: false,
    originalUrl: '/personal/rar?currency=dollar',
    _parsedUrl: [Url],
    _eventsCount: 1,
    [Symbol(shapeMode)]: true,
    [Symbol(kCapture)]: false,
    [Symbol(kHeaders)]: [Object],
    [Symbol(kHeadersCount)]: 32,
    [Symbol(kTrailers)]: null,
    [Symbol(kTrailersCount)]: 0
  },
```

Figure 5-14. (*continued*)

```
      response: ServerResponse {
        _events: [Object: null prototype],
        _eventsCount: 3,
        _maxListeners: undefined,
        outputData: [],
        outputSize: 0,
        writable: true,
        destroyed: false,
        _last: false,
        chunkedEncoding: false,
        shouldKeepAlive: true,
        maxRequestsOnConnectionReached: false,
        _defaultKeepAlive: true,
        useChunkedEncodingByDefault: true,
        sendDate: true,
        _removedConnection: false,
        _removedContLen: false,
        _removedTE: false,
        strictContentLength: false,
        _contentLength: null,
        _hasBody: true,
        _trailer: '',
        finished: false,
        _headerSent: false,
        _closed: false,
        socket: [Socket],
        _header: null,
        _keepAliveTimeout: 5000,
        _onPendingData: [Function: bound updateOutgoingData],
        req: [IncomingMessage],
        _sent100: false,
        _expect_continue: false,
        _maxRequestsPerSocket: 0,
        write: [Function (anonymous)],
        end: [Function (anonymous)],
        [Symbol(shapeMode)]: false,
        [Symbol(kCapture)]: false,
        [Symbol(kBytesWritten)]: 0,
        [Symbol(kNeedDrain)]: false,
        [Symbol(corked)]: 0,
        [Symbol(kOutHeaders)]: [Object: null prototype],
        [Symbol(errored)]: null,
        [Symbol(kHighWaterMark)]: 16384,
        [Symbol(kRejectNonStandardBodyWrites)]: false,
        [Symbol(kUniqueHeaders)]: null
      }
    },
    meta: { description: 'This is a test route to understand the {$urlpart}' },
    params: { user: 'rar' },
    route: '/personal/:user',
    serializedGlobals: { params: true, url: true }
}
```

Figure 5-14. (*continued*)

You will notice that from the **context** object, based on these logs, you can access a number of items that you would usually use in your processing or passing to downstream services. Some of them are logged in Figures 5-14 and 5-15.

```
console.log(context.request.headers);
console.log(context.request.url);
console.log(context.request.method);
console.log(context.url);
console.log(context.url.href);
console.log(context.url.pathname);
console.log(context.url.search);
console.log(context.meta);
console.log(context.params);
console.log(context.route);
console.log(context.serializedGlobals);
```

Figure 5-15. *Context property logs*

The **+meta.ts** is the route config, and you will notice that it's made available on the **context.meta** property.

```
Headers {
    host: 'localhost:3000',
    connection: 'keep-alive',
    'cache-control': 'max-age=0',
    'sec-ch-ua': '"Not A(Brand";v="8", "Chromium";v="132", "Google Chrome";v="132"',
    'sec-ch-ua-mobile': '?0',
    'sec-ch-ua-platform': '"macOS"',
    'upgrade-insecure-requests': '1',
    'user-agent': 'Mozilla/5.0 (Macintosh; Intel Mac OS X 10_15_7) AppleWebKit/537.36 (KHTML, like Gecko) Chrome/132.0.0.0 Safari/537.36',
    accept: 'text/html,application/xhtml+xml,application/xml;q=0.9,image/avif,image/webp,image/apng,*/*;q=0.8,application/signed-exchange;v=b3;q=0.7',
    'sec-fetch-site': 'same-origin',
    'sec-fetch-mode': 'navigate',
    'sec-fetch-dest': 'document',
    referer: 'http://localhost:3000/personal/rar?currency=dollar',
    'accept-encoding': 'gzip, deflate, br, zstd',
    'accept-language': 'en-US,en;q=0.9',
    cookie: 'marko-run-client-id=5c5yz37z'
}
http://localhost:3000/personal/rar?currency=dollar
GET
URL {
    href: 'http://localhost:3000/personal/rar?currency=dollar',
    origin: 'http://localhost:3000',
    protocol: 'http:',
    username: '',
    password: '',
    host: 'localhost:3000',
    hostname: 'localhost',
    port: '3000',
    pathname: '/personal/rar',
    search: '?currency=dollar',
    searchParams: URLSearchParams { 'currency' => 'dollar' },
    hash: ''
}
http://localhost:3000/personal/rar?currency=dollar
/personal/rar
?currency=dollar
{ description: 'This is a test route to understand the {$urlpart}' }
{ user: 'rar' }
/personal/:user
{ params: true, url: true }
```

Figure 5-16. *src/pages/personal/$user/+handler.ts logs for specific properties on* ***context***

371

Now if we instead had placed **$user** as a sibling to welcome, as shown in Figure 5-16

```
pages/
   $user/
      +handler.ts
      +page.marko
   welcome/
      +handler.ts
      +layout.marko
      +middleware.ts
      +page.marko
   +layout.marko
   +middleware.ts
   +page.marko
```

Figure 5-17. *When $user is a sibling to welcome*

If the route path was specifically /**welcome**, then +**page.marko** under **src**/**pages**/**welcome** will be rendered. If it was anything else, say /**copyright**, then +**page.marko** under **$user** will be rendered.

Lastly, what happens when your folder was named with just the **$** symbol? In that case, it will not capture the path param as it is empty. However, the route will still be matched by this handler to render the page under **src/pages/$/+page.marko**.

Note that we had previously mentioned about components being scoped to a folder. You can go pretty wild here by having a /components folder under src/pages/welcome.

```
src/
   pages/
      welcome/
         +page.marko
         components/
            +page.marko
            hello-world/
               index.marko
               +page.marko
```

Figure 5-18. *Scoping components locally*

- /welcome renders src/pages/welcome/+page.marko.

- Placing <hello-world/> as a component within src/pages/welcome/+page.marko renders <hello-world/>.

- /welcome/components renders src/pages/welcome/components/+page.marko.

- /welcome/components/hello-world renders src/pages/welcome/components/hello-world/+page.marko.

- <hello-world/> component renders within src/pages/welcome/components/hello-world/+page.marko.

- <hello-world/> not accessible to /terms rendered by src/pages/terms/+page.marko (assuming terms is a page folder within src/pages).

So **components/** not only can contain a **+page.marko** but can also contain components scoped to the route **welcome**/. But the general recommendation is not to put a components folder like this in a marko-run setup because you would literally have a route named welcome/components. It is recommended to place components under a **src/components** folder that is colocated alongside **src/pages** or **src/routes**.

There are some other variations of this as well.

For example, with the following folder structure

- pages/mystore/seller,buyer/dashboard

this implies the following routes:

- pages/mystore/seller/dashboard

- pages/mystore/buyer/dashboard

Next, with the following structure

- pages/mystore/messages/($id,)

this implies the following routes:

- pages/mystore/messages (maybe load a messages dashboard)

- pages/mystore/messages/$id (maybe load a specific message)

Catch-All Directories

These directories are similar to the dynamic directories seen in the previous section. They also introduce a dynamic parameter. The difference however lies in how they match. Instead of matching a single path fragment, they match to the end of the path.

Any directory that starts with two dollar symbols (**$$**) is a catch-all directory, and the remaining directory name will be the matched parameter at runtime. When the directory itself is named **$$**, the parameter name will not be captured, but it will match.

Catch-all directories are a good way to set up HTTP 404 routes at any level, including the root. However, you may note that at the root level (src/pages or src/routes), you can still configure a **404.marko** or a **500.marko** file as seen earlier.

An **important** note about nesting: Since catch-all directories match any path segment and consume the rest of the path, they cannot have nested route files (for more URL path fragments in them), and no further directories will be traversed. This also means the previous directory patterns can contain nested routes, and we have seen examples of them.

Let's look at this with an example.

```
pages/
    terms/
        +page.marko
        $$termid/
            +handler.ts
            +page.marko
    welcome/
        $$rest/
            +handler.ts
            +page.marko
    +page.marko
```

Figure 5-19. *Project structure for $$ catch-all directories*

Now running the app at

- /**terms** loads **pages/terms/+page.marko**.

- /**terms/and/conditions/2025** loads **pages/ terms/$$termid/+page.marko**.

- /**welcome** loads **pages/welcome/+page.marko**.

- /**welcome/to/my/profile** loads **pages/ welcome/$$rest/+page.marko**.

But an important part of this is what gets logged for the values *context.URL*, *context. params*, and *context.route*. This is shown in Figures 5-20 and 5-21.

```
url: URL {
  href: 'http://localhost:3000/terms/and/conditions/2025',
  origin: 'http://localhost:3000',
  protocol: 'http:',
  username: '',
  password: '',
  host: 'localhost:3000',
  hostname: 'localhost',
  port: '3000',
  pathname: '/terms/and/conditions/2025',
  search: '',
  searchParams: URLSearchParams {},
  hash: ''
},
meta: {},
params: { termid: 'and/conditions/2025' },
route: '/terms/:termid*',
serializedGlobals: { params: true, url: true }
```

Figure 5-20. *$$ catch-all directory logs*

```
url: URL {
  href: 'http://localhost:3000/welcome/to/my/profile',
  origin: 'http://localhost:3000',
  protocol: 'http:',
  username: '',
  password: '',
  host: 'localhost:3000',
  hostname: 'localhost',
  port: '3000',
  pathname: '/welcome/to/my/profile',
  search: '',
  searchParams: URLSearchParams {},
  hash: ''
},
  meta: {},
  params: { rest: 'to/my/profile' },
  route: '/welcome/:rest*',
  serializedGlobals: { params: true, url: true }
```

Figure 5-21. *$$ catch-all directory logs*

Note on Nested Directories That Match Nested Routes

- Static directories let you have nested subdirectories, which can be either static or pathless. If static, they contribute their folder name to the URL path parts of the nested subroute.

- Pathless directories can contain nested directories within them. As shown earlier, they help in organizing and scoping the code (say, you want to apply a middleware to a set of routes without the folder name contributing to the URL path fragment).

- Dynamic directories can contain nested directories within them. They will match nested subroutes with their dynamic part included in the URL path parts.

  - For example, say you have a tabbed view to switch between messages from buyers, sellers, and customer support within an inbox page. Your route is like

  - */profile/inbox/buyer/messages/bnty12678* which will map to marko-run via a folder path as pages/profile/inbox/$usertype/messages/$messageId

Flattened Routes

While nesting routes properly is certainly one way to look at whatever we have learned so far, they are also looked at as a pain because some routes can get really deep, causing a lot of friction for developers when code has to be moved around later, resulting in very large diffs in pull requests, etc. Nested subroutes certainly help with organizing the code better, but there are always downsides to everything especially when routes are really deep. Flattened routes help to alleviate that pain.

Flat routes allow you to achieve a lot of what was mentioned earlier without the folder structure–based routing, except that they now go into your file names. The folder structure can be defined either in the file or folder name. This lets you decouple the routes from the folder structure or colocate them as needed.

To define a flat route, use periods (.) to delineate each path segment.

This behaves exactly like creating a new folder (that originally contributed to the URL path parts), and each segment will be parsed using the rules described above for static, dynamic, and pathless routes. Flat route syntax can be used for both directories and routable files (e.g., pages, handlers.ts, middleware.ts, etc.). For these files, anything preceding the plus (+) will be treated as the flat route.

For example, to define a page at /friends/$friendId/followers/$followerId, alongside a root **+*layout.marko*** and a **friends/+*layout.marko***:

Without flat routes, you would have a nested file and directory structure, like the following, which can get unmaintainable and unwieldy.

> **routes/**
>> *+layout.marko*
>> **friends/**
>>> +page.marko
>>> *+layout.marko*
>>>> **$friendId/**
>>>>> +page.marko
>>>>> **followers/**
>>>>>> +page.marko
>>>>>> **$followerId/**
>>>>>>> +page.marko

Figure 5-22. *Project structure before flat routes*

With flat routes, move the path defined by the folders into the files and separate with a **period**.

> **routes/**
>> *+layout.marko*
>> friends+page.marko
>> friends+layout.marko
>> friends.$friendId+page.marko
>> friends.$friendId.followers+page.marko
>> friends.$friendId.followers.$followerId+page.marko

Figure 5-23. *Project structure after flat routes*

The way you would interpret it is

- friends+page.marko => the +page.marko file within the friends folder

- friends.$friendId+page.marko => the +page.marko file within the *$friendId* folder that is within the *friends* folder

Additionally, you can continue to organize the marko-run-specific files under folders for better organization and easier readability and combine it with the flat route syntax in the folder name.

In the following example, we have

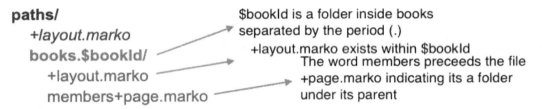

Figure 5-24. *Organize files under folders for better organization*

Now when you access the page as **/books/ISBN_1234/members**, it displays the page at *pages/books.$bookId/members+page.marko*, because this effectively means *pages/books/$bookId/members/+page.marko*.

Finally, flat routes and routes defined with directories are all treated equally and merged together. So, for example, if we had a couple of extra files highlighted in red

paths/
    +layout.marko
    books+page.marko
    books.$bookId+page.marko
    books.$bookId/
        +layout.marko
        members+page.marko

Figure 5-25. *Everything is merged*

these will all be merged together by Marko-run. So that for

- Request **/books**, it responds with **paths/books+page.marko**.

- Request **/books/ISBN_1234**, it responds with **paths/books.$bookId+page.marko**.

Multiple Paths, Grouping, and Optionality

We saw a glimpse of this with some earlier examples under the section "Dynamic Directories." But they can be extended to flat routes as well. Flat route syntax supports defining routes that match more than one path and segments that are optional.

To describe a route that matches multiple paths, **use a comma (,)** and define each route.

For example, for the routes **pages/$pageId/followers** and **pages/$pageId/following**, if they both end up sharing the same page template in the code, you do not have to duplicate them with two files. They can both share the same file via the multiple path syntax. They can thus be represented as

```
routes/
    pages.$pageId.followers,pages.$pageId.following+page.marko
```

Figure 5-26. *Comma-based multipath syntax*

If the file name is a bit long, you can also do

```
routes/
    pages.$pageId/
        following,followers+page.marko
```

Figure 5-27. *Folder name and comma-based multipath syntax*

This can be further simplified by **grouping**. Groups allow defining segments within a flat route that match multiple subpaths by surrounding them with parentheses ((and)). For example, this means you can therefore do

```
routes/
    pages.$pageId.(followers,following)+page.marko
```

Figure 5-28. *Groupings to distinguish multiple subpaths*

This is a simple example. You can obviously do nested routes and make it pretty complex.

The last is called **optionality**. This is done by introducing an empty segment or a pathless segment along with another value to make that segment optional. For example, if we want a page that matches /**pages/$pageId/followers** and /**pages/$pageId**, as a common landing page experience, you can create a flat route that optionally matches **followers**.

```
routes/
    pages.$pageId.(followers,)+page.marko
```

or you can also do

```
routes/
    pages.$pageId.(followers,_pathless)+page.marko
```

Figure 5-29. *Optionality*

While both of the above create a route that matches the two paths mentioned earlier, they have subtly different semantics. Using a ***_pathless*** segment is the same as creating a ***_pathless*** folder that allows you to scope +*middleware.t*s and +*layout.marko* files. Using an empty segment is the same as defining a file at the current location.

TypeScript Usage

Generated routes.d.ts File

If your project uses TypeScript (i.e., if you had scaffolded your project off the **basic-ts** template), you may have noticed a folder called ***.marko-run*** under the root project directory. This will have a generated file named ***routes.d.ts.*** This is updated every time there is a change to the directory folder structure or name and files involved in it when doing

`>> npm run build.`

It's also done lazily upon the first request when the dev server is running to serve the app in development mode via Vite. If the Marko-run meta framework is able to successfully generate this file, then it has successfully mapped your project layout, understood the structure, verified your compliance with the naming conventions, and determined all the associated files, handlers, and templates and is ready to serve the application. This is made possible via the validations run by Marko's type checker CLI called ***@marko/type-check*** or the ***mtc*** command, which you will learn in the subsequent chapters, to type-check Marko projects.

Also, you will notice that this has not been listed in the **tsconfig.json** file. This is because as long as you have the **Marko VS Code** plugin installed and **@marko/type-check,** this will get picked up automatically.

But What Is the Point of This?

This **routes.d.ts** file is a TypeScript declaration file automatically generated by the *marko-run* meta-framework that defines types and provides type information for the routes in a Marko-run app. It helps to validate the routing structure of your project. It's essentially a type system "blueprint" that describes

- **Routes**: The URL paths your app supports (e.g., */books*, */books/:bookId*, */books/:bookId/members*), which we were previously operating on.

- **HTTP Verbs**: The methods supported by these routes (in this case, only **GET** is defined)

- **Type Definitions**: Types for the route *handlers*, *contexts*, and utilities specific to Marko's runtime (*@marko/run*)

- **Module Declarations**: Type information for specific Marko *components* or *pages* (e.g., *books+page.marko*, *+layout.marko*) and their associated runtime behavior

The file uses TypeScript's **declare module** syntax to extend or define types for both the framework (*@marko/run*) and your project's source files (../src/paths/… or ../src/pages/… or ../src/routes/… based on whatever is in the *vite.config.js*). It ties together the routing system with Marko's component-based architecture, ensuring type safety when working with routes, context, handlers, and layouts.

Key parts

- **AppData**: Defines the app's route structure.

- **Route-Specific Declarations**: Each module corresponds to a Marko file (e.g., *books+page.marko*) and provides types for its route, context, and handler.

- **Routes Type**: A simple mapping of paths to their HTTP verbs (all get in this case).

- **Utility Types**: Things like GetPaths, PostPaths, etc., come from **@marko/run** and help with route handling that is taken care of under the hood by Marko-run.

Why Is This Required?

This file is required because

- **Type Safety**: TypeScript needs to know the shape of your project's routes, handlers, and contexts to catch errors at **compile** time. Without this, TypeScript wouldn't understand how your Marko pages map to routes that are based on the directory layout structure or what data they expect.

- **Framework Integration**: Marko's @marko/run runtime uses a specific routing system as we have seen, and this file bridges your app's structure to that system via types. It ensures your pages (e.g., books+page.marko) are properly typed as route handlers.

- **Auto-generation**: Since routes might change as you add or remove pages/layouts, manually maintaining this would be error-prone. The meta-framework generates it to reflect your src/paths directory accurately. If the generation fails, you know you have a problem. It's also a clear reflection of the various paths supported by your project.

- **Deprecation Handling**: It includes deprecated APIs (e.g., route: Run. HandlerTypeFn) with suggestions for modern alternatives, guiding you toward best practices.

In short, it's a contract between your code and the framework, enforced by TypeScript, to make development smoother and less buggy. This means this file also gets used by other IDE tooling and extensions to offer a seamless developer experience.

Where Will You Be Using All This?

You'll use this indirectly in your project wherever you

- **Define Route Handlers**: If you write logic for a route (e.g., in *books+page.marko* or a related file), you'll rely on these types to ensure your handler function matches the expected signature (e.g., Handler or Context).

- **Work with Context**: The Context type (e.g., *Run. MultiRouteContext<Route>* and *Marko.Global*) will be available when accessing route parameters (like *:bookId*) or global Marko data in your components via the $global prop.

– **Layouts**: For files like +layout.marko, the Input interface (with renderBody) ensures TypeScript knows what props your layout components expect.

– **IDE Support**: Your editor (e.g., VS Code) will use these declarations for autocompletion, error checking, and refactoring as you work with routes, handlers, or page-level Marko components.

You don't typically interact with **routes.d.ts** directly—it's a generated reference file. Instead, it's used by TypeScript behind the scenes as you write code in your directory or import utilities from **@marko/run**. In our example, the generated **routes.d.ts** file is shown in Figure 5-30.

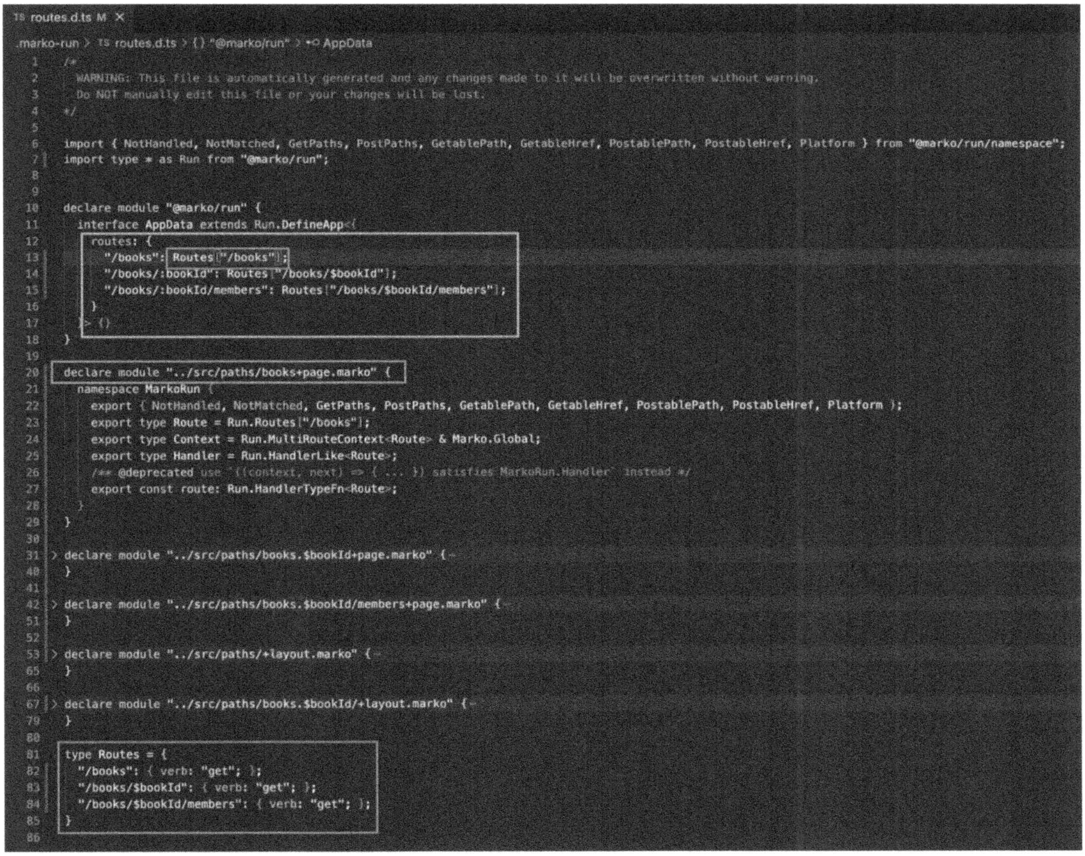

Figure 5-30. *Generated routes.d.ts file*

Why Is There a Namespace MarkoRun Defined Within Every Single Module?

The **MarkoRun** namespace is defined per module for a few reasons:

- **Module Isolation**: TypeScript's **declare module** syntax scopes the **MarkoRun** namespace to each specific file (e.g., *../src/paths/ books+page.marko*). This ensures that the types (like **Route**, **Context**, **Handler**) are tailored to that file's route, avoiding conflicts or overly generic definitions.

- **Route-Specific Types**: Each route has unique characteristics (e.g., / **books** vs. /**books/:bookId**), and the namespace customizes the types accordingly. For example, the Route type for *books.$bookId+page. marko* is **Run.Routes["/books/:bookId"]**, which might include a *bookId* parameter, unlike */**books**.

- **Framework Convention**: **@marko/run** likely uses this pattern to provide a consistent API surface for every route-related file. By namespacing MarkoRun, it avoids polluting the global scope and keeps related types (like **NotHandled** and **GetPaths**) grouped logically.

- **Reusability**: Repeating the namespace with exported utilities (e.g., **GetablePath**, **Platform**) ensures you can import them consistently from any Marko file, even if the exact route differs.

It might seem redundant, but it's a deliberate design to keep type definitions precise and modular, aligning with how Marko structures its runtime and file-based routing.

This **routes.d.ts** file is your project's routing backbone in TypeScript terms, generated to keep everything in sync with Marko's **@marko/run**. It saves you from writing boilerplate types manually, ensures your code aligns with the framework, and powers your IDE's intelligence. You'll "use" it implicitly as you build out pages and layouts, relying on its types to guide you. The **MarkoRun** repetition is just a way to keep things organized and route specific.

```
declare module "../src/paths/+layout.marko" {
  export interface Input {
    renderBody: Marko.Body;
  }
  namespace MarkoRun {
    export { NotHandled, NotMatched, GetPaths, PostPaths, GetablePath, GetableHref, PostablePath, PostableHref, Platform };
    export type Route = Run.Routes["/books" | "/books/:bookId" | "/books/:bookId/members"];
    export type Context = Run.MultiRouteContext<Route> & Marko.Global;
    export type Handler = Run.HandlerLike<Route>;
    /** @deprecated use `((context, next) => { ... }) satisfies MarkoRun.Handler` instead */
    export const route: Run.HandlerTypeFn<Route>;
  }
}
```

Figure 5-31. *A specific ../src/paths/+layout.marko*

The "../" is because it computes them with ./marko-run as the reference point.

What's Happening with the "declare module" Types?

The **declare module** "../src/paths/+layout.marko" block is telling TypeScript: "*Hey, the file +layout.marko (or its compiled output) has the following type information associated with it.*" This is a way to augment the module's type definition without altering the actual *.marko* template file itself, which is a template rather than a *.ts* file.

Within this declaration

- *export interface Input { renderBody:* Marko.Body; }

    - This defines the props (or "input") that the +layout.marko component expects. In this case, it's a renderBody prop of type Marko. Body, which is likely a render function or content block passed to the layout (common in Marko for nested content).

- *namespace MarkoRun { ... }*

    - This creates a MarkoRun namespace specific to this module, exposing types and utilities that you can use when working with this file in the context of Marko's routing runtime (@marko/run).

- Exported Members Inside *MarkoRun*

    - *export* { NotHandled, NotMatched, GetPaths, ... }: These are types/utilities re-exported from **@marko/run/namespace**. They're made available for use in this module.

- *export type Route = Run.Routes["/books" | "/books/:bookId" | "/books/:bookId/members"]*: Defines the Route type as a union of the three routes this layout applies to.

- *export type Context = Run.MultiRouteContext<Route>* and *Marko. Body*: Defines the Context type, combining route-specific context with Marko's global data.

- *export type Handler = Run.HandlerLike<Route>*: Defines the shape of a route handler function for these routes.

- *export const route: Run.HandlerTypeFn<Route>*: Declares a (deprecated) route constant that could be exported from this file as a handler.

Are NotHandled, Context, etc., Available in +layout.marko?

Yes, but with a nuance:

- **Direct Use in +layout.marko**: Since *+layout.marko* is a Marko template file (not a TypeScript file), you don't write TypeScript code like **NotHandled** or **Context** directly in it. Marko files typically focus on markup and logic using Marko's syntax, not raw TypeScript in this way. However, these types describe what's available to the file when it's processed by the underlying marko-run framework or referenced elsewhere.

- **Practical Availability**: These types and exports become usable in related TypeScript/JavaScript files or when you interact with *+layout. marko* programmatically. For example:

  - If *+layout.marko* has associated logic in a separate **.ts** or **.js** file (e.g., a handler), you can import and use these types there.

  - If you're defining a route handler for this layout, you'd use **MarkoRun.Handler** or **MarkoRun.Context** to type it correctly.

For example, in case we have a route /**schools** that returns the information of all schools nearby and generates the route's declarations files, through the *npm run build* command, we can import the types and use them as shown in Figure 5-32.

Exports like **NotHandled**, **Context**, and the rest are "available" to *./src/paths/+layout.marko* in the sense that they define the type environment for that file's interaction with the routing system. You'll use them most directly in TypeScript files or when typing logic associated with this layout, while Marko's runtime leverages them under the hood to tie everything together.

```
declare module "../src/paths/+layout.marko" {
  export interface Input {
    renderBody: Marko.Body;
  }
  namespace MarkoRun {
    export { NotHandled, NotMatched, GetPaths, PostPaths, GetablePath, GetableHref, PostablePath, PostableHref, Platform };
    export type Route = Run.Routes["/books" | "/books/:bookId" | "/books/:bookId/members" | "/schools"];
    export type Context = Run.MultiRouteContext<Route> & Marko.Global;
    export type Handler = Run.HandlerLike<Route>;
    /** @deprecated use `((context, next) => { ... }) satisfies MarkoRun.Handler` instead */
    export const route: Run.HandlerTypeFn<Route>;
  }
}
```

```
src > paths > schools > TS +handler.ts > ⊙ GET
1    // import type { MarkoRun } from "./+page.marko";
2    import type { NextFunction, Fetch, Match, Invoke } from "@marko/run";
3
4    export async function GET(context: MarkoRun.Context, next: NextFunction) {
5        console.log(context.customPropery);
6        return next();
7    }
```

Figure 5-32. *Example with the route /schools*

What's Being Declared?

Module declarations for files like *+layout.marko*, as shown in Figure 5-32, contain typings for template **Input** and include a ***renderBody*** property to allow transclusion of a *page.marko* into its body content. In TypeScript, the **declare module "some/path"** syntax is used to describe the shape of a module—here, **../src/paths/+layout.marko**—without actually implementing it. This declaration doesn't "live" inside the Marko file itself; it's a TypeScript construct in **routes.d.ts** that tells the type system what the module exports or makes available when imported elsewhere.

Are These Just Available Within the Module or Exported by It?

The contents here—**Input** and the **MarkoRun** namespace—are **exported** by the module *../src/paths/+layout.marko*, not just available for use within it. Here's why:

- **export** Keyword

    - The **export** interface, **Input**, and **export** within the **MarkoRun** namespace explicitly mark these items as part of the module's public API. In TypeScript, export means "*this is something the module provides to consumers when imported.*"

    - This aligns with how TypeScript declaration files work: they define what a module exports, not just what it internally uses.

- **Module Declaration Purpose**: The **declare module** syntax is about augmenting or defining the external interface of a module (in this case, a Marko file). It's telling TypeScript: "*When someone imports ../src/paths/+layout.marko, they can access these exported types and values.*"

- **Practical Implication**: For instance, with the example of *+layout. marko*, these types and values aren't "scoped" exclusively for internal use within *+layout.marko*. Instead, they're available to other modules that **import** *../src/paths/+layout.marko*.

How Does This Work in Practice?

- **Within +layout.marko**

    - The Marko file itself doesn't directly "see" these TypeScript declarations because it's not a TypeScript file—it's a template file processed by Marko's compiler. However, the runtime behavior of +layout.marko (e.g., accepting renderBody as input or acting as a route handler) is described by these types.

- **Outside +layout.marko**

    - When you import *../src/paths/+layout.marko* in a TypeScript file, you can access the exported ***Input*** interface and the ***MarkoRun*** namespace as shown in Figure 5-33. Here, ***MarkoRun*** (with its nested types like ***Context***, ***Handler***, etc.) and ***Input*** are explicitly exported by the module, so they're available to the importing code that uses them, as shown in the figure.

```
src > paths > schools > TS +handler.ts > ⬡ GET
  1     import type { MarkoRun } from "./+page.marko";
  2
  3     export async function GET(context: MarkoRun.Context, next: () => void) {
  4         console.log(context);
  5         return next();
  6     }
```

Figure 5-33. *Using the types*

Key Distinction: Exported By vs. Available Within

- **Exported By**: The **Input** interface and **MarkoRun** namespace (including its contents like **NotHandled**, **Context**, etc.) are part of the module's **export** surface. They're what *../src/paths/+layout.marko* provides to the outside world when imported.

- **Available Within**: Inside *+layout.marko*, you don't explicitly reference these TypeScript types in Marko syntax unless you are typing those args. However, the runtime environment aligns with these types. For instance:

  - The **renderBody** prop you pass to the *+layout.marko* matches **Input**.

Why Both Perspectives Matter

- **For the Module Itself**: The declaration ensures that Marko's compiler and runtime treat *+layout.marko* consistently with these types (e.g., expecting **renderBody** as input).

- **For Consumers**: Other parts of your codebase (like route handlers or components using this layout) can import and rely on these types for type safety. Besides this, it also gets used by the underlying framework for validation and for IDE tooling support.

The **Input** interface and **MarkoRun** namespace (with **NotHandled**, **Context**, etc.) are exported by *../src/paths/+layout.marko*, not just available within it. They're part of the module's public API, usable wherever you **import** this module in your TypeScript code. Inside +*layout.marko*, these types describe its behavior but aren't directly written out—they're enforced by the framework and TypeScript behind the scenes.

Namespace MarkoRun vs. declare module "@marko/run"

This gets to the heart of how TypeScript organizes and scopes type definitions in your **routes.d.ts** file. Let's break down the difference between the **declare module** "**@marko/run**" and **namespace MarkoRun**, why both appear, and why they're both needed in this context.

What Is the declare module "@marko/run"?

- **Purpose**: The declare module "@marko/run" syntax is used to define or extend the type definitions for the external @marko/run package.

- **Scope**: This declaration applies globally across your entire codebase. It's typically used to describe the public API of a library or module that doesn't ship with its own .d.ts files (or to augment it if it does).

- **What It Does Here**: In your routes.d.ts, it extends @marko/run with an AppData interface that defines your app's route structure.

```
declare module "@marko/run" {
  interface AppData extends Run.DefineApp<{
    routes: {
      "/books": Routes["/books"];
      "/books/:bookId": Routes["/books/$bookId"];
      "/books/:bookId/members": Routes["/books/$bookId/members"];
      "/schools": Routes["/schools"];
    }
  }> {}
}
```

Figure 5-34. *Declare module @marko/run*

- This says: "The **@marko/run** module includes an **AppData** type that reflects my app's routes." It ties your specific routes to the framework's runtime.

- **Usage**: Any file importing **@marko/run** (e.g., import * as Run from @marko/run) can access these types globally.

What Is the namespace MarkoRun?

- **Purpose**: The namespace **MarkoRun** syntax (as seen in Figure 5-32) defines a local namespace within a specific declare module block (e.g., *../src/paths/+layout.marko*). It's a way to group related types and values under a named scope, specific to that module.

- **Scope**: This namespace is scoped to the individual module it's declared in (e.g., *../src/paths/+layout.marko*). It doesn't affect the global namespace or other modules unless explicitly imported.

- **What It Does Here**: In each file-specific module declaration, namespace MarkoRun provides route-specific types and utilities:

  - This says: "For this specific file (+layout.marko), the MarkoRun namespace provides types like Route, Context, and Handler tailored to its routes, plus some utilities from @marko/run."

- **Usage**: You access these by importing from the specific module, for example, *import { MarkoRun } from "../src/paths/+layout.marko"*.

The Differences

Aspect	`declare module "@marko/run"`	`namespace MarkoRun`
Scope	Global, applies to the `@marko/run` package	Local, scoped to a specific file's module
Purpose	Defines/augments the framework's global API	Groups route-specific types for a single file
Location	Top-level in `routes.d.ts`	Inside each `declare module` for a Marko file
Access	Available via `import * as Run from "@marko/run"`	Available via `import { MarkoRun } from "path"`
Customization	Broad, app-wide route structure	Specific to the routes handled by that file

Figure 5-35. *The differences*

Why Are Both Needed?

They serve complementary purposes in your project:

– **declare module "@marko/run"**

  – **Why Needed**: This sets up the global foundation for how your app integrates with the *@marko/run* runtime. It defines the app's overall route structure (via *AppData*), so the framework knows all possible routes (*/books, /books/:bookId,* etc.) at a high level.

  – **Role**: It's a single, centralized place to tie your app's routes to the Marko runtime, ensuring the framework can map URLs to handlers and components correctly.

– **namespace MarkoRun**

  – **Why Needed**: Each Marko file (e.g., *+layout.marko, books+page. marko*) needs its own type definitions tailored to the specific routes it handles. The **MarkoRun** namespace provides this granularity, customizing types like **Route** and **Context** to match the file's role in the routing system.

- **Role**: It gives you type safety and IDE support when working with a specific file's logic (e.g., accessing *:bookId* in */books/:bookId*), without polluting the global scope.

- **Why Both Together?**

  - The global *declare module "@marko/run"* provides the big picture (all routes in the app), while the per-file *namespace MarkoRun* provides the details (types specific to each file's routes).

  - Without the *declare module "@marko/run"*, TypeScript wouldn't know how your app's routes fit into the @marko/run framework.

  - Without the *namespace MarkoRun*, you'd lack precise, file-specific types, making it harder to work with individual routes safely.

Why namespace MarkoRun in Every Module?

- **Route-Specific Customization**: Each file handles a subset of routes (e.g., *+layout.marko* handles all three, while *books.$bookId+page. marko* handles just */books/:bookId*). The **MarkoRun** namespace adapts the **Route**, **Context**, and **Handler** types to match those routes.

- **Modularity**: By scoping **MarkoRun** to each module, it avoids conflicts and keeps the types tightly coupled to the file they describe. You don't want a global **MarkoRun** namespace that tries to cover every route—it'd be too vague.

Available Types to Use

Global namespace **marko/run** (defined in the generated routes.d.ts) provides a global namespace **MarkoRun** with the following types:

- **MarkoRun.Handler**: Type that represents a handler function to be exported by a *+handler* or *+middleware* file.

- **MarkoRun.Route**: Type of the route's params and metadata.

- **MarkoRun.Context**: Type of the request context object in a handler and $global in your Marko files. This type can be extended using

TypeScript's module and interface merging by declaring a Context interface on the **@marko/run** module within your application code. For example, we have just placed a *types.d.ts* file with the *customProperty* on **context**.

```
src > TS types.d.ts > ...
1    import type * as Run from "@marko/run";
2    declare module "@marko/run" {
3        interface Context {
4            customPropery: string; // will be globally defined on MarkoRun.Context
5        }
6    }
```

Figure 5-36. *A customProperty on Context*

- **MarkoRun.Platform**: Type of the platform object provided by the adapter in use. We have logged this and shown its contents in Figure 5-38. This interface can be extended in that same way as **Context** (see above) by declaring a **Platform** interface.

```
src > TS types.d.ts > {} "@marko/run" > •○ Context > 🔧 customPropery
1    import type * as Run from "@marko/run";
2    declare module "@marko/run" {
3        interface Context {
4            customPropery: string; // will be globally defined on MarkoRun.Context
5        }
6        interface Platform {
7            awesomeAppProp: string; // will be globally defined on MarkoRun.Platform
8        }
9    }
```

Figure 5-37. *Interface platform*

In the above example, *customProperty* can now be picked by the IDE tooling.

```
src > paths > schools > TS +handler.ts > 🔷 GET
1    // import type { MarkoRun } from "./+page.marko";
2    import type { NextFunction } from "@marko/run";
3
4    export async function GET(context: MarkoRun.Context, next: NextFunction) {
5        console.log(context.customPropery);
6        return next();
7    }
```

Figure 5-38. *Logging the customProperty*

These common app-level types are replaced with more specific versions per routable file that is generated by Marko-run, as we have seen and covered in the previous section:

- **MarkoRun.Handler**: Overrides context with specific **MarkoRun. Context**.

- **MarkoRun.Route**: Adds specific parameters and meta types. In middleware and layouts which are used in many routes, this type will be a union of all possible routes that the file will see.

- **MarkoRun.Context**: In middleware and layouts which are used in many routes, this type will be a union of all possible routes that the file will see. When an adapter is used, it can provide types for the platform.

Runtime

This is about marko-run's runtime API. You will, for the most part, not be using this, and it will be used in cases of building adapters. However, there are a few that may be useful:

1. Fetch (we will refer to this as *fetch* going forward, and this is not the Fetch API of the browser)

2. match

3. invoke

The runtime is abstracted out when you use one of the adapters in your project. In the zero config mode—the non-connect-style marko-run app type that we have seen so far—there is little to no need for using this.

And these can be imported and used inside an existing server like

```
src > paths > schools > TS +handler.ts > ⊙ GET
   1    // import type { MarkoRun } from "./+page.marko";
   2    import type { NextFunction, Fetch, Match, Invoke } from "@marko/run";
   3
   4    export async function GET(context: MarkoRun.Context, next: NextFunction) {
   5        console.log(context.customPropery);
   6        return next();
   7    }
```

Figure 5-39. *Importing Fetch Match and Invoke from @marko/run*

Type Definition for Fetch, Match, and Invoke

```
export type Fetch<TPlatform extends Platform = Platform> = (request: Request, platform: TPlatform) => Promise<Response | void>;
export type Match = (method: string, pathname: string) => RouteWithHandler | null;
export type Invoke<TPlatform extends Platform = Platform> =
    (route: RouteWithHandler | null, request: Request, platform: TPlatform) => Promise<Response | void>;
```

Figure 5-40. *Types for Match Fetch and Invoke*

Fetch (Fetching a Response)

The async function takes a WHATWG Request object and a platform object containing some org platform–specific data and returns any of

- A WHATWG Response object (generated from executing any matched route files)

- Undefined (if the request was not explicitly handled)

- A 404 status code response (if no route matches the requested path)

- A 500 status code response (if an error occurs)

```
import express from "express";
import * as Run from "@marko/run";

const app = express();

app.use(async (req, res, next) => {
  // Example: Convert Express req to WHATWG Request (simplified)
  const request = new Request(`http://${req.headers.host}${req.url}`, {
    method: req.method,
    headers: req.headers,
    body: req.method !== "GET" && req.method !== "HEAD" ? req.body : undefined,
  });

  const response = await Run.fetch(request, {
    req,
    res,
  });

  if (response) {
    // 1. Set the status code
    res.status(response.status);

    // 2. Copy headers from the WHATWG Response to Express res
    for (const [key, value] of response.headers) {
      res.set(key, value);
    }

    // 3. Get the body and send it
    const body = await response.text(); // or response.json(), response.arrayBuffer(), et(
    res.send(body);
  } else {
    next();
  }
});

app.listen(3000, () => {
  console.log("Server running on port 3000");
});
```

Figure 5-41. *Explaining fetch*

In some cases, you might want more fine-grained control over when route matching and invocation (creating a response) occur. For instance, you may have a middleware in your server code which needs to know if there is a matched route. The runtime provides these additional methods.

Match (Matching a Route)

A route object is defined as

```
export interface Route<Params extends ParamsObject = ParamsObject, Meta = unknown, Path extends string = string> {
    path: Path;
    params: Params;
    meta: Meta;
}
```

Figure 5-42A. *Type route*

This is a sync function that takes an HTTP method and path name and returns an object representing the best match, or null if no match is found. params—a { key: value } collection of any path parameters for the route meta—metadata for the route.

- **Signature**: match(method: string, pathname: string) => Route | null

- **Purpose**: This sync function checks if a route matches the given HTTP method (e.g., "GET", "POST") and pathname (e.g., "/users/123") based on your @marko/run route configuration.

- It **returns**

  - A Route object if a match is found, containing params

    - A key-value object of path parameters (e.g., { id: "123" } for /users/:id)

    - meta: Metadata associated with the route (e.g., custom data defined in your route files)

  - *null* if no route matc   hes

- **Use Case**: Use match when you want to separate route matching from response generation, such as checking for a match before running middleware or custom logic.

Invoke (Response Creation to a Matched Route Object)

This is an async function that takes a Route object from the *match* operation, the *WHATWG Request*, and *platform* data object and returns a *WHATWG Response* in the same way the *fetch* does.

Let's look at an example that uses Match and Invoke.

```
import express from "express";
import * as Run from "@marko/run/router";

const app = express();

// Middleware to match routes and attach them to the request
app.use((req, res, next) => {
  // Use Run.match to find a matching route
  const matchedRoute = Run.match(req.method, req.path);
  if (matchedRoute) {
    // Attach the matched route to the request object for later use
    req.match = matchedRoute;
    console.log(`Matched route for ${req.method} ${req.path}:`, matchedRoute.params);
  } else {
    console.log(`No route matched for ${req.method} ${req.path}`);
  }
  next(); // Proceed to next middleware
});

// Example middleware that depends on route matching
app.use((req, res, next) => {
  if (req.match && req.match.params.id) {
    console.log(`Route has an ID parameter: ${req.match.params.id}`);
    // You could add logic here, e.g., fetching data based on params
  }
  next();
});

// Middleware to invoke the matched route and send the response
app.use(async (req, res, next) => {
  // If no route was matched earlier, skip to next middleware
  if (!req.match) {
    next();
    return;
  }

  // Convert Express req to a WHATWG Request object
  const request = new Request(`http://${req.headers.host}${req.url}`, {
    method: req.method,
    headers: req.headers,
    body: req.method !== "GET" && req.method !== "HEAD" ? req.body : undefined,
  });

  // Use Run.invoke to generate a response for the matched route
  const response = await Run.invoke(req.match, request, {
    req,
    res,
  });

  if (response) {
    // Apply the response to Express res (same as with Run.fetch)
    res.status(response.status);
    for (const [key, value] of response.headers) {
      res.set(key, value);
    }
    const body = await response.text(); // Adjust based on content type if needed
    res.send(body);
  } else {
    next(); // No response generated, pass to next middleware
  }
});

// Fallback for unmatched routes
app.use((req, res) => {
  res.status(404).send("404 - Not Found");
});

app.listen(3000, () => {
  console.log("Server running on port 3000");
});
```

Figure 5-42B. *Match and Invoke*

Explanation of the Example

- **Route Matching with *match***

    - *match*(req.method, req.path) is called in the first middleware to check if the request matches a route defined in @marko/run.

    - req.method is the HTTP method (e.g., "GET", "POST").

    - req.path is the URL pathname (e.g., "/users/123").

    - If a match is found, the Route object is stored in req.match for later use.

        - For example: For a route like /users/:id and a request to /users/123, matchedRoute.params might be { id: "123" }.

- **Middleware Flexibility**

    - The second middleware demonstrates how you can use req. match to access **route** parameters (e.g., id) or metadata (**meta**) before generating a response. This is useful for preprocessing, authentication, or logging.

- **Response Generation with *invoke***

    - invoke(req.match, request, { req, res }) takes the matched **Route** object, the *WHATWG* Request, and **platform** data (e.g., Express's req and res) to execute the route's logic and return a *WHATWG* **Response**.

    - This is similar to *fetch*, but it assumes you've already matched the route with *match*.

- **Applying the Response**

    - The **response** is applied to *res* using the same pattern as with *fetch*: set status, headers, and body. You can check the previous figure on how to apply a response to the *res* part you asked about earlier.

- **Fallback**

    - If no route matches (*req.match* is *undefined*) or *invoke* returns no response, the request falls through to a 404 handler.

Example of Using new Response(...) in Your Express Setup

Sometimes you may just want to use the **new Response(...)** to create a *WHATWG* Response object. You'd only use **new Response(...)** when you need to step outside the default behavior of *fetch* and take control of the response yourself.

In the context of *@marko/run* and its integration with an existing server like **Express**, you typically won't need to create a **new Response(...)** object yourself when handling incoming requests. The *fetch* function is responsible for generating and returning a WHATWG Response object based on the matched route or error conditions (e.g., 404 or 500 responses). You may just want to take that **Response** and apply it to the Express *res* object.

However, when you do not really want to interface with the Runtime's methods listed above, **new Response(...)** is a simple way to generate a WHATWG Response to an incoming request. And there are scenarios where you might use **new Response(...)** yourself when working with *@marko/run*. Here's where and why you might use it:

When to Use *new Response(...)*

- **Custom Middleware Logic**: If you need to intercept a request before it reaches *fetch* or after it returns undefined (i.e., no route matched), you might create a new Response to provide a custom response, for example, returning a custom 403 Forbidden or a maintenance page.

- **Testing or Mocking**: When writing unit tests for your application, you might create **new Response(...)** objects to simulate what *fetch* would return.

- **Dynamic Route Handling**: If you're extending *@marko/run* or writing custom logic outside its router (e.g., in a catch-all route), you might construct a **Response** manually.

- **Server-Side Rendering or API Responses**: If you're building an API endpoint or SSR logic alongside *@marko/run*, you might use **new Response** to craft responses directly.

Example of Using new Response(...) in Your Express Setup

```javascript
import express from "express";
import * as Run from "@marko/run";

const app = express();

app.use(async (req, res, next) => {
  // Convert Express req to WHATWG Request (simplified)
  const request = new Request(`http://${req.headers.host}${req.url}`, {
    method: req.method,
    headers: req.headers,
    body: req.method !== "GET" && req.method !== "HEAD" ? req.body : undefined,
  });

  let response = await Run.fetch(request, {
    req,
    res,
  });

  // If no response (undefined), create a custom one
  if (!response) {
    // Example: Return a custom "Not Found" response
    response = new Response("Sorry, nothing here!", {
      status: 404,
      statusText: "Not Found",
      headers: { "Content-Type": "text/plain" },
    });
  }

  // Apply the response to Express res
  res.status(response.status);
  for (const [key, value] of response.headers) {
    res.set(key, value);
  }
  const body = await response.text();
  res.send(body);
});

app.listen(3000, () => {
  console.log("Server running on port 3000");
});
```

Figure 5-43. *Using new Response(...)*

Explanation

- **new Response("Sorry, nothing here!", { ... })**: Creates a new
  WHATWG Response object with a plain text body, a 404 status, and a
  Content-Type header.

- **Use Case**: This runs if *fetch* returns undefined (no route matched),
  allowing you to provide a fallback response instead of calling **next()**.

Linked Mode

What Is It?

Linked mode is the default behavior of the marko/vite plugin when you're using Marko with Vite (a build tool and dev server). In this mode, the plugin does some heavy lifting for you:

- **Automatic Discovery**: It scans your project and finds all the .marko files that serve as entry points (basically, the starting points of your app's pages or components).

- **No HTML Files Needed**: Normally with Vite, you'd create .html files to tell it what to load in the browser. In linked mode, you skip that entirely—Marko files take over that role.

- **Auto-injection**: Things like scripts, styles, and other assets (stuff you'd typically put in an HTML file) get automatically added into your .marko templates without you having to manually wire them up.

- **Server-Side Rendering (SSR)**: You're required to use Vite's SSR API, which means your Marko templates are rendered on the server before being sent to the browser.

The example code shows this in action with Express in a *src/index.js* file:

- **In development**, it sets up a Vite dev server and loads the Marko template dynamically.

- **In production**, it uses prebuilt assets from the dist folder.

- **When someone visits the root URL (/)**, the server renders the Marko template (with a simple "hello world" data) and sends it to the browser, with Vite assets (like JavaScript and CSS) already included.

```
import { once } from "events";
import express from "express";
import markoMiddleware from "@marko/express";
import compressionMiddleware from "compression";

const devEnv = "development";
const { NODE_ENV = devEnv, PORT = 3000 } = process.env;
console.time("Start");

const app = express()
  .use(compressionMiddleware()) // Enable gzip compression for all HTTP responses.
  .use(markoMiddleware());

if (NODE_ENV === devEnv) {
  const { createServer } = await import("vite");
  const devServer = await createServer({
    appType: "custom",
    server: { middlewareMode: true },
  });
  app.use(devServer.middlewares);
  app.use(async (req, res, next) => {...
  });
} else {
  app
    .use("/assets", express.static("dist/assets")) // Serve assets generated from vite.
    .use((await import("./dist/index.js")).router);
}

await once(app.listen(PORT), "listening");

console.timeEnd("Start");
console.log(`Env: ${NODE_ENV}`);
console.log(`Address: http://localhost:${PORT}`);
```

Figure 5-44. *Example with express for linked mode*

So, *linked* mode is like an all-in-one solution: Marko drives everything, and Vite handles the assets behind the scenes.

What Happens When Linked Mode Is False?

If you set **linked: false** (in the plugin options for @marko/vite), you're opting out of this streamlined setup. Here's what changes:

- **No Automatic Discovery**: The plugin won't go looking for *.marko* files on its own. You'll need to explicitly tell Vite what to load, likely by creating *.html* files or manually specifying entry points in your Vite config.

- **Back to Standard Vite Behavior**: You're no longer "Marko all the way down." Instead, you'll use Vite's usual workflow, where *.html* files act as the entry points, and Marko files are just one part of the puzzle (like components or templates).

- **No Auto-injection**: Scripts, styles, and other assets won't magically appear in your *.marko* files. You'll have to manage that yourself, either in your *.html* files or through Vite's configuration.

- **Simpler Role for the Plugin**: The plugin's job shrinks to just two things:

  - **Resolving**: Figuring out where .marko files are and how they connect to other modules

  - **Transforming**: Converting .marko files into something Vite can work with (like JavaScript)

In this mode, you're not locked into Vite's SSR API. You could use Marko for client-side rendering only or mix and match with other setups, but you lose the tight integration that linked mode provides.

So, What Does It All Mean?

- **Linked Mode = true (Default)**: Everything is automated and Marko-centric. It's great if you're fully committed to server-side rendering with Marko and want Vite to stay out of your way. Think of it as a "set it and forget it" mode for Marko + Vite SSR.

- **Linked Mode = false**: You get more control but also more responsibility. It's closer to a standard Vite setup, where you might use **Marko** for some parts of your app but manage the bigger picture yourself. This is better if you don't need SSR or want a more traditional frontend workflow.

In short, *linked* mode is a convenience feature that ties Marko and Vite together tightly. Turning it off loosens that connection, giving you flexibility at the cost of doing more manual setup!

Adapters and "adapter" Prop

Adapters offer the means to change the development, build, and preview process to fit different deployment platforms and runtimes while allowing authors to focus on just writing code.

Currently, Marko-run supports three adapters:

1. For Netlify (*@marko/run-adapter-netlify*)

2. For Static site gen (*@marko/run-adapter-static*)

3. For Node JS (*@marko/run-adapter-node*)

The adapter can be passed into marko Vite options via the *adapter* prop.

```
import marko from "@marko/run/vite";
import adapter from "@marko/run-adapter-node";
import { defineConfig } from "vite";

export default defineConfig({
  plugins: [marko({ adapter: adapter() })],
});
```

Figure 5-45. *Setting up an adapter*

Other Ecosystem of Packages

1. *@marko/run* uses @marko/run-explorer and @marko/vite. Within the options of @Marko/vite, you can pass in an adapter optionally. This could be one of the adapters—node, static, netlify. (https://github.com/marko-js/run/tree/main/packages/run)

2. *@marko/run-explorer (https://github.com/marko-js/run/tree/main/packages/explorer)*

3. *@marko/vite (https://github.com/marko-js/vite)*

4. *@marko/run/vite (https://github.com/marko-js/run/tree/main/packages/run/src/vite)*

5. Adapter packages

a. *@marko/run-adapter-netlify (https://github.com/marko-js/ run/tree/main/packages/adapters/netlify)*

b. *@marko/run-adapter-static (https://github.com/marko-js/run/ tree/main/packages/adapters/static)*

c. *@marko/run-adapter-node (https://github.com/marko-js/run/ tree/main/packages/adapters/node)*

Previously in the subsection "Related Packages," we have already seen (1), (3), and (4), and in the section "Adapters," we have seen (5). *@marko/run-explorer* provides a way for you to explore the routes in your marko-run application. For example, in our case, when we start the dev server via *npm run dev*, you will notice this:

Figure 5-46. *Explore routes*

Marko offers a dedicated route, in this case under port **1234**, to preview the app routes. Hitting the given URL, you will notice a page with information about the routes.

Figure 5-47. *Route metadata for exploration*

Related Flavors of a marko-run App

So far, we have discussed non-connect-style Marko-run applications. In this, let's look at an example of a connect-style Marko-run application. This example will make use of the *@marko/run-adapter-node*. Note that when you scaffold a marko app via npx @marko/ create and choose the vite-express template, what comes there is just a plain Marko and Express setup. It does not use the marko-run meta framework. Let's call this app node-express-sample.

```
{} package.json > ...
  1    {
  2            "name": "node-express-example",
  3            "version": "0.0.1",
  4            "private": true,
  5            "type": "module",
         ▷ Debug
  6            "scripts": {
  7              "build": "marko-run build src/index.ts",
  8              "dev": "marko-run src/index.ts",
  9              "preview": "marko-run preview src/index.ts"
 10            },
 11            "dependencies": {
 12              "compression": "^1.7.5",
 13              "express": "^4.21.1",
 14              "marko": "^5.37.3"
 15            },
 16            "devDependencies": {
 17              "@marko/compiler": "^5.39.3",
 18              "@marko/run": "^0.5.17",
 19              "@marko/run-adapter-node": "^0.1",
 20              "@types/node": "^22.9.1",
 21              "prettier": "^3.3.3",
 22              "tsx": "^4.19.2",
 23              "typescript": "^5.7.2",
 24              "vite": "^6.0.0"
 25            }
 26    }
```

Figure 5-48. *Connect-style marko-run app example—package.json*

409

```json
tsconfig.json > ...
1  {
2      "include": ["src/**/*", "vite.config.ts", ".marko-run/*"],
3      "compilerOptions": {
4        "rootDir": "./",
5        "outDir": "./dist",
6        "noImplicitOverride": false,
7        "lib": ["DOM", "DOM.Iterable", "ESNext"],
8        "strict": true,
9        "target": "ESNext",
10       "module": "ESNext",
11       "sourceMap": false,
12       "composite": true,
13       "incremental": true,
14       "stripInternal": true,
15       "noUnusedLocals": true,
16       "isolatedModules": true,
17       "esModuleInterop": true,
18       "resolveJsonModule": true,
19       "moduleResolution": "bundler",
20       "noUnusedParameters": true,
21       "allowUnusedLabels": false,
22       "noImplicitReturns": false,
23       "emitDeclarationOnly": true,
24       "allowUnreachableCode": false,
25       "noFallthroughCasesInSwitch": true,
26       "allowSyntheticDefaultImports": true,
27       "forceConsistentCasingInFileNames": true,
28       "skipLibCheck": true
29     }
30  }
```

Figure 5-49. *Ts config*

```typescript
vite.config.ts > [∅] default
1  import { defineConfig } from "vite";
2  import marko from "@marko/run/vite";
3  import nodeAdapter from "@marko/run-adapter-node";
4
5  export default defineConfig({
6    plugins: [marko({ adapter: nodeAdapter() })]
7  });
```

Figure 5-50. *Vite config*

410

```
src > routes > ≡ +page.marko > 🔧 main
1    style {
2      main {
3        background: ■lightcyan;
4      }
5    }
6
7    class {
8      onMount() {
9        console.log('Mounted home')
10     }
11   }
12
13   <main>
14     <h1>Home</h1>
15   </main>
```

Figure 5-51. *src/routes/+page.marko*

```
src > routes > JS +middleware.js > ⊘ default
1    export default async function ({ request, url, meta }, next) {
2      const requestName = `${request.method} ${url.href}`;
3      let success = true;
4      console.log(`${requestName} request started`, { meta });
5      const startTime = performance.now();
6      try {
7        return await next();
8      } catch (err) {
9        success = false;
10       throw err;
11     } finally {
12       console.log(
13         `${requestName} completed ${
14           success ? "successfully" : "with errors"
15         } in ${performance.now() − startTime}ms`,
16       );
17     }
18   }
```

Figure 5-52. *src/routes+middleware.js*

411

```
src > routes > {} +meta.json > ...
  1    {
  2        "name": "foo"
  3    }
```

Figure 5-53. *src/routes/+meta.json*

```
src > routes > JS +handler.js > ⊗ GET
  1    export function POST() {
  2        return new Response("posted", { status: 200 });
  3    }
  4
  5    export function GET(_, next) {
  6      console.log(`'/' route GET handler`);
  7      return next();
  8    }
```

Figure 5-54. *src/routes/+handler.js*

```
src > routes > ☰ +404.marko > 🔧 main
  1    <main>
  2      <h1>Custom Not Found Page</h1>
  3      <a href="/">Go home</a>
  4    </>
```

Figure 5-55. *src/routes/+404.marko*

```
src > routes > ☰ +500.marko > 🔧 main
  1    <main>
  2      <h1>Custom Error Page</h1>
  3      <pre>${(input.error as Error).stack}</pre>
  4    </main>
```

Figure 5-56. *src/routes/+500.marko*

```
src > routes > ☰ +layout.marko > 🔧 html
 1    style {
 2      body {
 3        margin: 0;
 4        min-height: 100vh;
 5        display: flex;
 6        flex-direction: column;
 7        flex: 0 0 100%;
 8      }
 9
10      header {
11        background: ■pink;
12        padding: 1rem;
13      }
14
15      footer {
16        background: ■lightgray;
17        padding: 1rem;
18        margin-top: auto;
19      }
20
21      main {
22        padding: 1rem;
23      }
24    }
25
26    <!doctype html>
27    <html lang="en">
28      <head>
29        <meta charset="UTF-8">
30        <meta
31          name="description"
32          content="An example application showcasing Vite & Marko."
33        >
34        <meta name="viewport" content="width=device-width, initial-scale=1.0">
35        <title>@marko/run - Node Express</title>
36      </head>
37      <body>
38        <header>
39          <nav>
40            <a href="/">Home</a>
41            <a href="/users">Users</a>
42            <a href="/other/some/deep/path">Other</a>
43            <a href="/nowhere">Nowhere</a>
44          </nav>
45        </header>
46        <${input.renderBody} />
47        <footer>
48          <small>Footer</small>
49        </footer>
50      </body>
51    </html>
```

Figure 5-57. *src/routes/+layout.marko*

```
src > routes > other > $$rest > ≡ +page.marko > 🔧 main
1    <main>
2      <h1>Other</h1>
3      <p>Rest parameter matched <code>${$global.params.rest}</code></p>
4    </main>
```

Figure 5-58. *src/routes/other/$$rest/+page.marko*

```
src > routes > other > $$rest > TS +handler.ts > ...
1    export const GET: MarkoRun.Handler = ({ request }, next) => {
2      return request.headers.get("Accept")?.includes("text/html")
3        ? next()
4        : new Response(null, { status: 404 });
5    };
```

Figure 5-59. *src/routes/other/$$rest/+handler.ts*

```
src > routes > _two > users > foo > ≡ +page.marko > 🔧 p
1    <p>
2    This user page is in a different directory
3    than the other users pages and doesn't share a layout.
4    </p>
```

Figure 5-60. *src/routes/_two/users/foo/+page.marko*

```
src > routes > _one > users > ☰ +page.marko > 🔧 ul
   1    class {
   2      onMount() {
   3        console.log('Mounted users list')
   4      }
   5    }
   6
   7    <h2>User List</h2>
   8    <ul>
   9      <li><a href="users/234">John</a></li>
  10      <li><a href="users/451">Bob</a></li>
  11      <li><a href="users/986">Jane</a></li>
  12      <li><a href="users/foo">foo</a></li>
  13    </ul>
```

Figure 5-61. *src/routes/_one/users/+page.marko*

```
src > routes > _one > users > ☰ +layout.marko > 🔧 main
   1    <main>
   2      <h1>Users</h1>
   3      <${input.renderBody} />
   4    </main>
```

Figure 5-62. *src/routes/_one/users/+layout.marko*

```
src > routes > _one > users > components > thing > ☰ index.marko > 🔧 span
   1    <span>
   2      Hello
   3    </span>
```

Figure 5-63. *src/routes/_one/users/components/thing/index.marko*

```
src > routes > _one > users > $id >  ☰ +layout.marko > 🔧 div
1    <div>
2        <p>start</p>
3        <${input.renderBody}/>
4        <p>end</p>
5    </div>
```

Figure 5-64. *src/routes/_one/users/$id/+layout.marko*

```
src > routes > _one > users > $id > JS +middleware.js > 🝏 default
1    export default function ({ params }) {
2        if (parseInt(params.id, 10) % 2) {
3            throw new Error("An error thrown by middleware");
4        }
5    }
```

Figure 5-65. *src/routes/_one/users/$id/+middleware.js*

```
src > routes > _one > users > $id >  ☰ +page.marko > 🔧 div
1    <div>User Id = ${$global.params.id}</div>
```

Figure 5-66. *src/routes/_one/users/$id/+page.marko*

Now, next is the server entry file, which you would not have seen in the marko-run non-connect-style app, seen previously.

```
src > TS index.ts > [∅] __dirname
  1  import { routerMiddleware } from "@marko/run-adapter-node/middleware";
  2  import compressionMiddleware from "compression";
  3  import express from "express";
  4  import path from "path";
  5  import url from "url";
  6
  7  const __dirname = path.dirname(url.fileURLToPath(import.meta.url));
  8
  9  const { NODE_ENV = "development", PORT = 3000 } = process.env;
 10
 11  console.time("Start");
 12
 13  express()
 14    .use(compressionMiddleware())
 15    .use("/assets", express.static(path.join(__dirname, "assets")))
 16    .use(routerMiddleware())
 17    .listen(PORT, () => {
 18      console.log("listening");
 19      console.timeEnd("Start");
 20      console.log(`Env: ${NODE_ENV}`);
 21      console.log(`Address: http://localhost:${PORT}`);
 22  });
```

Figure 5-67. *src/index.ts*

This is how *@marko/run-adapter-node* is hooked into the Express Node setup.
You will notice that the folder routing directory structure continues to adhere to the
marko-run nomenclature and standard of things while still getting it to work with
Express and its connect-style middleware. Same as before, the three commands—**build**,
dev, and **preview**—exist here, and you can use them to run the app or preview it in
production mode.

Figure 5-68. *Project output*

Also, in this setup, same as before, you can set a property on ***globalThis*** to hold the resource server URL path (after uploading the generated assets to the resource server, maybe through a script or command which is executed after *npm run build*—that generates the assets for production mode). Marko and Vite are notified of this custom property name via the **basePathVar** option in the marko Vite plugin options within *vite. config.js*.

The obtained resource server URL path from the upload action is usually written into a file. While setting the value of the said property on ***globalThis***, the URL is read off the said file.

Conclusion

In this chapter, we have thus completed learning about the Marko-run meta framework that supercharges developer productivity and helps you focus on building Marko apps fast. In the subsequent chapters, we shall look at developer experience with Marko.

CHAPTER 6

Marko Ecosystem and Developer Experience

Introduction

In the previous chapters, we have learned about Marko, its unique features, and its meta framework marko-run. We saw how this makes developing Marko applications a breeze. In this chapter, we will delve deeper into the developer experience when using Marko and its ecosystem of plugins that power its seamless developer experience. For this, we will look at its plumbing with some of the most common developer tooling and tasks, essential for every framework today. These include

1. Authoring stories for Marko components using Storybook

2. Linting setup for Marko

3. TypeScript setup for Marko projects and writing Typed Marko code along with type checking Marko templates through its type checker CLI

4. Prettier as the formatter to quickly format Marko projects

5. Stylelint setup to lint for styles

6. PostCSS setup

7. Debugging Marko code

8. Introducing eBay's battle-tested core-ui component library suite that is also tested for accessibility compliance

9. Briefly looking into using Tailwind and CSS modules

© Damodaran Chingleput Sathyakumar 2025
D. Chingleput Sathyakumar, *Practical Marko*, https://doi.org/10.1007/979-8-8688-1483-9_6

While these are essential for the everyday developer in terms of quickly formatting the code to a said common style, easily previewing components during development and Lint checking of the code, they do not encompass the entire list. The two other items in this list, much needed for a great developer experience, are

1.   Being able to unit test Marko components

2.   Rapidly bootstrap and develop Marko applications
     (with hot module reloads)

In Chapter 7, we will look at testing marko components (#2) in detail. We have already seen how we can rapidly bootstrap and develop Marko applications in Chapter 5 (#1) through its meta framework marko-run. Given the prevalence of TypeScript and its popularity, we will be discussing all of the setups in the upcoming examples by incorporating TypeScript.

Note that while every bit of effort has been made here to have a working example, to get you going, the tooling land of Javascript is always evolving with potential breaking changes or entirely new set of tools or the related plumbing for them to play well together. So, it is possible that these examples get outdated pretty quickly. However, with Marko offering full support to play with Vite, you should always be able to find related plugins that work well with Vite and Marko to get you going or reach out to the ever-available Marko dev team.

PostCSS and CSS Modules

Scoped CSS refers to styling that is restricted to a specific component, preventing styles from unintentionally affecting other parts of the application. It's commonly used in component-based view JS frameworks where styles are automatically scoped to the component's DOM and requires support from the framework. CSS Modules, on the other hand, are a more explicit approach that are used in accordance with the bundler— like in Webpack-/ Vite-based setups. They compile CSS files into unique class names (e.g., button__3Xz8) to achieve isolation. While both aim to avoid global style conflicts, scoped CSS is often more declarative and seamless within frameworks, whereas CSS Modules provide a more programmatic, tooling-based isolation method. Also, only CSS Modules allow for access to class names within JavaScript via an exported object (made available when importing the scoped css source).

While the current version 5 of Marko doesn't allow for scoped CSS (`https://github.com/marko-js/marko/issues/666`), you can achieve it via CSS modules (scoped CSS for Marko lands in v6). In this simple example, we will look at CSS modules. CSS Modules achieve scoping by generating unique class names for each CSS rule within a module. This ensures that even if you use the same class name in different modules, the styles will not conflict because the generated class names will be different. The benefits of using CSS Modules include

- **Prevents CSS Conflicts**: By scoping styles locally, CSS Modules avoid the common problem of styles from one component accidentally affecting other parts of the application.

- **Improved Code Organization**: CSS Modules encourage a more modular and maintainable approach to styling, as styles are grouped with the components they belong to.

- **Easier Debugging**: When styles are scoped locally, it's easier to identify the source of styling issues and fix them.

- **Enhanced Reusability**: CSS Modules allow you to reuse the same class names in different modules without worrying about conflicts.

For this, let's spin up a marko-run app by scaffolding it via the **npx @marko/create** and choosing the **basic-ts** template as we have seen in earlier examples. To enable the usage of PostCSS, first install the following plugins postcss-auto-modules postcss-cli. This is illustrated in Figure 6-1.

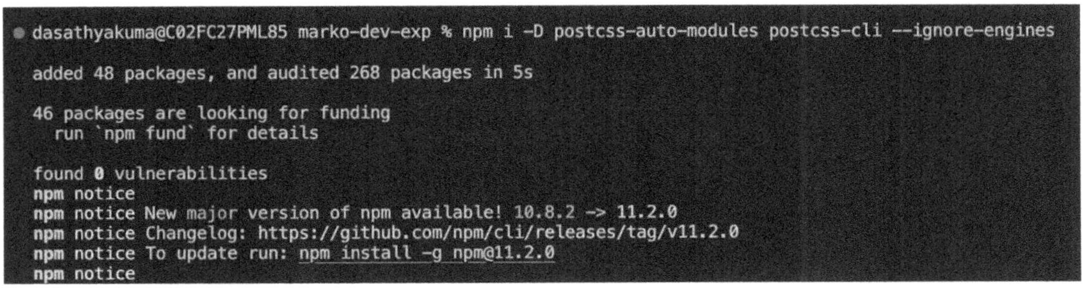

Figure 6-1. *Installing PostCSS dependencies for enabling CSS modules*

Following this, add a *.postcssrc.json* file to the project root as shown in Figure 6-2.

```
{} .postcssrc.json > ...
  1   {
  2        "$schema": "https://json.schemastore.org/postcssrc.json",
  3        "plugins": {
  4          "postcss-auto-modules": {}
  5        }
  6   }
  7
```

Figure 6-2. *Installing PostCSS dependencies for enabling CSS modules*

Next, let's add a new page to this marko-run app that can be accessed at /playground. For this, let's add a "playground" folder under src/routes/playground. Inside this, let's include a +page.marko file with the contents in Figure 6-3.

```
src > routes > playground >  +page.marko > count-down-timer
  1     <count-down-timer start=55/>
```

Figure 6-3. *Adding a +page.marko under src/routes/playground*

Next, let's add this component **<count-down-timer>** to the **src/components** folder.

```
src > components > count-down-timer >  index.marko > div
  1     import style from "./styles.module.css";
  2     <div>
  3         <h1>Countdown Timer</h1>
  4         <p>Timer originaly began from ${input.start}</p>
  5         <p class=style.test>${state.timeLeft} seconds remaining</p>
  6         <!-- Reset the counter as long as count is not 0 -->
  7         <button on-click("resetCounter")>
  8             ${(state.timeLeft === 0) ? "Restart counter" : "Reset counter"}
  9         </button>
 10     </div>
```

Figure 6-4. *Adding the count-down-timer under src/components/count-down-timer*

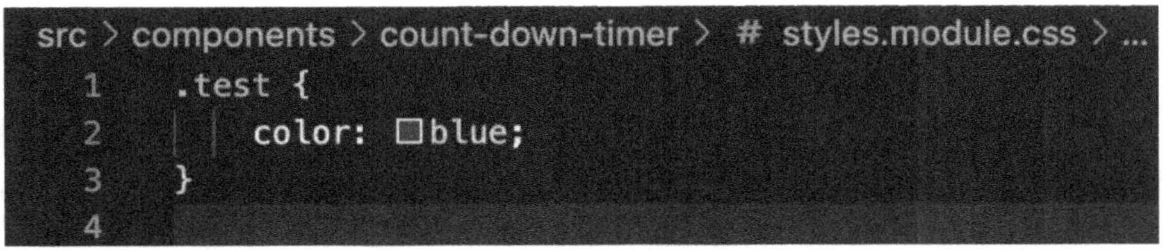

```
src > components > count-down-timer > # styles.module.css > ...
1     .test {
2         color: ☐blue;
3     }
4
```

Figure 6-5. *Adding a style file to the count-down-timer under src/components/ count-down-timer*

Notice the important line in Figure 6-4, at the top of the file, line 1:

```
import style from './styles.module.css';
```

and how the styles are accessed in line 5:

```
<p class=style.test
```

This line basically pulls in the associated styles.modules.css file. In earlier examples, you may have noticed that we never explicitly imported the style file into the template. As long as they co-existed and followed the naming convention as mentioned in Chapter 4, it just worked. However, now with scoped css as there are behind the scenes transformations involved with PostCSS and Vite, we explicitly include them. Let's next include the associated *component.ts* file as shown in Figure 6-6.

```
src > components > count-down-timer > TS component.ts > •O State
1    export interface State {
2        timeLeft: number;
3    };
4
5    export interface Input {
6        start: number;
7    };
8
9    export default class extends Marko.Component<Input, State> {
10       timerId: NodeJS.Timeout | undefined;
11       onCreate() {
12           this.state = {
13               timeLeft: 0
14           }
15       }
16       onInput(input:Input) {
17           this.state.timeLeft = input.start || 0;
18       }
19       beginCounter() {
20           this.timerId = setInterval(() => {
21               if (this.state.timeLeft === 0) {
22                   if (this.timerId !== null && this.timerId !== undefined) {
23                       clearInterval(this.timerId);
24                   }
25               } else {
26                   this.state.timeLeft = this.state.timeLeft - 1;
27               }
28           }, 1000);
29       }
30       onMount() {
31           this.beginCounter();
32       }
33       resetCounter () {
34           if (this.timerId !== null && this.timerId !== undefined) {
35               this.emit("reset");
36               clearInterval(this.timerId);
37           }
38           this.state.timeLeft = this.input.start;
39           this.beginCounter();
40       }
41   }
```

Figure 6-6. *Adding the component.ts file to the count-down-timer under src/ components/count-down-timer*

To recap, we have installed PostCSS dependencies, added a config file for PostCSS, built a component, and included it in our sample page. Now let's start the app via **npm run dev** and then access the page at http://localhost:3000/playground.

Figure 6-7. *The page is up!*

You can see in Figure 6-7 that the page with our sample component and post css-powered CSS modules that achieve scoped CSS is up. You will no longer see the original CSS class name .test that was used within the component **<simple-counter-marko>** on the <p> tag. Instead, you will see a scrambled version of it—something like **_test_1bx7o_1**. And the styles are properly applied.

You can also view the source maps for this by setting css : { devSourcemap: true } in the vite config file as shown in Figure 6-8.

```ts
vite.config.ts > [@] default
1   import { defineConfig } from "vite";
2   import marko from "@marko/run/vite";
3
4   // https://vite.dev/config/
5   export default defineConfig({
6     plugins: [marko()],
7     css: {
8       devSourcemap: true,
9     },
10  });
```

Figure 6-8. *Vite config for css source maps*

Doing this and restarting your dev server, you will be able to see the source maps for the CSS modules generated output via PostCSS.

Figure 6-9. *CSS source maps*

Click the styles.module.css in the developer tools (it is hyperlinked) and it will take you to the source-mapped output which will recreate the original css. This is shown in Figure 6-10.

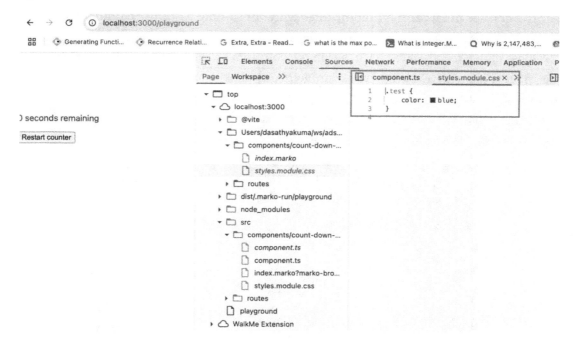

Figure 6-10. *Linked original file via CSS source maps*

To recap, a CSS Module is a CSS file. But all its associated class names and animation names are scoped locally to the component by default. All URLs (url(...)) and *@imports* are in module request format (./xxx and ../xxx mean relative, and xxx and xxx/yyy mean in modules folder, i.e., in node_modules). When importing a CSS Module into a JavaScript module, the setup exports a plain JS object with all mappings from local names to the scoped global names. This is why you are able to access it as styles.<property>.

One thing you may have noticed in Figure 6-4 is the squiggly lines for line #1:

```
import style from './styles.module.css';
```

This is because TypeScript isn't able to recognize this. To fix this, we will declare this as a module. For this, let's include a *types.d.ts* file under the src/ folder as shown in Figure 6-11A.

```
src > TS types.d.ts > ...
1    declare module "*.css" {
2        const content: { [className: string]: string };
3        export default content;
4    }
```

Figure 6-11A. *Including a types file with a declared module to handle TS errors for CSS modules*

After this, you will notice that there are no TS complaints by VS Code. This can be seen in Figure 6-11B.

```
src > components > count-down-timer > ≡ index.marko > 🔧 div
1    import style from "./styles.module.css";
2    <div>
3        <h1>Countdown Timer</h1>
4        <p>Timer originaly began from ${input.start}</p>
5        <p class=style.test>${state.timeLeft} seconds remaining</p>
6        <!-- Reset the counter as long as count is not 0 -->
7        <button on-click("resetCounter")>
8            ${(state.timeLeft === 0) ? "Restart counter" : "Reset counter"}
9        </button>
10   </div>
```

Figure 6-11B. *No more CSS Modules related TS errors*

Tailwind

Next will be the use of Tailwind. A very popular framework for authoring CSS in the web developer community. You will find all the popular view frameworks having their integrations with Tailwind. Marko can also be made to work with tailwind, and we will see that in the upcoming sections.

To get our Marko setup working with tailwind, we have a couple of plugins to install. These include "**tailwindcss**" and "**@tailwindcss/vite**". This is installed as shown in Figure 6-12.

```
○ dasathyakuma@C02FC27PML85 marko-dev-exp %
● dasathyakuma@C02FC27PML85 marko-dev-exp % npm i tailwindcss @tailwindcss/vite --ignore-engines

added 11 packages, and audited 279 packages in 15s

48 packages are looking for funding
  run `npm fund` for details

found 0 vulnerabilities
npm notice
npm notice New major version of npm available! 10.8.2 -> 11.2.0
npm notice Changelog: https://github.com/npm/cli/releases/tag/v11.2.0
npm notice To update run: npm install -g npm@11.2.0
npm notice
◇ dasathyakuma@C02FC27PML85 marko-dev-exp % []
```

Figure 6-12. *Installing tailwind dependencies*

Once this is done, let's update our Vite configs to include tailwind as shown in Figure 6-13.

```
⚡ vite.config.ts > ...
1   import { defineConfig } from "vite";
2   import marko from "@marko/run/vite";
3   import tailwindcss from '@tailwindcss/vite';
4
5   // https://vite.dev/config/
6   export default defineConfig({
7     plugins: [
8       tailwindcss(),
9       marko()
10    ],
11    css: {
12      devSourcemap: true,
13    },
14  });
```

Figure 6-13. *Vite configs updated with tailwind plugins*

Next, let's update some existing codes to use tailwind. For this, let's include a +*page. style.css* file, the src/routes/_index/ directory as shown in Figure 6-14, and update the existing code in +*page.marko* to use some classes from tailwind as shown in Figure 6-15.

```
src > routes > _index > # +page.style.css > img.logo
1    @import "tailwindcss";
2
3    .container {
4        display:flex;
5        flex-direction: column;
6        justify-content: center;
7        align-items: center;
8        font-size: clamp(1em, 2vw, 2em);
9        padding: 1em;
10       box-sizing: border-box;
11       height:100%;
12       width:100%;
13   }
14   img.logo {
15       width:12em;
16   }
```

Figure 6-14. *Moving the styles in src/routes/_index/+page.marko to this file and importing tailwind*

```
src > routes > _index > +page.marko > div > header > img
1    <div.container>
2      <header>
3        <img.logo src="./logo.svg" alt="Marko"/>
4      </header>
5      <h1 class="text-3xl font-bold underline" style="color: black">
6        Hello world!
7      </h1>
8      <main>
9        <p>Edit <code>./src/routes/_index/+page.marko</code> and save to reload.</p>
10       <a href="https://markojs.com/docs/getting-started">
11         Learn Marko
12       </a>
13     </main>
14   </div>
15   <mouse-mask/>
16
17 > <!-- style {…
32   } -->
```

Figure 6-15. *Including a <h1> tag with some css classes belonging to tailwind*

Note that the style block is commented out. It has been moved into a separate file as shown in Figure 6-16.

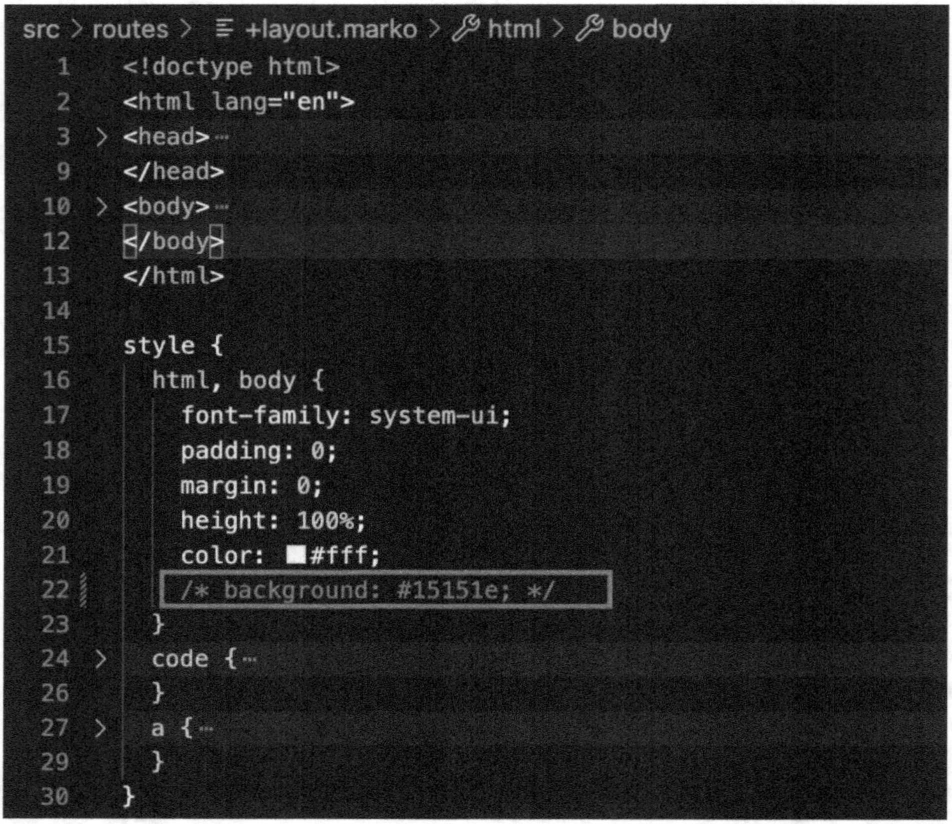

```
src > routes >  ≡ +layout.marko >  🔧 html >  🔧 body
 1      <!doctype html>
 2      <html lang="en">
 3  >   <head> ⋯
 9      </head>
10  >   <body> ⋯
12      </body>
13      </html>
14
15      style {
16        html, body {
17          font-family: system-ui;
18          padding: 0;
19          margin: 0;
20          height: 100%;
21          color: ■#fff;
22          /* background: #15151e; */
23        }
24  >     code { ⋯
26        }
27  >     a { ⋯
29        }
30      }
```

Figure 6-16. *In src/routes/+layout.marko, comment out the background css property*

Now start the dev server by running npm run dev in the terminal. This will bring up the page as shown in Figure 6-17. Notice the bold heading text "**Hello world!**". Once this is loaded, open up the developer tools of your browser to inspect the text, and you will find the classes from Tailwind being applied. This is indicated in Figure 6-18.

Figure 6-17. *The sample page with tailwind on it is loaded*

Figure 6-18. *Tailwind CSS and its classes are applied on to elements*

Notice that when using tailwind you can augment your CSS classes to be namespaced via the BEM (Block-Element-Modifier) syntax which also helps scope the CSS and avoid global collisions.

Marko and TypeScript

Marko offers a seamless developer experience with TypeScript. We have seen this briefly in Chapter 5, with Marko Run, where TS was discussed in the context of Marko-run. However, in this section, we will look deeper into how TS works with Marko itself in terms of components. This includes the following:

- Editor error checking when using VS Code.

- Refactoring is therefore less of a hassle.

- Verification if the data matches expectations.

- Helps with API design.

- Aids in autocompletion when using marko-tag.json descriptor files (seen in Chapter 4).

There are two ways to use TS in a given Marko project:

1. **When Building a Marko App:** When you're building an app, with marko-run and scaffolded from the **library-ts** template/starter, you will notice a **tsconfig.json** file already included at the project root. If you noticed the app we have scaffolded, you will notice the **tsconfig.json** as shown in Figure 6-19.

2. **When Building Marko Tag Library Packages:** The second way is when you are building a custom Marko tag library and you want to publish this as a package of Marko tags. Normally, you would do that by scaffolding the starter with the **library-ts**. In that case, include "script-lang": "ts" in your **marko.json** descriptor file. Doing so will automatically expose type checking and autocomplete for published tags.

```
TS tsconfig.json > ...
  1    {
  2      "include": ["src/**/*"],
  3      "compilerOptions": {
  4        "allowSyntheticDefaultImports": true,
  5        "lib": ["dom", "ESNext"],
  6        "module": "ESNext",
  7        "moduleResolution": "bundler",
  8        "noEmit": true,
  9        "noImplicitOverride": true,
 10        "noUnusedLocals": true,
 11        "outDir": "dist",
 12        "resolveJsonModule": true,
 13        "skipLibCheck": true,
 14        "strict": true,
 15        "target": "ESNext",
 16        "verbatimModuleSyntax": true
 17      }
 18    }
```

Figure 6-19. *TS config use in our projects*

This is a configuration file for the TypeScript compiler (tsc). It tells TypeScript how to compile your code, what rules to enforce, and which files to include or exclude. Let's break down what each part of this specific configuration means:

1. **"include"**: [*"src/**/*"*]:

   a. Specifies which files the TypeScript compiler should process.

   b. "src/**/*" means "include all files (with any extension) in the **src** directory and all its subdirectories."

   c. The ****** is a wildcard for any subdirectory, and * matches any file name.

2. **"compilerOptions"**: This section defines how TypeScript should compile your code and what rules to apply. The following properties are used:

    a. **"allowSyntheticDefaultImports"**: *true*

        i. Allows you to use default ES imports even if the module doesn't explicitly export a default value. This is useful for compatibility with tools like Webpack/Vite or when working with libraries (e.g., CommonJS modules) that don't have explicit default exports.

    b. **"lib"**: *["dom", "ESNext"]*

        i. Specifies the built-in TypeScript libraries (type definitions) to include

        1. "dom": Includes type definitions for browser APIs (e.g., document and window).

        2. "ESNext": Includes the latest ECMAScript features (e.g., modern JavaScript APIs like Promise, Map, etc.). This means your code can use both browser-specific APIs and cutting-edge JavaScript features.

    c. **"module"**: *"ESNext"*

        i. Defines the module system for the compiled output. "ESNext" uses the latest ECMAScript module syntax (e.g., **import** and **export**), which is typically used with modern bundlers like **Vite**, **Rollup**, or **ESbuild**.

    d. **"moduleResolution"**: *"bundler"*

        i. Specifies how TypeScript resolves module imports. **"bundler"** is a modern strategy optimized for tools like **Vite**, **Rollup**, or **Webpack**. It assumes the bundler will handle module resolution, allowing for more flexible import paths (e.g., omitting file extensions or resolving *package.json* fields like "**exports**").

    e. **"noEmit"**: *true*

        i. Tells TypeScript not to generate output files (e.g., .js files). This is common in projects where a separate tool (like a bundler) handles the compilation, and TypeScript is only used for type checking.

434

f. "**noImplicitOverride**": *true*

   i. Requires explicit use of the **override** keyword when a
       subclass method overrides a parent class method. Helps
       catch errors where you accidentally override a method
       without intending to.

g. "**noUnusedLocals**": *true*

   i. Flags an error if you declare a local variable or parameter
       but don't use it. Encourages cleaner code by preventing
       unused variables.

h. "**outDir**": "*dist*"

   i. Specifies the output directory for compiled files (e.g.,
       .js files). In this case, output would go to the **dist** folder.
       However, since "**noEmit**": **true** is also set, this option is
       effectively ignored unless **noEmit** is overridden.

i. "**resolveJsonModule**": *true*

   i. Allows importing *.json* files as modules (e.g., import
       data from './data.json'). TypeScript will also provide type
       checking for the JSON content.

j. "**skipLibCheck**": *true*

   i. Skips type checking of declaration files (**.d.ts**) from libraries.
       Speeds up compilation by avoiding checks on external
       libraries, which is useful if you trust the libraries or want
       faster builds.

k. "**strict**": *true*

   i. Enables all strict type-checking options (e.g., *noImplicitAny*,
       strictNullChecks, *strictFunctionTypes*, etc.). Enforces
       rigorous type safety, reducing the chance of runtime errors
       but requiring more explicit type annotations.

l. **"target"**: *"ESNext"*

i. Specifies the JavaScript version to compile to. *"ESNext"* targets the latest ECMAScript standard, meaning the output will use modern JavaScript syntax. This is often paired with a bundler or runtime that supports these features.

m. **"verbatimModuleSyntax"**: *true*

i. Enforces stricter rules for module syntax. Requires **imports** and **exports** to follow exact ESM (ECMAScript Module) rules, disallowing some CommonJS-specific patterns. This ensures compatibility with modern JavaScript runtimes and tools.

TL;DR;

– This *tsconfig.json* informs TS that this project uses a bundler (e.g., Vite in our case) instead of TypeScript's own compiler for output.

– Targets the latest JavaScript features (*ESNext*) for both input and output.

– Enforces strict type safety (**strict**) and clean code practices (*noUnusedLocals, noImplicitOverride*).

– Works in a browser environment (**dom**) with modern JavaScript features (**ESNext**).

– Includes all TypeScript files in the **src** directory and its subdirectories.

– Allows **JSON** imports and synthetic default imports for flexibility with external modules.

– Since **"noEmit"**: true is set, this setup is used for type checking only, with Vite handling the actual compilation and output.

One of the first things we will do is letting others know how our component (locally within a project) works. For this, we would be required to let TS know about what the tag takes as input props. Let's look at the **<count-down-timer/>** component in our current project. For this, any *.marko* file will use an exported **Input** type for that file's **input** object. This can be

- export type Input or

- export interface Input.

While this can be defined either in **Component.ts** or the **index.marko** files, it's always better to place them in the template (***index.marko***) file. Also, avoid placing them in both places as it would cause unnecessary issues when type checking.

Same as Input, the State also can be typed in a similar fashion. For this, any *.marko* file will use an exported **Input** type for that file's **input** object. This can be

- type State or

- interface State.

Note that there is no **export** here for the **State** type. The state is private to the component, and there is no need to export it. This is shown in Figure 6-20. In this figure, you will notice that the types are placed within the **component.ts** file. This is how you would do it for multi-file components. For single-file components where the *class { }* and template are in the same file, we declare State on the class itself. This is shown in Figure 6-21.

```
src > components > count-down-timer > TS component.ts > ⌂ default > ⊙ onCreate > 🔧 timeLeft
 1    interface State {
 2        timeLeft: number;
 3    };
 4
 5    export interface Input {
 6        start: number;
 7    };
 8
 9    export default class extends Marko.Component<Input, State> {
10        timerId: NodeJS.Timeout | undefined;
11        onCreate() {
12            this.state = {
13                timeLeft: 0
14            }
15        }
16        onInput(input:Input) {
17            this.state.timeLeft = input.start || 0;
18        }
19        beginCounter() {
20            this.timerId = setInterval(() => {
21                if (this.state.timeLeft === 0) {
22                    if (this.timerId !== null && this.timerId !== undefined) {
23                        clearInterval(this.timerId);
24                    }
25                } else {
26                    this.state.timeLeft = this.state.timeLeft - 1;
27                }
28            }, 1000);
29        }
30        onMount() {
31            this.beginCounter();
32        }
33        resetCounter () {
34            if (this.timerId !== null && this.timerId !== undefined) {
35                this.emit("reset");
36                clearInterval(this.timerId);
37            }
38            this.state.timeLeft = this.input.start;
39            this.beginCounter();
40        }
41    }
```

Figure 6-20. *Using TS within Marko templates to export Input and type the State*

```
src > components > count-up-timer > ≡ index.marko > 🔧 div > 🔧 h1
 1    import style from "./styles.module.css";
 2
 3    export type Input = {
 4        start: number;
 5        end: number;
 6    }
 7
 8    class {
 9        declare state: { count: number};
10        timerId: NodeJS.Timeout | undefined;
11        onCreate() {
12            this.state = {
13                count: 0
14            }
15        }
16        onInput(input:Input) {
17            this.state.count = input.end - input.start || 0;
18        }
19        beginCounter() {
20            this.timerId = setInterval(() => {
21                if (this.state.count === this.input.end) {
22                    if (this.timerId !== null && this.timerId !== undefined) {
23                        clearInterval(this.timerId);
24                    }
25                } else {
26                    this.state.count = this.state.count + 1;
27                }
28            }, 1000);
29        }
30        onMount() {
31            this.beginCounter();
32        }
33        resetCounter () {
34            if (this.timerId !== null && this.timerId !== undefined) {
35                this.emit("reset");
36                clearInterval(this.timerId);
37            }
38            this.state.count = this.input.start;
39            this.beginCounter();
40        }
41    }
42
43    <div>
44        <h1 style={color: "black"}>Countdown Up Timer</h1>
45        <p style={color: "black"}>Timer originaly began from ${input.start}</p>
46        <p class=style.test>${state.count} seconds remaining</p>
47        <!-- Reset the counter as long as count is not 0 -->
48        <button on-click("resetCounter")>
49            ${(state.count === input.end) ? "Restart counter" : "Reset counter"}
50        </button>
51    </div>
```

Figure 6-21. *Using TS within Marko templates when doing single-file components*

When we import this tag **<count-up-timer>** into *src/routes/playground/+page. marko* file, you will notice that the TS is in accordance with the IDE errors out as shown in Figure 6-22.

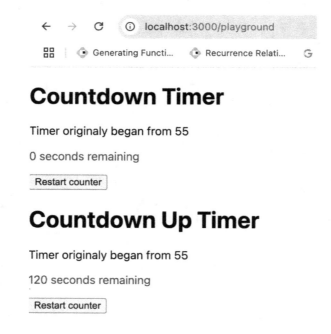

Figure 6-22. *TS works seamlessly with Marko components to notify missing input props*

Now, running this, you will see the output when you start the server via npm run dev and access the page at http://localhost:3000/playground.

Countdown Timer

Timer originaly began from 55

0 seconds remaining

Restart counter

Countdown Up Timer

Timer originaly began from 55

120 seconds remaining

Restart counter

Figure 6-23. *Count up and Count down timer*

So far, we have provided a way for consumers of our component to know what **Input** props our component accepts and so on. We have seen how TS works with the IDE and errors out if we dont pass the right Input props and their types. However, you can import the types exported from these index.marko files into other components and **.marko** files. This is shown in Figure 6-24, where you can **import** types and compose them to form **Union** types.

In our examples, since both <count-up-timer> and <count-down-timer> have the same start property, we can extend the Input of <count-down-timer> from within <count-up-timer>. This is shown in Figure 6-24.

```
src > components > count-up-timer >  ≡ index.marko > ...
  1    import { type Input as SimpleInput } from "../count-down-timer/index.marko";
  2    import style from "./styles.module.css";
  3
  4    export interface Input extends SimpleInput {
  5        end: number;
  6    }
  7
```

Figure 6-24. *Exporting and extending types*

Similar to typing **Input**, **State**, the **Marko Class**, and any other arguments within its lifecycle handlers, we can also type for the emitted events from these components. This is shown in Figure 6-25, where our **<count-up-timer>** that emitted a "**reset**" event when the "**Reset**" button was clicked now has its input including types for an optional event handler.

```
src > components > count-up-timer >  ≡ index.marko > ...
  1    import { type Input as SimpleInput } from "../count-down-timer/index.marko";
  2    import style from "./styles.module.css";
  3
  4    export interface Input extends SimpleInput {
  5        end: number;
  6        "on-reset"?: () => void;
  7    }
  8
```

Figure 6-25. *<count-up-timer> with typed handlers*

```
src > components > counter-wrapper > ☰ index.marko > ⅏ count-up-timer
  1    <count-down-timer start=100/>
  2    <count-up-timer start=1 end=59 on/>
                                    ⊘ on-reset?
                                    🔑 on<event>("<method>")?
                                    🔑 once<event>("<method>")?
```

Figure 6-26. *Typings for <count-up-timer> show the event handler*

In Figure 6-26, we have a sample component called **<counter-wrapper>** that attempts to use both the **<count-up-timer>** and **<count-down-timer>**, and you can see the IDE working with TS to showcase autocompletes for the possible optional event handler.

The next common use case in Marko components is handling body content. For this, we will see a basic example with a <fancy-label> component that takes in a heading and content to render it in a fancy way. This is shown in Figure 6-27.

```
src > components > fancy-label > ☰ index.marko > ⅏ .content
  1    export interface Input {
  2        heading: string;
  3        renderBody: Marko.Body
  4    }
  5
  6    style {
  7        .fancy {
  8            margin-top: 25px;
  9            border: 2px solid ▣chocolate;
 10            font-weight: 900;
 11        }
 12
 13        .title { color: ▣tomato;}
 14        .content { color: ☐saddlebrown;}
 15    }
 16
 17    <div.fancy>
 18        <div class="title">${input.heading}</div>
 19        <div.content>
 20            <${input.renderBody}/>
 21        </div>
 22    </div>
 23
```

Figure 6-27. *Typings for renderBody*

The output can be seen in Figure 6-28.

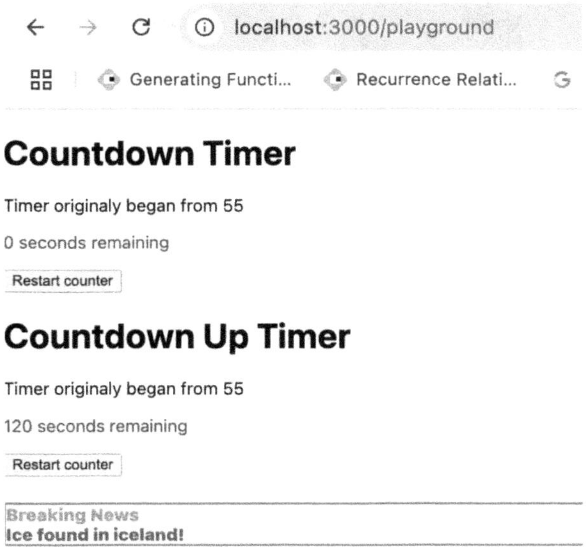

Figure 6-28. *Output for example using renderBody*

```marko
src > components > fake-tabs > ☰ index.marko > ...
 1  export type TabsEvent = {
 2      selectedIndex: number;
 3  }
 4  export interface Tab extends Omit<Marko.HTML.LI, `on${string}`> {}
 5  export interface Content extends Omit<Marko.HTML.Div, `on${string}`> {}
 6
 7  static interface FakeTabsInput {
 8      testid?: string;
 9      inputClass?: string;
10      selectedIndex?: number;
11      tab: Marko.AttrTag<Tab>;
12      content: Marko.AttrTag<Content>;
13      "on-select"?: (evt: TabsEvent) => void;
14  }
15
16  export interface Input extends FakeTabsInput {}
17
18  class {
19      declare state: { selectedIndex: number };
20      onInput(input: Input) {
21          this.state = {
22              selectedIndex: (input.selectedIndex || 0) as number
23          };
24      }
25      selectTab(index: number) {
26          this.setState("selectedIndex", index);
27          this.emit("select", {
28              selectedIndex: index
29          } as TabsEvent);
30      }
31  }
32  $ const {
33      inputClass,
34      tab: tabs = [],
35      content
36  } = input;
37
38  <div data-testid=input.testid class=["cdui fake-tabs", inputClass]>
39      <ul class="fake-tabs__items">
40          <for|tab, i| of=(tabs || [])>
41              $ const isSelected = state.selectedIndex === i;
42              $ const attrs: Record<string, string> = {};
43              $ if (isSelected) {
44                  attrs["aria-current"] = "true";
45              }
46              <li on-click("selectTab", i) class=[tab.class, "fake-tabs__item"]>
47                  <a ...attrs role="button">
48                      <${tab.renderBody}/>
49                  </a>
50              </li>
51          </for>
52      </ul>
53      <div class="fake-tabs__content">
54          <div class="fake-tabs__panel">
55              <div class="fake-tabs__cell">
56                  <div>
57                      <${content.renderBody}/>
58                  </div>
59              </div>
60          </div>
61      </div>
62  </div>
```

Figure 6-29. *<fake-tabs> component*

444

Next, we will see an example with a **<fake-tabs>** component. This is shown in Figure 6-29. One thing to note here is the namespace Marko being made globally available to all of Marko templates. This is why we are able to access **Marko.Body**, **Marko.Component**, etc. You can click them (they are hyperlinked) and access them to see in detail the type layout of Marko and various types it exposes. A partial portion of the same is replicated in Figure 6-30. You will find a similar one when hyperlinking **MarkoRun**.

```
Users > dasathyakuma > .vscode > extensions > marko-js.marko-vscode-1.5.20 > dist > TS marko.internal.d.ts > {} global > {} Marko
  1   // This is a typescript file which defines utilities used in the output of the typescript extractor.
  2   declare global {
  3     namespace Marko {
  4       export interface Directives {}
  5
  6       // Extend the Body type to keep track of what is yielded (used for scope hoisted types).
  7       export interface Body<
  8         in Params extends readonly any[] = [],
  9         out Return = void,
 10       > {
 11         (...params: Params): MarkoReturn<Return>;
 12       }
 13
 14       /**
 15        * Do not use or you will be fired.
 16        */
 17       namespace _ {
 18         export const voidReturn: MarkoReturn<void>;
 19         export const scope: unique symbol;
 20         export const out: Marko.Out;
 21         export const never: never;
 22         export const any: any;
 23
 24         export function getGlobal<Override>(
 25           override: Override
```

Figure 6-30. *A portion of Marko's type system*

Coming back to the **<fake-tabs>** component, it's a simple tab component, which takes in two attribute body tags **<@tab>** and **<@content>,** out of which <@tab> is repeatable and <@content> isn't. This can be seen from the way it's accessed from the input. The css for the same is included in Figure 6-32 as a style.css file. The output for the same can be seen in Figure 6-31.

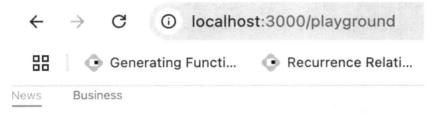

Figure 6-31. *Output of <fake-tabs>*

```
src > components > fake-tabs > # style.css > div.tabs__item[role="tab"] > span:after

1    .fake-tabs,
2    .tabs { margin-top: 16px; }
3    span.fake-tabs, span.tabs { display: inline-block; }
4    div.tabs__items[role="tablist"], ul.fake-tabs__items { font-size: 0.875rem; }
5    ul.fake-tabs__items { display: block; list-style: none; margin: 0; padding: 0; }
6    div.tabs__item[role="tab"] { cursor: default; }
7    div.tabs__item[role="tab"],
8    li.fake-tabs__item { display: inline-block; position: relative; -webkit-tap-highlight-color: ■#f7f7f7;}
9    div.tabs__item[role="tab"]:not(:last-child),
10   li.fake-tabs__item:not(:last-child) { margin-inline-end: 36px;}
11   li.fake-tabs__item > a { padding: 1px 0; text-decoration: none;}
12   div.tabs__item[role="tab"] > span { padding: 2px 0;}
13   div.tabs__item[role="tab"] > span,
14   li.fake-tabs__item > a { color: ■#707070; display: inline-block; }
15   div.tabs__item[role="tab"] > span:after,
16   li.fake-tabs__item > a:after { background-color: initial; border-radius: 6px;
17       content: ""; display: block; height: 2px; margin-top: 4px; position: absolute; width: 100%;}
18
19   div.tabs__item[role="tab"][aria-selected="true"] > span,
20   li.fake-tabs__item > a[aria-current] { color: ■darkgrey; }
21   div.tabs__item[role="tab"][aria-selected="true"] > span:after,
22   li.fake-tabs__item > a[aria-current]:after { background-color: ■grey; }
23   div.tabs__item[role="tab"]:focus:not(:focus-visible),
24   li.fake-tabs__item a:focus:not(:focus-visible) { outline: none;}
25   div.tabs__item[role="tab"]:not([aria-selected="true"]):focus > span,
26   div.tabs__item[role="tab"]:not([aria-selected="true"]):hover > span,
27   li.fake-tabs__item > a:not([aria-current]):focus,
28   li.fake-tabs__item > a:not([aria-current]):hover {
29       color: ■#707070;
30   }
31   div.tabs__item[role="tab"]:not([aria-selected="true"]):focus > span:after,
32   div.tabs__item[role="tab"]:not([aria-selected="true"]):hover > span:after,
33   li.fake-tabs__item > a:not([aria-current]):focus:after,
34   li.fake-tabs__item > a:not([aria-current]):hover:after {
35       background-color: currentColor;
36   }
37   .fake-tabs__cell,
38   .tabs__cell {
39       margin: 16px 0;
40   }
41   .fake-tabs__content {
42       color: □black;
43   }
```

Figure 6-32. *CSS for the <fake-tabs>*

When you look at Figure 6-29, line 36, where the **input** is accessed, **tab** will be accessed as "**tabs**" with **default as [ ]** and **content** will be accessed directly as **content**, indicating it's not repeating. Both **tab** and **content** props defined on the **Input** interface are of type Marko.AttrTag<Tab> and Marko.AttrTag<Content>, where Marko.AttrTag type is a generic type that now takes two different Input types—**Content** and **Tab** type.

Most importantly, Figure 6-33 showcases how we have used this tag in src/routes/playground/+page.marko.

```
src > routes > playground >  ≡ +page.marko > ...
 1    import type { TabsEvent } from "../../components/fake-tabs/index.marko";
 2    style {
 3        .m10 { margin-top: 10px;}
 4    }
 5
 6    class {
 7        declare state: { content: string }
 8        onCreate () {
 9            this.state = {
10                content: "This is the News Content"
11            }
12        }
13        changeTabContent(evt: TabsEvent) {
14            if(evt.selectedIndex === 0) {
15                this.state.content = "This is the News Content";
16            } else {
17                this.state.content = "This is the Business Content";
18            }
19        }
20    }
21
22    <!-- <count-down-timer start=55/>
23
24    <count-up-timer start=55 end=120/> -->
25
26    <!-- <fancy-label heading="Breaking News">
27        <div>
28            Ice found in iceland!
29        </div>
30    </fancy-label> -->
31
32    <fake-tabs inputClass="m10" on-select('changeTabContent') selectedIndex=0>
33        <@tab>News</@tab>
34        <@tab>Business</@tab>
35        <@content>${state.content}</@content>
36    </fake-tabs>
```

Figure 6-33. *Notice how we can even type the events being emitted*

As the tabs are clicked, the "**select**" event is emitted, which is listened by this parent as shown in Figure 6-33, in the *changeTabContent* method. Based on the **selectedIndex** found in the event, we switch the tab contents.

Note on some quirks: You can have the class { } exported from either the **index. marko** file or the **component.ts**. Don't try doing it in both places. It won't work. When you export the class { } from **component.ts** file, it will have to be a **default** export. There is no need to export the class { } when using it within the **index.marko** file. Export the **Input** from one place as well. In a similar way, you cannot have a style { } block and a style file. Only one is allowed.

In the same way as seen above, you can type tag parameters as well. Let's look at this with an example.

```
src > components > for-by-three >  ≡ index.marko > ⅔ for
1    export interface Input {
2      from: number;
3      to: number;
4      renderBody: Marko.Body<[number]>
5    }
6
7    <for|i| from=input.from to=input.to step=3>
8      <${input.renderBody}(i)/>
9    </for>
```

Figure 6-34. *A <for-by-three> component*

Including it in our src/routes/playground/+page.marko as shown in Figure 6-35, we have the following output as seen in Figure 6-36.

```
<for-by-three|index:number| from=10 to=20>
    <div>
        The number is ${index}
    </div>
</for-by-three>
```

Figure 6-35. *Including the <for-by-three> component*

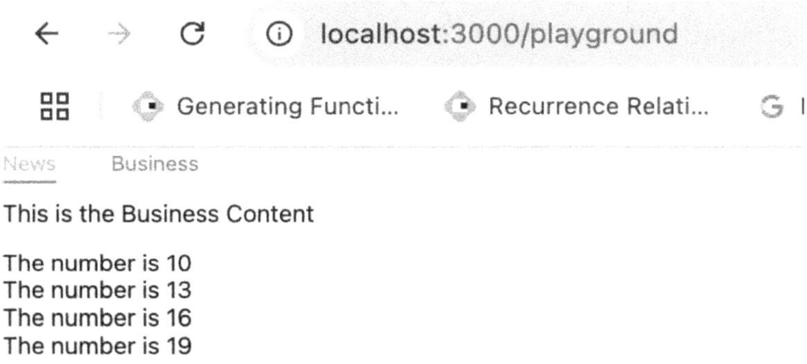

Figure 6-36. *Tag parameters output*

Some of the frequently used built-in Marko types that we previously saw in Figure 6-30 are listed below.

Built-in Marko type **Marko** exposes type definitions you can reuse in a TypeScript namespace called **Marko**:

1. **Marko.**Template<Input, Return>: The type of a **.marko** file. This is the *typeof* import("./template.marko") when importing a Marko template.

2. **Marko.**TemplateInput<Input>: The object accepted by the *.render* methods of a template. It includes the template's **Input** as well as **$global** values.

3. **Marko.**Body<Params, Return>: The type of the body content of a tag (**renderBody**).

4. **Marko.**Component<Input, State>: The base class for a class component. Every Marko component you will see will be extending this.

5. **Marko.**Renderable: Values accepted by the **<${dynamic}/>** tag. These include string | Marko.Template | **Marko.**Body | { renderBody: **Marko.**Body }.

6. **Marko.**Out: The render context which offers methods like *write*, *beginAsync*, etc. You will recall we used this as part of isomorphic progressive rendering. This is also the return type of template. render found as ReturnType<Template.render>.

7. **Marko.**Global: The type of the object in **$global** and **out.global** that can be passed to a template's render methods as the **$global** property. In Marko-run apps, the context is the same as **$global** and is typed as MarkoRun.context.

8. **Marko.**RenderResult: The result of rendering a Marko template. This is the return type ReturnType<template.renderSync>, Awaited<ReturnType<template.render>>.

9. **Marko.**Emitter: **EventEmitter** from **@types/node**. Every Marko component is an instance of the EventEmitter.

10. **Marko.**NativeTags: An object containing all native HTML tags and their associated types.

11. **Marko.**Input<TagName> and **Marko.**Return<TagName>: Helpers to extract the **Input** and **Return** types on native tags (when a string is passed) or a custom tag.

12. **Marko.**BodyParameters<Body> and **Marko.**BodyReturnType<Body>: Helpers to extract the parameters and return types from the specified **Marko.**Body.

13. **Marko.**AttrTag<**T**>: Used to represent types for attributes tags. A single attribute tag, with a [Symbol.iterator] to consume any repeated tags.

Coming back to our journey of types, you can extend and augment native HTML tags as well. This is seen in Figure 6-37 where we pull in the **Input** type of the native button HTML tag and use that (extend it) to build a fancy button.

```
src > components > fancy-button >  ≡ index.marko > 🔧 button
  1    export interface Input extends Marko.Input<"button"> {
  2      color: string;
  3      bgColor: string;
  4      renderBody?: Marko.Body;
  5    }
  6
  7    $ const { color, bgColor, renderBody, ...restOfInput } = input;
  8
  9    <button style=`color: ${color}; background-color: ${bgColor}` ...restOfInput>
 10      <${renderBody}/>
 11    </button>
```

Figure 6-37. *<fancy-button> builds upon by extending the native HTML button Input*

```
<fancy-button color="#FFF" bgColor="red">
    <span>Fancy Button!</span>
</fancy-button>
```

Figure 6-38. *Using the <fancy-button> within src/routes/ playground/+page.marko*

You can also register custom css properties. For example, within the same <fancy-button> we can register a custom CSS prop as shown in Figure 6-39.

```
src > components > fancy-button > ≡ index.marko > ...
  1    static declare global {
  2      namespace Marko {
  3        namespace CSS {
  4          interface Properties {
  5            // adds a support for a custom `--foo` css property.
  6            "--font-weight-casual"?: string;
  7          }
  8        }
  9      }
 10    }
 11
 12    style {
 13      .fancy-button {
 14        --font-weight-casual: ☐black;
 15        font-weight: var(--font-weight-casual);
 16      }
 17    }
```

Figure 6-39. *Registering custom CSS props*

This code extends Marko's own TypeScript type definitions to recognize custom CSS properties within Marko's ecosystem. Instead of modifying a generic *csstype* module (which is used by libraries like React), this targets Marko's specific Marko.CSS.Properties interface.

Here's why this matters:

- Marko has its own way of handling styles (via style { } blocks in .marko files or other styling mechanisms).

- By extending Marko.CSS.Properties, you ensure TypeScript understands your custom properties when they're used in Marko-specific contexts, like Marko templates or components.

The declare global syntax means it modifies the **global** TypeScript namespace, so it doesn't need to be imported—it's automatically available everywhere in your project once included. Because it's mentioned as declare global, this applies project wide. Any Marko component or TypeScript file in your project will recognize **--font-weight-casual** as a valid CSS property.

When using Marko with Custom Elements, you may want to register them as a new native tag. Let's look at this with an example, as shown in Figure 6-40.

```
src > components > fancy-label > ≡ index.marko > 🔧 div
 1    // @ts-check
 2  > export interface Input {…
 5    }
 6
 7    static interface MyCustomElementAttributes extends Marko.HTML.Div {
 8      // ...
 9    }
10
11    static declare global {
12      namespace Marko {
13        interface NativeTags {
14          // By adding this entry, you can now use `my-custom-element` as a native html tag.
15          "my-custom-element": MyCustomElementAttributes;
16        }
17      }
18    }
19
20  > style {…
29    }
30
31    <div.fancy>
32      <my-custom-element class="title">${input.heading}</my-custom-element>
33      <div.content>
34        <${input.renderBody}/>
35      </div>
36    </div>
```

Figure 6-40. *Registering custom elements as native tags*

When using Marko with custom HTML attributes, you can register them as well. This is shown with an example in Figure 6-41.

```
src > components > fancy-button > ≡ index.marko > button
  1 > static declare global {~
 10   }
 11
 12   static declare global {
 13     namespace Marko {
 14       interface HTMLAttributes {
 15         "track"?: string; // Adds this attribute as available on all HTML tags.
 16       }
 17     }
 18   }
 19
 20   style {
 21     .fancy-button {
 22       --font-weight-casual: □black;
 23       font-weight: var(--font-weight-casual);
 24     }
 25   }
 26
 27 > export interface Input extends Marko.Input<"button"> {~
 31   }
 32       (property) Marko.HTMLAttributes<T extends Element = Element>["track"]?: string | undefined
 33   $ const
 34       "track"?: string;
 35   button track="123.ptyu" style=`color: ${color}; background-color: ${bgColor}` ...restOfInput class="fancy-button">
 36     <${renderBody}/>
 37   </button>
```

Figure 6-41. *Registering custom HTML attributes*

Here, we have just included a "**track**" attribute to be present across HTML tags in our repo to include some tracking information. Marko autocompletes the same by working along with the IDE and the type system.

You can do type assertions as well, just as you would in normal TS code as shown in Figure 6-42A.

```
                                          const TEN: 10
static const TEN = 10 as const
                                          const TEN = 10 as const

<for-by-three index:number  from=TEN to=20>
    <div style="color: black">
        The number is ${index}
    </div>
</for-by-three>
```

Figure 6-42A. *Type assertions*

We have seen **inline Javascript and Static Javascript** in Chapter 4—Marko language and syntax. These are Javascript expressions. Any valid JS expression can be typed, which means all the JS codes in those blocks can also be typed.

Also, we can have Tag parameters and Tag arguments. This is shown with an example in Figures 6-42B and 6-42C, where we have a <print-and-log> component that prints the value on the page and logs the value on the console.

```
src > components > print-and-log > ≡ index.marko > 🔧 div
1    static type LoggerFunc<T> = (a: T) => string;
2
3    export interface Input<T> {
4      value: T;
5      renderBody: Marko.Body<[T]>;
6      process: LoggerFunc<T>;
7    }
8
9    <div style={color: "black"}>
10       <${input.renderBody}(input.value)/>
11       $ console.log(input.process(input.value));
12    </div>
```

Figure 6-42B. *Type parameters and arguments*

This can now be used in our src/routes/playground/+page.marko as shown in Figure 6-42C.

```
<print-and-log<number>|value: number| value=55 process(data: number){
    return `The processed data is ${data}`;
}>
    <div>
        The message is: ${value}
    </div>
</print-and-log>
```

Figure 6-42C. *Using type parameters and arguments*

Sometimes, engineers opt into TypeScript progressively, cautiously in the case of existing projects. Marko handles this by allowing for incremental typing via JSDoc.

After setting up TypeScript into the project through

1. Installing typescript

2. Installing @marko/type-check (for type checking Marko files)

3. Adding the tsconfig.json (configuration file for TS)

one can progressively implement type checking as well by

1. Setting // @ts-check to the top of any file that you want to be
   type checked

2. Setting // @ts-nocheck to the top of any file that you don't want to
   be type checked

If you want to enable type checking for all Marko and JavaScript files in a JavaScript project, you can switch to using a jsconfig.json (`https://www.typescriptlang.org/docs/handbook/tsconfig-json.html#using-tsconfigjson-or-jsconfigjson`).

```
1  // @ts-check
2
3  /**
4   * @typedef {{
5   *   age: string,
6   *   name: string,
7   * }} Input
8   */
9
10 <div>${name} ${age}</div>
```

Figure 6-43. *Using JSDoc to type Input*

After enabling it, we can type the input with JSDoc. An example of this is shown in Figure 6-43. For projects that use multi-file components, even that is also handled by Marko. An example for that is shown in Figures 6-44 and 6-45.

```
// @ts-check
/**
 * @typedef {{
 *   colors: string[],
 *   renderBody: Marko.Renderable
 * }} Input
 * @typedef {{
 *   colorIndex: number
 * }} State
 * @extends {Marko.Component<Input, State>}
 */
export default class extends Marko.Component {
  onCreate() {
    this.state = {
      colorIndex: 0,
    };
  }

  loopColor() {
    this.state.colorIndex =
      (this.state.colorIndex + 1) % this.input.colors.length;
  }
}
```

Figure 6-44. *Using JSDoc to type multi-file components*

This example shows a color-switcher tag that, given a list of colors, builds out a button and loops the colors. This is built as a multi-file component and has a *component. js* shown in Figure 6-44 and an *index.marko* file shown in Figure 6-45.

```
// @ts-check

/* Input will be automatically imported from `component.js`! */

<button
  onClick('loop')
  style=`color: white; background-color: ${input.colors[state.colorIndex]}`>
  <${input.renderBody}/>
</button>
```

Figure 6-45. *Using JSDoc to type multi-file components*

For type validation/checking both locally and on the CI, we will use the @marko/ type-check package which we shall look into in the next section.

One last thing to look at is the types offered by installed Marko components. For this, we will look at a **<lib-count-down-timer>** component, which we will get by installing the **lib-marko@latest** package. If you will recall, this was a sample custom marko component we published to NPM. First, let's install this into this project by doing an

npm i lib-marko@latest

Upon installing this, let's explore this package, which you will find within the **node_ modules** folder (that contains all the installed dependencies for a NodeJS project). You will notice the structure as shown in Figure 6-46.

Figure 6-46. *Installed lib-marko package's <lib-count-down-marko> tag*

This is the same <count-down-timer> that was renamed as <lib-count-down-timer> and published to avoid tag namespace collision since we already have a <count-down-timer>. The following are the lists of files and are shown in Figures 6-47 to 6-51:

1. *component.js*: This is the original component.ts file, with the types stripped out and the file transformed to Javascript.

2. *index.marko*: This is the template file with all types stripped out (even the ones within static and inline JS).

3. *index.marko.d.ts*: This is the declaration file that is output for *index.marko*. In our case since we have gone with the multi-file component approach and that there are no types within JS expressions, this file is empty.

4. *component.d.ts*: This is the declaration file that is output for
   component.ts.

5. *styles.modules.dist.css*: This contains the css modules file output.

6. *styles.modules.css.js*: This contains the CSS modules
   mapped output.

```
node_modules › lib-marko › dist › components › lib-count-down-timer › TS component.d.ts ›
1    export interface State {
2        timeLeft: number;
3    }
4    export interface Input {
5        start: number;
6    }
7    export default class extends Marko.Component<Input, State> {
8        timerId: NodeJS.Timeout | undefined;
9        onCreate(): void;
10       onInput(input: Input): void;
11       beginCounter(): void;
12       onMount(): void;
13       resetCounter(): void;
14   }
```

Figure 6-47. *component.d.ts*

```
node_modules › lib-marko › dist › components › lib-count-down-timer › JS styles.module.css.js › ...
1    import "./styles.module.dist.css";
2    export default {"test":"_test_1bx7o_1"};
```

Figure 6-48. *styles.modules.css.js*

```
node_modules › lib-marko › dist › components › lib-count-down-timer › # styles.module.dist.css › ...
1    ._test_1bx7o_1 {
2        color: ☐blue;
3    }
```

Figure 6-49. *styles.module.dist.css*

```
node_modules > lib-marko > dist > components > lib-count-down-timer >  ☰ index.marko > ...
1    import style from "./styles.module.css";
2    <div>
3      <h1>
4        Countdown Timer
5      </h1>
6      <p>
7        Timer originaly began from ${input.start}
8      </p>
9      <p class=style.test>
10       ${state.timeLeft} seconds remaining
11     </p>
12     <!-- Reset the counter as long as count is not 0 -->
13     <button on-click("resetCounter")>
14       ${state.timeLeft === 0 ? "Restart counter" : "Reset counter"}
15     </button>
16   </div>
```

Figure 6-50. *index.marko*

```
node_modules > lib-marko > dist > components > lib-count-down-timer >  JS component.js > ...
1    ;
2    ;
3    export default class extends Marko.Component {
4        timerId;
5        onCreate() {
6            this.state = {
7                timeLeft: 0
8            };
9        }
10       onInput(input) {
11           this.state.timeLeft = input.start || 0;
12       }
13       beginCounter() {
14           this.timerId = setInterval(() => {
15               if (this.state.timeLeft === 0) {
16                   if (this.timerId !== null && this.timerId !== undefined) {
17                       clearInterval(this.timerId);
18                   }
19               }
20               else {
21                   this.state.timeLeft = this.state.timeLeft - 1;
22               }
23           }, 1000);
24       }
25       onMount() {
26           this.beginCounter();
27       }
28       resetCounter() {
29           if (this.timerId !== null && this.timerId !== undefined) {
30               this.emit("reset");
31               clearInterval(this.timerId);
32           }
33           this.state.timeLeft = this.input.start;
34           this.beginCounter();
35       }
36   }
```

Figure 6-51. *component.js*

As a next step, when we use this in our +page.marko,

```
src > routes > playground > ≡ +page.marko > ⅍ lib-count-down-timer
 38    static const TEN = 10 as const
 39
 40  > <for-by-three index:number  from=TEN to=20>
 44    </for-by-three>
 45
 46  > <fancy-button color="#FFF" bgColor="red">
 48    </fancy-button>
 49
 50  <  Object literal may only specify known properties, and '["renderBody"/*lib-count-down-timer*/]' does
 51       not exist in type 'Directives & Input'. script(2353)
 52  }
 53     Custom Marko tag discovered from the "lib-marko" npm package.
 54     (property) ["renderBody"/*lib-count-down-timer*/]: () => MarkoReturn<void>
 55
 56  <  Click to show 2 definitions.
 57     View Problem (⌥F8)    Quick Fix... (⌘.)    Fix using Copilot (⌘I)
 58  <lib-count-down-timer>
 59  </lib-count-down-timer>
```

Figure 6-52A. *Including <lib-count-down-timer> into the +page.marko*

You will notice that when it's included, VS Code and TS and marko work together to produce completions and validations. In this case, it highlights missing props. Sometimes, you may have to restart your TS server locally (Cmd+SHIFT+P) and choose Restart TypeScript server or restart your IDE for it to pick up the types for the newly installed tag.

Another important part of using TS is the one that is tied to the Marko-run meta framework. We have briefly seen them in Chapter 5. To revisit, you can type other aspects of Marko code such as **$global** as seen in the list of types Marko exposes. In Marko Run, whatever you set on context within the HTTP handlers (+handler.ts) is what you get on **$global.** Also, as before, to serialize it, you will need to explicitly whitelist them via

```
context.serializedGlobals.<prop_on_context> = true.
```

A sample usage of this value along with type is shown in Figure 6-52B.

```
src > routes > ☰ +layout.marko > ...
  1    // will be globally defined on MarkoRun.Context
  2
  3    static declare module "@marko/run" {
  4      interface Context {
  5        pageTitle: string;
  6      }
  7    }
  8    <!doctype html>
  9    <html lang="en">
 10      <head>
 11        <meta charset="UTF-8">
 12        <link rel="icon" type="image/png" sizes="32x32" href="./favicon.png">
 13        <meta name="viewport" content="width=device-width, initial-scale=1.0">
 14        <meta name="description" content="A basic Marko app.">
 15        <title>${($global as MarkoRun.Context).pageTitle || "Marko"}</title>
 16      </head>
```

Figure 6-52B. *Using MarkoRun types within templates*

Lint (Stylelint and ESLint and TypeScript Lint) and Formatting via Prettier

There are multiple pieces that we would like to lint: marko files, JS files, and style files. For this, we would require the support of plugins to type check marko files, ESLint to type check style files, and stylelint to type check styles files. You can add JSON lint to this if your project uses JSON files. To enable this, we will be installing the following plugins as *development dependencies*. They are grouped together by their function:

1. **Lint Styles**

    a. stylelint

    b. stylelint-checkstyle-formatter

    c. stylelint-config-standard

2. **Lint Javascript**

    a. @eslint/js

    b. eslint

    c. eslint-formatter-checkstyle

  d. eslint-formatter-unix

  e. eslint-plugin-simple-import-sort

3. **Lint TypeScript**

  a. @types/node

  b. @marko/type-check

  c. typescript

  d. typescript-eslint

4. **Lint Marko**

5. **Vite Related**

  a. vite

  b. @marko/vite

6. **Other**

  a. Globals

7. **PostCSS**

  a. postcss

  b. postcss-preset-env

Besides this, to enable us to quickly format and fix the issues that we would run into while lint fails, we will install Prettier—a formatter for the entire project. For this, we will install the following dependencies:

1. prettier

2. prettier-plugin-marko

3. prettier-plugin-packagejson

Next, we will add some files. These include

1. stylelint-format.js

2. .stylelintignore

3. .stylelintrc.json

4. eslint-format.js

5. eslint.config.js

6. .prettierignore

7. .prettierrc.json

These are shown in Figures 6-53 to 6-59.

```js
JS .stylelint-format.js > ⊙ default
1    // Custom stylelint formatter to output checkstyle format for ci
2    // and unix format for local development
3
4    import fs from "fs";
5    import stylelint from "stylelint";
6    import checkStyleFormatter from "stylelint-checkstyle-formatter";
7    const unixFormatter = await stylelint.formatters.unix;
8
9    export default function (results) {
10       fs.writeFileSync("stylelint-warnings.xml", checkStyleFormatter(results));
11       return unixFormatter(results);
12   }
```

Figure 6-53. *stylelint-format.js*

```
▽ .stylelintignore
1    __snapshots__
2    .beans
3    .cache
4    *actual*
5    *expected*
6    coverage
7    dist
8    node_modules
```

Figure 6-54. *.stylelintignore*

```json
 .stylelintrc.json > ...
1    {
2        "$schema": "http://json.schemastore.org/stylelintrc.json",
3        "extends": "stylelint-config-standard",
4        "allowEmptyInput": true,
5        "cache": true,
6        "rules": {
7          "import-notation": "string"
8        }
9    }
```

Figure 6-55. *.stylelintrc.json*

```js
JS eslint-format.js > ...
1    // Custom eslint formatter to output checkstyle format for ci
2    // and unix format for local development
3
4    import { ESLint } from "eslint";
5    import fs from "fs";
6    const eslint = new ESLint();
7
8    export default async function (results) {
9      const format = async (id) => (await eslint.loadFormatter(id)).format(results);
10     fs.writeFileSync("eslint.xml", await format("checkstyle"));
11     return format("unix");
12   }
```

Figure 6-56. *eslint-format.js*

```json
{} .prettierrc.json > ...
1    {
2        "$schema": "https://json.schemastore.org/prettierrc",
3        "plugins": ["prettier-plugin-packagejson", "prettier-plugin-marko"]
4    }
5
```

Figure 6-57. *.prettierrc.json*

```
.prettierignore
.marko-run
.nvm
.vscode
*actual*
*expected*
build-ebay
CHANGELOG.md
coverage
dependencies.json
dependencyTree.json
dist
jenkins.json
node_modules
package-lock.json
platform_modules_dependency.json
routes.json
telemetry.json
yarn-installables.json
swu.json
package.json
```

Figure 6-58. *.prettierignore*

Next, let's update the "**scripts**" section of *package.json* to trigger **lint** via the command

*"**lint**": "mtc && eslint --format ./eslint-format.js . && stylelint --custom-formatter ./.stylelint-format.js '**/*.css' && prettier . --check --log-level=warn"*

For example, let's add an inline JS expression $ { const x = 10 } in <fake-tabs> component, and when linting, you will see the error shown in Figures 6-60 and 6-61. As more TS rules and ESLint and stylelint rules are added to the project, you will find manually formatting them becomes a tedious job, just to keep the linter happy. For this purpose, we can use Prettier. Prettier works along with the other tooling linters to properly format the code. We have already installed prettier.

Now, let's run prettier over the project to format the project per the style guides we have used. For this, include the following command named "**format**" in your **package.json** file:

```
"format": "eslint --format unix --fix .; stylelint --formatter unix --fix '**/*.css'; prettier . --write --log-level=warn",
```

Since we have used the tabs css, it runs into some issues, and we can skip that for now by including

```
/* stylelint-disable selector-class-pattern */
/* stylelint-disable rule-empty-line-before */
```

at the top of the src/components/fake-tabs/style.css.

Running prettier again, we get the result shown in Figure 6-60.

```
eslint.config.js > [∅] default > 🔧 languageOptions > 🔧 globals > 🔧 <unknown>
 5
 6    export default tseslint.config(
 7      {
 8        ignores: [
 9          "__snapshots__",
10          ".beans",
11          ".cache",
12          ".marko-run",
13          "build-ebay",
14          "coverage",
15          "dist",
16          "node_modules",
17          "*actual*",
18          "*expected*",
19        ],
20      },
21      eslint.configs.recommended,
22      ...tseslint.configs.recommended,
23      {
24        languageOptions: {
25          globals: {
26            ...globals.browser,
27            ...globals.node,
28          },
29        },
30        plugins: {
31          "simple-import-sort": sortImportPlugin,
32        },
33        rules: {
34          "simple-import-sort/imports": "error",
35          "simple-import-sort/exports": "error",
36          "@typescript-eslint/no-import-type-side-effects": "error",
37          "@typescript-eslint/no-non-null-assertion": "off",
38          "@typescript-eslint/no-empty-function": "off",
39          "@typescript-eslint/no-explicit-any": "off",
40        },
41      },
42    );
```

Figure 6-59. *eslint.config.js*

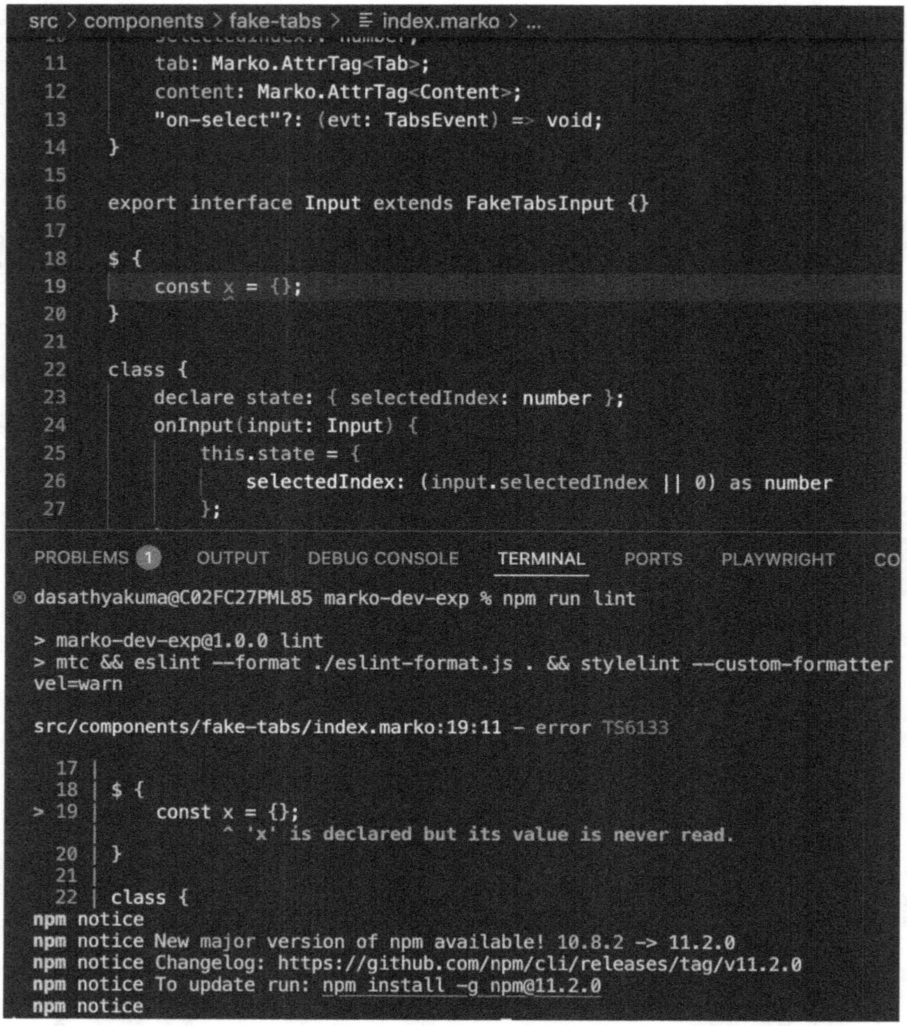

Figure 6-60. *Forcing an error to see if lint works*

Remove that **const** line and you will see the other lint errors as shown in Figure 6-61.

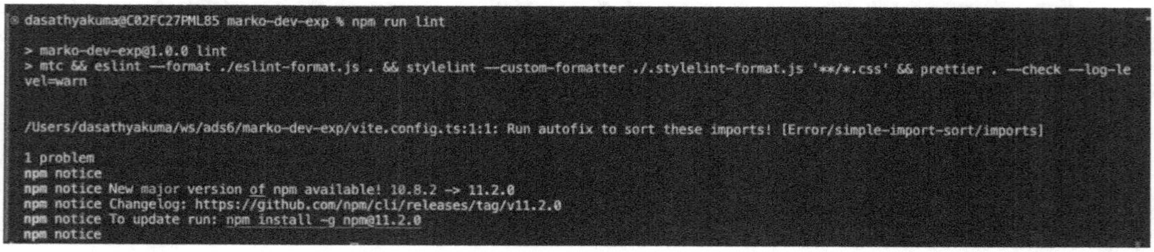

Figure 6-61. *Removing it to see other lint errors*

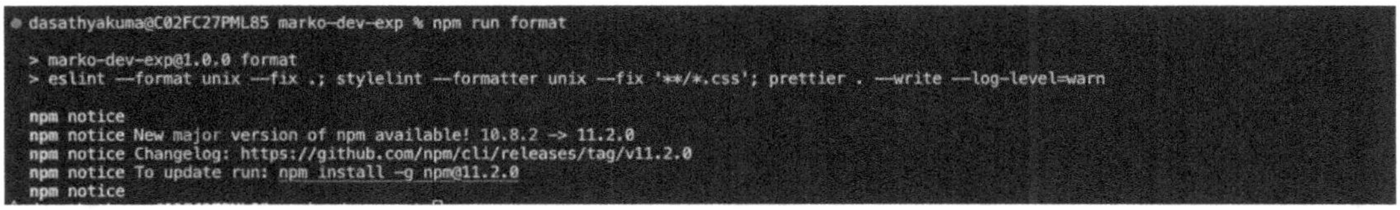

Figure 6-62. *Running format*

Now, look at all the files in the repo and you will find it to be neatly formatted per the chosen formatting guides. This completes Marko's tooling with **TypeScript**, the lint world via **ESLint, Stylelint**, and **Marko type check**, and formatting via **Prettier**.

The results of these are the files like **eslint.xml** and **stylelint-warnings.xml** being the output. Some enterprises log this to determine actionable insights. Else, you can ignore these files through **.gitignore**.

Marko and Storybook

While all of the sections we have seen until now form an important part of the developer experience, nothing comes close to **Storybook** that helps preview our UX changes in development. Marko plays well with **storybook** and goes one step ahead by letting you use the authored stories, as part of your tests via the component story format, which we shall look into in Chapter 7. For now, let's set up marko with **storybook** and write a sample story for the **count-down-timer** and **fake-tabs** components.

To set up storybook, install the following dependencies:

1. storybook

2. @storybook/addon-essentials

3. @storybook/addon-interactions

4. @storybook/marko

5. @storybook/marko-vite

These are either **storybook** plugins or plugins of **Marko** to work with **storybook** or **vite** integrations that let you author and instantly refresh your Marko Storybook stories. Next, after installing the aforementioned development dependencies, we will add a couple of files to a **.storybook/** folder under the project root. This is shown in Figures 6-63 and 6-64.

```
.storybook > TS main.ts > ...
1    import type { StorybookConfig } from "@storybook/marko-vite";
2
3    export default {
4      framework: "@storybook/marko-vite",
5      stories: ["../src/**/{,*.}stories.ts"],
6      addons: ["@storybook/addon-essentials", "@storybook/addon-interactions"],
7      core: {
8        disableTelemetry: true,
9        disableWhatsNewNotifications: true,
10     },
11     docs: {
12       autodocs: true,
13       defaultName: "Documentation",
14     },
15   } satisfies StorybookConfig;
16
```

Figure 6-63. *.storybook/main.ts*

```
.storybook > TS preview.ts > [∅] default
1    import type { Parameters } from "@storybook/marko";
2
3    export const parameters = {
4      actions: { argTypesRegex: "^on[A-Z].*" },
5      options: {
6        storySort: {
7          method: "alphabetical",
8        },
9      },
10   } satisfies Parameters;
11
12   export default {
13     parameters,
14     loaders: [],
15   };
```

Figure 6-64. *.storybook/preview.ts*

After this, let's add some stories to see them in action! First, let's add the **count-down-timer** shown in Figure 6-65 and then the **fake-tabs** shown in Figure 6-66. These will be part of a **stories.ts** file.

```
src > components > count-down-timer > TS stories.ts > ...
  1    import type { Meta, Story } from "@storybook/marko";
  2
  3    import type { Input } from "./component";
  4    import Template from "./index.marko";
  5
  6    export default {
  7      title: "count-down-timer",
  8      component: Template,
  9      argTypes: {
 10        start: {
 11          control: {
 12            type: "number",
 13          },
 14        },
 15      },
 16    } as Meta<Input>;
 17
 18    export const Default: Story<Input> = {
 19      args: {
 20        start: 10,
 21      },
 22    };
 23
```

Figure 6-65. *src/components/count-down-timer/stories.ts*

```
src > components > fake-tabs > TS stories.ts > ...
  1    import type { Meta, Story } from '@storybook/marko';
  2
  3    import type { Input } from './fixtures/story.marko';
  4    import Component from './fixtures/story.marko';
  5
  6    export default {
  7      title: 'ads-fake-tabs',
  8      component: Component
  9    } as Meta<Input>;
 10
 11    export const Basic = {
 12      args: {}
 13    } as Story<Input>;
```

Figure 6-66. *src/components/fake-tabs/stories.ts*

```
src > components > fake-tabs > fixtures > ≡ story.marko > ⁂ fake-tabs
 1    export interface Input {
 2        selectedIndex?: number;
 3    }
 4
 5    <fake-tabs on-select("emit", "select")>
 6        <@tab>Tab one</@tab>
 7        <@tab>Tab two</@tab>
 8        <@content>
 9            <div>content</div>
10        </@content>
11    </fake-tabs>
```

Figure 6-67. *src/components/fake-tabs/fixtures/story.marko*

Now, to run storybook and view the stories, include the "**storybook**" command to your "**scripts**" section of the **package.json** file of this project:

"**storybook**": "storybook dev -p 6006",

You can see the output as shown in Figure 6-68.

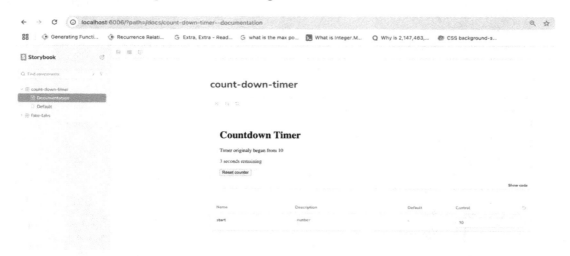

Figure 6-68. *Storybook output for count-down-timer*

Debugging Marko code

This was briefly touched upon in Chapter 3 when showcasing progressive rendering where we saw the source-mapped output provided by Webpack. The same thing is also offered by Vite. When starting up the dev server using the command npm run dev, start it via the Javascript Debug Terminal as shown in Figure 6-69.

Figure 6-69. *Storybook output for count-down-timer*

Now just keep breakpoints even in your template code and you should be able to get the debugger to halt there. This is shown in Figure 6-70.

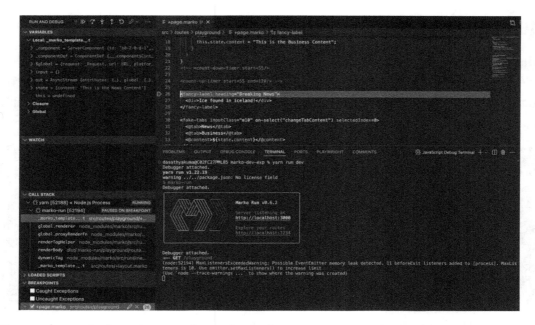

Figure 6-70. *Debugging Marko code and stepping through Marko components on the server*

Another way to do this is via the Chrome Debugger. But with the VS Code setup, you can easily inspect values and also switch to the browser for debugging the client side part of the code as it comes with source maps. This is shown in Figure 6-71.

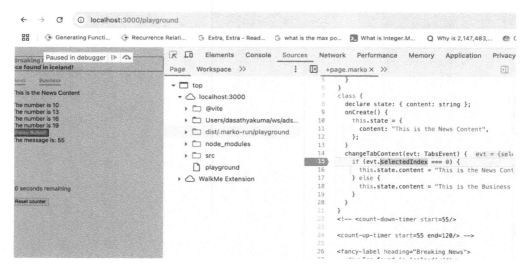

Figure 6-71. *Debugging Marko code and stepping through Marko components on the client*

The source map recreates the files back on the Chrome ➤ Sources tab as shown in Figure 6-72. In prod mode, ensure you have the "download sourcemaps enabled" option selected in Chrome settings.

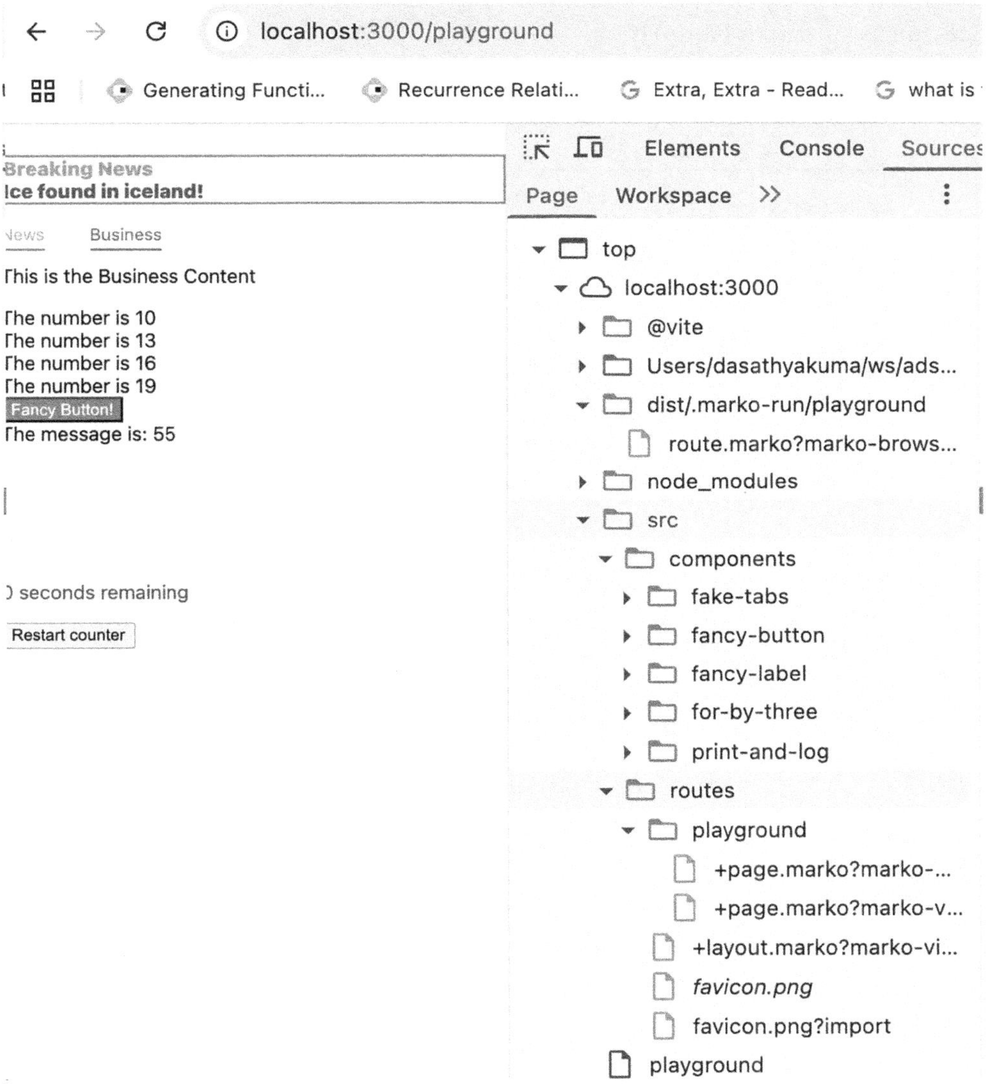

Figure 6-72. *Source maps*

Using CSS Preprocessors with Marko

CSS preprocessors are easy to work with Marko and Vite. For instance, you can use LESS css by just installing the LESS css dependency via *npm i less*. Then, just update the vite. config.ts file as shown in Figure 6-73.

```ts
import marko from "@marko/run/vite";
import tailwindcss from "@tailwindcss/vite";
import { defineConfig } from "vite";

// https://vite.dev/config/
export default defineConfig({
  plugins: [tailwindcss(), marko()],
  css: {
    devSourcemap: true,
    preprocessorOptions: {
      less: {
        math: "always",
        javascriptEnabled: true,
      },
    },
  },
});
```

Figure 6-73. *Using preprocessors like LESS with Marko*

In the same manner, you can use other CSS preprocessors like SCSS. If you are using the webpack setup of Marko scaffolded via *npx @marko/create*, you may have to use a loader like less-loader to resolve LESS files.

To check if this works, let's go back to the print-and-log component and include a style.less file.

```
src > components > print-and-log > {} style.less > ⅓ .print-and-log
1    .print-and-log {
2        color: "black" ;
3        & .logger {
4            color: "red";
5        }
6    }
```

Figure 6-74. *style.less with <print-and-log>*

Next, restart your dev server and hit the http://localhost:3000/playground page and you will see everything works fine!

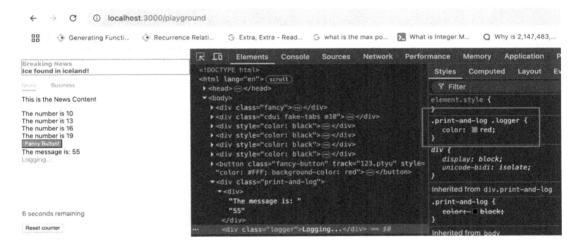

Figure 6-75. *Resolved LESS css styles from the file*

Reusable Core UX Components Library from eBay

Finally, we come to core UX components! What is a framework that doesn't have a set of components to get you immediately started and playing with? Marko has you covered here via eBay's Core UX component repository (**https://github.com/eBay/evo-web**).

These components are fully battle tested for responsiveness and accessibility and cover a variety of use cases. You can consider them as atomic components or the core building blocks of a given page.

They can be accessed at `https://opensource.ebay.com/evo-web/`. eBay takes accessibility very seriously. Therefore, all components are built in accordance with the eBay MIND Patterns (`https://ebay.gitbooks.io/mindpatterns/content/`). These patterns, in turn, build on from the specifications provided by the WAI-ARIA Authoring Practices (`https://w3c.github.io/aria-practices/`).

The **MIND** (**M**essaging, **I**nput, **N**avigation, and **D**isclosure) patterns are not to be confused with a visual design system, CSS framework, or JavaScript library. These patterns are instead intended to complement those systems by acting as foundational accessibility guidance.

As mentioned in the MIND patterns GIT book, there are four principles of accessibility known by the acronym **POUR,** listed below:

- **Perceivable**: People experience content in different ways (sight, hearing, and touch). Content needs to be transferable into recognizable (or perceivable) formats.

- **Operable**: Content needs to be navigable (or operable) by multiple methods—not just a mouse.

- **Understandable**: Web content needs to be understandable. Language should be simple and concise; functionality should be consistent and intuitive.

- **Robust**: Create web content that works for all (or most!) technologies. This includes operating systems, browsers, and mobile devices.

Testing for Accessibility: Accessibility testing is performed with latest versions of Chrome and JAWS, Firefox and NVDA, and Safari and VoiceOver.

These MIND patterns are built on top of the foundational pattern called **BONES** as defined at `https://github.com/ianmcburnie/bones`. Bones provide just the lean, mean, and semantic HTML markup for widgets, ensuring maximum accessibility, SEO, and site speed performance. Bones markup uses ARIA only where strictly necessary. Bones are not intended to be an exhaustive set of instructions for creating accessible components. The primary intention of bones is to detail the structural and semantic markup requirements.

Building for accessibility: Most of the common accessibility logic required for components built with the MIND pattern methodologies is made possible via the dependency **MakeupJS**—a suite of vanilla, headless UI JavaScript modules—tailored specifically for building accessible user interfaces in a frontend framework agnostic manner, for example, implementing a keyboard roving tab index (`https://github.com/makeup/makeup-js`).

Along with this comes the in-house theming framework called **SKIN** (`https://opensource.ebay.com/skin/`) that powers all the theming behind these components. SKIN is a pure CSS framework. Skin's default stylesheet represents eBay Evo—eBay's evolved brand and design system. But SKIN also offers token-based configuration to enable non-eBay branded experiences. You can look them up at `https://opensource.ebay.com/skin/#token-system`.

Skin adheres to the following core principles:

- **Accessible**: Skin leverages semantic HTML, SVG, and ARIA to apply our styles wherever possible, thus enforcing correct and accessible markup.

- **Declarative**: Skin follows the BEM methodology ("Block, Element, and Modifier") for structured human-readable code which embraces the power and efficiency of the cascade.

- **Decoupled**: Skin is decoupled from the JavaScript layer, meaning the HTML and CSS is agnostic of the frontend framework (BYOJ = Bring Your Own Javascript!)*.

- **Scalable**: Skin is built on a system of design tokens (implemented as CSS variables), enabling a scalable and consistent visual system for UI development.

The work is all open source, which means you can always contribute! Let's look at some examples of building with eBayUI and SKIN.

Using eBayUI Components

Using eBayUI components on your page is pretty simple. You just have to install two dependencies:

- @ebay/ebayui-core@latest

- @ebay/skin@latest

The other related dependencies are brought in by these.

There are a couple of dependencies to pull into your top-level page template. These include

1. @import "~@ebay/skin/marketsans.css";

2. @import '~@ebay/skin/index.css';

3. @import '~@ebay/skin/global.css';

4. @import '~@ebay/skin/less.less';

5. @import "~@ebay/skin/tokens.css";

6. @import "~@ebay/skin/utility.css";

The second one is needed only if your bundler is unable to pull all the related component CSS. But with Vite, it won't be required. Now, for instance, if we want to use the <ebay-menu-button> component, all we have to do is just include and use it.

You can refer to this component here:

https://opensource.ebay.com/evo-web/ebayui-core/?path=/docs/buttons-ebay-menu-button--documentation

Let's create a <sample-menu> component and include this eBayUI component in it as shown in Figure 6-76.

```
src > components > sample-menu > ≡ index.marko > ⁙ ebay-menu-button
  1    <ebay-menu-button
  2        text='eBay Menu'
  3        on-collapse('emit', 'collapse')
  4        on-expand('emit', 'expand')
  5        on-change('emit', 'change')
  6        on-select('emit', 'select')
  7    >
  8        <@item badgeNumber=1 aria-label="1 item unread">item 1 that has very long text</@item>
  9        <@item badgeNumber=99 aria-label="99 items unread">item 2</@item>
 10        <@item badgeNumber=10 aria-label="10 item unread">item 3</@item>
 11    </ebay-menu-button>
```

Figure 6-76. *Using eBayUI's <ebay-menu-button> component via sample-menu/index.marko*

Our associated style file will be as shown in Figure 6-77.

```
src > components > sample-menu > {} style.less
1    @import "~@ebay/skin/marketsans.css";
2    // @import '@ebay/skin/index.css';
3    @import '~@ebay/skin/global.css';
4    @import '~@ebay/skin/less.less';
5    @import "~@ebay/skin/tokens.css";
6    @import "~@ebay/skin/utility.css";
```

Figure 6-77. *sample-menu/style.less*

Let's include this <sample-menu> into our src/routes/playground/+page.marko and you will see it on the page as shown in Figure 6-78. Other previously used components have been commented out.

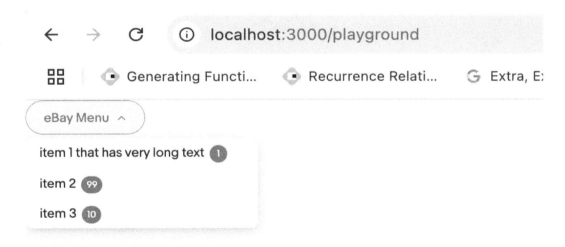

Figure 6-78. *The menu component shows up!*

Conclusion

In this chapter, we have seen all the tooling ecosystems surrounding Marko from TypeScript to CSS preprocessors, Lint, format, Storybook, debugging, and the core UX components. In the next chapter, let's look at another important aspect of the developer experience—testing Marko components and see how Marko plays with some of the most popular testing frameworks.

CHAPTER 7

Testing Marko Components and Pages

Introduction

Testing forms a very important facet in being able to deliver reliable UX. So, it's important for any view framework to be able to address this, and Marko is no different. Marko plays well with every popular testing framework in the market today. In this chapter, we will look at testing Marko components on the browser and server.

There are other additional forms of testing, like Visual regression testing through tools like Percy, and external solutions like BrowserStack to test on multiple devices. While our focus is not on these tools, as they are not free, we will look at other forms of testing Marko components—testing on the browser, server, snapshot testing, and end-to-end testing through Playwright.

In the examples in this chapter, we will be using **Vitest** as the test runner under the hood for unit testing Marko components. This will run the tests in both the server environment and browser environment. It simulates the browser environment via JSDOM. We will be using the ***@marko/testing-library*** plugin to make use of Testing Library to test Marko components as part of the unit tests.

We will also see how to import and use Stories defined for the components via **Storybook** into test cases and use them. If you are used to writing tests with **Jest**, **Vitest** should be pretty straightforward for you and, in most cases, a drop-in replacement with its Jest-compatible API.

Note that while every bit of effort has been made here to have a working example, to get you going, the tooling land of Javascript is always evolving with potential breaking changes or entirely new set of tools or the related plumbing for them to play well together. So, it is possible that these examples get outdated pretty quickly.

© Damodaran Chingleput Sathyakumar 2025
D. Chingleput Sathyakumar, *Practical Marko*, https://doi.org/10.1007/979-8-8688-1483-9_7

However, with Marko offering full support to play with Vite, you should always be able to find related plugins that play well with Vite and Marko to get you going. Given the prevalence of TypeScript and its popularity, we will be discussing all of this, incorporating TypeScript along with the setup.

Unit Testing Marko Components

The frameworks we will be using include

1. **Vitest**: A next-generation, fast, and simple testing framework (and runner) designed to work seamlessly with Vite (the module bundler that we have seen in all our examples so far)

2. **Testing-library**: A family of libraries that help developers write tests for user interfaces, focusing on simulating user interactions and verifying the behavior of components rather than relying on implementation details

3. **JSDOM**: A pure-JavaScript implementation of many web standards, notably the WHATWG DOM and HTML Standards, designed for use with Node.js, allowing you to emulate a browser environment for testing and scraping purposes

4. **Storybook**: A frontend tool for building UI components and pages in isolation, allowing developers to develop, test, and document UI components without needing to run the entire application

The associated Marko plugins that we will be relying on include

- **@marko/testing-library**: Bindings of testing-library using Marko

- **@marko/vite**: The Marko Vite plugin that helps Vite interface with the Marko compiler

- **@vitest/coverage-v8**: The Vitest coverage package

- **@vitest/ui**: The vitest package that creates a UI tool

- **Vitest**: The testing framework

- **Jsdom**: The environment we will be running client-side tests on

- **@testing-library/user-event**: To help simulate user events

- **@testing-library/jest-dom**: Helps testing library to interface with JSDOM

- **@storybook/testing-library**: Helps storybook interface with testing library

Note that this setup is intentionally kept minimal to help you get started. There are numerous other vitest and testing-library plugins that you can install depending on your use case.

Getting Started

To begin with, let's scaffold a Marko application via the

```
>> npx @marko/create.
```

Figure 7-1. *Scaffolding a basic Marko-run non-connect-style app via the basic-ts template*

Choose the **basic-ts** template, and this should get you with a minimalist non-connect-style Marko-run application. If you noticed in this basic setup, you will see a src/components/mouse-mask.marko component that is used as <mouse-mask/>.

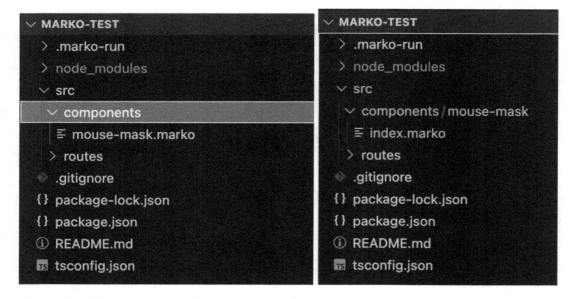

Figure 7-2. *Re-org the mouse-mask template*

To begin with, we shall move this to its own separate folder, as shown in Figure 7-2. To check if our changes are fine, just do npm run dev, and you will find the sample application up and running at http://localhost:3000.

Now, let's install the following libraries as development dependencies:

- **@marko/testing-library**

- **@marko/vite**

- **@vitest/coverage-v8**

- **@vitest/ui**

- **Vitest**

- **Jsdom**

- **@testing-library/user-event**

- **@testing-library/jest-dom**

- **@storybook/testing-library**

```
dasathyakuma@C02FC27PML85 marko-test % npm install -D @marko/testing-library @marko/vite
@vitest/coverage-v8 @vitest/ui vitest jsdom @testing-library/user-event @testing-library/
jest-dom @storybook/testing-library --ignore-engines

added 210 packages, and audited 430 packages in 41s

107 packages are looking for funding
  run `npm fund` for details

found 0 vulnerabilities
npm notice
npm notice New major version of npm available! 10.8.2 -> 11.2.0
npm notice Changelog: https://github.com/npm/cli/releases/tag/v11.2.0
npm notice To update run: npm install -g npm@11.2.0
npm notice
```

Figure 7-3. *First set of dependencies installed*

Next, we are required to add a few configuration files as listed below:

1. **vitest.config.ts**: A configuration file for vitest

2. **vitest.workspace.ts**: A configuration file to designate server- and client-side tests

3. **vite.config.ts**: The vite configuration

4. **vitest-setup.ts**: Any basic code to be executed as part of the test bootstrap

These files are listed in Figures 7-4 to 7-7.

```ts
TS vitest.config.ts > ...
1   import marko from "@marko/vite";
2   import { defineConfig } from "vitest/config";
3
4   export default defineConfig({
5     plugins: [marko()],
6     define: {
7       "process.env": process.env,
8     },
9     test: {
10      globals: true,
11      outputFile: "test-results.xml",
12      reporters: ["default", "junit"],
13      setupFiles: ["./vitest-setup.ts"],
14      coverage: {
15        exclude: [
16          "**/integration-tests/**",
17          "**/*stories.ts",
18          "**/*fixtures.ts",
19          "**/test/**/*",
20          "**/__test__/**",
21          "**/__tests__/**",
22          "**/__mocks__/**",
23          "**/fixtures/**",
24        ],
25        include: ["src/**/*"],
26        reporter: ["text", "html", "cobertura", "lcov"],
27        thresholds: {
28          statements: 90,
29          functions: 90,
30          lines: 90,
31          // branches: 90
32        },
33      },
34      ...(process.env.CI && {
35        outputFile: "test-results.xml",
36        reporters: ["default", "junit"],
37      }),
38    },
39    resolve: {
40      alias: {
41        "@": "/src",
42        "@pages": "/src/pages",
43        "@components": "/src/components",
44        "~@types": "/@types",
45        "~@": "/node_modules/@",
46      },
47    },
48  });
```

Figure 7-4. *vitest.config.ts*

```ts
TS vitest.workspace.ts > [∅] default
1    import { defineWorkspace } from "vitest/config";
2
3    export default defineWorkspace([
4      {
5        extends: "vitest.config.ts",
6        test: {
7          name: "server",
8          environment: "node",
9          include: ["src/**/{,*.}server.test.ts"],
10         setupFiles: ["src/test/setup/server.ts"],
11       },
12     },
13     {
14       extends: "vitest.config.ts",
15       test: {
16         name: "browser",
17         environment: "jsdom",
18         include: ["src/**/{,*.}browser.test.ts"],
19         setupFiles: ["src/test/setup/browser.ts"],
20         environmentOptions: {
21           jsdom: { url: "https://localhost:8082" },
22         },
23       },
24     },
25   ]);
26
```

Figure 7-5. *vitest.workspace.ts*

```ts
vite.config.ts > ...
1    import { defineConfig } from "vite";
2
3    const isDev = process.env.NODE_ENV === "development";
4
5    export default defineConfig({
6      build: {
7        rollupOptions: {
8          output: {
9            sourcemap: isDev,
10         },
11       },
12     },
13     server: {
14       port: 3000,
15     },
16   });
17
```

Figure 7-6. *vite.config.ts*

```ts
TS vitest-setup.ts > ⬡ vi.fn() callback
 1   import "@testing-library/jest-dom/vitest";
 2
 3   import { vi } from "vitest";
 4
 5   if (typeof window !== "undefined") {
 6     global.matchMedia = vi.fn((query: string) => ({
 7       matches: false,
 8       media: query,
 9       onchange: null,
10       addListener: vi.fn(),
11       removeListener: vi.fn(),
12       addEventListener: vi.fn(),
13       removeEventListener: vi.fn(),
14       dispatchEvent: vi.fn(),
15     }));
16
17     window.navigator = window.navigator || {};
18     window.navigator.sendBeacon = vi.fn();
19     Object.defineProperty(window, "scrollTo", {
20       value: vi.fn(),
21       writable: true,
22     });
23     Object.defineProperty(window, "location", {
24       value: {
25         ...window.location,
26         reload: vi.fn(),
27       },
28       writable: true,
29     });
30   }
```

Figure 7-7. *vitest-setup.ts*

With this, we have our basic configuration files set up. Now, to trigger testing with Vite and this ecosystem of plugins, we have to enable a few commands in the "**scripts**" section of our **package.json**. This is shown in Figure 7-9.

We also have missed out on one package—*vite*. While this will be available, it's good to have it explicitly installed. This is shown in Figure 7-8.

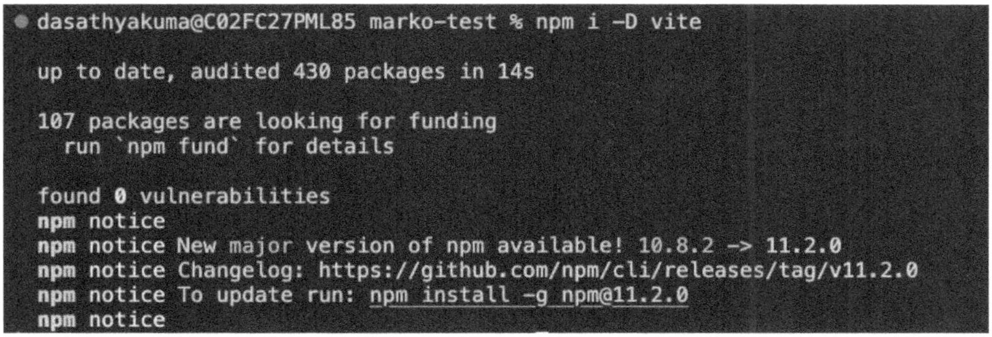

Figure 7-8. *Install vite*

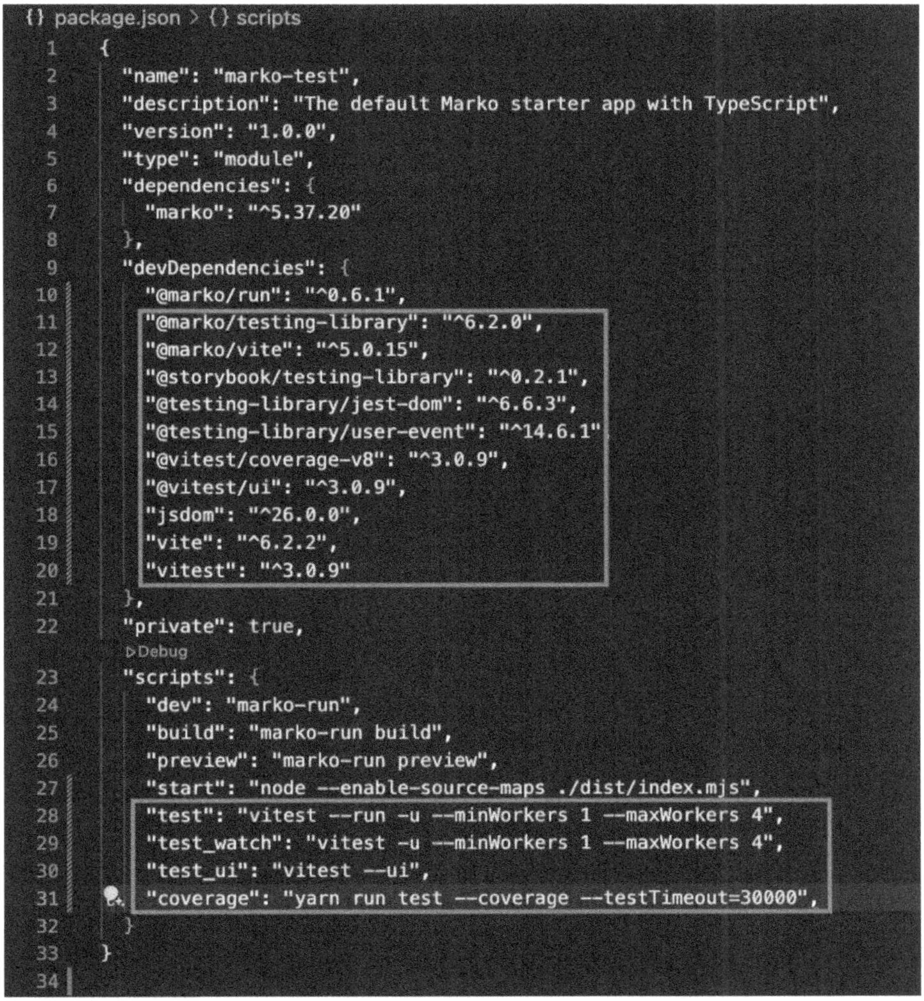

Figure 7-9. *Installed dev dependencies and updated "scripts" section*

Now that we have our setup ready, all we are left now is to add some tests. We will add some tests to the **<mouse-mask/>** component that is provided in this scaffolded setup.

Adding Tests

Before adding tests, we will revisit some of our setup in the previous section. In Figure 7-4, we have mentioned **vite** to make use of the **@marko/vite** plugin in its list of *plugins*. We have instructed it to use **process.env**; provided an output file in **test-results.xml**; instructed it to use **default** and **junit** reporters; provided **vitest-setup.ts** as the setup file; instructed it to resolve any aliases such as **@pages/****, **@components/****, etc.; and added some configuration for coverage as to what files have to be included or excluded and thresholds for coverage (anything less than that will be reported a failure!).

In Figure 7-5, we have mentioned **vite** to use separate configurations for the browser and server while still extending from vitest.config.ts. The server environment uses "node," while the browser environment uses JSDOM. We also have specific setup files for the browser and server environments included here.

In Figure 7-6, we have mentioned the configuration for **vite**. In Figure 7-7, we have included a setup file that mocks some of the important browser APIs. Now let's include the two other server and browser environment–specific setup files as shown in Figure 7-10.

```
src > test > setup > TS server.ts
  1       import "@testing-library/jest-dom/vitest";
  2
```

Figure 7-10A. *src/test/setup/server.ts*

Next, we will organize the test files in a __tests__ folder, under the specific components. Every component within the components/ folder will have a __tests__ in it. This is not necessarily restricted to components but carries on for all the unit tests we shall write. Also, we will be testing snapshots for the server side if there are no API calls involved. This tests the rendered snapshot of the component.

To distinguish between server- and client-side test files, they have been designated with a specific pattern as indicated in Figure 7-5. Server files will be detected by the pattern "src/**/{,*.}server.test.ts", and the client-side test files will be detected by the pattern "src/**/{,*.}browser.test.ts".

```
src > test > setup > TS browser.ts > ...
 1    import "@testing-library/jest-dom/vitest";
 2
 3    import { vi } from "vitest";
 4
 5    // https://vitest.dev/api/vi.html#vi-mock
 6
 7    if (typeof window.navigator.sendBeacon === "undefined") {
 8      Object.defineProperty(window.navigator, "sendBeacon", {
 9        value: vi.fn(),
10      });
11    }
12
13    Object.defineProperty(window, "scrollTo", { value: () => {}, writable: true });
14
15    Object.defineProperty(window, "matchMedia", {
16      writable: true,
17      value: vi.fn().mockImplementation((query) => ({
18        matches: false,
19        media: query,
20        onchange: null,
21        addListener: vi.fn(),
22        removeListener: vi.fn(),
23        addEventListener: vi.fn(),
24        removeEventListener: vi.fn(),
25        dispatchEvent: vi.fn(),
26      })),
27    });
28
29    global.Range = function Range() {} as any;
30    global.document.createRange = () =>
31      ({
32        setStart: () => {},
33        setEnd: () => {},
34        commonAncestorContainer: {
35          nodeName: "BODY",
36          ownerDocument: document,
37        } as Node,
38      }) as any;
39    global.document.getSelection = vi.fn();
40    Range.prototype.selectNodeContents = () => {};
41    Range.prototype.getBoundingClientRect = () => ({ right: 0 }) as DOMRect;
42    window.history.replaceState = vi.fn();
```

Figure 7-10B. *src/test/setup/browser.ts*

In Figure 7-11, we have included the server-side test file for the mouse-mask component.

```
src > components > mouse-mask > __tests__ > TS server.test.ts > ...
  1   import { render } from "@marko/testing-library";
  2   import { expect, test } from "vitest";
  3
  4   import template from "../index.marko";
  5
  6   test("Mouse-mask", async () => {
  7     const { container } = await render<any>(template, {});
  8     expect(container).toMatchSnapshot();
  9   });
 10
```

Figure 7-11. *src/components/mouse-mask/__tests__/server.test.ts*

In Figures 7-12A and 7-12B, we have included the browser-side test file for the mouse-mask component.

```
src > components > mouse-mask > __tests__ > TS browser.test.ts > ...
  1   import { fireEvent, render } from "@marko/testing-library";
  2   import { describe, expect, it, vi } from "vitest";
  3
  4   import MouseMask from "../index.marko";
  5
  6   describe("MouseMask Component", () => {
  7     it("renders with initial center position", async () => {
  8       const { container } = await render(MouseMask);
  9       const element = container.querySelector(".mouse-mask");
 10
 11       expect(element).toBeInTheDocument();
 12       expect(element).toHaveStyle({
 13         "--mouse-x": "center",
 14         "--mouse-y": "center",
 15       });
 16     });
 17
 18     it("updates position on mouse move", async () => {
 19       const { container } = await render(MouseMask);
 20       const element = container.querySelector(".mouse-mask");
 21
 22       // Simulate mouse move
 23       await fireEvent.mouseMove(window, {
 24         clientX: 100,
 25         clientY: 200,
 26       });
 27
 28       expect(element).toHaveStyle({
 29         "--mouse-x": "100px",
 30         "--mouse-y": "200px",
 31       });
 32     });
 33
```

Figure 7-12A. *src/components/mouse-mask/__tests__/browser.test.ts*

```
src > components > mouse-mask > __tests__ > TS browser.test.ts > ✪ describe("MouseMask Compone
  6      describe("MouseMask Component", () => {
 33
 34        it("adds mousemove event listener on mount", async () => {
 35          const addEventListenerSpy = vi.spyOn(window, "addEventListener");
 36
 37          await render(MouseMask);
 38
 39          expect(addEventListenerSpy).toHaveBeenCalledWith(
 40            "mousemove",
 41            expect.any(Function),
 42          );
 43
 44          addEventListenerSpy.mockRestore();
 45        });
 46
 47        it("removes mousemove event listener on destroy", async () => {
 48          const removeEventListenerSpy = vi.spyOn(window, "removeEventListener");
 49
 50          const { instance } = await render(MouseMask);
 51          await instance.destroy();
 52
 53          expect(removeEventListenerSpy).toHaveBeenCalledWith(
 54            "mousemove",
 55            expect.any(Function),
 56          );
 57
 58          removeEventListenerSpy.mockRestore();
 59        });
 60
 61        it("emits updated-position event with new coordinates", async () => {
 62          const { emitted } = await render(MouseMask);
 63
 64          await fireEvent.mouseMove(window, {
 65            clientX: 150,
 66            clientY: 250,
 67          });
 68
 69          const emittedEvents = emitted("updated-position");
 70          expect(emittedEvents).toHaveLength(1);
 71          expect(emittedEvents[0]).toEqual([{ x: "150px", y: "250px" }]);
 72        });
 73      });
```

Figure 7-12B.   *src/components/mouse-mask/__tests__/browser.test.ts*
(continued...)

Now to make our tests meaningful, we have made some small changes to the
<mouse-mask/> component by letting it emit events with the coordinates that can be
tested. This is achieved via *this.emit* as you will remember that every Marko component
is an event emitter. The lines related to styles are the same and have been collapsed for
convenience as indicated in Figure 7-13.

```
src > components > mouse-mask >  ≡ index.marko > ...
  1    export interface Input {}
  2
  3    <div
  4      role="presentation"
  5      style=`--mouse-x:${state.x};--mouse-y:${state.y};`
  6      class="mouse-mask"
  7    />
  8    class {
  9      declare state: { x: string; y: string };
 10      declare boundMove: (e: MouseEvent) => void;
 11      onCreate() {
 12        this.state = { x: "center", y: "center" };
 13        this.boundMove = this.move.bind(this);
 14      }
 15      onMount() {
 16        window.addEventListener("mousemove", this.boundMove);
 17      }
 18      onDestroy() {
 19        window.removeEventListener("mousemove", this.boundMove);
 20      }
 21      move(e: MouseEvent) {
 22        this.state.x = e.clientX + "px";
 23        this.state.y = e.clientY + "px";
 24        this.emit("updated-position", { x: this.state.x, y: this.state.y });
 25      }
 26    }
 27
 28  > style { ...
 53    }
 54
```

Figure 7-13. *src/components/mouse-mask/index.marko*

The server test in Figure 7-11 consisted of just snapshot testing offered by **vitest** along
with **@marko/testing-library**. This basically rendered the mouse-mask template (***index.
marko*** file) and placed the generated **vitest** output into a __*snapshots*__ folder inside
__*tests*__ in a file named server.test.ts.snap. This basically contains a Vite understandable
descriptive snapshot of the rendered component output for the given input. We provided

the render function with the template and an empty input as seen in Figure 7-11, line #7. Next time, when the render changes either due to a different input or structural changes in the template, the snapshots will not match, and Vite will flag it with an error. It will also offer you an option (-u) to update the snapshots automatically in case your update to the component was indeed correct. This is what we call snapshot testing.

When you integrate it with paid solutions like Percy, this will be an additional step in bullet-proofing your UX components by being able to indulge in visual regression testing.

Next comes the client-side test in Figure 7-12. This checks for the following:

- Mouse move event listener is wired on mount.

- Mouse move event listener is cleaned up on destroy.

- When position changes, the updated position is emitted.

- When there is mouse move, it updates the position with the right coordinates.

- Initial render has the center position.

This uses the "render," "fireEvent," and "screen" APIs of testing-library while using them to render the mouse-mask template.

Now that we have our setup ready, script commands added, and tests and test files ready, let's execute the following command:

>> npm run test

```
dasathyakuma@C02FC27PML85 marko-test % npm run test

> marko-test@1.0.0 test
> vitest --run -u --minWorkers 1 --maxWorkers 4


 RUN  v3.0.9 /Users/dasathyakuma/ws/ads4/marko-test

 ✓  browser  src/components/mouse-mask/__tests__/browser.test.ts (5 tests) 83ms
 ✓  server   src/components/mouse-mask/__tests__/server.test.ts (1 test) 74ms

 Snapshots  1 updated
 Test Files  2 passed (2)
      Tests  6 passed (6)
   Start at  21:38:33
   Duration  1.69s (transform 354ms, setup 320ms, collect 1.48s, tests 157ms, environment 690ms, prepare 220ms)

JUNIT report written to /Users/dasathyakuma/ws/ads4/marko-test/test-results.xml
npm notice
npm notice New major version of npm available! 10.8.2 -> 11.2.0
npm notice Changelog: https://github.com/npm/cli/releases/tag/v11.2.0
npm notice To update run: npm install -g npm@11.2.0
npm notice
```

Figure 7-14. *Tests executed!*

It will indicate that one snapshot was generated, two test files were executed, and six tests in total were run and all passed successfully. You can check for the generated snapshot file under __snapshots__ within __tests__ as shown in Figure 7-15.

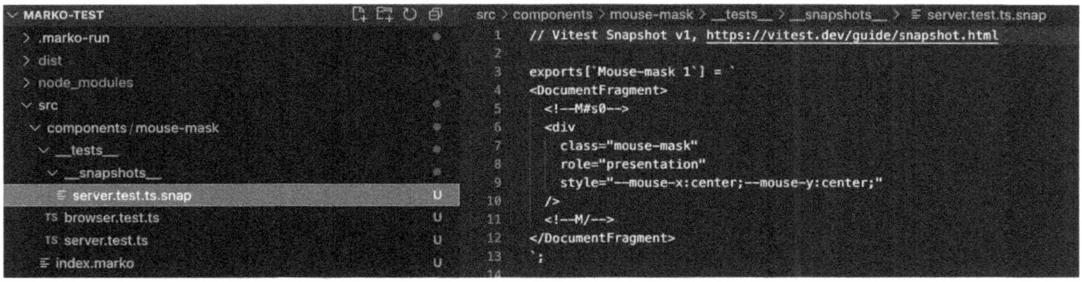

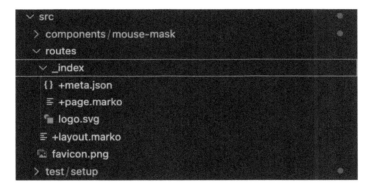

Figure 7-15. *Snapshot file generated*

Next, let us look at adding tests for the src/routes folder. These contain our pages as they belong to the Marko-run setup, as shown in Figure 7-16.

Figure 7-16. *src/routes directory of pages*

We will place two __**tests**__ folders: one under **src/routes** and the second under **src/routes/_index**. This is illustrated in Figure 7-17. For the one under *src/routes*, since it's a +*layout.marko* that transcludes any +*page.marko*, we will have to test for the transclusion of content as well. For this, let's create a fixtures folder within src/routes/__tests__ with an index.marko file that will just be used for testing purposes.

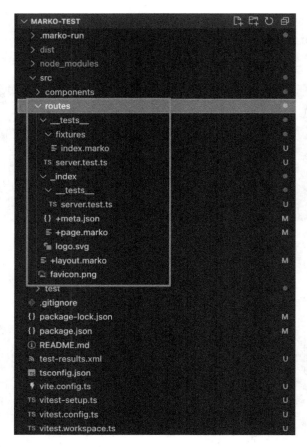

Figure 7-17. *src/routes directory (new files)*

```
src > routes > _index > {} +meta.json > ...
1    {
2        "pageTitle": "Welcome to Marko"
3    }
4
```

Figure 7-18. *src/routes/_index/+meta.json*

```
src > routes > _index > ☰ +page.marko > ...
 1    <div class="container">
 2      <header>
 3        <img src="./logo.svg" alt="Marko" class="logo">
 4      </header>
 5      <main>
 6        <p>
 7          Edit
 8          <code>./src/routes/_index/+page.marko</code>
 9          and save to reload.
10        </p>
11        <a data-testid="Learn" href="https://markojs.com/docs/getting-started">
12          Learn Marko
13        </a>
14      </main>
15    </div>
16    <mouse-mask/>
17
18 > style {¬
33    }
34
```

Figure 7-19. *src/routes/_index/+page.marko*

```
src > routes > __tests__ > fixtures > ☰ index.marko > ...
 1    import Layout from "../../+layout.marko";
 2    export interface Input {
 3      name: string;
 4    }
 5
 6    <Layout>
 7      <div>Greetings ${input.name}</div>
 8    </Layout>
 9
```

Figure 7-20. *src/routes/__tests__/fixtures/index.marko*

501

```
src > routes > ≡ +layout.marko > ...
  1    <!doctype html>
  2    <html lang="en">
  3      <head>
  4        <meta charset="UTF-8">
  5        <link rel="icon" type="image/png" sizes="32x32" href="./favicon.png">
  6        <meta name="viewport" content="width=device-width, initial-scale=1.0">
  7        <meta name="description" content="A basic Marko app.">
  8        <title>${$global.meta.pageTitle || "Marko"}</title>
  9      </head>
 10      <body>
 11        <${input.renderBody}/>
 12      </body>
 13    </html>
 14
 15    style {
 16      html,
 17      body {
 18        font-family: system-ui;
 19        padding: 0;
 20        margin: 0;
 21        height: 100%;
 22        color: ■#fff;
 23        background: □#15151e;
 24      }
 25      code {
 26        color: ■#fc0;
 27      }
 28      a {
 29        color: ■#09c;
 30      }
 31    }
```

Figure 7-21. *src/routes/+layout.marko*

The two test files we will be including are server-side test files. This is because we are talking about the app in the context of an MPA where +layout and +page are rendered on the server. Also, notice that components not required for our test case like the <mouse-mask/> has been mocked out.

As part of the test, we are checking if the render contains some text that we have used from +meta.json. Also, we have checked for the presence of the Learn link.

```
src > routes > __tests__ > TS server.test.ts > ...
  1    import { render } from "@marko/testing-library";
  2    import { expect, test, vi } from "vitest";
  3
  4    import meta from "../_index/+meta.json";
  5    import Test, { type Input } from "./fixtures/index.marko";
  6
  7    vi.mock("@components/mouse-mask");
  8
  9    test("+layout.marko", async () => {
 10      const { container } = await render<any>(Test, {
 11        name: "John Doe",
 12        $global: {
 13          meta: {
 14            ...meta,
 15          },
 16        },
 17      } as Input);
 18      expect(container).toMatchSnapshot();
 19      expect(container.querySelector("div")).toHaveTextContent(/John Doe/);
 20      expect(container.querySelector("title")).toHaveTextContent(
 21        "Welcome to Marko",
 22      );
 23    });
```

Figure 7-22. *src/routes/__tests__/server.test.ts*

```
src > routes > _index > __tests__ > TS server.test.ts > ...
  1    import { render } from "@marko/testing-library";
  2    import { expect, test, vi } from "vitest";
  3
  4    import Page from "../+page.marko";
  5
  6    vi.mock("@components/mouse-mask");
  7
  8    test("+layout.marko", async () => {
  9      const { container } = await render<any>(Page, {});
 10      expect(container).toMatchSnapshot();
 11      const link = container.querySelector('[data-testid="Learn"]');
 12      expect(link).toHaveTextContent("Learn Marko");
 13    });
 14
```

Figure 7-23. *src/routes/_index/__tests__/server.test.ts*

With all the new files added, we see two new files being written when executing the tests as shown in Figure 7-24. These are the snapshot files for the two new test files we have added.

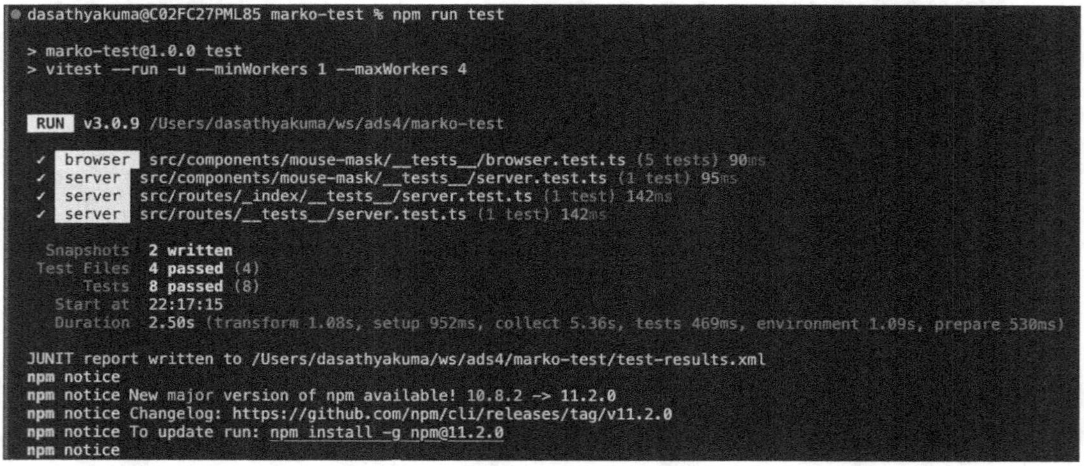
dasathyakuma@C02FC27PML85 marko-test % npm run test
> marko-test@1.0.0 test
> vitest --run -u --minWorkers 1 --maxWorkers 4
RUN v3.0.9 /Users/dasathyakuma/ws/ads4/marko-test
✓ browser src/components/mouse-mask/__tests__/browser.test.ts (5 tests) 90ms
✓ server src/components/mouse-mask/__tests__/server.test.ts (1 test) 95ms
✓ server src/routes/_index/__tests__/server.test.ts (1 test) 142ms
✓ server src/routes/__tests__/server.test.ts (1 test) 142ms
Snapshots 2 written
Test Files 4 passed (4)
Tests 8 passed (8)
Start at 22:17:15
Duration 2.50s (transform 1.08s, setup 952ms, collect 5.36s, tests 469ms, environment 1.09s, prepare 530ms)
JUNIT report written to /Users/dasathyakuma/ws/ads4/marko-test/test-results.xml
npm notice
npm notice New major version of npm available! 10.8.2 -> 11.2.0
npm notice Changelog: https://github.com/npm/cli/releases/tag/v11.2.0
npm notice To update run: npm install -g npm@11.2.0
npm notice

***Figure 7-24.** Test execution output with new files being written*

The two new snapshot files are included in Figures 7-25 and 7-26.

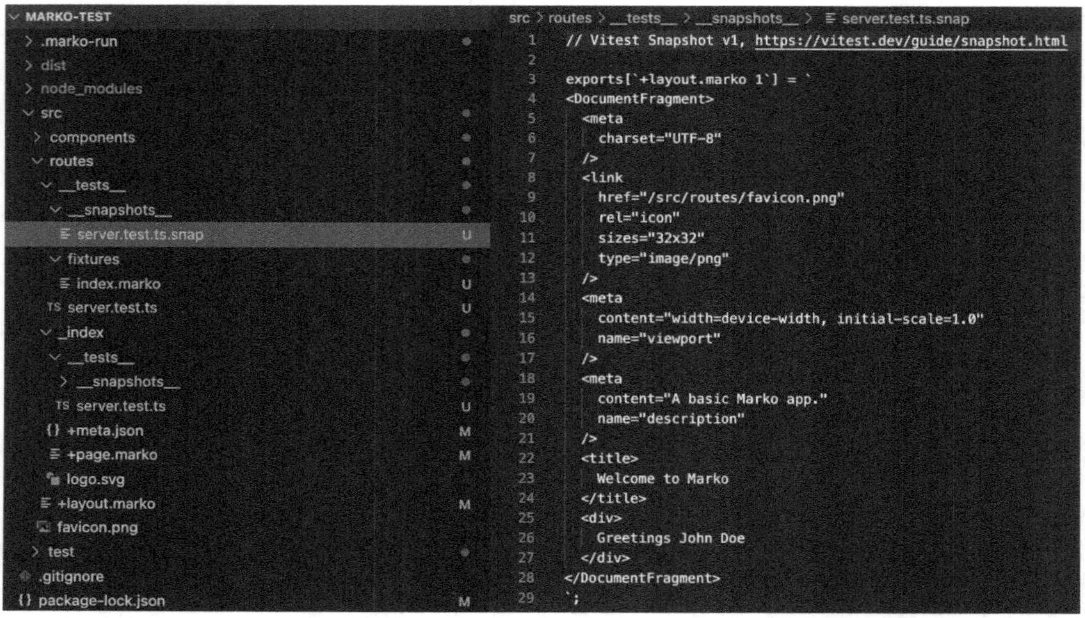
MARKO-TEST
.marko-run
dist
node_modules
src
components
routes
__tests__
__snapshots__
server.test.ts.snap U
fixtures
index.marko U
server.test.ts U
_index
__tests__
__snapshots__
server.test.ts U
+meta.json M
+page.marko M
logo.svg
+layout.marko M
favicon.png
test
.gitignore
package-lock.json M
src > routes > __tests__ > __snapshots__ > server.test.ts.snap
// Vitest Snapshot v1, https://vitest.dev/guide/snapshot.html
exports[`+layout.marko 1`] = `
<DocumentFragment>
<meta
charset="UTF-8"
/>
<link
href="/src/routes/favicon.png"
rel="icon"
sizes="32x32"
type="image/png"
/>
<meta
content="width=device-width, initial-scale=1.0"
name="viewport"
/>
<meta
content="A basic Marko app."
name="description"
/>
<title>
Welcome to Marko
</title>
<div>
Greetings John Doe
</div>
</DocumentFragment>
`;

***Figure 7-25.** Generated snapshots*

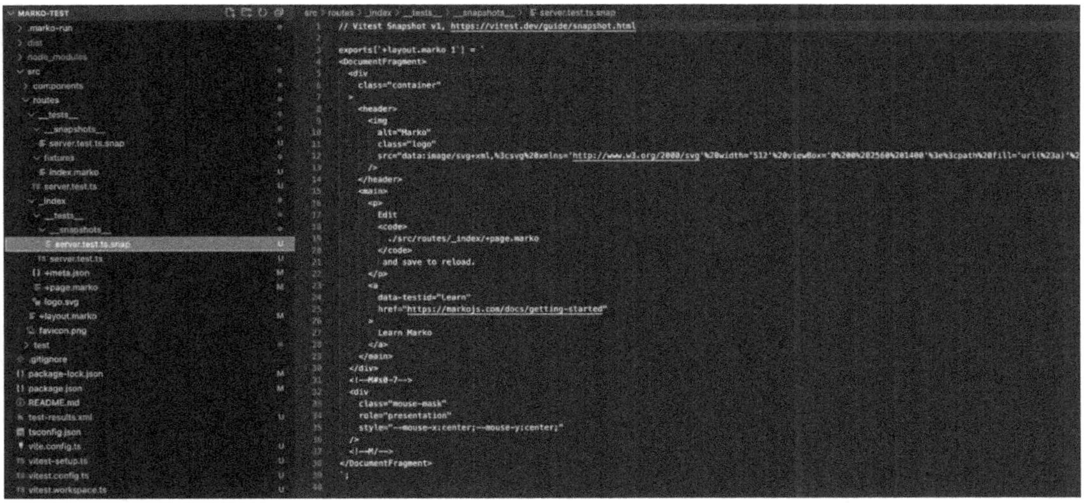

Figure 7-26. *Generated snapshots*

You will also notice this file test-results.xml (JUNIT XML) output being generated, which you can use to upload to other additional tooling.

Figure 7-27. *test-results.xml*

This can be ignored by placing an entry within the ***.gitignore*** file. So, our overall changeset is shown in Figure 7-28.

```
dasathyakuma@C02FC27PML85 marko-test % git status
On branch main
Changes not staged for commit:
  (use "git add/rm <file>..." to update what will be committed)
  (use "git restore <file>..." to discard changes in working directory)
        modified:    .gitignore
        modified:    .marko-run/routes.d.ts
        modified:    package-lock.json
        modified:    package.json
        deleted:     src/components/mouse-mask.marko
        modified:    src/routes/+layout.marko
        modified:    src/routes/_index/+meta.json
        modified:    src/routes/_index/+page.marko

Untracked files:
  (use "git add <file>..." to include in what will be committed)
        src/components/mouse-mask/
        src/routes/__tests__/
        src/routes/_index/__tests__/
        src/test/
        vite.config.ts
        vitest-setup.ts
        vitest.config.ts
        vitest.workspace.ts
```

Figure 7-28. *changeset*

Generating Coverage

Coverage basically computes what parts of our code have been covered or run via the unit tests that we have. In the context of *vitest*, which runs server- and client-side test cases, **@vitest/coverage-v8** helps *vitest* to determine the coverage of our code. In this case, it is able to determine the line, function, branch coverage, and more. This is illustrated in Figures 7-29 and 7-30. This can be triggered by the command "yarn run coverage".

Be sure to include **coverage/** in the project's *.gitignore* file, so that the **coverage/** folder doesn't get accidentally checked into GIT. You can also open and view the coverage report.

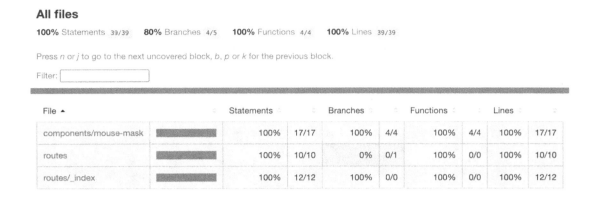

Figure 7-29. *Coverage report*

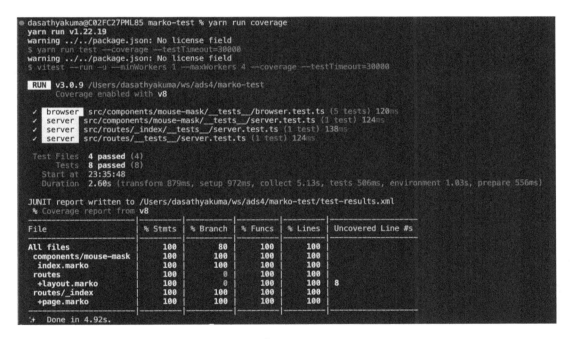

Figure 7-30. *Coverage report generation*

Watch Mode

You can also execute the tests in watch mode. This means, as you edit and make modifications to the test files or source code, the impacted tests shall be re-executed. This can be executed via the command "npm run test_watch". This is shown in Figure 7-31.

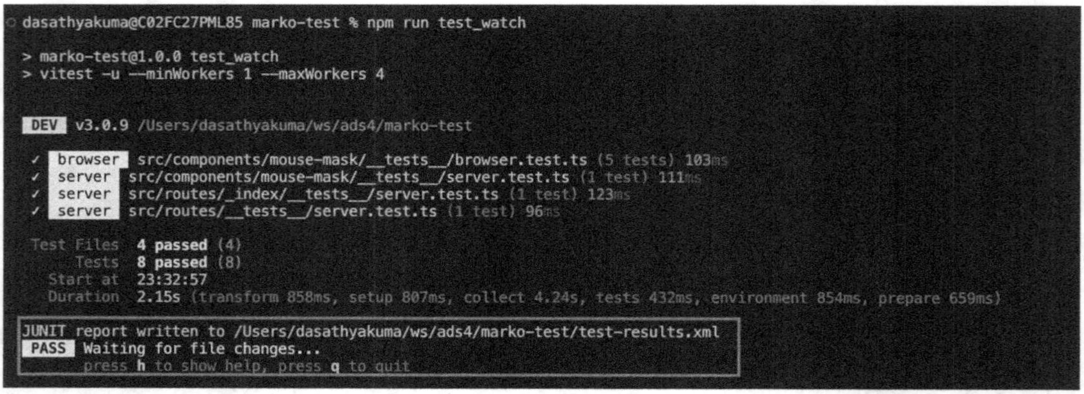

Figure 7-31. *Watch mode*

UI Mode

This mode is offered by Vite, where it provides us with a UI shell to interact with the tests. You can get a closer look at the execution of tests and failures, execute individual tests, and so on. This is shown in Figure 7-32.

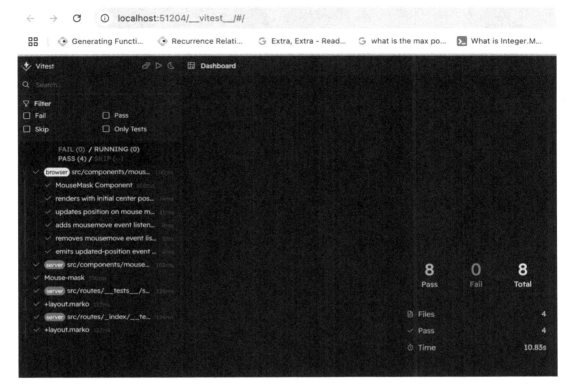

Figure 7-32. *vitest UI mode*

Visualizing Vite Bundles

An important part of ensuring performance is keeping tabs on the bundle sizes and contents of the generated bundles. While vite generates the bundles, you can pair up with solutions like BundleSize to set performance budget (I don't want my app's bundles to exceed 500KB and so on). This, when integrated with CI, will generate a failure if the size is exceeded. Pair that with solutions like the Vite bundle visualizer, and it will provide you with a detailed analysis of why the size is so large and what constitutes the generated bundles.

To see this, we will first require to install the *rollup-plugin-visualizer*. Note that Vite uses rollup under the hood. And then we include the command shown in Figure 7-33A.

```
24    "scripts": {
25      "dev": "marko-run",
26      "build": "marko-run build",
27      "preview": "marko-run preview",
28      "start": "node --enable-source-maps ./dist/index.mjs",
29      "test": "vitest --run -u --minWorkers 1 --maxWorkers 4",
30      "test_watch": "vitest -u --minWorkers 1 --maxWorkers 4",
31      "test_ui": "vitest --ui",
32      "coverage": "yarn run test --coverage --testTimeout=30000",
33      "visualizer": "yarn build --config vite.visualizer.config.ts"
34    }
```

Figure 7-33A. *Vite visualizer*

And then we include the associated configuration file for this plugin to work with Vite.

```
TS vite.visualizer.config.ts > ...
1   import { visualizer } from "rollup-plugin-visualizer";
2   import { defineConfig, type PluginOption } from "vite";
3
4   const plugins: PluginOption[] = [];
5
6   plugins.push(
7     visualizer({
8       template: "treemap", // or sunburst
9       open: true,
10      gzipSize: true,
11      filename: "stats.html",
12    }) as PluginOption,
13  );
14
15  export default defineConfig({
16    plugins,
17  });
18
```

Figure 7-33B. *Vite visualizer config*

Now running "npm run visualizer" will generate the bundles and provide the analysis in this fashion. You can drill deeper and take a look at the various pieces of the bundle and what is being included/excluded. This will generate a **stats.html** file as part of the output. You can place it as part of the GIT ignore.

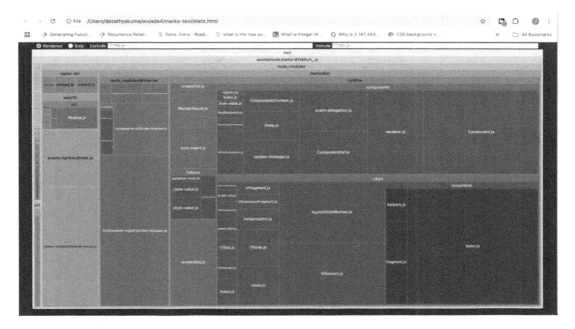

Figure 7-33C. *Vite visualizer output*

Figures 7-33A to 7-33C illustrate visualizing vite bundles.

Writing End-to-End Tests for Marko Pages with Playwright

Playwright is an open source automation library developed by Microsoft for browser testing and web scraping, allowing you to automate tasks across Chromium, Firefox, and WebKit browsers with a single API. Playwright enables reliable end-to-end testing for modern web apps. · Any browser • Any platform.

We will be using playwright to run automation tests (end-to-end tests) on our sample page accessible at http://localhost:3000. These tests will be executed for now on our local code. For this, while on one side we start playwright on a port, we also start our development vite server on port 3000 as usual. Then we run the automation by letting playwright work with our dev server on port 3000 to load the pages and test them.

To start, we will include the following files:

1. **playwright.config.ts**: Playwright configuration file

2. **global-setup.ts**: A setup file to bootstrap playwright-related stuff

3. **.env**: Environment variables file)

Figures 7-34A and 7-34B shows the *playwright.config.ts* file.

```ts
ts playwright.config.ts > ...
1    import { defineConfig, devices } from "@playwright/test";
2    /**
3     * Read environment variables from file.
4     * https://github.com/motdotla/dotenv
5     */
6    import dotenv from "dotenv";
7    // Configure dotenv to load environment variables from a .env file.
8    // `override: true` allows overriding existing environment variables.
9    dotenv.config({
10     path: ".env",
11     override: false,
12   });
13
14   const environmentUrls = {
15     local: "http://localhost:3000",
16     // other environments like QA / Prod / go here ...
17   };
18   // Default environment if PLAYWRIGHT_ENV is not defined
19   const defaultEnvironment = "local";
20   const playwrightEnv = process.env.PLAYWRIGHT_ENV || defaultEnvironment;
21   const playwrightEnvUrl = environmentUrls[playwrightEnv];
22   // Determine the baseURL
23   const baseUrl = process.env.FEATURE_POOL_URL || playwrightEnvUrl;
24   /**
25    * See https://playwright.dev/docs/test-configuration.
26    */
27 > export default defineConfig({ ...
75   });
76
```

Figure 7-34A. *playwright.config.ts*

The playwright configuration file contains a lot of details and is quite descriptive. It indicates the reporter to be used for coverage—allure. It also indicates the directory that contains end-to-end tests. What to do when there is an error? Should it take videos, screen grabs, etc.? It offers a place for the *global-setup.ts* file and then the browser to run the tests on. You can include other browsers in that list. There is also the *storageState*.

When you call storageState, Playwright will make all the current cookie and localStorage entries accessible to you. If you will, storageState returns an entire browser storage session dump.

```ts
 ts playwright.config.ts > ...
 26     */
 27    export default defineConfig({
 28      testDir: "./integration-tests",
 29      /* Run tests in files in parallel */
 30      fullyParallel: true,
 31      /* Fail the build on CI if you accidentally left test.only in the source code. */
 32      forbidOnly: !!process.env.CI,
 33      /* Retry on CI only */
 34      retries: process.env.CI ? 2 : 0,
 35      /* Opt out of parallel tests on CI. */
 36      workers: process.env.PLAYWRIGHT_WORKERS
 37        ? parseInt(process.env.PLAYWRIGHT_WORKERS, 10)
 38        : "50%",
 39      /* Reporter to use. See https://playwright.dev/docs/test-reporters */
 40      reporter: [["allure-playwright"]],
 41      /* Shared settings for all the projects below. See https://playwright.dev/docs/api/class-testoptions. */
 42      use: {
 43        /* Base URL to use in actions like `await page.goto('/')`. */
 44        baseURL: baseUrl,
 45        storageState: {
 46          origins: [],
 47          cookies: [],
 48        },
 49
 50        /* Collect trace when retrying the failed test. See https://playwright.dev/docs/trace-viewer */
 51        trace: "on-first-retry",
 52        ignoreHTTPSErrors: true,
 53        screenshot: "only-on-failure",
 54        video: "retry-with-video",
 55        testIdAttribute: "data-testid",
 56        actionTimeout: 100000,
 57      },
 58      expect: { timeout: 45000 },
 59      timeout: 100000,
 60      /* Configure projects for major browsers */
 61      projects: [
 62        {
 63          name: "setup",
 64          testMatch: /global\.setup\.ts/,
 65          use: {
 66            navigationTimeout: 120000,
 67          },
 68        },
 69        {
 70          name: "chromium",
 71          use: { ...devices["Desktop Chrome"] },
 72          dependencies: ["setup"],
 73        },
 74      ],
 75    });
 76
```

Figure 7-34B. *playwright.config.ts (continued...)*

Note that we will be placing all the end-to-end tests under the **integration-tests** folder. This is indicated in the .env file and the **playwright.config.ts** file.

```
⚙ .env
1    # Available environment variables:
2    ENVIRONMENT=local
3    CLIENT=dweb,mweb
4    PRIORITY=P1,P2,P3,P4
5    # Test spec folder paths
6    TEST_AUTOMATION_FOLDER=integration-tests
7    # Other configurations
8    MAX_INSTANCES=1
```

Figure 7-35. *.env file*

Figure 7-35 shows the .env file, and Figure 7-36 shows the **global-setup.ts** file. All end-to-end tests are placed under the **integration-tests/** folder under the project root. This is also mentioned in the **playwright.config.ts** file and the **.env** file.

```
integration-tests > TS global-setup.ts > ...
1    import os from "node:os";
2
3    import { test as setup } from "@playwright/test";
4
5    // eslint-disable-next-line no-empty-pattern
6    setup("System config", async ({}, testInfo) => {
7      const cpuCount = os.cpus().length;
8      const workerCount = testInfo.config.workers;
9
10     console.log(`Available CPU cores: ${cpuCount}`);
11     console.log(`Configured parallel workers: ${workerCount}`);
12   });
13
```

Figure 7-36. *integration-tests/global-setup.ts file*

And we shall install the following packages:

1. @playwright/test

2. Playwright

3. Allure-playwright
4. Concurrently (helps executing terminal commands concurrently)

Allure is the reporting tool that will be used with playwright for reporting the coverage.

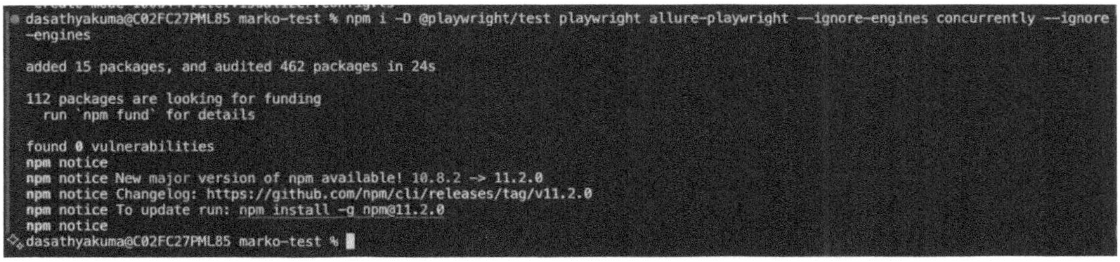

```
dasathyakuma@C02FC27PML85 marko-test % npm i -D @playwright/test playwright allure-playwright --ignore-engines concurrently --ignore-engines

added 15 packages, and audited 462 packages in 24s

112 packages are looking for funding
  run `npm fund` for details

found 0 vulnerabilities
npm notice
npm notice New major version of npm available! 10.8.2 -> 11.2.0
npm notice Changelog: https://github.com/npm/cli/releases/tag/v11.2.0
npm notice To update run: npm install -g npm@11.2.0
npm notice
dasathyakuma@C02FC27PML85 marko-test %
```

Figure 7-37. *Installing playwright dependencies*

Now let us add an end-to-end test for the index page that loads the <mouse-mask/> component with the Learn marko link. We will test the click of this and if it navigates to a new page. This is shown in Figure 7-40. The commands to invoke playwright are updated in the "scripts" section of the package.json file and is indicated in Figure 7-38.

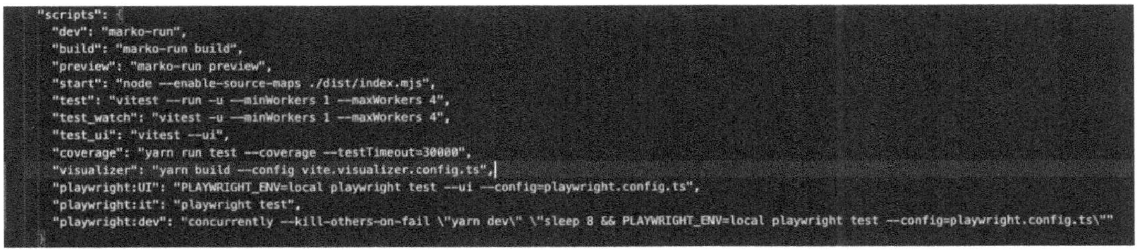

```
"scripts": {
  "dev": "marko-run",
  "build": "marko-run build",
  "preview": "marko-run preview",
  "start": "node --enable-source-maps ./dist/index.mjs",
  "test": "vitest --run -u --minWorkers 1 --maxWorkers 4",
  "test_watch": "vitest -u --minWorkers 1 --maxWorkers 4",
  "test_ui": "vitest --ui",
  "coverage": "yarn run test --coverage --testTimeout=30000",
  "visualizer": "yarn build --config vite.visualizer.config.ts",
  "playwright:UI": "PLAYWRIGHT_ENV=local playwright test --ui --config=playwright.config.ts",
  "playwright:it": "playwright test",
  "playwright:dev": "concurrently --kill-others-on-fail \"yarn dev\" \"sleep 8 && PLAYWRIGHT_ENV=local playwright test --config=playwright.config.ts\""
}
```

Figure 7-38. *Playwright commands in "scripts"*

Now when you run the "npm run playwright:UI", it will open up a nice visualizer as shown in Figure 7-39. This is the same as the Vite test visualizer we saw earlier, but for playwright. With this, you can execute individual tests and have a better look at the logs, source code failing, etc. If this is up, your playwright setup is good to go.

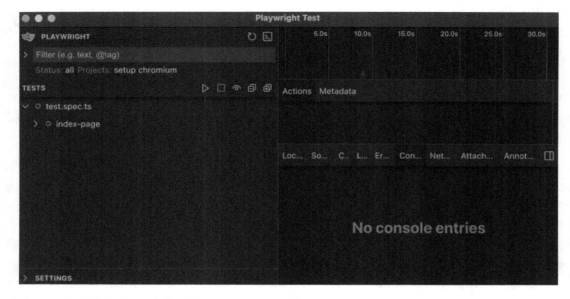

Figure 7-39. *Playwright UI*

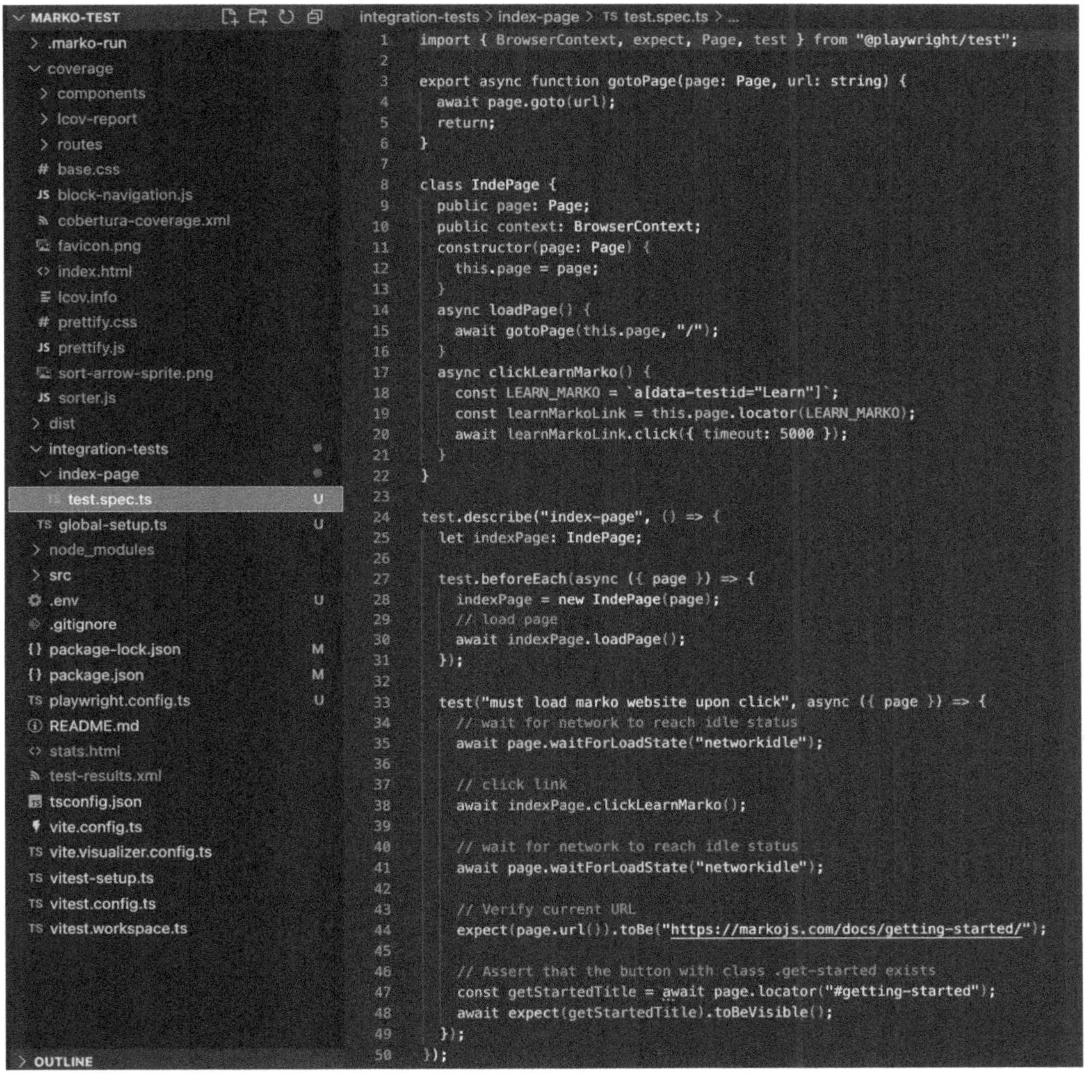

Figure 7-40. *Playwright end-to-end test*

Now to begin testing, start your local development vite dev server on port 3000. Once that is done, and your page is up on http://localhost:3000, click the > button on the playwright UI. You can see the execution happening and the tests passing. The snapshots taken by playwright will also be made visible as seen in Figure 7-41.

In case you are executing playwright for the first time, it may error out and ask you to run "npm playwright install," which will download all the requisite browsers needed for the execution and install them.

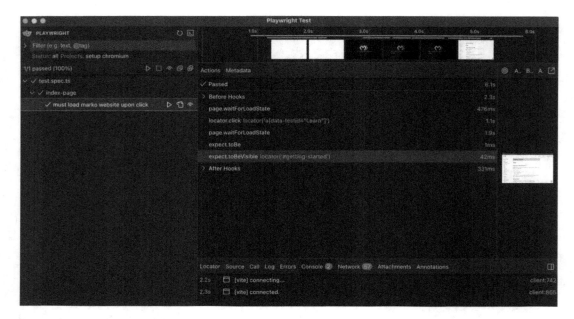

Figure 7-41. *Playwright execution*

Coming back to the contents of the end-to-end test case, in Figure 7-40, we have basically opened the page at http://localhost:3000, clicked the "Learn marko" link, validated if the page redirected to the correct URL, then proceeded to check for an element on the page.

The coverage results of the end-to-end testing can be found in the **allure-results/** folder, and the test results are formally documented in the **test-results/** folder. These can be GIT ignored.

Adding Component Stories into Unit Tests via the Component Story Format

The Component Story Format (CSF) (`https://storybook.js.org/docs/api/csf`) is a standardized way to write stories for UI components in Storybook, a popular tool for developing and testing UI components in isolation, as seen in the previous chapter. CSF is an ES6 module–based format that makes it easy to define stories (examples or use cases) for a component, including its props, states, and behaviors. It's designed to be simple, declarative, and reusable, which makes it particularly useful for integrating with unit testing frameworks. Here's a breakdown of what CSF is and how it helps reuse stories in unit tests for components.

What Is the Component Story Format (CSF)?

CSF is essentially a JavaScript (or TypeScript) file that exports an object with metadata about a component and its stories. Each story represents a specific state or variant of the component, such as different prop combinations or user interactions. The format is structured as shown in Figure 7-42.

```
export default {
    title: 'Components/Button',
    component: Button,
};

export const Primary = {
  args: {
    label: 'Click me',
    primary: true,
  },
};

export const Secondary = {
  args: {
    label: 'Click me',
  },
};
```

Figure 7-42. *CSF*

- **default Export**: Contains metadata like the component name, title, and sometimes additional configuration (e.g., decorators or parameters).

- **Named Exports**: Each named export (e.g., Primary, Secondary) is a story that defines how the component should be rendered with specific props or conditions.

Here, args automatically passes props to the component, reducing boilerplate.

How CSF Helps Reuse Stories in Unit Tests?

When testing UI components (e.g., in React, Marko, Vue, etc.), you often want to verify how they behave under different conditions—like the ones defined in your stories. CSF makes this reusable by providing a machine-readable, consistent structure that testing tools can leverage. Here's how it works:

1. **Stories As Test Cases**: Each story in CSF represents a specific use case or state of the component (e.g., a button in its primary state or disabled state). These stories can be imported into unit tests (e.g., with Jest or Vitest) and used to render the component with the exact same props or setup as in Storybook.

2. **DRY (Don't Repeat Yourself)**: Without CSF, you'd have to manually redefine these test cases in your unit tests, duplicating effort and risking inconsistencies between what's tested and what's displayed in Storybook. With CSF, the stories serve as a single source of truth. You define the component's states once in the .stories.js file and reuse them in both Storybook and tests.

3. **Integration with Testing Libraries**: Tools like @storybook/testing-library or Marko's testing utilities can directly consume CSF stories. For example, in Marko, you can use the *composeStories* utility via the *@storybook/mark*o to extract all stories from a CSF file and test them.

4. **Consistency Across Development and Testing**: Since Storybook stories are visual representations of your component's states, reusing them in tests ensures that what developers see in Storybook matches what's being validated in the test suite. This reduces bugs caused by mismatched assumptions between development and testing phases.

5. **Args for Dynamic Testing**: The *args* feature in CSF allows you to define reusable prop combinations. Testing tools can iterate over these args or combine them with additional test-specific variations, making it easy to test edge cases without rewriting stories.

@storybook/marko

@storybook/marko makes it possible to consume component stories as test fixtures while supporting many of the shorthands and features not taken care of automatically. Features such as **args**, **decorators/global decorators**, and **meta** from your story will be composed and returned to you in a component, which you can render directly or using **@marko/testing-library**.

Example

We will look at this with an example using the stories we previously created for <mouse-mask/> in the previous chapter. Before that, let's install the following dependencies into our project:

1. @storybook/addon-essentials

2. @storybook/addon-interactions

3. @storybook/marko

4. @storybook/marko-vite

5. @storybook/testing-library

6. storybook

```
dasathyakuma@C02FC27PML85 marko-test % npm i -D @storybook/addon-essentials @storybook/ad]
don-interactions @storybook/marko @storybook/marko-vite @storybook/testing-library storyb
ook --ignore-engines


added 108 packages, and audited 570 packages in 53s

155 packages are looking for funding
  run `npm fund` for details

found 0 vulnerabilities
npm notice
npm notice New major version of npm available! 10.8.2 -> 11.2.0
npm notice Changelog: https://github.com/npm/cli/releases/tag/v11.2.0
npm notice To update run: npm install -g npm@11.2.0
npm notice
dasathyakuma@C02FC27PML85 marko-test %
```

Figure 7-43. *Installing storybook dependencies*

Following this, we shall include the following files:

1.   .storybook/main.ts

2.   .storybook/preview.ts

```ts
.storybook > TS main.ts > ...
1    import type { StorybookConfig } from "@storybook/marko-vite";
2
3    export default {
4      framework: "@storybook/marko-vite",
5      stories: ["../src/**/{,*.}stories.ts"],
6      addons: ["@storybook/addon-essentials", "@storybook/addon-interactions"],
7      core: {
8        disableTelemetry: true,
9        disableWhatsNewNotifications: true,
10     },
11     docs: {
12       autodocs: true,
13       defaultName: "Documentation",
14     },
15   } satisfies StorybookConfig;
16
```

Figure 7-44.   *.storybook/main.ts*

```ts
.storybook > TS preview.ts > [⊘] default
1    import type { Parameters } from "@storybook/marko";
2
3    export const parameters = {
4      actions: { argTypesRegex: "^on[A-Z].*" },
5      options: {
6        storySort: {
7          method: "alphabetical",
8        },
9      },
10   } satisfies Parameters;
11
12   export default {
13     parameters,
14     loaders: [],
15   };
```

Figure 7-45.   *.storybook/preview.ts*

Following this, let's look at the stories for the <mouse-mask/> component. This is reproduced again in Figure 7-46. In this, you will notice the stories—Default, Mouse Moved, Top Left, Bottom Left, etc. These capture the various use cases or scenarios of this component. Now, as mentioned before, we would like to use these pre-created scenarios or stories and test them by incorporating our tests around them and asserting their expected behavior.

```ts
src > components > mouse-mask > __tests__ > TS stories.ts > ...
1    import type { Meta, Story } from "@storybook/marko";
2
3    import type { Input } from "../index.marko";
4    import MouseMask from "../index.marko"; // Adjust the path to your component
5
6    export default {
7      title: "Components/MouseMask", // Storybook hierarchy
8      component: MouseMask, // The Marko component
9      parameters: {
10       // Optional: Configure the story canvas size for better visualization
11       layout: "fullscreen", // Makes the story take up the full Storybook canvas
12     },
13   } as Meta<Input>;
14
15   // Default story: Mouse at center (initial state)
16   export const Default: Story<Input> = {
17     args: {},
18     name: "Default (Centered)",
19   };
20
21   // Mouse at a specific position (e.g., 200px, 200px)
22   export const MouseMoved: Story<Input> = {
23     args: {},
24     name: "Mouse Moved (200px, 200px)",
25     play: async ({ canvasElement }) => {
26       // Simulate a mouse move event (Storybook's play function for interactions)
27       const event = new MouseEvent("mousemove", {
28         clientX: 200,
29         clientY: 200,
30         bubbles: true,
31       });
32       canvasElement.dispatchEvent(event);
33     },
34   };
35
```

Figure 7-46. *Stories of <mouse-mask/> component*

```
36   // Mouse at top-left corner (0px, 0px)
37   export const TopLeft: Story<Input> = {
38     args: {},
39     name: "Top Left Corner",
40     play: async ({ canvasElement }) => {
41       const event = new MouseEvent("mousemove", {
42         clientX: 0,
43         clientY: 0,
44         bubbles: true,
45       });
46       canvasElement.dispatchEvent(event);
47     },
48   };
49
50   // Mouse at bottom-right corner (simulating a 1280x720 viewport)
51   export const BottomRight: Story<Input> = {
52     args: {},
53     name: "Bottom Right Corner",
54     play: async ({ canvasElement }) => {
55       const event = new MouseEvent("mousemove", {
56         clientX: 1280,
57         clientY: 720,
58         bubbles: true,
59       });
60       canvasElement.dispatchEvent(event);
61     },
62   };
```

Figure 7-47. *Stories of <mouse-mask/> component (continued...)*

Next, let's look at the stories.browser.test.ts in Figure 7-48 at a high level and dig deeper into each test, which will be each Story previously catalogued in Figure 7-47.

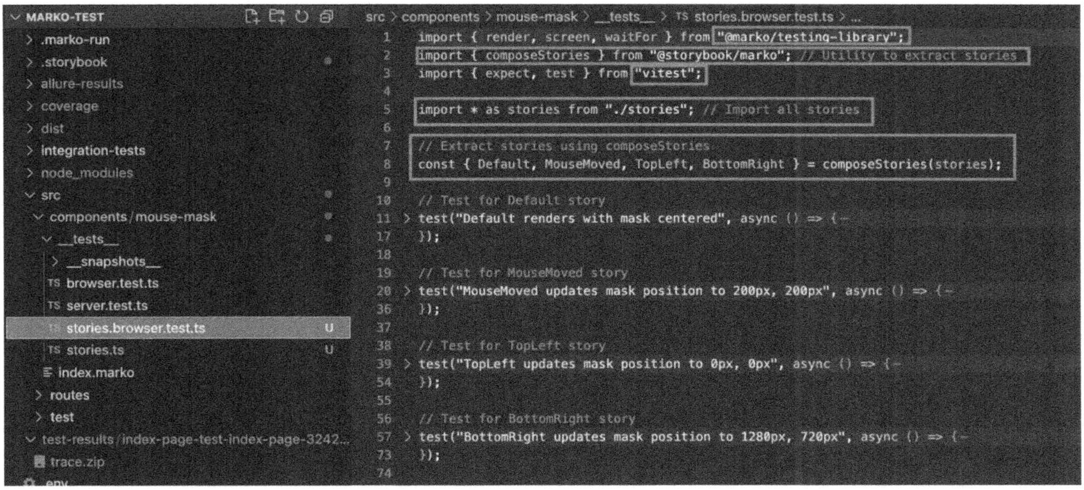

Figure 7-48. *Stories used in tests*

Notice how all stories are being imported and reused. You no longer have to spend time creating a setup for the tests. They just reuse your previously created setup in stories. Now let's explore deeper into each test in Figure 7-49.

```
// Test for Default story
test("Default renders with mask centered", async () => {
  await render(Default);
  const mask = screen.getByRole("presentation"); // Assuming the div is a presentation element
  const styles = getComputedStyle(mask);
  expect(styles.getPropertyValue("--mouse-x")).toBe("center");
  expect(styles.getPropertyValue("--mouse-y")).toBe("center");
});
```

Figure 7-49. *stories.browser.test.ts (continued…)*

```
// Test for MouseMoved story
test("MouseMoved updates mask position to 200px, 200px", async () => {
  const { container, cleanup } = await render(MouseMoved);
  // Simulate the mousemove event as in the story's play function
  const event = new MouseEvent("mousemove", {
    clientX: 200,
    clientY: 200,
    bubbles: true,
  });
  container.dispatchEvent(event);
  await waitFor(() => {
    const mask = screen.getByRole("presentation");
    const styles = getComputedStyle(mask);
    expect(styles.getPropertyValue("--mouse-x")).toBe("200px");
    expect(styles.getPropertyValue("--mouse-y")).toBe("200px");
  });
  cleanup();
});
```

Figure 7-50. *stories.browser.test.ts (continued...)*

```
// Test for TopLeft story
test("TopLeft updates mask position to 0px, 0px", async () => {
  const { container, cleanup } = await render(TopLeft);
  const event = new MouseEvent("mousemove", {
    clientX: 0,
    clientY: 0,
    bubbles: true,
  });
  container.dispatchEvent(event);
  await waitFor(() => {
    const mask = screen.getByRole("presentation");
    const styles = getComputedStyle(mask);
    expect(styles.getPropertyValue("--mouse-x")).toBe("0px");
    expect(styles.getPropertyValue("--mouse-y")).toBe("0px");
  });
  cleanup();
});
```

Figure 7-51. *stories.browser.test.ts (continued...)*

```
// Test for BottomRight story
test("BottomRight updates mask position to 1280px, 720px", async () => {
  const { container, cleanup } = await render(BottomRight);
  const event = new MouseEvent("mousemove", {
    clientX: 1280,
    clientY: 720,
    bubbles: true,
  });
  container.dispatchEvent(event);

  await waitFor(() => {
    const mask = screen.getByRole("presentation");
    const styles = getComputedStyle(mask);
    expect(styles.getPropertyValue("--mouse-x")).toBe("1280px");
    expect(styles.getPropertyValue("--mouse-y")).toBe("720px");
  });
  cleanup();
});
```

Figure 7-52. *stories.browser.test.ts (continued…)*

One thing to note is that the ***play*** that we saw in the previous chapter, where the stories play themselves, basically is not triggered here. Instead, we supply the **mousemove** event via **dispatchEvent**, and that causes the component to trigger its functionality. Finally, we use the ***waitFor*** function of **testing-library** to wait and observe resolution. The results are seen in Figure 7-53.

```
dasathyakuma@C02FC27PML85 marko-test % npm run test

> marko-test@1.0.0 test
> vitest --run -u --minWorkers 1 --maxWorkers 4


 RUN  v3.0.9 /Users/dasathyakuma/ws/ads4/marko-test

 ✓ browser  src/components/mouse-mask/__tests__/browser.test.ts (5 tests) 98ms
 ✓ browser  src/components/mouse-mask/__tests__/stories.browser.test.ts (4 tests) 106ms
 ✓ server   src/routes/_index/__tests__/server.test.ts (1 test) 110ms
 ✓ server   src/routes/__tests__/server.test.ts (1 test) 108ms
 ✓ server   src/components/mouse-mask/__tests__/server.test.ts (1 test) 74ms

 Test Files  5 passed (5)
      Tests  12 passed (12)
   Start at  01:49:05
   Duration  4.06s (transform 884ms, setup 1.15s, collect 5.49s, tests 495ms, environment 2.84s, prepare 878ms)

JUNIT report written to /Users/dasathyakuma/ws/ads4/marko-test/test-results.xml
npm notice
npm notice New major version of npm available! 10.8.2 -> 11.2.0
npm notice Changelog: https://github.com/npm/cli/releases/tag/v11.2.0
npm notice To update run: npm install -g npm@11.2.0
npm notice
dasathyakuma@C02FC27PML85 marko-test %
```

Figure 7-53. *Unit test execution with stories included*

Conclusion

As we come to the end of this chapter, it must be evident how seamless Marko is for testing purposes and how well it plays with all of the existing testing libraries and frameworks that are popular in the JS ecosystem today. While the marko-run setup gets you rapidly bootstrapped into authoring marko components and pages with ease, the Vitest, testing-library, and playwright setup discussed in this chapter should help you test your Marko components confidently and ensure you author reliable UX. Note that while we have discussed Vitest here, you can always swap this with Jest, testing-library, and other end-to-end testing frameworks of your choice like Cypress or WebdriverIO. In the same manner, you can always easily integrate solutions like Percy/Browserstack.

CHAPTER 8

The Marko RealWorld App

Introduction

In this chapter, we will look at Marko's take on the RealWorld application that is built per the RealWorld app specs—the mother of all demo apps as mentioned here: `https://github.com/gothinkster/realworld`. **You will find all the code at** `https://github.com/Apress/Practical-Marko`.

The RealWorld App

What Is It?

The RealWorld app, hosted at github.com/gothinkster/realworld, is an open source project designed to provide a comprehensive, full-stack example application that mirrors the functionality of Medium.com. It serves as a practical reference for developers to understand how to build real-world applications using various frontend and backend technologies.

More docs about the thinkster project are here:

`https://realworld-docs.netlify.app/specifications/frontend/api/#run-the-official-backend-implementation-locally`. Here is the RealWorld starter kit:

`https://github.com/gothinkster/realworld-starter-kit`.

The RealWorld backend API Postman collection can be got from here:

`https://github.com/gothinkster/realworld/blob/main/api/Conduit.postman_collection.json`

So any backend implementation you have must pass this RealWorld spec.

© Damodaran Chingleput Sathyakumar 2025
D. Chingleput Sathyakumar, *Practical Marko*, https://doi.org/10.1007/979-8-8688-1483-9_8

RealWorld is often referred to as "the mother of all demo apps" because it goes beyond simplistic examples like "TodoMVC" by offering a full-fledged application that includes

- **CRUD Operations**: Create, Read, Update, and Delete functionalities for articles and comments

- **Authentication**: User registration, login, and JWT-based authentication

- **Routing**: Client-side or server-side routing for seamless navigation

- **Pagination**: Efficient handling of large lists of articles

- **User Interactions**: Features like favoriting articles and following other users

The application is built around a standardized API specification, allowing developers to mix and match different frontend and backend implementations while maintaining consistent functionality and user experience.

The Core Components

- **Frontend Implementations**: RealWorld offers frontend examples built with frameworks such as React, Angular, Vue.js, and more. Each implementation adheres to the same design and functionality guidelines, making it easier to compare and learn different technologies.

- **Backend Implementations**: On the server side, RealWorld provides backend examples using Node.js, Django, ASP.NET Core, Laravel, Spring Boot, and others. These implementations follow the same API spec, ensuring interoperability with any of the frontend projects.

- **API Specification**: A detailed API spec defines the endpoints, request/response formats, and authentication methods, serving as a contract between the frontend and backend.

The Marko RealWorld App

For our example, given the focus of this book is about Marko, we will go over the frontend implementation of the RealWorld app spec with Marko. You will find all the code at `https://github.com/practical-marko` chapterwise. The contents of this chapter are kept intentionally minimum to focus on the implementation. The repository on GitHub contains ample README files to help you follow the code along the journey. However, it is important that you actually step away from the book and fork the project to try it out so that you get a first hand experience of how it is to work with Marko.

All our earlier examples were intentionally kept minimal to focus on the various concepts. We have already seen full-fledged examples of server and client progressive rendering, along with isomorphic progressive rendering. If you read this book at a time when Marko's version 6 is released, you can continue to try all these examples as they will be backward compatible (thanks to the presence of a compiler in Marko). Moreover, you may never have to feel that the code you write will not be useful because Marko's migration utilities will be updated to auto migrate applications from version 5 to version 6.

This Marko RealWorld app will be built using Marko-run—the meta framework of Marko. It will be fully operational as a multi-page application (the only difference from most of the existing RealWorld app implementations, which are focused on a SPA experience). For our backend, we have chosen `https://github.com/gothinkster/node-express-realworld-example-app` as our backend implementation, which is one of the officially maintained versions of the backend implementations of the RealWorld app spec.

The application we will be building is called conduit (a minimalist clone of medium.com). We will be using the aforementioned backend implementation running on port 3000, while our application runs on 3001. The backend implementation will be up and running, providing endpoints that our frontend application shall be querying or writing into. The backend implementation is however dependent on us having a working PostgreSQL database running. Earlier, the RealWorld application had free hosting for implementations to be able to query freely hosted endpoints, but at the time of writing this book, those endpoints were not operational.

So our use of the backend application is just to be able to provide us with an endpoint that the frontend application can query or write to and talk to the database behind the scenes. You will be required to have installed and running PostgreSQL for this to work. While this is fairly easy, the installation will vary depending on the OS you are on. The installation instructions provided are for Mac OS.

Once you get this up and running, please direct all your attention to the Marko RealWorld application. We will be building this application as an MPA for a change and set it up with cross-document view transitions to showcase how snappy the app and its interactions can be. As you author this and work through the application development, you will realize what a breeze it is to work with Marko, unlike many of the competitive offerings in the market today. Moreover, while the Marko dev team is hard at work regarding version 6, post launch you will find Marko coming up with integrations with many of the mainstream libraries related to routing, form handling, state management, and other UI integrations via ShadCN, etc.

The Frontend Components of the RealWorld App

The screens and functionalities that we shall be building include the following:

- Sign Up screen
- Login screen
- Profile page
    - Author page (same as profile page, except that it's your own information)
- Settings page
- Home page
    - Loads the tags
    - Loads the feed
        - Global feed
        - Personal feed
    - Click on the tag, loads articles with those specific tags
- Click on an article
    - Load article page
    - Edit/Update an existing article
    - Delete an existing article

- Favorite an article

- Unfavorite an article

- Follow an author

- Unfollow an author

- Comment on an article

- Load all comments

- Delete a posted comment

- Click on Author

- Click on an author

    - Authors articles

    - Articles favorited by the author

    - Authors followers

    - Other users that the author follows

    - A favorite button to favorite the author if not already

    - Pagination

    - Click on articles takes the user back to articles flow

Figure 8-1 is an example of how the home page will look.

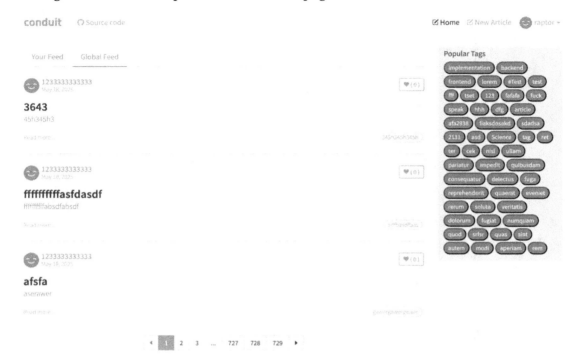

Figure 8-1. *The home page of the Marko RealWorld app (conduit/clone of medium.com)*

The spec uses JWT (JSON Web Tokens) for auth.

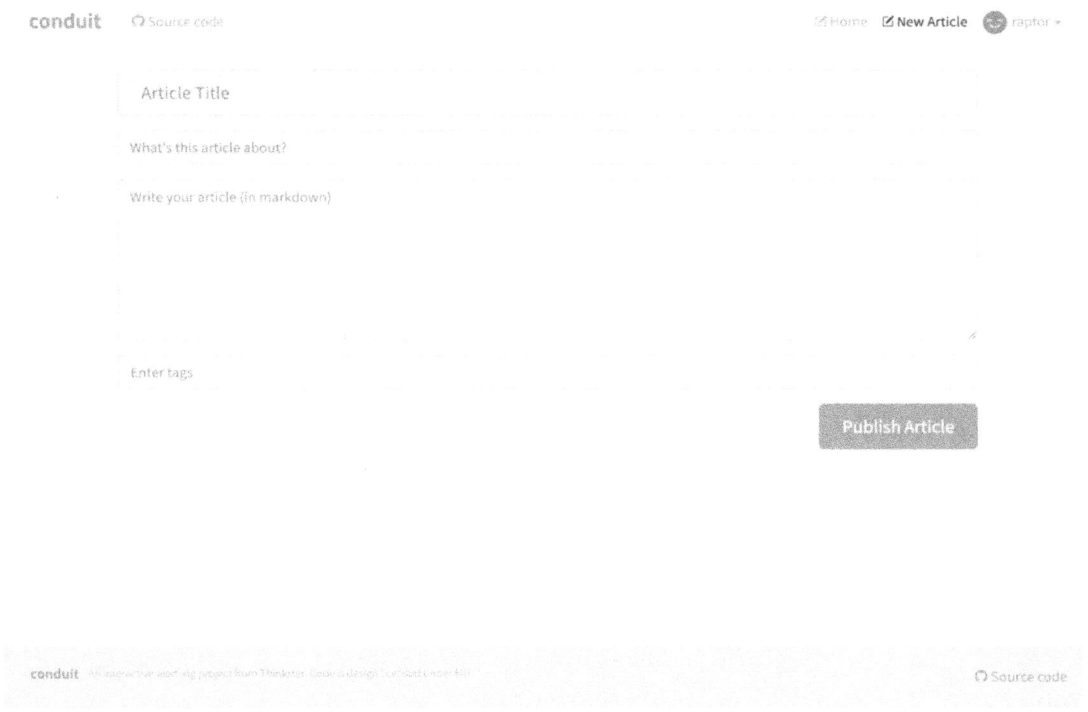

Figure 8-2. *The article authoring page of the Marko RealWorld app (conduit/ clone of medium.com)*

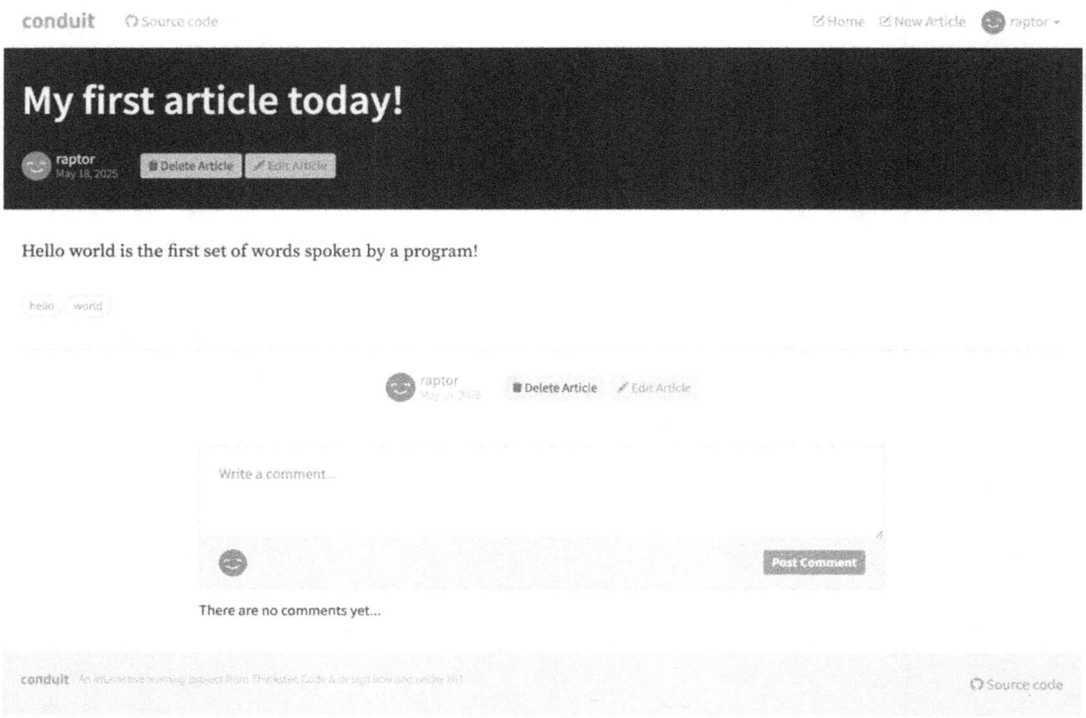

Figure 8-3. *The article page of the Marko RealWorld app (conduit/clone of medium.com)*

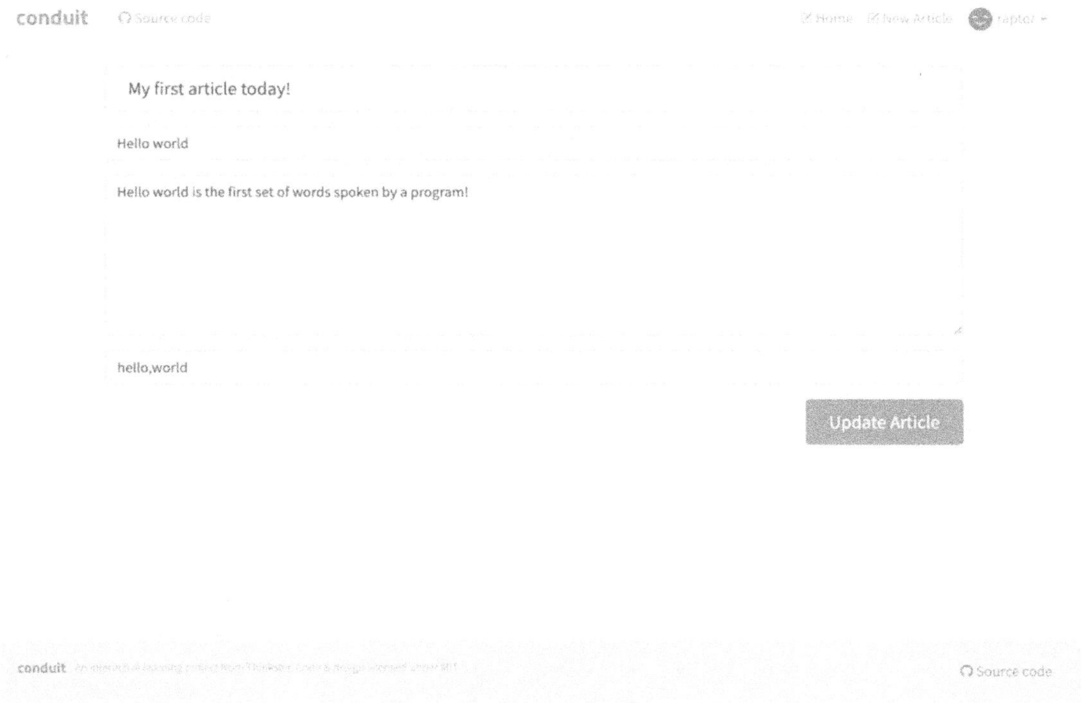

Figure 8-4. *Edit the article page of the Marko RealWorld app (conduit/clone of medium.com)*

As before, since this is a marko-run application, it will use the following structure:

- src/pages => powers all the pages in the application

- src/components => powers all the components used in the application

- src/services => location that takes care of api requests to the backend app

- src/utils => any utilities used by the application

- **/__tests__*.browser.test.ts => client-side unit tests

- **/__tests__*.server.test.ts => server-side unit tests

- integration-tests/** => contains integration tests for the entire app

- *.stories.ts => stories for the components

- **/__mocks__/**/*.ts => folder with the mocks

- **/__fixtures__/**/*.ts => folder with the fixtures that may be needed for testing

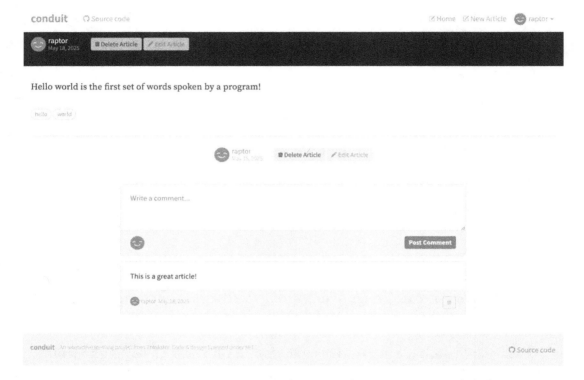

Figure 8-5. *Post a comment on the article page of the Marko RealWorld app (conduit/clone of medium.com)*

The entire application is built as a marko-run application scaffolded with the TypeScript template. It uses the following tools:

- TypeScript

- ESLint

- Stylelint

- Marko-run, Marko

- Prettier

- Testing-library, Vitest for unit testing

- Vite as the bundler

- Playwright for end-to-end testing

However, above all, you will need the following:

- Node JS, NPM

- Git

- An IDE like VS Code with the Marko VS Code extension installed (if VS Code)

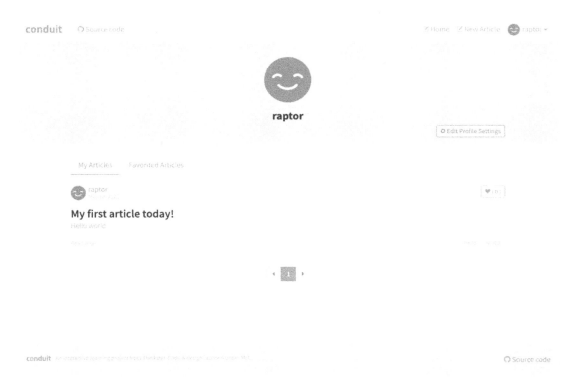

Figure 8-6. *Profile page in the Marko RealWorld app (conduit/clone of medium.com)*

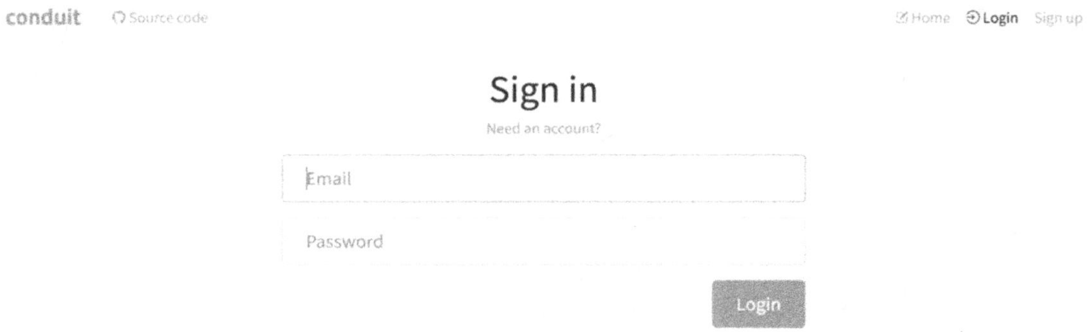

Figure 8-7. *Sign-in page of the Marko RealWorld app (conduit/clone of medium.com)*

Figure 8-8. *Other author profile page in the Marko RealWorld app (conduit/clone of medium.com)*

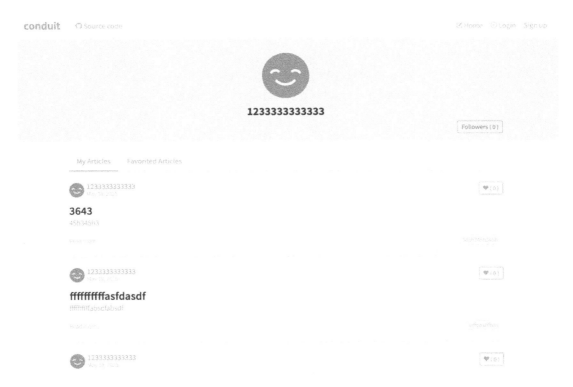

Figure 8-9. *Sign-up page in the Marko RealWorld app (conduit/clone of medium.com)*

Figure 8-10. *Viewing the Marko RealWorld app unsigned in (conduit/clone of medium.com)*

The Backend Components of the RealWorld Application

As earlier mentioned, we will be using `https://github.com/gothinkster/node-express-realworld-example-app` as the backend application that talks to the database and offers our frontend application with endpoints to query from or write to. Once you set this app and have it up and running, you can import and use the postman collection at `https://github.com/gothinkster/realworld/blob/main/api/Conduit.postman_collection.json` (modify your host information in postman) and then query the backend application to see if everything works. If all the endpoints work, then your backend application is up and running, ready to power your frontend application that will be with Marko.

The backend application uses Prisma. It is an open source Object-Relational Mapping (ORM) tool for Node.js and TypeScript. It simplifies database interactions by providing a type-safe query builder and an intuitive data modeling language. It acts as an intermediary between your backend application code and the database, abstracting away the complexities of raw SQL queries.

The repository has docs to help you get started with both the applications. It's now time for you to take a step away from the book and try the sample application!

Conclusion

By the end of building this application, you will begin to appreciate the hassle-free and seamless developer experience offered by Marko in the context of server rendering and building MPAs—something that many of the frameworks promise to offer today only to cause a lot of developer friction ultimately. This is, however, not our only sample application. As we delve deeper into micro frontends in Chapters 9 and 10, you will notice a new form of micro frontends that Marko introduces, which lets you achieve transcluded and embeddable applications. Besides this, in Chapter 11, before we conclude, we shall see a number of tiny examples that illustrate how Marko plays with other libraries and frameworks in a number of practical contexts, which will help you gain more confidence toward using Marko in production.

While this example application doesn't explicitly focus much on HTML streaming and progressive rendering, we have already seen examples of them in the earlier chapters and will continue to see more when we learn about micro frontends with Marko in Chapters 9 and 10.

CHAPTER 9

Decoupled MPA Micro Frontends: App Federation via @micro-frame/marko

Introduction

All through this book we have emphasized about Marko—the framework—and through various examples have illustrated how it's a fabulous solution for building multi-page applications (MPA's) rapidly through all of its performance-oriented features like out-of-order progressive rendering, streaming, async rendering, etc.

We have also seen via numerous examples of how Marko helps you rapidly develop applications and test them easily so that you can be confident of your code. The rapid application development was made possible because of Marko's meta framework—marko-run as we have seen in Chapter 5 and with the sample application in Chapter 8. We have also seen both the connect-style and non-connect flavors of this meta framework.

The rest of the developer experience is made possible via its ecosystem of plugins that integrate with Vite, Storybook, ESLint, Stylelint, TypeScript, Prettier, PostCSS, etc. Features like ease of debugging, hot module reloads (all seen in Chapter 6), confident testing (seen in Chapter 7) via its integration with testing-library, Vitest, and ease of use with end-to-end test frameworks like Playwright make Marko a very practical framework that can take on the toughest of use cases.

© Damodaran Chingleput Sathyakumar 2025
D. Chingleput Sathyakumar, *Practical Marko*, https://doi.org/10.1007/979-8-8688-1483-9_9

We also saw this in practice via the simple sample application in Chapter 8. This helped us appreciate the great developer experience that the Marko dev team has always prioritized alongside top-notch performance (server-side rendering, streaming, async and progressive rendering, and client-side performance).

Factors Besides Performance and Developer Experience

However, in the context of a large organization, when making architectural decisions, besides considering just the performance, learning curve, ecosystem support, and developer experience, there are some other factors to consider as well.

These include *interoperability, maintainability, failure isolation, building reusable modules or UX, independent releases, decoupled development, product velocity,* etc. In short, we are coming to micro frontends. For example, when building MPAs, let's say you had a "Similar Items" module that you had to show up on the Item Page, Checkout Page, etc.

While the React world took on to solve this problem via the introduction of *Module Federation* (by the ever awesome *Zach Jackson*) to the **webpack** architecture and subsequently build on this concept for other view frameworks and bundlers, Marko took on an entirely different approach to solve for micro frontends, which we shall see in this chapter, theoretically as a concept, to gain an initially understanding of it. Following this, in Chapter 10, we shall look at it with a sample app that helps achieve this.

Although Marko and React had started pretty much around the same time, Marko was put on trial (at eBay scale of a billion renders) pretty quickly. This meant it had to solve for Micro frontends (for cases like item listing promotions, ads, site-wide widgets, header and navigation, recommendations, guidances, etc.) so much before "micro frontends" as a term was coined or even considered a thing! So, rest assured you do not have to worry about the efficacy of this technique.

The Beginnings of Micro Frontends

Before we delve into Marko's approach, it would be worth the read to understand a bit of history around this.

The History

Most applications begin as "monoliths". A monolithic application is one application that contains all of the pages, UX components, core business logic, data aggregation, etc. to render every single page (as a route) for an enterprise website. They are called "monoliths" because at some point everything from maintainability, failure isolation (e.g., when the "terms" page is down, the failure must be isolated to it and must not bring down the whole app), code health, scaling (some pages get more traffic), etc. takes a hit. Even deploy time and product velocity (how fast features can be released) go for a toss.

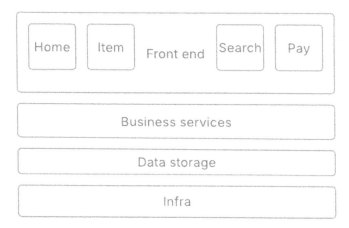

Figure 9-1. *Monolith with multiple pages in the same application*

Once apps reach this stage, companies indulge in large-scale rewrites by splitting out features from the monolith app, usually by page (tied to a route), to create a portfolio of applications that correspond to every single page and that are independently deployable and maintainable. The resulting architecture is the "multi-page multi-application architecture."

This means the app is composed of multiple pages where every page is now powered by an individual application in the enterprise's infrastructure environment. Note that we are not talking of the render type here. You can have MPAs that are fully client rendered or server rendered. In this context, we are talking about every page inside the previous monolith app, now being managed by an entirely focused and isolated application and a corresponding team.

The problems with monolith applications include tech debt, bloat, runtime performance degradation, maintenance issues, lack of failure isolation (one thing can bring the app down), poor product velocity, very long build, deploy, and rollback times. That being said, not all monoliths are bad either. It depends on the size and the use case. Sometimes simplicity still wins. A sample monolith is illustrated in Figure 9-1.

The Evolution to a Multi-page and Multi-application Architecture

We have already seen this with Marko-run. But here, we are specifically talking about multi-page and multi-application. This means every major route in the enterprise application is an application by itself (rather than just another route in a single Marko-run app that is rendered on the server). Of course, you will still use solutions like Marko-run overall. For example, the home page and the search page will be two different Marko-run applications, but navigations contained with those pages will be hosted on the respective Marko-run apps as individual routes.

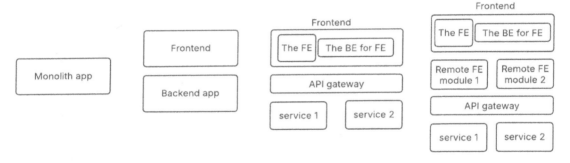

Figure 9-2. *Evolution from a Monolith to a multi-page*

This means, if one page went down, it would not bring down the others. Product managers and engineers can focus on those respective individual apps that they are responsible for and rapidly release features. They can run focused migrations and software upgrades and plan for the respective releases without having to coordinate with other teams that own the other pages (via other apps) through a train-like build system. Maintenance also is enhanced, and engineers no longer have to focus on other apps. This evolution is illustrated in Figure 9-2. The remotes mentioned here can be remote modules or remote apps.

What Are Micro Frontends?

Having seen monoliths and how they eventually get broken down into a multi-page multi-application architecture, a simple analogy regarding micro frontends would be to think of them as something akin to the concept of microservices of the backend, but for the frontend.

Micro services are independent services that when deployed collectively form the overall backend system for a given application. When you take e-commerce sites, every domain like buying, selling, advertising, shipping, etc. will have numerous microservices that comprise its overall function.

Similarly, for frontends, micro frontends help in dividing the overall frontend of the entire application (think of a large-scale shopping site like eBay) into numerous pages, sometimes to even the level of individual modules so that they are easier to maintain, individually scale, operate, and reduce/contain failures. Micro frontends are therefore independent applications (as seen in the previous section), operated by multiple independent teams, that have their own roadmaps, code rollouts, releases, etc. These apps/modules are self-contained, independently hosted, and assembled within an application.

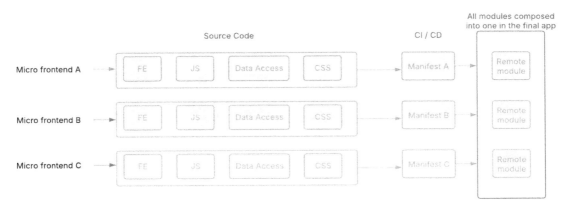

Figure 9-3. *Micro frontends visualized*

For example, reverting back to the example of an e-commerce website, when built as a multi-page application, home, search, item, product, checkout, etc. are page-level micro frontend applications. Also, common shareable modules (referred as horizontal UX) like guidance modules, recommendation modules, advertising, promotions, site-wide UX, etc. are examples of modules as micro frontends. Think you have to build a coupon system that shows the coupons on the various aforementioned pages at different points along the users' journey.

Going from a Monolith, How Are They Split?

We have already seen the benefits of splitting large monoliths, and decoupling them helps us solve the various organizational issues listed earlier. But how do we split those tightly coupled applications into multiple, composable parts that can be deployed independently? To make the right choices, we must understand the infrastructure and cloud offerings being used by the enterprise. However, at a very high level, as described earlier, you can do either horizontal or vertical splitting.

By horizontal splitting what we mean is use cases like the guidance modules, recommendation modules, etc. that are present across multiple pages of the large enterprise applications, and you have teams that are fully working on catering it to the other "host" applications like Search, Home page, Checkout page, etc. By vertical splitting what we mean is the original use case where every major route in your enterprise application is now powered by an entire application and is managed by an entire team that solely exists for it.

Deciding the split strategy is an important decision in terms of achieving composable decoupled frontends. However, in practice, we usually start with one and ultimately end up in a hybrid strategy of composition—using both vertical and horizontal splits. Another highly popular strategy is the API first micro frontend, where every block of UX on the page that is powered by an API under the hood is an isolated unit. These isolated units are then composed to build the page. This takes the hybrid split strategy to the extreme. These strategies (hybrid and vertical and horizontal splits) are illustrated in Figures 9-3 and 9-4, respectively.

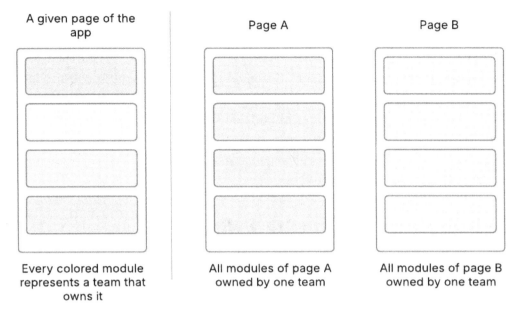

Figure 9-4. *Micro frontend split strategies*

These aforementioned strategies are besides the render strategy. You can have a single-page application—from the point of view of the end user—but still serve every single shell page within the single page app as an individually hosted application.

Why Does All This Need to Be Done?

In the context of large-scale enterprises, aspects of software development like reusability, rapid deploy, failure isolation, rapid rollbacks, maintainability, rapid scaling, product velocity, ease of debugging, independent code rollouts, feature roadmaps, ease of making fixes and upgrades, isolated migrations, etc. have an equal measure of importance alongside performance and developer experience.

These are the operational considerations in running large-scale enterprises. When a chief architect or a principal engineer is tasked into building something, it's not just about the performance and great quality of code, it's all of these operational considerations that are taken into account when designing the system.

Product velocity is the measure of how quickly the engineering team can release new features, fix bugs, roll out enhancements, and A/B test new features. If the entire enterprise was one large codebase (monolith), how would you run software migrations or apply software upgrades on it reliably? How would you scale the app given that it's more prone to failures that cannot be isolated—one failure and the entire app goes down.

The answer to this as we have seen all along this book is the multi-page application architecture. But even that comes with some more questions—code sharing, reusability, interoperability, etc. For example, how would you build a reusable item recommendation module that shows up at multiple places along the customers' journey (horizontal split)—think of modules like *"Items similar to X"*, *"Buyers who purchase X also purchased Y"*, *"Related items to X"*, etc.

What Was Being Done to Start With?

So as we have seen, what was a single application managed by say 30 or so frontend engineers became four to five teams of engineers now managing individual applications that power every major route (of the original monolith) in a multi-page multi-application setting. These may include a team that manages a shared core UI library, different teams that manage the home page, search page, item page, checkout page, payments page, order history page, messaging page, notifications, site navigation (think header, footer, and navigation system), etc. This perhaps implies that application is already a micro frontend now. Teams no longer wait for a **"train"** to hop on and launch their code (as was the initial build system at eBay in the early 2000s).

With the prevalence of NPM, the various teams publish their modules which the other teams consume, thereby resulting in code reuse, better code organization, independent development cycles, rapid iteration, etc. This formed the initial days of micro frontends where teams piggybacked on the **NPM** package manager system as the means to deliver micro frontends. It worked initially and works even now to a large extent. The first big advantage is now the app is broken down and can be independently worked on, deployed, scaled, and released. Now, each of these teams can deploy the respective apps without having to coordinate with the other teams. But then, this setup or system isn't without its own problems. But these were the initial footprints into the world of micro frontends. This is what Zack Jackson refers to as build time deploys.

In the illustration shown in Figure 9-5, you will see the <item-recommendation> module now being distributed to the various multi-page multi-application setups as NPM modules which are installed within them.

Figure 9-5. *Initial micro frontends through NPM modules distributed*

What Were the Problems with the Build Time Deploy Approach?

This means, for instance, consider you had a Marko-run app that consumed a specific version of a published custom Marko component (say a <customer-preferences-selector/>) that contained a certain functionality (tied down to an associated underlying API that helped customers store their selected preferences).

The important part is that the Marko compiler was able to resolve this at build/compile time, despite being a separate module, as it was installed and is now available. We have seen the operational advantages already, but ultimately it deploys as one unit. But the problem is that each of the respective host pages of your enterprise application—home, search, item, profile, checkout, etc.—may run independent versions of this module.

Remember the workflow here. The <customer-preferences-selector/> component was published by the corresponding team to an artifact repo like **NPM**, **Bit**, etc. to start with. Then, they had to work with individual teams and coordinate its release. Otherwise, every team would be on a different version of this component. The component owners had to do this for every single thing—feature enhancements, feature launches, software upgrades, software migrations, bug fixes, etc. This slowly became a churn for both the teams that owned it and for the teams that consumed it. In an enterprise setting, we are talking of this one team having to coordinate with a few hundred teams.

So, What Solutions Do We Have for the Issues Posed by the Build Time Approach?

It obviouzsly is having runtime dependencies instead of build time dependencies. This means that the <customer-preferences-selector/> would now be deployed independently to production and are consumed at runtime by the various host applications like home page, search page, item page, etc.

551

This is usually done within the app through ESM dynamic imports and solutions like Vite when this dependency is within the application. However, when you rely on solutions published by other teams within your enterprise (as is the case of <customer-preferences-selector/>) that is now made available as a runtime dependency (to be consumed at runtime), solutions like module federation shine here and help you with it.

The important thing being the host application doesn't need to be redeployed for a change to be reflected now. When the <customer-preferences-selector/> redeploys itself, the host application—the search page—will get the changes instantly. In the same way, the team that manages the <customer-preferences-selector/> doesn't have to coordinate its release with the few hundred teams within the enterprise for every single aspect of development—upgrades, migrations, enhancements, bug fixes, and feature launches.

Both runtime and build time deployed micro frontends have their own benefits and complexities. So, just because a new solution is touted, you shouldn't be jumping the bandwagon. A thorough round of exhaustive evaluation will help you nail down the right solution for your needs. Sometimes, build time dependencies via NPM work just fine.

How Were Runtime Dependencies Done Earlier?

Previously, runtime dependencies weren't a major issue before module bundlers. Before static bundlers, like Webpack and others where JS was deployed as individual files with the collective code, dependencies were managed by module loaders like Require JS that ensured global dependencies were available before the associated code loads.

eBay's in-house module bundler (now open sourced and retired) Lasso JS took this to the next level with runtime bundling and easily resolved async dependencies at runtime via a module called lasso-async by prebuilding them at compile time and having them ready. This was later retired in favor of modern toolchains like Webpack, Rollup, Vite, etc. to expand Marko's adoption and embrace more of open-source toolchains given that a lot of them are now being written in Rust and Go for performance.

However, bundlers offered the advantage of having a single file to deploy and later with solutions like code splitting to better manage and load dependencies. But this advantage came at the cost of losing the ability to load runtime dependencies, as they now required prior knowledge, at compile time, about the various modules that comprised the app.

With the earlier example of build time deployments through NPM/Bit, enterprises were constrained by the fact they had to coordinate releases and every change was a redeployment of the host app.

They got around this to some extent by deploying the <custom-preferences-selector/> independently and then employing a package, as a shim layer, to consume this (load the module). The shim was tasked with loading the right version by supplying them as environment variables into the host application, which passed it down to the shim. Even this required older copies of the modules to be ever present, just in case a host application wasn't able to consume it. The responsibility was always partially on the host app, which needed to be inverted. This is illustrated in Figure 9-6. While they were decoupled, they still had issues with versioning.

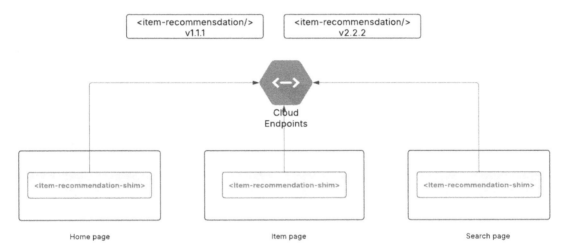

Figure 9-6. *Load NPM modules through a shim*

This is where solutions like module federation come in. Module federation was initially built into Webpack 5 that helped in easier code sharing between applications. These applications were either the host application (consumer) or the remote application (provider). Module federation helps with multiple things—solving the aforementioned problem and also code sharing/reuse both for the server side and the client side (universal federation plugin). For example, if your page already loaded a copy of Lodash (a popular JS utility module), why do you have to load it again when consuming the remote application?

What About Module Federation?

As mentioned earlier, module federation lets you organize apps as remote apps and host apps. The host app is the consumer, while the remote app is the provider that exposes a remote module. A given app can be both the host and a remote app (for some other apps). For example, <custom-preferences-selector/> will be exposed as the remote runtime dependency. And a host application like the home page will import it and use it.

How Does It Do This?

Module federation is a way to share code between different JavaScript projects at runtime rather than having everything bundled together at build time. Imagine you have multiple small apps (like a dashboard, a shopping cart, and a user profile page) that need to work together as one big app. Normally, you'd bundle all their code into a single file, but that can get messy and slow, especially if different teams are working on each part.

With module federation, each app can stay separate. One app (called the "host") can load pieces of code (like components or functions) from other apps (called "remotes") only when needed, over the internet, while the user is interacting with the app. It's like ordering food from different restaurants instead of cooking everything yourself—you just grab what you need when you need it. This makes apps faster and easier to update and allows teams to work independently.

In simpler terms, module federation lets apps share and use each other's code live without needing to mash everything into one big package beforehand.

Advantages

Besides some of the advantages we have already seen with runtime dependencies like independent deployments and code releases, reduced to no coordination, there are some other features that make the module federated solution stand out. These include

1. **Code Is Contained**: For the host applications, the rendering code remains within its control.

2. **Sharing the Framework Runtimes**: When both applications use the same view framework, they share the runtimes.

3. **No Code Loaders**: SPA Frameworks usually rely on code loaders that work alongside the babel and Webpack imports. Importing a federated module works just like any normal import. Just that the module is remote now.

4. **Pull Any Javascript Module**: When we talk of micro frontend frameworks, we usually talk in the context of UI components. But module federation lets you do it for any type of JS module—UI components, business logic, core functions, etc. Any Javascript can now be shared between apps.

5. **Pull Non-Javascript Modules**: While many frameworks focus heavily on the Javascript aspects, module federation will work with any file that Webpack can process today into JS.

6. **Use It Universally:** Module federation can be used on any platform that uses the Javascript runtime: Browser, Node, Electron, Web Workers, etc. Module federation can work with any module loading system like UMD, ESM, Common JS, System JS, and so on.

7. **Composability**: Basically implies breaking down entire apps into pages and then pages into modules (powered by underlying APIs) that when composed together offer the overall experience to the end consumer. For the end consumer, they cannot really tell if these are independent applications and others. However, we have broken them down into independent units that are operationally maintainable and scalable. Basically, you have to start looking at beyond apps, beyond pages up to the level of individual display elements on the page.

8. **Framework Neutrality**: Initial footprints into module federation will usually be loading different modules that rely on the same framework (say React). However, in practice this is seldom the case. Developers are very passionate and opinionated toward frameworks, and you will usually encounter a mix of frameworks being used (depending on the developers in the team) to author the various modules. This means you need interoperability— load a remote Svelte module into a host page written with Solid

JS/React and so on. Module federation recommends relying on solutions like single-spa for the same. This lets you write them in your framework of choice but package them as a framework agnostic parcel that can be consumed. While single-spa lets you embed such remote modules into incompatible host apps, you will still need a solution like module federation for loading them.

Module federation is illustrated in Figure 9-7.

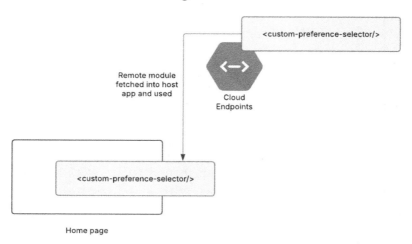

Figure 9-7. *Module federation as a concept*

Disadvantages

While we have seen these advantages with module federation, there are disadvantages as mentioned by its creators such as requiring great debugging skills for resolving issues that may arise due to CORS (cross-origin resource sharing), the usage of singletons (sharing runtimes in a way that, e.g., only one copy of React is loaded), and compatibility issues between different versions of libraries when sharing code, which add a new dimension of complexity. Note that these aren't inherent issues with the module federation package or as a solution but issues related to compatibility, deployments, versioning, singletons, etc.

Final Thoughts on Module Federation

When learning module federation, you will be repeatedly driven a point. That being, federated modules are just JS files or any files that can be processed into JS by module bundlers like Webpack. They aren't connected to an application server, and they should be deployed to an asset store like Amazon S3. Whether a server runs or not, it should not affect their availability.

Per the architectural philosophy of federated modules, serving files from an Express server or any other server is a waste of CPU cycles, and one must rely on solutions like CDN or Amazon S3 for the same. And it is super smart in being able to resolve shared dependencies between host and remote or multiple remote modules. They also include support for circular imports and nested imports.

When you look at module federation as a concept, you will realize this has its beginnings from the single-page application philosophy, client-side renders (although with universal federation, you can use it on the server now). Now add into this our previous learnings about busting a monolith SPA into a multi-page (multi-shell pages) multi-application architecture from the viewpoint of a client-side rendering, yet a single-page application design, you will arrive at module federation as a solution.

It helps you achieve a single-page experience, with the various shell pages being built and deployed by teams independently (as a multi-page, multi-team, or multi-application). You then use module federation as a solution to consume these independently deployed modules on the client or the server (based on the renders), use it to make API calls on your application, use the data, and render the experience.

This means, with the single-page app philosophy, in practice your app would usually have a copy of the view framework, say React already loaded initially. This requires you to avoid loading other copies of React as it's both redundant and can interfere with each other. Also these view frameworks aren't small in their bundle sizes (which impact performance), and you have to take great care in loading other related dependencies for the same concern of duplicates and redundancies requiring greater focus on code sharing/reuse.

This is exactly where @micro-frame/marko differs.

What Is @micro-frame/marko?

Note that just like module federation, micro-frame as a concept can be extended to any other view framework or library. It doesn't have to be specifically tied to Marko. But it was pioneered by the Marko team long before micro frontends were even considered a thing.

The Beginnings

The beginnings for micro-frame within the Marko ecosystem also began at eBay when eBay had to render its header and footer in a resilient manner, with a p95 of under 50ms, as part of the first flush of the page. Along with this, another project about delivering site-wide coupons across eBay's various pages, at various points along the customer journey, meant targeted rendering of widgets into specific locators on the page. The collection of techniques used to achieve the same was then abstracted out into this concept of micro-frame that now lets any app achieve the same result without all the hassle while still maintaining all the goodness of server-side rendering and streaming of Marko.

Regarding the problems and beginnings for micro-frame, they differ from the beginnings of module federation in that it all began with the multi-page application and server-side rendering philosophy from the start. This means how can micro frontends be achieved in the context of MPAs? Marko already has solutions like Marko-run which make building MPAs a breeze. Now, if you want to achieve vertical splitting of your monolith, all you have to do is deploy each route as an individual independent marko-run application that is managed by the associated product engineering team. Sub-page navigation will be contained within the respective marko-run apps. This means achieving vertical splitting is super simple already with Marko.

So, the next is horizontal splitting and ultimately a hybrid composition, where both these techniques are used. This is where micro-frames come into the picture. Marko's micro-frame is a different solution for splitting up frontend apps, and it's worth comparing to module federation. Micro-frame lets you break a Marko app into smaller, independent pieces (apps instead of modules) (micro frontends) that can be developed and deployed separately. You define "frames" (small app sections) in your Marko project. These frames are rendered on the respective application server or client and stitched (transcluded) into the host application using a lightweight runtime.

It's Different with Marko

One aspect to remember about Marko is that it's not distributed as a single-file runtime. Marko relies on a super optimizing compiler that does all the work at compile time. This means that the runtime dependencies of Marko required for your app's build are very unique to your build and only those required portions of the Marko runtime will be included.

For instance, just because both the host and remote apps are on version 5.37.0, it does not imply they will work and are compatible. This is because the compiler on the host app may have produced a build, where a specific runtime dependency (that is needed by the remote app) may not have been packaged into the host app, as it was not required at the time of bundling the host app and was therefore tree-shaken away.

So, thinking that you no longer have to load the Marko runtime for the remote app because it's already loaded by the host app and that they share the same version is not something that works within the Marko world (as a specific runtime dependency may have never been included). You may think but wouldn't loading multiple copies of Marko cause issues? No, they won't. Marko lets you encapsulate different Marko runtimes via its **runtimeId** as seen in the Marko-run examples.

While module federation focuses on runtime code loading that lets apps dynamically fetch and use code from other apps (code reuse/sharing), no matter the framework is, micro-frame focuses on runtime rendering and transcluding the rendered content from a remote app into the host app. So, it's less about code sharing and more about actual rendering.

This is partially also because of the tiny runtime Marko has (13KB Gzipped and expected to be 7KB Gzipped with the upcoming Marko 6 through reactivity and resumability). Also, with the app navigations being multi-page (navigations reload) and layout that way, there is never really the need to focus super heavily on code sharing just for the sake of performance.

With assets being cached by the browser, served from CDN servers, script loading strategies like above the fold and below the fold, async loading via dynamic imports, the HTTP early hints API, the resource hints APIs like (pre-render, prefetch, preload, etc.), background APIs, effective treeshaking with Vite, and code splitting by routes, apps using Marko can make use of all the goodness of the various loading strategies by the browser, before having to resort to any techniques like module federation for code reuse/sharing.

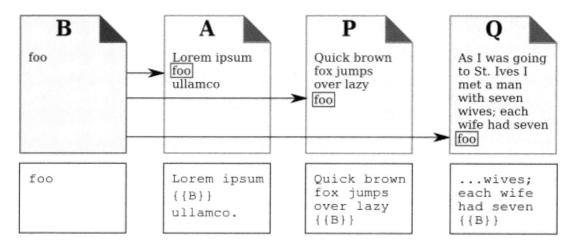

Figure 9-8. *Micro frontends as remote apps instead of remote modules doing remote rendering and content transclusion*

You can think of each of these apps (A, P, Q) as independent host apps. The app B is the remote app. Micro-frame helps the host apps talk to the remote apps, do the rendering of the requisite UX on the remote app (letting the remote app do all the API talking), bring in the rendered content from the remote app, and transclude them into the host app at the required targets with all the goodness of streaming. Figure 9-8 shows content transclusion achieved via micro-frame by embedding content rendered from remote applications into the host application.

How It Compares with Module Federation

With module federation, the browser or the server grabs the module from the remote app's URL and runs it live in the host app. This means the host application is in charge of the render. It's all about pulling in code on demand from a "remote" app to use in your "host" app, whether that happens in the browser or on the server. Universal federation just means it can work in both places seamlessly—browser and server. Your application is still responsible for dealing with service orchestration for fetching the required data.

Micro-frame inverts this completely. It's not about code reuse or sharing. It's about the actual rendering. The remote app is the one that renders. The remote application is responsible for the various API calls and service orchestration needed to fetch the data required for its render. The host app is fully decoupled and just informs the remote application of the placeholder, and micro-frame takes care of interfacing with the remote application, getting back the rendered output and transcluding it at the spot designated by the host application.

So, micro-frame does not drive the point of modules or everything being a remote module that can be fetched. Instead, it's about every micro frontend fragment being an independent application that can be conversed with and rendered.

Main Differences

Feature	Module Federation	Micro-Frame
Integration	JS modules dynamically imported at runtime	HTML content fetched from a remote source
Performance	Optimized for modern SPAs (React, Vue, Angular)	Optimized for SSR and streaming
Best For	Sharing components, business logic, and dependencies	Embedding micro frontends with independent lifecycles
Complexity	Requires Webpack and JavaScript bundling	Works via HTTP requests, no need for a bundler

To Recap

Module Federation

- **What It Is**: A feature in Webpack 5 that allows JavaScript modules to be dynamically loaded from different builds at runtime.

- **How It Works**: Applications (or "remotes") expose specific modules, and other applications (or "hosts") can consume them on demand without requiring separate bundling.

- **Use Case**: Ideal for sharing React/Vue/Angular components, business logic, or utilities between independently deployed frontend applications.

- **Key Advantages**

    - **Runtime Dependency Resolution**: No need to redeploy the entire app when a module changes.

    - **Shared Dependencies**: Ensures that applications use the same version of React, lodash, etc.

    - Works within JavaScript ecosystems (React, Vue, and Angular).

Micro-Frame (Marko)

- **What It Is**: A Marko component (<micro-frame>) designed to embed micro frontends using server-side rendering (SSR), streaming, and HTTP requests.

- **How It Works**: Instead of bundling and importing JavaScript modules, it fetches and streams the content of a micro frontend from a URL and injects it into the page.

- **Use Case**: Best suited for embedding standalone applications or UI fragments without requiring shared dependencies or JavaScript bundlers.

- **Key Advantages**

    - **SSR-Friendly**: It streams content from another service as part of the initial page load.

    - Works like an <iframe> but without the hassles.

    - Supports timeouts, error handling, and loading states.

Which to Use?

- **Use module federation if**

    - You are working with React, Vue, Angular, or another JS-based framework.

    - You need to share libraries and dependencies across multiple applications.

- You want to dynamically update parts of your frontend without full-page reloads.

- **Use micro-frame if**

  - You want a simpler micro frontend solution with SSR and streaming capabilities.

  - You don't need shared JavaScript dependencies.

  - Your embedded micro frontend is more content driven.

But Don't Both Rely on HTTP?

Yes, you're right to notice that in **both module federation and micro-frame**, there are **HTTP calls involved** to fetch the remote content. However, the key difference lies in **what** is being fetched and **how** it is integrated into the main app (in terms of who does the **render**).

Module federation loads JS code dynamically so that the host app can execute it as if it were their local code. **Micro-frame** loads HTML content from another server and embeds it in the DOM, much like an iframe, as if the content was rendered by the remote app itself.

Feature	Module Federation	Micro-Frame
What is fetched?	JavaScript **modules** (e.g., React components, functions)	Entire **HTML fragments** from a remote URL
How is it used?	JS modules are loaded dynamically and executed inside the main app	HTML is inserted into the DOM (like an iframe but streamed)
When is HTTP called?	Only when the module is needed	Every time the component is rendered as the ownership of render lies with the remote app (both components and data fetching)

Performance Differences

- **Module Federation**: Once a module is loaded, it behaves like a local component on the SPA. This however still implies you have to make calls to fetch data, to use the component, and to render every time. Great in the context of a SPA.

- **Micro-Frame**: Always fetches fresh content (both data, the HTML and the code). Great in the context of an MPA.

Is Micro-frame App Federation?

Comparing micro-frame to module federation, **you can consider micro-frame as app federation**, along the lines of module federation. *Where module federation helps you consume federated remote modules, micro-frame helps you consume federated remote applications.* That is, you are composing applications through remote apps (instead of modules) that all work together to render the UX.

The term "federated" in module or app federation (micro-frame) refers to the concept of independent, yet interconnected, modules or applications that can be dynamically shared and loaded across different applications at runtime. In simple terms, federation means distributed ownership and collaboration between separate applications without tight coupling. This is illustrated in Figure 9-9.

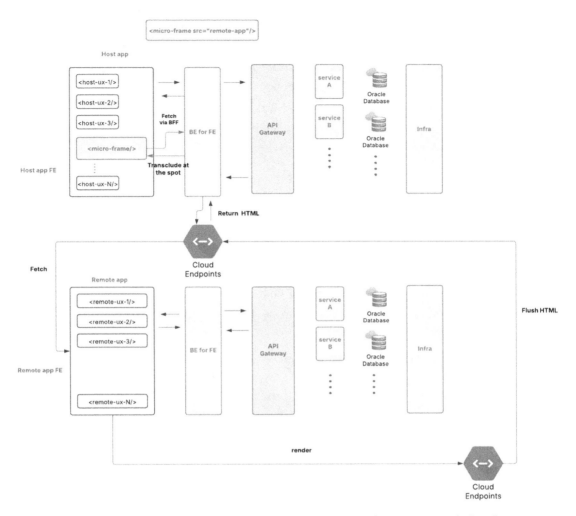

Figure 9-9. *Micro frontends as remote apps instead of remote modules doing remote rendering and content transclusion via micro-frame to achieve app federation*

A Deeper Look into @micro-frame/marko

Note that micro-frame isn't a core concept within Marko. This means it's not just "available" and you will have to install a package to use it. To use, install

```
>> npm i @micro-frame/marko
```

@micro-frame/marko (`https://github.com/marko-js/micro-frame/tree/main`) internally uses the core **<await>** tag that we are now used to seeing. Aside from it, it also relies on a package called the **@marko/writable-dom** which uses the **writeableStream** API, with a fallback API in case of legacy browsers.

This package exposes a **<micro-frame>** Marko component that in many ways is similar to a traditional **<iframe>**. However, unlike an iframe, the content from the **src** is loaded, with **streaming** support, directly into the existing document.

When Used on the Server Side

When **@micro-frame/marko** is rendered on the server side, it will make a request to load the embedded html resource from the remote source. The response is then streamed alongside the content for the host page. It does this by internally using the **make-fetch-happen** module to perform HTTP requests from the host BFF server to the remote server. This also implies you can leverage HTTP Cache-Control.

When Used on the Client Side

When **@micro-frame/marko** is rendered on the client side, a normal **fetch** request is made to the remote server to fetch and load the embedded html resource. The content of the response will be rendered within the page as if it was a server-side render. This includes full streaming support. Any time the **src** attribute is changed, a new request will be made to load updated html content.

Note

App federation via **@micro-frame/marko** is another solution to achieve micro frontends. It by no means aims to be a replacement for module federation, which solves for a different use case. There will always be some forms of complexity involved when dealing with a micro frontend setup. This could be in terms of debugging or the deployment and others as seen in the case of module federation. But, at least, in the case of **@micro-frame/marko**, you do not have to worry about singletons, resource sharing, CORS, library versioning, loading multiple copies of a view framework, etc. because they are all encapsulated away. Every load is a HTTP call to a remote server that fetches HTML rendered on the remote server itself.

Benefits

1. This is framework agnostic, meaning you can build one for your own view framework of choice.

2. Helps you achieve embedded micro frontends that are server rendered with full streaming support.

3. You can stream content irrespective of where the tag is rendered—server/browser.

4. Both the host and the remote app respond with HTML.

5. Great for interoperability. You don't need solutions like **single-spa** to have parceled manifests on a given page so as to make different view frameworks work together. Your remote app can be on a different view framework. It just has to respond with HTML, same as how it would when invoked directly.

6. When compared to iframes, you get the following usability benefits:

    a. You get control over loading and error state rendering.

    b. Modifying the src attribute of the micro-frame tag will cause it to reload.

    c. Doesn't impact SEO.

    d. No issues when using native browser APIs that are sometimes restricted with iframes.

    e. Doesn't render differently for screen readers, which means great for accessibility.

    f. Can be rendered along with the rest of the content on the page.

    g. Doesn't break the back navigation button.

7. Great for performance

    a. Iframes receive lower priority than the page assets. No issues like that.

    b. Doesn't impact SEO.

    c. Shares a single connection with the host.

    d. Less memory used because additional browser/window context is avoided.

    e. Avoids all the boilerplate HTML that you would see when using iframes. It just loads the UX fragment as HTML.

    f. Caches in both the client and the host server.

8. Just because the package is named **@micro-frame/marko**, it doesn't imply that the remote app must also be built on Marko. This is just a convenience utility for the calling host application. Your remote application can be on any stack. Ultimately it has to respond with HTML.

9. Same as module federation in the aspect, the remote app can be both a remote app and a host app at the same time.

The Caveat

As with all the goodness, there is a caveat when using it with respect to CORS. Embedded apps should be served from the same origin/TLD to prevent CORS issues. This means this setup works great when you have a BFF (backend for the frontend) setup. You can then send all your calls from the client side to this backend for frontend setup/layer which then handles orchestrating the calls to further downstream systems within your infra, to connect to the remote application and then fetch the remotely rendered HTML. Else, you would be dealing with preflights and configuring your servers for the same.

Two Tags

This is a two-tag solution. What you are looking at is the simple use case that uses the basic tag. We will look at the streaming tag in the next section after dissecting this tag's API. Note that there is <@then> block as in the case of core <await>. This is because whatever HTML is fetched through the HTTP call is just embedded, so there is nothing actionable to be done in a <@then>, warranting a block for the same.

Using @micro-frame/marko

<**micro-frame**> tag can be used as shown in Figure 9-10.

```
<micro-frame src="my-remote-app">
  <@loading>
    <!-- Render a loading message -->
    Hold on. We are loading...
  </@loading>
  <@catch|err|>
    <!-- Render alternative UX -->
    Boom! ${err.message}
  </@catch>
</micro-frame>
```

Figure 9-10.   *Sample use of <micro-frame>*

<micro-frame> Tag API

src

Type: It's an attribute type on the tag.

Required: Yes

Description: A path to an embedded remote application that will respond with HTML. This is resolved from the origin of the host application that triggers the call.

Caveat: So, to avoid CORS issues, sometimes it is best to route the client-side fetch requests also to the host application servers and then let the host application server make the HTTP call to the remote application and respond with the fetched HTML. In this manner, you get around the CORS issues as the HTTP call to the remote app is made within the confines of your server environment.

Sample usage:

```
<micro-frame src="my-remote-app"/>
```

With the above, assuming the host application is rendered at `https://ebay.com/n/all-categories`, the embedded application will resolve to `https://ebay.com/my-remote-app`.

headers

Type: It's an attribute type on the tag.

Required: Optional

Description: Optionally provide additional HTTP headers to the request. Only the object form shown below is supported.

Sample usage:

```
<micro-frame src="..." headers={ "X-My-Header": "Hello", "X-Another-Header": "World" }/>
```

Note that by default, on the server side, headers are copied from the current incoming request; the headers option will be merged with existing headers.

cache

Type: It's an attribute type on the tag.

Required: Optional

Description: Mirrors the Request.cache (https://developer.mozilla.org/en-US/docs/Web/API/Request/cache) options (works on both server and client renders).

Sample usage:

```
<!-- This example will always show cached content
     when available and fallback to the network
     otherwise -->
<micro-frame src="..." cache="force-cache"/>
```

timeout

Type: It's an attribute type on the tag.

Required: Optional

Description: A timeout in ms. If not provided, it defaults to 30s. Once the timeout is reached, it will prematurely abort the request. Hitting the timeout will cause it to trigger the <@catch> block. *If set to 0, the request will not time out.*

Sample usage:

```
<!-- This example will disable the default 30s timeout. -->
<micro-frame src="..." timeout=0/>
```

class

Type: It's a Marko Class attribute type on the tag.

Required: Optional

Description:
Optional class attribute which works the same way as how class works on any other Marko tags.

Sample usage:

```
<micro-frame src="..." class="a c"/>
<micro-frame src="..." class={ a:true, b:false, c:true }/>
```

style

Type: It's a Marko Style attribute type on the tag.

Required: Optional

Description: Optional style attribute which works the same way as a Marko style attribute.

Sample usage:

```
<micro-frame src="..." style="display:block;margin-right:16px"/>
<micro-frame src="..." style={ display: "block", color: false,
marginRight: 16 }/>
```

fetch

Type: It's an attribute type on the tag.

Required: Optional

Description: Optionally provide the tag with a function to use for making the fetch. It will override default fetch logic.

Sample usage:

```
<micro-frame src="..." fetch(url, options, fetch) {
    // The 3rd parameter allows us to continue to
    // use micro-frames fetch implementation
    // (which is different server/browser).
    // We can use this override to do things like a POST request, eg:
    const myHeaders = {};
    return fetch(url, {
        ...options,
        method: "POST",
        headers: {
            ...myHeaders,
            "Content-Type": "application/json"
        },
        body: JSON.stringify({ "hello": "world" })
    });
}
/>
```

Figure 9-11. Sample use of fetch in <micro-frame>

client-reorder

Type: It's an attribute type on the tag.

Required: Optional

Description: Similar to the core **<await>** tag's client-reorder attribute, this tells the **<micro-frame/>** to avoid blocking content coming later in the document. This means it lets other contents of the page continue to render out of order without blocking them and even flush them out of order while doing in-order paint (in case the other parts of the host page content are also wrapped in other <await> fragments).

However, with respect to itself, micro-frame will buffer the content it controls, instead of streaming and finally insert it, once it's ready.

<@catchlerrl>

Type: It's an attribute type on the tag.

Required: Optional

Description: An optional attribute tag rendered when there is a network error or timeout. If there is no **@catch** handler, the error will be emitted to the stream, similar to the **<await>** tag. This can be used to render a fallback UX.

Sample Usage:

```
<micro-frame src="...">
    <@catch|err|>
        <!-- Displays if request to service fails or times out -->
        <div>Sorry we could not process your request at this timee.</div>
        $ window.log(${err.message})
    </@catch>
</micro-frame>
```

Figure 9-12. *Sample use of <@catch> in <micro-frame>*

In the sample usage shown above, besides rendering a fallback UX, it logs the error to the upstream systems for tracking.

<@loading>

Type: It's an attribute type on the tag.

Required: Optional

Description: An optional attribute tag that is rendered when the request is still being streamed or processed. It is removed after the request has either errored or successfully loaded. You can consider using it to render a Loading UX placeholder like silhouettes.

Sample usage:

```
<micro-frame src="...">
    <@loading>
        <div>
            We are loading the nested app... <my-spinner/>
        </div>
    </@loading>
</micro-frame>
```

Figure 9-13. *Sample use of <@loading> in <micro-frame>*

Communicating Between the Host and the Remote (Post-Render, Within the Page)

Communicating with the embedded application happens in the following ways:

- Do a full reload of and get new HTML.

- Orchestrate a client-side rendered update to the existing HTML.

Full Reload

To perform a full reload of the embedded application, it works best to pass a query string in the src attribute or replace the src attribute itself entirely with a new URL. Sometimes a query param as a time stamp also just works. Whenever **src** updates, a full reload will happen automatically to the content fragment (not the whole page). In the following example, when *state.page* changes, there is a reload of the fragment.

```
1   export interface Input {};
2
3   interface State {
4       page: number
5   };
6
7   export default class extends Marko.Component<Input, State> {
8     onCreate() {
9       this.state = { page: 0 };
10    }
11
12    nextPage() {
13      this.state.page++;
14    }
15  }
16
```

```
1   <micro-frame src=`my-remote-app?page=${state.page}`/>
2
3   <button onClick("nextPage")>Next Page</button>
```

Figure 9-14. *Reloading <micro-frame>*

Client-Side Update

Client-side communication between the host app and the remote-child application can be done through mechanisms like a global store, stored data on the dom (perhaps even use web components), or other solutions like a publish-subscribe mechanism. The following example showcases just using a plain custom event solution, where the nested application's script is expected to listen to an emitted custom event and react by opening the modal accordingly.

```
1   import raptorPubsub from 'raptor-pubsub';
2   export interface Input{}
3
4   class {
5     declare state: { page: number };
6
7     onCreate() {
8       this.state = { page: 0 };
9     }
10
11    openModal() {
12      if (window.remoteApp) {
13        // assuming that "remoteApp" registers itself on window
14        window.remoteApp.openModal();
15      }
16
17      // alternatively
18      raptorPubsub.emit("remoteApp-openModal");
19
20      // alternatively
21      document.body.dispatchEvent(new CustomEvent('remoteApp-openModal'))
22    }
23  }
24
25  <micro-frame src="my-nested-app"/>
26
27  <button onClick("openModal")>Open nested app modal</button>
```

Figure 9-15. *Updating <micro-frame> on the client*

Caveats When Building This for Other Frameworks

As mentioned earlier, this is something you can extend for other frameworks too. An important part of it is making it isomorphic and also ensuring that the parent component of the host application into which the fetched HTML is embedded does not diff it as part of its diffing process in response to change of state of input, because this is content rendered and transcluded from an external source.

Two More Tags

In the previous section when talking about the **<micro-frame/>** tag, we said two tags. This is the second tag called **<micro-frame-sse/>**. It comes associated with another **<micro-frame-slot/>**. In the next section, let's look at them and see how they differ from **<micro-frame/>**.

<micro-frame-sse> Tag API

The **<micro-frame-sse/>** component enhances the existing **<micro-frame>** functionality by introducing support for Server-Sent Events (SSE) streams. **<micro-frame-sse>** is used to initiate the SSE stream, and **<micro-frame-slot>** governs the placement of the incoming chunk of streaming content.

In addition to the benefits from **<micro-frame>**, **<micro-frame-sse>** allows for short-lived Server-Sent Events to stream content into designated slots within a single HTTP request. In another word, **<micro-frame-sse>** enables multiplexing of **<micro-frame>**.

Note that SSE is one possible stream format. There are others like JSON stream, multi-part JSON, etc., and with a proper parser, this can potentially support all of these formats.

<micro-frame-sse> tag is to be placed as perhaps the first tag in your top-level server-side page template so that it is present in the early stage of page rendering. This will initiate the SSE request as soon as the page render starts.

<micro-frame-slot> is where the fetched content will be injected and can be placed at any desired location. An SSE endpoint usually responds with multiple chunks. In that case, you can map each chunk to a **<micro-frame-slot>** and embed them/transclude them in any place within the HTML document of the host application.

With these two tags, you govern both the data fetching and also the placement of the fetched data. Let's look at <micro-frame-sse> tag's API.

headers

Type: It's an attribute type on the tag.

Required: Optional

Description: Include any additional HTTP headers you want to be sent as part of the request. Only the object form shown below is supported.

576

Sample usage:

```
<micro-frame-sse
    src="..." name="..." headers={ "X-My-Header": "Hello", "X-Another-
    Header": "World" }/>
```

Note that by default on the server side headers are copied from the current incoming request, the headers option will be merged with existing headers.

cache

Type: It's an attribute type on the tag.

Required: Optional

Description: Mirrors the Request.cache (`https://developer.mozilla.org/en-US/docs/Web/API/Request/cache`) options (works on both server and client renders).

Sample usage:

```
<!-- This example will always show cached content
    when available and fallback to the network
    otherwise -->
<micro-frame-sse src="..." name="..." cache="force-cache"/>
```

timeout

Type: It's an attribute type on the tag.

Required: Optional

Description: A timeout in ms. If not provided, it defaults to 30s. Once the timeout is reached, it will prematurely abort the request. Hitting the timeout will cause it to trigger the **<@catch>** block. *If set to 0, the request will not time out.* Note that, if it times out, besides triggering the **<@catch>** block within itself, it will trigger the **<@catch>** of all the **<micro-frame-slot>** tags waiting on this.

Sample usage:

```
<!-- This example will disable the default 30s timeout. -->
<micro-frame-sse src="..." name="..." timeout=0/>
```

read

Type: It's an attribute type on the tag.

Required: Optional

Description: The **read** function in **<micro-frame-sse>** is responsible for parsing SSE (Server-Sent Event) messages from the server and extracting where the streamed content should go in the client-side HTML. It's a function to parse the MessageEvent (argument of the read function `https://developer.mozilla.org/en-US/docs/Web/API/EventSource/message_event#event_properties`) which returns the slot ID and streamed content as an array (optionally an **isDone** flag).

The **read** function takes in a **MessageEvent** object from the SSE stream. It extracts two important pieces of data from the event: **Slot ID** (which identifies where the received content should be placed) and **HTML content** (the streamed data that should be inserted). Optionally, it sets an **isDone** flag to indicate whether the slot is finished receiving content.

When no **read** function is provided, by default, the following logic will be used if no **read** provided in the attribute.

```
// default logic if read not provided
function read(ev: MessageEvent) {
    return [ev.lastEventId, ev.data, true];
}
```

```
<micro-frame-sse src="..." name="..." read(ev) {
  // logic to fetch slot ID and html_content from event
  return [slot, html_content];

  // if the isDone flag is set to true, slot will be closed after reading.
  // const isDone = true;
  // return [slot, html_content, isDone];
} />
```

Figure 9-16. *Using <micro-frame-sse> with a read*

How It Works

- ev.lastEventId

  - This is the event ID sent by the SSE server.

  - It helps track which message is being processed.

  - If "someId" is detected, the function ignores that message (return;).

- ev.data

  - This contains the actual HTML content streamed from the server.

- return [ev.lastEventId, ev.data, true];

  - The function returns an array:

    - **Slot ID** (ev.lastEventId): Identifies which part of the page to update.

    - **HTML** content (ev.data): The streamed HTML that should be rendered.

    - **true (isDone Flag)**: Indicates that this slot is fully loaded and will not receive more updates. This is because once a slot begins to receive chunks of content, it can be followed by contents for other slots. That is, the contents for a given single slot may not be continuously obtained. So it's important to be informed when the slot is closed and will no longer receive any content.

Why Is the isDone Flag Important?

If a slot is not marked as **done (isDone = false)**, the browser will keep waiting for more data for that slot. If progressive rendering is happening in order, an unfinished slot can block other contents from rendering below it. Setting **isDone = true** allows streaming to complete properly.

What if you did not want to listen to some messages?

To skip a specific message, just return undefined in the **read** function.

```
function read(ev: MessageEvent) {
  if (ev.lastEventId === "someId") {
    // event with id: someId will be skipped
    return;
  }
  return [ev.lastEventId, ev.data, true];
}
```

Figure 9-17. *Discarding a message*

Note   *MessageEvent extends from Event and is the eventType for EventSource events. It comes with some additional properties like lastEventId, data, ports, origin, source.*

---

fetch

Type: It's an attribute type on the tag.

Required: Optional

Description: Optionally provide the tag with a function to use for making the fetch. It will override default fetch logic via make-fetch-happen.

Sample usage:

```
<micro-frame-sse src="..." name="..." fetch(...args) {
  return new Promise(resolve => {
    resolve({
      ok: true,
      body: new Readable({read() {}}).push('some data..').push(null)
    })
    // more basic usage:
    // invoke your own fetch
    // const response = customFetch(...args);
    // resolve(response);
  })
} />
```

Figure 9-18. *A sample fetch usage*

src

Type: It's an attribute type on the tag.

Required: Yes

Description: A path to the SSE endpoint to fetch the content.

Sample usage:

```
<micro-frame-sse src="sse-source" name="..." />
```

name

Type: It's an attribute type on the tag.

Required: Yes

Description: A unique name for the stream which matches a corresponding <micro-frame-slot> tag's **from** attribute. A page can have multiple streams, so multiple <micro-frame-sse> tags and correspondingly associated **<micro-frame-slot>** tags.

Sample usage:

```
<micro-frame-sse src="..." name="stream_name" />
```

An important part of the **<micro-frame-sse>** tag is the lack of **<@placeholder>** and **<@catch>** named body tags as seen in **<micro-frame>**. This is because they just initiate the call and do not serve as the placeholder for the content. You will instead find these named body tags with **<micro-frame-slot>**.

<micro-frame-slot> Tag API

If you recall, in the case of **<micro-frame/>** there was no **slot tag** needed. This is because the place where the HTML is embedded is lexical—in the sense, the **<micro-frame/>** tag acts as both *fetcher* and the *placeholder* of the fetched HTML. The HTML will be embedded/transcluded right at the spot in the HTML document/Marko template where you placed the tag.

But, with SSE, given that the responses from a SSE endpoint appear in chunks and that you can have more than one chunk, with each of them occupying its own position in the HTML document, you need placeholders that let you control where every chunk is embedded/transcluded into the HTML document. This is where **<micro-frame-slot/>** finds its use.

<micro-frame-slot/> is where the fetched content chunk from an SSE endpoint is injected, and this can be placed at any desired location in the HTML document.

slot

Type: It's an attribute type on the tag.

Required: Yes

Description: It's a unique ID for the **slot** which is used to receive streaming content from an SSE endpoint.

Sample usage:

```
<micro-frame-slot from="..." slot="slot_id" />
```

from

Type: It's an attribute type on the tag.

Required: Yes

Description: Given that your page can have multiple **<micro-frame-sse/>** tags which map to multiple SSE endpoints that fetch different content, you need a way to map a given **<micro-frame-slot/>** tag to a specific **<micro-frame-sse/>** provider/source. This attribute helps with it. The **<micro-frame-sse/>** (stream provider) **name** attribute must match the **from** attribute of **<micro-frame-slot>** (stream source).

Sample usage:

```
<micro-frame-slot from="stream-source-name" slot="..." />
```

client-reorder="after-first-chunk"

Type: It's an attribute type on the tag.

Required: Optional

Description: This is one of the additional values that the **client-reorder** attribute can take. When set with "*after-first-chunk*", the slot will be rendered in order before the first chunk and will convert to out of order while streaming. This is useful when the loading indicator is controlled inside the stream.

Sample usage:

```
<micro-frame-slot from="..." slot="..." client-reorder="after-first-
chunk" />
```

no-refresh

Type: It's an attribute type on the tag.

Required: Optional

Description: It's a Boolean value that controls whether the **<micro-frame-slot**/> slot should refresh itself when its stream source's **src** attribute changes and gets new content. This lets you exclusively control the slot as well, as to whether or not it accepts new content when its provider changes.

Sample usage:

```
<micro-frame-slot from="..." slot="..." no-refresh />
```

timeout

Type: It's an attribute type on the tag.

Required: Optional

Description: A timeout in ms for the slot. If not provided, it defaults to 30s. Note that a **<micro-frame-slot**/> maps to a specific chunk from its provider SSE endpoint managed by the **<micro-frame-sse**/> tag. So, once the timeout for the slot is reached, it will cause it to trigger the **<@catch>** block. *If set to 0, the slot will not time out*. Note that this cannot abort the request or cause the **<micro-frame-sse**/> tag to timeout as that has its own **timeout** attribute. This lets you exclusively control the slot as well as to when it can choose to stop waiting.

Sample usage:

```
<!-- This example will disable the default 30s timeout. -->
<micro-frame-slot from="..." timeout=0/>
```

class

Type: It's a Marko Class attribute type on the tag.

Required: Optional

Description: Optional class attribute which works the same way as how class works on any other Marko tag.

Sample usage:

```
<micro-frame-slot from="..." class="a c"/>
<micro-frame-slot from="..." class={ a:true, b:false, c:true }/>
<micro-frame-slot from="..." class=["a", null, { c:true }]/>
```

style

Type: It's a Marko Style attribute type on the tag.

Required: Optional

Description: Optional style attribute which works the same way as a Marko style attribute.

Sample usage:

```
<micro-frame-slot from="..." style="display:block;margin-right:16px"/>
<micro-frame-slot from="..." style={ display: "block", color: false,
marginRight: 16 }/>
<micro-frame-slot from="..." style=["display:block", null, {
marginRight: 16 }]/>
```

<@catchlerrl>

Type: It's an attribute type on the tag.

Required: Optional

Description: An optional attribute tag rendered when there is a network error or timeout. If there is no **@catch** handler, the error will be emitted to the stream, similar to the **<await>** tag. Errors that occur in the **<micro-frame-sse>** tag will be emitted to all of its associated **<micro-frame-slot>** tags which can be caught here. This can be used to render a fallback UX.

Sample usage:

```
<micro-frame-slot from="custom-preference-provider" slot="metrics-preference">
  <@catch|err|>
    We are sorry. Please refresh
  </@catch>
</micro-frame-slot>
```

Figure 9-19. *<micro-frame-slot> with <@catch>*

<@loading>

Type: It's an attribute type on the tag.

Required: Optional

Description: An optional attribute tag that is rendered when the request is still being streamed or processed for the specific slot. It is removed after the response chunk mapped to that slot has either errored or successfully arrived (loaded). You can consider using it to render a Loading UX placeholder like silhouettes in the meantime.

Sample usage:

```
<micro-frame-slot from="custom-preference-provider" slot="metrics-preference">
  <@loading>
    We are loading the your preferences..
    <loading-silhouettes/>
  </@loading>
</micro-frame-slot>
```

Figure 9-20. *<@loading> with <micro-frame-slot>*

client-reorder

Type: It's an attribute type on the tag.

Required: Optional

Description: Similar to the Marko's core **<await>** tag's client-reorder attribute and the client-reorder attribute of **<micro-frame/>**, but at a slot level. This instructs the **<micro-frame-slot/>** if that specific slot is needed to be streamed out of order.

Communicating between the host app and the remote app (HTML fragments within the slots post-render within the page) follows the same methodologies as **<micro-frame/>.**

585

Conclusion

With this, you should have got a considerable understanding of the differences between module federation and app federation via micro-frame. We have also visited the micro-frame solution and the slot tags in the context of rendering content from Server-Sent Event streams. You would have also been able to better appreciate the path taken by Marko in the development of the micro-frame solution in contrast to the capabilities offered by module federation as a micro frontend solution. We also learned how both have their places and use cases and aren't intended to be a replacement for one another. We have also seen the syntax and the various tags and their use cases.

In the next chapter, let's use this knowledge of micro-frame to build a remote micro frontend application and start it on another port locally, which we will then use to render HTML and consume it from a host application. You will see usage of this both on the server side and client side and how it transcludes contents (embeds HTML in the right targets) and makes building micro frontends seamless and mostly a hassle-free experience.

CHAPTER 10

App Federation–Based Micro Frontends with Marko

Introduction

In the previous chapter, we had a brief conceptual aside on what **app federation** is and how it has its own place in the arena of micro frontend practices currently popularized by **module federation**. We also saw the benefits of app federation and how it contrasts itself in comparison to module federation. It was also emphasized that it isn't aimed to be a replacement for module federation and that both takes have their unique places in the way micro frontends are built. We also had a brief overview of how Marko achieves it via @micro-frame/marko. In this chapter, let's examine this with sample apps and different use cases that will help drive this point and better appreciate this methodology of achieving micro frontends. It will help you realize decoupled releases, maintain distributed codebases, and not have to worry about sharing runtimes and dependencies, doing upgrades, rolling out feature enhancements, coordinating releases between hosts and remote, extensive debugging, etc.

@micro-frame/marko

In this section, let's walk through a simple setup that will drive the point of this tag within the **@micro-frame/marko** package. We will create two Marko-run applications running on different ports. Let's call the first app **marko-host-app**. This is the host application.

© Damodaran Chingleput Sathyakumar 2025
D. Chingleput Sathyakumar, *Practical Marko*, https://doi.org/10.1007/979-8-8688-1483-9_10

Let's call the second app **marko-remote-app**. This is the remote application. We will build a page notification UX in marko-remote-app via **Marko**, **@ebay/skin**, and **@ebay/ebayui-core**.

Using **@micro-frame/marko**, we will let the **marko-host-app** talk with the **marko-remote-app**, fetch the server-rendered HTML from **marko-remote-app**, and transclude/embed it into the host **marko-host-app**. Then, we will perform some interactions and re-render them on the client side.

The important thing to note is that the render of the embedded HTML is fully owned by the remote app: **marko-remote-app**. It is responsible for the render, fetching the data needed for the render, API orchestration, etc.; **marko-host-app** knows nothing of all this. It just fetches the rendered response and embeds it. No Marko runtime is shared here as app federation does not aim at solving the problem of shared dependencies. And yes, you can have multiple copies of Marko on the page—its footprint is tiny, outputs bundles unique to every build/app, and is sandboxed from each other via its **runtimeID**.

To get started, let's scaffold the marko-host-app, which is shown in Figure 10-1. It is the same default codebase scaffolded with the **basic** template. We have a number of files, but let us focus on the src/routes/_index directory. Let's make some changes to the files within this. First, let's update the **+page.marko** as shown in Figure 10-2.

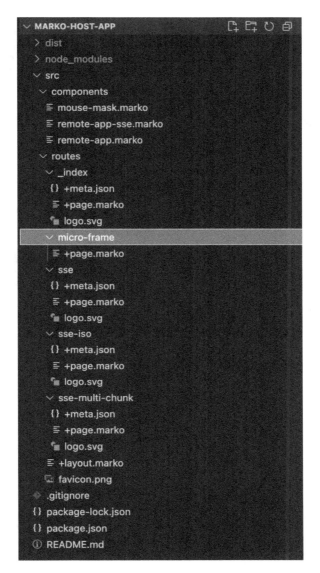

Figure 10-1. *Marko-host-app project layout*

```
src > routes > _index > ☰ +page.marko > ...
 1    <div class="container">
 2      <header>
 3        <div>
 4          <remote-app/>
 5        </div>
 6        <div>
 7          <img src="./logo.svg" alt="Marko" class="logo">
 8        </div>
 9      </header>
10      <main>
11        <p>
12          Edit
13          <code>./src/routes/_index/+page.marko</code>
14          and save to reload.
15        </p>
16        <a href="https://markojs.com/docs/getting-started">
17          Learn Marko
18        </a>
19      </main>
20    </div>
21    <mouse-mask/>
22
23  > style {…
38  }
```

Figure 10-2. *src/routes/_index/+page.marko*

The +page.marko file has some changes with a new component being included: **<remote-app/>**. Before checking what the **<remote-app/>** does, let's also do an npm install for the package **@micro-frame/marko**. Next, the component **<remote-app/>** is shown in Figure 10-3.

```
src > components > ☰ remote-app.marko > 𝒫 div > 𝒫 div > 𝕔 micro-frame
 1    <div id="remote-app">
 2      <div class="remote-app__content">
 3        <micro-frame
 4          src=`http://localhost:3001/remote-app-fragment?dt=${Date.now()}`
 5          timeout=0
 6          client-reorder
 7        >
 8          <@loading>We're still loading...</@loading>
 9          <@catch|err|>
10            Uh-oh! ${err.message}
11          </@catch>
12        </micro-frame>
13      </div>
14    </div>
```

Figure 10-3. *src/components/remote-app.marko*

If you will notice in Figure 10-3, the **@micro-frame/marko** tag is used with its source set as a URL that points to a route path that is handled by the **marko-remote-app** running on port **3001**. The current marko-run app named **marko-host-app** is running on port **3000**. So, in effect, we are making an HTTP call on the server side to another application that is running on a different port (**3001**) to fetch some content. This content is entirely owned by the **marko-remote-app** running on port **3001**, and the **marko-host-app** has nothing to do with the content in terms of its render, API orchestration, etc.

We have seen the details of the **@micro-frame/marko** tag in Chapter 9. But to help you recall, **src** is the URL to the remote application. **client-reorder** indicates that when the host app is being server-rendered, it doesn't have to wait for the micro-frame to be rendered and flushed. This is the same as async rendering and out-of-order render and out-of-order flush set to true, but in-order paint. There is a placeholder text provided via the **<@loading>** named body tag, and the **<@catch>** named body tag is used to render some content in the case of an error.

Next, let's see the remote application (**marko-remote-app**) running on port 3001. For this, we will be required to make some configuration changes to let Vite know to run the remote app on port **3001**. Besides, given that both the apps are being run simultaneously and served locally, we will need a mechanism to handle **CORS** here (specifically for **JS** and **CSS** assets belonging to the remote app when it's accessed with the host app as the origin). In the real world, ideally these assets will be served from a CDN server with the necessary **CORS** provisions like (*Access-Control-Allow-Origin* header). For instance, with eBay, the CDN server would respond with an allowed list of URL patterns for the same header, enabling assets to be accessed on any eBay-rendered page.

This marko-remote-app is also another marko-run application scaffolded as a connect-style application for fine-grained control. To start with, Figure 10-4 shows the **Vite.config.js** of the **marko-remote-app** application.

```
vite.config.js > [∅] default > plugins > basePathVar
 1   import marko from "@marko/run/vite";
 2   import nodeAdapter from "@marko/run-adapter-node";
 3   import { defineConfig } from "vite";
 4
 5   // https://vite.dev/config/
 6   export default defineConfig({
 7     preview: {
 8       port: 3001
 9     },
10     server: {
11       port: 3001
12     },
13     plugins: [marko({
14       adapter: nodeAdapter(),
15       runtimeId: 'mr',
16       basePathVar: "__MY_ASSET_BASE_PATH__"
17     })],
18     css: {
19       devSourcemap: true,
20       preprocessorOptions: {
21         less: {
22           math: "always",
23           javascriptEnabled: true,
24         },
25       },
26     },
27   });
28
```

Figure 10-4. *marko-remote-app/vite.config.js*

As shown in Figure 10-4, the sections highlighted in red are to inform Vite to start this app on port **3001** (both the **dev** mode and **preview** mode). Next, we have configured this app as a connect-style marko-run application (refer to Chapter 5 for connect and non-connect-style marko-run apps).

While the **marko-host-app** was configured as a non-connect-style marko-run app, this is specifically being configured as a connect-style marko-run app to gain finer control in handling static assets, which we will look at shortly. For this purpose, the adapter is set as **run-adapter-node** to make this a connect-style marko app. Next, as earlier mentioned, loading different marko runtimes on a given page is not an issue as long as their runtimes are properly sandboxed. This is achieved via the **runtimeId** prop.

Finally, we will be serving this UX (from the remote app) as proper static assets and not via the dev server from port 3001. For this case, we will be required to provide the base URL from which the assets have to be served. Given that the baseURL of the app is http://localhost:3001/ and when Marko-run is triggered with npm run build and its assets output under **dist/public/assets** and accessed via the /**assets** route, we have configured a variable **__MY_ASSET_BASE_PATH__** to hold the URL information. Marko-run will read the base URL (in production, this is the base URL of the CDN server) information from this variable, so we are required to set this variable next.

Before we get started, let's install some dependencies that will help us with getting over the CORS issue when running two apps locally. Also, let's install some dependencies that will help us quickly build some UX which we will send to the host application. For this, install the following dependencies in the marko-remote-app:

- less
- @ebay/skin
- @ebay/ebayui-core
- express
- compression
- cors
- marko

The development dependencies to be installed include

- run-adapter-node

In Figure 10-5, let's look at the server startup code under src/index.js. In this file, the **cors** and **compression** middlewares are imported and used with **express** to start the server. The project directory structure continues to adhere to the marko-run standards.

In the CORS middleware, we have whitelisted the origin http://localhost:3000 (belonging to the calling application—**marko-host-app** which calls the **marko-remote-app** on port 3001). We have also explicitly ensured that the **Access-Control-Allow-Origin** response header is set with the host app whitelisted (http://localhost:3000). This is because, although the content is rendered by the **marko-remote-app**, it gets embedded (transcluded) into the **marko-host-app** and is served under the domain of the **marko-host-app** which is running on port 3000.

However, since it was rendered by the **marko-remote-app**, the URLs of the generated assets that come with the remote app rendered HTML continue to point to http://localhost:3001/assets/, which makes those asset (script, css, images, etc.) URLs from the remote app a cross-origin request.

This will be marked with a **CORS** error by the browser despite having an HTTP status 200. This is because, although the marko-remote-app responds with the assets, if the **marko-remote-app** doesn't respond with the necessary **CORS** response headers set (like *Access-Control-Allow-Origin*), it will be marked as an error by the browser. The browser needs this from the **marko-remote-app** server. This indicates to the browser that the specific resource can be trusted from another domain (**remote**) and run in the context of the **host** domain.

```js
src > JS index.js > ...
    1   import { routerMiddleware } from "@marko/run-adapter-node/middleware";
    2   import compressionMiddleware from "compression";
    3   import express from "express";
    4   import path from "path";
    5   import url from "url";
    6   import cors from 'cors';
    7
    8   const __dirname = path.dirname(url.fileURLToPath(import.meta.url));
    9
   10   const { NODE_ENV = "development", PORT = 3001 } = process.env;
   11
   12   console.time("Start", PORT);
   13
   14   express()
   15   .use(cors({
   16     origin: 'http://localhost:3000'
   17   }))
   18     .use(compressionMiddleware())
   19     // .use("/assets", express.static(path.join(__dirname, "public/assets")))
   20     .use("/assets", express.static(path.join(__dirname, "public/assets"), {
   21       setHeaders: (res, path) => {
   22         console.log("setting headers.....");
   23         res.set('Access-Control-Allow-Origin', 'http://localhost:3000');
   24       }
   25   }))
   26     .use(routerMiddleware())
   27     .listen(PORT, () => {
   28       console.log("listening");
   29       console.timeEnd("Start");
   30       console.log(`Env: ${NODE_ENV}`);
   31       console.log(`Address: http://localhost:${PORT}`);
   32   });
```

Figure 10-5. *marko-remote-app/src/index.js*

Now that we have installed the dependencies; configured the PORT, runtimeID, adapter, and base path variable; updated the vite.config.js; and seen the starter code which gives us finer control in being able to set response headers for assets to handle CORS (given that we are getting the setup to run locally by running two different apps), let's look at what the remote app renders.

Think of a hypothetical use case where your entire enterprise is an MPA, and you are to inform your users that browsers which don't support the TLS 1.2 protocol (mandatory for payments) will no longer be supported. Although easy, you now have to work with each of the teams that own the respective pages of your app—home page, search page, item page, product page, profile page, settings page, checkout page, and deals page, to name a few. The simple job now becomes a massive undertaking as you now have to coordinate releases, rollouts, bug fixes, enhancements, new features, software upgrades, code migrations, and so on. In an operational scale of a setup like eBay, you can see how this soon becomes a major hassle. With over 700 application pools managed by hundreds of teams, this simple task of showing a notification becomes a massive undertaking.

These are the scenarios that micro-frame solves easily by fully inverting the dependencies between teams. All you now need is a one-time integration with the respective pages as shown in Figures 10-2 and 10-3. You can even render backward-compatible UIs by passing an expected version (on the host app) in the query params to the remote app. Given that it's an HTTP call, you are now free to roll out upgrades, bug fixes, and enhancements on your production pool. Gone are the days of having to coordinate releases and manage code rollouts. You don't have to be worried about runtimes clashing as they are properly sandboxed or resort to extensive debugging about dependencies being shared, incompatible versions, CORS issues, bringing the render of remote modules into the host app, and so on.

Enough talk now! Let's see the code for the component we are to render in Figures 10-6 and 10-7. This is a notification component which we have built with **@ebay/skin** and **@ebayui/ebayui-core**. You will recall it being introduced in Chapter 6. These are eBay's open source CSS theme framework and a suite of core UX components battle-tested across devices that are accessibility compliant and responsive. They are built with Marko.

```
src > components > notice-bar > ☰ index.marko > ⁂ ebay-page-notice > ⌔ div
 1    <ebay-page-notice ...input on-dismiss('emit', 'dismiss') status=input.type a11yDismissText="Dismiss Notice">
 2        <@title>
 3            <div>Outdated browser alert</div>
 4        </@title>
 5        <p>
 6            Your experience on our website will be degraded and minimal as we have
 7            detected you are on an outdated browser with potential security vulnerabilities.
 8        </p>
 9        <div>
10            <a href="https://www.ebay.com">Click here to read about our browser policy</a>
11        </div>
12    </ebay-page-notice>
```

Figure 10-6. *marko-remote-app/src/components/notice-bar/index.marko*

Before we access this via the micro-frame, let's see if it renders well as a page. For this, we will include the **<notice-bar>** component within **marko-remote-app/src/routes/remote-app-fragment**, as shown in Figures 10-8 and 10-9. Incidentally, given that **marko-remote-app** is a marko-run app that follows the file and directory structure–based routing of the marko-run meta framework, this page can be accessed at http://localhost:3001/remote-app-fragment. Let's start the remote app in the **dev** mode via npm run dev. This output is shown in Figure 10-10.

```
src > components > notice-bar > {} style.less
 1    @import "~@ebay/skin/marketsans.css";
 2    // @import '@ebay/skin/index.css';
 3    @import '~@ebay/skin/global.css';
 4    @import '~@ebay/skin/less.less';
 5    @import "~@ebay/skin/tokens.css";
 6    @import "~@ebay/skin/utility.css";
```

Figure 10-7. *marko-remote-app/src/components/notice-bar/style.less*

```
src > routes > remote-app-fragment > ☰ +page.marko > ...
 1    $ console.log("Rendering....")
 2
 3    $ const { type } = $global;
 4
 5    <notice-bar type=type/>
```

Figure 10-8. *marko-remote-app/src/routes/remote-app-fragment/+page.marko*

```
src > routes > remote-app-fragment > JS +handler.js > ⊗ GET
  1    export async function GET(context, next) {
  2        const request = context.platform.request;
  3        const response = context.platform.response;
  4        response.setHeader("Access-Control-Allow-Origin", "http://localhost:3000")
  5        const query = request.query;
  6        const type = query.type || "confirmation";
  7        context.type = type;
  8    }
```

Figure 10-9. *marko-remote-app/src/routes/remote-app-fragment/+handler.js*

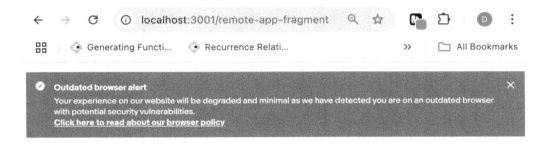

Figure 10-10. *Remote app output of /remote-app-fragment route*

Note that we have configured this route to respond based on the **type** query param. From Figure 10-9, if nothing is passed, it defaults to a confirmation type message. Next, let's pass the **type=attention**. This is shown in Figure 10-11.

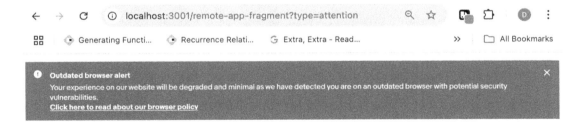

Figure 10-11. *Remote app output of /remote-app-fragment route with query param type=attention*

Given that we have now established that the remote app works fine in an isolated manner and that we have properly set up all our bindings between the host app and the remote app, let's start the remote app in preview mode after building it. For this, do npm

597

run build followed by an npm run preview. After this, head to the **marko-host-app** and start that with **npm run dev** or the same npm run build followed by an npm run preview.

You now have two apps running—**marko-host-app** on PORT **3000** and **marko-remote-app** on PORT **3001**. Hit the default route of the host app at http://localhost:3000/.

The output is shown in Figure 10-12.

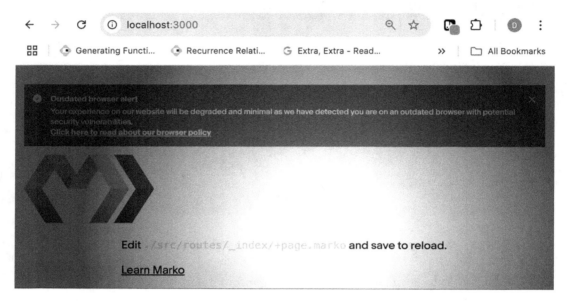

Figure 10-12. *Remote app–rendered component is transcluded (embedded) into the host app*

Notice how the outdated browser alert rendered by the remote app gets embedded into the host app! You have thus achieved the basic use case of app federation–based micro frontends! Instead of federating modules, you are federating apps now! This is of course a very basic case. There is so much more to app federation–based micro frontends. But this is a great start to understand how simple it all is. Notice that from Figures 10-2 and 10-3, we have used the URL to the **marko-remote-app**, within the **marko-host-app**. You can see this within the invocation of the <micro-frame> component's **src** attribute.

The example is kept intentionally simple, which is why in Figure 10-9 you don't see any API calls being made to fetch some data to render this notification component. However, in practice, you would be making API calls within the **marko-remote-app/src/routes/remote-app-fragment/handler.js**, fetching data to render the component.

Figure 10-13 shows how the host app is on 3000 and loads the content from the remote app, with the contents of the remote app (assets) being served from 3001. Also, you will see when inspecting the network tab that there was no fetch and the content was entirely rendered from the server.

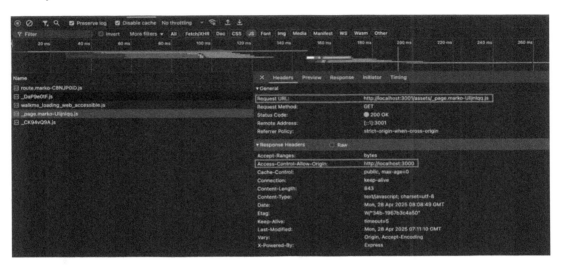

Figure 10-13. *Remote app from 3001 called from the host app on 3000*

One thing to note here in the **marko-remote-app** is that the following files that came when the project was scaffolded have been removed:

- src/routes/favicon.png

- src/routes/_index/logo.svg

- src/routes/_index/+page.marko

- src/routes/_index/+meta.json

- src/routes/+layout.marko

- src/components/mouse-mask.marko

But is our setup capable of re-rendering on the client? We can test that out with a small change to the **<remote-app>** component of the **marko-host-app**, as shown in Figure 10-14. A **type** is being passed in the URL query params—which is in effect passing some props to a component being rendered remotely on another application.

```
src > components > ≡ remote-app.marko > ...
  1    class {
  2        onCreate() {
  3            this.state = {
  4                type: "confirmation",
  5            };
  6        }
  7        reload() {
  8            this.state.type="attention";
  9        }
 10    }
 11
 12    <div id="remote-app">
 13        <div class="remote-app__content">
 14            <micro-frame
 15                src=`http://localhost:3001/remote-app-fragment?dt=${Date.now()}&type=${state.type}`
 16                timeout=0
 17                client-reorder
 18            >
 19                <@loading>We're still loading...</@loading>
 20                <@catch|err|>
 21                    Uh-oh! ${err.message}
 22                </@catch>
 23            </micro-frame>
 24        </div>
 25        <div class="remote-app__content">
 26            <button on-click("reload")>Refresh</button>
 27        </div>
 28    </div>
```

Figure 10-14. *marko-host-app/src/components/remote-app.marko updated with a mechanism to reload on the client*

From Figure 10-14, you will notice we have just included a button that updates the **state** property **type**, which will then cause the micro-frame tag to be re-rendered on the client side. When you click the Reload button, the initial render (which was a notification of type confirmation—green) now switches to notification type attention—red. This is shown in Figures 10-15 and 10-16.

One detail that was missed in all this is where the __MY_ASSET_BASE_PATH__ variable was set. This is set in the +middleware.js of the **marko-remote-app** as shown in Figure 10-17.

Also, as you noticed in Figure 10-8, our **marko-remote-app/src/routes/+page. marko** does not have all the additional wrapper HTML elements (like <html><body>, etc.). The **+layout.marko** that is usually present in a marko-run app (which adds all the layout) has also been deleted. This means the page acts as a template partial (a fragment of HTML) that marko can render without the need for all the surrounding wrappers.

Before we look at the next section, it would be helpful to take a look at how Marko can be used to render Server-Sent Event streams. Let's look at this with a simple example. As an extension to this example, in Chapter 11, an example with consuming

Server-Sent Event streams from the client side to render Marko templates on the client is presented via the **EventSource** API. But in the following example, in the next section of this chapter, let's look at how Marko templates can be rendered on the server while consuming Server-Sent Event streams on the server side.

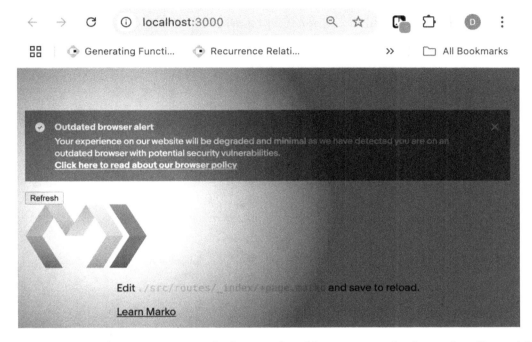

Figure 10-15. *The page now includes a Reload button to refresh on the client side*

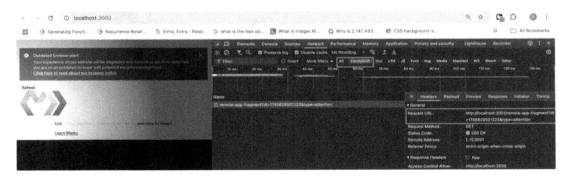

Figure 10-16. *Clicking Reload makes a fetch call to server-render the UX and update on the client*

But before we get to this, we would need a way for Marko to be able to handle streams of data. We saw a primitive version of this in Chapter 3 while dealing with progressive rendering, in the **<server-await>** tag, which was part of an **<iso-await>** component. This tag was able to handle async resolvables (promises) passed into the template, await them, and render them in a non-blocking way. We can use that component and build an enhanced version of it, which now takes in event emitters instead of async resolvables, where it now listens for a stream of data instead of one async value. Let's call this take **<server-stream>.**

```js
src > routes > JS +middleware.js > ...
 1    globalThis.__MY_ASSET_BASE_PATH__ = "http://localhost:3001/assets/"
 2
 3    export default async function ({ request, url, meta }, next) {
 4        const requestName = `${request.method} ${url.href}`;
 5        let success = true;
 6        console.log(`${requestName} request started`, { meta });
 7        const startTime = performance.now();
 8        try {
 9          return await next();
10        } catch (err) {
11          success = false;
12          throw err;
13        } finally {
14          console.log(
15            `${requestName} completed ${
16              success ? "successfully" : "with errors"
17            } in ${performance.now() - startTime}ms`,
18          );
19        }
20    }
```

Figure 10-17. *marko-remote-app/src/routes/+middleware.js containing the __ MY_ASSET_BASE_PATH__ variable setting*

Let's place the code for this component under marko-remote-app/src/components/ stream-input.

The code is shown in Figures 10-18 to 10-20 (expanded portions).

This tag is currently written as a server-only render tag. We will do a couple of things next.

1. We will use this to server-render a test page. In this test page

    a. This tag will be used to consume messages/events from an SSE API (that returns data as a Server-Sent Event stream) and render them on the server side.

    b. In this case, the invocation to the API will be done on the server side.

    c. The stream itself will be passed into the Marko template. So, this example would be to use Marko templates in the context of Server-Sent Events to consume an SSE API stream and progressively render HTML.

2. Next, we will expand upon #1 to serve the progressively rendered HTML itself as SSE chunks.

3. In Chapter 11, we will expand upon #1 to do the invocation to the SSE API from the client side via the **EventSource** API available on the web. Followed by rendering the API stream data that is mapped to Marko components on the client side.

```
src > components > stream-input > {} marko-tag.json > ...
  1    {
  2        "renderer": "./renderer.js"
  3    }
```

Figure 10-18. *<stream-input> marko-tag.json*

```
src > components > stream-input > JS renderer.js > ...
  1    export default function (input, out) {
  2      const emitter = input.dataProvider;
  3
  4      let isFinished = false;
  5      let isFirstFlush = false;
  6
  7      // This async fragment doesn't have timeout handling
  8      const asyncOut = out.beginAsync({ timeout: 0, name: input.name });
  9
 10 >    emitter.on("data", (data) => {…
 17      });
 18
 19 >    emitter.on("error", (err) => {…
 22      });
 23
 24 >    emitter.on("done", () => {…
 27      });
 28
 29 >    function closeFragment() {…
 37      }
 38
 39 >    function renderFragment(renderer, data) {…
 49      }
 50
 51      renderFragment(input.placeholder);
 52    }
```

Figure 10-19. *<stream-input> renderer.js*

In Figures 10-19 and 10-20, the renderer of the **<stream-input>** component is shown. If you will recall, it follows the same approach as of **<server-await>**, but now, instead of the input being an async resolvable (that resolves to one value), we have the input as a stream.

So, handlers are wired on to render the fragment every time there is a "**data**" event. Similarly, the catch block is rendered when there is an "**error**" event. If it's the last chunk of the SSE stream, then the **closeFragment** function is invoked to close the async stream. Before the first chunk arrives, the placeholder fragment (if any) is flushed. Upon the first chunk, an inline-style placeholder is flushed to hide the placeholder that was previously flushed.

Let's assume we host this app on the http://localhost:3001/ssr-sse-page, so we would be required to place the following routes-related files like this:

- marko-remote-app/src/routes/ssr-sse-page/+page.marko shown in Figure 10-21

- marko-remote-app/src/routes/ssr-sse-page/+handler.js shown in Figure 10-22

- marko-remote-app/src/routes/ssr-sse-page/+page.style.css shown in Figure 10-24

- marko-remote-app/src/routes/ssr-sse-page/utils.js shown in Figure 10-25

```
10    emitter.on("data", (data) => {
11      if (!isFirstFlush) {
12        isFirstFlush = true;
13        renderFragment(input.placeholderhidestyle)
14      }
15      console.log("isnide then", data);
16      renderFragment(input.then, data);
17    });
18
19    emitter.on("error", (err) => {
20      console.log("isnide err");
21      renderFragment(input.catch, err);
22    });
23
24    emitter.on("done", () => {
25      isFinished = true;
26      closeFragment();
27    });
28
29    function closeFragment() {
30      console.log("closeFrag");
31      if (isFinished) {
32        console.log("finished");
33        console.log("closing...");
34        asyncOut.flush();
35        asyncOut.end();
36      }
37    }
38
39    function renderFragment(renderer, data) {
40      console.log("render frag");
41      if (!isFinished) {
42        console.log("!finished");
43        if (renderer) {
44          console.log("render fragment....");
45          renderer.renderBody(asyncOut, data);
46        }
47        asyncOut.flush();
48      }
49    }
```

Figure 10-20. <stream-input> renderer.js expanded segments of the code

Figure 10-21 shows the page template for this route http://localhost:3001/ssr-sse-page. The page template takes an input property, **messageStream**, which is an SSE stream, as its input. This stream is passed to the **<stream-input>** tag, and the template fragment we would require to render is included within it as part of the **<@then>** named body tag. There are also other named body tags for placeholder (**<@placeholder>**), handling errors (**<@catch>**) and handling hiding the placeholder when a chunk arrives (**<@placeholderhidestye>**). When the stream begins emitting a **data** event, for every **data** event emitted, the template partial contained within the **<@then>** block will be rendered. The content we plan on rendering here is a section notice UX that holds a message.

```
src > routes > ssr-sse-page > ≡ +page.marko > 𝒫 html > 𝒫 body > ⅗ stream-input
1     $ const { messageStream } = input;
2
3     <html lang="en-US">
4         <head>
5             <title>App Page</title>
6         </head>
7         <body>
8             <h1>Messages from SSE API</h1>
9             <stream-input dataProvider=messageStream>
10                <@placeholder>
11                    <div class="placeholder">Loading...</div>
12                </@placeholder>
13                <@placeholderhidestyle>
14                    <style>.placeholder{display: none}</style>
15                </@placeholderhidestyle>
16                <@then|message|>
17                    <html-comment>${message.id}</html-comment>
18                    <div style={margin: "10px 0 10px 0"}>
19                        <ebay-section-notice status="information" a11y-dismiss-text="close">
20                            <span>${message.message} </span>
21                        </ebay-section-notice>
22                    </div>
23                </@then>
24                <@catch|err|>
25                    $ console.log(err);
26                    <div>A error occurred!</div>
27                </@catch>
28            </stream-input>
29        </body>
30    </html>
```

Figure 10-21. *marko-remote-app/src/route/ssr-sse-page/+page.marko*

```
src > routes > ssr-sse-page > # +page.style.css
  1    @import '~@ebay/skin/marketsans.css';
  2    /* @import '~@ebay/skin/less.css'; */
  3    @import '~@ebay/skin/tokens.css';
  4    @import '~@ebay/skin/global.css';
  5    @import '~@ebay/skin/utility.css';
  6    @import "~@ebay/skin/section-notice.css";
```

Figure 10-22. *marko-remote-app/src/route/ssr-sse-page/+page.style.css*

In Figure 10-22, the page styles are included, and in Figure 10-23 the associated handler file for this page is provided. Before we get here, let's install **undici** for making API calls. This is done via an npm install **undici**. We are making a request to the same marko-remote-app, but to a different route: http://localhost:3001/api. This API is our mock API that provides data as SSE chunks and is shown in Figure 10-24.

```
src > routes > ssr-sse-page > JS +handler.js > ⊘ GET
  1   import { createMessageEmitter } from "./utils";
  2   import { fetch } from "undici"; // undici's fetch
  3   import template from "./+page.marko"; // Compiled Marko template
  4
  5   export async function GET({ platform: { request } }) {
  6     try {
  7       // Fetch the SSE data from /api
  8       const response = await fetch("http://localhost:3001/api", {
  9         headers: {
 10           Accept: "text/event-stream",
 11         },
 12       });
 13
 14       // Validate response
 15       if (!response.ok) {
 16         throw new Error(`Fetch failed with status ${response.status}`);
 17       }
 18       if (!response.body) {
 19         throw new Error("response.body is null or undefined");
 20       }
 21
 22       // Render the template with the message stream
 23       if (typeof template.stream !== "function") {
 24         throw new Error("template.stream is not a function");
 25       }
 26       const emitter = createMessageEmitter(response);
 27       const stream = template.stream({ messageStream: emitter });
 28
 29       // const stream = template.stream({ messageStream: messageStream() });
 30
 31       // Return Response
 32       return new Response(stream, {
 33         headers: {
 34           "Content-Type": "text/html",
 35           "Transfer-Encoding": "chunked", // Ensure streaming
 36         },
 37       });
 38     } catch (err) {
 39       console.error("Error in /ssr-sse handler:", err);
 40       return new Response("Internal Server Error: " + err.message, {
 41         status: 500,
 42         headers: { "Content-Type": "text/html" },
 43       });
 44     }
 45   }
```

Figure 10-23. marko-remote-app/src/route/ssr-sse-page/+handler.js

In Figure 10-23, when you look at the handler, you will see we do the following:

- Make an API call to the SSE endpoint via **undici's fetch**.

- This API is also a sample mock API that is housed within the same **marko-remote-app** under **src/routes/api/+handler.js** and responds to requests made to http://localhost:3001/api.

- While the API is awaited, it will move to the next line of execution as it's an SSE endpoint that will respond over time in chunks of data.

```
src > routes > api > JS +handler.js > ⊙ GET
1    export async function GET({ platform: { request }}) {
2        const query = request.query || {};
3        const chunkId = query.slotName || 'defaultID';
4
5        console.log(`chunkId= `, chunkId);
6
7        // Create a readable stream for SSE
8        const stream = new ReadableStream({
9          start(controller) {
10           let count = 0; // Track number of emissions
11           const maxEmissions = 5; // Stop after 5 messages
12
13           // Set up an interval to send data every 2 seconds
14           const interval = setInterval(() => {
15             const data = {
16               id: `${chunkId}`,
17               message: `Server time: ${new Date().toISOString()} (#${count + 1})`,
18             };
19             // Encode the data as SSE format (data: JSON\n\n)
20             const text = `data: ${JSON.stringify(data)}\n\n`;
21             controller.enqueue(new TextEncoder().encode(text));
22
23             // Increment count and check if limit is reached
24             count++;
25             if (count >= maxEmissions) {
26               clearInterval(interval); // Stop the interval
27               controller.close(); // Close the stream
28             }
29           }, 2000);
30
31           // Store interval for cleanup
32           request._interval = interval;
33         },
34         cancel() {
35           // Clean up when the stream is canceled (client disconnects)
36           if (request._interval) {
37             clearInterval(request._interval);
38           }
39         },
40       });
41
42       // Return a Response with SSE headers
43       return new Response(stream, {
44         headers: {
45           'Content-Type': 'text/event-stream',
46           'Cache-Control': 'no-cache',
47           'Connection': 'keep-alive',
48         },
49       });
50     }
```

Figure 10-24. *marko-remote-app/src/route/api/+handler.js*

- The response stream received from the SSE endpoint is passed into the **createMessageEmitter** function which wraps the response stream and returns an event emitter (from data stream to event streams).

- This event emitter is passed into the template's render method (*.stream*) as input via the **messageStream** property.

- The render method used here is **template.stream** (briefly discussed in Chapter 5).

- The returned stream from this is piped into the response stream via **new Response(..)**.

- This setup allows for HTML to be streamed to the browser while being rendered on the server.

- Notice the response headers with "**Content-Type**" set to "**text/html**" along with the "**Transfer-Encoding**" header set to "**chunked**". This is because we are running the app on HTTP. Ideally, when you use HTTPS, you would not be required to set this, as HTTPS by default supports chunking when the response size header is not set.

```
src > routes > ssr-sse-page > JS utils.js > ⊙ createMessageEmitter
  1    import { EventEmitter } from "events";
  2  |
  3    export function createMessageEmitter(response) {
  4      const emitter = new EventEmitter();
  5      const reader = response.body.getReader();
  6      const decoder = new TextDecoder();
  7      let buffer = "";
  8
  9  >   (async () => {...
 66    })();
 67
 68      return emitter;
 69    }
 70
```

Figure 10-25. *marko-remote-app/src/route/ssr-sse-page/utils.js*

We have two final pieces of the puzzle pending before we can start the server to test server-side rendering of a template that consumes SSE on the server. They are

- **marko-remote-app/src/routes/ssr-sse-page/utils.js** which contains the **createMessageEmitter** function. This is shown in Figures 10-25 and 10-26.

- The route handler for the http://localhost:3001/api contained at **marko-remote-app/src/routes/api**. This is shown in Figure 10-24.

```
 9   (async () => {
10     try {
11       while (true) {
12         // Remove the messageCount limit
13         const { done, value } = await reader.read();
14         if (done) break;
15
16         buffer += decoder.decode(value, { stream: true });
17
18         // Split messages on double newlines (SSE message delimiter)
19         const messages = buffer.split("\n\n");
20
21         // Process all complete messages except potentially incomplete last one
22         for (let i = 0; i < messages.length - 1; i++) {
23           const msg = messages[i].trim();
24
25           // Only process lines that start with data:
26           if (msg.startsWith("data: ")) {
27             const dataLine = msg.slice(6); // remove "data: "
28             try {
29               const data = JSON.parse(dataLine);
30               console.log(`data=`, data);
31               emitter.emit("data", data);
32             } catch (err) {
33               emitter.emit(
34                 "error",
35                 new Error("Failed to parse JSON: " + dataLine)
36               );
37             }
38           }
39         }
40
41         // Preserve potentially incomplete message for next read
42         buffer = messages[messages.length - 1];
43       }
44
45       // Final flush of remaining buffer
46       const finalMsg = buffer.trim();
47       if (finalMsg.startsWith("data: ")) {
48         const dataLine = finalMsg.slice(6);
49         try {
50           const data = JSON.parse(dataLine);
51           emitter.emit("data", data);
52         } catch (err) {
53           emitter.emit(
54             "error",
55             new Error("Failed to parse final JSON: " + dataLine)
56           );
57         }
58       }
59
60       emitter.emit("done");
61     } catch (err) {
62       emitter.emit("error", err);
63     } finally {
64       await reader.cancel();
65     }
66   })();
```

Figure 10-26. *marko-remote-app/src/route/ssr-sse-page/utils.js (expanded)*

In Figure 10-24, let's see the API route handler, and in Figures 10-25 and 10-26, let's see the utils file. In the API route handler, we return a new response which is a readable stream. We begin the readable stream via the **start()** function and do cleanup within the **cancel()** function. Basically, what this does is enqueue a chunk of data wired via a **setInterval** function, which triggers every two seconds, pushing in a chunk of data into the stream every two seconds. It emits five such chunks (governed by the **maxEmissions** variable).

Once it hits this limit, the **controller** param closes the stream, causing it to be cleaned up. When writing data into the readable stream, it ensures that the SSE data format is maintained. While this data is being pushed into the readable stream, the receiver (or the invoker of the API call, which is the **src/routes/ssr-sse-page/+handler. js**) will read from this and send these individual chunks to the template which will process it.

Also, the SSE format is of type **text/event-stream**, so when flushing the chunks, we use the **TextEncoder** to send data in the text format. Finally, the associated response headers are set up:

- "**Content-Type**" as "**text/event-stream**"

- "**Connection**" as "**Keep-Alive**"

- "**Cache-Control**" as "**no-cache**"

Pro tip: While chunking responses is good (flushing responses as they become available to the stream ensures that the frontend can begin processing them as they arrive), care should be taken not to go overboard and over-chunk the responses. You could perhaps do a left nav, river, header and top-nav and footer and so on.

Figures 10-25 and 10-26 illustrate the utils file which contains the **createMessageEmitter** function, which takes the response stream from the API call, wraps it over an event emitter, and returns the event emitter which is then passed as input to the Marko template. This enables us to create a bridge between a data stream and an event stream. The response data stream is now handled via the event emitter, which is able to serve data (as an event stream) to the template.

This code in Figures 10-25 and 10-26 (expanded), defines a utility function, **createMessageEmitter**, which processes a stream of data from a response stream object and emits structured events using the Node JS's **EventEmitter**.

It is designed to handle **Server-Sent Events (SSE)**, where messages are delimited by double newlines (**\n\n**) and typically prefixed with **data:**. The function begins by creating an **EventEmitter** instance and initializing a **ReadableStream** reader from the **response.body**.

A **TextDecoder** is used to decode the binary chunks of data into strings. A **buffer** variable is maintained to accumulate data chunks, and a **messageCount** variable tracks how many messages have been successfully processed. The core logic is encapsulated in an asynchronous self-invoking function.

It reads chunks of data from the stream in a loop using **reader.read()**. Each chunk is decoded and appended to the buffer. The buffer is then split into individual messages using the double newline delimiter. Complete messages are processed, while the last (potentially incomplete) message is preserved in the buffer for the next iteration.

For each complete message, the code checks if it starts with **data:**. If so, it extracts the content after **data:**, attempts to parse it as JSON, and emits a data event with the parsed object. If JSON parsing fails, an error event is emitted with a descriptive error message. The loop stops after processing five messages, at which point a **done** event is emitted, and the stream reader is canceled.

Finally, after exiting the loop, the code performs a "final flush" of the remaining buffer to handle any leftover data. If the buffer contains a valid message, it is processed and emitted. The function ensures proper cleanup by canceling the reader in a finally block, regardless of whether the loop exited normally or due to an error.

Note that we have introduced the following files overall:

- marko-remote-app/src/components/stream-input/marko-tag.json
- marko-remote-app/src/components/stream-input/renderer.js
- marko-remote-app/src/routes/api/+handler.js
- marko-remote-app/src/routes/ssr-sse-page/+handler.js
- marko-remote-app/src/routes/ssr-sse-page/+page.style.css
- marko-remote-app/src/routes/ssr-sse-page/+page.marko
- marko-remote-app/src/routes/ssr-sse-page/+utils.js

Now, restart the app on port 3001 and hit http://localhost:3001/ssr-sse-page, and you will see how each chunk of data is emitted by the API call /api and how each chunk is processed by **createMessageEmitter**, which responds to every chunk by emitting a data event.

Every time a **data** event is emitted with the data, the **<stream-input>** listens for it and renders the section within the **<@then>**. The **<@then>** block contains the **<ebay-section-notice>** component which uses the content within the data event.

Once you load the page, you will see these section notice messages appearing on the screen (streamed, one by one). A total of five chunks are emitted, causing five data events to be triggered, causing the <@then> block to be rendered five times, bringing the output of five messages on the screen, one by one. Isn't that fabulous? The output is shown in Figure 10-27.

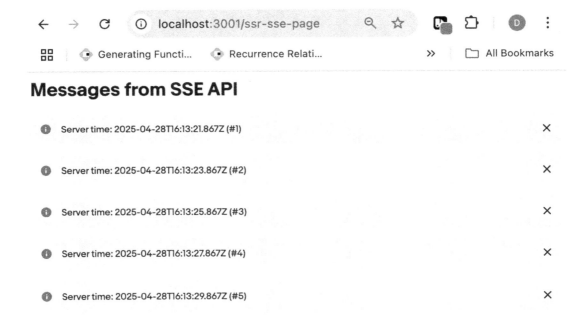

Figure 10-27. *Output of the page*

If you will recall, we have used the <stream-input> tag that operates by directly employing the Marko's async render APIs, which the marko team generally advises against. So, let's modify that. This is shown in Figure 10-28. There are no modifications to any of the code except for the file **marko-remote-app/src/routes/ssr-sse-page/+handler.js**.

Instead of directly modifying it, the code is duplicated under **ssr-sse-page-v2** with all the existing code remaining intact and the only change being the **+handler.js**. If you will notice in Figure 10-28, the **<stream-input>** tag is removed and replaced with a **<macro>** that uses an **<await>** within it, which recursively calls itself.

Promise.any also takes an array of promises and returns a single promise that resolves as soon as any of the promises in the input array fulfills. It is used here to check the resolution of the two values—either a resolve or a reject. Every time, it waits for the done event and then proceeds to recursively call itself if the current chunk is successful.

This proceeds until the stream is ended.

```
src > routes > ssr-sse-page-v2 > ☰ +page.marko > ⅋ macro > ⅋ await > ⅋ n
 1    import { once } from "events"
 2    $ const { messageStream } = input;
 3
 4
 5    <macro name="wait">
 6        <await(Promise.any([
 7            once(messageStream, "done"),
 8            once(messageStream, "data")
 9        ])) timeout=0>
10            <@placeholder>
11                <div class="placeholder">Loading...</div>
12            </@placeholder>
13            <@catch|err|>
14                $ console.log(err);
15                <div>A error occurred!</div>
16            </@catch>
17            <@then|messages|>
18                <if(messages && Array.isArray(messages) && messages.length)>
19                    <html-comment>${messages[0].id}</html-comment>
20                    <div style={margin: "10px 0 10px 0"}>
21                        <ebay-section-notice status="information" a11y-dismiss-text="close">
22                            <span>${messages[0].message} </span>
23                        </ebay-section-notice>
24                    </div>
25                    <wait/>
26                </>
27            </>
28        </>
29    </>
30
31    <html lang="en-US">
32        <head>
33            <title>App Page</title>
34        </head>
35        <body>
36            <h1>Messages from SSE API</h1>
37            <wait/>
38        </body>
39    </html>
```

Figure 10-28. *A declarative version of the <stream-input> tag via <macro> and <await>*

What did we achieve from this exercise so far? Well, we have achieved #1 from the list mentioned earlier:

1. We will use this to server-render a test page. In this test page

   a. This tag will be used to consume messages/events from an SSE API (that returns data as a Server-Sent Event stream) and render them on the server side.

   b. In this case, the invocation to the API will be done on the server side.

   c. The stream itself will be passed into the Marko template. So, this example would be to use Marko templates in the context of Server-Sent Events to consume an SSE API stream and progressively render HTML.

2. Next, we will expand upon #1 to serve the progressively rendered HTML itself as SSE chunks.

For #2, we have so far achieved progressive HTML rendering via streaming of SSE API chunks. That is, HTML was also being streaming rendered. However, HTML was being sent as HTML and not as HTML in the SSE format.

But to use the next **@microframe/marko** tag, the **<micro-frame-sse>** tag and the **<micro-frame-slot>** tags, we would need to be able to serve this progressively rendered/ streamed HTML (which is already rendering HTML in chunks) as an SSE response.

This means, while the earlier /**api** call returned JSON within the **data:** property of the SSE frame, this next change will make HTML be returned as part of the **data:** property of the SSE frame when accessed via /**remote-app-sse-single-slot**. This is the type of endpoint that **<micro-frame-sse>** and **<micro-frame-slot>** deal with.

To achieve #2, we have to make minor changes to the +**page.marko** and the associated +**handler.js** within **marko-remote-app/src/routes/ssr-sse-page**. But instead of touching them, let's copy them to a new folder titled **remote-app-sse-single-slot** under **src/routes**. In the template, we will get rid of the **<html>** and **<body>** tag wrappers, etc., so that only the partial is rendered and served.

To the +**handler.js**, there is an elaborate change because we have to now serve the HTML itself as SSE chunks. This is covered in Figures 10-29 and 10-30. The changes to the host app to be able to consume the SSE HTML via the **@microframe/marko** are covered in Figure 10-32 onward.

Notice that there is no change to the +page.style.css, utils.js, or the api handler. The only change is with the +page.marko and +handler.js files of the page. We will be adding the following files now:

- **marko-remote-app/src/routes/remote-app-sse-single-slot/+page.marko**

- marko-remote-app/src/routes/remote-app-sse-single-slot/+page.style.css

- **marko-remote-app/src/routes/remote-app-sse-single-slot/+handler.js**

- marko-remote-app/src/routes/remote-app-sse-single-slot/utils.js

```
src > routes > remote-app-sse-single-slot > Ξ +page.marko > ⌘ stream-input
 1    $ const { messageStream } = input;
 2
 3    <h1>Messages from SSE API</h1>
 4    <stream-input dataProvider=messageStream>
 5        <@placeholder>
 6            <div class="placeholder">Loading...</div>
 7        </@placeholder>
 8        <@placeholderhidestyle>
 9            <style>.placeholder{display: none}</style>
10        </@placeholderhidestyle>
11        <@then|message|>
12            <html-comment>${message.id}</html-comment>
13            <div style={margin: "10px 0 10px 0"}>
14                <ebay-section-notice status="information" a11y-dismiss-text="close">
15                    <span>${message.message} </span>
16                </ebay-section-notice>
17            </div>
18        </@then>
19        <@catch|err|>
20            $ console.log(err);
21            <div>A error occurred!</div>
22        </@catch>
23    </stream-input>
```

Figure 10-29. *marko-remote-app/src/routes/remote-app-sse-single-shot /+page.marko*

As shown in Figure 10-30, the only difference lies in how the response is served finally. Comparing this with what we saw earlier in Figure 10-23, the difference is

- In Figure 10-23, the output from **template.stream** was directly piped into the response stream.

- In Figure 10-29, the output from **template.stream** is wrapped over another ReadableStream named **sseWrappedStream**. And this readable stream is then piped to the response stream.

Basically, we listen for **data** events from within **markoNodeStream** (the output of *template.stream*), and as we get chunks of data, we convert it to the SSE format and enqueue it after encoding it via **TextEncoder**.

Let's do an npm run build and npm run preview to see how it would now emit by accessing the route http://localhost:3001/remote-app-sse-single-slot. The output is shown in Figure 10-31. As you load the page, same as before, chunks of data arrive on the browser in a streaming fashion. But this time, unlike actual UI components, you will see text chunks arriving one by one, formatted per the SSE format (SSE'd HTML).

```
src > routes > remote-app-sse-single-slot > JS +handler.js > ⊕ GET
 1  import { fetch } from "undici"; // undici's fetch
 2  import template from "./+page.marko"; // Compiled Marko template
 3  import { createMessageEmitter } from "./utils"
 4
 5  export async function GET({ platform: { request } }) {
 6    try {
 7      const query = request.query || {};
 8      const slotName = query.slotName || 'defaultID';
 9
10      console.log(`slotName= `, slotName);
11
12      // Fetch the SSE data from /api
13      const response = await fetch(`http://localhost:3001/api?slotName=${slotName}`, {
14        headers: {
15          Accept: "text/event-stream",
16        },
17      });
18
19      // Validate response
20      if (!response.ok) {
21        throw new Error(`Fetch failed with status ${response.status}`);
22      }
23      if (!response.body) {
24        throw new Error("response.body is null or undefined");
25      }
26
27      // Render the template with the message stream
28      if (typeof template.stream !== "function") {
29        throw new Error("template.stream is not a function");
30      }
31      const emitter = createMessageEmitter(response);
32      const markoNodeStream = template.stream({ messageStream: emitter });
33
34      const sseWrappedStream = new ReadableStream({
35        start(controller) {
36          const encoder = new TextEncoder();
37
38          markoNodeStream.on('data', (chunk) => {
39            const html = chunk.toString(); // buffer -> string
40            console.log(`html=`, html);
41            // const sseChunk = `data: ${JSON.stringify(html)}\n\n`;
42            // const sseChunk = `id: defaultID\ndata: ${JSON.stringify(html)}\n\n`;
43            const sseChunk = `id: ${slotName}\ndata: ${JSON.stringify(html)}\n\n`;
44            controller.enqueue(encoder.encode(sseChunk));
45          });
46
47          markoNodeStream.on('end', () => {
48            controller.close();
49          });
50
51          markoNodeStream.on('error', (err) => {
52            const errorChunk = `event: error\ndata: ${JSON.stringify(err.message)}\n\n`;
53            controller.enqueue(encoder.encode(errorChunk));
54            controller.close();
55          });
56        }
57      });
58
59      return new Response(sseWrappedStream, {
60        headers: {
61          'Content-Type': 'text/event-stream',
62          'Cache-Control': 'no-cache',
63          'Connection': 'keep-alive',
64          "Access-Control-Allow-Origin": "http://localhost:3000"
65        },
66      });
67
68    } catch (err) {
69      console.error("Error in /ssr-sse handler:", err);
70      const errorMsg = `event: error\ndata: ${JSON.stringify(err.message)}\n\n`;
71      return new Response(errorMsg, {
72        status: 500,
73        headers: { 'Content-Type': 'text/event-stream' },
74      });
75    }
76  }
```

Figure 10-30. *marko-remote-app/src/routes/remote-app-sse-single-shot /+handler.js*

If you will notice in Figure 10-31, we originally had five chunks, but we see seven chunks. This is because, for every template, there are common chunks—assets and hydration data. The first chunk you see contains the asset information. The last chunk contains the initialization code and the hydration information.

Between these chunks is our rendered HTML that is mapped to the slot **defaultID**. You will also notice the component boundary markers as comments within the rendered HTML, which also contain our updated **runtimeID—mr.**

These hydration data pointers are generated by the sophisticated **warp10** module of MarkoJS, all using the **runtimeId** *mr* that we set (**mr** for marko remote) in **vite.config.js** of **marko-remote-app**. This could be any unique identifier that helps sandbox our runtime from any marko runtimes that may be loaded by the host application.

We have now achieved #2 from the previously mentioned list. The next step is to consume this SSE output from **marko-host-app** via **<micro-frame-sse>** and **<micro-frame-slot>** tags of **@micro-frame/marko**. We have earlier seen the **<micro-frame>** tag used in **marko-host-app**.

We briefly saw these other tags in Chapter 9. We will see them now in the next section being used in the **marko-host-app**. The usage of **<micro-frame-sse>** and **<micro-frame-slot>** with this **defaultID** is shown in Figures 10-32 and 10-33. The output is shown in Figure 10-34.

id: defaultID
data: "<script>$mbp_mr=\"http://localhost:3001/assets/\"</script><script async type=\"module\" crossorigin
src=\"http://localhost:3001/assets/_page.marko-ddGir89H.js\"></script><link rel=\"modulepreload\" crossorigin
href=\"http://localhost:3001/assets/_CK94vQ9A.js\"><link rel=\"modulepreload\" crossorigin
href=\"http://localhost:3001/assets/_D1a4o7MU.js\"><link rel=\"stylesheet\" crossorigin href=\"http://localhost:3001/assets/index-
D9ugJnRL.css\"><link rel=\"stylesheet\" crossorigin href=\"http://localhost:3001/assets/index-C8vaF62D.css\"><link rel=\"stylesheet\"
crossorigin href=\"http://localhost:3001/assets/_page-CIzs3r6b.css\"><h1>Messages from SSE API</h1><div class=placeholder>Loading...
</div>"

id: defaultID
data: "<style>.placeholder{display: none}</style><!--defaultID--><div style=\"margin:10px 0 10px 0\"><!--mr#s0-2-5--><section aria-
labelledby=s0-2-5-0-status aria-roledescription=Notice class=section-notice role=region><div class=section-notice__header id=s0-2-5-0-
status><svg class=\"icon--information-filled icon icon--information-filled\" focusable=false aria-hidden=true><defs><symbol
viewbox=\"0 0 16 16\" id=icon-information-filled-16><path d=\"M8 0a8 8 0 1 0 0 16A8 8 0 0 0 8 0Zm1 11a1 1 0 1 1-2 0V8a1 1 0 0 1 2
0v3ZM8 6a1 1 0 1 1 0-2 1 1 0 0 1 0 2Z\"></path></symbol></defs><use href=\"#icon-information-filled-16\" /></svg></div><span
class=section-notice__main><!--F#13--><span>Server time: 2025-04-28T16:50:16.022Z (#1) </span><!--F/--></span><div class=\"section-
notice__footer\"><button aria-label=\"close\" class=\"fake-link section-notice__dismiss\"><svg class=\"icon icon--close-16 icon icon-
-16\" focusable=false aria-hidden=true><defs><symbol viewbox=\"0 0 16 16\" id=icon-close-16><path d=\"M2.293 2.293a1 1 0 0 1 1.414 0L8
6.586l4.293-4.293a1 1 0 1 1.414 1.414L9.414 8l4.293 4.293a1 1 0 0 1-1.414 1.414L8 9.414l-4.293 4.293a1 1 0 0 1-1.414-1.414L6.586 8
2.293 3.707a1 1 0 0 1 0-1.414Z\"></path></symbol></defs><use href=\"#icon-close-16\" /></svg></button></div></section><!--mr/--></div>"

id: defaultID
data: "<!--defaultID--><div style=\"margin:10px 0 10px 0\"><!--mr#s0-2-5_1--><section aria-labelledby=s0-2-5_1-0-status aria-
roledescription=Notice class=section-notice role=region><div class=section-notice__header id=s0-2-5_1-0-status><svg class=\"icon--
information-filled icon icon--16 icon--information-filled\" focusable=false aria-hidden=true><use href=\"#icon-information-filled-16\"
/></svg></div><span class=section-notice__main><!--F#13--><span>Server time: 2025-04-28T16:50:18.023Z (#2) </span><!--F/--></span><div
class=\"section-notice__footer\"><button aria-label=\"close\" class=\"fake-link section-notice__dismiss\"><svg class=\"icon icon--
close-16 icon icon--16\" focusable=false aria-hidden=true><use href=\"#icon-close-16\" /></svg></button></div></section><!--mr/-->
</div>"

id: defaultID
data: "<!--defaultID--><div style=\"margin:10px 0 10px 0\"><!--mr#s0-2-5_2--><section aria-labelledby=s0-2-5_2-0-status aria-
roledescription=Notice class=section-notice role=region><div class=section-notice__header id=s0-2-5_2-0-status><svg class=\"icon--
information-filled icon icon--16 icon--information-filled\" focusable=false aria-hidden=true><use href=\"#icon-information-filled-16\"
/></svg></div><span class=section-notice__main><!--F#13--><span>Server time: 2025-04-28T16:50:20.024Z (#3) </span><!--F/--></span><div
class=\"section-notice__footer\"><button aria-label=\"close\" class=\"fake-link section-notice__dismiss\"><svg class=\"icon icon--
close-16 icon icon--16\" focusable=false aria-hidden=true><use href=\"#icon-close-16\" /></svg></button></div></section><!--mr/-->
</div>"

id: defaultID
data: "<!--defaultID--><div style=\"margin:10px 0 10px 0\"><!--mr#s0-2-5_3--><section aria-labelledby=s0-2-5_3-0-status aria-
roledescription=Notice class=section-notice role=region><div class=section-notice__header id=s0-2-5_3-0-status><svg class=\"icon--
information-filled icon icon--16 icon--information-filled\" focusable=false aria-hidden=true><use href=\"#icon-information-filled-16\"
/></svg></div><span class=section-notice__main><!--F#13--><span>Server time: 2025-04-28T16:50:22.024Z (#4) </span><!--F/--></span><div
class=\"section-notice__footer\"><button aria-label=\"close\" class=\"fake-link section-notice__dismiss\"><svg class=\"icon icon--
close-16 icon icon--16\" focusable=false aria-hidden=true><use href=\"#icon-close-16\" /></svg></button></div></section><!--mr/-->
</div>"

id: defaultID
data: "<!--defaultID--><div style=\"margin:10px 0 10px 0\"><!--mr#s0-2-5_4--><section aria-labelledby=s0-2-5_4-0-status aria-
roledescription=Notice class=section-notice role=region><div class=section-notice__header id=s0-2-5_4-0-status><svg class=\"icon--
information-filled icon icon--16 icon--information-filled\" focusable=false aria-hidden=true><use href=\"#icon-information-filled-16\"
/></svg></div><span class=section-notice__main><!--F#13--><span>Server time: 2025-04-28T16:50:24.025Z (#5) </span><!--F/--></span><div
class=\"section-notice__footer\"><button aria-label=\"close\" class=\"fake-link section-notice__dismiss\"><svg class=\"icon icon--
close-16 icon icon--16\" focusable=false aria-hidden=true><use href=\"#icon-close-16\" /></svg></button></div></section><!--mr/-->
</div>"

id: defaultID
data: "<script>$mr_C=(window.$mr_C||[]).concat({\"w\":[[\"s0-2-5\",0,{\"status\":\"information\",\"a11yDismissText\":\"close\"},
{\"f\":3}],[\"s0-2-5_1\",0,{\"status\":\"information\",\"a11yDismissText\":\"close\"},{\"f\":3}],[\"s0-2-5_2\",0,
{\"status\":\"information\",\"a11yDismissText\":\"close\"},{\"f\":3}],[\"s0-2-5_3\",0,
{\"status\":\"information\",\"a11yDismissText\":\"close\"},{\"f\":3}],[\"s0-2-5_4\",0,
{\"status\":\"information\",\"a11yDismissText\":\"close\"},{\"f\":3}]],\"t\":[\"$qBp9fg\"]})</script>"

Figure 10-31. *Output of the SSE'd HTML*

Now back to our marko-host-app, let's add some route files to access this SSE'd HTML. The code snippets for this are shown in Figures 10-32 and 10-33.

```
src > routes > sse >  ≡ +page.marko > ⅋ micro-frame-sse
 1    <!-- The following end point is only for testing purposes -->
 2    <!-- src=`http://localhost:3001/mock-api-html?dt=${Date.now()}` -->
 3    <micro-frame-sse
 4        timeout=0
 5        src=`http://localhost:3001/remote-app-sse-single-slot?dt=${Date.now()}&slotName=defaultID`
 6        name="remote-stream-source"
 7        read(ev) {
 8            console.log("readingding...", ev);
 9            return [ev.lastEventId, JSON.parse(ev.data), false];
10        }
11    />
12
13    <div class="container">
14        <header>
15            <div id="remote-app">
16                <div class="remote-app__content">
17                    <!-- if client-reorder is set it will render in a non-blocking manner -->
18                    <!-- if client-reorder is removed it will render in a blocking manner -->
19                    <micro-frame-slot from="remote-stream-source" slot="defaultID" timeout=0 client-reorder>
20                        <@loading>
21                            $ console.log("LOAAAAAAAAAAAADDDDD");
22                            We're still loading...
23                        </@loading>
24                        <@catch|err|>
25                            $ console.log("ERRRRRRRRRRRR");
26                            Uh-oh! ${err.message || err}
27                        </@catch>
28                    </micro-frame-slot>
29                </div>
30            </div>
31
32            <div>
33                <img src="./logo.svg" alt="Marko" class="logo">
34            </div>
35        </header>
36        <main>
37            <p>
38                Edit
39                <code>./src/routes/_index/+page.marko</code>
40                and save to reload.
41            </p>
42            <a href="https://markojs.com/docs/getting-started">
43                Learn Marko
44            </a>
45        </main>
46    </div>
47    <mouse-mask/>
48
49    style {
50        .container {
51            display: flex;
52            flex-direction: column;
53            justify-content: center;
54            align-items: center;
55            font-size: clamp(1em, 2vw, 2em);
56            padding: 1em;
57            box-sizing: border-box;
58            height: 100%;
59            width: 100%;
60        }
61        img.logo {
62            width: 12em;
63        }
64    }
```

Figure 10-32. *marko-host-app/src/routes/sse/+page.marko*

In Figure 10-32, if you will notice we have replaced the original **<micro-frame>** tag with the **<micro-frame-sse>** tag. We have also included the new **<micro-frame-slot>** tag that tells exactly where we want our SSE'd HTML to go. The src attribute also points now to http://localhost:3001/remote-app-sse-single-slot.

The **slotName** is passed as a query param. The same **slotName** is also included as part of the slot attribute of the **<micro-frame-slot>** tag. The **<micro-frame-slot>** tag and the **<micro-frame-sse>** tag are tied together via the **from** attribute.

This is because you can be consuming similar SSE'd HTML that can go into other parts or locations of this page from other remote apps. So it's important to map the source and the slots.

The output is shown in Figure 10-33. This is fully rendered on the server. However, just as before, what if we wanted to re-render this on the client side? We absolutely can. This is covered inside the marko-host-app, under the route sse-iso. That is, we have created another folder, marko-host-app/src/routes/sse-iso, and placed the code with some slight modifications that are shown in Figures 10-34 and 10-35. The output of this isomorphic SSE setup is included in Figure 10-36.

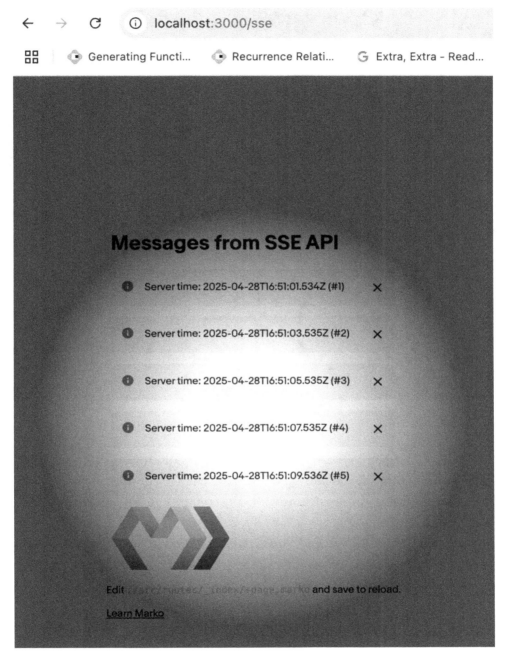

Figure 10-33. *Accessing streaming SSE'd HTML from remote app into host app*

```
src > routes > sse-iso >  ☰ +page.marko > ⌗ div > ⌗ main > ⌗ p
 1    <div class="container">
 2        <header>
 3            <remote-app-sse/>
 4
 5            <div>
 6                <img src="./logo.svg" alt="Marko" class="logo">
 7            </div>
 8        </header>
 9        <main>
10            <p>
11                Edit
12                <code>./src/routes/_index/+page.marko</code>
13                 and save to reload.
14            </p>
15            <a href="https://markojs.com/docs/getting-started">
16                Learn Marko
17            </a>
18        </main>
19    </div>
20    <mouse-mask/>
21
22    style {
23        .container {
24            display: flex;
25            flex-direction: column;
26            justify-content: center;
27            align-items: center;
28            font-size: clamp(1em, 2vw, 2em);
29            padding: 1em;
30            box-sizing: border-box;
31            height: 100%;
32            width: 100%;
33        }
34        img.logo {
35            width: 12em;
36        }
37    }
```

Figure 10-34. *marko-host-app/src/routes/sse-iso/+page.marko*

The changes are again to the **+page.marko**, and we now have a new component **<remote-app-sse>** that fully encapsulates the state changes needed for the re-render of **<micro-frame-sse>** and **<micro-frame-slot>** tags on the client side. This is shown in Figures 10-34 and 10-35.

Same as before, there is a reload button that is mapped to a click handler—reload. This, when clicked, just updates the time stamp, causing the URL of the micro-frame-sse tag to be changed and thereby causing it to re-render.

```marko
src > components >  remote-app-sse.marko >  micro-frame-sse
 1   class {
 2       onCreate() {
 3           this.state = {
 4               time: Date.now(),
 5           };
 6       }
 7       reload() {
 8           this.state.time = Date.now();
 9       }
10   }
11   <!-- The following end point is only for testing purposes -->
12   <!-- src=`http://localhost:3001/mock-api-html?dt=${Date.now()}` -->
13   <micro-frame-sse
14       timeout=0
15       src=`http://localhost:3001/remote-app-sse-single-slot?dt=${state.time}&slotName=defaultID`
16       name="remote-stream-source"
17       read(ev) {
18           console.log("readingding...", ev);
19           return [ev.lastEventId, JSON.parse(ev.data), false];
20       }
21   />
22
23   <div id="remote-app">
24       <div class="remote-app__content">
25           <!-- if client-reorder is set it will render in a non-blocking manner -->
26           <!-- if client-reorder is removed it will render in a blocking manner -->
27           <micro-frame-slot
28               from="remote-stream-source"
29               slot="defaultID"
30               timeout=0
31               client-reorder
32           >
33               <@loading>
34                   $ console.log("LOAAAAAAAAAAAADDDDD");
35                   We're still loading...
36               </@loading>
37               <@catch|err|>
38                   $ console.log("ERRRRRRRRRRRR");
39                   Uh-oh! ${err.message || err}
40               </@catch>
41           </micro-frame-slot>
42       </div>
43       <div class="remote-app__content">
44           <button on-click("reload")>
45               Refresh
46           </button>
47       </div>
48   </div>
```

Figure 10-35. *marko-host-app/src/components/remote-app-sse/index.marko*

Stop the server. Rebuild the app via npm run build and restart via npm run preview. The output can be seen in Figure 10-36. Clicking the Refresh button will cause it to reload and be re-rendered on the client side. If you will notice the figure, the fetch call happens on the client side, and you will also be able to notice the presence of the **EventStream** tab that shows the SSE'd HTML chunks arriving along with the data contained in them and their time stamps of arrival.

You can now delete the notifications and play with it, and you will notice everything works magically because the runtimes do not interfere with each other, thus making micro frontends very seamless and hassle-free, instead of an afterthought, and then working all through the code to achieve them.

One more thing is that our example uses the **client-reorder** prop. You can remove it and load the page. You will find that the content following the micro-frame-slot tag is being blocked. **client-reorder** helps to load the page in a non-blocking fashion.

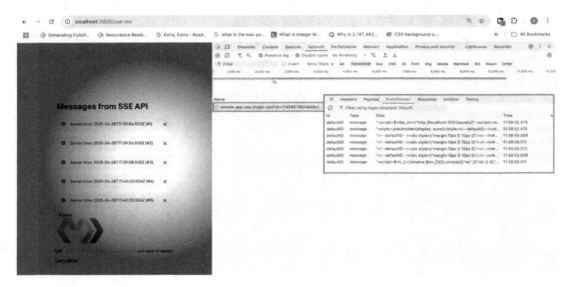

Figure 10-36. *Isomorphically rendered micro-frame-sse and micro-frame-slot tags*

While you can have multiple micro-frame-sse tags that fetch such content from multiple remote resources, the point of micro-frame SSE is to stream content from one source into multiple parts of the DOM simultaneously.

And these parts of the DOM can be distributed (across the template) and don't have to be together. In our earlier example, we saw a basic use case where every chunk was streamed to one slot named **defaultID**. Ideally, we would be doing something like every chunk being mapped to a separate slot, and thereby we are able to paint multiple portions of a given page with data from one source.

But first, before we get to this advanced use case, let's modify the SSE response we got to suit what **<micro-frame-sse>** and **<micro-frame-slot>** tags need. This means different chunks are representative of content to be shown in different parts of the page, from one stream source.

The **<micro-frame-slot>** is required, as we use that to specify the exact spot on the page where we want content streamed into. Also, given that there could be multiple points on the page where you want to serve the data, every slot tag has a slot ID. And unless your chunk's ID matches the slotID, it will not be rendered well. For this, we would need to fix the output from marko-remote-app to emit in SSE format, with differing chunk IDs.

In our earlier example, with the **defaultID**, we were rendering a top-level page template while streaming fragments within it upon every chunk of data from the API. However, for this example, we will need to render a template partial for every chunk of data from the API rather than a portion of a template within a top-level template. With that, we will be able to create different SSE chunk IDs.

First, let's introduce the setup in the host app. The code for this example will be found in the host app under marko-host-app/src/routes/sse-multi-chunk. The page is represented by the +page.marko as shown in Figure 10-38. You will notice there are multiple app-slot components that now encapsulate the micro-frame-slot tag, making it configurable and reusable.

The app-slot component used in this is shown in Figure 10-37.

```
src > components > ☰ app-slot.marko > ⟨⟩ micro-frame-slot

1    <!-- if client-reorder is set it will render in a non-blocking manner -->
2    <!-- if client-reorder is removed it will render in a blocking manner -->
3    <micro-frame-slot from=input.from slot=input.slot timeout=0 client-reorder>
4        <@loading>
5            $ console.log("LOAAAAAAAAAAAADDDDD");
6            We're still loading...
7        </@loading>
8        <@catch|err|>
9            $ console.log("ERRRRRRRRRRRR");
10           Uh-oh! ${err.message || err}
11       </@catch>
12   </micro-frame-slot>
```

Figure 10-37.   marko-host-app/src/components/app-slot.marko containing the micro-frame-slot tags

Note in Figure 10-38, the +page.marko is now configured to use its micro-frame-sse tag to accept content from a different remote endpoint source: http://localhost:3001/remote-app-sse-multi-slot.

The <app-slot> tags are placed at multiple points in the page—three different places. Now we are looking at the example where one source is used to stream content into three different places in the page/DOM.

As before, the entire setup is isomorphic, and you can render it on the client and server.

```
src > routes > sse-multi-chunk > ☰ +page.marko > 𝒫 div > 𝒫 header > 𝒫 div

1    <!-- The following end point is only for testing purposes -->
2    <!-- src=`http://localhost:3001/mock-api-html?dt=${Date.now()}` -->
3    <micro-frame-sse
4        timeout=0
5        src=`http://localhost:3001/remote-app-sse-multi-slot?dt=${Date.now()}`
6        name="remote-stream-source"
7        read(ev) {
8            console.log("readingding...", ev);
9            return [ev.lastEventId, JSON.parse(ev.data), false];
10       }
11   />
12
13   <div class="container">
14       <header>
15           <div id="remote-app">
16               <div class="remote-app__content">
17                   <app-slot slot="module_1" from="remote-stream-source" />
18               </div>
19           </div>
20
21           <div>
22               <img src="./logo.svg" alt="Marko" class="logo">
23               <app-slot slot="module_2" from="remote-stream-source" />
24           </div>
25       </header>
26       <main>
27           <p>
28               Edit
29               <code>./src/routes/_index/+page.marko</code>
30               and save to reload.
31           </p>
32           <app-slot slot="module_3" from="remote-stream-source" />
33           <a href="https://markojs.com/docs/getting-started">
34               Learn Marko
35           </a>
36       </main>
37   </div>
38   <mouse-mask/>
39
40 > style {-
55   }
```

Figure 10-38. *marko-host-app/src/routes/sse-multi-chunk/+page.marko containing the <app-slot> tags which make the micro-frame-slot tags configurable*

Next, let us head to the **marko-remote-app** and check out the endpoint /**remote-app-sse-multi-slot**, which now emits SSE'd HTML (same as before), but renders different templates for every chunk emitted by the API.

632

The API used to emit data also needed slight modifications to emit different chunk IDs for every data event. Earlier, the **/api** route was emitting only one chunk or defaulted to **defaultID** as the chunk ID. Now, we will have different ones for each of the three slots. The api we will use for **/remote-app-sse-multi-slot** is **/api-multi-chunk-id** (also within the marko-remote-app) shown in Figure 10-39.

```
src > routes > api-multi-chunk-id > JS +handler.js > ⊙ GET > [∅] stream > ⊙ start
 1    export async function GET({ platform: { request }}) {
 2      // Create a readable stream for SSE
 3      const stream = new ReadableStream({
 4        start(controller) {
 5          let count = 1; // Track number of emissions
 6          const maxEmissions = 4; // Stop after 5 messages
 7
 8          // Set up an interval to send data every 2 seconds
 9          const interval = setInterval(() => {
10            const data = {
11              id: `${count}`,
12              message: `Server time: ${new Date().toISOString()} (Module #${count})`,
13            };
14            // Encode the data as SSE format (data: JSON\n\n)
15            const text = `data: ${JSON.stringify(data)}\n\n`;
16            controller.enqueue(new TextEncoder().encode(text));
17
18            // Increment count and check if limit is reached
19            count++;
20            if (count >= maxEmissions) {
21              clearInterval(interval); // Stop the interval
22              controller.close(); // Close the stream
23            }
24          }, 2000);
25
26          // Store interval for cleanup
27          request._interval = interval;
28        },
29        cancel() {
30          // Clean up when the stream is canceled (client disconnects)
31          if (request._interval) {
32            clearInterval(request._interval);
33          }
34        },
35      });
36
37      // Return a Response with SSE headers
38      return new Response(stream, {
39        headers: {
40          'Content-Type': 'text/event-stream',
41          'Cache-Control': 'no-cache',
42          'Connection': 'keep-alive',
43        },
44      });
45    }
```

Figure 10-39. *marko-remote-app/src/routes/api-multi-chunk-id/+handler.js*

In Figure 10-39, you will notice that three data events with chunk IDs 1, 2, and 3 are being emitted. Each of these chunks will be mapped to render different templates. Let's call them fragment-one, fragment-two, and fragment-three and place them with their associated index.marko files, as components, under the components folder. This is shown in Figures 10-42 to 10-44. Each of these components has a common style.less file placed alongside their templates, as shown in Figures 10-40 and 10-41.

```
src > components > fragment-three > {} style.less
  1    @import "../../common/style.less";
```

Figure 10-40. *marko-remote-app/src/components/fragment-three/style.less (common for fragment-one and fragment-two as well)*

```
src > common > {} style.less
  1    @import '~@ebay/skin/marketsans.css';
  2    /* @import '~@ebay/skin/less.css'; */
  3    @import '~@ebay/skin/tokens.css';
  4    @import '~@ebay/skin/global.css';
  5    @import '~@ebay/skin/utility.css';
  6    @import "~@ebay/skin/section-notice.css";
```

Figure 10-41. *marko-remote-app/src/common/style.less*

```marko
src > components > fragment-one > ☰ index.marko > 🔧 div
  1   $ const { message, id } = input.messages;
  2   $ console.log("======= fragment-one =========")
  3   $ console.log(message, id, "Template_1_information");
  4   $ console.log("======= fragment-one =========")
  5   $ const chunkID = `module_${id}`;
  6
  7   <div style={margin: "10px 0 10px 0"}>
  8       <html-comment>${chunkID}</html-comment>
  9       <html-comment>Template_1_information</html-comment>
 10       // <div id="one"><span>${message} </span></div>
 11       <ebay-section-notice status="information" a11y-dismiss-text="close">
 12           <span>${message} </span>
 13       </ebay-section-notice>
 14   </div>
```

Figure 10-42. *marko-remote-app/src/components/fragment-one/index.marko*

```marko
src > components > fragment-two > ☰ index.marko > 🔧 div
  1   $ const { message, id } = input.messages;
  2   $ console.log("======= fragment-two =========")
  3   $ console.log(message, id, "Template_2_confirmation");
  4   $ console.log("======= fragment-two =========")
  5   $ const chunkID = `module_${id}`;
  6
  7   <div style={margin: "10px 0 10px 0"}>
  8       <html-comment>${chunkID}</html-comment>
  9       <html-comment>Template_2_confirmation</html-comment>
 10       // <div id="two"><span>${message} </span></div>
 11       <ebay-section-notice status="confirmation" a11y-dismiss-text="close">
 12           <span>${message} </span>
 13       </ebay-section-notice>
 14   </div>
```

Figure 10-43. *marko-remote-app/src/components/fragment-two/index.marko*

```
src > components > fragment-three >  ☰ index.marko > 🔧 div
1    $ const { message, id } = input.messages;
2    $ console.log("======= fragment-three =========")
3    $ console.log(message, id, "Template_3_attention");
4    $ console.log("======= fragment-three =========")
5    $ const chunkID = `module_${id}`;
6
7    <div style={margin: "10px 0 10px 0"}>
8        <html-comment>${chunkID}</html-comment>
9        <html-comment>Template_3_attention</html-comment>
10       // <div id="three"><span>${message} </span></div>
11       <ebay-section-notice status="attention" a11y-dismiss-text="close">
12           <span>${message} </span>
13       </ebay-section-notice>
14   </div>
```

Figure 10-44. *marko-remote-app/src/components/fragment-three/index.marko*

Now comes the route handler for /**remote-app-sse-multi-slot**. Note that this route does not have a +page.marko, +page.style.css, etc. This is because they are now rendering the components shown in Figures 10-42 to 10-44. The utils.js file is however present here to map the data stream into an event stream (from api to the templates). But this is the same as the one previously shown. The only difference is the +handler.js file as shown in Figure 10-45.

```
src > routes > remote-app-sse-multi-slot > JS +handler.js > ...
  1  import { fetch } from "undici";
  2  import templateOneInformation from "../../components/fragment-one/index.marko";
  3  import templateTwoConfirmation from "../../components/fragment-two/index.marko";
  4  import templateThreeAttention from "../../components/fragment-three/index.marko";
  5  import { createMessageEmitter } from "./utils";
  6
  7  export async function GET({ platform: { request } }) {
  8    const response = await fetch("http://localhost:3001/api-multi-chunk-id", {
  9      headers: {
 10        Accept: "text/event-stream",
 11      },
 12    });
 13
 14    if (!response.ok || !response.body) {
 15      return new Response("event: error\ndata: Failed to connect\n\n", {
 16        status: 500,
 17        headers: { "Content-Type": "text/event-stream" },
 18      });
 19    }
 20
 21    const encoder = new TextEncoder();
 22    const emitter = createMessageEmitter(response);
 23
 24    const sseStream = new ReadableStream({
 25      start(controller) {
 26        const pendingRenders = new Set();
 27
 28        emitter.on("data", async (dataChunk) => {
 29          let selectedTemplate;
 30          const newId = parseInt(dataChunk.id, 10);
 31
 32          switch (newId % 3) {
 33            case 2:
 34              selectedTemplate = templateTwoConfirmation;
 35              break;
 36            case 1:
 37              selectedTemplate = templateOneInformation;
 38              break;
 39            default:
 40              selectedTemplate = templateThreeAttention;
 41              break;
 42          }
 43
 44          const renderPromise = (async () => {
 45            try {
 46              for await (const chunk of selectedTemplate.render({
 47                messages: dataChunk,
 48                $global: { componentIdPrefix: Date.now().toString(36) }
 49              })) {
 50                controller.enqueue(
 51                  encoder.encode(`id: module_${dataChunk.id}\ndata: ${JSON.stringify(chunk)}\n\n`)
 52                );
 53              }
 54            } catch (err) {
 55              const errorChunk = `event: error\ndata: ${JSON.stringify(err.message)}\n\n`;
 56              controller.enqueue(encoder.encode(errorChunk));
 57            }
 58          })();
 59
 60          pendingRenders.add(renderPromise);
 61          renderPromise.finally(() => pendingRenders.delete(renderPromise));
 62        });
 63
 64        emitter.on("done", async () => {
 65          // Wait for all in-progress renders to complete before closing the stream
 66          await Promise.all([...pendingRenders]);
 67          controller.close();
 68          console.log('closing the stream....')
 69        });
 70
 71        emitter.on("error", (err) => {
 72          const errMsg = `event: error\ndata: ${JSON.stringify(err.message)}\n\n`;
 73          controller.enqueue(encoder.encode(errMsg));
 74          controller.close();
 75        });
 76      },
 77    });
 78
 79    return new Response(sseStream, {
 80      headers: {
 81        "Content-Type": "text/event-stream",
 82        "Cache-Control": "no-cache",
 83        "Connection": "keep-alive",
 84        "Access-Control-Allow-Origin": "http://localhost:3000",
 85      },
 86    });
 87  }
```

Figure 10-45. *marko-remote-app/src/routes/remote-app-sse-multi-slot /+handler.js*

637

There are some minor differences when compared to the +handler.js that we had earlier seen with the route /remote-app-sse-single-slot. They are

- The api is now /api-multi-chunk-id.

- The **template.render** function is used, instead of **template.stream**, as we now have different fragments to be rendered for every chunk emitted. These have the extra information about the assets and the hydration data.

- The template.render returns an async iterable here, which we then use to enqueue SSE HTML with chunk IDs mapped to module_. So we have SSE HTML chunks as module_1, module_2, and module_3. If you recall, these were names for the slots in the micro-frame-slot tags.

- Based on the chunk ID, we choose a template to be rendered.

- Instead of one template being rendered for all the chunks, each chunk now gets a unique template to be rendered.

- In total, we are rendering three different templates.

We can test this change locally by building it via npm run build and npm run preview and accessing it on http://localhost:3001/remote-app-sse-multi-slot. The output is as shown in Figure 10-46.

Figure 10-46. *Remote app SSE multi-chunk ID output*

Now let's attempt to access this from the host app at http://localhost:3000/sse-multi-chunk. This is shown in Figure 10-47. You will see three different modules (ebay-section-notice of types "attention," "confirmation," and "information") streamed to three different placeholders (locators) in the DOM that are managed by the **micro-frame-slot** tags.

Conclusion

With this, we have seen the various use cases of the **@micro-frame/marko** tags and how it helps us build micro frontends in a hassle-free manner in the context of MPAs. Note that this is not necessarily MPAs. In Chapter 11, we will see an example of how Marko can be used to build SPAs too, and even in the SPA context, the **@micro-frame/marko** tags can help you achieve decoupled micro frontends as they are an ismorphic solution. One thing to note is that while runtimeID helps to sandbox Javascript, other solutions like CSS Modules (shown in Chapter 6) will help to sandbox CSS so that CSS from remote apps and host apps do not interfere and cause issues.

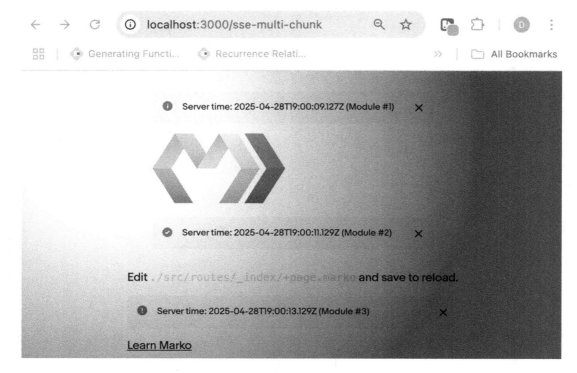

Figure 10-47. *Remote app SSE multi-chunk ID output from within the host app*

CHAPTER 11

Recipes with Marko

Introduction

In this chapter, we will look at some of the most common use cases developers face when having to deal with building applications with view frameworks like Marko. These use cases are pretty standard ones that most view frameworks face, and you will see queries for the same requesting for sample starter apps for the same. These use cases include

- *Client-side rendering and single-page applications, with client-side routing.*

- *Using a data store solution like Redux.*

- *Using a library (that is closely tied to the view framework) to communicate with GraphQL APIs. (Note that you don't necessarily need this if you resort to other GraphQL data fetching solutions like Apollo.)*

- Static site generation.

- *Form handling.*

- *Dynamic imports.*

- *SSE Endpoints via the EventSource API.*

As before, through all these apps, we will be operating with mock data. This is to keep the setup simple and focus only on the view layer portion of it. Marko remains un-opinionated with regard to data fetching. You are free to use a library of choice to fetch data and any of the popular ORM solutions you would otherwise use to talk to the various databases.

© Damodaran Chingleput Sathyakumar 2025
D. Chingleput Sathyakumar, *Practical Marko*, https://doi.org/10.1007/979-8-8688-1483-9_11

As long as the fetched data is passed into Marko components, the render just happens as always. In the same way, authentication and authorization are not the focus points of these examples; you are free to use any solutions of your choice and have them wired on along with the *+middleware.ts* files to handle route-based auth.

Using a Data Store Solution like Redux

Redux is a very popular data store solution (among others like recoil, mobx, easy peasy, etc.) whose need is felt when you have a lot of cross-app state updates to be done. With the case of Marko, we have usually stayed away from Redux due to

1.   The availability of other minimalist solutions like a simple channel-based **publish-subscribe** (check *raptor-pubsub* package) where every component can just wire on event handlers to this publish-subscribe utility, emit and listen to events, and take corresponding action. This simplifies cross component state updates **on the client side**.

2.   Every Marko component is an event emitter, and so, hierarchical updates are easy in that, child components can emit events to their parent components, and the parent can then decide on a course of action (making API calls, updating state, etc.)

However, we understand the need for a solution like Redux from purists and Marko plays well with redux. Let us look at this simple example.

This example also follows from scaffolding a Marko application via **npx @marko/create** and the template as **basic**. Let's get away from focusing on types for the moment and focus on getting redux up.

For this example, we will load a basic page, initialize store on the server, dispatch actions, render the UX on the server using the updated state, flush the rendered HTML along with the final serialized state, and bootstrap the application and the store on the client with the latest state.

Upon scaffolding the application, we have deleted src/components/mouse-mask. marko. Following that, let's add some files as shown in Figure 11-1 per the updated project layout.

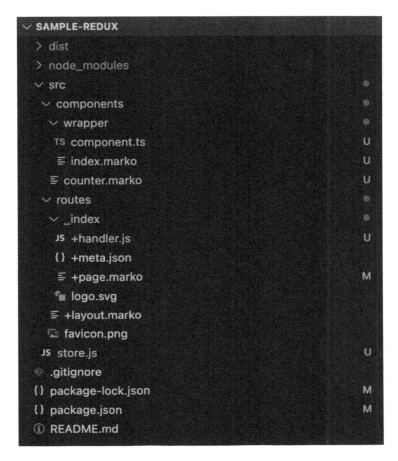

Figure 11-1. *sample-redux application project layout*

Next, let's install redux via **npm i redux.** This will bring in the latest dependency of redux into the sample application. After this, the first file we will include is src/store.js. This is basic with utility functions to initialize and interact with the redux store. For this example, we will use a simple counter to increment decrement count on the server and the client such that the state is shared by two instances of the counter. For this create a reducer for this counter. Similarly you can have other reducers and combine them via the *combineReducers* function. This is shown in Figure 11-2.

```
src > JS store.js > ⦿ configureStore
  1   import { combineReducers } from 'redux';
  2   import { createStore } from "redux";
  3
  4   let store;
  5
  6   export function getStore(){
  7       return store;
  8   }
  9
 10   export function setStore(reduxStore) {
 11       if (store) {
 12           throw new Error('storeRegistry - ReduxStore already set');
 13       }
 14
 15       store = reduxStore;
 16   }
 17
 18   // Reducer for the counter
 19   function counterReducer(state = { count: 0 }, action) {
 20     switch (action.type) {
 21       case "INCREMENT":
 22         return { count: state.count + 1 };
 23       case "DECREMENT":
 24         return { count: state.count - 1 };
 25       default:
 26         return state;
 27     }
 28   }
 29
 30   export const increaseCounter = () => {
 31       return {
 32           type: "INCREMENT"
 33       };
 34   };
 35
 36   export const decreaseCounter = (payload) => {
 37       return {
 38           type: "DECREMENT",
 39       };
 40   };
 41
 42
 43   const mainPageRootReducer = combineReducers({
 44       counter: counterReducer
 45   });
 46
 47   // Function to initialize store with preloaded state (for server-side rendering)
 48   export function configureStore(preloadedState = { counter: { count: 0 }}) {
 49     store = createStore(mainPageRootReducer, preloadedState)
 50     return store;
 51   }
```

Figure 11-2. *sample-redux/src/store.js*

We will use the functions configureStore, getStore, and setStore to configure the store, getStore, etc.

```
src > routes > _index > JS +handler.js > ⊘ GET
  1    import { configureStore, increaseCounter } from "../../store";
  2
  3    export async function GET(context) {
  4       const initialState = {
  5          counter: {
  6             count: 55
  7          }
  8       };
  9       const store = configureStore(initialState);
 10       store.dispatch(increaseCounter())
 11       const state = store.getState()
 12       context.initialState = state;
 13    }
```

Figure 11-3. *sample-redux/src/routes/_index/+handler.js*

This is the basic controller/handler provided by the marko-run setup as shown in Figure 11-3. We start with an initialState. Then we configure the store on the server with this initial State. Note that you can also ease this setup via the **@redux/toolkit**. Finally, we dispatch some action to increment the count (originally 55) and after this 56. You can use all of redux async actions/thunk and others. Finally, we get the updated state from the store and set it on context (which is also **$global**) causing it to be available across all templates during server-side rendering. We don't explicitly serialize it because it's also passed into the top-level component as **input**, which enables it to be serialized by default (as input is serialized for hydration purposes). This is shown in Figure 11-4.

```
src > routes > _index > ☰ +page.marko > ...
  1    $ const { initialState } = $global;
  2
  3    <div.container>
  4       <wrapper initialState=initialState>
  5          <counter/>
  6          <counter/>
  7       </wrapper>
  8    </div>
```

Figure 11-4. *sample-redux/src/routes/_index/+page.marko*

The input is passed into the top-level <wrapper> component via the prop **initialState.**
Figures 11-5 and 11-6 show the <wrapper> component.

```
src > components > wrapper > ☰ index.marko > ...
  1    <div class="main-content" id="mainContent" role="main">
  2        <if(input.renderBody)>
  3            <${input.renderBody}/>
  4        </if>
  5    </div>
  6
```

Figure 11-5. *sample-redux/src/components/wrapper/index.marko*

```
src > components > wrapper > TS component.ts > ...
  1    import { getStore, configureStore } from "../../store";
  2
  3    export default class {
  4        onCreate(input) {
  5            let store = getStore();
  6
  7            if (!store) {
  8                store = configureStore(input.initialState || {});
  9            }
 10        }
 11
 12        onMount() {
 13            debugger;
 14            console.log(getStore().getState());
 15        }
 16    }
 17
```

Figure 11-6. *sample-redux/src/components/wrapper/component.js*

The **onCreate** block helps to recreate the redux store on the client side with the final latest state from the server. We have created two instances of <counter> within the +page. marko. Both these counters utilize the shared state. The <counter> is shown in Figure 11-7.

Clicking the increment button in one counter will cause it to **dispatch** an **action** to the **redux store**, causing it to update the central counter state within the redux store. Once this central store state is updated, the other counter which is also subscribed to the store is notified to update its state, and you will notice the state being synced across both the components. The same occurs when clicking Decrement.

```
src > components > ☰ counter.marko > ...
 1    import { decreaseCounter, getStore, increaseCounter } from "../store";
 2
 3    class {
 4        onCreate() {
 5          const store = getStore();
 6          const state = store.getState();
 7          this.state = { count: state.counter.count || 0 };
 8        }
 9        onMount() {
10          const store = getStore();
11          // Subscribe to store updates
12          this.unsubscribe = store.subscribe(() => {
13            const state = store.getState();
14            this.setState('count', state.counter.count);
15          });
16
17          // Set initial state
18          const initialState = store.getState();
19          this.setState('count', initialState.counter.count);
20        }
21        onDestroy() {
22          this.unsubscribe();
23        }
24        increment() {
25          const store = getStore();
26          store.dispatch(increaseCounter());
27        }
28        decrement() {
29          const store = getStore();
30          store.dispatch(decreaseCounter());
31        }
32    }
33
34    <div>
35      <h1>Counter: ${state.count}</h1>
36      <button on-click("increment")>Increment</button>
37      <button on-click("decrement")>Decrement</button>
38    </div>
```

Figure 11-7. *sample-redux/src/components/counter.marko*

The output for the counters example is shown in Figure 11-8.

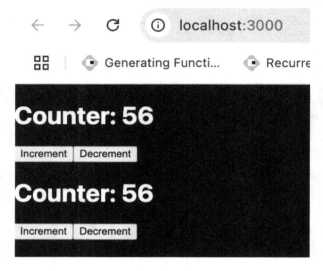

Figure 11-8. *Page loads with count value as 56 after being rendered on server*

Subsequent updates will cause the components state to be synced together as shown in Figure 11-9.

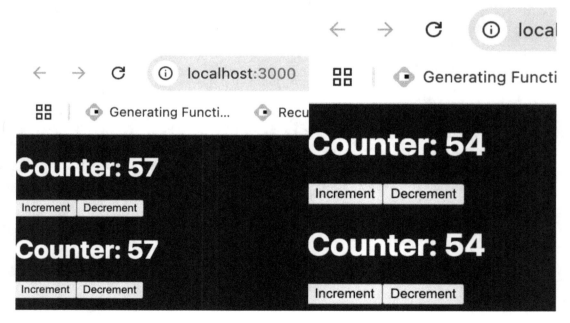

Figure 11-9. *Counters synced via central Redux Store state*

This completes our simple example for using redux with marko to maintain central state via a store and subscribe to it across components.

Static Site Generation with Marko

This example also follows from scaffolding a Marko application via **npx @marko/create** and the template as **basic**.

Static site generation is a common use case, and you will find full-fledged frameworks on the React world that offer this—Gatsby and Astro. While Marko's solution is not as super full fledged as these, it can still get the job done for you.

The project layout is as shown in Figure 11-10.

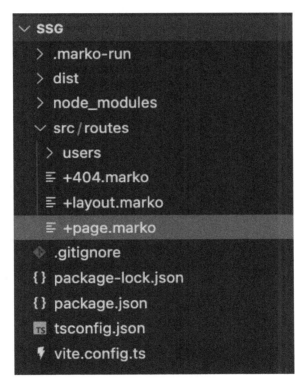

Figure 11-10. *Project layout for static site generation example*

In our sample app (named **ssg**), we shall add the following files shown in Figures 11-11 to 11-17. An important part of static site generation in Marko is via the Marko-run setup using its adapter **run-adapter-static**.

So, what does this adapter do? It basically outputs html files into the **dist/** directory. This means you just get to work with plain HTML files and you are free to deploy these HTML files with the required wiring into any server environment that now serves HTML files.

Marko makes no assumptions about which server environment you work in. Instead it provides you with all the resolved and compiled HTML files for you to be able to use it and deploy it into any environment you see fit.

```
 ☰ +page.marko ✕

src > routes > ☰ +page.marko > 🔧 main
   1     style {
   2       main {
   3         background:  ■lightcyan;
   4       }
   5     }
   6
   7     class {
   8       onMount() {
   9         console.log('mounted home!')
  10       }
  11     }
  12
  13     <main>
  14       <h1>Home</h1>
  15     </main>
```

Figure 11-11. *ssg/src/routes/+page.marko*

```
src > routes > ☰ +404.marko > 🔧 main
   1     <main>
   2       <h1>Custom Not Found Page</h1>
   3       <a href="/">Go home</a>
   4     </>
```

Figure 11-12. *ssg/src/routes/+404.marko*

```
src > routes > users >  ≡ +page.marko >  🔧 h1
    1        <h1>Users</h1>
```

Figure 11-13. *ssg/src/routes/users/+page.marko*

Lastly, let's include a ***+layout.marko*** file to handle the basic layout into which these pages and components go into.

```
src > routes >  ≡ +layout.marko >  🔧 html
 1    export interface Input {
 2        renderBody: Marko.Body
 3    }
 4
 5    style {
 6      body { margin: 0; min-height: 100vh; display: flex; flex-direction: column; flex: 0 0 100%; }
 7      header { background: ■pink; padding: 1rem; }
 8      footer { background: ■lightgray; padding: 1rem; margin-top: auto; }
 9      main { padding: 1rem; }
10    }
11
12    <!doctype html>
13    <html lang="en">
14      <head>
15        <meta charset="UTF-8">
16        <meta
17          name="description"
18          content="An example application showcasing Vite & Marko."
19        >
20        <meta name="viewport" content="width=device-width, initial-scale=1.0">
21        <title>@marko/run - Static</title>
22      </head>
23      <body>
24        <header>
25          <nav>
26            <a href="/">Home</a>
27            <a href="/users">Users</a>
28            <a href="/nowhere">Nowhere</a>
29          </nav>
30        </header>
31        <${input.renderBody} />
32        <footer>
33          <small>Footer</small>
34        </footer>
35      </body>
36    </html>
```

Figure 11-14. *ssg/src/routes/+layout.marko*

651

```
⚡ vite.config.ts > [∅] default
1    import { defineConfig } from "vite";
2    import marko from "@marko/run/vite";
3    import staticAdapter from "@marko/run-adapter-static";
4
5    export default defineConfig({
6      plugins: [
7        marko({
8          adapter: staticAdapter()
9        })
10     ]
11   });
```

Figure 11-15. *ssg/vite.config.js*

In **vite.config.js**, you will notice the adapter **run-adapter-static** being included as an option into the marko plugin from **@marko/run/vite**.

```
{} package.json > ...
1    {
2      "name": "static-example",
3      "version": "0.0.1",
4      "private": true,
5      "type": "module",
     ▷Debug
6      "scripts": {
7        "build": "marko-run build",
8        "dev": "marko-run",
9        "preview": "marko-run preview"
10     },
11     "dependencies": {
12       "marko": "^5.37.4"
13     },
14     "devDependencies": {
15       "@marko/compiler": "^5.39.4",
16       "@marko/run": "^0.6.2",
17       "@marko/run-adapter-static": "^1.0.1",
18       "@types/mocha": "^10.0.10",
19       "@types/node": "^22.9.1",
20       "prettier": "^3.3.3",
21       "tsx": "^4.19.2",
22       "typescript": "^5.7.2",
23       "vite": "^6.0.0"
24     }
25   }
```

Figure 11-16. *ssg/package.json*

Lastly, let's also take a look at the tsconfig.json file shown in Figure 11-17.

You can run this application locally via **npm run dev** (the usual command you will with all other marko-run apps). For production build, to output the files, run the **npm run build** command. Once you run this, you will see actual HTML files being output into the **dist/** folder. You are now free to take this rendered build and wire it into any deploy server pipeline of your choice to get your site up and running.

```
tsconfig.json > ...
 1    {
 2        "include": ["src/**/*", "vite.config.ts", ".marko-run/*"],
 3        "compilerOptions": {
 4          "rootDir": "./",
 5          "outDir": "./dist",
 6          "lib": ["DOM", "DOM.Iterable", "ESNext"],
 7        "strict": true,
 8        "target": "ESNext",
 9        "module": "ESNext",
10        "sourceMap": false,
11        "composite": true,
12        "incremental": true,
13        "stripInternal": true,
14        "noUnusedLocals": true,
15        "isolatedModules": true,
16        "esModuleInterop": true,
17        "resolveJsonModule": true,
18        "moduleResolution": "bundler",
19        "noUnusedParameters": true,
20        "allowUnusedLabels": false,
21        "noImplicitReturns": false,
22        "noImplicitOverride": true,
23        "emitDeclarationOnly": true,
24        "allowUnreachableCode": false,
25        "noFallthroughCasesInSwitch": true,
26        "allowSyntheticDefaultImports": true,
27        "forceConsistentCasingInFileNames": true,
28        "skipLibCheck": true
29        },
30    }
```

Figure 11-17. *ssg/tsconfig.json*

The output of running the build command is included here in Figure 11-18.

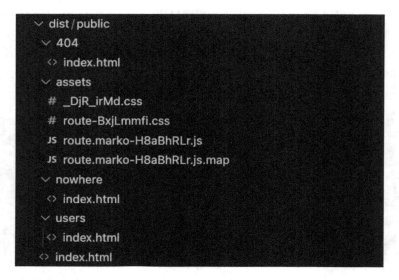

Figure 11-18. *output of* *dist/*

This completes our simple example for static site generation. You will notice how the output includes HTML files which can now be used as part of a post-build processing step to deploy into any server of choice to realize statically generated sites based out of pure HTML from Marko instead of compiled templates.

Using Marko-urql for Talking to GraphQL APIs

This example also follows from scaffolding a Marko application via **npx @marko/create** and the template as **basic**. This is a sample application using Marko Run and **@marko/urql** (https://github.com/marko-js/urql) to query and mutate data. For simplicity, we'll use a local SQLite-based GraphQL server with a public API-like structure, leveraging **graphql-yoga** and **sqlite3**. This example will demonstrate a basic todo list app where you can query todos and add new ones via mutations. The project layout is as shown in Figure 11-19.

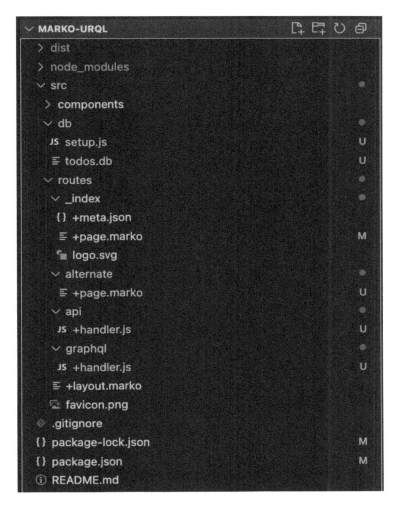

Figure 11-19. Layout of sample project using @marko/urql

The project package.json is in Figure 11-20.

```
{} package.json > ...
  1    {
  2      "name": "marko-urql",
  3      "description": "The default Marko starter app",
  4      "version": "1.0.0",
  5      "type": "module",
  6      "dependencies": {
  7        "@marko/urql": "^2.5.5",
  8        "graphql": "^16.10.0",
  9        "graphql-yoga": "^5.13.2",
 10        "marko": "^5.37.20",
 11        "sqlite3": "^5.1.7"
 12      },
 13      "devDependencies": {
 14        "@marko/run": "^0.6.1"
 15      },
 16      "private": true,
       ▷Debug
 17      "scripts": {
 18        "dev": "marko-run",
 19        "build": "marko-run build",
 20        "preview": "marko-run preview",
 21        "start": "node --enable-source-maps ./dist/index.mjs"
 22      }
 23    }
```

Figure 11-20. *package.json*

We'll use SQLite to store todos locally. Install **graphql**, **@marko/urql**, **graphql-yoga**, and **sqlite3** packages. Create a simple schema and seed it with some data. This is done via the initial setup file **db/setup.js** as shown in Figure 11-21.

```
src > db > JS setup.js > ...
   1    import sqlite3 from 'sqlite3';
   2    const db = new sqlite3.Database('./src/db/todos.db');
   3
   4    db.serialize(() => {
   5      db.run(`
   6        CREATE TABLE IF NOT EXISTS todos (
   7          id INTEGER PRIMARY KEY AUTOINCREMENT,
   8          text TEXT NOT NULL,
   9          completed BOOLEAN DEFAULT 0
  10        )
  11      `);
  12
  13      // Seed some initial data
  14      db.run("INSERT INTO todos (text, completed) VALUES ('Learn Marko', 1)");
  15      db.run("INSERT INTO todos (text, completed) VALUES ('Build a todo app', 0)");
  16    });
  17
  18    db.close();
```

Figure 11-21. *src/db/setup.js*

This is run once to create a database. This can be run via node src/db/setup.js.

Once you run this, you will notice the **src/db/todos.db** file being created.

To talk to the server, which again is our own application, we will create the **src/routes/api/+handler.ts**.

```js
src > routes > api > JS +handler.js > ...
1    import { createYoga } from 'graphql-yoga';
2    import { makeExecutableSchema } from '@graphql-tools/schema';
3    import sqlite3 from 'sqlite3';
4
5    const db = new sqlite3.Database('./src/db/todos.db', { readonly: false });
6
7    const typeDefs = `
8      type Todo {
9        id: ID!
10       text: String!
11       completed: Boolean!
12     }
13     type Query {
14       todos: [Todo!]!
15     }
16     type Mutation {
17       addTodo(text: String!): Todo!
18     }
19   `;
20
```

```js
src > routes > api > JS +handler.js > ...
21   const resolvers = {
22     Query: {
23       todos: () => new Promise((resolve, reject) => {
24         db.all('SELECT * FROM todos', (err, rows) => {
25           if (err) reject(err);
26           else resolve(rows);
27         });
28       }),
29     },
30     Mutation: {
31       addTodo: (_, { text }) => new Promise((resolve, reject) => {
32         db.run('INSERT INTO todos (text) VALUES (?)', [text], function (err) {
33           if (err) reject(err);
34           else resolve({ id: this.lastID, text, completed: false });
35         });
36       }),
37     },
38   };
39
40   const schema = makeExecutableSchema({ typeDefs, resolvers });
41   const yoga = createYoga({ schema, graphqlEndpoint: '/api' });
42
```

```js
src > routes > api > JS +handler.js > ...
43   export async function POST(context) {
44     // Convert Marko Run context to a Yoga-compatible response
45     const response = await yoga.handleRequest(context.request, {
46       ...context,
47       req: context.request, // Ensure Yoga sees the request
48       res: null,            // Let Yoga handle the response directly
49     });
50
51     // Convert stream to text for debugging
52     const bodyText = await streamToString(response.body);
53     console.log('Response body:', bodyText);
54
55     return new Response(bodyText, {
56       status: response.status,
57       headers: {
58         ...response.headers,
59         'Content-Type': 'application/json', // Ensure correct MIME type
60       },
61     });
62   }
63
64   export async function GET(context) {
65     return POST(context); // Handle GET requests the same way for simplicity
66   }
67
68   // Helper to read stream
69   async function streamToString(stream) {
```

Figure 11-22. *src/routes/api/+handler.js*

The **todos.db** file is an SQLite database that contains a single table called **todos**. This table has the following schema, as defined in the **CREATE TABLE** statement:

```
CREATE TABLE IF NOT EXISTS todos (
    id INTEGER PRIMARY KEY AUTOINCREMENT,
    text TEXT NOT NULL,
    completed BOOLEAN DEFAULT 0
);
```

id: An auto-incrementing integer that serves as the unique identifier for each todo item (e.g., 1, 2, 3...)

text: A text field that stores the description of the todo item (e.g., "Learn Marko")

completed: A boolean field that indicates whether the todo is completed (defaults to 0, meaning false in SQLite)

After the table is created, the script seeds it with two initial todo items using **INSERT** statements:

```
text: "Learn Marko", completed: 1 (true)
text: "Build a todo app", completed: 0 (false)
```

So, after running node src/db/setup.js, the **todos.db** file will contain a **todos** table with these two rows. The **src/db/setup.js** script uses the **sqlite3** Node package to interact with **SQLite**. Here's a breakdown of what it does:

- **Database Connection**: **new sqlite3.Database('....')** creates or opens an SQLite database file at **db/todos.db**. If the directory **db/** doesn't exist, you'll need to create it manually (mkdir db) before running the script, or it will throw an error.

- **Table Creation**: The **CREATE TABLE** statement defines the structure of the todos table.

- **Data Seeding**: The **INSERT** statements add two rows to the table.

- **Close Connection**: **db.close()** ensures the database connection is properly closed after setup. Once this script runs successfully, **todos. db** is a binary SQLite database file stored on your filesystem.

You won't see the contents of **todos.db** as plain text since it's a binary file. To inspect it, you can use an **SQLite** client like the **sqlite3** command-line tool or a GUI like DB Browser for SQLite.

You will also notice from Figures 11-21 and 11-22

```
const db = new sqlite3.Database('./src/db/todos.db');
```

The only differentiating factor is that the one in **src/routes/api/+handler.js** will have a second argument that takes an option `{ readonly: false }`.

The similarity stems from the fact that both files are using the **sqlite3** Node module to interact with the same **SQLite** database file (**todos.db**). The **sqlite3.database** constructor is the standard way to establish a connection to an SQLite database in Node. js, so it's natural that both files use it. However, their purposes and execution contexts differ, which explains why the syntax appears in both places.

In db/setup.js

Purpose: This file is a one-time setup script to create and initialize the **todos.db** database.

Syntax: `const db = new sqlite3.Database('./src/db/todos.db');` No options like `{ readonly: false }` are specified, so it defaults to read-write mode (which is fine since it needs to create the table and insert data).

Execution: You run this manually once with node db/setup.js to set up the database. After that, it's not used again unless you need to reset or modify the initial state.

Scope: The db object is local to this script, used for setup, and closed with db.close() when done.

In routes/api/+handler.js

Purpose: This file is part of the Marko Run application and defines the GraphQL API endpoint. It needs ongoing access to todos.db to handle queries and mutations during runtime.

Syntax: `const db = new sqlite3.Database('./src/db/todos.db', { readonly: false });` explicitly includes `{ readonly: false }` to emphasize that the connection must support both reading (for queries) and writing (for mutations). While this is the default behavior, adding it makes the intent clear.

Execution: This runs as part of the Marko Run server. The **db** object is created when the file is loaded and persists for the lifetime of the server, handling requests dynamically.

Scope: The db object is module scoped and reused across all API requests.

Why Repeat the Syntax?

The repetition occurs because

1. **Separate Responsibilities**

   a. src/db/setup.js is a standalone script for initialization.

   b. src/routes/api/+handler.js is a runtime component of the app.

   c. They don't share a connection because the setup script is not part of the running application—it's a one-off task.

2. **No Shared Connection**

   a. In this simple example, there's no shared database module or connection pool. Each file independently opens its own connection to **todos.db**.

   b. In a more sophisticated app, you might create a separate module (e.g., db.js) to manage a single connection or pool, which both setup and runtime could import. For simplicity, this example keeps them separate.

3. **SQLite's Nature**

   a. SQLite is a file-based database, and each call to **sqlite3.database** opens a new connection to the same file. SQLite handles concurrent access internally (via file locking), so multiple connections to **todos.db** are safe, though not optimal for performance in a real app.

The Subtle Difference: `{ readonly: false }`

- In src/db/setup.js, the absence of `{ readonly: false }` doesn't change the behavior—it's implicitly read-write, which is sufficient for creating tables and inserting data.

- In src/routes/api/+handler.js, `{ readonly: false }` is explicitly added for clarity since the API needs both read (querying todos) and write (adding todos) capabilities. It's technically redundant (since read-write is the default), but it documents the intent.

If you removed { readonly: false } from src/routes/api/+handler.js, the code would still work because **SQLite** defaults to read-write mode unless specified otherwise (e.g., with { readonly: false }).

And no, we're not creating the database twice. The syntax **new sqlite3.Database('...')** opens a connection to the same **todos.db** file in both **src/db/setup.js** and **src/routes/api/+handler.js**.

- **src/db/setup.js** creates the database file and table if it doesn't exist (one-time setup).

- **src/routes/api/+handler.js** connects to the existing file to read/ write data during runtime. The database itself (**todos.db**) is created only once; the similar syntax just establishes separate connections to it at different times.

The next file we will look at is src/routes/_index/+page.marko (continued in multiple screenshots).

```marko
src > routes > _index > ☰ +page.marko > ...
 1    import { gql } from "@marko/urql";
 2
 3    static const TODOS_QUERY = gql`
 4      query {
 5        todos {
 6          id
 7          text
 8          completed
 9        }
10      }
11    `;
12
13    static const ADD_TODO_MUTATION = gql`
14      mutation addTodo($text: String!) {
15        addTodo(text: $text) {
16          id
17          text
18          completed
19        }
20      }
21    `;
22
```

```marko
src > routes > _index > ☰ +page.marko > ...
23    class {
24      onCreate() {
25        this.state = { newTodo: '' };
26      }
27
28      handleInput(e) {
29        this.state.newTodo = e.target.value;
30      }
31
32      async handleAdd(mutate) {
33        await mutate({ text: this.state.newTodo });
34        this.state.newTodo = ''; // Clear input
35      }
36    }
37
```

Figure 11-23. *src/routes/_index/+page.marko*

```
src > routes > _index > ≡ +page.marko > ...
  38   <gql-client url="http://localhost:3000/api"/>
  39
  40   <div>
  41     <h1>Todo List</h1>
  42
  43     <!-- Query Todos -->
  44   <gql-query query=TODOS_QUERY>
  45     <@then|{ data, fetching }|>
  46       <if(fetching)>
  47         <p>Loading...</p>
  48       </if>
  49       <else>
  50         <ul>
  51           <for|todo| of=data.todos>
  52             <li>
  53               ${todo.text} - ${todo.completed ? 'Done' : 'Pending'}
  54             </li>
  55           </for>
  56         </ul>
  57       </else>
  58     </@then>
  59     <@placeholder>
  60       <p>Loading todos...</p>
  61     </@placeholder>
  62   </gql-query>
  63
  64     <!-- Add Todo Mutation -->
  65   <gql-mutation|mutate| mutation=ADD_TODO_MUTATION>
  66     <input
  67       type="text"
  68       value=state.newTodo
  69       on-input("handleInput")
  70       placeholder="New todo"
  71     />
  72     <button
  73       on-click("handleAdd", mutate)
  74       disabled=!state.newTodo
  75     >
  76       Add Todo
  77     </button>
  78   </gql-mutation>
  79   </div>
```

Figure 11-23. *(continued)*

Now let us run the marko-run application via **npm run dev**. Doing this will bring up the page at http://localhost:3000/ with pre-created todos.

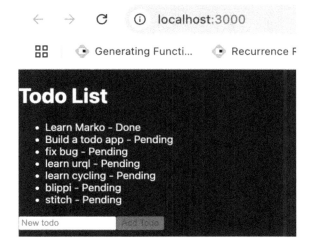

Figure 11-24. *Bringing the page up!*

Next, add a todo via the input text field. And refresh the page. The new todo you had added will now show up.

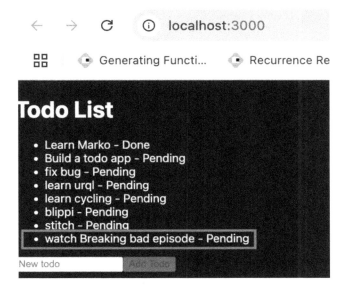

Figure 11-25. *New todo added*

This completes a basic demo of using **@marko/urql**. The tags highlighted in Figure 11-23 are the following:

- **<graphql-query>** is used to query the graphql API via the *src/routes/api+handler.js* file we have created, which talks to the **todos.db** and gets the todos.

- **<graphql-client>** indicates which is the API to query and performs some behind-the-scenes task to set it all up.

- **<graphql-mutation>** performs a mutation action on the same GraphQL API by taking our todo, inserting a new record into the database.

As an update to this example, we will create a similar flow via

- *src/routes/grapqhl/+handler.js*

- *src/routes/alternate/+page.marko*

wherein we will add some filtering logic to demonstrate usage of variables. This page can be accessed at http://localhost:3000/alternate.

```
src > routes > alternate >  ≡ +page.marko > ...
 1    import { gql } from "@marko/urql";
 2
 3    static const TODOS_QUERY = gql`
 4      query Todos($completed: Boolean) {
 5        todos(completed: $completed) {
 6          id
 7          text
 8          completed
 9        }
10      }
11    `;
12
13
14    static const ADD_TODO_MUTATION = gql`
15      mutation addTodo($text: String!) {
16        addTodo(text: $text) {
17          id
18          text
19          completed
20        }
21      }
22    `;
23
```

```
src > routes > alternate >  ≡ +page.marko > ...
24    class {
25      onCreate() {
26        this.state = { newTodo: '', filter: 'all' };
27      }
28
29      handleFilterChange(e) {
30        this.state.filter = e.target.value;
31      }
32
33      handleInput(e) {
34        this.state.newTodo = e.target.value;
35      }
36
37      async handleAdd(mutate) {
38        await mutate({ text: this.state.newTodo });
39        this.state.newTodo = ''; // Clear input
40      }
41
42      getVariables() {
43        return this.state.filter === 'all'
44          ? {} // No completed variable, fetch all
45          : { completed: this.state.filter === 'completed' };
46      }
47    }
48
```

Figure 11-26. *src/routes/alternate/+page.marko*

```
src > routes > alternate >  +page.marko > ...
49    <gql-client url="http://localhost:3000/graphql"/>
50
51    <div>
52      <h1>Todo List</h1>
53
54      <!-- Filter Dropdown -->
55      <select on-change("handleFilterChange") value=state.filter>
56        <option value="all">All</option>
57        <option value="completed">Completed</option>
58      </select>
59
60      <!-- Query with Variables -->
61      <gql-query query=TODOS_QUERY variables=component.getVariables()>
62        <@then|{ data, fetching }|>
63          <if(fetching)>
64            <p>Loading...</p>
65          </if>
66          <else>
67            <ul>
68              <for|todo| of=data.todos>
69                <li>${todo.text} - ${todo.completed ? 'Done' : 'Pending'}</li>
70              </for>
71            </ul>
72          </else>
73        </@then>
74        <@placeholder>
75          <p>Loading todos...</p>
76        </@placeholder>
77      </gql-query>
78
79      <!-- Add Todo Mutation -->
80      <gql-mutation|mutate| mutation=ADD_TODO_MUTATION>
81        <input
82          type="text"
83          value=state.newTodo
84          on-input("handleInput")
85          placeholder="New todo"
86        />
87        <button
88          on-click("handleAdd", mutate)
89          disabled=!state.newTodo
90        >
91          Add Todo
92        </button>
93      </gql-mutation>
94    </div>
```

Figure 11-26. *(continued)*

Note that in Figure 11-26 the <graphql-client> tag points to the new handler API. Next, we shall see the *src/routes/grapqhl/+handler.js* which contains some updates to handling the variables. This is shown in Figure 11-27.

```
src > routes > graphql > JS +handler.js
 1  import { createYoga } from 'graphql-yoga';
 2  import { makeExecutableSchema } from '@graphql-tools/schema';
 3  import sqlite3 from 'sqlite3';
 4
 5  const db = new sqlite3.Database('./src/db/todos.db', { readonly: false });
 6
 7  const typeDefs = `
 8    type Todo {
 9      id: ID!
10      text: String!
11      completed: Boolean!
12    }
13    type Query {
14      todos(completed: Boolean): [Todo!]!
15    }
16    type Mutation {
17      addTodo(text: String!): Todo!
18    }
19  `;
20
21  const resolvers = {
22    Query: {
23      todos: (_, { completed }) => new Promise((resolve, reject) => {
24        const query = completed !== undefined
25          ? 'SELECT * FROM todos WHERE completed = ?'
26          : 'SELECT * FROM todos';
27        const params = completed !== undefined ? [completed ? 1 : 0] : [];
28        db.all(query, params, (err, rows) => {
29          if (err) reject(err);
30          else resolve(rows);
31        });
32      }),
33    },
34    Mutation: {
35      addTodo: (_, { text }) => new Promise((resolve, reject) => {
36        db.run('INSERT INTO todos (text) VALUES (?)', [text], function (err) {
37          if (err) reject(err);
38          else resolve({ id: this.lastID, text, completed: false });
39        });
40      }),
41    },
42  };
43
44  const schema = makeExecutableSchema({ typeDefs, resolvers });
45  const yoga = createYoga({ schema, graphqlEndpoint: '/graphql' });
46
47  export async function POST(context) {
48    console.log('inside /graphql post.');
49    // const text = await context.request.text();
50    // console.log('Request body:', text);
51    // Convert Marko Run context to a Yoga-compatible response
52    const response = await yoga.handleRequest(context.request, {
53      ...context,
54      req: context.request, // Ensure Yoga sees the request
55      res: null,            // Let Yoga handle the response directly
56    });
57
58    // Convert stream to text for debugging
59    const bodyText = await streamToString(response.body);
60    console.log('Response body:', bodyText);
61
62    return new Response(bodyText, {
63      status: response.status,
64      headers: {
65        ...response.headers,
66        'Content-Type': 'application/json', // Ensure correct MIME type
67      },
68    });
69  }
70
71  export async function GET(context) {
72    return POST(context); // Handle GET requests the same way for simplicity
73  }
74
75  // Helper to read stream
76  async function streamToString(stream) {
77    const chunks = [];
78    for await (const chunk of stream) {
79      chunks.push(Buffer.from(chunk));
80    }
81    return Buffer.concat(chunks).toString('utf-8');
82  }
83
```

Figure 11-27A. *src/routes/graphql/+handler.js*

Now restart the server to hit the page at http://localhost:3000/alternate. This is shown in Figure 11-28. Now select between the options and you will see the filtered list as shown in Figure 11-30. When you inspect your browser tab for the network requests, you will notice these additional variables getting passed as shown in Figure 11-27B.

Figure 11-27B. *Network requests with variables*

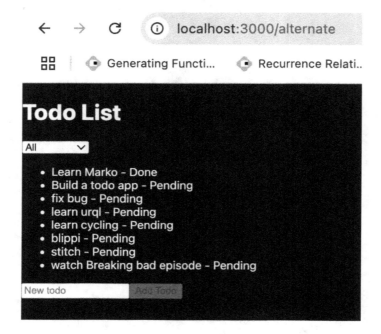

Figure 11-28. *Showing the updated page with a filter to choose the status of todos*

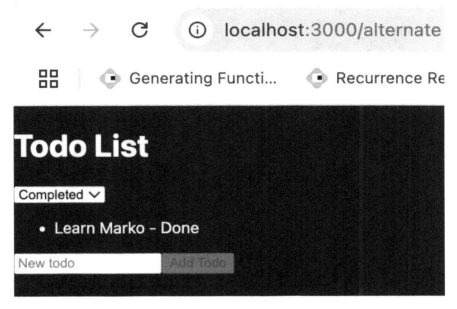

Figure 11-29. *Showing the updated page with a filter to choose the status of todos*

This completes our example of using Marko with URQL for interfacing with GraphQL APIs.

Form Handling with Marko

This example also follows from scaffolding a Marko application via **npx @marko/ create** and the template as **basic**. Note that Marko doesn't have a full-blown solution like Formik of React. However, other framework agnostic solutions should play well with marko. This includes **@tanstack/form** or **final-form**. In this example, we will look at how **Marko** works with **final-form** using the same vanilla final-form example, but using Marko. For this, let's first install the **final-form** package. The project dependencies are shown in Figures 11-30A and 11-30B.

```
{} package.json > ...
 1    {
 2       "name": "marko-form",
 3       "description": "The default Marko starter app",
 4       "version": "1.0.0",
 5       "type": "module",
 6       "dependencies": {
 7         "final-form": "^4.20.10",
 8         "marko": "^5.37.20"
 9       },
10       "devDependencies": {
11         "@marko/run": "^0.6.1"
12       },
13       "private": true,
      ▷Debug
14       "scripts": {
15         "dev": "marko-run",
16         "build": "marko-run build",
17         "preview": "marko-run preview",
18         "start": "node --enable-source-maps ./dist/index.mjs"
19       }
20    }
21
```

Figure 11-30. *package.json*

```
src > routes > ≡ +layout.marko > ...
 1    <!doctype html>
 2    <html lang="en">
 3    <head>
 4      <meta charset="UTF-8">
 5      <link rel="icon" type="image/png" sizes="32x32" href="./favicon.png">
 6      <meta name="viewport" content="width=device-width, initial-scale=1.0">
 7      <meta name="description" content="A basic Marko app.">
 8      <title>${$global.meta.pageTitle || 'Marko'}</title>
 9    </head>
10    <body>
11      <${input.renderBody}/>
12    </body>
13    </html>
14
15 > <!-- style {…
30    } -->
```

Figure 11-30A. *src/routes/+layout.marko (styles commented out)*

672

```
src > routes > _index > ≡ +page.marko > ⅏ sample-form
  1   <sample-form/>
```

Figure 11-31. *src/routes/_index/+page.marko*

```
src > components > sample-form > # style.css > ...
  1   body { font-family: sans-serif; }
  2   form {
  3     max-width: 600px; margin: 10px auto; border: 1px solid ■#ccc; border-radius: 3px;
  4     box-shadow: 1 1 2px □rgba(0, 0, 0, 0.3); padding: 10px; display: flex; flex-flow: column nowrap;
  5   }
  6   h1 { text-align: center; color: □#333; }
  7   p { margin: 10px auto; line-height: 1.2em; max-width: 500px; }
  8   div { margin: 10px; display: flex; flex-flow: row nowrap; justify-content: center; }
  9   label { width: 120px; text-align: right; margin-right: 15px; padding: 5px; }
 10   input { padding: 5px; flex: 1; border: 1px solid ■#ccc; border-radius: 3px; }
 11   select { flex: 1; height: 24px; border: 1px solid ■#ccc; border-radius: 3px; }
 12   span { color: □#600; font-weight: bold; margin: 0 0 0 10px; line-height: 26px; }
 13   button { width: 80px; display: block; margin: 0 auto; }
 14
```

Figure 11-32. *src/components/sample-form/style.css*

As you will see in Figures 11-31 to 11-33, we just have a simple <sample-form> component that is included into the page. This contains a couple of form fields like a select, text fields, checkboxes, etc. We are using final-form to handle validations, provide error messages, and so on. If you are not familiar with final-form, please read the API at https://final-form.org/docs/final-form/api.

The submit button is to submit the form and reset is to reset the fields to default. The error fields are placed with **_error** type span fields right next to the various elements. This will be populated with the various error messages as needed.

The associated functionality is part of the component.js file shown in Figure 11-34. In this, as part of the **onMount** phase, we create the form by taking the various form fields within the given form. This is done via **final-form's createForm** API. This method also provides a **validate** function that is called when submitting the form, and we can place all our validations in it. It also takes in an **onSubmit** function which just shows an alert with the string-based representation of the values in the form. There is a handler to submit the form and a handler to reset the form. In the submit handler, we prevent the default form submit action and instead invoke the **submit** within the **this.form** which contains the final-form's form object that was assigned to it in the **onMount** phase.

673

Next, we also register all the fields in an object. The **registerField** method is invoked for every field element and contains a method that takes the field state and gets triggered for the various actions like blur, change, focus, etc. This is invoked after the validation is complete, and within this, the error messages are set.

```marko
src > components > sample-form >  ☰ index.marko >  🔧 form >  🔧 div >  🔧 select >  🔧 option
1    <form id="form" key="sample-form" on-submit('handleSubmit')>
2        <h1>※ Final Form - Vanilla JS Demo</h1>
3        <p>
4            Uses record level validation. Errors don't show up until a field is
5            "touched" or a submit is attempted. Errors disappear immediately as
6            the user types.
7        </p>
8        <div>
9            <label>First Name</label>
10           <input type="text" name="firstName" placeholder="First Name">
11           <span id="firstName_error" key="firstName_error"/>
12       </div>
13       <div>
14           <label>Last Name</label>
15           <input type="text" name="lastName" placeholder="Last Name">
16           <span id="lastName_error" key="lastName_error"/>
17       </div>
18       <div>
19           <label>Favorite Color</label>
20           <select name="color">
21               <option value="#FF0000">
22                   Red
23               </option>
24               <option value="#00FF00">
25                   Green
26               </option>
27               <option value="#0000FF">
28                   Blue
29               </option>
30           </select>
31           <span id="color_error" key="color_error"/>
32       </div>
33       <div>
34           <label>Employed?</label>
35           <input type="checkbox" name="employed">
36           <span id="employed_error" key="employed_error"/>
37       </div>
38       <div>
39           <button type="submit">
40               Submit
41           </button>
42           <button type="reset" id="reset" on-reset('handleReset')>
43               Reset
44           </button>
45       </div>
46   </form>
47
```

Figure 11-33. *src/components/sample-form/index.marko*

```
src > components > sample-form > JS component.js > ✦ default > ⊙ onMount > ⊙ onSubmit
1    import { createForm } from "final-form";
2
3    export default class {
4      registered = {};
5      form = undefined;
6      // called when form is submitted
7      onMount() {
8        this.registered = {};
9
10       this.form = createForm({
11         onSubmit: (values) => window.alert(JSON.stringify(values, undefined, 2)),
12         initialValues: {
13           color: "#0000FF",
14         },
15         // values is of type FormValues
16         validate: (values) => {
17           const errorMessages = {};
18           if (!values.firstName) {
19             errorMessages.firstName = "Required";
20           }
21           if (!values.lastName) {
22             errorMessages.lastName = "Required";
23           }
24           if (values.color === "#00FF00") {
25             errorMessages.color = "Gross! Not green! 🤮";
26           }
27           return errorMessages;
28         },
29       });
30
31       this.registerFields();
32     }
33     registerFields() {
34       [...this.getEl("sample-form")].forEach((input) => {
35         if (input.name) {
36           this.registerField(input);
37         }
38       });
39     }
40     handleSubmit(e) {
41       debugger;
42       e.preventDefault();
43       this.form.submit();
44     }
45     handleReset(e) {
46       debugger;
47       this.form.reset();
48     }
```

Figure 11-34. *src/components/sample-form/component.js*

```
49      registerField(input) {
50        const { name } = input;
51        this.form.registerField(
52          name,
53          (fieldState) => {
54            const { blur, change, error, focus, touched, value } = fieldState;
55            // const errorElement = document.getElementById(name + "_error");
56            const errorElement = this.getEl(name + "_error");
57            if (!this.registered[name]) {
58              // first time, register event listeners
59              this.subscribeTo(input).on("blur", () => blur());
60              this.subscribeTo(input).on("input", (event) =>
61                change(
62                  input.type === "checkbox"
63                    ? event.target.checked
64                    : event.target.value
65                )
66              );
67              this.subscribeTo(input).on("focus", () => focus());
68              this.registered[name] = true;
69            }
70
71            // update value
72            if (input.type === "checkbox") {
73              input.checked = value;
74            } else {
75              input.value = value === undefined ? "" : value;
76            }
77
78            // show/hide errors
79            if (errorElement) {
80              if (touched && error) {
81                errorElement.innerHTML = error;
82                errorElement.style.display = "block";
83              } else {
84                errorElement.innerHTML = "";
85                errorElement.style.display = "none";
86              }
87            }
88          },
89          {
90            value: true,
91            error: true,
92            touched: true,
93          }
94        );
95      }
```

Figure 11-34. *(continued)*

When you start the app via npm run dev and hit http://localhost:3000/, you get the page as shown in Figure 11-35.

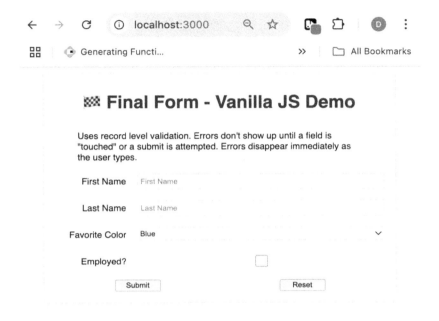

Figure 11-35. *Sample page using final-form*

Now submit the form and you will see fields marked with error messages as they are required. If you made a bad selection, the message will show up next to the select box. Fixing all that and submitting will submit the form. Clicking Reset will reset the form. This is shown in Figures 11-35 and 11-36.

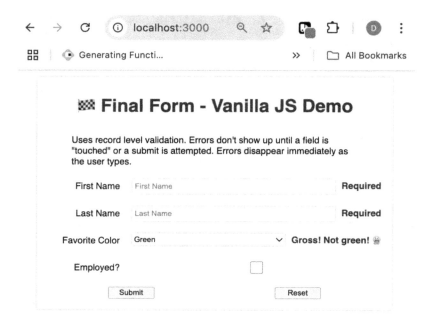

Figure 11-36. *Sample page using final-form with errors*

This completes our example of showcasing external libraries used in other framework land for form handling also works well with Marko. There are other form handling libraries by tanstack, formik, etc. that can be adapted and used to make it work with Marko.

Dynamic Loading of Marko Components

This example also follows from scaffolding a Marko application via **npx @marko/create** and the template as **basic**. In this example, we will just demonstrate dynamic/lazy loading of Marko components on a need to be basis. In our simple example, we will add the following files:

- src/routes/dynamic/+page.marko
- src/components/nested-component/index.marko
- src/components/variant-1/index.marko
- src/components/variant-2/index.marko

To keep it simple, the style in +layout.marko is commented out.

```
src > routes > dynamic >  ☰ +page.marko > ❖ nested-component
  1      <nested-component variant=1/>
  2      <nested-component variant=2/>
```

Figure 11-37. *src/routes/dynamic/+page.marko*

```
src > components > nested-component >  ☰ index.marko > ◈ div > ◈ button
  1   class {
  2       onInput(input) {
  3           this.state = {
  4               variant: input.variant,
  5               open: false,
  6               dynamicRenderer: null
  7           };
  8
  9       }
 10       async toggle() {
 11           const currentVal = !this.state.open;
 12           this.state.open = currentVal;
 13           this.contentEl = this.getEl('content');
 14           if (currentVal) {
 15               let dynamicRenderer = this.state.variant ===  ? await import('../variant-1/index.marko') : await import('../variant-2/index.marko');
 16               this.state.dynamicRenderer = dynamicRenderer.default;
 17           } else {
 18               this.state.dynamicRenderer = null;
 19           }
 20       }
 21   }
 22
 23   <div>
 24       <button on-click('toggle')>
 25           Click me to open a dialog
 26       </button>
 27       <div key="content">
 28       <${state.dynamicRenderer}/>
 29       </div>
 30   </div>
```

Figure 11-38. *src/components/nested-component/index.marko*

As you will notice in Figure 11-28, ESM dynamic imports are used here. This will cause Vite to bundle it as a separate bundle that is loaded dynamically and assimilated into the page along with the existing marko runtime and is then rendered or destroyed.

Let's next look at **<variant-1>** and **<variant-2>** in Figures 11-39 and 11-40.

```
src > components > variant-1 >  ☰ index.marko > ◈ div
  1      <div>
  2          Hello im variant 1
  3      </div>
```

Figure 11-39. *src/components/variant-1/index.marko*

```
src > components > variant-2 >  ☰ index.marko > 🔧 div
1   <div>
2        Hello im variant 2
3   </div>
```

Figure 11-40. *src/components/variant-2/index.marko*

Now, start the app via npm run dev and hit the page at http://localhost:3000/dynamic.

You will see it as shown in Figure 11-41.

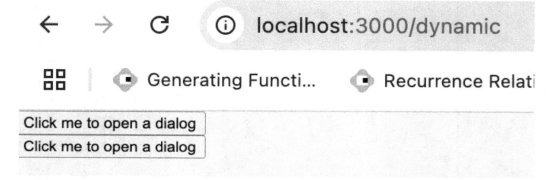

Figure 11-41. *Load the page*

When you click the button (first is mapped to load variant 1 and second is mapped to load variant 2), you will see a separate request in the network tab to fetch the associated component and render it. This is shown in Figures 11-42 and 11-43.

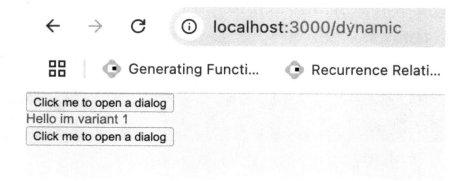

Figure 11-42. *Clicking button 1 renders variant 1*

Figure 11-43. *Variant 1's template is fetched lazily and the component is rendered*

Clicking the same button again triggers the same **toggle** function, and this time the component is removed. Figure 11-43 shows the highlighted "Hello Im variant 1" text included in the fetched template, compiled for client-side usage.

This makes dynamic fetching and rendering possible with Marko components. This means you can code split your bundles to fetch them dynamically by planning out your application's use cases. Note that this is not inherently a feature in Marko but something offered by the underlying bundler, with Marko supporting the use case.

Client-Side Rendering and SPAs with Marko

This example also follows from scaffolding a Marko application via **npx @marko/create** and the template as **basic**. In this example, we will use

- **@preact/signals-core** as our client-side data store solution

- **axios** for data fetching

- **immer** for doing immutable state updates

- **Router5** as our client-side routing solution

- **Router5-plugin-browser** (to automatically update the page URL in changes to the state)

Although this is a simple project, the amount of files is slightly on the higher side, and we will therefore keep everything as simple as possible to illustrate the core aspects of client-side rendering, client-side routing, and history management that is usually involved with SPAs.

The project layout is as shown in Figure 11-44.

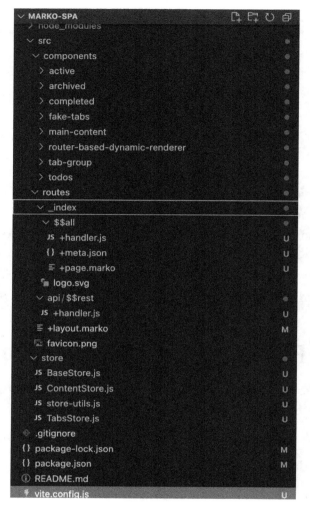

Figure 11-44. *Marko SPA example project layout*

The application we are building is a basic todo application. When the server starts up, we load some basic todos and keep the todos in memory. As todos are added or removed, we update this in-memory object (to keep it simple).

Once the code is complete, our application will look as shown in Figure 11-45.

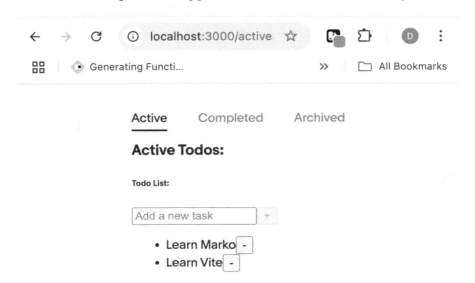

Figure 11-45. *Marko SPA example project layout*

First, let's get to the server side of the changes. For this, while the client-side router manages routing on the client side, we would want to handle any URL to the server. For example, on the client side, the page initially loads with

- http://localhost:3000

- The client-side router sees there are no other fragments in the URL, so defaults to loading the Active tab. You will see it update the client-side URL to http://localhost:3000/active.

- Next, when you click either of Completed or Archived, you will see the client router updating the URL to http://localhost:3000/completed and http://localhost:3000/archived, respectively, without reloading the page but fetching the contents for the respective tabs via fetch calls to the server.

- Now, if you copied one of these URLs and entered them, the server must now be able to understand that you wanted to land on a specific tab and will have to render the initial page on the server, with that tab selected. The client router bootstraps now with this URL.

This is why we moved our server routes originally under *src/routes/_index* to load the page at http://localhost:3000 to be under src/routes/_index/$$all. If you will recall, these are catch-all directories configured in the marko-run setup. This means any URL to the server will go here.

```
src > routes > _index > $$all > JS +handler.js > [∅] tabs
1    const tabs = [
2        {
3            content: "Active",
4            value: "active",
5            selected: false,
6        },
7        {
8            content: "Completed",
9            value: "completed",
10           selected: false,
11       },
12       {
13           content: "Archived",
14           value: "archived",
15           selected: false,
16       }
17   ];
18
19   function checkUrlPath(url) {
20       // Parse URL using URL constructor
21       const parsedUrl = new URL(url);
22       const path = parsedUrl.pathname;
23
24       // Remove leading/trailing slashes and split into fragments
25       const pathFragments = path.replace(/^\/|\/$/g, '').split('/');
26
27       // Possible status fragments
28       const statusFragments = ['active', 'completed', 'archived'];
29
30       // Find the first matching status fragment (if any)
31       const matchedFragment = pathFragments.find(fragment =>
32           statusFragments.includes(fragment)
33       );
34
35       // Return matched fragment or empty string if no match
36       return matchedFragment || '';
37   }
38
39   export async function GET(context) {
40       const pathFragFromUrl = checkUrlPath(context.request.url);
41       context.viewName = pathFragFromUrl || "active";
42       const clonedTabs = JSON.parse(JSON.stringify(tabs));
43       const indexFromPathFrag =
44           clonedTabs.findIndex((tab) => tab.value === pathFragFromUrl) || 0
45       const index = indexFromPathFrag === -1 ? 0 : indexFromPathFrag;
46       clonedTabs[index].selected = true;
47       context.tabs = clonedTabs;
48       context.serializedGlobals.viewName = true;
49   }
```

Figure 11-46. *src/routes/_index/$$all/+handler.js*

As shown in Figure 11-46, we have a GET route wired on, and based on the incoming URL, we set one of the tabs as selected and set this as the input data on the **context.** This will be available within the templates as **$global**.

```
src > routes > _index > $$all >  ≡ +page.marko > ...
 1     $ const { tabs } = $global;
 2
 3     <div.container>
 4       <main-content tabs=tabs/>
 5     </div>
 6
 7     style {
 8       .container {
 9         display:flex;
10         flex-direction: column;
11         justify-content: center;
12         align-items: center;
13         font-size: clamp(1em, 2vw, 2em);
14         padding: 1em;
15         box-sizing: border-box;
16         height:100%;
17         width:100%;
18       }
19       img.logo {
20         width:12em;
21       }
22     }
```

Figure 11-47.   *src/routes/_index/$$all/+page.marko*

As shown in Figure 11-47, we read the tabs from the **$global** prop (originally set on **context** in the **+handler.js**) and pass it down as props to **<main-content/>**. This component shown in Figure 11-48 serves as a wrapper to the **<tab-group>** component.

```
src > components > main-content >  ≡ index.marko > 🔧 div
 1     <div class='router-container'>
 2        <tab-group tabs=input.tabs/>
 3     </div>
```

Figure 11-48.   *src/components/main-content/index.marko*

Next the <tab-group> is mentioned in Figure 11-49.

```
src > components > tab-group > Ξ index.marko > ...
  1   import { effect } from '@preact/signals-core';
  2   import { navigate } from "../router-based-dynamic-renderer/route-util";
  3   import { activeTodosStore, completedTodosStore, archivedTodosStore } from "../../store/ContentStore";
  4   import { tabsStore } from "../../store/TabsStore";
  5   import { routeNames } from "../router-based-dynamic-renderer/routes";
  6
  7   class {
  8       onCreate(input) {
  9           const defaultSelectedIndex =
 10               input.tabs?.findIndex((tab) => tab.selected === true) || 0;
 11           this.state = {
 12               selectedIndex: defaultSelectedIndex,
 13               tabs: input.tabs
 14           };
 15           tabsStore.setTabIndex(defaultSelectedIndex);
 16       }
 17       onMount() {
 18           debugger;
 19           this.tabIndexSubscription();
 20       }
 21       tabIndexSubscription() {
 22           effect(() => {
 23               this.setState('selectedIndex', tabsStore.getTabIndex());
 24           });
 25       }
 26       onTabChanged({ selectedIndex }) {
 27           tabsStore.setTabIndex(selectedIndex);
 28           // reset
 29           activeTodosStore.resetAll();
 30           // reset
 31           completedTodosStore.resetAll();
 32           // reset
 33           archivedTodosStore.resetAll();
 34
 35           navigate(routeNames[this.state.tabs[selectedIndex].value.toUpperCase()]);
 36       }
 37   }
 38
 39   <fake-tabs selectedIndex=state.selectedIndex on-select('onTabChanged')>
 40       <@tab>Active</@tab>
 41       <@tab>Completed</@tab>
 42       <@tab>Archived</@tab>
 43       <@content>
 44           <span/>
 45       </@content>
 46   </fake-tabs>
 47
 48   <router-based-dynamic-renderer/>
```

Figure 11-49. *src/components/tab-group/index.marko*

Notice how in the **onCreate** phase we set the selected tab to a global store (powered with **@preact/signals-core**). Then subscriptions are wired on to the central store by this component, in the onMount phase, to listen to changes in the store. The **effect** method wires on subscriptions to the store.

Any tab selection change is first updated to the store and then listened to by the component to update its own central state. We maintain four stores here which you consider as slices similar to what Redux offers:

- The **tab store** slice which holds the tab state

- The **active store** slice which holds the active todos

- The **completed store** slice which holds the completed todos

- The **archived store** slice which holds the archived todos

Every time a new tab selection occurs, the contents of the current tab are cleared away via the **resetAll()**. Next, every time a new selection is done, the **navigate()** is invoked on the router.

Finally, you will notice the **<router-based-dynamic-renderer/>** which basically configures the client-side router (powered by **router5**) and renders components based on what route the router selects. The imported **routes.js** file is shown in Figure 11-50. It's just a mapping of the route, route name, and the associated component to render.

```
src > components > router-based-dynamic-renderer > JS routes.js > [@] rc
 1    import activeTodos from '../active/index.marko';
 2    import archivedTodos from '../archived/index.marko';
 3    import completedTodos from '../completed/index.marko';
 4
 5    const BASE_URL = '/';
 6
 7    export const routeNames = {
 8        ACTIVE: 'active',
 9        ARCHIVED: 'archived',
10        COMPLETED: 'completed'
11    };
12
13    export const routes = [
14        {
15            name: routeNames.ACTIVE,
16            path: `${BASE_URL}${routeNames.ACTIVE}`,
17            component: activeTodos
18        },
19        {
20            name: routeNames.ARCHIVED,
21            path: `${BASE_URL}${routeNames.ARCHIVED}`,
22            component: archivedTodos
23        },
24        {
25            name: routeNames.COMPLETED,
26            path: `${BASE_URL}${routeNames.COMPLETED}`,
27            component: completedTodos
28        }
29    ];
```

Figure 11-50. *src/components/router-based-dynamic-renderer/routes.js*

We will look at the three components (**<active>**, **<archived>**, and **<completed>**) next in Figures 11-51 to 11-53, respectively.

```
src > components > active > ☰ index.marko > ...
  1    import { effect } from '@preact/signals-core';
  2    import { activeTodosStore } from "../../store/ContentStore";
  3
  4    class {
  5        onCreate() {
  6            this.state = {
  7                todos: [],
  8                pending: false
  9            };
 10        }
 11        onMount() {
 12            debugger;
 13            // 1. wire subscriptions
 14            this.todosSubscription();
 15            this.pendingSubscription();
 16
 17            // 2. Trigger the call
 18            if (typeof document !== 'undefined' && document.readyState !== 'loading') {
 19                // tab switch use case
 20                activeTodosStore.fetchContents("active");
 21            } else {
 22                // page load use case
 23                this.subscribeTo(window).on('DOMContentLoaded', () => {
 24                    activeTodosStore.fetchContents("active", "/api/active")
 25                });
 26            }
 27        }
 28        todosSubscription() {
 29            effect(() => {
 30                this.setState('todos', activeTodosStore.getTodos());
 31            });
 32        }
 33        pendingSubscription() {
 34            effect(() => {
 35                this.setState('pending', activeTodosStore.getPending());
 36            });
 37        }
 38    }
 39
 40    <div>
 41        <h3>
 42            Active Todos:
 43        </h3>
 44        <todos todos=state.todos/>
 45    </div>
```

Figure 11-51. *src/components/active/index.marko*

The basic setup in all these components is the same. They have an internal state but wire on subscriptions for their slice of the state from the central store and update their state. They also trigger fetch in the onMount phase to the server to fetch the todos and store them in the central state. This is done via the **fetchContents** method in their respective stores. The only difference in these components is the store slice they are wired to listen to.

```
src > components > archived > ≡ index.marko > ...
 1    import { effect } from '@preact/signals-core';
 2    import { archivedTodosStore } from "../../store/ContentStore";
 3
 4    class {
 5        onCreate() {
 6            this.state = {
 7                todos: [],
 8                pending: false
 9            };
10        }
11        onMount() {
12            debugger;
13            // 1. wire subscriptions
14            this.todosSubscription();
15            this.pendingSubscription();
16
17            // 2. Trigger the call
18            if (typeof document !== 'undefined' && document.readyState !== 'loading') {
19                // tab switch use case
20                archivedTodosStore.fetchContents("archived");
21            } else {
22                // page load use case
23                this.subscribeTo(window).on('DOMContentLoaded', () => {
24                    archivedTodosStore.fetchContents("archived", "/api/archived")
25                });
26            }
27        }
28        todosSubscription() {
29            effect(() => {
30                this.setState('todos', archivedTodosStore.getTodos());
31            });
32        }
33        pendingSubscription() {
34            effect(() => {
35                this.setState('pending', archivedTodosStore.getPending());
36            });
37        }
38    }
39
40    <div>
41        <h3>
42            Active Todos:
43        </h3>
44        <todos todos=state.todos/>
45    </div>
```

Figure 11-52. *src/components/archived/index.marko*

```marko
src > components > completed > ☰ index.marko > ...
1    import { effect } from '@preact/signals-core';
2    import { completedTodosStore } from "../../store/ContentStore";
3
4    class {
5        onCreate() {
6            this.state = {
7                todos: [],
8                pending: false
9            };
10       }
11       onMount() {
12           debugger;
13           // 1. wire subscriptions
14           this.todosSubscription();
15           this.pendingSubscription();
16
17           // 2. Trigger the call
18           if (typeof document !== 'undefined' && document.readyState !== 'loading') {
19               // tab switch use case
20               completedTodosStore.fetchContents("completed");
21           } else {
22               // page load use case
23               this.subscribeTo(window).on('DOMContentLoaded', () => {
24                   completedTodosStore.fetchContents("completed", "/api/completed")
25               });
26           }
27       }
28       todosSubscription() {
29           effect(() => {
30               this.setState('todos', completedTodosStore.getTodos());
31           });
32       }
33       pendingSubscription() {
34           effect(() => {
35               this.setState('pending', completedTodosStore.getPending());
36           });
37       }
38   }
39
40   <div>
41       <h3>
42           Active Todos:
43       </h3>
44       <todos todos=state.todos/>
45   </div>
```

Figure 11-53. *src/components/completed/index.marko*

Before heading back to Figure 11-49 to see the other imports used in <tab-group>, let's peek into the **<todos>** component in Figure 11-54.

```
src > components > todos > ≡ index.marko > ...
 1   import {produce} from "immer"
 2
 3   class {
 4       onInput(input) {
 5           this.state = {
 6               todos: input.todos || [],
 7               task: ""
 8           }
 9       }
10       updateTaskValue(evt) {
11           this.state.task = evt.target.value;
12       }
13       addTodo() {
14           if ((this.state.task || "").trim()) {
15               const nextTodos = produce(this.state.todos, (draftTodos) => {
16                   draftTodos.push(this.state.task)
17               });
18               this.state.todos = nextTodos;
19               this.state.task = "";
20           }
21       }
22       removeTask(index) {
23           if (index < this.state.todos.length) {
24               const nextTodos = produce(this.state.todos, (draftTodos) => {
25                   draftTodos.splice(index, 1);
26               });
27               this.state.todos = nextTodos;
28           }
29       }
30   }
31
32   style {
33       .font {font-size: 14px;}
34   }
35
36   <div.font>
37       <h6>Todo List:</h6>
38       <input
39           type="text"
40           value=state.task
41           on-change("updateTaskValue")
42           placeholder="Add a new task"
43       />
44       <button on-click("addTodo") disabled=(state.task === "")>+</button>
45       <ul>
46           <for|todo, index| of=state.todos>
47               <li key={index}>
48                   ${todo}
49                   <button on-click("removeTask", index)>-</button>
50               </li>
51           </for>
52       </ul>
53   </div>
54
```

Figure 11-54. *src/components/todos/index.marko*

This builds a basic todo list component with todos passed via its input props. It offers basic functions like displaying the list of todos, a button to add todos, and a button to remove todos. While we ideally will have to send an update (POST) to the server, let's leave this free for now to reduce complexity in the code. Notice that we have again used **immer** to perform immutable state updates here.

Having seen the routes.js and all the associated Marko components—**active**, **archived**, and **completed**—let's head back to Figure 11-49 to see the **navigate()** function defined as part of **route-util.js**. This is illustrated in Figure 11-55.

```
src > components > router-based-dynamic-renderer > JS route-util.js > ...
1   import { createRouter } from 'router5';
2   import browserPlugin from 'router5-plugin-browser';
3
4   export function configureRouter(routes, defaultRoute) {
5       const router = createRouter(routes, {
6           defaultRoute,
7           queryParamsMode: 'loose'
8       });
9       router.usePlugin(
10          browserPlugin({
11              // Set queryParamsMode to 'loose' to retain query parameters
12              queryParamsMode: 'loose'
13          })
14      );
15      return router;
16  }
17
18  export function navigate(name, searchFrag = window?.location?.search) {
19      const router = window.router;
20      const queryParams = {};
21
22      router.navigate(name, queryParams);
23  }
```

Figure 11-55. *src/components/router-based-dynamic-renderer/route-util.js*

This **route-util.js** has two functions defined:

- One is to trigger navigation via the **navigate()** and cause the router to navigate, update the URL via the history API, and thereby cause the corresponding component mapped to that route (within our **routes. js** file) to render. We have used this within the **<tab-group>** when there is a change to the tab selection.

- Second is to configure the router itself. This is done via the **<router-based-dynamic-renderer>**.

Let's look at the **<router-based-dynamic-renderer>** next as part of Figure 11-56.

```marko
src > components > router-based-dynamic-renderer > ≡ index.marko > ...
1   import { configureRouter } from './route-util';
2   import { routes } from './routes';
3   class {
4       onCreate(input, out) {
5           this.state = {
6               componentToRender: null
7           };
8           this.routes = input.routes || routes;
9           this.router = configureRouter(this.routes, out.global.viewName);
10
11          // listener for route change
12          const listener = ({ route, previousRoute }) => {
13              this.setComponentToRender(route);
14          };
15
16          this.unsubscribe = this.router.subscribe(listener);
17      }
18
19      onMount() {
20          debugger;
21          window.router = this.router;
22          this.router.start();
23      }
24
25      setComponentToRender(selectedRoute) {
26          const comp = this.routes.find(
27              (route) => {
28                  console.log(route, selectedRoute);
29                  return route.name === selectedRoute.name
30              }
31          );
32          if (comp && comp.component) {
33              this.setState({
34                  componentToRender: comp.component
35              });
36          }
37      }
38
39      onDestroy() {
40          if (this.unsubscribe) {
41              this.unsubscribe();
42          }
43      }
44  }
45
46  <div id="shell-page">
47      <${state.componentToRender}/>
48  </div>
```

Figure 11-56. *src/components/router-based-dynamic-renderer/index.marko*

This is a simple component which maintains a state prop about the component to render. It configures the router in the **onCreate** phase, via the **configureRouter(),** from within the **route-util.js**, and also creates a **listener** and wires it to the router, to listen for any navigational changes to the router (this navigation is triggered when **navigate()** is invoked when tab selection changes) and get the latest route for navigation. Within the listener, it invokes **setComponentToRender**, where it picks the associated component based on the route, from the array of routes in **routes.js** and renders that component. It triggers initial navigation in the **onMount** phase via the **start()** invocation. The associated components can be loaded upfront or lazily as seen in the previous section of dynamic loading.

Next let's look at the <fake-tabs> component in Figures 11-57 and 11-58. This is the same as the **<fake-tabs>** we have seen in the earlier chapters. It relies on styles from eBay's open source CSS framework Skin.

```less
src > components > fake-tabs > {} style.less
1    @import "~@ebay/skin/marketsans.css";
2    // @import '@ebay/skin/index.css';
3    @import '~@ebay/skin/global.css';
4    @import '~@ebay/skin/less.less';
5    @import "~@ebay/skin/tokens.css";
6    @import "~@ebay/skin/utility.css";
7    @import "~@ebay/skin/tabs.css";
```

Figure 11-57. *src/components/fake-tabs/style.css*

Having seen all the components and the render part of the server code, let's also take a look at the data stores defined via **@preact/signals-core**. As mentioned earlier, there are multiple stores, and these are put together via the following files:

1. src/store/TabStore

2. src/store/ContentStore (for Active, Archived, and Completed)

3. src/store/BaseStore (#1, #2 extends from this, which wires on convenience methods get and set to the state props)

4. src/store/store-utils.js (basic utilities for extending)

These are covered in Figures 11-59 to 11-62.

```
src > components > fake-tabs > ≡ index.marko > ...
  1    class {
  2        onInput(input) {
  3            this.state = {
  4                selectedIndex: input.selectedIndex || 0,
  5            };
  6        }
  7        selectTab(index) {
  8            this.setState("selectedIndex", index);
  9            this.emit("select", {
 10                selectedIndex: index,
 11            });
 12        }
 13    }
 14    $ const {
 15        inputClass,
 16        tab: tabs = [],
 17        content,
 18    } = input;
 19
 20    <div data-testid=input.testid class=["cdui fake-tabs", inputClass]>
 21        <ul class="fake-tabs__items">
 22            <for|tab, i| of=tabs || []>
 23                $ const isSelected = state.selectedIndex === i;
 24                $ const attrs = {};
 25                $ if (isSelected) {
 26                    attrs["aria-current"] = "true";
 27                }
 28                <li on-click("selectTab", i) class=[tab.class, "fake-tabs__item"]>
 29                    <a ...attrs role="button">
 30                        <${tab.renderBody}/>
 31                    </a>
 32                </li>
 33            </for>
 34        </ul>
 35        <div class="fake-tabs__content">
 36            <div class="fake-tabs__panel">
 37                <div class="fake-tabs__cell">
 38                    <div>
 39                        <${content.renderBody}/>
 40                    </div>
 41                </div>
 42            </div>
 43        </div>
 44    </div>
 45
```

Figure 11-58. *src/components/fake-tabs/index.marko*

```
src > store > JS TabsStore.js > ⁣ TabsStore > ⊙ resetAll
 1   import { signal } from '@preact/signals-core';
 2   import { getBaseStore } from './BaseStore';
 3   import { proxyClass } from './store-utils';
 4
 5   export class TabsStore extends proxyClass(getBaseStore()) {
 6       static #instance;
 7       constructor(initialState) {
 8           if (TabsStore.#instance) {
 9               throw new TypeError('TabsStore is not constructable');
10           }
11           super(initialState);
12           TabsStore.#instance = this;
13       }
14       static getInstance(initialState) {
15           if (TabsStore.#instance) {
16               return TabsStore.#instance;
17           }
18           return new TabsStore(initialState);
19       }
20       resetAll() {
21           super.setTabIndex(null);
22       }
23   }
24
25   export const tabsStore = TabsStore.getInstance({
26       tabIndex: signal(0)
27   });
28
```

Figure 11-59. *src/store/TabsStore.js*

```
src > store > JS BaseStore.js > ⊙ getBaseStore
 1    export function getBaseStore() {
 2        if (new.target) {
 3            throw new Error('Cannot instantitate getBaseStore with "new"');
 4        }
 5        class BaseStore {
 6            #state = {};
 7            constructor(initialState) {
 8                this.#state = initialState;
 9            }
10            setState(queryPath, value) {
11                let wasSet = false;
12
13                // value can be null too. So just check typeof
14                if (!queryPath || typeof value === 'undefined') {
15                    return wasSet;
16                }
17
18                const propParts = queryPath.split('.');
19                if (propParts && propParts) {
20                    const finalObj = propParts.reduce((acc, currentVal) => {
21                        if (acc && typeof acc[currentVal] !== 'undefined') {
22                            return acc[currentVal];
23                        }
24                    }, this.#state);
25                    // dont check for value. check for 'value' in finalObj
26                    if (finalObj && 'value' in finalObj) {
27                        finalObj.value = value;
28                        wasSet = true;
29                    }
30                }
31
32                return wasSet;
33            }
34            getState(queryPath) {
35                // only access to props and not like index elems of arrays
36                const propParts = queryPath.split('.');
37                if (propParts && propParts.length) {
38                    const finalFrag = propParts[propParts.length - 1];
39                    return propParts.reduce((acc, currentVal) => {
40                        if (acc && typeof acc[currentVal] !== 'undefined') {
41                            if (currentVal === finalFrag) {
42                                return acc[currentVal].value;
43                            }
44                            return acc[currentVal];
45                        }
46                    }, this.#state);
47                }
48            }
49        }
50        return BaseStore;
51    }
52
```

Figure 11-60. *src/store/BaseStore.js*

```
src > store > JS ContentStore.js > ⬡ ContentStore > ⬡ fetchContents
 1    import axios from 'axios';
 2    import { signal } from '@preact/signals-core';
 3    import { getBaseStore } from './BaseStore';
 4    import { proxyClass } from './store-utils';
 5
 6    export class ContentStore extends proxyClass(getBaseStore()) {
 7        static #instance;
 8        constructor(initialState) {
 9            if (ContentStore.#instance) {
10                throw new TypeError('ContentStore is not constructable');
11            }
12            super(initialState);
13            ContentStore.#instance = this;
14        }
15  >     static getInstance(initialState) {···
20        }
21        async fetchContents(view) {
22            try {
23                // we are not explicitly clearing pageNotifications here
24                // because that would be taken care of when switching between tabs.
25                super.setPending(true);
26
27                const { data, status, headers } = await axios.get(
28                    `/api/${view}`
29                );
30
31                const todos = data.todos;
32
33                if (todos) {
34                    super.setTodos(todos);
35                }
36            } catch (error) {
37                // will trigger for 4xx and 5xx
38
39            } finally {
40                super.setPending(false);
41            }
42        }
43        resetAll() {
44            super.setTodos([]);
45            super.setPending(false);
46        }
47    }
48
49    export const activeTodosStore = ContentStore.getInstance({
50        todos: signal([]),
51        pending: signal(false)
52    });
53
54    export const completedTodosStore = ContentStore.getInstance({
55        todos: signal([]),
56        pending: signal(false)
57    });
58
59    export const archivedTodosStore = ContentStore.getInstance({
60        todos: signal([]),
61        pending: signal(false)
62    });
63
```

Figure 11-61. *src/store/ContentStore.js*

```
src > store > JS store-utils.js > ...
 1    const decorateAccessorsAndMutators = (newTarget, obj) => {
 2        if (!newTarget || !obj) {
 3            return;
 4        }
 5        const wireOnHandlers = (currentObj, accKey = '') => {
 6            const stateKeys = Object.keys(currentObj);
 7            stateKeys.forEach((stateKey) => {
 8                const updatedStateKey =
 9                    stateKey.charAt(0).toUpperCase() + stateKey.slice(1);
10                const currentPropObj = currentObj[stateKey];
11                if ('subscribe' in currentPropObj) {
12                    const parentObj = Object.getPrototypeOf(
13                        Object.getPrototypeOf(newTarget)
14                    );
15                    Object.defineProperty(parentObj, `get${updatedStateKey}`, {
16                        enumerable: true,
17                        configurable: false,
18                        writable: false,
19                        value: ((fulKeyPath) =>
20                            function () {
21                                return this.getState(fulKeyPath);
22                            })(`${accKey}${stateKey}`)
23                    });
24                    Object.defineProperty(parentObj, `set${updatedStateKey}`, {
25                        enumerable: true,
26                        configurable: false,
27                        writable: false,
28                        value: ((fulKeyPath) =>
29                            function (value) {
30                                return this.setState(fulKeyPath, value);
31                            })(`${accKey}${stateKey}`)
32                    });
33                }
34                if (
35                    typeof currentPropObj === 'object' &&
36                    !('subscribe' in currentPropObj)
37                ) {
38                    wireOnHandlers(currentPropObj, `${accKey}${stateKey}.`);
39                }
40            });
41        };
42        // top level obj is not a signal
43        wireOnHandlers(obj);
44        return;
45    };
46
47    export const proxyClass = (clazz) =>
48        new Proxy(clazz, {
49            construct(target, args, newTarget) {
50                const targetInstance = Reflect.construct(target, args, newTarget);
51                if (
52                    args &&
53                    Array.isArray(args) &&
54                    args[0] &&
55                    typeof args[0] === 'object'
56                ) {
57                    decorateAccessorsAndMutators(targetInstance, args[0]);
58                }
59                return targetInstance;
60            }
61        });
62
```

Figure 11-62. *src/store/store-utils.js*

From Figure 11-62, the store-util.js code is designed to automatically add **getter** and **setter** methods to an object's prototype based on the structure of a passed object, specifically for properties that have a **subscribe** attribute (the preact signals state props all have this). These methods allow access and modification of the object's state through **getState** and **setState** functions. The **proxyClass** function wraps a class to apply this decoration logic whenever an instance is created. Overall, the use of proxy classes for automatic method generation based on an object's structure is a powerful technique that enhances flexibility, reduces code complexity, and supports reactive programming paradigms.

From Figures 11-60, 11-59, and 11-61, we have the **TabsStore** and **ContentStore**, each extending from a **BaseStore** wrapped via the Proxies in **store-util.js**. Also, individual stores are created for active, archived, and completed from within **ContentStore**. Within the ContentStore is a fetchContents method which triggers API calls to fetch the todos for the respective tab views from the server. This is the only API call we have yet to see. There are no API calls for modifying todos—adding/removing. This is intentional to reduce complexity. We will next look at the one final API call in Figure 11-64. The output of all of this is visible in Figure 11-63.

The folder directory path is src/routes/api/$$rest/+handler.js. This is again a catch-all directory which means anything /**api**/ has to go here, while anything else will go to the previous route we defined under _**index/$$all**/.

Right now there is only one file here and that is configured to return some todos held in memory. However, you can always extend this to POST/UPDATE/DELETE todos—HTTP verb-based methods, per the marko-run spec. You will notice this in Figure 11-63.

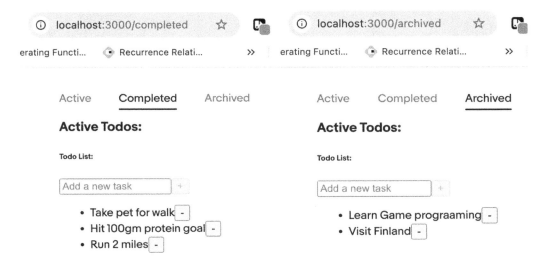

Figure 11-63. *Routing between different tab routes*

```
src > routes > api > $$rest > JS +handler.js > ⊘ GET > [◎] response
 1    const dataStore = {
 2        active: [
 3            "Learn Marko",
 4            "Learn Vite"
 5        ],
 6        completed: [
 7            "Take pet for walk",
 8            "Hit 100gm protein goal",
 9            "Run 2 miles"
10        ],
11        archived: [
12            "Learn Game prograaming",
13            "Visit Finland"
14        ]
15    };
16
17    export async function GET(context) {
18        let response = {};
19
20        if (context.params.rest === "active") {
21            response.todos = dataStore.active;
22        } else if (context.params.rest === "completed") {
23            response.todos = dataStore.completed;
24        } else if (context.params.rest === "archived") {
25            response.todos = dataStore.archived;
26        } else {
27            response.todos = dataStore.active;
28        }
29
30        return new Response(JSON.stringify(response), {
31            headers: { 'Content-Type': 'application/json' },
32            status: 200
33        });
34    }
35
36    export async function POST(context) {
37        return new Response(JSON.stringify(response), {
38            headers: { 'Content-Type': 'application/json' },
39            status: 200
40        });
41    }
```

Figure 11-64. *src/routes/api/$$rest/+handler.js*

702

This completes our single-page application demonstrating how simple it can be to build SPAs with Marko. You can use any router of choice such as TanStack Router (`https://tanstack.com/router/latest`) or Router5 (`https://router5.js.org/`). Router5 also supports subpath navigations. However, while a SPA is a favorite use case, Marko was intended for building MPAs. Couple that with view transitions and you will realize how simple, performant, and snappy apps can be!

Marko and the Event Source APIs

This example also follows from scaffolding a Marko application via **npx @marko/create** and the template as **basic**.

In this simple example, we will look at how Marko works with Server-Sent Events by accessing an endpoint that sends events accessed from the client via the EventSource API. For this app, we will have the following files:

- *src/routes/api/events/+handler.js*

- *src/routes/_index/+page.marko*

- *src/components/sse-display/component.js*

- *src/components/sse-display/index.marko*

```
src > routes > api > events > JS +handler.js > ⊘ GET
 1    export async function GET({ request }) {
 2      // Create a readable stream for SSE
 3      const stream = new ReadableStream({
 4        start(controller) {
 5          // Set up an interval to send data every 2 seconds
 6          const interval = setInterval(() => {
 7            const data = {
 8              id: Date.now(),
 9              message: `Server time: ${new Date().toISOString()}`,
10            };
11            // Encode the data as SSE format (data: JSON\n\n)
12            const text = `data: ${JSON.stringify(data)}\n\n`;
13            controller.enqueue(new TextEncoder().encode(text));
14          }, 2000);
15
16          // Store interval for cleanup
17          request._interval = interval;
18        },
19        cancel() {
20          // Clean up when the stream is canceled (client disconnects)
21          if (request._interval) {
22            clearInterval(request._interval);
23          }
24        },
25      });
26
27      // Return a Response with SSE headers
28      return new Response(stream, {
29        headers: {
30          'Content-Type': 'text/event-stream',
31          'Cache-Control': 'no-cache',
32          'Connection': 'keep-alive',
33        },
34      });
35    }
```

Figure 11-65. *src/routes/api/events/+handler.js*

```marko
src > components > sse-display > ≡ index.marko > ...
 1    style {
 2        ul {
 3            list-style: none;
 4            padding: 0;
 5        }
 6        li {
 7            padding: 10px;
 8            border-bottom: 1px solid ■#eee;
 9        }
10    }
11
12    <div>
13        <if(state.error)>
14            <p style="color: red;">
15                ${state.error}
16            </p>
17        </if>
18        <else>
19            <if(!state.isloading)>
20                <if(state.messages.length !== 0)>
21                    <h2>Messages</h2>
22                    <ul>
23                        <for|msg| of=state.messages>
24                            <li key=msg.id>
25                                ${msg.message}
26                            </li>
27                        </for>
28                    </ul>
29                </if>
30                <else-if(state.messages.length === 0)>
31                    <h2>No messages available!</h2>
32                </else-if>
33            </if>
34            <else>
35                <h2>Loading....</h2>
36            </else>
37            <div>
38                <button on-click("subscribeEvt") disabled=(state.isreceiving)>
39                    Subscribe
40                </button>
41                <button on-click("stop") disabled=(!state.isreceiving)>
42                    Stop
43                </button>
44            </div>
45        </else>
46    </div>
47
```

Figure 11-66. *src/components/sse-display/index.marko*

```
src > components > sse-display > JS component.js > ⚙ default > ⊙ triggerEventSource > ⊙ onmessage
1   export default class {
2     onCreate() {
3       this.state = { messages: [], isloading: false, error: null, isreceiving: false};
4     }
5     onMount() {
6       this.triggerEventSource();
7     }
8     triggerEventSource() {
9       this.state.messages = [];
10      this.state.isloading = true;
11      this.state.isreceiving = false;
12
13      const eventSource = new EventSource("http://localhost:3000/api/events");
14      let messageCount = 0;
15
16      eventSource.onmessage = (event) => {
17        if (messageCount === 0) {
18          this.state.isloading = false;
19          this.state.isreceiving = true;
20        }
21
22        const data = JSON.parse(event.data);
23        this.setState("messages", [
24          ...this.state.messages.slice(-9),
25          { id: data.id, message: data.message },
26        ]);
27      };
28
29      eventSource.onerror = () => {
30        console.error("SSE error occurred");
31
32        this.setState("error", "Failed to connect to the server.");
33        this.state.isreceiving = false;
34        this.state.isloading = false;
35        this.state.messages = [];
36
37        eventSource.close();
38      };
39
40      this.eventSource = eventSource;
41    }
42    onDestroy() {
43      this.eventSource.close();
44    }
45    stop() {
46      this.onDestroy();
47
48      this.state.isreceiving = false;
49      this.state.isloading = false;
50      this.state.messages = [];
51    }
52    subscribeEvt() {
53      this.triggerEventSource();
54    }
55  }
```

Figure 11-67. *src/components/sse-display/component.js*

```
src > routes > _index > ≡ +page.marko > ᛘ .container
1    <div.container>
2      <header>
3        SSE Example With Marko via EventSource API
4      </header>
5      <main>
6        <sse-display/>
7      </main>
8    </div>
9
10   style {
11     .container {
12       display:flex;
13       flex-direction: column;
14       justify-content: center;
15       align-items: center;
16       font-size: clamp(1em, 2vw, 2em);
17       padding: 1em;
18       box-sizing: border-box;
19       height:100%;
20       width:100%;
21     }
22   }
```

Figure 11-68. *src/routes/_index/+page.marko*

In Figure 11-65, we see a +handler.js file set up to handle requests that come to the route /api/events. For this, it responds with a stream and writes to the stream, in an interval of every two seconds, a message that contains a Date string. This is queued and written into the response stream. This API can be accessed directly at http:// localhost:3000/api/events. You will notice the SSE stream as seen in the developer console shown in Figure 11-69.

Figure 11-69. *Developer console indicating the SSE stream*

Our page is accessed via http://localhost:3000/. Initially nothing is there as the API fetch happens onMount via the EventSource API that connects to our API at http://localhost:3000/api/events. Once this connection is successful, you will notice that the server API begins to write messages which our component now receives and parses to include within the list. The moment data starts arriving, the STOP button is enabled, letting you stop the stream at any point when clicked. The moment the stream is stopped receiving, the SUBSCRIBE button is enabled, clicking on which causes you to re-subscribe. There are some minor error handling setups along with a loading indicator and also a possible case when there are no messages to read. The output is as shown in Figure 11-70.

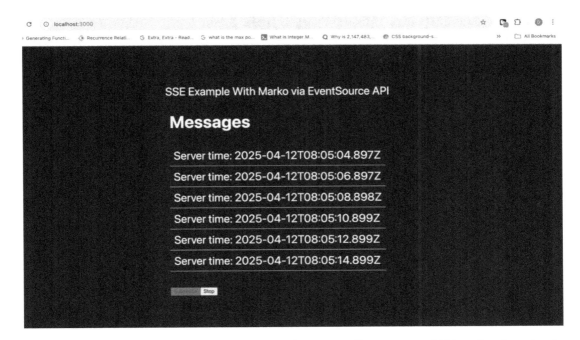

Figure 11-70. *Output of the sample Marko app talking to an SSE endpoint via the EventSource API*

The important pieces in getting an SSE endpoint to work are shown in Figure 11-71.

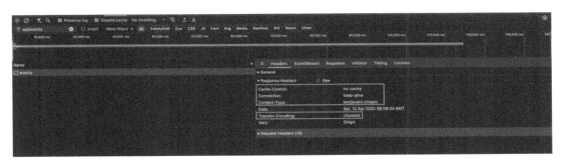

Figure 11-71. *Response headers in getting SSE to work*

If you will note in Figure 11-65, at the **+handler.js**, the **Transfer-Encoding** header was not set. This is added by default when the response size cannot be determined. The other headers highlighted are set in the **+handler.js**.

Some Tips While Working with Marko

1. When serializing state from server to browser via

   ```
   context.serializedGlobals.<property> = true,
   ```

   Marko can serialize only top-level props (one level deep). So if you specifically try to serialize a nested prop like

   ```
   context.serializedGlobals.<my>.<nested>.<property>
   = true;
   ```

   this will not work.

2. When serializing state props from server to browser via

   ```
   context.serializedGlobals.<property> = true,
   ```

   ensure that <property> is not marked with **_Object.freeze_**.

3. Sometimes multiple versions of Marko installed can cause issues in your codebase; for this do a yarn list marko to ensure you have only one version of Marko installed. Having multiple sandboxed runtimes of Marko (as seen with micro-frames) that load on a page is okay, but on the server side, a project is expected to contain only one version.

4. Same as #3, when doing upgrades to marko and its ecosystem of dependencies, ensure you upgrade all versions collectively together to avoid any issues caused by versions being incompatible. For this, you can do something like

   yarn upgrade marko "@marko/" @storybook/marko-vite --latest && npx yarn-deduplicate && yarn*

   For #4 and #5, the commands yarn and npm are interchangeable. Both are package managers for Node JS.

5. When having web component-based custom elements, Marko will have to understand them as custom elements belonging to the web components spec. For this, within the **marko.json** of a given project, do the following to **register** the web component custom element so that marko can understand it:

```
{
    "tags": {
        "my-custom-element": { }
    }
}
```

Or, with a shorthand:

```
{
    "<my-custom-element>": { }
}
```

However, note that you cannot server render web components.

6. When writing tests, as you will have known by now, Marko
   generates component ID markers (which should most likely
   stay the same between test runs). However, if your code has
   some pathways for non-deterministic renders, it's possible these
   component markers will be different between test runs causing
   snapshot updates to be done every time. To avoid this, use the
   normalize function which is provided by Marko testing library.
   This will help you around the issue of internal markers: `https://`
   `github.com/marko-js/testing-library?tab=readme-ov-`
   `file#normalize`

7. When working with Marko, all the starter apps within the
   scaffolder **npx @marko/create** will work. These apps are well
   tested with Webpack, Rollup, and Vite as the module bundlers (for
   the various starters). However, Vite is generally the recommended
   starter these days due to its superior support for HMR. The same
   is for testing. @testing-library/marko works well with both Jest
   and Vitest as the test runners, although the Marko dev team
   recommends working with Vitest. In case you are on the webpack
   setup, Jest will serve as a seamless solution for your testing needs.

Index

A

API, *see* Application programming interface (API)

App federation, *see* Module federation

Application programming interface (API)
  accessing global values, 248
  component instance, 245
  components
    destruction, 252
    DOM manipulation methods, 252
    event handling, 250
    method/property access, 250
    this keyword, 249–252
  context tag, 203
  event sources, 703–710
  getStudentName(), 245
  globalMessage, 246, 248
  graphql-yoga, 654
  +handler.ts, 246
  Hello world, 249
  input/output stream, 245
  keywords/templates, 245
  real world application, 530
  rendering process
    child/parent mount, 340
    compiler options, 321
    countdown-timer, 337
    DOM manipulation utilities, 322
    event handlers, 334
    getComponent() method, 338
    getOutput/afterInsert, 328
    interfaces, 318
    lifecycle events, 333–335, 338
    Node.js extension, 320–323
    render(input), 323, 324
    render(input, callback(err,result)), 324, 325
    render(input, out), 325, 326
    render(input, stream), 324
    renderSync, 323
    renderToString(input), 326
    renderToString(input, callback (err, html)), 327
    serializedGlobals, 330
    server render data, 328–333
    stream(input), 327, 328
    terminology, 319
  rich contexts, 7
  state management, 198, 199
  state properties, 245
  value accessing, 247

Application types
  categorization, 45
  history, 48
  hybrid apps, 48
  multi-page apps (MPAs), 47
  render (*see* Rendering techniques)
  single-page application, 45–47

B

Binary data, 77

Body content
  attributes, 270
  attribute tags, 270, 273–275

© Damodaran Chingleput Sathyakumar 2025
D. Chingleput Sathyakumar, *Practical Marko*, https://doi.org/10.1007/979-8-8688-1483-9

D

H

N, O

P, Q

U, V

W, X, Y

GPSR Compliance
The European Union's (EU) General Product Safety Regulation (GPSR) is a set
of rules that requires consumer products to be safe and our obligations to
ensure this.

If you have any concerns about our products, you can contact us on

ProductSafety@springernature.com

In case Publisher is established outside the EU, the EU authorized
representative is:

Springer Nature Customer Service Center GmbH
Europaplatz 3
69115 Heidelberg, Germany